Robert Plotkin's
The Bartender's Companion — 4th Edition

The Original Guide to
American Cocktails and Drinks

Our hearts go out to everyone affected by the tragic events of September 11th.

This printing is dedicated to

— The World Trade Center —

The lives lost, their families, and the dedication
of Americans to help those in need.

A portion of the profits from this printing will be
donated to the Twin Towers Fund.

BarMedia
September 2001

OTHER BOOKS BY ROBERT PLOTKIN

Drinks for All Ages: The Original Guide to Alcohol-Free Beverages and Drinks (2002)
The Professional Bartender's Training Manual — 3rd Edition (2002)
Caribe Rum: The Original Guide to Caribbean Rum and Drinks (2001)
Successful Beverage Management: Proven Strategies for the On-Premise Operator (2000)
¡Toma! Margaritas! The Original Guide to Margaritas and Tequila (1999)
Preventing Internal Theft: A Bar Owner's Guide — 2nd Edition (1998)
Increasing Bar Sales: Creative Twists to Bigger Profits (1997)
Reducing Bar Costs: A Survival Guide for the '90s (1993)
501 Questions Every Bartender Should Know How to Answer:
    A Unique Look at the Bar Business (1993)
The Professional Guide to Bartending: The Encyclopedia of American Mixology (1991)
The Intervention Handbook: The Legal Aspects of Serving Alcohol — 2nd Edition (1990)

Publishers:	Carol Plotkin, Robert Plotkin
Editors:	Sheila Berry, Elisa Carrizoza, Miguel Castillo, Karen Schmidt
Managing Editor:	Robert Plotkin
Production Manager:	Carol Plotkin
Cover Design:	Miguel Castillo, Carol Plotkin
Book Design:	Miguel Castillo
Product Photography:	Erik Hinote Photography
Additional Photography:	Artwork comes from archival sources and may not be reproduced without the written consent of the respective companies.
Published by:	**BarMedia**

BarMedia
P.O. Box 14486
Tucson, AZ 85732
520.747.8131
www.BarMedia.com

Copyright 2001 BarMedia
Third Printing

All rights reserved. No part of this book may be reproduced or transmitted in any form or by any means, electronic or mechanical, including photocopy, recording or any information storage or retrieval system, without written permission from the publisher, except by a reviewer who may quote brief passages.

Notice: The information in this book is true and correct to the best of our knowledge. It is offered with no guarantees on the part of the authors or BarMedia. The authors and publisher disclaim all liability in connection with the use of this book.

Library of Congress Card Catalog Number: 2001 130648
ISBN: 0-945562-23-3

Printed in China

M.S.
Over 35 years my friend and mentor.
RP

Contents

Responsible Service

The editors of this book advocate moderation in the consumption of alcohol. In addition, we strongly urge responsibility when serving alcohol. The information contained herein is intended to assist in the responsible service of alcohol with the understanding that certification from an alcohol-awareness program is beneficial for all servers of alcohol. Responsibility falls on each individual who serves alcohol. Whether at home or commercially, serve conscientiously and responsibly.

Furthermore, we would like to advance the following:

- A "strong drink" is not necessarily a "good drink." Increasing a drink's liquor portion from 1 ounce to 1 1/2 ounces, for example, increases both its alcoholic potency and cost by 50%. Over-portioning alcohol is an expensive and liability-laden practice.

- Not all drinks are created equally. For instance, a Martini served straight-up is more potent than one served on-the-rocks. Alcohol is soluble in water and will increase the rate at which ice melts. As a result, the melting ice will dilute the drink's alcohol, rendering it less potent.

- Similarly, a blended drink is less potent than one served on-the-rocks. Blending a drink with ice makes it more diluted. In most instances, the dominant ingredient in a blended drink is water (the ice).

- Neat drinks are prepared directly into the glass in which they are served. They are undiluted and high in alcohol concentration. Care should be taken with respect to their service.

- Shooters and layered cordials are conventionally consumed in one swallow, thereby dramatically increasing the rate the alcohol is absorbed into a person's bloodstream. Increased rate of consumption tends to accelerate intoxication.

- A "double" highball, containing 2 ounces of liquor instead of the standard one ounce, is more than twice as potent as two prepared regularly. A "double" will profoundly impact intoxication. Conversely, a "tall" highball, one prepared in a tall glass with significantly more mixer, is less potent than the same drink prepared in the regular manner.

Recipes

ABBEY ROAD
Coffee mug, heated
Build in glass
3/4 oz. Chambord Liqueur
1/2 oz. Disaronno Amaretto Liqueur
1/2 oz. Kahlúa Coffee Liqueur
Near fill with hot coffee
Whipped cream garnish
Dust powdered cocoa

ABERDEEN ANGUS
Coffee mug, heated
Build in glass
1 1/2 oz. Dewar's White Label
   Scotch Whisky
3/4 oz. Drambuie Liqueur
1 tbsp. honey
1/2 oz. fresh lemon juice
Fill with hot water
Lemon wedge garnish

ABSOLUT GRAND
Cocktail glass, chilled
Pour ingredients into iced mixing glass
1 1/2 oz. Absolut Vodka
3/4 oz. Grand Marnier Liqueur
1/2 oz. fresh lime juice
Stir and strain

ABSOLUT MANDRINADE
Bucket glass, ice
Build in glass
1 1/2 oz. Absolut Mandrin Vodka
1/2 oz. Chambord Liqueur
Fill with lemonade
Lemon slice garnish

ABSOLUT MANDRIN MIMOSA
Champagne glass, chilled
Build in glass
1 oz. Absolut Mandrin Vodka
1 1/2 oz. orange juice
Fill with Champagne
Lemon twist garnish

ABSOLUT SAMURAI
Rocks glass, ice
Build in glass
1 1/2 oz. Absolut Citron Vodka
1/2 oz. DJ Dotson Triple Sec
Lemon wedge garnish

ABSOLUT TROUBLE
Cocktail glass, chilled
Pour ingredients into iced mixing glass
1 1/2 oz. Absolut Citron Vodka
1 oz. Grand Marnier Liqueur
1/2 oz. grenadine
1 oz. orange juice
Shake and strain

ACAPULCO
House specialty glass, ice
Pour ingredients into iced mixing glass
1 oz. Farias Silver Tequila
1 oz. Bacardi Light Rum
1 oz. grapefruit juice
3 oz. pineapple juice
Shake and strain
Pineapple wedge and cherry garnish

ACAPULCO BREEZE
House specialty glass, ice
Pour ingredients into iced mixing glass
1 1/2 oz. Sauza Hornitos Tequila
1/2 oz. Midori Melon Liqueur
2 oz. sweet 'n' sour
3 oz. cranberry juice
Shake and strain
Lemon wedge garnish

ACAPULCO GOLD
Highball glass, ice
Build in glass
3/4 oz. Bacardi Gold Rum
3/4 oz. DeKuyper Peachtree Schnapps
Fill with orange juice

ACAPULCO SUNBURN
Bucket glass, ice
Build in glass
1 3/4 oz. Sauza Conmemorativo
   Añejo Tequila
1/2 oz. Midori Melon Liqueur
1/4 oz. fresh lime juice
1 oz. pineapple juice
1/2 fill cranberry juice
1/2 fill lemonade
Lemon wedge garnish

ACHING BACH
Presentation shot glass, chilled
Build in glass
1/3 fill Brandy
1/3 fill Kahlúa Coffee Liqueur
1/3 fill Tequila

VOX® VODKA

VOX VODKA from the Netherlands is a pristine, ultra-premium spirit bred for a chilled cocktail glass and the unhurried time to enjoy it. VOX is made from 100% wheat selected for its mild taste, and demineralized water repeatedly filtered to remove all traces of color, taste and odor. The vodka is distilled five times, then filtered numerous times through screens made of inert material to achieve its essential purity.

VOX is a meticulously produced, wonderfully neutral vodka. It possesses brilliant clarity, a nearly weightless body, a surgically clean palate and a cool, crisp finish. It's packaged in a striking, sculpted bottle made of Austrian glass to accentuate the spirit within.

Ultra-premium VOX earned double gold medals at the *2000 World Spirits Competition* in San Francisco. It is a marvelous addition to Jim Beam's Master's Collection. They recommend that to avoid compromising the vodka's clean profile that VOX be served slightly chilled, or featured in an extra dry martini garnished with a black olive, which is lighter in taste than its green counterpart.

VOX is a product with an unlimited universe of creative possibilities. While fabulous served as a cocktail, it is also primed and ready for a vodka-related assignment.

A CILLO MIA
Tea cup or coffee mug, heated
Build in glass
2 oz. Giori Lemoncillo Cream Liqueur
3/4 oz. Cointreau Liqueur
Fill with hot herbal tea
Lemon wedge garnish

ADAM'S APPLE
Cocktail glass, chilled
Pour ingredients into iced mixing glass
1 1/2 oz. Sauza Hornitos Tequila
1/2 oz. DeKuyper Pucker Sour Apple
1 oz. sweet 'n' sour
1 oz. orange juice
Shake and strain
Green apple wedge garnish

A DAY AT THE BEACH
House specialty glass, ice
Pour ingredients into iced mixing glass
1 oz. Bacardi Light Rum
1 oz. Cruzan Coconut Rum
1/2 oz. Disaronno Amaretto Liqueur
1/2 oz. grenadine
4 oz. orange juice
Shake and strain
Pineapple wedge and orange slice garnish

ADIOS MOTHER
House specialty glass, ice
Pour ingredients into iced mixing glass
1/2 oz. Pearl Vodka
1/2 oz. Damrak Amsterdam Gin
1/2 oz. Bacardi Light Rum
1/2 oz. Blue Curaçao
2 oz. sweet 'n' sour
Shake and strain
Fill with Seven-Up

ADONIS
Cocktail glass, chilled
Pour ingredients into iced mixing glass
1/2 oz. Sweet Vermouth
1 1/2 oz. Dry Sherry
2 dashes orange bitters
Stir and strain
Orange twist garnish

AFTERBURNER
Presentation shot glass, chilled
Build in glass
3/4 oz. Kahlúa Coffee Liqueur
3/4 oz. Jägermeister Liqueur
1/2 oz. 151 proof Rum

AFTER EIGHT
Presentation shot glass, chilled
Layer ingredients
1/3 fill Kahlúa Coffee Liqueur
1/3 fill Green Crème de Menthe
1/3 fill half & half cream

AFTER FIVE
Presentation shot glass, chilled
Layer ingredients
1/3 fill Kahlúa Coffee Liqueur
1/3 fill DeKuyper Peppermint Schnapps
1/3 fill Baileys Irish Cream

AFTER HOURS COCKTAIL
Cocktail glass, chilled
Pour ingredients into iced mixing glass
1 1/2 oz. Beefeater London Dry Gin
1/2 oz. Cointreau Liqueur
1/2 oz. fresh lime juice
1/2 oz. orange juice
Stir and strain
Orange twist garnish

AFTER TAN (1)
House specialty glass, chilled
Pour ingredients into blender
3/4 oz. Cruzan Coconut Rum
3/4 oz. Cruzan Orange Rum
1/2 oz. Dark Crème de Cacao
2 scoops vanilla ice cream
Blend ingredients (with ice optional)
Whipped cream garnish
Drizzle 1/2 oz. Disaronno
    Amaretto Liqueur

AFTER TAN (2)
House specialty glass, chilled
Pour ingredients into blender
1/2 oz. Malibu Rum
1/2 oz. White Crème de Cacao
2 scoops vanilla ice cream
Blend ingredients (with ice optional)
Whipped cream garnish
Drizzle 1/2 oz. Disaronno
    Amaretto Liqueur

AGGRAVATION
Rocks glass, ice
Build in glass
1 1/2 oz. Scotch Whisky
1/2 oz. Kahlúa Coffee Liqueur
1/2 oz. half & half cream

ALABAMA SLAMMER (1)
Presentation shot glass, chilled
Layer ingredients
1/3 fill Southern Comfort Liqueur
1/3 fill Sloe Gin
1/3 fill orange juice

ALABAMA SLAMMER (2)
Rocks glass, ice
Build in glass
1 oz. Disaronno Amaretto Liqueur
1 oz. Southern Comfort Liqueur
1/2 oz. Rose's Lime Juice
1/2 oz. grenadine

ALABAMA SLAMMER (3)
Bucket glass, ice
Pour ingredients into iced mixing glass
1 1/2 oz. Brilliant Vodka
1/2 oz. Southern Comfort Liqueur
1/2 oz. Rémy Red
1 1/2 oz. sweet 'n' sour
1 1/2 oz. orange juice
Shake and strain

ALABAMA SLAMMER (4)
Bucket glass, ice
Build in glass
1 oz. Southern Comfort Liqueur
3/4 oz. Disaronno Amaretto Liqueur
1/2 oz. Sloe Gin
Fill with orange juice

ALABAMA SLAMMER (5)
Rocks glass, chilled
Pour ingredients into iced mixing glass
1/2 oz. Southern Comfort Liqueur
1/2 oz. Disaronno Amaretto Liqueur
1/2 oz. Sloe Gin
1/4 oz. orange juice
1/4 oz. sweet 'n' sour
1/4 oz. Seven-Up
Shake and strain

ALASKA
Cocktail glass, chilled
Pour ingredients into iced mixing glass
1 1/2 oz. Gin
1/2 oz. Yellow Chartreuse
1/2 oz. Dry Sherry
Stir and strain
Lemon twist garnish

ALEXANDER THE GREAT
Cocktail glass, chilled
Pour ingredients into iced mixing glass
1 oz. Metaxa 5 Star Brandy
1/2 oz. Dark Crème de Cacao
1 1/2 oz. half & half cream
Shake and strain
Sprinkle nutmeg

SAUZA® TRES GENERACIONES® AÑEJO TEQUILA

Popularly referred to as "Three Gs" or "Tres," SAUZA TRES GENERACIONES AÑEJO is a 100% agave tequila double-distilled in copper alembic stills and then aged a minimum of 3 years in 180-liter white oak barrels. It has for years ranked high among the ultra-premium elite.

Tres Generaciones Añejo is an understated, sophisticated tequila. It has the pale, golden hue of white wine and a lush, smooth body and texture. The tequila has an alluring, somewhat floral bouquet interlaced with the aromas of earthy agave, caramel and spice. Tres Generaciones is rich and supple, possessing a soft palate amply endowed with the flavors of citrus, pepper and toasted oak. The finish is warm and satisfying.

In 1998, Tres Generaciones Añejo was awarded the coveted gold medal at the *International Wine & Spirits Competition*. It should come as no surprise that Tres Generaciones Añejo Tequila is at its finest when served neat so that it can properly oxygenate and be savored slowly.

Do not miss out on the opportunity of using Tres Generaciones Añejo in a specialty margarita. The time honored adage "the better the tequila, the better the margarita" definitely applies here.

Tres Generaciones Añejo definitely deserves its top-shelf status.

ALICE IN WONDERLAND
aka **A.M.F., Dallas Alice**
Rocks glass, chilled
Pour ingredients into iced mixing glass
3/4 oz. Tia Maria
3/4 oz. Grand Marnier 100th Anniversary
3/4 oz. El Tesoro Añejo Tequila
Stir and strain

ALIEN SECRETION
Bucket glass, ice
Build in glass
1 oz. Midori Melon Liqueur
1 oz. Malibu Rum
Fill with pineapple juice

ALI-TRON
Cocktail glass, chilled
Pour ingredients into iced mixing glass
1 oz. Absolut Citron Vodka
2 oz. Alizé Red Passion
Stir and strain
Lemon twist garnish

ALIZÉ COCKTAIL
Cocktail glass, chilled
Pour ingredients into iced mixing glass
1 1/2 oz. Alizé Red Passion
1 oz. Apricot Brandy
1 oz. fresh lemon juice
Shake and strain
Lemon wheel garnish

ALIZÉ DAY
House specialty glass, chilled
Pour ingredients into blender
3/4 oz. Sauza Conmemorativo
    Añejo Tequila
3/4 oz. Alizé de France
1/2 oz. Crème de Banana
1/2 oz. Razzmatazz Raspberry Liqueur
1/2 cup strawberries
1 1/2 oz. sweet 'n' sour
1 1/2 oz. orange juice
Blend with ice
Strawberry garnish

ALIZÉ DREAM MAKER
House specialty glass, ice
Pour ingredients into iced mixing glass
2 1/4 oz. Alizé de France
1 oz. Artic Vodka & Strawberry Liqueur
3/4 oz. Chambord Liqueur
1 1/4 oz. pineapple juice
1 1/2 oz. coconut cream syrup
2 oz. orange juice
Shake and strain
Pineapple wedge garnish

ALIZÉ ORCHID COCKTAIL
Cocktail glass, chilled
Pour ingredients into iced mixing glass
1 1/2 oz. Alizé V.S.O.P. Cognac
1/2 oz. Chambord Liqueur
3/4 oz. sweet 'n' sour
Shake and strain
Lemon wheel garnish

ALL AMERICAN WHISTLER
Bucket glass, ice
Build in glass
1 1/4 oz. Cascade Mountain Gin
Near fill with Squirt
Float 3/4 oz. DeKuyper Peachtree Schnapps
Lemon wedge garnish

ALL STAR CAST
Brandy snifter, ice
Build in glass
1 1/2 oz. Sauza Tres Generaciones
    Añejo Tequila
3/4 oz. Mandarine Napoléon Liqueur
1/2 oz. Godiva Chocolate Liqueur

ALMOND JOY
Rocks glass, ice
Build in glass
1 1/2 oz. Disaronno Amaretto Liqueur
1/2 oz. Dark Crème de Cacao
1/2 oz. half & half cream

ALPINE GLOW
House specialty glass, ice
Pour ingredients into iced mixing glass
1 1/2 oz. Bacardi Gold Rum
1 1/2 oz. Christian Brothers Brandy
1/2 oz. Gran Gala Orange Liqueur
1/2 oz. grenadine
2 oz. sweet 'n' sour
Shake and strain
Float 3/4 oz. Gosling's Black Seal Rum
Lemon twist garnish

AMANGANI
INDIAN PAINTBRUSH
House specialty glass, chilled
Pour ingredients into blender
2 oz. Bacardi Light Rum
6 strawberries
1 oz. orange juice
2 oz. pineapple juice
Blend with ice
Strawberry garnish

AMARETTO CRUISE
House specialty glass, chilled
Pour ingredients into blender
1 1/4 oz. Bacardi Gold Rum
1 oz. Disaronno Amaretto Liqueur
3/4 oz. Mount Gay Eclipse Rum
1/2 oz. DeKuyper Peachtree Schnapps
1 oz. sweet 'n' sour
1 oz. half & half cream
2 oz. orange juice
2 oz. cranberry juice
Blend with ice

AMBER CLOUD
Brandy snifter, heated
Build in glass
1 1/2 oz. V.S. Cognac
1/2 oz. Galliano Liqueur

AMBROSIA (1)
Champagne glass, chilled
Build in glass
1/2 fill apricot puree
1/2 fill Champagne

AMBROSIA (2)
Champagne glass, chilled
Pour ingredients into iced mixing glass
1 1/4 oz. Laird's Applejack Brandy
1/2 oz. Cointreau Liqueur
3/4 oz. sweet 'n' sour
Shake and strain
Fill with Champagne
Orange twist garnish

AMBUSH
Coffee mug, heated
Build in glass
1 oz. Knappogue Castle Irish Whiskey
1 oz. Disaronno Amaretto Liqueur
Near fill with hot coffee
Whipped cream garnish

AMERICAN DREAM
Presentation shot glass, chilled
Build in glass
1/4 fill Kahlúa Coffee Liqueur
1/4 fill Disaronno Amaretto Liqueur
1/4 fill Godiva Chocolate Liqueur
1/4 fill Frangelico Liqueur

GRAND MARNIER®
LIQUEUR

GRAND MARNIER ranks among the finest liqueurs on the planet. It is the creation of the Lapostolle family, who in 1827, founded a distillery to produce liqueurs in the chateau country of France. By 1870, the firm was experimenting with different blends of cognac-based liqueurs at their distillery in Cognac. Family member Louis-Alexandre Marnier hit on the notion of combining the peels of bitter Haitian oranges with Fine Champagne cognac. After a decade in development, Grand Marnier was introduced to the world in 1880.

The liqueur is made in Neauphle-le-Château and crafted exactly as it was 120 years ago. The orange peels are first slowly macerated in cognac. The infused-spirit is redistilled, blended with the finest cognacs from each of the growing regions. The liqueur is then barrel-aged at the Marnier-Lapostolle cognac cellars at Château de Bourg.

To describe Grand Marnier as exquisite may be underselling it a bit. The liqueur has the captivating color of cognac with radiant yellow and gold highlights. Its lightweight body has the texture of satin and the generous citrus bouquet is laced with the aroma of brandy. The palate is an elegant array of sweet and sour orange flavors followed closely by a lingering cognac finish. Grand Marnier is unsurpassed in cocktails.

AMERICAN GRAFFITI
Bucket glass, ice
Pour ingredients into iced mixing glass
1 1/4 oz. Bacardi Light Rum
3/4 oz. Mount Gay Eclipse Rum
1/2 oz. Sloe Gin
1/2 oz. Southern Comfort Liqueur
1/4 oz. Rose's Lime Juice
1 1/2 oz. pineapple juice
1 1/2 oz. sweet 'n' sour
Shake and strain
Orange slice and cherry garnish

AMERICANO
Rocks glass, ice
Build in glass
1 oz. Campari Aperitivo
1 oz. Sweet Vermouth
Lemon twist garnish

AMERICANO HIGHBALL
Highball glass, ice
Build in glass
3/4 oz. Campari Aperitivo
3/4 oz. Sweet Vermouth
Fill with club soda
Lemon twist garnish

A.M.F.
aka **Alice in Wonderland, Dallas Alice**
Brandy snifter (ice optional)
Build in glass
3/4 oz. Tia Maria
3/4 oz. Grand Marnier Liqueur
3/4 oz. Jose Cuervo Especial Tequila

ANCIENT MARINER (1)
Brandy snifter, ice
Build in glass
1 1/4 oz. Bacardi 8 Reserva Rum
1 oz. Grand Marnier 100th Anniversary

ANCIENT MARINER (2)
Brandy snifter, ice
Build in glass
1 1/4 oz. Pyrat Cask 23 Rum
1 oz. Grand Marnier 100th Anniversary

ANDALUSIA
Brandy snifter, heated
Build in glass
1 1/2 oz. Bacardi 8 Reserva Rum
1/2 oz. V.S. Cognac
1/2 oz. Dry Sherry
1-2 dashes Angostura Bitters
Lemon twist garnish

ANDES SUMMIT
House specialty glass, chilled
Pour ingredients into blender
1 1/2 oz. Dr. McGillicuddy's
    Mentholmint Schnapps
1 1/2 oz. Godiva Chocolate Liqueur
3 oz. milk
2 scoops vanilla ice cream
Blend ingredients (with ice optional)
Shaved chocolate garnish

ANGEL KISS
Rocks glass, ice
Build in glass
1 oz. Vodka
1 oz. Frangelico Liqueur
Lime wedge garnish

ANGEL'S KISS
aka **Angel's Tip**
Cordial or sherry glass, chilled
Layer ingredients
3/4 fill Dark Crème de Cacao
1/4 fill half & half cream

APPENDECTOMY
Cocktail glass, chilled
Pour ingredients into iced mixing glass
1 oz. Damrak Amsterdam Gin
1/2 oz. Grand Marnier Liqueur
1 1/2 oz. sweet 'n' sour
Shake and strain

APPENDICITIS
aka **White Lady**
Cocktail glass, chilled
Pour ingredients into iced mixing glass
1 oz. Gin
1/2 oz. Hiram Walker Triple Sec
1 1/2 oz. sweet 'n' sour
Shake and strain

APPETIZER
Cocktail glass, chilled
Pour ingredients into iced mixing glass
3/4 oz. Tanqueray Nº Ten Gin
3/4 oz. Dubonnet Rouge
2-3 dashes Angostura Bitters
1 1/2 oz. orange juice
Shake and strain

APPLE A GO-GOGH
Cocktail glass, chilled
Rim glass with sugar
Pour ingredients into iced mixing glass
1 1/2 oz. Vincent Van Gogh
    Wild Appel Vodka
1/2 oz. Kahlúa Coffee Liqueur
1/4 oz. DeKuyper Buttershots Schnapps
Shake and strain
Apple wedge garnish

APPLE BRANDY COOLER
House specialty glass, ice
Pour ingredients into iced mixing glass
1 oz. Bacardi Light Rum
1 oz. Brandy
4 oz. apple juice
Shake and strain
Float 3/4 oz. Cockspur V.S.O.R. Rum
Lime wedge garnish

APPLE CART
Cocktail glass, chilled
Pour ingredients into iced mixing glass
1 oz. Laird's 12-Year Apple Brandy
1/2 oz. Cointreau Liqueur
1 1/2 oz. sweet 'n' sour
Shake and strain

APPLE COOLER
Bucket glass, ice
Build in glass
1 1/4 oz. DeKuyper Pucker Sour Apple
1/2 oz. Zone Melon Italian Vodka
2 oz. cranberry juice
Fill with club soda

APPLE GRAND MARNIER
Cappuccino cup, heated
Build in glass
3/4 oz. Grand Marnier Liqueur
3/4 oz. Calvados Apple Brandy
3/4 oz. V.S. Cognac
Near fill with hot espresso coffee
Top with frothed milk
Dust powdered cocoa

APPLEJACK CREAM
Cocktail glass, chilled
Pour ingredients into iced mixing glass
1 1/2 oz. Laird's Applejack Brandy
1 oz. apple cider
1 tsp. sugar
2 oz. half & half cream
Shake and strain
Sprinkle cinnamon

APPLE SPICE
Bucket glass, ice
Build in glass
1 1/4 oz. Jim Beam White Label Bourbon
1/2 oz. DeKuyper Pucker Sour Apple
1/4 oz. Hot Damn Cinnamon Schnapps
Fill with apple cider
Apple wedge garnish

APPLE STING
Brandy snifter (ice optional)
Build in glass
1 1/2 oz. Laird's Applejack Brandy
1/2 oz. DeKuyper Peppermint Schnapps

TIPS ON PROPER HANDLING AND STORING OF GLASSWARE

Glassware Handling

Avoid handling any part of a glass that might come into contact with a person's mouth. Touching the rim or the inside of a clean glass is unsanitary and must be avoided.

Practice holding two or more glasses at a time in your hand. This can make a big difference in productivity, since the less time it takes to select and fully ice down glassware, the less time it takes to prepare a drink order.

Never use a glass to scoop ice from the bin. In the process the glass could chip or break in the ice, causing someone to be served a drink with a shard of glass in it. Obviously, this is something that must be avoided at all costs.

Finally, inspect each glass before adding ice or committing products to it. Inspect the glass for spots, lipstick smudges, greasy or oily deposits, chips, cracks, off-odors, or anything that may be unappealing in any way.

Glassware Storage

Clean glasses must be stored properly in order to keep them clean. Glassware should be inverted and stored on level shelves covered with open matting that allows air to circulate within the glass. Rotate the glassware occasionally to prevent them from becoming dusty or sticking to the matting.

Glasses should never be stored in a refrigerator or glass-chiller that is not clean and odor-free. Lingering odors in a glass will negatively affect the flavor of a drink, or the taste of wine and beer.

Glasses should be stored in areas away from smoke, which will create a film on glass. This is the significant drawback to storing stemmed glassware in hanging racks over the bar.

APPLE TINKER
Cocktail glass, chilled
Pour ingredients into iced mixing glass
1 3/4 oz. Tanqueray № Ten Gin
1/2 oz. DeKuyper Pucker Sour Apple
1/2 oz. Rose's Lime Juice
1 1/2 oz. sweet 'n' sour
Shake and strain
Lemon twist garnish

APPLE TODDY
Coffee mug, heated
Build in glass
1 oz. Laird's Applejack Brandy
1/2 oz. simple syrup
Fill with frothed milk
Sprinkle nutmeg

APPLE WORKS
Coffee mug, heated
Build in glass
1 1/4 oz. Bacardi Light Rum
3/4 oz. Mount Gay Extra Old Rum
1/2 oz. Laird's 12-Year Apple Brandy
1/2 fill warm cranberry juice
1/2 fill warm apple cider
Cinnamon stick garnish

APPLETON BLAST
House specialty glass, ice
Build in glass
1 1/2 oz. Appleton Estate V/X Jamaica Rum
1/2 oz. Disaronno Amaretto Liqueur
1/2 oz. DeKuyper Peachtree Schnapps
Fill with cranberry juice
Orange slice garnish

APPLETON BREEZE
House specialty glass, ice
Build in glass
1 1/2 oz. Appleton Special Jamaica Rum
1/2 oz. Rose's Lime Juice
3 oz. cranberry juice
3 oz. grapefruit juice
Lime wedge garnish

APRÉS SKI
Coffee mug, heated
Build in glass
1 oz. Laird's Applejack Brandy
3/4 oz. Laird's 12-Year Apple Brandy
Fill with hot apple cider
Cinnamon stick garnish

APRIL IN PARIS
Champagne glass, chilled
Build in glass
1 oz. Grand Marnier 100th Anniversary
Swirl and coat inside of glass
Fill with Champagne
Orange twist garnish

AQUA ZEST
Bucket glass, ice
Build in glass
1 1/4 oz. Sauza Hornitos Tequila
3/4 oz. Blue Curaçao
1/2 oz. Rose's Lime Juice
1/2 fill orange juice
1/2 fill lemonade

ARCTIC MINT
House specialty glass, chilled
Rim glass with powdered cocoa (optional)
Pour ingredients into blender
1 oz. Peppermint Schnapps
3/4 oz. chocolate syrup
3 oz. milk
2 scoops chocolate mint ice cream
Blend ingredients (with ice optional)
Chocolate covered pretzel garnish

AREA 151
Rocks glass, ice
Build in glass
3/4 oz. Sauza Conmemorativo
   Añejo Tequila
3/4 oz. 151 proof Rum
1/2 oz. Kahlúa Coffee Liqueur
1/2 oz. DeKuyper Peppermint Schnapps

ARIANA'S DREAM
House specialty glass, chilled
Pour ingredients into blender
1 oz. Bacardi Light Rum
1 oz. Alizé Red Passion
1 oz. White Crème de Cacao
3 oz. orange juice
Blend with ice
Orange slice and strawberry garnish

ARTIFICIAL INTELLIGENCE
House specialty glass, ice
Pour ingredients into iced mixing glass
3/4 oz. Mount Gay Eclipse Rum
3/4 oz. Bacardi Select Rum
3/4 oz. Appleton Estate V/X Jamaica Rum
3/4 oz. Cruzan Coconut Rum
1 oz. fresh lime juice
3 oz. pineapple juice
Shake and strain
Float 3/4 oz. Midori Melon Liqueur
Lime, lemon and orange wedge garnish

A.S. MACPHERSON
House specialty glass, ice
Pour ingredients into iced mixing glass
3 oz. orange juice
2 oz. apple cider
1 1/2 oz. sweet 'n' sour
3 dashes Angostura Bitters
Shake and strain
Fill with club soda
Orange slice and cherry garnish

ASPEN COFFEE
Coffee mug, heated
Build in glass
1/2 oz. Kahlúa Coffee Liqueur
1/2 oz. Baileys Irish Cream
1/2 oz. Frangelico Liqueur
Near fill with hot coffee
Whipped cream garnish
Sprinkle shaved chocolate

AUGUST MOON
Presentation shot glass, chilled
Build in glass
1/3 fill DJ Dotson Triple Sec
1/3 fill Disaronno Amaretto Liqueur
Near fill with orange juice
Whipped cream garnish

AUNT BEA'S CURE-ALL
HOT MILK PUNCH
Coffee mug, heated
Build in glass
1 oz. Christian Brothers Brandy
1 oz. Foursquare Spiced Rum
1/2 oz. Dr. McGillicuddy's Vanilla Liqueur
Fill with hot milk
Sprinkle nutmeg

AUTUMN SIDECAR
Cocktail glass, chilled
Rim glass with sugar (optional)
Pour ingredients into iced mixing glass
1 1/2 oz. Hennessy V.S. Cognac
1/2 oz. Tuaca
1/2 oz. Frangelico Liqueur
1 3/4 oz. sweet 'n' sour
Shake and strain
Orange slice garnish

AVIATION COCKTAIL
Cocktail glass, chilled
Pour ingredients into iced mixing glass
2 oz. Bombay Sapphire London Dry Gin
1/2 oz. Chambord Liqueur
1 3/4 oz. sweet 'n' sour
Shake and strain
Lemon twist garnish

ABERLOUR®
A'BUNADH SPEYSIDE
SINGLE MALT WHISKY

Aberlour is one of the classic, most esteemed whisky distilleries in Scotland. It is located in the heart of the Highlands, an easy walk from the river Spey, ensconced among towering trees and a gurgling natural spring. Master distiller, Douglas Cruickshank, leads the small group of craftsmen, and together they have created a line of world-class single malt whiskies ranging up to the 30-year-old Stillman's Dram.

Once only sold in Duty Free shops around the world, ABERLOUR A'BUNADH SPEYSIDE SINGLE MALT is certainly one of the most singular whiskies sold in a bottle. It is a robust, unadulterated, natural whisky. It is left pristine, unfiltered and undiluted. It is bottled at cask strength; our tasting sample was 59.6% abv (119.2 proof).

For whisky aficionados, Aberlour a'bunadh is a mother lode, definitely in the "too good to share" category. It has an expansive nose, and a full, creamy palate that features the malty, smoky flavors of sherry, chocolate and fruit. This magnificent whisky has one of the truly memorable finishes.

Aberlour a'bunadh was bred to be savored after dinner and should be served neat, or with a splash of spring water to be fully appreciated.

BABY GRAND COCKTAIL
Brandy snifter, heated
Build in glass
3/4 oz. B & B Liqueur
1/2 oz. Baileys Irish Cream

BACARDI COCKTAIL
Cocktail glass, chilled
Pour ingredients into iced mixing glass
1 1/2 oz. Bacardi Light Rum
3/4 oz. grenadine
2 oz. sweet 'n' sour
Shake and strain

BACARDI TROPICO DREAM
House specialty glass, chilled
Pour ingredients into blender
1 3/4 oz. Bacardi Gold Rum
1 1/4 oz. Tropico
3/4 oz. Disaronno Amaretto Liqueur
1/2 oz. Rose's Lime Juice
1 1/2 oz. sweet 'n' sour
2 oz. orange juice
Blend with ice
Lime, lemon and orange wedge garnish

BADDA-BING
House specialty glass, ice
Pour ingredients into iced mixing glass
3/4 oz. Stolichnaya Russian Vodka
3/4 oz. Bacardi Gold Rum
1/2 oz. Gran Gala Orange Liqueur
1/2 oz. Razzmatazz Raspberry Liqueur
1/2 oz. sweet 'n' sour
1 oz. orange juice
1 oz. cranberry juice
1 oz. pineapple juice
Shake and strain
Pineapple wedge garnish

BAFFERTS REVIVER
House specialty glass, chilled
Pour ingredients into blender
1 3/4 oz. Bafferts Gin
3/4 oz. Villa Massa Limoncello
3/4 oz. DeKuyper Triple Sec
3 oz. limeade
Blend with ice
Float 3/4 oz. DeKuyper Watermelon Pucker
Lime wedge, orange slice and
    cherry garnish

BAHAMA MAMA (1)
House specialty glass, ice
Pour ingredients into iced mixing glass
1 1/2 oz. Bacardi Light Rum
3 oz. pineapple juice
Shake and strain
Float 1/2 oz. Appleton Estate V/X
    Jamaica Rum and 1/2 oz. Gosling's
    Black Seal Rum

BAHAMA MAMA (2)
House specialty glass, ice
Pour ingredients into iced mixing glass
1 1/4 oz. Bacardi Light Rum
1/2 oz. Bacardi 151° Rum
1/2 oz. Cruzan Coconut Rum
1/2 oz. Kahlúa Coffee Liqueur
1/2 oz. Rose's Lime Juice
1 1/2 oz. sweet 'n' sour
3 oz. pineapple juice
Shake and strain
Lime, lemon and orange wedge garnish

BAILEYS BUTTERBALL
Presentation shot glass, chilled
Build in glass
3/4 oz. Baileys Irish Cream
3/4 oz. DeKuyper Buttershots Schnapps
1/2 oz. Kahlúa Coffee Liqueur

BAILEYS COMET
Rocks glass, ice
Build in glass
1 1/2 oz. Stolichnaya Russian Vodka
1/2 oz. Baileys Irish Cream

BAILEYS EXPRESS
Coffee mug, heated
Build in glass
1 1/4 oz. Baileys Irish Cream
Near fill with hot espresso coffee
Whipped cream garnish
Dust powdered cocoa

BAILEYS FIZZ
Highball glass, ice
Build in glass
1 1/4 oz. Baileys Irish Cream
Fill with club soda

BAILEYS MALIBU RUM YUM
Rocks glass, chilled
Pour ingredients into iced mixing glass
1 oz. Baileys Irish Cream
1 oz. Malibu Rum
1 oz. half & half cream
Shake and strain

BAILEYS MINT KISS
Coffee mug, heated
Build in glass
3/4 oz. Baileys Irish Cream
3/4 oz. Kahlúa Coffee Liqueur
3/4 oz. Rumple Minze Schnapps
Near fill with hot coffee
Whipped cream garnish
Dust powdered cocoa

BALALAIKA
Cocktail glass, chilled
Pour ingredients into iced mixing glass
1 1/2 oz. Jewel of Russia
    Wild Bilberry Infusion
1/2 oz. DJ Dotson Triple Sec
1 1/2 oz. sweet 'n' sour
Shake and strain
Lime wedge garnish

BALASHI BREEZE
House specialty glass, chilled
Pour ingredients into blender
1 1/2 oz. Midori Melon Liqueur
1/2 oz. Blue Curaçao
1/2 oz. Light Rum
1 oz. cranberry juice
2 1/2 oz. coconut cream syrup
4 oz. pineapple juice
Blend with ice

BALL BEARING
Presentation shot glass, chilled
Build in glass
1/2 fill Cherry Marnier
1/2 fill Champagne

BALL JOINT
House specialty glass, chilled
Pour ingredients into iced mixing glass
1 oz. Absolut Vodka
3/4 oz. Grand Marnier Liqueur
3 oz. orange juice
Shake and strain

BALTIMORE ZOO
House specialty glass, ice
Pour ingredients into iced mixing glass
1 oz. VOX Vodka
1/2 oz. Sea Wynde Pot Still Rum
3/4 oz. DeKuyper Triple Sec
1/2 oz. Sloe Gin
1/2 oz. Rose's Lime Juice
2 oz. orange juice
Shake and strain
Fill with Guinness Stout

BAM BE
Presentation shot glass, chilled
Layer ingredients
1/3 fill Tia Maria
1/3 fill Baileys Irish Cream
1/3 fill B & B Liqueur

ROYALE CHAMBORD®
LIQUEUR DE FRANCE

It is hard to imagine sipping something more luscious than ROYALE CHAMBORD LIQUEUR DE FRANCE. Long a favorite of King Louis the XIV, Chambord is an elegant and refined crème de framboise. It became an overnight success when introduced in the United States and was a fixture on back bars moments after its arrival. Now twenty years later, the liqueur is the featured performer in a large repertoire of cocktails and permanently enrolled in the "must have" class.

Appropriately enough, Chambord Liqueur is made in the town of Chambord, which is located in the center of France. The liqueur is crafted on a base of premium grape spirits that is infused with a mixture of fresh *framboise noires* (small black raspberries), herbs, and other fruits. The liqueur is then sweetened with honey, filtered and bottled at 33 proof.

Everything about Chambord is sensational. The intrigue begins with its opaque appearance and extremely deep, ruby/purple hue. The liqueur has a luxuriously textured, medium-weight body and a wafting herbal and fruit bouquet. The semi-sweet palate is a lavish affair featuring raspberries, spice, herbs and a taste of honey. The flavors persist on the palate for a remarkably long finish.

In the hands of the inspired, Chambord has no creative limitations.

BANALINI
Champagne glass, chilled
Build in glass
3/4 oz. DeKuyper Peach Pucker
3/4 oz. Cruzan Banana Rum
Fill with Champagne
Banana slice garnish

BANANA BAY
Bucket glass, ice
Build in glass
1 1/2 oz. Cruzan Banana Rum
Fill with cola

BANANA COW
House specialty glass, chilled
Pour ingredients into blender
1 1/2 oz. Royal Oak Extra Old Rum
1 oz. Cruzan Banana Rum
1 oz. Cruzan Orange Rum
1/2 oz. grenadine syrup
1/2 oz. half & half cream
2 scoops vanilla ice cream
Blend ingredients (with ice optional)
Banana slice garnish

BANANA FROST
House specialty glass, chilled
Pour ingredients into blender
1 oz. Disaronno Amaretto Liqueur
1 oz. Whaler's Hawaiian Vanille Rum
1 ripe banana
1 oz. half & half cream
2 scoops vanilla ice cream
Blend ingredients (with ice optional)
Banana slice garnish

BANANA FRUIT PUNCH
(makes two servings)
2 house specialty glasses, chilled
Pour ingredients into blender
2 1/2 oz. Bacardi Gold Rum
1 3/4 oz. Mount Gay Eclipse Rum
4-5 slices cored, peeled pineapple
3 ripe bananas
5 oz. orange juice
4 oz. sweet 'n' sour
2 oz. fresh lime juice
1/2 tsp. nutmeg
Blend with ice
Float into each 3/4 oz. Cockspur
   V.S.O.R. Rum
Pineapple wedge and cherry garnish

BANANA MILKSHAKE
House specialty glass, chilled
Pour ingredients into blender
1 1/2 oz. Bacardi Gold Rum
3/4 oz. Gosling's Black Seal Rum
2 ripe bananas
1 oz. honey
1 cup milk
2 scoops vanilla ice cream
Blend ingredients (with ice optional)
Whipped cream garnish
Drizzle chocolate syrup

BANANA MONKEY
House specialty glass, chilled
Pour ingredients into iced mixing glass
2 oz. Royal Oak Extra Old Rum
1 oz. Mount Gay Eclipse Rum
1 oz. Crème de Banana
1 oz. fresh lime juice
3/4 oz. grenadine
Shake and strain
Lime wedge garnish

BANANA NUTS
Cocktail glass, chilled
Rim glass with sugar (optional)
Pour ingredients into iced mixing glass
1 1/4 oz. Cruzan Banana Rum
3/4 oz. Crème de Banana
1/2 oz. Frangelico Liqueur
1/2 oz. orange juice
1/2 oz. grapefruit juice
Shake and strain
Orange slice garnish

BANANA POPSICLE
House specialty glass, chilled
Pour ingredients into blender
1 oz. Crème de Banana
3/4 oz. Cruzan Banana Rum
1 1/2 oz. orange juice
1 ripe banana
1 oz. half & half cream
Blend with ice

BANANA SANDWICH
aka **Monkey's Lunch**
Presentation shot glass, chilled
Layer ingredients
1/3 fill Kahlúa Coffee Liqueur
1/3 fill Crème de Banana
1/3 fill Baileys Irish Cream

BANANAS BARBADOS
House specialty glass, chilled
Pour ingredients into blender
1 oz. Mount Gay Eclipse Rum
1/2 oz. Crème de Banana
2 oz. sweet 'n' sour
1 dash vanilla extract
1 ripe banana
Blend with ice
Float 1 oz. Mount Gay Extra Old Rum

BANANAS FOSTER
Rocks glass, ice
Build in glass
1 1/2 oz. Dr. McGillicuddy's Vanilla Liqueur
3/4 oz. Crème de Banana
3-4 drops Hot Damn Cinnamon Schnapps
Splash half & half cream

BANANA STIGMA
Cocktail glass, chilled
Pour ingredients into iced mixing glass
2 oz. Original Polish Vodka
1/2 oz. Cruzan Banana Rum
Stir and strain
Lime wedge garnish

BANANAS OVER YOU
House specialty glass, chilled
Pour ingredients into blender
1 oz. Frangelico Liqueur
1 oz. Crème de Banana
1/2 oz. White Crème de Cacao
1 ripe banana
2 oz. half & half cream
2 scoops vanilla ice cream
Blend ingredients (with ice optional)
Strawberry garnish

BANANA SPLIT
House specialty glass, chilled
Pour ingredients into blender
3/4 oz. White Crème de Menthe
3/4 oz. White Crème de Cacao
3/4 oz. Crème de Banana
2 scoops strawberry ice cream
Blend ingredients (with ice optional)
Whipped cream garnish

BANILLA BOAT
House specialty glass, chilled
Pour ingredients into blender
1 oz. B & B Liqueur
3/4 oz. Crème de Banana
2 scoops vanilla ice cream
Blend ingredients (with ice optional)
Float 3/4 oz. Chambord Liqueur
Banana slice garnish

STOLICHNAYA® VODKA

One of the most widely recognized spirit brands in the world, STOLICHNAYA VODKA is made in the heart of Moscow and is a classic, Russian-built vodka. This famed spirit is double-distilled from hearty winter wheat. It is filtered five times through crushed quartz and charcoal before being rested in stainless-steel holding tanks.

The reasons Stolichnaya attained world-class status are quickly evident. It is crystal clear with a light, herbal and pine bouquet. The fun really begins when the medium-weight, satiny body glides over the palate, immediately filling the mouth with warmth and sweet, slightly peppery flavors. It has a long, lemon-citrus finish.

The distillers raised the bar with the 1994 release of STOLICHNAYA GOLD VODKA. This award-winning spirit is quadruple-distilled from late harvest wheat and glacial water. It is an elegant vodka—expansive, warming and loaded with a herbal, peppery palate and lingering finish.

In 1997, Stolichnaya introduced the martini-starved world to a line of six flavored vodkas, including STOLICHNAYA VANIL (vanilla), STOLICHNAYA STRASBERI (strawberry) and STOLICHNAYA PERSIK (peach). These overnight successes joined their existing flavored vodka line of STOLICHNAYA LIMONNAYA (lemon), and STOLICHNAYA OHRANJ (orange).

BANK SHOT
Rocks glass, chilled
Pour ingredients into iced mixing glass
1 1/4 oz. Absolut Kurant Vodka
1/2 oz. Chambord Liqueur
1 1/2 oz. orange juice
Shake and strain

BANSHEE
aka **White Monkey**
Cocktail glass, chilled
Pour ingredients into iced mixing glass
1/2 oz. Crème de Banana
1/2 oz. White Crème de Cacao
2 oz. half & half cream
Shake and strain
Banana slice garnish (optional)

BARBARY COAST
Cocktail glass, chilled
Pour ingredients into iced mixing glass
3/4 oz. Dewar's White Label Scotch Whisky
3/4 oz. Beefeater London Dry Gin
3/4 oz. White Crème de Cacao
3/4 oz. half & half cream
Shake and strain

BARCELONA COFFEE
Coffee mug, heated
Build in glass
1 3/4 oz. Licor 43 (Cuarenta y Tres)
1 oz. Christian Brothers Brandy
Near fill with hot coffee
Top with frothed milk
Dust powdered cocoa

BARN RAISER
House specialty glass, ice
Build in glass
1 oz. VOX Vodka
1 oz. Light Rum
1/2 oz. grenadine
2 oz. orange juice
2 oz. pineapple juice
Float 3/4 oz. Cruzan Estate
    Single Barrel Rum

BASIN STREET BALM
Cocktail glass, chilled
Pour ingredients into iced mixing glass
1 oz. Brandy
3/4 oz. DeKuyper Peachtree Schnapps
1 1/2 oz. sweet 'n' sour
Shake and strain
Orange slice and cherry garnish

BAT BITE
Highball glass, ice
Build in glass
1 1/4 oz. Bacardi Select Rum
Fill with cranberry juice

BATIDA
Bucket glass, ice
Build in glass
1 1/2 oz. Ypioca Cachaça
1/2 fill orange juice
1/2 fill pineapple juice

BAY AREA GARTER
Coffee mug, heated
Build in glass
1/2 oz. Kahlúa Coffee Liqueur
1/2 oz. Frangelico Liqueur
1/2 oz. Godiva Chocolate Liqueur
1/2 oz. chocolate syrup
Near fill with hot coffee
Whipped cream garnish
Dust powder cocoa

BAYBREEZE
aka **Downeaster**
Highball glass, ice
Build in glass
1 1/4 oz. Vodka
1/2 fill cranberry juice
1/2 fill pineapple juice

BAY BRIDGE COMMUTER (1)
Bucket glass, ice
Pour ingredients into iced mixing glass
1 3/4 oz. VOX Vodka
1/2 tsp. horseradish
3-4 dashes Tabasco Sauce
4 oz. gazpacho
Shake and strain
Lime wedge and prawn garnish

BAY BRIDGE COMMUTER (2)
Bucket glass, ice
Pour ingredients into iced mixing glass
1 1/2 oz. Aquavit
1/2 tsp. horseradish
3-4 dashes Tabasco Sauce
4 oz. gazpacho
Shake and strain
Lime wedge and prawn garnish

BAY BRIDGE COMMUTER SHOOTER
Rocks glass, chilled
Build in glass
1 1/2 oz. Aquavit
1/2 tsp. horseradish
2 dashes Tabasco Sauce
2 oz. gazpacho
Lime wedge and prawn garnish

BBC
Presentation shot glass, chilled
Build in glass
1/3 fill Baileys Irish Cream
1/3 fill B & B Liqueur
1/3 fill Cointreau Liqueur

BEACH BLONDE
House specialty glass, ice
Pour ingredients into iced mixing glass
1 1/2 oz. Bacardi Light Rum
1 oz. Disaronno Amaretto Liqueur
3/4 oz. grenadine
3/4 oz. Rose's Lime Juice
2 1/2 oz. orange juice
Shake and strain
Near fill with Seven-Up
Float 3/4 oz. Cockspur V.S.O.R. Rum

BEACH BUM BLUE
House specialty glass, ice
Rim glass with sugar (optional)
Pour ingredients into iced mixing glass
1 1/4 oz. Hussong's Reposado Tequila
1 oz. Blue Curaçao
1/2 oz. DeKuyper Peach Pucker
1 1/2 oz. sweet 'n' sour
Shake and strain
Lime wedge garnish

BEACHCOMBER (1)
House specialty glass, ice
Pour ingredients into iced mixing glass
1 1/2 oz. Cruzan Estate Light Rum
1/2 oz. DJ Dotson Triple Sec
1/2 oz. Chambord Liqueur
1/2 oz. Rose's Lime Juice
1 1/2 oz. sweet 'n' sour
Shake and strain

BEACHCOMBER (2)
Cocktail glass, chilled
Pour ingredients into iced mixing glass
1 1/4 oz. Bacardi Light Rum
3/4 oz. Mount Gay Eclipse Rum
1/2 oz. DeKuyper Triple Sec
1/2 oz. grenadine
1 oz. sweet 'n' sour
Shake and strain
Lime wedge garnish

BEAM ME UP, SCOTTIE
Presentation shot glass, chilled
Layer ingredients
1/3 fill Kahlúa Coffee Liqueur
1/3 fill Crème de Banana
1/3 fill Baileys Irish Cream

TANQUERAY® N° TEN GIN

TANQUERAY N° TEN is unlike any gin that has preceded it. Instead of using botanicals such as dried roots, berries, rinds, barks and seeds to derive its flavor, this innovative spirit is made using only fresh ingredients, such as ripe, hand picked grapefruits, oranges, and limes. In addition, the recipe calls for fresh juniper berries from Tuscany and herbs such as coriander and chamomile.

The whole fruit and other botanicals are then distilled in an elegant, swan-necked, small batch still designated "N° Ten." This distinctive spirit, lovingly referred to as "the heart of the gin," is added to a larger batch of premium botanicals and redistilled for a total of four distillations.

The gin tastes and smells like no other. It has an immense bouquet, comprised of layers of luscious citrus, spice and evergreen aromas. The light bodied gin has a dry, crisp palate, one that completely fills the mouth with a delicate medley of fresh fruit, juniper and a slight hint of chamomile. Tanqueray N° TEN is so smooth and refreshing that you won't even notice that it's 94.6 proof.

Tanqueray N° TEN was seemingly bred for a chilled cocktail glass and a crisp dry martini. In the right hands, it knows no creative limitations.

BEARING STRAIT
Cocktail glass, chilled
Pour ingredients into iced mixing glass
1 1/2 oz. Stolichnaya Russian Vodka
1/2 oz. Grand Marnier Liqueur
1/2 oz. Rose's Lime Juice
Stir and strain
Lime wedge garnish

BEAURITA
Presentation shot glass, chilled
Build in glass
Rim glass with salt (optional)
2 dashes Tabasco Sauce
1/4 oz. fresh lime juice
2 oz. Tequila

BEAUTIFUL THING
Rocks glass, ice
Build in glass
1 oz. Baileys Irish Cream
1 oz. Rumple Minze Schnapps

BEAUTY AND THE BEAST
Brandy snifter, heated
Build in glass
3/4 oz. B & B Liqueur
3/4 oz. Opal Nera Black Sambuca

BEER BUSTER
Beer glass or mug, chilled
Build in glass
1 oz. Van Hoo Belgium Vodka
3 dashes Tabasco Sauce
Fill with Draft Beer

BEE'S KNEES
Cocktail glass, chilled
Pour ingredients into iced mixing glass
1 oz. Gin
1/2 oz. honey
1 1/2 oz. sweet 'n' sour
Shake and strain

BELGIAN WAFFLE
Tankard or pilsner glass, chilled
Build in glass
1/2 fill Tommyknocker Maple Nut Ale
1/2 fill Pete's Strawberry Blonde Ale

BELLINI
Champagne glass, chilled
Build in glass
1/2 fill peach puree
1/2 fill Champagne

BELLINISIMO

Champagne glass, chilled
Build in glass
1 oz. Chambord Liqueur
1 oz. pear puree
Fill with Champagne
Lemon twist garnish

BELLISIMO

House specialty glass, ice
Pour ingredients into iced mixing glass
3/4 oz. Alizé Red Passion
1 1/4 oz. Bacardi Limón Rum
2 dashes orange bitters
1 1/2 oz. sweet 'n' sour
3 oz. orange juice
Shake and strain
Orange slice garnish

BELVEDERE MILK CHOCOLATE

Cocktail glass, chilled
Pour ingredients into iced mixing glass
2 oz. Vodka
3/4 oz. Godiva Chocolate Liqueur
Stir and strain
Float 3/4 oz. Baileys Irish Cream

B & B

Sherry glass or brandy snifter, heated
Build in glass
1/2 fill Brandy
1/2 fill Benedictine

BENSON BOMBER

Bucket glass, ice
Build in glass
1/2 oz. Dark Crème de Cacao
1/2 oz. Brandy
1/2 oz. Kahlúa Coffee Liqueur
1/2 oz. Disaronno Amaretto Liqueur
1/2 fill cola
1/2 fill half & half cream

BERLIN WALL

Rocks glass, ice
Build in glass
1 1/2 oz. Rumple Minze Schnapps
1/2 oz. Baileys Irish Cream

BERMUDA TRIANGLE (1)

Bucket glass, ice
Build in glass
1 1/2 oz. Gosling's Black Seal Rum
1 oz. DeKuyper Peachtree Schnapps
1/2 oz. Bacardi Spiced Rum
Fill with orange juice
Orange slice garnish

BERMUDA TRIANGLE (2)

Bucket glass, ice
Build in glass
1 1/2 oz. Gosling's Black Seal Rum
2 oz. cranberry juice
2 oz. orange juice
Orange slice garnish

BERMUDA TRIANGLE (3)

Cocktail glass, chilled
Pour ingredients into iced mixing glass
1 1/2 oz. Mount Gay Eclipse Rum
3/4 oz. Cointreau Liqueur
1/2 oz. Rose's Lime Juice
1/2 oz. cranberry juice
Stir and strain
Lime wedge garnish

BERRIES JUBILEE

House specialty glass, chilled
Pour ingredients into blender
1 3/4 oz. Chambord Liqueur
1/2 oz. coconut cream syrup
1 oz. half & half cream
2 1/2 oz. pineapple juice
Blend with ice
Whipped cream garnish (optional)

BERRY COOLER

House specialty glass, ice
Build in glass
3/4 oz. DeKuyper Raspberry Pucker
1/4 oz. Disaronno Amaretto Liqueur
Fill with Seven-Up

BETELGEUSE

Champagne glass, chilled
Pour ingredients into iced mixing glass
1 oz. Stolichnaya Vanil Russian Vodka
1 oz. Whaler's Hawaiian Vanille Rum
1/2 oz. Rose's Lime Juice
1 oz. White Zinfandel
Shake and strain
Fill with Champagne
Orange slice garnish

BETSY ROSS

Cocktail glass, chilled
Pour ingredients into iced mixing glass
1 oz. Brandy
1 oz. Tawny Port
1/2 oz. Cointreau Liqueur
2 dashes Angostura Bitters
Stir and strain

BAILEYS® ORIGINAL IRISH CREAM LIQUEUR

The makers of BAILEYS ORIGINAL IRISH CREAM LIQUEUR are justifiably proud of being the "original" brand of cream liqueur. Now often imitated, Baileys was indeed the world's first and it became an instant success upon its 1979 introduction. It is now the best selling liqueur in the world.

Created by R. & A. Bailey Company of Dublin, Ireland, the liqueur is made from a base of dairy cream not more than 2 hours old. The cream is infused with aged, triple distilled Irish whiskey and natural vanilla and chocolate flavorings. The liqueur is homogenized to ensure that the flavors fully amalgamate, then pasteurized and bottled at 34 proof.

Baileys Irish Cream is an elegant taste sensation that is well deserving of its international preeminence. The liqueur has a beige hue and a luscious, medium-weight body. The creamy bouquet has engaging whiskey and chocolate notes. It spreads a wealth of flavors over the palate, alternating notes of vanilla, chocolate and whiskey. The dairy-wrapped flavors persist long into the luxurious finish.

Baileys Irish Cream is absolutely marvelous served chilled, straight-up or over ice. To overlook its versatility behind the bar would be to deny it of its pub heritage. Baileys is a liqueur with unlimited creative uses, as evidenced by the long list of cocktails in which it is featured.

BETTOR'S DREAM
Cocktail glass, chilled
Pour ingredients into iced mixing glass
1 1/2 oz. Gooderham & Worts
  Canadian Whisky
1/2 oz. Extase XO Liqueur
2 oz. sweet 'n' sour
Shake and strain
Orange slice and cherry garnish

BETTY GRABLE
Coffee mug, heated
Build in glass
1 1/4 oz. Bacardi Select Rum
1/2 oz. Disaronno Amaretto Liqueur
1/2 oz. Chambord Liqueur
Near fill with hot apple cider
Whipped cream and
  cinnamon stick garnish
Sprinkle nutmeg

BETWEEN THE SHEETS
Bucket glass, ice
Pour ingredients into iced mixing glass
1 oz. Brandy
3/4 oz. Light Rum
1/2 oz. Triple Sec
2 oz. sweet 'n' sour
Shake and strain

BEVERLY HILLBILLY
Presentation shot glass, chilled
Layer ingredients
1/2 fill Goldschläger
1/2 fill Jägermeister Liqueur

BEVERLY HILLS COOLER
Champagne glass, chilled
Pour ingredients into iced mixing glass
1 oz. Courvoisier V.S.O.P. Cognac
1/2 oz. B & B Liqueur
3 oz. orange juice
Shake and strain
Fill with Champagne
Orange twist garnish

B-52
Presentation shot glass, chilled
Layer ingredients
1/3 fill Kahlúa Coffee Liqueur
1/3 fill Baileys Irish Cream
1/3 fill Grand Marnier Liqueur

BIBLE BELT (1)
Cocktail glass, chilled
Pour ingredients into iced mixing glass
1 oz. Southern Comfort Liqueur
1/2 oz. DeKuyper Triple Sec
1 1/2 oz. sweet 'n' sour
Shake and strain
Lime wedge garnish

BIBLE BELT (2)
Cocktail glass, chilled
Rim glass with sugar (optional)
Pour ingredients into iced mixing glass
1 1/4 oz. Jack Daniel's Tennessee Whiskey
3/4 oz. Grand Marnier Liqueur
1/2 oz. Rose's Lime Juice
1 1/4 oz. sweet 'n' sour
Shake and strain

BIG BACARDI BAMBOO
House specialty glass, ice
Pour ingredients into iced mixing glass
1 oz. Bacardi Gold Rum
1 oz. Bacardi 151° Rum
3/4 oz. Chambord Liqueur
1 oz. pineapple juice
1 oz. orange juice
1 oz. fresh lime juice
Shake and strain
Float 3/4 oz. Grand Marnier Liqueur
Orange slice garnish

BIG BAMBOO, THE
House specialty glass, ice
Pour ingredients into iced mixing glass
1 1/4 oz. KéKé Beach Cream Liqueur
3/4 oz. Cruzan Estate Diamond Rum
3/4 oz. Cruzan Banana Rum
1 1/2 oz. sweet 'n' sour
1 1/2 oz. pineapple juice
Shake and strain

BIG BLUE SHOOTER
Rocks glass, chilled
Pour ingredients into iced mixing glass
1 1/4 oz. Pyrat Pistol Rum
1 oz. Malibu Rum
3/4 oz. Captain Morgan Spiced Rum
3/4 oz. Blue Curaçao
3 oz. pineapple juice
Shake and strain
Lime wedge garnish

BIG CHILL
House specialty glass, chilled
Pour ingredients into blender
1 1/2 oz. Bacardi Select Rum
1 oz. Cruzan Coconut Rum
3/4 oz. Rose's Lime Juice
1 oz. pineapple juice
1 1/2 oz. cranberry juice
1 1/2 oz. orange juice
Blend with ice
Float 3/4 oz. J. Bally Rhum Vieux 7-Year
Pineapple wedge and cherry garnish

BIG FAT MONKEY KISS
Presentation shot glass, chilled
Build in glass
1/2 oz. Disaronno Amaretto Liqueur
1/2 oz. DeKuyper Peachtree Schnapps
1/2 oz. Crème de Banana
1/2 oz. cranberry juice

BIKINI LINE
Presentation shot glass, chilled
Build in glass
1/3 fill Tia Maria
1/3 fill Chambord Liqueur
1/3 fill Vodka

BISMARK
Tankard or pilsner glass, chilled
Build in glass
1/2 fill Beck's Dark Lager
1/2 fill Champagne

BITCHES FROM HELL
Presentation shot glass, chilled
Build in glass
1/3 fill Jägermeister Liqueur
1/3 fill Crème de Banana
1/3 fill half & half cream

BLACK & BLUE BAYOU
Bucket glass, ice
Build in glass
1 1/2 oz. Blavod Black Vodka
3/4 oz. Blue Curaçao
1/2 fill pineapple juice
1/2 fill grapefruit juice

BLACK AND BROWN
Tankard or pilsner glass, chilled
Build in glass
1/2 fill Guinness Stout
1/2 fill Newcastle Brown Ale

BLACK AND TAN
Beer or ale glass, chilled
Build in glass
1/2 fill Bass Ale
1/2 fill Guinness Stout

BLACK AND WHITE
Presentation shot glass, chilled
Layer ingredients
1/2 fill Kahlúa Coffee Liqueur
1/2 fill Chambord Liqueur

BLACK APE
Tankard or pilsner glass, chilled
Build in glass
1/2 fill Guinness Stout
1/2 fill Pyramid Apricot Ale

CRUZAN® SINGLE BARREL ESTATE RUM

CRUZAN SINGLE BARREL ESTATE RUM is a limited production, handcrafted rum made from a blend of triple-distilled rums that are aged between 5 and 12 years in American oak bourbon barrels.

After blending, the rum is placed in new, American white oak casks for secondary aging, the insides of which are heavily charred. This extended aging allows the elements of the blend to "marry" and fully integrate.

Each bottle bears the handwritten number of the cask in which the rum was aged. No batch is bottled until a panel of tasters, headed by master blender Hardy Nelthropp, deems the rum ready for release.

The result of the "double casking" can be perceived in every aspect of the rum's character. It has a lustrous, tawny red color and a trim, compact body. Cruzan Single Barrel Estate Rum is impressively similar to an aged brandy with rum notes on the palate and finish.

The brand's preeminent status was solidified when it was named the "Best Rum in the World" at the World Spirits Competition.

This is a spirit that should be doted over, sipped straight-up or on-the-rocks. If you're in the mood for a cocktail, however, Cruzan Single Barrel Estate Rum is more than ready to play.

BLACKBEARD'S TREASURE
House specialty glass, chilled
Pour ingredients into blender
1 1/2 oz. Bacardi Spiced Rum
1 oz. Mount Gay Eclipse Rum
1 oz. Chambord Liqueur
2 oz. raspberry puree
2 oz. sweet 'n' sour
Blend with ice
Pineapple wedge and cherry garnish

BLACK BEAUTY
Rocks glass, ice
Build in glass
1/2 oz. Blavod Black Vodka
1/2 oz. Frangelico Liqueur
1/2 oz. Kahlúa Coffee Liqueur
1/2 oz. Dark Crème de Cacáo
1/2 oz. half & half cream

BLACK CAT
Bucket glass, ice
Build in glass
1 1/2 oz. DeKuyper Cherry Pucker
1/2 oz. Blavod Black Vodka
1/2 fill cranberry juice
1/2 fill cola

BLACK DEATH
Pilsner glass, chilled
Build in glass
1/2 fill Guinness Stout
1/2 fill Woodchuck Cider

BLACK DIAMOND
Cocktail glass, chilled
Pour ingredients into iced mixing glass
1 3/4 oz. Jameson Irish Whiskey
1/2 oz. Alizé de France
1/2 oz. Vya California Dry Vermouth
Stir and strain
Lemon twist garnish

BLACK-EYED SUSAN
aka **Kentucky Screwdriver**
Highball glass, ice
Build in glass
1 1/4 oz. Jim Beam Black Label Bourbon
Fill with orange juice

BLACK HOOTER
Rocks glass, chilled
Pour ingredients into iced mixing glass
1 oz. Blackberry Brandy
1 oz. Chambord Liqueur
Shake and strain
Splash Seven-Up

BLACK JACK
Coffee mug, heated
Build in glass
1 oz. Jack Daniel's Tennessee Whiskey
1 oz. Rumple Minze Schnapps
Fill with hot coffee

BLACK JAMAICAN
Rocks glass, ice
Build in glass
1 1/2 oz. Appleton Estate V/X Jamaica Rum
1/2 oz. Tia Maria

BLACK MARIA
Coffee mug, heated
Build in glass
1 1/2 oz. Bacardi Select Rum
1 1/2 oz. Tia Maria
3/4 oz. Dark Crème de Cacao
Near fill with hot coffee
Whipped cream garnish

BLACK MASS
Presentation shot glass, chilled
Layer ingredients
1/3 fill X.O. Café Coffee Liqueur
1/3 fill Sambuca
1/3 fill Matusalem Classic Black Rum

BLACK 'N' BLUE
Cocktail glass, chilled
Pour ingredients into iced mixing glass
1 1/2 oz. Original Polish Vodka
1/2 oz. Blue Curaçao
1/2 oz. cranberry juice
Stir and strain
Lime wedge garnish

BLACK ORCHID
Bucket glass, ice
Pour ingredients into iced mixing glass
1 oz. Bacardi Select Rum
1 oz. Blue Curaçao
1 1/2 oz. grenadine
1 1/2 oz. cranberry juice
Shake and strain
Float 3/4 oz. Gosling's Black Seal Rum
Orange slice garnish

BLACK RUBY
Coffee mug, heated
Build in glass
1 oz. Opal Nera Black Sambuca
3/4 oz. Tuaca
1 pinch each, sugar and cinnamon
Add lemon and orange zest
Fill with hot coffee

BLACK RUSSIAN
Rocks glass, ice
Build in glass
1 1/2 oz. Vodka
3/4 oz. Kahlúa Coffee Liqueur

BLACK JEWELED RUSSIAN
Rocks glass, ice
Build in glass
1 1/2 oz. Jewel of Russia Classic Vodka
1/2 oz. Drambuie Liqueur
1/2 oz. Kahlúa Coffee Liqueur

BLACK STOCKINGS
Cocktail glass, chilled
Pour ingredients into iced mixing glass
2 oz. Chopin Polish Vodka
3/4 oz. Chambord Liqueur
3/4 oz. Godiva Chocolate Liqueur
Stir and strain
Lemon twist garnish

BLACK SUN
Bucket glass, ice
Build in glass
1 1/2 oz. Mount Gay Eclipse Rum
3/4 oz. Cointreau Liqueur
3/4 oz. sweet 'n' sour
Fill with cola
Lime wheel garnish

BLACK TEQUILA ROSE
Brandy snifter
Layer in bottom of glass
1 oz. Razzmatazz Raspberry Liqueur
Add ice
Pour into center of glass
1 1/4 oz. Tequila Rose Cream Liqueur

BLACK VELVET
Tankard or pilsner glass, chilled
Build in glass
1/2 fill Guinness Stout
1/2 fill Champagne

BLACK VELVETEEN
Tankard or pilsner glass, chilled
Build in glass
1/2 fill Guinness Stout
1/2 fill hard apple cider

BLACK WATCH
Rocks glass, ice
Build in glass
1 1/2 oz. Dewar's White Label
   Scotch Whisky
1/2 oz. Kahlúa Coffee Liqueur
Lemon twist garnish

POURING TECHNIQUES

There are three, generally accepted methods of pouring liquor quickly and accurately behind the bar.

- **Free Pouring** is most often used with fast-paced drink making. Liquor is poured without the use of a measuring device and portioning is dependent on keeping an internal count. For example, a silent count of "one-thousand-one, one-thousand-two, one-thousand-three" will typically yield a 1 1/2 oz. portion. Liqueurs, because of their viscosity, will pour through the same spout at a slower rate.

  The real time savings of free pouring is that while one hand is holding the liquor bottle, the other hand is free to add mixer or a second product to the drink at the same time.

- **Hand-Measured Pouring** entails the use of a jigger, and while slower than free pouring, is more precise. The best way to master hand-measuring is to use a technique of visualizing an imaginary hinge between the lip of the glass and the jigger. As liquor begins filling the measure, the device is brought to the side of the glass as if a hinge existed between the two. The instant the portion is reached, the jigger is tipped into the glass and the bottle turned upright. The technique should be executed in one smooth motion and performed as quickly as possible.

- **Bottle-Attached Measures** are innovative control devices that are precise and easy-to-use. They rely on a series of three-ball bearings within the pour spout that work together to cut-off the flow of liquor at the prescribed measure. These spouts are available in a range of different portion sizes.

BLACK WIDOW
Bucket glass, ice
Build in glass
1 oz. Grey Goose Vodka
1 oz. Disaronno Amaretto Liqueur
Near fill with orange juice
Splash club soda
Orange slice garnish

BLAST FROM THE PAST
Cappuccino cup, heated
Build in glass
1/2 oz. Tia Maria
1/2 oz. Grand Marnier Liqueur
1/2 oz. Chambord Liqueur
Near fill with hot espresso coffee
Top with frothed milk
Sprinkle shaved chocolate

BLAST-OFF PUNCH
House specialty glass, ice
Pour ingredients into iced mixing glass
3/4 oz. Bacardi Light Rum
3/4 oz. Bacardi Gold Rum
3/4 oz. Blue Curaçao
1/2 oz. Cruzan Orange Rum
1 1/2 oz. sweet 'n' sour
1 1/2 oz. orange juice
Shake and strain
Float 3/4 oz. Mount Gay Extra Old Rum
Lime, lemon and orange wedge garnish

BLEACHER'S TWIST
Presentation shot glass, chilled
Layer ingredients
1/3 fill Kahlúa Coffee Liqueur
1/3 fill Chambord Liqueur
1/3 fill Baileys Irish Cream

BLENDED FROG
House specialty glass, chilled
Pour ingredients into blender
1 oz. Artic Vodka & Peach Liqueur
1 oz. DeKuyper Raspberry Pucker
3 oz. cranberry juice
2 scoops vanilla ice cream
Blend ingredients (with ice optional)

BLIZZARD (1)
House specialty glass, chilled
Pour ingredients into blender
2 oz. Jim Beam White Label Bourbon
1/2 oz. Rose's Lime Juice
1/2 oz. grenadine
1 1/2 oz. cranberry juice
2 oz. sweet 'n' sour
Blend with ice
Orange slice and cherry garnish

BLIZZARD (2)

House specialty glass, chilled
Pour ingredients into blender
1 1/4 oz. Matusalem Classic Black Rum
3/4 oz. Brandy
3/4 oz. Cruzan Rum Cream
3/4 oz. half & half cream
2 scoops chocolate ice cream
Blend ingredients (with ice optional)
Whipped cream garnish
Drizzle 3/4 oz. X.O. Café Coffee Liqueur
Sprinkle nutmeg

BLONDE TEASER (1)

Bucket glass, ice
Build in glass
3/4 oz. Ketel One Dutch Vodka
3/4 oz. DeKuyper Buttershots Schnapps
Fill with cola

BLONDE TEASER (2)

Bucket glass, ice
Build in glass
3/4 oz. Whaler's Hawaiian Vanille Rum
3/4 oz. DeKuyper Buttershots Schnapps
Fill with cola

BLOOD AND SAND (1)

Highball glass, ice
Build in glass
3/4 oz. Scotch Whisky
3/4 oz. Cherry Brandy
Fill with orange juice

BLOOD AND SAND (2)

Cocktail glass, chilled
Pour ingredients into iced mixing glass
1 1/4 oz. Scotch Whisky
1/2 oz. Sweet Vermouth
1/2 oz. Cherry Brandy
1 oz. orange juice
Shake and strain
Orange twist garnish

BLOOD ORANGE
CHAMPAGNE COCKTAIL

Champagne glass, chilled
Build in glass
1/2 fill blood orange juice
1/2 fill Champagne
Lemon twist garnish

BLOODY BRAIN

Presentation shot glass, chilled
Build in glass
1 oz. Baileys Irish Cream
1 oz. DeKuyper Peach Pucker
3 drops grenadine

BLOODY MARIA

Bucket glass, ice
Rim glass with salt (optional)
Build in glass
1 1/4 oz. Tequila
Fill with Bloody Mary mix
Lime wedge and celery garnish

BLOODY MARY

Bucket glass, ice
Rim glass with salt (optional)
Build in glass
1 1/4 oz. Vodka
Fill with Bloody Mary mix
Lime wedge and celery garnish

BLOODY MARY, BLOODHOUND

Bucket glass, ice
Build in glass
Rim glass with salt (optional)
1 oz. Zubrówka Bison Brand Vodka
1 oz. Dry Sack Sherry
Fill with Bloody Mary mix
Lime wedge and celery garnish

BLOODY MARY,
BLOODY BASTARD

Bucket glass, ice
Build in glass
Rim glass with salt (optional)
1/2 fill Bass Ale
1/2 fill Bloody Mary mix
1/2 tbsp. horseradish
Lime wedge and shrimp garnish

BLOODY MARY, BLOODY BISON

Bucket glass, ice
Rim glass with salt (optional)
Build in glass
1 1/4 oz. Zubrówka Bison Brand Vodka
Fill with Bull Shot
Lime wedge and celery garnish
Note: "Bull Shot" is 1/2 Bloody Mary mix
and 1/2 beef broth

BLOODY MARY, BLOODY BULL

Bucket glass, ice
Rim glass with salt (optional)
Build in glass
1 1/4 oz. Vodka
Fill with Bull Shot
Lime wedge and celery garnish
Note: "Bull Shot" is 1/2 Bloody Mary mix
and 1/2 beef broth

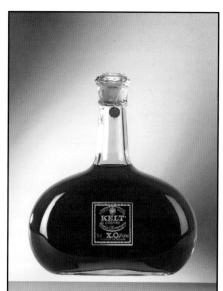

KELT® XO TOUR DU MONDE GRANDE CHAMPAGNE COGNAC

If you haven't had a vacation in years, you're not going to want to read any further. One of the highest rated brandies in the world—KELT XO TOUR DU MONDE GRANDE CHAMPAGNE COGNAC—takes a leisurely cruise around the world before being bottled.

The cognac takes this three-month sea voyage shortly after blending. While en route, the brandy is stored in small, 72-liter Limousin oak barrels that are lashed to the ship's deck. The gentle rolling of the ship at sea allows the blended cognac to fully integrate, while the constantly changing climate and fresh ocean air positively influence the aging brandy. Upon its return to France, the cognac is aged an additional year in oak casks.

Kelt XO Tour du Monde is an extraordinarily luxurious Grande Champagne cognac with an average age of 42 years. The brandy has a lush texture and medium-weight body. It has an expansive, alluring bouquet with rich fruity and floral aromas. The palate is a lavish affair featuring the delectable flavors of fruit, vanilla, spice and oak. The lingering, warm finish is a sublime pleasure.

Kelt XO Tour du Monde is a singular cognac worthy of the critical acclaim it has received.

BLOODY MARY, BLOODY CAESAR
House specialty glass, ice
Rim glass with salt (optional)
Build in glass
1 1/4 oz. VOX Vodka
Fill with Clamato juice
Lime wedge and celery garnish
Note: "Bloody Clam" may be substituted
   for Clamato juice (a mix of 1 1/2 oz. clam
   juice per serving of Bloody Mary mix)

BLOODY MARY, BLOODY CAJUN
Bucket glass, ice
Rim glass with salt (optional)
Build in glass
1 1/2 oz. Vodka
1/2 tsp. onion powder
1/4 tsp. crushed thyme leaves
1 pinch red pepper
2 pinches paprika
Fill with Bloody Mary mix
Lime wedge and celery garnish

BLOODY MARY, BLOODY ITALIAN
Bucket glass, ice
Rim glass with salt (optional)
Build in glass
1 1/2 oz. Vodka
1/4 tsp. Italian seasoning
2 pinches each, garlic powder and paprika
Fill with Bloody Mary mix
Lime wedge and celery garnish

BLOODY MARY, BLOODY FRENCH GOOSE
Bucket glass, ice
Rim glass with salt (optional)
Build in glass
1 1/2 oz. Grey Goose Vodka
1/4 tsp. Italian seasoning
2 pinches each, garlic powder and paprika
1/2 oz. fresh lime juice
Fill with Bloody Mary mix
Roasted garlic and celery garnish

BLOODY MARY, BLOODY MOOSE
Bucket or house specialty glass, ice
Rim glass with salt (optional)
Build in glass
1 1/2 oz. Zubrówka Bison Brand Vodka
Fill with Bloody Mary mix
Lime wedge and beef jerky garnish

BLOODY MARY, BLOODY NOSE (1)

Bucket or house specialty glass, ice
Rim glass with salt (optional)
Build in glass
1 1/2 oz. Zubrówka Bison Brand Vodka
Near fill with Bloody Mary mix
Float raw oyster
Lime wedge and celery garnish

BLOODY MARY, BLOODY NOSE (2)

Bucket or house specialty glass, ice
Rim glass with salt (optional)
Build in glass
1 1/2 oz. Absolut Peppar Vodka
1/2 tbsp. horseradish
Near fill with Bloody Mary mix
Float raw oyster
Lime wedge and celery garnish

BLOODY MARY, BLOODY RUSSIAN BASTARD

Bucket or house specialty glass, ice
Rim glass with salt (optional)
Build in glass
1 1/4 oz. Stolichnaya Limonnaya
   Russian Vodka
2 oz. Bass Ale
1/2 tbsp. horseradish
Fill with Bloody Mary mix
Lime wedge and shrimp garnish

BLOODY MARY, BLOODY TEX-MEX

Bucket or house specialty glass, ice
Rim glass with salt (optional)
Build in glass
1 1/2 oz. Dirty Olive Vodka
1/2 oz. chili powder
2 pinches each, ground cumin and paprika
Fill with Bloody Mary mix
Lime wedge and celery garnish

BLOODY MARY, BLOODY WRIGHT

Bucket glass, ice
Rim glass with salt (optional)
Build in glass
1 1/2 oz. Cruzan Estate Light Rum
Fill with Bloody Mary mix
Lime wedge and celery garnish

BLOODY MARY, DANISH (1)

Bucket glass, ice
Rim glass with salt (optional)
Build in glass
1 1/2 oz. Aquavit
1/2 tsp. horseradish
2 oz. Clamato juice
Fill with Bloody Mary mix
Lime wedge and celery garnish

BLOODY MARY, DANISH (2)

Bucket glass, ice
Rim glass with salt (optional)
Build in glass
1 1/4 oz. Aquavit
Fill with Bloody Mary mix
Lime wedge and celery garnish

BLOODY MARY, DIRTY

Bucket glass, ice
Rim glass with salt (optional)
Build in glass
1 1/2 oz. Dirty Olive Vodka
Fill with Bloody Mary mix
Olive and celery garnish

BLOODY MARY, DIRTY BLOODY CAJUN

Bucket glass, ice
Rim glass with salt (optional)
Build in glass
1 1/2 oz. Dirty Olive Vodka
1/2 tsp. onion powder
1/4 tsp. crushed thyme leaves
1 pinch red pepper
2 pinches paprika
Fill with Bloody Mary mix
Lime wedge, olive and celery

BLOODY MARY, GIN

aka **Gin Mary, Red Snapper**
Bucket glass, ice
Rim glass with salt (optional)
Build in glass
1 1/4 oz. Gin
Fill with Bloody Mary mix
Lime wedge and celery garnish

BLOODY MARY, JÄGER SALSA

House specialty glass, ice
Rim glass with salt (optional)
Build in glass
1 1/4 oz. Jägermeister Liqueur
2 tsp. salsa, medium-hot
Fill with Bloody Mary mix
Lime wedge and celery garnish

ORIGINAL CRISTALL® RUSSIAN VODKA

The centuries old Cristall Distillery in the heart of Moscow is at the center of the Russian vodka universe. Before the end of the cold war, Stolichnaya Cristall was the finest vodka available in the United States. The Kremlin kept a tight rein on how much of the good stuff was exported to the West.

This incomparable vodka is again available in the United States, and we as a country are better for it. It is now labeled as ORIGINAL CRISTALL RUSSIAN VODKA. Its appealing taste is the result of being triple-distilled from winter wheat and glacier water. The vodka is filtered through quartz crystals and birch charcoal to achieve its impeccable quality and ultra-clean finish.

Original Cristall is an exceptional vodka. It has pristine clarity and an enticing floral bouquet. The vodka's full, supple body immediately warms the mouth, then it slowly ebbs away in a finish marked with notes of chocolate and vanilla. While often showcased in cocktails, Original Cristall is ideally served straight-up or over ice.

To add to their already long list of accomplishments, the distillery has released CRISTALL LEMON TWIST RUSSIAN VODKA, a silky smooth spirit imbued with a delightful citrus personality.

BLOODY MARY, MANGO
Bucket glass, ice
Rim glass with salt (optional)
Build in glass
1 1/4 oz. Mango-infused Vodka
Fill with Mango Bloody Mary mix
Lime wedge, celery and mango slice garnish
Note: See **Mars Mango Infusion** and
Mango Bloody Mary Mix

BLOODY MARY, MICHILATA
Pint glass, ice
Rim glass with salt (optional)
Pour ingredients into iced mixing glass
1 1/2 oz. Herradura Reposado Tequila
3/4 oz. fresh lime juice
1/2 oz. fresh lemon juice
4 dashes Tabasco Sauce
1/4 oz. white wine vinegar
2 pinches each, salt, black pepper, and
    seasoned salt
3 oz. tomato juice
Shake and strain
Fill with Tecate Mexican Beer
Lime wedge garnish

BLOODY MARY MIX
Large covered jar
Mix per instructions
46 oz. tomato juice
2 oz. Worcestershire sauce
6 dashes Tabasco Sauce
2 tbsp. celery salt
1 tbsp. black pepper
1/2 tbsp. salt
2 dashes Angostura Bitters
Thoroughly mix ingredients and taste-test over ice. Keep refrigerated.
Optional ingredients: prepared horseradish; V-8; clamato juice; clam juice; pureed Mexican salsa; Mexican hot sauce; fresh lemon juice; fresh lime juice; beef bouillon; seasoned salt; cayenne pepper; onion powder; garlic salt/powder; diced or pureed jalapeño pepper; cilantro; A-1 sauce; chili powder; Italian seasonings; paprika; red pepper; crushed thyme leaves; ground cumin.

BLOODY MARY MIX, MANGO
Large covered jar
Pour ingredients into blender
2 cups mango cubes
1 tsp. chili powder
1 tsp. ginger powder
1 tbsp. black pepper, cracked
1 dash Tabasco Sauce
1/2 tsp. horseradish
4 cups V-8 juice
Thoroughly blend ingredients
Taste test, serve over ice
Note: See **Mango Bloody Mary**

BLOODY MARY, VIRGIN
aka **Bloody Shame**
Bucket or house specialty glass, ice
Rim glass with salt (optional)
Build in glass
Fill with Bloody Mary mix
Lime wedge and celery garnish

BLOODY MARY,
WHAT? ME WORRY
House specialty glass, ice
Rim glass with salt (optional)
Build in glass
4 oz. Alcohol-free Beer
Fill with Bloody Mary mix
Lime wedge and shrimp garnish

BLOODY MARY, WHARF POPPER
Bucket glass, ice
Build in glass
1 1/2 oz. Aquavit
1/2 oz. fresh lemon juice
2 pinches basil
Fill with Bloody Mary mix
Lime wedge and scallion garnish

BLOW JOB (1)
Presentation shot glass, chilled
Build in glass
1/3 fill Grand Marnier Liqueur
1/3 fill Crème de Banana
Near fill with Tia Maria
Whipped cream garnish

BLOW JOB (2)
Presentation shot glass, chilled
Build in glass
1/2 fill Grand Marnier Liqueur
Near fill with Baileys Irish Cream
Whipped cream garnish

BLUE BAYOU (1)
Bucket glass, ice
Build in glass
1 1/2 oz. Artic Vodka & Melon Liqueur
3/4 oz. Blue Curaçao
1/2 fill pineapple juice
1/2 fill grapefruit juice

BLUE BAYOU (2)
House specialty glass, chilled
Pour ingredients into blender
1 1/2 oz. Bacardi Light Rum
1 oz. Blue Curaçao
3/4 oz. half & half cream
2 scoops French vanilla ice cream
Blend ingredients (with ice optional)
Orange slice and cherry garnish

BLUEBERRY LEMON FIZZ
House specialty glass, chilled
Pour ingredients into blender
6 oz. blueberry yogurt
1/2 oz. grenadine
2 oz. lemon-lime soda
2 scoops lemon sherbet
Blend ingredients (with ice optional)
Pineapple wedge garnish

BLUEBERRY TEA
Tea cup or coffee mug, heated
Build in glass
3/4 oz. Grand Marnier Liqueur
3/4 oz. Disaronno Amaretto Liqueur
Fill with hot tea
Lemon wedge garnish

BLUE BLAZER
Mug or tankard
Build in glass
2 oz. Scotch Whisky
3/4 oz. honey
1/4 oz. fresh lemon juice
3 oz. hot water
*Combine ingredients and bring slowly
to a boil allowing honey to dissolve
before serving.*
Note: Traditionally prepared aflame,
this is an extremely dangerous and
highly discouraged practice.

BLUE DEVIL
aka **Blue Moon**
Cocktail glass, chilled
Pour ingredients into iced mixing glass
1 oz. Gin
1/2 oz. Blue Curaçao
1 1/2 oz. sweet 'n' sour
Shake and strain

DISARONNO®
ORIGINALE AMARETTO

Legend has it that the recipe for DISARONNO ORIGINALE AMARETTO originated in Saronno, Italy in 1525. Known as the "liqueur of love," it was passed through the creator's family for generations until it was acquired in 1817 by Carlo Dominico Reina, who began selling the liqueur in his apothecary. It wasn't until after World War I that the liqueur was marketed outside of Saronno.

In 1939, the century-old firm of Illva Saronno began producing the famous liqueur under the name Amaretto di Saronno. Its proprietary recipe is still made with a base of premium Italian grape spirits, which is patiently steeped with 17 herbs and fruits, including apricot kernel oil. Once fully infused with flavor, the liqueur is sweetened with caramelized sugar and bottled at 56 proof.

Disaronno Originale Amaretto is a *grand dame* of liqueurs; one often imitated yet never equaled. It has a burnished, copper hue and medium-weight, satiny smooth body. The generous bouquet is laced with the aromas of marzipan and citrus zest. Its palate rapidly fills the mouth with the marvelous, semi-sweet flavors of almonds, oranges and vanilla. The finish is long and flavorful.

Disaronno Originale Amaretto is altogether indispensable behind the bar, as evidenced by the exceptionally large numbers of drinks in which it is featured.

BLUE DUCK
Bucket glass, ice
Build in glass
1 1/2 oz. Stolichnaya Russian Vodka
3/4 oz. Beefeater London Dry Gin
3/4 oz. Briottet Crème de Pêche
1/4 oz. Blue Curaçao
1/4 oz. fresh lemon juice
Fill with tonic water
Lime wheel garnish

BLUE FLUTE
Champagne glass, chilled
Build in glass
1 1/4 oz. Disaronno Amaretto Liqueur
3/4 oz. Blue Curaçao
Fill with Champagne
Orange twist garnish

BLUE HAWAII
House specialty glass, chilled
Pour ingredients into blender
1 1/2 oz. Cruzan Estate Light Rum
1 oz. Blue Curaçao
3/4 oz. White Crème de Cacao
3/4 oz. half & half cream
2 scoops vanilla ice cream
Blend ingredients (with ice optional)
Orange slice and cherry garnish

BLUE HAWAIIAN
Collins or bucket glass, ice
Pour ingredients into iced mixing glass
1 1/2 oz. Bacardi Light Rum
1 oz. Mount Gay Eclipse Rum
1 oz. Blue Curaçao
1 1/2 oz. sweet 'n' sour
1 1/2 oz. pineapple juice
1 1/2 oz. coconut cream syrup
Shake and strain
Pineapple wedge and orange slice garnish

BLUE LADY
Cocktail glass, chilled
Pour ingredients into iced mixing glass
1 1/2 oz. Bombay Sapphire London Dry Gin
1/2 oz. Blue Curaçao
1 1/2 oz. sweet 'n' sour
Shake and strain

BLUE LAGOON (1)
Bucket glass, ice
Build in glass
1 1/2 oz. Cruzan Coconut Rum
3/4 oz. Cruzan Pineapple Rum
Near fill with pineapple juice
Float 3/4 oz. Blue Curaçao

BLUE LAGOON (2)
Bucket glass, ice
Build in glass
1 oz. Malibu Rum
Near fill with pineapple juice
Float 3/4 oz. Blue Curaçao

BLUE LEMONADE
Bucket glass, ice
Build in glass
1 1/2 oz. Absolut Citron Vodka
3/4 oz. Blue Curaçao
Fill with lemonade

BLUE MARLIN
Cocktail glass, chilled
Pour ingredients into iced mixing glass
1 1/2 oz. Appleton Estate V/X Jamaica Rum
1 1/4 oz. Mount Gay Eclipse Rum
3/4 oz. Blue Curaçao
1/2 oz. Citrónge Orange Liqueur
1 oz. fresh lime juice
Shake and strain
Lime wedge garnish

BLUE MOON CAFÉ
Sherry glass, chilled
Build in glass
1/3 fill Blue Curaçao
1/3 fill orange juice
1/3 fill Champagne

BLUE TAIL FLY
Cocktail glass, chilled
Pour ingredients into iced mixing glass
1/2 oz. White Crème de Cacao
1/2 oz. Blue Curaçao
2 oz. half & half cream
Shake and strain

BLUE TRAIN SPECIAL
Champagne glass, chilled
Pour ingredients into iced mixing glass
1 oz. Christian Brothers Brandy
1 oz. pineapple juice
Shake and strain
Fill with Champagne
Lemon twist garnish

BLUE WAVE
Bucket glass, ice
Build in glass
1 1/2 oz. El Jimador Reposado Tequila
3/4 oz. Blue Curaçao
Fill with lemonade
Orange slice and cherry garnish

BLUE WHALE
Bucket glass, ice
Build in glass
1 1/2 oz. DeKuyper Peachtree Schnapps
3/4 oz. Blue Curaçao
Fill with Seven-Up

BLUSH
Cocktail glass, chilled
Pour ingredients into iced mixing glass
2 oz. Belvedere Polish Vodka
1/2 oz. Briottet Crème de Cassis
Stir and strain
Lemon twist garnish

BLUSHING ANGEL
Champagne glass, chilled
Pour ingredients into iced mixing glass
1 1/2 oz. Dubonnet Rouge
2 1/2 oz. cranberry juice
Shake and strain
Fill with Champagne
Lemon twist garnish

BLUSHING BERRY COOLER
House specialty glass, chilled
Pour ingredients into blender
1 1/2 oz. Kahlúa Coffee Liqueur
4 oz. strawberry puree or
   1/2 cup frozen strawberries
2 1/2 oz. milk
2 oz. plain lowfat yogurt
2 oz. orange juice concentrate, frozen
Blend with ice

BOBBY BURNS
Cocktail glass, chilled
Pour ingredients into iced mixing glass
1 1/2 oz. Scotch Whisky
1/2 oz. Sweet Vermouth
1/2 oz. Drambuie Liqueur
Stir and strain

BOBSLEDDER'S BANSHEE
House specialty glass, chilled
Pour ingredients into blender
1 oz. Dr. McGillicuddy's
   Mentholmint Schnapps
1 oz. Baileys Irish Cream
1/2 oz. half & half cream
2 chocolate chip cookies
2 scoops vanilla ice cream
Blend ingredients (with ice optional)
Chocolate chip cookie garnish

BOCCI BALL
Highball glass, ice
Build in glass
1 1/4 oz. Disaronno Amaretto Liqueur
Near fill with orange juice
Splash club soda

EL TESORO DE DON FELIPE®
SILVER TEQUILA

EL TESORO DE DON FELIPE 100% AGAVE TEQUILAS are handmade at a small distillery named La Alteña located high in the Los Altos mountains. There the Camarena family makes tequila the same way they have for over 50 years, using time-honored traditions long since abandoned by others as too expensive.

The EL TESORO SILVER TEQUILA is a remarkable spirit. It is aromatic, peppery and loaded with the robust character and clean, crisp flavor of blue agave. The tequila is distilled to proof with no water added and bottled within 24 hours of distillation—unfiltered and unaltered, exactly as it came out of the still.

The EL TESORO AÑEJO is aged for 2 to 3 years in oak bourbon barrels. It has a deep, satisfying bouquet, an exceptionally rich, well-rounded flavor and a long, lingering finish.

EL TESORO PARADISO is an innovative style of tequila. It is a 5-year-old añejo, hand-crafted from a blend of El Tesoro tequilas that are further aged in French oak barrels previously used to age A. de Fussigny Cognac.

Paradiso strikes a sublime balance between the elegance of cognac and the sultry character of tequila, both of which are deeply imbued in its bouquet, body, flavor and finish.

El Tesoro was one of the first boutique tequilas, sample some and see why.

BOCCI SHOOTER
Presentation shot glass, chilled
Build in glass
1/2 fill Disaronno Amaretto Liqueur
Near fill with orange juice
Splash club soda

BODY WARMER
Tea cup or coffee mug, heated
Build in glass
1 1/4 oz. Grand Marnier Liqueur
1/2 oz. simple syrup (optional)
Fill with hot tea

BOG FOG
Highball glass, ice
Build in glass
1 1/4 oz. Bacardi Light Rum
1/2 fill cranberry juice
1/2 fill orange juice

BOGS & BUBBLES
Champagne glass, chilled
Build in glass
1/2 fill cranberry juice
1/2 fill Champagne

BOILERMAKER
Shot glass and beer mug
Build in shot glass
1 1/2 oz. Whiskey
Build in mug
Fill with Draft Beer

BOINA ROJA
House specialty glass, ice
Pour ingredients into iced mixing glass
1 1/2 oz. Bacardi Light Rum
3/4 oz. Bacardi Gold Rum
1/2 oz. grenadine
1 oz. fresh lime juice
1 1/2 oz. sweet 'n' sour
Shake and strain
Mint sprig and cherry garnish

BOMB
House specialty glass, ice
Pour ingredients into iced mixing glass
1 oz. Dewar's White Label Scotch Whisky
1 oz. Jim Beam Black Label Bourbon
1/2 oz. Foursquare Spiced Rum
1 1/2 oz. orange juice
1 1/2 oz. pineapple juice
Shake and strain
Float 3/4 oz. Razzmatazz Raspberry Liqueur

BOMBAY GRAND
Cocktail glass, chilled
Pour ingredients into iced mixing glass
1 oz. Bombay Sapphire London Dry Gin
1/2 oz. Grand Marnier Liqueur
1 1/2 oz. sweet 'n' sour
Shake and strain
Orange twist garnish

BOMBAY SPIDER
Bucket glass, ice
Build in glass
1 1/4 oz. Bombay Sapphire London Dry Gin
3 dashes Angostura Bitters
Fill with ginger ale

BOMB POP
Bucket glass, ice
Build in glass
1 oz. Artic Vodka & Melon Liqueur
1 oz. Midori Melon Liqueur
1 oz. DeKuyper Watermelon Pucker
3/4 oz. sweet 'n' sour
Fill with Seven-Up

BONAPARTE
Brandy snifter, heated
Build in glass
1 3/4 oz. Courvoisier V.S.O.P. Cognac
3/4 oz. Mandarine Napoléon Liqueur

BORINQUEN
House specialty glass, chilled
Pour ingredients into blender
1 1/2 oz. Cruzan Estate Light Rum
1 oz. Rhum Barbancourt 5-Star
3/4 oz. Rose's Lime Juice
2 oz. orange juice
2 oz. passion fruit syrup
2 oz. fresh lime juice
Blend with ice
Float 3/4 oz. Matusalem Red Flame Rum
Pineapple wedge and cherry garnish

BOSOM CARESSER
Cocktail glass, chilled
Pour ingredients into iced mixing glass
1 1/2 oz. Brandy
1/2 oz. Triple Sec
3 dashes grenadine
1 egg yolk (optional)
Shake and strain

BOSSA NOVA
House specialty glass, ice
Pour ingredients into iced mixing glass
2 oz. Bacardi Limón Rum
1 1/2 oz. fresh lime juice
2 oz. sweet 'n' sour
2 oz. passion fruit juice
Shake and strain
Float 1 oz. Bacardi Select Rum
Lime wedge and orange slice garnish

BOTTOM BOUNCER
Presentation shot glass, chilled
Build in glass
1 oz. Baileys Irish Cream
1 oz. DeKuyper Buttershots Schnapps

BRAHMA BULL
Rocks glass, ice
Build in glass
1 1/2 oz. Jose Cuervo Especial Tequila
3/4 oz. Tia Maria

BRAIN SHOOTER
Cordial or sherry glass, chilled
Build in glass
3/4 oz. Baileys Irish Cream
1/2 oz. DeKuyper Peppermint Schnapps
3 drops grenadine in center

BRAINSTORM COCKTAIL
Cocktail glass, chilled
Pour ingredients into iced mixing glass
1 1/2 oz. Irish (or Rye) Whiskey
1/2 oz. B & B Liqueur
1/2 oz. Dry Vermouth
Stir and strain
Orange twist garnish

BRANDY ALEXANDER
Cocktail glass, chilled
Pour ingredients into iced mixing glass
3/4 oz. Brandy
3/4 oz. Dark Crème de Cacao
1 1/2 oz. half & half cream
Shake and strain
Sprinkle nutmeg

BRANDY EGG NOG (1)
House specialty glass, ice
Pour ingredients into iced mixing glass
1 1/2 oz. Christian Brothers Brandy
1 tsp. sugar
1 egg (optional)
3 dashes vanilla extract
4 oz. half & half cream
Shake and strain
Sprinkle nutmeg

GENTLEMAN JACK RARE TENNESSEE WHISKEY

GENTLEMAN JACK RARE TENNESSEE WHISKEY is the first new whiskey released by Jack Daniel's Distillery in almost 100 years. It is handcrafted from a recipe created by Jack Daniel himself at the turn of the century, and the result is an American masterpiece.

The exact mash bill used to make this superb whiskey is a closely guarded secret, however, it is no doubt still made with the same limestone spring water that helped make Jack Daniel's a worldwide brand.

The whiskey is aged in oak barrels for 4 years, and then mellowed twice in Tennessee sugar maple charcoal, once before being put in wood and once again after.

A whiskey this wonderful could only have been conceived by Jack Daniel himself. The bouquet is a complex affair with ribbons of honey, raisins, oak and a hint of smoke. The whiskey has a medium-weight body that slides effortlessly over the palate, leaving behind a marvelous array of sweet honey and maple flavors. The finish is warm, flavorful and lingering.

To best appreciate how rare Gentleman Jack really is, present it neat with some spring water on the side. But don't stop there, this whiskey is spry enough to be the featured attraction in numerous cocktails.

BRANDY EGG NOG (2)
Coffee mug, heated
Build in glass
3/4 oz. Brandy
3/4 oz. Dark Crème de Cacao
Fill with hot milk
Sprinkle nutmeg

BRANDY GUMP
Cocktail glass, chilled
Pour ingredients into iced mixing glass
1 oz. Brandy
1/2 oz. grenadine
1 1/2 oz. sweet 'n' sour
Shake and strain

BRASS MONKEY
Cocktail glass, chilled
Pour ingredients into iced mixing glass
1 1/2 oz. Sea Wynde Pot Still Rum
1 1/2 oz. Grey Goose Vodka
3/4 oz. orange juice
Shake and strain

BRAVE BULL
Rocks glass, ice
Build in glass
1 1/2 oz. Tequila
3/4 oz. Kahlúa Coffee Liqueur

BRAWNY BROTH
Coffee mug, heated
Build in glass
1 1/4 oz. Zubrówka Bison Brand Vodka
Fill with hot beef bouillon
1 dash lemon pepper
Lemon wedge garnish

BRAZIL
Cocktail glass, chilled
Pour ingredients into iced mixing glass
1 oz. Dry Vermouth
1 oz. Dry Sherry
1/4 oz. Pernod
2-3 dashes Angostura Bitters
Stir and strain
Lemon twist garnish

BRILLIANT LEMON DROP
Cocktail glass, chilled
Rim glass with sugar
Pour ingredients into iced mixing glass
2 oz. Brilliant Vodka
1/2 tsp. sugar
1/2 oz. fresh lemon juice
Shake and strain
Sprinkle 1/2 tsp. sugar
Lemon wheel garnish

BRILLIANT SONIC
Highball glass, ice
Build in glass
1 1/4 oz. Brilliant Vodka
1/2 fill club soda
1/2 fill tonic water
Lime wedge garnish

BROOKLYN
Cocktail glass, chilled
Pour ingredients into iced mixing glass
1/2 oz. Dry Vermouth
1 1/2 oz. Gentleman Jack Tennessee Whiskey
1 dash Amer Picon or Angostura Bitters
Stir and strain

BROWN COW
Rocks glass, ice
Build in glass
1 1/2 oz. W.L. Weller Bourbon
3/4 oz. Hershey's chocolate syrup
3/4 oz. half & half cream

BROWN COW MILKSHAKE
House specialty glass, chilled
Pour ingredients into blender
2 oz. W.L. Weller Bourbon
1 1/2 oz. Hershey's chocolate syrup
1 oz. half & half cream
2 scoops vanilla ice cream
Blend ingredients (with ice optional)
Whipped cream garnish
Sprinkle shaved chocolate

BROWN DRINK
House specialty glass, ice
Build in glass
1 1/2 oz. Stolichnaya Razberi Russian Vodka
3 oz. Dr. Pepper
Fill with Guinness Stout

BROWN SQUIRREL
Cocktail glass, chilled
Pour ingredients into iced mixing glass
1/2 oz. Disaronno Amaretto Liqueur
1/2 oz. Dark Crème de Cacao
2 oz. half & half cream
Shake and strain

BROWN VELVET
Tankard or pilsner glass, chilled
Build in glass
2 oz. Tawny Port
Fill with Anchor Steam Beer

BRUT 'N' BOGS
Champagne glass, chilled
Build in glass
1 oz. Chambord Liqueur
1/2 fill cranberry juice
1/2 fill Champagne

B-STING
Cocktail glass, chilled
Pour ingredients into iced mixing glass
1 1/2 oz. B & B Liqueur
1/2 oz. DeKuyper Peppermint Schnapps
Stir and strain

BUBBLE GUM
Rocks glass, chilled
Pour ingredients into iced mixing glass
1/2 oz. Southern Comfort Liqueur
1/2 oz. Disaronno Amaretto Liqueur
1/2 oz. Crème de Banana
1/2 oz. milk
2 dashes grenadine
Shake and strain

BUBBLE ZAZA
Champagne glass, chilled
Pour ingredients into iced mixing glass
3/4 oz. Zone Peach Italian Vodka
3/4 oz. DeKuyper Watermelon Pucker
3/4 oz. orange juice
Shake and strain
Fill with Champagne
Lemon twist garnish

BUCK
Highball glass, ice
Build in glass
1 1/4 oz. requested liquor
Fill with ginger ale
Lemon wedge garnish

BUCKHEAD ROOT BEER
Highball glass, ice
Build in glass
1 1/4 oz. Jägermeister Liqueur
Fill with club soda
Lime wedge garnish

BUCKING BRONCO
Rocks glass, chilled
Pour ingredients into iced mixing glass
3/4 oz. Jägermeister Liqueur
3/4 oz. Myers's Jamaican Rum
3/4 oz. Tropico
3/4 oz. pineapple juice
Shake and strain
Lime wedge garnish

KAHLÚA® COFFEE LIQUEUR

The exact origins of the KAHLÚA COFFEE LIQUEUR recipe are a matter of debate. Those that contend it originated in Morocco, point to the Moorish archway depicted on the label as one piece of evidence.

What is known, however, is that Kahlúa has been made in Mexico for nearly a century and that it steadfastly remains one of the best-selling liqueurs in the world.

Kahlúa is made from a base of distilled sugar cane that is steeped with vanilla and mountain-grown Mexican coffee. The liqueur has a deep brown color, a velvety smooth texture and a freshly ground coffee bouquet. Kahlúa's well-rounded body delivers the rich flavors of roasted coffee, cocoa and mint. While moderately sweet, it is never cloying or overbearing. The liqueur has a long, flavorful finish.

Kahlúa was first imported into the United States after the repeal of Prohibition and quickly became a favorite with this country's mixologists. One of the liqueur's strong suits is that it mixes with a seemingly endless combination of products.

As testimony to its nearly universal mixability, Kahlúa is one of the most frequently used ingredients in this or any other drink guide. Obviously this is a "must have" product.

BUDDHA SHOOTER
Presentation shot glass, chilled
Build in glass
1 oz. NapaSaki Saké
1 oz. La Piz Añejo Tequila

BUFFALO SWEAT
Presentation shot glass, chilled
Build in glass
1 3/4 oz. Wild Turkey 101° Bourbon
3 dashes Tabasco Sauce

BUKHARA COFFEE
House specialty glass, chilled
Pour ingredients into blender
1 1/4 oz. Stolichnaya Vanil Russian Vodka
3/4 oz. Baileys Irish Cream
1/2 oz. White Crème de Cacao
2 oz. coffee
2 scoops vanilla ice cream
Blend ingredients (with ice optional)
Whipped cream garnish
Sprinkle shaved chocolate

BULL AND BEAR
Cocktail glass, chilled
Pour ingredients into iced mixing glass
1 1/2 oz. W.L. Weller Bourbon
3/4 oz. Mandarine Napoléon Liqueur
1/4 oz. Briottet Crème de Cassis
1/2 oz. Rose's Lime Juice
Stir and strain
Orange slice and cherry garnish

BULLFIGHTER
Presentation shot glass, chilled
Layer ingredients
1/2 fill Kahlúa Coffee Liqueur
1/2 fill Tequila

BULLFROG (1)
Highball glass, ice
Build in glass
1 1/4 oz. Van Hoo Belgium Vodka
Fill with lemonade
Lemon twist garnish

BULLFROG (2)
Bucket glass, ice
Build in glass
1 1/2 oz. Southern Comfort Liqueur
3/4 oz. Midori Melon Liqueur
2 1/2 oz. sweet 'n' sour
Fill with Seven-Up

BUMBLE BEE
Pilsner glass, chilled
Build in glass
1/2 fill with Honey Lager
1/2 fill with Guinness Stout

BURGUNDY BISHOP
Bucket glass, ice
Pour ingredients into iced mixing glass
1 1/2 oz. Bacardi Light Rum
2 oz. sweet 'n' sour
3 oz. Dry Red Wine
Shake and strain
Lime, lemon and orange wedge garnish

BURGUNDY COCKTAIL
Wine glass, chilled
Pour ingredients into iced mixing glass
3 oz. Dry Red Wine
3/4 oz. V.S. Cognac
1/2 oz. Chambord Liqueur
Stir and strain
Lemon twist garnish

BURNT SIENNA
House specialty glass, ice
Pour ingredients into iced mixing glass
3/4 oz. Jim Beam White Label Bourbon
3/4 oz. Yukon Jack Liqueur
3/4 oz. Midori Melon Liqueur
1/4 oz. Chambord Liqueur
1 oz. orange juice
1 oz. cranberry juice
2 oz. sweet 'n' sour
Shake and strain
Lime wedge garnish

BUSH TICKLER
House specialty glass, chilled
Pour ingredients into blender
1 1/2 oz. Bacardi Select Rum
1 oz. Mount Gay Eclipse Rum
3/4 oz. Dark Crème de Cacao
1/2 oz. half & half cream
2 oz. coconut cream syrup
3 oz. pineapple juice
Blend with ice
Float 3/4 oz. Kahlúa Coffee Liqueur
Pineapple wedge and cherry garnish

BUSHWACKER
House specialty glass, chilled
Pour ingredients into blender
1 1/4 oz. Bacardi Light Rum
1 oz. Gosling's Black Seal Rum
3/4 oz. half & half cream
2 1/2 oz. coconut cream syrup
Blend with ice
Float 3/4 oz. Kahlúa Coffee Liqueur
Pineapple wedge and cherry garnish

BUSTED RUBBER
Presentation shot glass, chilled
Layer ingredients
1/3 fill DeKuyper Raspberry Pucker
1/3 fill Baileys Irish Cream
1/3 fill Grand Marnier Liqueur

BUTTERFINGER
Presentation shot glass, chilled
Layer ingredients
1/3 fill Godiva Chocolate Liqueur
1/3 fill DeKuyper Buttershots Schnapps
1/3 fill Baileys Irish Cream

BUTTERSCOTCH HOP
House specialty glass, chilled
Pour ingredients into blender
3/4 oz. DeKuyper Buttershots Schnapps
3/4 oz. Kahlúa Coffee Liqueur
3/4 oz. Whaler's Hawaiian Vanille Rum
2 scoops vanilla ice cream
Blend ingredients (with ice optional)

BUTTERSCOTCH SLIDE
House specialty glass, chilled
Pour ingredients into blender
3/4 oz. Baileys Irish Cream
3/4 oz. Kahlúa Coffee Liqueur
3/4 oz. DeKuyper Buttershots Schnapps
2 oz. milk
Blend with ice

BUZZ BOMB
Champagne glass, chilled
Pour ingredients into iced mixing glass
1/2 oz. Cognac
1/2 oz. B & B Liqueur
1/2 oz. Cointreau Liqueur
1/2 oz. sweet 'n' sour
Shake and strain
Fill with Champagne
Lemon wheel garnish

BYRRH COCKTAIL
Cocktail glass, chilled
Pour ingredients into iced mixing glass
1 oz. Byrrh
1 oz. Gin
1/2 oz. Dry Vermouth (optional)
Stir and strain
Lemon twist garnish

CABIN FEVER CURE
Coffee mug, heated
Build in glass
1/2 oz. Finlandia Vodka
1/2 oz. Foursquare Spiced Rum
1/2 oz. Rumple Minze Schnapps
Near fill with hot chocolate
Whipped cream garnish
Sprinkle shaved chocolate

DRINK ORIGINS
How's Your Linkage with the Past?

1. What classic rum drink was named for a mine located near Santiago, Cuba at the turn of the century?
2. This famous drink was created by Fernand Petiot at Harry's New York Bar in Paris in 1924.
3. This drink originated in France during World War I and was named after a famed artillery piece.
4. This classic cocktail originated in San Francisco in the 1880's as the "Martinez Cocktail."
5. What classic tropical drink was invented by Trader Vic Bergeron and originally garnished with a fresh orchid?
6. This classic mixed drink originated at the Louisville Pendernis Club and was first served to famed bourbon producer, Colonel James Pepper.
7. The Buena Vista Cafe located at Fisherman's Wharf in San Francisco is credited with popularizing what famous hot drink?
8. This colorful tropical concoction actually originated at the Zanzibar Club in London.
9. The combination of Pernod and champagne was popularized by what great American author?
10. What classic cocktail was introduced at an exclusive New York club in 1874?
11. Which wine-based drink is named after a mayor of Dijon, France?
12. This famous rum based drink originated in 1954 at the Caribe Hilton Hotel.
13. What legendary mixologist invented the Blue Blazer?
14. This effervescent concoction was first devised at Harry's Bar in Venice during World War II.
15. What drink is closely associated with the running of the Kentucky Derby?

Answers
1. Daiquiri
2. Bloody Mary
3. French 75
4. Martini
5. Mai Tai
6. Old Fashioned
7. Irish Coffee
8. Blue Hawaiian
9. Ernest Hemingway
10. Manhattan
11. Kir
12. Piña Colada
13. Professor Jerry Thomas
14. Bellini
15. Mint Julep

CACTUS JUICE
Bucket glass, ice
Build in glass
1 1/4 oz. El Tesoro Silver Tequila
3/4 oz. Disaronno Amaretto Liqueur
Fill with lemonade
Lemon wedge garnish

CACTUS MOON
Bucket glass, ice
Build in glass
1 1/2 oz. Original Cristall Russian Vodka
1/2 oz. Mandarine Napoléon Liqueur
1/2 oz. Villa Massa Limoncello
Fill with lemonade
Lemon wedge garnish

CADENHEAD'S KNIGHT
Cocktail glass, chilled
Pour ingredients into iced mixing glass
2 1/2 oz. Old Raj Dry Gin
1/8 oz. fresh lime juice
Stir and strain
Lemon twist garnish

CAFÉ A LA CABANA
Coffee mug, heated
Build in glass
3/4 oz. Matusalem Gran Reserva Rum
3/4 oz. Licor 43 (Cuarenta y Tres)
1/2 oz. Godiva Chocolate Liqueur
Near fill with hot coffee
Whipped cream garnish

CAFÉ AMORE
Coffee mug, heated
Build in glass
1/2 oz. Godiva Chocolate Liqueur
1/2 oz. Disaronno Amaretto Liqueur
1/2 oz. Tia Maria
1/2 oz. V.S. Cognac
Near fill with hot coffee
Whipped cream garnish

CAFÉ BRÛLOT
2 Demitasse cups, heated
Heat in a shallow bowl
1 oz. Laird's 12-Year Apple Brandy
1 oz. Cointreau Liqueur
Lemon and orange horse's neck
   (a continuous peel)
1 cinnamon stick
4 cloves
Ignite mixture
Ladle flaming liquid over orange peel
1 1/2 cups hot coffee
*Slowly pour hot coffee into bowl
   to extinguish flame*
Pour into demitasse cups

CAFÉ CHARLES
2 Irish coffee glasses, heated
Build in one glass
3/4 oz. Metaxa 5 Star Brandy
3/4 oz. Galliano Liqueur
3/4 oz. Kahlúa Coffee Liqueur
Ignite and split flaming mixture
between glasses
Near fill each glass with hot coffee
to extinguish flames
Whipped cream garnish
Sprinkle shaved chocolate

CAFÉ CHOCOLATE (1)
Coffee mug, heated
Build in glass
3/4 oz. Kahlúa Coffee Liqueur
3/4 oz. Baileys Irish Cream
1/2 oz. Dark Crème de Cacao
1/2 oz. Grand Marnier Liqueur
1 oz. chocolate syrup
Near fill with hot coffee
Whipped cream garnish
Sprinkle shaved chocolate

CAFÉ CHOCOLATE (2)
Coffee mug, heated
Build in glass
3/4 oz. Gran Gala Orange Liqueur
3/4 oz. Kahlúa Coffee Liqueur
3/4 oz. Baileys Irish Cream
1/2 oz. Dark Crème de Cacao
1 oz. Hershey's chocolate syrup
Near fill with hot coffee
Whipped cream garnish
Sprinkle shaved chocolate

CAFÉ CHOPIN
Cocktail glass, chilled
Pour ingredients into iced mixing glass
1 3/4 oz. Chopin Polish Vodka
1/2 oz. Kahlúa Coffee Liqueur
1/2 oz. Ballylarkin Irish Liqueur
Stir and strain

CAFÉ CONTENTÉ
Coffee mug, heated
Build in glass
3/4 oz. Cruzan Estate Diamond Rum
3/4 oz. Kahlúa Coffee Liqueur
3/4 oz. Chambord Liqueur
Fill with hot coffee
Whipped cream garnish

CAFÉ CORRECTO
Coffee mug, heated
Build in glass
1 oz. Brandy
Near fill with hot espresso coffee
Whipped cream garnish
Dust powdered cocoa

CAFÉ DIABLO
Coffee mug, heated
Build in glass
3/4 oz. V.S. Cognac
3/4 oz. Grand Marnier Liqueur
3/4 oz. Sambuca
1/2 oz. simple syrup
Fill with hot coffee
Sprinkle grated orange rind,
cloves, cinnamon and allspice
Orange twist garnish

CAFÉ DUBLIN
Coffee mug, heated
Build in glass
1 oz. Irish Whiskey
1 oz. Irish Mist
1/2 oz. Kahlúa Coffee Liqueur
Near fill with hot coffee
Top with frothed milk
Dust powdered cocoa

CAFÉ FOSTER
Coffee mug, heated
Build in glass
1 1/2 oz. Bacardi Select Rum
3/4 oz. Godiva Chocolate Liqueur
3/4 oz. Crème de Banana
Near fill with hot coffee
Whipped cream garnish
Drizzle chocolate syrup

CAFÉ GATES
Presentation shot glass, chilled
Build in glass
1/3 fill Grand Marnier Liqueur
1/3 fill Tia Maria
1/3 fill Dark Crème de Cacao

CAFÉ KINGSTON
Coffee mug, heated
Build in glass
1/2 oz. Appleton Estate V/X Jamaica Rum
1/2 oz. Angostura Caribbean Rum Cream
1/2 oz. Tia Maria
1/2 oz. Hershey's chocolate syrup
Near fill with hot coffee
Whipped cream garnish
Sprinkle shaved chocolate

CAFÉ REGGAE
Coffee mug, heated
Build in glass
3/4 oz. Bacardi Gold Rum
1/2 oz. Tia Maria
1/2 oz. Dark Crème de Cacao
Near fill with hot coffee
Whipped cream garnish
Drizzle 3/4 oz. Pusser's British Navy Rum

ABSOLUT® VODKA

Lars Olsson Smith was a giant in the Swedish vodka industry, who by the 1870s, controlled the majority of the country's spirits production. Armed with a state of the art facility equipped with a revolutionary new column still, Smith began bottling a vodka of unprecedented purity in 1879. Appropriately labeled *Absolut Rent Bränvin* (Absolutely pure vodka), it is this spirit that inspired the creation of ABSOLUT VODKA.

The world-renowned brand is distilled in Ahus, a picturesque town on the southern coast of Sweden, by the state-consortium V. & S. Vin and Sprit AB. Company. Absolut Vodka is made entirely from a mash of locally grown wheat and purified well water. It is continuously distilled in a six-column still and emerges at extremely high proof. The vodka is not subjected to filtration before being reduced with water to 80 proof.

Introduced in the United States in 1979, Absolut is now the best selling imported vodka in this country. It has pristine clarity and a lightweight body with the lush texture of velvet. The vodka has a subtle bouquet of citrus, pine and clover, and a clean, marvelously neutral palate. The finish is crisp and refreshing.

The famed Absolut line of vodkas also includes CITRON (citrus), PEPPAR (pepper), KURANT (currant) and MANDRIN (mandarine orange).

CAFÉ ROYALE
Coffee mug, heated
Build in glass
1/2 oz. simple syrup (optional)
1 oz. V.S. Cognac
Fill with hot coffee
Note: May be requested made with Brandy

CAFÉ ST. ARMANDS
Coffee mug, heated
Build in glass
1 oz. Dark Crème de Cacao
1/2 oz. Licor 43 (Cuarenta y Tres)
Near fill with hot coffee
Whipped cream garnish

CAIPIRINHA (1)
Rocks or old fashion glass
Build in glass
4 large lime wedges
3/4 oz. simple syrup
Muddle contents
2 1/2 oz. Ypioca Cachaça
Add cracked ice

CAIPIRINHA (2)
Rocks or old fashion glass
Build in glass
4 large lime wedges
3/4 oz. simple syrup
Muddle contents
1 1/2 oz. Licor 43 (Cuarenta y Tres)
1 1/2 oz. Light Rum
Add cracked ice

CAIPIRISSMA
Rocks or old fashion glass
Build in glass
4 large lime wedges
3/4 oz. simple syrup
Muddle contents
2 1/2 oz. Bacardi Light Rum
Add crushed ice
Lime wedge garnish

CAIPIROSHKA
Rocks or old fashion glass
Build in glass
4 large lime wedges
3/4 oz. simple syrup
Muddle contents
2 1/2 oz. Belvedere Polish Vodka
Add cracked ice

CAJUN MIMOSA
Champagne glass, chilled
Build in glass
1/2 fill Champagne
1/4 oz. jalapeño pepper juice
Fill with orange juice
Orange slice and pepper garnish

CALIFORNIA LEMONADE
Bucket glass, ice
Pour ingredients into iced mixing glass
1 1/2 oz. Seagram's 7 Whisky
1/2 oz. Rose's Lime Juice
1/2 oz. grenadine
1 1/2 oz. sweet 'n' sour
Shake and strain
Fill with club soda
Orange slice and cherry garnish

CALIFORNIAN
Highball glass, ice
Build in glass
1 1/4 oz. Artic Vodka & Strawberry Liqueur
1/2 fill orange juice
Near fill with sweet 'n' sour
Splash Seven-Up

CALIFORNIA ROOT BEER
Highball glass, ice
Build in glass
3/4 oz. Kahlúa Coffee Liqueur
3/4 oz. Galliano Liqueur
Fill with club soda

CALIFORNIA SCREW
aka **California Split, Desert Screw**
Highball glass, ice
Build in glass
1 1/4 oz. Vodka
1/2 fill orange juice
1/2 fill grapefruit juice

CALYPSO COFFEE
aka **Spanish Coffee**
Coffee mug, heated
Build in glass
1 oz. Bacardi Light Rum
1 oz. Tia Maria
Near fill with hot coffee
Whipped cream garnish
Sprinkle shaved chocolate

CALYPSO HIGHWAY
House specialty glass, ice
Pour ingredients into iced mixing glass
1 oz. Bacardi Select Rum
1 oz. Cruzan Banana Rum
3/4 oz. Blue Curaçao
2 dashes vanilla extract
1 oz. coconut cream syrup
2 oz. pineapple juice
2 oz. orange juice
Shake and strain
Float 3/4 oz. Bacardi 151° Rum
Pineapple wedge and cherry garnish

CAMPARI & SODA
Highball glass, ice
Build in glass
1 1/4 oz. Campari Aperitivo
Fill with club soda
Lemon twist garnish

CANADIAN
aka **Canada**
Cocktail glass, chilled
Pour ingredients into iced mixing glass
1 1/2 oz. Canadian Whisky
1/2 oz. DeKuyper Triple Sec
2 dashes Angostura Bitters
1/2 oz. simple syrup
1 oz. sweet 'n' sour
Shake and strain

CANADIAN BLISS
Rocks glass, ice
Build in glass
2 oz. Lot No. 40 Canadian Whisky
3/4 oz. Villa Massa Limoncello
Lemon twist garnish

CANADIAN FOOT WARMER
Coffee mug, heated
Build in glass
1 1/4 oz. Lot No. 40 Canadian Whisky
3/4 oz. Fireball Cinnamon Canadian Whisky
1/2 oz. Kahlúa Coffee Liqueur
Near fill with hot chocolate
Whipped cream garnish
Dust powdered cocoa

CANADIAN STONE FENCE
House specialty glass, ice
Pour ingredients into iced mixing glass
1 1/2 oz. Canadian Whisky
1/2 oz. DJ Dotson Triple Sec
1/2 oz. sugar syrup
2 oz. apple cider
Shake and strain

CANADIAN TART
Rocks glass, ice
Build in glass
2 oz. Pike Creek Canadian Whisky
3/4 oz. Rémy Red
Cherry garnish

C. & C.
Brandy snifter, heated
Build in glass
1 1/2 oz. V.S. Cognac
1/2 oz. Green Chartreuse

JAMESON®
IRISH WHISKEY

Irish whiskey remains one of the most popular types of spirits in the world, and the best-selling brand of Irish whiskey—by a wide margin—is JAMESON. The brand's namesake, John Jameson, began crafting whiskey at the distillery he built in the heart of Dublin in 1780, and the whiskey has become something of a phenomenon ever since.

Jameson Irish Whiskey is a blend of grain, and malted and unmalted barley whiskies, triple-distilled in both pot and continuous stills. The blend is aged a minimum of 6 years in American oak barrels and sherry casks.

As a result, Jameson is a magnificently light and accessible whiskey. Its lush bouquet is an alluring mix of honey and fruit. On the palate, the whiskey presents a delicious array of semi-sweet flavors, including toasted oak, vanilla, fruit and a hint of caramel. The finish is soft, relaxed and of medium-duration.

Jameson has extended its line with the release of several other stellar Irish whiskies, including JAMESON 1780, an elegant 12-year-old blend with higher proportions of pot still and sherry cask finished whiskies; and the appropriately named JAMESON GOLD, an ultra-premium blend of pure pot still whiskies aged in both new and seasoned oak casks.

CANDY APPLE
Bucket glass, ice
Build in glass
1 3/4 oz. Dr. McGillicuddy's Vanilla Liqueur
3/4 oz. DeKuyper Pucker Sour Apple
Near fill with club soda
Float 1/2 oz. grenadine

CANNONBALL
Bucket glass, ice
Build in glass
2 oz. Pusser's British Navy Rum
1/2 oz. Rose's Lime Juice
1 oz. cranberry juice
1 oz. pineapple juice
1 oz. orange juice
Lime wedge garnish

CANYON QUAKE (1)
House specialty glass, chilled
Pour ingredients into blender
3/4 oz. Baileys Irish Cream
3/4 oz. Christian Brothers Brandy
3/4 oz. Kahlúa Coffee Liqueur
2 oz. half & half cream
Blend with ice

CANYON QUAKE (2)
Rocks glass, chilled
Pour ingredients into iced mixing glass
1 oz. Disaronno Amaretto Liqueur
3/4 oz. Baileys Irish Cream
3/4 oz. Brandy
1/2 oz. half & half cream
Shake and strain

CANYON SLIDER
Presentation shot glass, chilled
Layer ingredients
1/2 fill Dr. McGillicuddy's
   Mentholmint Schnapps
1/2 fill Jim Beam White Label Bourbon

CAPE CODDER
aka **Cape Cod**
Highball glass, ice
Build in glass
1 1/4 oz. Vodka
Fill with cranberry juice

CAPERS COCKTAIL
House specialty glass, ice
Rim glass with salt (optional)
Build in glass
1 oz. Absolut Citron Vodka
3/4 oz. Giori Lemoncillo Liqueur
Fill with lemonade
Lemon wheel garnish

CAPO DI SOPRANOS
Coffee mug or glass, heated
Build in glass
1 oz. Giori Lemoncillo Liqueur
3/4 oz. Giori Lemoncillo Cream Liqueur
1/2 oz. Sambuca
Fill with hot coffee
Whipped cream garnish
Drizzle 1/2 oz. Kahlúa Coffee Liqueur

CAPPA 21
Cappuccino cup, heated
Build in glass
1 1/2 oz. Bacardi Select Rum
1/2 oz. Tia Maria
1/2 oz. Brandy
Square of Ghirardelli chocolate
Near fill with hot espresso coffee
Top with frothed milk
Sprinkle shaved chocolate

CAPPO de TUTTI CAPPI
Cappuccino cup, heated
Build in glass
1/2 oz. Tia Maria
1/2 oz. Brandy
1/2 oz. Bacardi Select Rum
1 piece Ghirardelli chocolate
Near fill with hot espresso coffee
Top with frothed milk
Sprinkle shaved chocolate

CAPTAIN'S COFFEE (1)
Coffee mug, heated
Build in glass
1 1/2 oz. Pusser's British Navy Rum
1 oz. X.O. Café Coffee Liqueur
Near fill with hot coffee
Whipped cream garnish (optional)
Drizzle 1/2 oz. X.O. Café Coffee Liqueur

CAPTAIN'S COFFEE (2)
Coffee mug, heated
Build in glass
1 oz. Captain Morgan Spiced Rum
1 oz. Kahlúa Coffee Liqueur
2 dashes Angostura Bitters
Near fill with hot coffee
Whipped cream garnish
Sprinkle nutmeg

CAPTAIN'S COOLER
Bucket glass, ice
Pour ingredients into iced mixing glass
1 1/4 oz. Captain Morgan Spiced Rum
1 oz. DJ Dotson Triple Sec
1/2 oz. Rose's Lime Juice
1/2 oz. cranberry juice
1 oz. orange juice
Shake and strain
Fill with Seven-Up

CAR BOMB
Shot glass and tankard glass, chilled
Build in shot glass
1 1/2 oz. Baileys Irish Cream
Build in tankard glass
3/4 fill Guinness Stout
Drop shot glass of Baileys into Guinness

CARDINALI
Bucket glass, ice
Pour ingredients into iced mixing glass
3 oz. cranberry juice
2 oz. sweet 'n' sour
Shake and strain
Lime wheel garnish

CARDINAL PUNCH
Bucket glass, ice
Pour ingredients into iced mixing glass
3 oz. cranberry juice
1 1/2 oz. orange juice
1 oz. sweet 'n' sour
Shake and strain
Fill with ginger ale

CARIBBEAN BERRY
House specialty glass, chilled
Pour ingredients into blender
3/4 oz. Bacardi Gold Rum
3/4 oz. Disaronno Amaretto Liqueur
1/2 oz. Crème de Banana
1/2 cup strawberries
1 1/2 oz. sweet 'n' sour
Blend with ice
Float 3/4 oz. Gosling's Black Seal Rum
Banana slice and strawberry garnish

CARIBBEAN CHAMPAGNE
Champagne glass, chilled
Build in glass
3/4 oz. Bacardi Light Rum
3/4 oz. Crème de Banana
Fill with Champagne
Banana slice and cherry garnish

CARIBBEAN CONTESSA
Champagne glass, chilled
Pour ingredients into iced mixing glass
1/2 oz. Original Cristall Russian Vodka
1/2 oz. Grand Marnier Liqueur
1/2 oz. cranberry juice
1/2 oz. orange juice
Shake and strain
Fill with Champagne
Lemon twist garnish

B & B® LIQUEUR

B & B LIQUEUR is a timeless classic, an elegant combination of aged cognac and BENEDICTINE LIQUEUR. Thought to be the oldest surviving proprietary liqueur, Benedictine was created in 1510 at the monastery in Fecamp, France. The legendary elixir is made with 27 fragrant herbs, spices, plants, tea and fruits, each distilled individually and matured in oak barrels for 3 months before blending. The liqueur is made on a base of aged cognac and rested in oak casks before being bottled at 80 proof.

B & B Liqueur was created in the 1930s. The inspiration behind the liqueur came from a veteran barman at the famous 21 Club in Manhattan who concocted a cocktail made with Benedictine and brandy.

Its soaring popularity prompted the distillery to devise its own version, and to ensure its longevity, created the now famous liqueur on a base of old Fine Champagne cognac.

B & B Liqueur is endowed with a flawlessly textured body and a wafting bouquet of spicy, herbal aromas highlighted by notes of cognac. The sumptuous palate is a feast of zesty flavors mellowed with the refined taste of Benedictine. The lingering finish is sensational.

As great as B & B Liqueur is served neat, it is equally fabulous featured in a cocktail.

CARIBBEAN CRUISE (1)
House specialty glass, chilled
Pour ingredients into blender
1 oz. Appleton Estate V/X Jamaica Rum
1 oz. Mount Gay Eclipse Rum
3/4 oz. Kahlúa Coffee Liqueur
1/2 oz. half & half cream
2 oz. coconut cream syrup
3 oz. pineapple juice
Blend with ice
Float 3/4 oz. Cockspur V.S.O.R. Rum
Pineapple wedge and cherry garnish

CARIBBEAN CRUISE (2)
House specialty glass, ice
Pour ingredients into iced mixing glass
1 1/2 oz. Bacardi Select Rum
3/4 oz. Gran Gala Orange Liqueur
1 1/2 oz. sweet 'n' sour
1 1/2 oz. orange juice
Shake and strain
Float 3/4 oz. Royal Oak Extra Old Rum
Orange slice garnish

CARIBBEAN CRUISE (3)
Cocktail glass, chilled
Pour ingredients into iced mixing glass
1 1/2 oz. Light Rum
3/4 oz. Gran Gala Orange Liqueur
1 oz. sweet 'n' sour
Shake and strain
Orange twist garnish

CARIBBEAN DREAM
Coffee mug, heated
Build in glass
1 oz. Mount Gay Eclipse Rum
1/2 oz. Myers's Jamaican Rum
1/2 oz. Crème de Banana
1/2 oz. White Crème de Cacao
Near fill with hot coffee
Whipped cream garnish

CARIBBEAN GRIDLOCK
House specialty glass, chilled
Pour ingredients into blender
3/4 oz. Appleton Estate V/X Jamaica Rum
3/4 oz. Bacardi Light Rum
3/4 oz. Mount Gay Eclipse Rum
3/4 oz. Rose's Lime Juice
2 oz. sweet 'n' sour
2 oz. orange juice
Blend with ice
Float 3/4 oz. Gosling's Black Seal Rum
Lime, lemon and orange wedge garnish

CARIBBEAN ROMANCE
House specialty glass, ice
Pour ingredients into iced mixing glass
1 1/2 oz. Bacardi Light Rum
1 oz. Disaronno Amaretto Liqueur
1 1/2 oz. orange juice
1 1/2 oz. pineapple juice
1/2 oz. grenadine
Shake and strain
Float 3/4 oz. Mount Gay Extra Old Rum
Lime, lemon and orange wedge garnish

CARIBBEAN SUNSET
Presentation shot glass, chilled
Build in glass
1/3 fill Kahlúa Coffee Liqueur
1/3 fill Chambord Liqueur
1/3 fill Tia Maria

CARIBE SUNSET
Presentation shot glass
Build in glass
1/4 fill Chambord Liqueur
1/4 fill Dark Crème de Cacao
1/4 fill Tia Maria
1/4 fill hot coffee

CARIBE SURFSIDER
House specialty glass, chilled
Pour ingredients into blender
3/4 oz. Bacardi Light Rum
3/4 oz. Bacardi Gold Rum
1/2 oz. Crème de Banana
1/2 oz. Blackberry Brandy
3/4 oz. grenadine
3/4 oz. fresh lime juice
1/2 cup strawberries
2 oz. sweet 'n' sour
Blend with ice
Pineapple wedge and strawberry garnish

CARMALITA
Rocks glass, chilled
Build in glass
1/2 oz. Stolichnaya Russian Vodka
1/2 oz. Baileys Irish Cream
1/2 oz. Frangelico Liqueur
1/2 oz. Kahlúa Coffee Liqueur

CARTE BLANCHE
Coffee mug, heated
Build in glass
1/2 oz. Christian Brothers Brandy
1/2 oz. White Crème de Menthe
1/2 oz. Godiva Chocolate Liqueur
Near fill with hot chocolate
Whipped cream garnish
Drizzle 1/2 oz. Green Crème de Menthe

CARTEL BUSTER
Presentation shot glass, chilled
Layer ingredients
1/3 fill Tia Maria
1/3 fill Grand Marnier Liqueur
1/3 fill Jose Cuervo Especial Tequila

CARTEL SHOOTER
Presentation shot glass, chilled
Build in glass
1/2 oz. Chambord Liqueur
1/2 oz. Artic Vodka & Strawberry Liqueur
1/2 oz. grapefruit juice
1/2 oz. lemonade

CARTLAND CURE
House specialty glass, chilled
Pour ingredients into blender
3 oz. milk
1 egg (optional)
1 ripe banana
2 tbsp. yogurt, plain
1 tbsp. powdered cocoa
1 tsp. honey
1 tsp. wheat germ
Blend with ice

CASTLE COFFEE
Coffee mug, heated
Build in glass
1 oz. Knappogue Castle Irish Whiskey
1 oz. Celtic Crossing Irish Liqueur
1/2 oz. Mandarine Napoléon Liqueur
Near fill with hot coffee
Whipped cream garnish
Drizzle 1/2 oz. Kahlúa Coffee Liqueur

CASTLE IN THE CLOUDS
Cocktail glass, chilled
Pour ingredients into iced mixing glass
2 oz. Knappogue Castle Irish Whiskey
1/2 oz. Dubonnet Rouge
1/2 oz. Giori Lemoncillo Liqueur
Stir and strain
Lemon twist garnish

CATHERINE WAS GREAT
House specialty glass, chilled
Pour ingredients into blender
1 3/4 oz. Jewel of Russia Berry Infusion
1/2 oz. Disaronno Amaretto Liqueur
1/2 oz. Bacardi Limón Rum
2 oz. orange juice
2 oz. sweet 'n' sour
Blend with ice
Orange slice garnish

DUBONNET® ROUGE

DUBONNET is the best-selling aperitif in America. Best described as a sweetened and fortified wine, its original calling was as an aperitif wine, one typically consumed before dinner to awaken and stimulate the appetite. While still popular as an aperitif, the brand has also become an ingredient in many contemporary cocktails.

Considered the *Grand Dame* of aperitifs, Dubonnet was created by Frenchman Joseph Dubonnet in 1846 as a restorative elixir for the French Foreign Legion on their missions to Africa and Asia. The brand's two versions are still made according to the same secret recipe.

DUBONNET ROUGE is produced on a base of premium red wine that is infused with a proprietary blend of herbs, spices, peels and quinine. The wine is fortified with grape spirits to an elevated strength of 19% alcohol by volume (38 proof).

DUBONNET BLANC is crafted on a base of white wine, fortified with grape spirits and infused with botanicals. It is drier than its red wine counterpart.

Dubonnet Rouge is characteristically aromatic with a light, delicate body and a palate of tangy fruit. While a pleasure to sip neat, it is even more interesting to explore its creative potential in cocktails.

CAYMAN COCKTAIL
Cocktail glass, chilled
Pour ingredients into iced mixing glass
1 1/2 oz. Zone Peach Italian Vodka
1 1/2 oz. DeKuyper Peach Pucker
1/2 oz. orange juice
1/2 oz. pineapple juice
1/2 oz. grenadine
Shake and strain
Splash Seven-Up
Orange slice garnish

C.C. RIDER
Presentation shot glass, chilled
Build in glass
1/2 fill Chambord Liqueur
1/2 fill Champagne

CECIL'S DREAM
House specialty glass, chilled
Pour ingredients into blender
1 oz. Bacardi Light Rum
1/2 oz. Disaronno Amaretto Liqueur
1/2 oz. White Crème de Cacao
1/2 oz. simple syrup
3 oz. pineapple juice
Blend with ice
Float 3/4 oz. Dillon Dark Rhum
Pineapple wedge and cherry garnish

CELESTE'S COCKTAIL
House specialty glass, ice
Pour ingredients into iced mixing glass
1 oz. Forty Creek Canadian Whisky
1 oz. Fireball Cinnamon Canadian Whisky
1/2 oz. Tropico
1/2 oz. Rémy Red
1 1/2 oz. Hawaiian Punch
Shake and strain

CELESTIAL FIZZ
Champagne glass, chilled
Pour ingredients into iced mixing glass
1 oz. Cognac
3/4 oz. Grand Marnier Liqueur
1 oz. sweet 'n' sour
1 1/2 oz. cranberry juice
Shake and strain
Fill with Champagne
Orange slice garnish

CELTIC KISS
Rocks glass, ice
Build in glass
1 1/2 oz. Celtic Crossing Irish Liqueur
3/4 oz. Baileys Irish Cream

CEMENT MIXER
Presentation shot glass, chilled
Build in glass
1 oz. Baileys Irish Cream
1 oz. Absolut Citron Vodka
Swirl in mouth before swallowing

CENSORED ON THE BEACH
Highball glass, ice
Build in glass
1 oz. DeKuyper Peach Pucker
1 oz. Zone Peach Italian Vodka
1/2 fill cranberry juice
1/2 fill orange juice

CESAR RITZ
Champagne glass, chilled
Pour ingredients into iced mixing glass
1/2 oz. Armagnac
1/2 oz. DeKuyper Peachtree Schnapps
1/4 oz. grenadine
1 tbsp. vanilla ice cream
Shake and strain
Fill with Champagne
Lemon twist garnish

CHAMBORD DREAM
Cocktail glass, chilled
Pour ingredients into iced mixing glass
1/2 oz. Chambord Liqueur
1/2 oz. Dark Crème de Cacao
2 oz. half & half cream
Shake and strain

CHAMBORD REPOSE
Coffee mug, heated
Build in glass
3/4 oz. Chambord Liqueur
1/2 oz. Dark Crème de Cacao
1/2 oz. Tia Maria
Near fill with hot coffee
Top with frothed milk
Sprinkle shaved chocolate

CHAMPAGNE COCKTAIL
Champagne glass, chilled
Build in glass
Sugar cube soaked w/Angostura Bitters
Fill with Champagne
Lemon twist garnish

CHAMPAGNE CORNUCOPIA
House specialty glass, chilled
Pour ingredients into blender
1 oz. Artic Vodka & Peach Liqueur
3/4 oz. DeKuyper Peachtree Schnapps
1 1/2 oz. cranberry juice
2 scoops orange sorbet
Blend ingredients (with ice optional)
Fill with Champagne
Orange slice and cherry garnish

CHAMPAGNE FRAMBOISE
Champagne glass, chilled
Build in glass
Near fill with Champagne
Float 3/4 oz. Chambord Liqueur
Lemon twist garnish

CHAMPAGNE IMPERIAL
Champagne glass, chilled
Build in glass
Sugar cube soaked w/Angostura Bitters
1/2 oz. Courvoisier V.S.O.P. Cognac
1/2 oz. Grand Marnier 100th Anniversary
Fill with Champagne
Lemon twist garnish

CHAMPAGNE JUBILEE
Champagne glass, chilled
Build in glass
1 1/2 oz. Disaronno Amaretto Liqueur
2 oz. cranberry juice
Fill with Champagne
Orange twist garnish

CHAMPAGNE MARSEILLE
Champagne glass, chilled
Pour ingredients into iced mixing glass
3/4 oz. Grand Marnier Liqueur
3/4 oz. Disaronno Amaretto Liqueur
1/2 oz. Stolichnaya Russian Vodka
1 1/2 oz. orange juice
Shake and strain
Fill with Champagne

CHAMPAGNE NORMANDE
Champagne glass, chilled
Build in glass
1 oz. Calvados Apple Brandy
1/2 oz. simple syrup
2 dashes Angostura Bitters
Fill with Champagne
Orange twist garnish

CHAMPS ELYSEES COCKTAIL (1)
Cocktail glass, chilled
Pour ingredients into iced mixing glass
1 oz. Christian Brothers Brandy
1/2 oz. B & B Liqueur
2 dashes Angostura Bitters
1 1/2 oz. sweet 'n' sour
Shake and strain

CHAMPS ELYSEES COCKTAIL (2)
Champagne glass, chilled
Pour ingredients into iced mixing glass
1 oz. Courvoisier V.S.O.P. Cognac
1 oz. B & B Liqueur
2 dashes Angostura Bitters
1 1/2 oz. sweet 'n' sour
Shake and strain
Fill with Champagne

BOMBAY SAPPHIRE®
LONDON DRY GIN

BOMBAY SAPPHIRE LONDON DRY GIN took the world by storm with its release in 1988, quickly shooting up the charts as the category's first and only super-premium entry. It has become the popular favorite of the discriminating martini-craving public.

The secret behind Bombay Sapphire's spectacular success can be found in the singular way in which it is produced. The gin is crafted at the Greenall Distillery using a series of Carter Head stills, the only examples of this type in the world. Neutral grain spirits are double-distilled, then during their final distillation, the rising vapours pass through a perforated copper basket holding the gin's 10 botanicals. This vapour infusion process allows the subtle aroma of each botanical to be absorbed. The recipe mix includes fragrant herbs, spices, roots, fruit and juniper berries from around the world. It is bottled at 94 proof.

Bombay Sapphire richly deserves its uninterrupted ranking as a "must have" brand. The gin is crystal clear with a plush, medium-weight body. Its mesmerizing bouquet is a sensational melange of citrus, spice and juniper. Sapphire is brimming with crisp, mouth-filling flavors that linger on the palate for a consummate finish.

Also highly desirable is BOMBAY DRY GIN, which is made similarly to Sapphire, although it contains fewer botanicals.

CHEAP SHADES
House specialty glass, chilled
Pour ingredients into blender
1 oz. Midori Melon Liqueur
1 oz. DeKuyper Peachtree Schnapps
1 oz. sweet 'n' sour
2 oz. orange juice
2 oz. pineapple juice
Blend with ice
Fill with Seven-Up

CHEAP SUNGLASSES
Bucket glass, ice
Build in glass
1 1/4 oz. Van Hoo Belgium Vodka
1/2 fill cranberry juice
1/2 fill Seven-Up

CHEESY CHEERLEADER
House specialty glass, ice
Pour ingredients into iced mixing glass
1 1/2 oz. KéKé Beach Cream Liqueur
3/4 oz. Bacardi Limón Rum
3/4 oz. Giori Lemoncillo Liqueur
1 1/2 oz. pink lemonade
1 1/2 oz. pineapple juice
Shake and strain

CHEF DIETER'S
APPLE PIE COCKTAIL
Coffee mug, heated
Build in glass
1 oz. Laird's Applejack Brandy
1 oz. Bärenjäger Honey Liqueur
1/4 tsp. mulling spices
4 oz. hot apple cider
Cinnamon stick garnish

CHERRILLO
Presentation shot glass, chilled
Build in glass
1 oz. Giori Lemoncillo Cream Liqueur
1 oz. Chambord Liqueur
Cherry garnish

CHERRY AMORE
Champagne glass, chilled
Pour ingredients into iced mixing glass
1 1/4 oz. Christian Brothers Brandy
1/2 oz. maraschino cherry juice
2 oz. sweet 'n' sour
Shake and strain
Fill with Champagne

CHERRY BEAN
Presentation shot glass, chilled
Layer ingredients
1/2 fill Anisette
1/2 fill Cherry Brandy

CHERRY BLOSSOM
Cocktail glass, chilled
Pour ingredients into iced mixing glass
1 1/2 oz. Cherry Brandy
1 oz. Brandy
3/4 oz. sweet 'n' sour
1 dash Triple Sec
1 dash grenadine
Shake and strain
Cherry garnish

CHERRY BOMB
Presentation shot glass, chilled
Layer ingredients
1/4 fill Kahlúa Coffee Liqueur
1/4 fill Crème de Banana
1/4 fill Baileys Irish Cream
1/4 fill DeKuyper Cherry Pucker

CHICAGO
Champagne glass, chilled
Rim glass with salt (optional)
Pour ingredients into iced mixing glass
1 oz. Brandy
1/2 oz. Hiram Walker Triple Sec
2 dashes Angostura Bitters
Stir and strain
Fill with Champagne
Lemon twist garnish

CHICAGO TIMES
Coffee mug, heated
Build in glass
1/2 oz. Disaronno Amaretto Liqueur
1/2 oz. Tuaca
1/2 oz. Baileys Irish Cream
1/2 fill hot coffee
Near fill with hot chocolate
Whipped cream garnish
Drizzle 1/2 oz. Frangelico Liqueur
Dust powdered cocoa

CHI-CHI
House specialty glass, chilled
Pour ingredients into blender
1 oz. Vodka
2 oz. coconut cream syrup
3 oz. pineapple juice
1/2 oz. half & half cream (optional)
Blend with ice
Pineapple wedge and cherry garnish

CHIHUAHUA
Bucket glass, ice
Rim glass with salt (optional)
Build in glass
1 1/4 oz. Sauza Tres Generaciones
    Plata Tequila
Fill with grapefruit juice

CHILLER
Highball glass, ice
Build in glass
1 1/4 oz. requested liquor/liqueur
Fill with ginger ale

CHILL-OUT CAFÉ
Coffee mug or glass, ice
Build in glass
1/2 oz. Kahlúa Coffee Liqueur
1/2 oz. Disaronno Amaretto Liqueur
1/2 oz. Dark Crème de Cacao
Fill with iced coffee
Mint sprig garnish

CHIMAYO COCKTAIL
House specialty glass, ice
Pour ingredients into iced mixing glass
1 oz. Sauza Conmemorativo Añejo Tequila
1/2 oz. Briottet Crème de Cassis
1/2 oz. fresh lime juice
3 oz. unfiltered apple cider
Shake and strain

CHIP SHOT
Presentation shot glass
Layer ingredients
1/3 fill Kahlúa Coffee Liqueur
1/3 fill Disaronno Amaretto Liqueur
1/3 fill hot coffee

CHIQUITA PUNCH
House specialty glass, chilled
Pour ingredients into blender
1 oz. Crème de Banana
1/2 oz. Kahlúa Coffee Liqueur
1/2 oz. Dark Crème de Cacao
3/4 oz. grenadine
1 1/2 oz. half & half cream
1 1/2 oz. orange juice
Blend with ice
Banana slice garnish

CHOCOLATE ALMOND KISS
House specialty glass, chilled
Pour ingredients into blender
1 oz. Frangelico Liqueur
1/2 oz. Dark Crème de Cacao
1/2 oz. Chopin Polish Vodka
2 scoops vanilla ice cream
Blend ingredients (with ice optional)
Sprinkle shaved chocolate

KETEL ONE® DUTCH VODKA

KETEL ONE DUTCH VODKA originated in 1691, when the Nolet family built a distillery in Schiedam, Holland. Within decades they gained international fame and became the purveyor of spirits to the czars. In 1804, the Nolet distillery was granted the right to display the Romanoff family crest on their labels.

Handcrafted Ketel One Vodka is made in small batches entirely from wheat. The final distillation occurs in a 137-year-old, copper alembic still, referred to as "Ketel #1." The water used in production is purified through sand filtration. After distillation, the vodka is rested in tile-lined tanks for 6 weeks. Every batch of vodka is tasted by Carl Nolet, Sr. prior to bottling.

Ketel One is an exemplary vodka. It has pristine clarity and a gloriously round, flawlessly textured body. The vodka's subtle yet pleasing bouquet is laced with citrus and toasted cereal aromas. The real treat awaits you upon first taste. It immediately fills the mouth with a rich palate layered with sweet and spicy flavors. The finish is elegant and long lasting.

Citrus-infused KETEL ONE CITROEN VODKA has a pale yellow hue and a wafting bouquet of fresh limes and lemons. The zesty palate is endowed with a refreshing, bona fide citrus flavor that persists well into the extended finish.

The Ketel One sisters are sophisticated vodkas that know no creative limitations.

CHOCOLATE BANANA (1)
House specialty glass, chilled
Pour ingredients into blender
1 1/4 oz. Crème de Banana
1 oz. chocolate syrup
1 ripe banana
2 scoops vanilla ice cream
Blend ingredients (with ice optional)
Whipped cream garnish
Sprinkle shaved chocolate

CHOCOLATE BANANA (2)
Presentation shot glass, chilled
Build in glass
1 oz. Cruzan Banana Rum
1 oz. Godiva Chocolate Liqueur
1/2 oz. half & half cream

CHOCOLATE COVERED BANANA (1)
House specialty glass, chilled
Pour ingredients into blender
1 1/2 oz. Appleton Estate V/X Jamaica Rum
1 1/2 oz. Godiva Chocolate Liqueur
2 ripe bananas
1/2 oz. half & half cream
2 scoops vanilla ice cream
Blend ingredients (with ice optional)
Whipped cream garnish
Drizzle 3/4 oz. St. James Extra Old Rhum
Sprinkle shaved chocolate

CHOCOLATE COVERED BANANA (2)
House specialty glass, chilled
Pour ingredients into blender
1 3/4 oz. Baileys Irish Cream
1 oz. Cruzan Banana Rum
1 oz. chocolate syrup
1 ripe banana
2 scoops banana ice cream
Blend ingredients (with ice optional)
Whipped cream garnish
Drizzle chocolate syrup
Banana slice garnish

CHOCOLATE CREAM SODA
Bucket glass, ice
Build in glass
1 1/2 oz. Godiva Chocolate Liqueur
2 oz. milk
Fill with club soda

CHOCOLATE ICE CREAM FLOAT
House specialty glass, chilled
Pour ingredients into blender
1 3/4 oz. Jack Daniel's Tennessee Whiskey
2 oz. Hershey's chocolate syrup
2 scoops chocolate ice cream
Blend ingredients (with ice optional)
Pour into glass
Near fill with club soda
Float 1 scoop chocolate ice cream
Drizzle chocolate syrup
Graham cracker garnish

CHOCOLATE MILK COOLER
House specialty glass, chilled
Pour ingredients into blender
1 1/2 oz. Kahlúa Coffee Liqueur
1 1/4 oz. Christian Brothers Brandy
8 oz. chocolate milk
1 tsp. vanilla extract
Blend with ice
Whipped cream garnish
Sprinkle shaved chocolate

CHOCO LATÉ ORANGE
Brandy snifter, ice
Build in glass
1 oz. Vincent Van Gogh Vodka
1 oz. Vincent Van Gogh Oranje Vodka
1 oz. Godiva Chocolate Liqueur
1/2 oz. Extase XO Liqueur
Orange twist garnish

CHOCOLATE SQUIRREL
Cocktail glass, chilled
Pour ingredients into iced mixing glass
3/4 oz. Disaronno Amaretto Liqueur
3/4 oz. Frangelico Liqueur
1/2 oz. Dark Crème de Cacao
1/2 oz. Brandy
1 1/2 oz. half & half cream
Shake and strain

CHOCOLATE WHITE RUSSIAN
Rocks glass, ice
Build in glass
1 oz. Jewel of Russia Classic Vodka
1 1/2 oz. Godiva Chocolate Liqueur
1 oz. milk

CHOPIN'S RIVER
Rocks glass, ice
Build in glass
2 oz. Chopin Polish Vodka
1/2 oz. Celtic Crossing Irish Liqueur
Lemon twist garnish

CIAO BELLO
Coffee mug or glass, heated
Build in glass
1 1/2 oz. Giori Lemoncillo Cream Liqueur
3/4 oz. Kahlúa Coffee Liqueur
Near fill with hot coffee
Whipped cream garnish
Sprinkle shaved chocolate

CILLO AMORE
Cocktail glass, chilled
Rim glass with powdered cocoa
Pour ingredients into iced mixing glass
1 3/4 oz. Giori Lemoncillo Cream Liqueur
1 oz. Disaronno Amaretto Liqueur
1 oz. Kahlúa Coffee Liqueur
Shake and strain

CILLO BLANCO
Cocktail glass, chilled
Pour ingredients into iced mixing glass
1 3/4 oz. Giori Lemoncillo Liqueur
3/4 oz. White Crème de Cacao
3/4 oz. Southern Comfort Liqueur
Stir and strain
Lemon wheel garnish

CILLO FELLOW
Bucket glass, ice
Build in glass
1 3/4 oz. Giori Lemoncillo Cream Liqueur
1 oz. Finlandia Vodka
3/4 oz. Disaronno Amaretto Liqueur
Fill with orange juice
Orange slice garnish

CINDERELLA
House specialty glass, chilled
Pour ingredients into blender
1/2 oz. grenadine
1 1/2 oz. orange juice
1 1/2 oz. sweet 'n' sour
1 1/2 oz. pineapple juice
Blend with ice
Fill with club soda

CINNAMON SLING
Bucket glass, ice
Pour ingredients into iced mixing glass
1 oz. Gin
1 oz. Hot Damn Cinnamon Schnapps
2 1/2 oz. sweet 'n' sour
Shake and strain
Fill with club soda
Orange slice and cherry garnish

CINNFUL APPLE
Highball glass, ice
Build in glass
1 1/4 oz. Hot Damn Cinnamon Schnapps
Fill with apple cider

HIGHBALL DRINKS
A Popular Mainstay

Highball drinks are typically a combination of a liquor or liqueur and a mixer, such as water, tonic, soda, juice, etc. They are most frequently prepared with a 1 to 1 1/4 oz. portion of liquor, yielding a liquor to mix proportion of 1:2, one part liquor to two parts mixer. A proportion of 1:1, or equal parts of liquor to mixer, is too strong tasting of a drink for most people. A proportion of 1:3 or 1:4 will make a drink over-diluted and weak tasting.

There are four standard variations of the highball:

- A **Double Highball** is prepared in a standard 9 ounce highball glass using 2 ounces of the liquor and a fill of the requested mixer. This will yield a relatively potent proportion of two parts liquor to one part mixer. A word of caution, drinking a double highball is more potent than consuming two regularly prepared highballs.

- A **Tall Highball** is prepared in a 10 or 12 ounce bucket glass using one ounce of liquor and a fill of the specified mixer. This combination will produce a relatively weak tasting drink, an approximate proportion of 1:4 or 1:5.

- A **Short Highball** is prepared in a 7 ounce glass using 1 ounce of liquor and a fill of the specified mixer. This combination will yield a strong tasting drink with a proportion of about 1:1, or equal parts of liquor to mix.

- A **Double Tall Highball** is prepared in a 10 or 12 ounce bucket glass using 2 ounces of requested liquor and a fill of the specified mixer. This combination will usually create a standard 1:2 proportion. A double tall highball is like preparing two regular highballs drinks in the same glass.

CIRCUS PEANUT
Presentation shot glass, chilled
Build in glass
1/3 fill Midori Melon Liqueur
1/3 fill Crème de Banana
1/3 fill half & half cream

CITRON NEON
House specialty glass, chilled
Pour ingredients into blender
1 1/2 oz. Absolut Citron Vodka
1 oz. Midori Melon Liqueur
3/4 oz. Blue Curaçao
1/2 oz. Rose's Lime Juice
2 oz. sweet 'n' sour
Blend with ice

CITY TAVERN COOLER
Bucket glass, ice
Build in glass
1 1/2 oz. Appleton Estate V/X Jamaica Rum
1 oz. Bourbon
3/4 oz. DeKuyper Peachtree Schnapps
4 oz. apple cider
Apple wedge garnish

CLAM DIGGER
Bucket glass, ice
Rim glass with salt (optional)
Build in glass
1 1/2 oz. Gin
3 dashes red pepper sauce
Fill with clam juice

CLAM FOGGER
Highball glass, ice
Build in glass
1 1/4 oz. Finlandia Vodka
1/3 fill cranberry juice
1/3 fill grapefruit juice
1/3 fill orange juice

CLASSIC VETTE
Cocktail glass, chilled
Rim glass with sugar (optional)
Pour ingredients into iced mixing glass
1 oz. Brandy
3/4 oz. Cointreau Liqueur
1/2 oz. Giori Lemoncillo Liqueur
2 oz. sweet 'n' sour
Shake and strain
Lemon twist garnish

CLOVER CLUB
Cocktail glass, chilled
Pour ingredients into iced mixing glass
1 1/2 oz. Gin
1/2 oz. grenadine
1 1/2 oz. sweet 'n' sour
1 egg white (optional)
Shake and strain

CLUB MACANUDO
Cocktail glass, chilled
Pour ingredients into iced mixing glass
2 oz. Grey Goose Vodka
1/2 oz. Alizé V.S.O.P. Cognac
1/2 oz. Dubonnet Rouge
Shake and strain
Splash Champagne

CLUB SHERRY
Rocks glass, ice
Build in glass
1 1/2 oz. Canadian Club Whisky
3/4 oz. Sherry

C-NOTE A-FLOAT
Cocktail glass, chilled
Pour ingredients into iced mixing glass
1 1/2 oz. Ballylarkin Irish Liqueur
1/2 oz. Godiva Chocolate Liqueur
1/2 oz. Green Crème de Menthe
1/2 oz. Kahlúa Coffee Liqueur
Shake and strain

COCAINE SHOOTER (1)
Rocks glass, chilled
Pour ingredients into iced mixing glass
3/4 oz. Vodka
3/4 oz. Chambord Liqueur
1/2 oz. Southern Comfort Liqueur
3/4 oz. orange juice
3/4 oz. cranberry juice
Shake and strain

COCAINE SHOOTER (2)
Rocks glass, chilled
Pour ingredients into iced mixing glass
1 1/2 oz. Vodka
3/4 oz. Chambord Liqueur
1/4 oz. sweet 'n' sour
1/4 oz. Seven-Up
Shake and strain

COCO LOCO
House specialty glass, chilled
Pour ingredients into blender
1 oz. Sauza Tres Generaciones Añejo Tequila
2 oz. coconut cream syrup
3 oz. pineapple juice
1/2 oz. Rose's Lime Juice
Blend with ice
Pineapple wedge and cherry garnish

COCOMACOQUE
House specialty glass, ice
Pour ingredients into iced mixing glass
1 1/2 oz. Bacardi Gold Rum
1 1/2 oz. Red Wine
1 1/2 oz. sweet 'n' sour
1 1/2 oz. pineapple juice
1 1/2 oz. orange juice
Shake and strain
Float 3/4 oz. Cockspur V.S.O.R. Rum
Pineapple wedge and cherry garnish

COCO MOCHA
House specialty glass or
   large coffee mug, chilled
Pour ingredients into blender
3 oz. cold coffee
1/2 tsp. chocolate syrup
4 oz. coconut cream syrup
Blend with ice
Whipped cream garnish
Sprinkle nutmeg

COCOMOTION
House specialty glass, chilled
Pour ingredients into blender
1 1/2 oz. Mount Gay Eclipse Rum
1 oz. Bacardi Gold Rum
3/4 oz. Tia Maria
1 oz. fresh lime juice
2 oz. coconut cream syrup
3 oz. pineapple juice
Blend with ice
Float 3/4 oz. Dillon Dark Rhum
Pineapple wedge and cherry garnish

COCONUT BREEZE
House specialty glass, ice
Pour ingredients into iced mixing glass
1 1/4 oz. Bacardi Light Rum
1 oz. Cruzan Coconut Rum
1/2 oz. simple syrup
1 oz. fresh lime juice
2 oz. mango juice
2 oz. pineapple juice
Shake and strain
Fill with Seven-Up
Lime wedge garnish

COCONUT COFFEE POT
Cocktail glass, chilled
Pour ingredients into iced mixing glass
1 3/4 oz. Ketel One Dutch Vodka
1/2 oz. Cruzan Coconut Rum
1/2 oz. Tia Maria
Stir and strain

COINTREAU® LIQUEUR

Recognized around the world as one of the transcendent liqueurs, COINTREAU was created in 1849 by Frenchman Edouard Cointreau in the historic city of Angers in the Loire Valley. The recipe for Cointreau has remained a secret and been passed down from generation to generation. Today only five members of the immediate family know the recipe.

Cointreau is crafted from a blend of sweet orange peels from Spain, France and Brazil, and bitter, unripe orange peels from South America. A portion of the peels are dried in the sun prior to distillation, the rest are used fresh. The peels are macerated in alcohol, and when the infusions have reached peak flavor, they are double-distilled in copper alembic stills. The distillery has nineteen stills, each designed specifically to produce Cointreau.

The liqueur must be tasted neat to be fully appreciated. It is perfectly clear with a satiny textured, medium-weight body. Cointreau is impressively aromatic with a highly focused bouquet of freshly cut oranges. It glides over the palate with a tingling wash of sweet orange flavor. The citrus experience continues long into the lingering finish.

Cointreau is particularly versatile in drink making. It has a starring role in an impressively long list of cocktails, both classic and contemporary.

COCONUT CREAM PIE
Cocktail glass, chilled
Pour ingredients into iced mixing glass
1 oz. Dr. McGillicuddy's Vanilla Liqueur
1 oz. Malibu Rum
1 1/2 oz. half & half cream
Shake and strain
Shredded coconut garnish

CODE RED
Champagne glass, chilled
Build in glass
2 1/2 oz. Rémy Red
Fill with Champagne
Orange twist garnish

COFFEE NUTCAKE
House specialty glass, chilled
Pour ingredients into blender
1 1/2 oz. Kahlúa Coffee Liqueur
3/4 oz. Frangelico Liqueur
1/2 oz. Dark Crème de Cacao
2 dashes grenadine
2 scoops French vanilla ice cream
Blend ingredients (with ice optional)

COGNAC RITZ
Champagne glass, chilled
Pour ingredients into iced mixing glass
1 oz. Courvoisier V.S.O.P. Cognac
1 oz. orange juice
1 oz. sweet 'n' sour
Shake and strain
Fill with Champagne
Lemon twist garnish

COLD FUSION
House specialty glass, ice
Pour ingredients into iced mixing glass
3/4 oz. Stolichnaya Russian Vodka
3/4 oz. Midori Melon Liqueur
1/2 oz. DJ Dotson Triple Sec
1/2 oz. Rose's Lime Juice
1/2 oz. fresh lemon juice
1 1/2 oz. sweet 'n' sour
Shake and strain
Lime wedge garnish

COLD GOLD
Highball glass, ice
Build in glass
3/4 oz. Cruzan Orange Rum
Near fill with orange juice
Float 3/4 oz. Blue Curaçao

COLLINS

Collins or bucket glass, ice
Pour ingredients into iced mixing glass
1 1/4 oz. requested liquor/liqueur
2 oz. sweet 'n' sour
Shake and strain
Fill with club soda
Orange slice and cherry garnish

COLLINS, BEVERLY

Collins or bucket glass, ice
Pour ingredients into iced mixing glass
1 1/4 oz. Cascade Mountain Gin
2 oz. sweet 'n' sour
Shake and strain
Fill with Perrier mineral water
Orange slice and cherry garnish

COLLINS, FIFI

Collins or bucket glass, ice
Pour ingredients into iced mixing glass
1 1/4 oz. Courvoisier V.S. Cognac
2 oz. sweet 'n' sour
Shake and strain
Fill with club soda
Orange slice and cherry garnish

COLLINS, JACK
aka **Apple Collins**

Collins or bucket glass, ice
Pour ingredients into iced mixing glass
1 1/4 oz. Laird's Applejack Brandy
2 oz. sweet 'n' sour
Shake and strain
Fill with club soda
Orange slice and cherry garnish

COLLINS, JAMIE

Collins or bucket glass, ice
Pour ingredients into iced mixing glass
1 1/4 oz. Jim Beam Black Label Bourbon
1/2 oz. Giori Lemoncillo Liqueur
2 oz. sweet 'n' sour
Shake and strain
Fill with Squirt
Orange slice and cherry garnish

COLLINS, JEFF

Collins or bucket glass, ice
Pour ingredients into iced mixing glass
1 1/4 oz. Absolut Citron Vodka
3/4 oz. cranberry juice
1 1/2 oz. sweet 'n' sour
Shake and strain
Fill with club soda
Lemon wedge garnish

COLLINS, JIM

Collins or bucket glass, ice
Pour ingredients into iced mixing glass
1 1/4 oz. Scotch Whisky
2 oz. sweet 'n' sour
Shake and strain
Fill with club soda
Orange slice and cherry garnish

COLLINS, JOE
aka **Mike Collins**

Collins or bucket glass, ice
Pour ingredients into iced mixing glass
1 1/4 oz. Irish Whiskey
2 oz. sweet 'n' sour
Shake and strain
Fill with club soda
Orange slice and cherry garnish

COLLINS, JOHN
aka **Colonel Collins**

Collins or bucket glass, ice
Pour ingredients into iced mixing glass
1 1/4 oz. Bourbon
2 oz. sweet 'n' sour
Shake and strain
Fill with club soda
Orange slice and cherry garnish

COLLINS, PEDRO

Collins or bucket glass, ice
Pour ingredients into iced mixing glass
1 1/4 oz. Light Rum
2 oz. sweet 'n' sour
Shake and strain
Fill with club soda
Orange slice and cherry garnish

COLLINS, PIERRE

Collins or bucket glass, ice
Pour ingredients into iced mixing glass
1 1/4 oz. Cognac
2 oz. sweet 'n' sour
Shake and strain
Fill with club soda
Orange slice and cherry garnish

COLLINS, RED TURKEY

Collins or bucket glass, ice
Pour ingredients into iced mixing glass
1 1/4 oz. Wild Turkey 101° Bourbon
1/2 oz. Rémy Red
2 oz. sweet 'n' sour
Shake and strain
Fill with club soda
Orange slice and cherry garnish

BACARDI LIMÓN® RUM

Bacardi clearly places a premium on innovation. In 1995, the company launched BACARDI LIMÓN, a revolutionary new style of rum that turned the rum-drinking world on end. Limón is an imaginative infusion of Bacardi Carta Blanca Rum and a proprietary, all-natural blend of lemon, lime and grapefruit essence. It was an immediate success and continues to be an extremely popular rum.

Made in San Juan, Puerto Rico, Limón is a blend of continuous-distilled and pot distilled rums that are twice filtered through charcoal and aged a year in charred oak barrels. Fresh citrus extracts are added to the rum during blending. It is marketed in the United States at 70 proof.

Limón has achieved "must have" status for good reason. The rum is crystal clear with a lightweight, satiny smooth texture. The engaging bouquet is saturated with luscious, citrus aromas that set the stage for the mouth-watering flavors to come. Its broad, fresh palate is brimming with the tangy flavors of sun-ripened citrus. The rum finishes long, warm and flavorful.

Frankly, everything about Limón is refreshing. Its singular flavor makes it exceptionally mixable. Bacardi Limón is a natural with lemonade, fresh juice or blended in a daiquiri. It's also excellent when featured in a martini, gimlet or Cosmopolitan.

COLLINS, RODEO DRIVE
House specialty glass, ice
Build in glass
2 oz. Damrak Amsterdam Gin
3/4 oz. Cointreau Liqueur
Fill with Perrier mineral water
Float 3/4 oz. Oro di Mazzetti
   Grappa Liqueur
Orange slice and lemon garnish

COLLINS, TOM
aka **Gin Fizz**
Collins or bucket glass, ice
Pour ingredients into iced mixing glass
1 1/4 oz. Gin
2 oz. sweet 'n' sour
Shake and strain
Fill with club soda
Orange slice and cherry garnish

COLLINS, VODKA
Collins or bucket glass, ice
Pour ingredients into iced mixing glass
1 1/4 oz. Vodka
2 oz. sweet 'n' sour
Shake and strain
Fill with club soda
Orange slice and cherry garnish

COLOMBIAN NECKTIE
Rocks glass, chilled
Build in glass
3/4 oz. Rumple Minze Schnapps
3/4 oz. Bacardi 151° Rum
2-3 dashes Tabasco Sauce
1/2 oz. Hot Damn Cinnamon Schnapps

COLORADO AVALANCHE
Coffee mug, heated
Build in glass
1/2 oz. Kahlúa Coffee Liqueur
1/2 oz. Dark Crème de Cacao
1/2 oz. Chambord Liqueur
Near fill with hot Nestle's
   Alpine White Cocoa
Whipped cream garnish
Dust powdered cocoa

COLORADO BULLDOG
Bucket glass, ice
Build in glass
1 1/2 oz. Vodka
3/4 oz. Kahlúa Coffee Liqueur
1/2 fill cola
1/2 fill half & half cream

COLORADO RIVER COOLER
Brandy snifter, ice
Build in glass
4 oz. White Zinfandel Wine
1 oz. Midori Melon Liqueur
Fill with club soda

COME-ON-I-WANNA-LEI-YA
House specialty glass, chilled
Pour ingredients into blender
1 1/4 oz. Whaler's Hawaiian Vanille Rum
3/4 oz. Cruzan Coconut Rum
3/4 oz. Cruzan Orange Rum
2 scoops vanilla ice cream
Blend ingredients (with ice optional)
Whipped cream garnish
Drizzle 1/2 oz. Disaronno Amaretto Liqueur

COMFORTABLE CRUSH
Bucket glass, ice
Build in glass
3/4 oz. Chambord Liqueur
3/4 oz. Southern Comfort Liqueur
1/2 oz. Artic Vodka & Peach Liqueur
Fill with lemonade
Lemon wedge garnish

COMFORTABLE SCREW
aka **Southern Screw**
Highball glass, ice
Build in glass
1 1/4 oz. Southern Comfort Liqueur
Fill with orange juice

COMFORT KIT
Bucket glass, ice
Build in glass
1 oz. Hussong's Reposado Tequila
Near fill with orange juice
Float 3/4 oz. Southern Comfort Liqueur

COMMODORE
Cocktail glass, chilled
Pour ingredients into iced mixing glass
1 1/2 oz. Gold Rum
2 dashes grenadine
1 egg white (optional)
1/2 oz. simple syrup
1 1/2 oz. sweet 'n' sour
Shake and strain

CONCORDE
Champagne glass, chilled
Build in glass
1 1/2 oz. Stolichnaya Limonnaya
    Russian Vodka
Near fill with Champagne
Float 3/4 oz. Grand Marnier Liqueur

CONGO COOLER
Bucket glass, ice
Build in glass
1 1/2 oz. Jewel of Russia
    Wild Bilberry Infusion
3/4 oz. half & half cream
Near fill with orange juice
Float 3/4 oz. Crème de Banana

COOKIE
Rocks glass, ice
Build in glass
1 1/2 oz. Chopin Polish Vodka
1/2 oz. Kahlúa Coffee Liqueur
1/2 oz. DeKuyper Peppermint Schnapps

COOKIES 'N' CREAM
House specialty glass, chilled
Pour ingredients into blender
1 oz. Dark Crème de Cacao
1 oz. half & half cream
2-3 Oreo cookies
2 scoops vanilla ice cream
Blend ingredients (with ice optional)

COOL CAPTAIN
Presentation shot glass, chilled
Build in glass
1 oz. Captain Morgan Spiced Rum
3/4 oz. DeKuyper Peppermint Schnapps
1/4 oz. grenadine

COOL CARLOS
House specialty glass, ice
Pour ingredients into iced mixing glass
1 1/2 oz. Matusalem Classic Black Rum
1 oz. Orange Curaçao
1 1/2 oz. sweet 'n' sour
2 oz. cranberry juice
2 oz. pineapple juice
Shake and strain
Float 3/4 oz. St. James Extra Old Rhum
Pineapple wedge and orange slice garnish

COOL MINT LISTERINE
Presentation shot glass, chilled
Build in glass
1/3 fill Pearl Vodka
1/3 fill DeKuyper Peppermint Schnapps
1/3 fill Blue Curaçao

CORK STREET COFFEE (1)
Coffee mug, heated
Build in glass
1 1/2 oz. Bacardi Gold Rum
1/2 oz. Cruzan Rum Cream
1/2 oz. Frangelico Liqueur
Near fill with hot coffee
Whipped cream garnish
Drizzle chocolate syrup

SAUZA® HORNITOS® TEQUILA

Sauza struck pay dirt with the introduction of HORNITOS REPOSADO 100% AGAVE TEQUILA. It has for years been the best selling reposado in the United States. More importantly, Sauza Hornitos is likely the best value in the entire category, earning it the distinction of being the "most tequila for the buck."

Hornitos is distilled entirely from mature blue agave at the Sauza La Perseverancia Distillery in Jalisco, Mexico. The harvested agaves are baked, shredded, fermented, and double distilled in both an alembic still and a stainless steel column still. Sauza then ages Hornitos for 4- to 6-months in large oak vats, which is just enough time to soften its character without being appreciably affected by the tannins in the wood. As a result, Hornitos has the exuberance and fresh agave character of a blanco tequila with a touch of mellow refinement of an añejo.

A quick sniff, sip and swallow will reveal why Hornitos has become such a run-away success. The pale, golden color belies its complexity and full, rounded body. The tequila has an alluring bouquet concentrated with the aromas of pepper, caramel and citrus. Its semisweet palate features the flavors of caramel, pepper, ripe fruit and the herbaceous taste of agave.

Sauza Hornitos Reposado is a tequila that knows no creative limitations and is fit for any tequila-based assignment.

CORK STREET COFFEE (2)
Coffee mug, heated
Build in glass
3/4 oz. Baileys Irish Cream
3/4 oz. Frangelico Liqueur
1/2 oz. Gold Rum
Near fill with hot coffee
Whipped cream garnish
Dust powdered cocoa

CORONATION
Wine goblet (ice optional)
Build in glass
1 oz. Dry Vermouth
1 1/2 oz. Dry Sherry
1 dash Maraschino Liqueur
2 dashes Angostura Bitters
5 oz. White Wine
Fill with club soda

CORPSE REVIVER (1)
Cocktail glass, chilled
Pour ingredients into iced mixing glass
3/4 oz. Calvados Apple Brandy
3/4 oz. V.S. Cognac
1/2 oz. Sweet Vermouth
Stir and strain
Lemon twist garnish

CORPSE REVIVER (2)
Cocktail glass, chilled
Pour ingredients into iced mixing glass
1 oz. Fernet Branca
1 oz. Brandy
1 oz. White Crème de Cacao
Stir and strain

COSMOPOLITAN
Cocktail glass, chilled
Pour ingredients into iced mixing glass
1 1/2 oz. Absolut Citron Vodka
1/2 oz. Cointreau Liqueur
1/2 oz. Rose's Lime Juice
1/2 oz. cranberry juice
Stir and strain
Orange twist garnish

COSMOPOLITAN, ALIZÉ
Cocktail glass, chilled
Pour ingredients into iced mixing glass
1 oz. Alizé de France
1 oz. Absolut Citron Vodka
1/4 oz. fresh lemon juice
1 oz. cranberry juice
Stir and strain
Lime wheel garnish

COSMOPOLITAN, ARTIC PEACH

Cocktail glass, chilled
Pour ingredients into iced mixing glass
2 oz. Artic Vodka & Peach Liqueur
1 1/2 oz. cranberry juice
1/2 oz. Rose's Lime Juice
Stir and strain
Peach slice garnish

COSMOPOLITAN, BLACK

Cocktail glass, chilled
Pour ingredients into iced mixing glass
1 1/2 oz. Blavod Black Vodka
1/2 oz. DeKuyper Triple Sec
1/2 oz. cranberry juice
1/2 oz. fresh lime juice
Stir and strain
Lime wedge garnish

COSMOPOLITAN, CILLO

Cocktail glass, chilled
Pour ingredients into iced mixing glass
1 1/2 oz. Giori Lemoncillo Cream Liqueur
1/2 oz. Cointreau Liqueur
1/2 oz. Rose's Lime Juice
1/2 oz. cranberry juice
Stir and strain
Lime wedge garnish

COSMOPOLITAN, CHI CHI

Cocktail glass, chilled
Pour ingredients into iced mixing glass
1 1/2 oz. Cruzan Coconut Rum
3/4 oz. Artic Vodka & Peach Liqueur
1/2 oz. Gran Gala Orange Liqueur
1/2 oz. cranberry juice
3/4 oz. sweet 'n' sour
Stir and strain
Frozen cranberry garnish

COSMOPOLITAN, COSMORITA

Cocktail glass, chilled
Pour ingredients into iced mixing glass
1 1/2 oz. Sauza Tres Generaciones
   Plata Tequila
3/4 oz. DeKuyper Peachtree Schnapps
1/2 oz. Rose's Lime Juice
1/2 oz. cranberry juice
Stir and strain
Lime wedge garnish

COSMOPOLITAN, CRISTALL LEMON TWIST

Cocktail glass, chilled
Pour ingredients into iced mixing glass
2 oz. Cristall Lemon Twist Russian Vodka
1 oz. Triple Sec
1/2 oz. fresh lime juice
Splash cranberry juice
Shake and strain
Lemon twist garnish

COSMOPOLITAN, DIRTY

Cocktail glass, chilled
Pour ingredients into iced mixing glass
2 oz. Jewel of Russia Berry Infusion
3/4 oz. Cointreau Liqueur
1/2 oz. fresh lime juice
Stir and strain
Lemon wheel garnish

COSMOPOLITAN, DISARONNO

Cocktail glass, chilled
Pour ingredients into iced mixing glass
1 oz. Disaronno Amaretto Liqueur
1 oz. Bacardi Limón Rum
1/2 oz. cranberry juice
Stir and strain
Lime wedge garnish

COSMOPOLITAN, DUBONNET

Cocktail glass, chilled
Pour ingredients into iced mixing glass
1 1/4 oz. Absolut Citron Vodka
3/4 oz. Dubonnet Rouge
1/2 oz. Cointreau Liqueur
1/2 oz. Rose's Lime Juice
1/2 oz. cranberry juice
1/4 oz. fresh lime juice
Stir and strain
Lime wheel garnish

COSMOPOLITAN, LIMÓN

Cocktail glass, chilled
Pour ingredients into iced mixing glass
1 1/2 oz. Bacardi Limón Rum
1/2 oz. Cointreau Liqueur
1/2 oz. Rose's Lime Juice
1/2 oz. cranberry juice
Stir and strain
Orange twist garnish

COSMOPOLITAN, LONDON

Cocktail glass, chilled
Pour ingredients into iced mixing glass
1 1/2 oz. Beefeater London Dry Gin
1/2 oz. Cointreau Liqueur
1/2 oz. Rose's Lime Juice
1/2 oz. cranberry juice
Stir and strain
Orange twist garnish

COSMOPOLITAN, MARGARITA COSMO

Cocktail glass, chilled
Rim glass with salt (optional)
Pour ingredients into iced mixing glass
2 oz. Sauza Tres Generaciones Plata Tequila
3/4 oz. Grand Marnier Liqueur
1/2 oz. Rose's Lime Juice
3/4 oz. cranberry juice
Stir and strain
Lime wedge garnish

FRANGELICO® LIQUEUR

Introduced in the early 1980s, premium FRANGELICO LIQUEUR immediately shot up the pop charts. Nothing like it had appeared on American back bars before. Its brilliant hazelnut flavor quickly became the featured attraction in many contemporary classics.

Legend has it that in the early 1600s an Italian Christian named Fra. Angelico concocted a liqueur out of wild hazelnuts nuts and natural flavorings. This was the inspiration for the Frangelico Liqueur recipe, as interpreted by the renowned firm G. Barbero of Canale, located near Turin, Italy. The award-winning liqueur is made with a base of Italian grape spirits, which are steeped with the natural extracts, including hazelnuts, cocoa, coffee, vanilla, rhubarb and orange blossoms. It is then filtered for purity, sweetened and bottled at 48 proof.

The reasons for Frangelico's meteoric success are perfectly evident. It has an attractive amber hue and a lightweight, lushly textured body. The liqueur's bouquet is about the most seductive in the business, a wafting affair of vanilla, honey, and nuts. The bakery fresh aromas expertly prepare the palate for chocolate, spicy herbs and toasted hazelnuts. The flavorful finish is warm and relaxed.

Frangelico is now firmly entrenched in the "must have" category. It is as versatile as it is delicious; an indispensable liqueur in a mixologist's repertoire.

COSMOPOLITAN, MELON
Cocktail glass, chilled
Pour ingredients into iced mixing glass
1 3/4 oz. Artic Vodka & Melon Liqueur
1/2 oz. Cointreau Liqueur
1/2 oz. Rose's Lime Juice
1/2 oz. cranberry juice
Stir and strain
Lime wedge garnish

COSMOPOLITAN, MEXICALI
Cocktail glass, chilled
Pour ingredients into iced mixing glass
1 1/2 oz. Sauza Hornitos Tequila
3/4 oz. Cointreau Liqueur
1/2 oz. Rose's Lime Juice
1/2 oz. cranberry juice
Stir and strain
Lime wedge garnish

COSMOPOLITAN, RASPBERRY
Cocktail glass, chilled
Pour ingredients into iced mixing glass
2 oz. Pearl Vodka
3/4 oz. Cointreau Liqueur
1/2 oz. DeKuyper Raspberry Pucker
1/2 oz. fresh lime juice
Stir and strain
Lemon wheel garnish

COSMOPOLITAN, TRES COSMO
Cocktail glass, chilled
Pour ingredients into iced mixing glass
1 1/2 oz. Sauza Tres Generaciones
    Añejo Tequila
1 oz. Cointreau Liqueur
1 oz. fresh lime juice
1 oz. cranberry juice
Shake and strain
Lime twist garnish

COVE COOLER
Bucket glass, ice
Build in glass
1 1/4 oz. Pusser's British Navy Rum
1 1/2 oz. sweet 'n' sour
Near fill with pineapple juice
Splash club soda
Orange slice garnish

COWBOY KILLER
House specialty glass, ice
Pour ingredients into iced mixing glass
1/2 oz. Disaronno Amaretto Liqueur
1/2 oz. DeKuyper Cherry Pucker
1/2 oz. Southern Comfort Liqueur
1/2 oz. grenadine
1 oz. sweet 'n' sour
2 oz. orange juice
Shake and strain
Orange slice and cherry garnish

CRABAPPLE
Bucket glass, ice
Build in glass
1 1/2 oz. DeKuyper Pucker Sour Apple
1/2 oz. Zone Peach Italian Vodka
Near fill with Squirt
Float 1/2 oz. grenadine

CRAB HOUSE SHOOTER
Rocks glass, chilled
Pour ingredients into iced mixing glass
1/2 oz. Disaronno Amaretto Liqueur
1/2 oz. Southern Comfort Liqueur
1/2 oz. Chambord Liqueur
1/4 oz. sweet 'n' sour
1/4 oz. Rose's Lime Juice
1/4 oz. pineapple juice
1/4 oz. cranberry juice
1/4 oz. orange juice
Shake and strain

CRANBERRY SQUEEZE
Bucket glass, ice
Build in glass
1 1/4 oz. Stolichnaya Limonnaya
    Russian Vodka
3/4 oz. Chambord Liqueur
Fill with lemonade
Lemon wedge garnish

CREAM OF GIN
Cocktail glass, chilled
Pour ingredients into iced mixing glass
3/4 oz. Beefeater London Dry Gin
1/2 oz. White Crème de Menthe
1/2 oz. White Crème de Cacao
2 oz. half & half cream
Shake and strain

CREAMSICLE (1)
Cocktail glass, chilled
Pour ingredients into iced mixing glass
3/4 oz. Crème de Banana
3/4 oz. DeKuyper Triple Sec
1 oz. orange juice
1 oz. half & half cream
Shake and strain

CREAMSICLE (2)
House specialty glass, chilled
Pour ingredients into blender
1 1/4 oz. Disaronno Amaretto Liqueur
3/4 oz. Gran Gala Orange Liqueur
2 oz. orange juice
1 scoop each, vanilla ice cream and
    orange sorbet
Blend ingredients (with ice optional)
Whipped cream garnish

CREAMY BULL
Cocktail glass, chilled
Pour ingredients into iced mixing glass
3/4 oz. Tequila
3/4 oz. Kahlúa Coffee Liqueur
2 oz. half & half cream
Shake and strain

CREAMY DREAMY ISOTOPE
Bucket glass, ice
Pour ingredients into iced mixing glass
3/4 oz. Tropico
3/4 oz. B & B Liqueur
3/4 oz. Galliano Liqueur
3/4 oz. Brandy
1 oz. orange juice
1 oz. half & half cream
Shake and strain

CREOLE
Rocks glass, ice
Pour ingredients into iced mixing glass
1 1/2 oz. Bacardi Light Rum
2 dashes Tabasco Sauce
1 tsp. fresh lemon juice
1 1/2 oz. beef bouillon
Salt and pepper to taste
Shake and strain
Lemon wedge garnish

CRIMSON ROSE
House specialty glass, chilled
Pour ingredients into blender
1 1/4 oz. Tequila Rose Cream Liqueur
2 oz. DeKuyper Triple Sec
3 oz. frozen strawberries
Blend with ice
Strawberry garnish

CRUZAN GLIDE SLIDE
Bucket glass, ice
Build in glass
1 1/2 oz. Cruzan Coconut Rum
3/4 oz. Kahlúa Coffee Liqueur
3/4 oz. Baileys Irish Cream
2 oz. milk
2 oz. pineapple juice
Float 3/4 oz. Matusalem Classic Black Rum

CRYPTO NUGGET
Rocks glass, chilled
Pour ingredients into iced mixing glass
3/4 oz. DeKuyper Pucker Sour Apple
1/2 oz. Finlandia Vodka
1/4 oz. Blue Curaçao
1/4 oz. Rose's Lime Juice
Shake and strain

BELVEDERE® POLISH VODKA

Since its American debut in 1996, BELVEDERE POLISH LUXURY VODKA has caught on in a seriously big way. It can be found on the back bar of any self-respecting martini bar, and with good reason. Belvedere is a full-bodied, character-laden spirit that gives substance and meaning to any martini or vodka-inspired cocktail.

Belvedere Vodka is crafted at the Polmos Zyrardów from 100% Polish rye and purified water. It is first distilled in an alembic still, a costly and relatively laborious step, but one that imbues the vodka with a substantial body and a robust character. That spirit is then triple-distilled in a continuous still, which lightens it significantly. The vodka is free of any trace congeners as a result of being purified four times through a complex of filter screens.

Belvedere is genuinely deserving of its world-class reputation. The vodka has pristine clarity and a subtle, pleasant bouquet of pine and dried herbs. Its velvety smooth body has heft and substance as it glides over the palate, completely filling the mouth with notes of vanilla and citrus zest. The protracted, slightly sweet finish is flawless.

This uptown vodka is a perfect candidate for serving straight-up, over ice, or in any contemporary cocktail that showcases vodka.

CRYSTAL CLEAR

House specialty glass, ice
Pour ingredients into iced mixing glass
1 oz. Brilliant Vodka
3/4 oz. Midori Melon Liqueur
3/4 oz. DeKuyper Peach Pucker
3/4 oz. grape juice
1 1/2 oz. cranberry juice
2 oz. orange juice
Shake and strain

CUBAN COCKTAIL

Cocktail glass, chilled
Pour ingredients into iced mixing glass
2 oz. Matusalem Light Dry Rum
2 oz. sweetened lime juice
Shake and strain
Lime wedge garnish

CUBA LIBRE

Highball glass, ice
Build in glass
1 1/4 oz. Light Rum
Fill with cola
Lime wedge garnish

CUBAN PEACH

Cocktail glass, chilled
Pour ingredients into iced mixing glass
1 1/2 oz. Matusalem Light Dry Rum
1 oz. DeKuyper Peachtree Schnapps
1/2 oz. Rose's Lime Juice
1 dash simple syrup
Shake and strain
Mint sprig garnish

CUBAN SIDECAR

Cocktail glass, chilled
Pour ingredients into iced mixing glass
1 1/2 oz. Matusalem Light Dry Rum
1 oz. DeKuyper Triple Sec
1 oz. fresh lime juice
Shake and strain
Lime wedge garnish

CUBAN SPECIAL

Cocktail glass, chilled
Pour ingredients into iced mixing glass
1 1/2 oz. Matusalem Light Dry Rum
1/2 oz. DeKuyper Triple Sec
1/2 oz. fresh lime juice
3/4 oz. pineapple juice
Shake and strain
Lime wedge garnish

CULTURE SHOCK
House specialty glass, chilled
Pour ingredients into blender
1/2 oz. Cruzan Coconut Rum
1/2 oz. Cruzan Banana Rum
1/2 oz. Cruzan Estate Diamond Rum
1/2 oz. Alizé Red Passion
1 1/2 oz. orange juice
1 1/2 oz. pineapple juice
Blend with ice
Float 3/4 oz. Cruzan Estate Diamond Rum
Orange slice and cherry garnish

CURAÇAO COOLER
House specialty glass, ice
Pour ingredients into iced mixing glass
1 1/2 oz. Mount Gay Eclipse Rum
1 1/4 oz. Blue Curaçao
3/4 oz. Citrónge Orange Liqueur
1 oz. fresh lime juice
1 1/2 oz. orange juice
1 1/2 oz. sweet 'n' sour
Shake and strain
Near fill with club soda
Float 3/4 oz. St. James Extra Old Rhum
Lime wedge garnish

CYRANO
Rocks glass, chilled
Pour ingredients into iced mixing glass
1 oz. Baileys Irish Cream
1 oz. Grand Marnier 100th Anniversary
Shake and strain
Splash Chambord Liqueur

DACTYL NIGHTMARE
Presentation shot glass, chilled
Layer ingredients
1/2 fill Baileys Irish Cream
1/2 fill Midori Melon Liqueur
4 drops grenadine

DAIQUIRI
House specialty glass, ice
Pour ingredients into iced mixing glass
1 1/4 oz. Light Rum
1/2 oz. Rose's Lime Juice
2 oz. sweet 'n' sour
Shake and strain
Lime wedge garnish

DAIQUIRI, BANANA
House specialty glass, chilled
Pour ingredients into blender
1 1/4 oz. Light Rum
1 oz. Cruzan Banana Rum
Peeled ripe banana
1/2 oz. Rose's Lime Juice
2 oz. sweet 'n' sour
Blend with ice
Orange and banana slice garnish

DAIQUIRI, BERRY
House specialty glass, chilled
Pour ingredients into blender
1 1/4 oz. Bacardi Light Rum
1/2 cup raspberries or strawberries
1/2 oz. Rose's Lime Juice
2 oz. sweet 'n' sour
Blend with ice
Float 3/4 oz. Chambord Liqueur
Pineapple wedge and cherry garnish

DAIQUIRI, CALYPSO
House specialty glass, chilled
Pour ingredients into blender
1 1/2 oz. Appleton Estate V/X Jamaica Rum
1 ripe banana
1 tsp. vanilla extract
1/2 oz. half & half cream
2 1/2 oz. sweet 'n' sour
Blend with ice
Float 3/4 oz. Rhum Barbancourt
    3-Star Rum
Pineapple wedge and cherry garnish

DAIQUIRI, CHARLES
Cocktail glass, chilled
Pour ingredients into iced mixing glass
1 1/2 oz. Bacardi Light Rum
3/4 oz. Royal Oak Extra Old Rum
3/4 oz. Cointreau Liqueur
1/2 oz. Rose's Lime Juice
1 1/2 oz. sweet 'n' sour
Shake and strain
Lime wedge garnish

DAIQUIRI, COCONUT
Cocktail glass, chilled
Pour ingredients into iced mixing glass
1 1/2 oz. Bacardi Light Rum
1 oz. Cruzan Coconut Rum
3/4 oz. coconut cream syrup
1/2 oz. Rose's Lime Juice
1 1/2 oz. sweet 'n' sour
Shake and strain
Lime wedge garnish

DAIQUIRI, DEMERARA
Cocktail glass, chilled
Pour ingredients into iced mixing glass
1 1/4 oz. Cadenhead's Green Label
    Demerara Rum
1/2 oz. Rose's Lime Juice
2 oz. sweet 'n' sour
Shake and strain
Orange slice garnish

CHOPIN® POLISH VODKA

Frederic Chopin's musical masterpieces are timeless classics. CHOPIN POLISH LUXURY VODKA is an opus worthy of the revered composer's name.

Chopin is imported from Poland where its ancestry can be traced back five centuries. This elegant vodka is distilled four times in small batches, and is made exclusively from Stobrawa potatoes grown in the Mazovic region of Poland. These hand-cultivated potatoes give Chopin its robust character and distinctively delicious flavor. The water used in its production is drawn from deep, underground wells repeatedly filtered for purity.

Chopin Polish Vodka has a light, flawlessly smooth texture and a subtle, yet inviting bouquet with the semi-sweet aromas of apple, caramel and citrus. The vodka immediately expands in the mouth and sizzles just slightly on the palate. It is lightly flavored with the semi-sweet taste of cocoa and toffee flavors that persist throughout the medium length finish.

The vodka's eye-catching, cork-finished bottle is the same type used to market best-selling BELVEDERE VODKA. These two luxury vodkas are typical sisters, related, yet dissimilar. Where Chopin has a bold, zesty character, Belvedere is softer, with a rounder, more sedate personality. Both are absolutely exemplary and deserving of top-shelf status.

DAIQUIRI de PIÑA
House specialty glass, chilled
Pour ingredients into blender
1 1/2 oz. Bacardi Light Rum
1 oz. Cruzan Pineapple Rum
2-3 slices cored and peeled pineapple
1/2 oz. Rose's Lime Juice
2 oz. sweet 'n' sour
Blend with ice
Orange slice, pineapple wedge and cherry garnish

DAIQUIRI, DERBY
Cocktail glass, chilled
Pour ingredients into blender
1 1/2 oz. Bacardi Select Rum
1/2 oz. Rose's Lime Juice
1 oz. orange juice
1 1/2 oz. sweet 'n' sour
Blend with ice
Float 3/4 oz. Pyrat Pistol Rum
Pineapple wedge and cherry garnish

DAIQUIRI, DON ROLAND
Cocktail glass, chilled
Pour ingredients into iced mixing glass
1 1/2 oz. Bacardi Light Rum
1/2 oz. Green Crème de Menthe
1/2 oz. Cointreau Liqueur
2 mint leaves
1/2 oz. Rose's Lime Juice
1 1/2 oz. sweet 'n' sour
Shake and strain
Mint sprig garnish

DAIQUIRI, FLORIDA
Cocktail glass, chilled
Pour ingredients into iced mixing glass
1 1/2 oz. Bacardi Light Rum
1/4 oz. grenadine
1/2 oz. Rose's Lime Juice
1/2 oz. grapefruit juice
1 1/2 oz. sweet 'n' sour
Shake and strain
Lime wedge garnish

DAIQUIRI, FRENCH (1)
Cocktail glass, chilled
Pour ingredients into iced mixing glass
1 3/4 oz. St. James Extra Old Rhum
3/4 oz. Briottet Crème de Cassis
1/2 oz. Rose's Lime Juice
2 oz. sweet 'n' sour
Shake and strain
Orange twist garnish

DAIQUIRI, FRENCH (2)
Cocktail glass, chilled
Pour ingredients into iced mixing glass
1 3/4 oz. J. Bally Rhum Vieux 7-Year
1/2 oz. Rose's Lime Juice
1 oz. passion fruit juice
2 oz. sweet 'n' sour
Shake and strain
Orange twist garnish

DAIQUIRI, FLIGHT OF FANCY
House specialty glass, chilled
Pour ingredients into blender
2 oz. Gosling's Black Seal Rum
1/2 oz. Rose's Lime Juice
1/2 cup raspberries
3 oz. sweet 'n' sour
Blend with ice

DAIQUIRI, FRUIT (BASIC)
House specialty glass, chilled
Pour ingredients into blender
1 1/2 oz. Light Rum
1/2 cup requested fruit
1/2 oz. Rose's Lime Juice
1 1/2 oz. sweet 'n' sour
Blend with ice
Fresh fruit garnish

DAIQUIRI, HEMINGWAY
Cocktail glass, chilled
Pour ingredients into iced mixing glass
1 3/4 oz. Light Rum
1/2 oz. Maraschino Liqueur
1 oz. grapefruit juice
1 1/2 oz. fresh lime juice
Shake and strain
Lime wheel garnish

DAIQUIRI, LA FLORIDITA
Cocktail glass, chilled
Pour ingredients into iced mixing glass
1 1/2 oz. Bacardi Light Rum
3/4 oz. Cointreau Liqueur
3/4 oz. fresh lime juice
2 oz. sweet 'n' sour
Shake and strain
Lime wedge garnish

DAIQUIRI, LECHTHALER'S
House specialty glass, chilled
Pour ingredients into iced mixing glass
1 oz. Bacardi Light Rum
1 oz. Bacardi Gold Rum
1/2 oz. Rose's Lime Juice
2 oz. sweet 'n' sour
Shake and strain
Lime wedge and orange slice garnish

DAIQUIRI, MULATTA
House specialty glass, chilled
Pour ingredients into iced mixing glass
1 oz. Appleton Estate V/X Jamaica Rum
1 oz. Mount Gay Eclipse Rum
3/4 oz. Dark Crème de Cacao
3/4 oz. Maraschino Liqueur
1/2 oz. Rose's Lime Juice
2 oz. sweet 'n' sour
Shake and strain
Lime wedge garnish

DAIQUIRI, PAPA HEMINGWAY
Cocktail glass, chilled
Pour ingredients into iced mixing glass
1 1/2 oz. Bacardi Light Rum
1/2 oz. Maraschino Liqueur
1 oz. fresh lime juice
1 1/2 oz. grapefruit juice
Shake and strain
Lime wedge garnish

DAIQUIRI, PASSION
Cocktail glass, chilled
Pour ingredients into iced mixing glass
1 1/2 oz. Bacardi Light Rum
1/2 oz. Rose's Lime Juice
1 1/2 oz. passion fruit juice
1 1/2 oz. sweet 'n' sour
Shake and strain
Orange twist garnish

DAIQUIRI, PRICKLY PEAR
House specialty glass, chilled
Pour ingredients into iced mixing glass
2 oz. Bacardi Limón Rum
1/2 oz. grenadine
1 oz. sweetened lime juice
1 oz. sweet 'n' sour
2 oz. prickly pear syrup (puree)
Shake and strain
Lime wedge garnish

DAIQUIRI, PYRAT
Cocktail glass, chilled
Pour ingredients into iced mixing glass
1 3/4 oz. Pyrat X.O. Reserve Rum
1 oz. orange juice
1 1/4 oz. sweetened lime juice
Shake and strain
Orange twist garnish

DAIQUIRI, RASPBERRY
Cocktail glass, chilled
Pour ingredients into iced mixing glass
1 1/2 oz. Gosling's Black Seal Rum
3/4 oz. DeKuyper Raspberry Pucker
1/2 oz. Rose's Lime Juice
2 oz. sweet 'n' sour
Shake and strain
Berry garnish

HIGHBALL DRINKS
Preparation Tips

Highballs are popular and easy to prepare drinks, and yet they account for a high percentage of mistakes and waste created behind the bar. These drinks require concentration to remember three or four highball combinations in the same drink order.

The most frequently committed error is inadvertently switching the mixers. For example, in the order "gin & tonic, scotch & soda, and bourbon & water", it would be easy to mistakenly prepare instead "gin & tonic, scotch & water, and bourbon & soda." This type of mistake results in two of the drinks being returned, liquor being wasted, and extra time needed to remake the drinks.

To minimize mistakes, be sure you hear the drink order correctly and silently repeat it until the drinks have been prepared. Preparing the drinks in the same sequence that they are ordered will also reduce the likelihood of making a costly mistake.

Another helpful technique when preparing several highball drinks at the same time is to pour the liquor portions for all of the drinks first, and then finishing the order with the specified mixers.

Another commonly heard complaint from highball drinkers is that a drink is too "weak." One explanation may be that the glass was not filled with enough ice prior to making the drink. An insufficient amount of ice will result in the use of too much mixer, thereby over-diluting the drink.

It is equally important to fill the glass to the proper level. If too much mixer is added, the glass will become too full and difficult to move without creating a mess. If too little mixer is added the drink will appear short and taste too strong.

DAIQUIRI, RHUM
Cocktail glass, chilled
Pour ingredients into iced mixing glass
1 1/2 oz. Rhum Barbancourt 5-Star Rum
3/4 oz. Chambord Liqueur
3/4 oz. Crème de Banana
2 oz. sweetened lime juice
Shake and strain
Lime wedge and orange slice garnish

DAIQUIRI, SUMMER SKY
Cocktail glass, chilled
Pour ingredients into iced mixing glass
1 3/4 oz. Mount Gay Eclipse Rum
1 1/2 oz. orange juice
1 1/2 oz. sweetened lime juice
Shake and strain
Orange twist garnish

DAIQUIRI, SWEET TART
House specialty glass, ice
Pour ingredients into iced mixing glass
1 1/4 oz. Doorly's XO Barbados Rum
3/4 oz. Giori Lemoncillo Liqueur
1/2 oz. Rose's Lime Juice
2 oz. sweet 'n' sour
Shake and strain
Strawberry garnish

DAIQUIRI, WHALE SMOOCH
House specialty glass, ice
Pour ingredients into iced mixing glass
1 1/4 oz. Matusalem Gran Reserva Rum
3/4 oz. Whaler's Hawaiian Vanille Rum
1/2 oz. Rose's Lime Juice
2 oz. sweet 'n' sour
Shake and strain
Lime wedge garnish

DALE'S SOUR APPLE
Cocktail glass, chilled
Pour ingredients into iced mixing glass
1 1/2 oz. Luksusowa Polish Vodka
1/2 oz. DeKuyper Pucker Sour Apple
1/2 oz. DeKuyper Triple Sec
3/4 oz. fresh lemon juice
Shake and strain
Green apple wedge garnish

DAMRAK BLUE LADY
Cocktail glass, chilled
Pour ingredients into iced mixing glass
1 1/2 oz. Damrak Amsterdam Gin
3/4 oz. Blue Curaçao
1 tsp. sugar
1 oz. fresh lemon juice
Shake and strain
Lime wheel and lemon twist garnish

DAMRAK 75 (1)
Champagne glass, chilled
Pour ingredients into iced mixing glass
1 3/4 oz. Damrak Amsterdam Gin
1/2 oz. Cointreau Liqueur
2 oz. sweet 'n' sour
Shake and strain
Fill with Champagne
Lemon twist garnish

DANGEROUS LIAISONS
Cocktail glass, chilled
Pour ingredients into iced mixing glass
1 oz. Christian Brothers Brandy
1 oz. Cointreau Liqueur
2 oz. sweet 'n' sour
Shake and strain
Lemon wheel garnish

DARK'n STORMY®
House specialty glass, ice
Build in glass
1 3/4 oz. Gosling's Black Seal Rum
Fill with Ginger Beer
Lime wedge garnish

DARK WATERS
House specialty glass, ice
Pour ingredients into iced mixing glass
1 oz. Blavod Black Vodka
1 oz. Bacardi Limón Rum
1/2 oz. grenadine
2 oz. orange juice
2 oz. pineapple juice
Shake and strain
Float 3/4 oz. Matusalem Gran Reserva Rum

DC-3 SHOOTER
Rocks glass, chilled
Pour ingredients into iced mixing glass
1 oz. Campari Aperitivo
1 oz. Jewel of Russia Wild Bilberry Infusion
1 oz. grapefruit juice
1 oz. orange juice
Shake and strain
Orange twist garnish

DEAD EYE DICK'S RED EYE
Pilsner glass, chilled
Build in glass
3/4 fill Draft Beer
Near fill with Bloody Mary mix
Float whole egg on top (optional)

DEAD GRIZZLY
Rocks glass, ice
Build in glass
3/4 oz. Yukon Jack Liqueur
3/4 oz. El Jimador Añejo Tequila
3/4 oz. W.L. Weller Bourbon
2 dashes Tabasco Sauce

DEAD GRIZZLY SHOOTER
Presentation shot glass, chilled
Build in glass
1/2 oz. Yukon Jack Liqueur
1/2 oz. El Jimador Añejo Tequila
1/2 oz. W.L. Weller Bourbon
2 dashes Tabasco Sauce

DEATH BY CHOCOLATE
House specialty glass, chilled
Pour ingredients into blender
1 oz. Baileys Irish Cream
1 oz. Godiva Chocolate Liqueur
1/2 oz. Vodka
1 scoop chocolate ice cream
Blend ingredients (with ice optional)

DEATH OF A VIRGIN
Bucket glass, ice
Build in glass
1 1/4 oz. Artic Vodka & Melon Liqueur
1 1/4 oz. DeKuyper Peach Pucker
1/2 oz. Rose's Lime Juice
1/2 fill orange juice
1/2 fill Seven-Up
Orange slice and cherry garnish

DEATHWISH
Presentation shot glass, chilled
Build in glass
1/2 oz. Wild Turkey 101° Bourbon
1/2 oz. Bacardi Gold Rum
1/2 oz. DeKuyper Peppermint Schnapps
1/2 oz. grenadine

DEAUVILLE
Cocktail glass, chilled
Pour ingredients into iced mixing glass
1 1/4 oz. Laird's Applejack Brandy
1/2 oz. Cointreau Liqueur
1/2 oz. grenadine
1 1/2 oz. sweet 'n' sour
Shake and strain

DEBONAIR
Brandy snifter, ice
Build in glass
1 1/2 oz. Ballylarkin Irish Liqueur
3/4 oz. Baileys Irish Cream

DEBUTANTE
Cocktail glass, chilled
Pour ingredients into iced mixing glass
1/2 oz. Tequila
1/2 oz. DeKuyper Peachtree Schnapps
1/2 oz. White Crème de Menthe
1 1/2 oz. sweet 'n' sour
Shake and strain
Lemon twist garnish

LAIRD'S® 12-YEAR-OLD RARE APPLE BRANDY

As the country's oldest distiller and holder of federal liquor license #1, Laird & Company is an American institution. The company's founder, Robert Laird, not only fought in the American Revolution under the command of General George Washington, but his family's inn in Colt's Neck, New Jersey provided apple brandy to the beleaguered Continental soldiers.

The company has introduced LAIRD'S 12-YEAR-OLD RARE APPLE BRANDY, a sumptuous spirit worthy of international recognition and acclaim. Distilled from a blend of five varieties of American apples, the brandy is aged in American white oak barrels for a minimum of 12 years.

This classic American brandy is handcrafted in extremely limited quantity. It has an alluring, expansive bouquet laced with the aromas of fresh fruit. The luscious palate is dominated by the flavors of ripe apples and vanilla that slowly taper off into a lingering, flavorful finish.

Laird's 12-year-old Rare Apple Brandy is a triumphant accomplishment. It compares favorably with the finest Calvados from Normandy costing 2 to 3 times as much. Every bottle of 88 proof brandy is hand-filled and inscribed with a batch number, bottling date and bottle number.

Need we mention what your mother told you about an apple a day?

DEEP SEA DIVER
House specialty glass, ice
Pour ingredients into iced mixing glass
1 1/4 oz. Bacardi Gold Rum
3/4 oz. Mount Gay Eclipse Rum
3/4 oz. Citrónge Orange Liqueur
1/2 oz. Rose's Lime Juice
2 oz. sweet 'n' sour
Shake and strain
Float 3/4 oz. Bacardi Select Rum
Lime, lemon and orange wedge garnish

DEEP THROAT
Presentation shot glass, chilled
Build in glass
3/4 oz. Stolichnaya Russian Vodka
3/4 oz. Tia Maria
1/2 oz. Baileys Irish Cream
Whipped cream garnish

DEFROSTER (1)
House specialty glass, chilled
Pour ingredients into blender
2 oz. Forty Creek Canadian Whisky
1/2 oz. Villa Massa Limoncello
1/2 oz. Alizé Red Passion
1 1/2 oz. peach puree
2 oz. sweet 'n' sour
Blend with ice

DE GAULLE COCKTAIL
Champagne glass, chilled
Pour ingredients into iced mixing glass
3/4 oz. V.S. Cognac
3/4 oz. Chambord Liqueur
1 1/2 oz. sweet 'n' sour
Shake and strain
Fill with Champagne
Lemon wheel garnish

DE GAULLE'S DESSERT
House specialty glass, chilled
Pour ingredients into blender
1 1/2 oz. B & B Liqueur
1/2 oz. simple syrup
1/2 oz. grenadine
2 scoops vanilla ice cream
Blend ingredients (with ice optional)
Sprinkle shaved chocolate

DELICIAS de LA HABANA
House specialty glass, chilled
Pour ingredients into blender
1 1/4 oz. Matusalem Light Dry Rum
1 1/4 oz. Matusalem Golden Dry Rum
1 oz. Midori Melon Liqueur
3/4 oz. Blue Curaçao
1 oz. coconut cream syrup
1 oz. pineapple juice
2 oz. peach nectar
Blend with ice
Pineapple and peach wedge garnish

DEPTH CHARGE
Shot glass and beer mug, chilled
Build in shot glass
1 1/2 oz. Whiskey
Build in mug
3/4 fill Draft Beer
Drop shot glass of whiskey into beer

DESERT PASSION
House specialty glass, ice
Pour ingredients into iced mixing glass
1 oz. Alizé Red Passion
1 oz. Alizé de France
1 oz. Midori Melon Liqueur
1/2 oz. grenadine
1/2 oz. Rose's Lime Juice
1 oz. tangerine juice
3 oz. pineapple juice
Shake and strain
Pineapple wedge garnish

DESERT STORM
Bucket glass, ice
Pour ingredients into iced mixing glass
1 1/2 oz. Cruzan Pineapple Rum
1 oz. Disaronno Amaretto Liqueur
1 1/2 oz. pineapple juice
1 1/2 oz. orange juice
1/2 oz. sweet 'n' sour
Shake and strain

DESERT SUNRISE
Bucket glass, ice
Build in glass
1 1/4 oz. Hussong's Reposado Tequila
3/4 oz. Blue Curaçao
1/2 fill orange juice
1/2 fill lemonade
Lime wedge garnish

DESIGNER JEANS
Presentation shot glass, chilled
Build in glass
1/3 fill Baileys Irish Cream
1/3 fill DeKuyper Raspberry Pucker
1/3 fill Myers's Jamaican Rum

DEWAR'S HIGHLAND COOLER
Bucket glass, ice
Build in glass
2 oz. Dewar's White Label Scotch Whisky
1/4 oz. simple syrup
Near fill with club soda
Long spiral lemon twist garnish

DEWAR'S TANGO
Cocktail glass, chilled
Pour ingredients into iced mixing glass
1 oz. Dewar's White Label Scotch Whisky
1 oz. sweet 'n' sour
1 oz. orange juice
Shake and strain
Orange slice and cherry garnish

DEW DROP DEAD
Mason jar, ice
Build in glass
2 1/2 oz. Georgia Moonshine Corn Whiskey
1/2 oz. DJ Dotson Triple Sec
Fill with white grape juice

DHARAMA RUM
House specialty glass, chilled
Pour ingredients into blender
1 1/2 oz. Appleton Estate V/X Jamaica Rum
3/4 oz. Dark Crème de Cacao
3/4 oz. Crème de Banana
Peeled, ripe banana
2 scoops vanilla ice cream
Blend ingredients (with ice optional)
Pineapple wedge and banana slice garnish

DIABLO
Cocktail glass, chilled
Pour ingredients into iced mixing glass
1 1/2 oz. Brandy
1/2 oz. Dry Vermouth
1/2 oz. Hiram Walker Triple Sec
2 dashes Angostura Bitters
Stir and strain
Lemon twist garnish

DIKI-DIKI
Cocktail glass, chilled
Pour ingredients into iced mixing glass
1 1/2 oz. Laird's Applejack Brandy
3/4 oz. Plymouth Dry Gin
2 oz. grapefruit juice
Shake and strain

JIM BEAM®
BLACK LABEL BOURBON

Long considered by those in the know as one of the top two or three best values in the category, JIM BEAM BLACK LABEL BOURBON has grown up some. The Jim Beam Distillery has relaunched venerable Black Label Bourbon with an additional year of aging to its credit. It is now matured in oak a minimum of 8 years.

What Jim Beam didn't change is Black Label's tremendous personality and character. The bourbon has always been crammed full with taste, so much so that the mere mention of its name is enough to get a sly grin out of enthusiasts. Considering how little the bourbon costs, it almost feels as if you're ripping Jim Beam off.

This new Black Label bottling is similar, yet different than its predecessor. The bouquet is still irresistible—sweet and brimming with the aromas of corn, vanilla and toasted oak. While the whiskey remains enormously flavorful, the additional time in the barrel has tempered some of its natural exuberance. The finish is warm and long.

Jim Beam Black Label Bourbon has genuinely come of age, proving once again that leaving well enough alone isn't always the best policy. Use it in any bourbon-based cocktail you'd like to ascend into the great range.

DINGO
House specialty glass, ice
Pour ingredients into iced mixing glass
1 oz. Bacardi Light Rum
3/4 oz. Disaronno Amaretto Liqueur
1/2 oz. Southern Comfort Liqueur
3/4 oz. grenadine
2 oz. sweet 'n' sour
2 oz. orange juice
Shake and strain
Float 3/4 oz. Gosling's Black Seal Rum
Orange slice garnish

DINGY GINGER
Highball glass, ice
Build in glass
1 1/4 oz. Wild Turkey 101° Bourbon
Fill with ginger ale
Float 3/4 oz. Rémy Red
Lemon wedge garnish

DIPLOMATIC IMMUNITY
Cocktail glass, chilled
Pour ingredients into iced mixing glass
1 3/4 oz. Knappogue Castle Irish Whiskey
3/4 oz. Cruzan Banana Rum
3/4 oz. Gran Gala Orange Liqueur
1 1/2 oz. sweet 'n' sour
Shake and strain
Speared banana slice and cherry garnish

DIRE STRAITS
aka **Dirty Mother F'er**
Rocks glass, ice
Build in glass
1 1/2 oz. Brandy
1/2 oz. Kahlúa Coffee Liqueur
1/2 oz. Galliano Liqueur
1/2 oz. half & half cream

DIRTY BANANA
Cocktail glass, chilled
Pour ingredients into iced mixing glass
3/4 oz. Dark Crème de Cacao
3/4 oz. Crème de Banana
2 oz. half & half cream
Shake and strain

DIRTY BULL
Bucket glass, ice
Build in glass
1 1/2 oz. Dirty Olive Gin
Near fill with Red Bull
Splash cranberry juice

DIRTY DOG
Bucket glass, ice
Build in glass
1 1/4 oz. Dirty Olive Vodka
Fill with grapefruit juice

DIRTY GIN 'N' JUICE
Bucket glass, ice
Build in glass
1 1/4 oz. Dirty Olive Gin
Fill with grapefruit juice

DIRTY HARRY
Presentation shot glass, chilled
Build in glass
1 oz. Tia Maria
1 oz. Grand Marnier Liqueur

DIRTY LEMONADE
Bucket glass, ice
Build in glass
1 1/4 oz. Dirty Olive Gin
1/2 oz. DeKuyper Triple Sec
2 1/2 oz. sweet 'n' sour
Splash cranberry juice
Splash club soda

DIRTY MOTHER
aka **Dirty White Mother**
Rocks glass, ice
Build in glass
1 1/2 oz. Brandy
1/2 oz. Kahlúa Coffee Liqueur
1/2 oz. half & half cream

DIZZY LIZZY
Bucket glass, ice
Pour ingredients into iced mixing glass
1 1/2 oz. Maker's Mark Bourbon
1 1/2 oz. Sherry
1 oz. sweet 'n' sour
Shake and strain
Fill with club soda

DOCTOR'S ADVICE
Cocktail glass, chilled
Pour ingredients into iced mixing glass
1 oz. Dr. McGillicuddy's Mentholmint
    Schnapps
1 oz. Kahlúa Coffee Liqueur
1 oz. White Crème de Cacao
Shake and strain

DOCTOR'S ELIXIR
Rocks glass, ice
Build in glass
1 oz. Chambord Liqueur
1 oz. Dr. McGillicuddy's Mentholmint
    Schnapps

DOCTOR'S ORDERS
Presentation shot glass, chilled
Build in glass
1/2 fill Dr. McGillicuddy's Vanilla Liqueur
1/2 fill Canadian Club Whisky

DOG SLED
Rocks glass, chilled
Pour ingredients into iced mixing glass
1 1/2 oz. Canadian Club Whisky
1/2 oz. fresh lemon juice
1/2 oz. grenadine
2 oz. orange juice
Shake and strain

DOLLAR BILL
Cocktail glass, chilled
Pour ingredients into iced mixing glass
1 3/4 oz. Jameson Irish Whiskey
1/2 oz. Sweet Vermouth
1/2 oz. Dubonnet Rouge
Stir and strain
Lemon twist garnish

DONE & BRADSTREET
Cocktail glass, chilled
Pour ingredients into iced mixing glass
1 oz. Absolut Vodka
1/2 oz. Absolut Citron Vodka
1/2 oz. Blue Curaçao
1/2 oz. Midori Melon Liqueur
1/4 oz. Rose's Lime Juice
Stir and strain
Lime wheel garnish

DOUBLE AGENT
Bucket glass, ice
Pour ingredients into iced mixing glass
1 1/2 oz. Jewel of Russia Berry Infusion
1/2 oz. Rose's Lime Juice
1/2 oz. grenadine
1 oz. sweet 'n' sour
Shake and strain
Fill with Seven-Up

DOUBT RAISER
Champagne glass, chilled
Build in glass
3/4 oz. Chambord Liqueur
3/4 oz. Grand Marnier Liqueur
1/2 oz. Belvedere Polish Vodka
1 dash grenadine
Fill with Champagne
Lemon twist garnish

DOWNEASTER
Highball glass, ice
Build in glass
1 1/4 oz. Finlandia Vodka
1/2 fill cranberry juice
1/2 fill pineapple juice

69

KNAPPOGUE CASTLE®
IRISH SINGLE MALT
WHISKEY~1993

Irish whiskies continue to flourish in the United States and the 1993 vintage of KNAPPOGUE CASTLE IRISH SINGLE MALT WHISKEY will certainly fan the flames.

This sensational whiskey is double-distilled in small batches at the famed Bushmill's Distillery in Dundalk. The malt whiskies selected for this prestigious bottling are aged in 180-liter, American oak bourbon casks for a minimum of 8 years. Each cask is evaluated by world-renowned whiskey expert Jim Murray before bottling.

This is an extraordinary single malt whiskey. Unlike many Scotch single malts, Knappogue (pronounced nah-POG) Castle '93 is not dominated by a smoky, peaty character, rather it is light and eminently drinkable. It has an alluring bouquet with notes of malt, grain and just a hint of smoke. On the palate, the silky textured whiskey is ideally balanced with the delightfully sweet flavor of malt and the dry, chewy taste of grain. The finish is long, relaxed and flavorful.

It is an affordable, highly versatile whiskey, one as equally at home served neat in a snifter as it is mixed in a cocktail. Knappogue Castle '93 is a lot of whiskey for the money.

DOWN UNDER
House specialty glass, ice
Pour ingredients into iced mixing glass
1 1/2 oz. Disaronno Amaretto Liqueur
1 1/2 oz. orange juice
1 1/2 oz. sweet 'n' sour
Shake and strain
Fill with Champagne

DOWN UNDER SNOWBALL
House specialty glass, chilled
Pour ingredients into blender
1 1/2 oz. Bacardi Light Rum
3/4 oz. DeKuyper Peachtree Schnapps
1 oz. grenadine
4 oz. orange juice
Blend with ice
Orange slice garnish

DRAGOON
Sherry glass, chilled
Build in glass
1/3 fill Opal Nera Black Sambuca
1/3 fill Kahlúa Coffee Liqueur
1/3 fill Baileys Irish Cream

DR. BERRY VANILLA
Bucket glass, ice
Build in glass
1 3/4 oz. Dr. McGillicuddy's Vanilla Liqueur
3/4 oz. Razzmatazz Raspberry Liqueur
Near fill with club soda
Splash half & half cream

DREAM CATCHER
Champagne glass, chilled
Build in glass
3/4 oz. Gran Gala Orange Liqueur
3/4 oz. Chambord Liqueur
1/2 oz. Jewel of Russia Berry Infusion
1/4 oz. grenadine
Fill with Champagne
Lemon twist garnish

DREAMSICLE (1)
Highball glass, ice
Build in glass
1 1/4 oz. Disaronno Amaretto Liqueur
1/2 oz. half & half cream
Near fill with orange juice
Float 3/4 oz. Galliano Liqueur (optional)

DREAMSICLE (2)
House specialty glass, chilled
Pour ingredients into blender
1 1/4 oz. Disaronno Amaretto Liqueur
3/4 oz. DJ Dotson Triple Sec
2 oz. orange juice
2 scoops vanilla ice cream
Blend ingredients (with ice optional)
Vanilla wafer garnish

DREAMSICLE (3)
Bucket glass, ice
Build in glass
1 1/4 oz. Licor 43 (Cuarenta y Tres)
1/2 fill half & half cream
1/2 fill orange juice
Orange slice garnish

DREAMSICLE (4)
Bucket glass, ice
Build in glass
1 3/4 oz. Licor 43 (Cuarenta y Tres)
3/4 oz. Giori Lemoncillo Cream Liqueur
Fill with orange juice
Orange slice garnish

DR. PEPPER (1)
aka **Easy Rider**
Highball glass, ice
Build in glass
1 1/4 oz. Disaronno Amaretto Liqueur
Fill with club soda

DR. PEPPER (2)
Shot glass and beer mug, chilled
Build in shot glass
1 1/4 oz. Disaronno Amaretto Liqueur
Build in mug
3/4 fill Draft Beer
Drop shot glass of Amaretto into beer

DR. PEPPER FROM HELL
Shot glass and beer mug, chilled
Build in shot glass
1/2 fill Disaronno Amaretto Liqueur
1/2 fill 151 proof Rum
Build in mug
3/4 fill Draft Beer
Drop shot glass into beer mug

DR. SEUSS GO-GO JUICE
House specialty glass, ice
Pour ingredients into iced mixing glass
1 1/2 oz. Farias Reposado Tequila
1/2 oz. Razzmatazz Raspberry Liqueur
1/2 oz. Rose's Lime Juice
1 1/2 oz. cranberry juice
1 1/2 oz. sweet 'n' sour
Shake and strain
Lime wedge garnish

DR. VANILLA DREAMSICLE
House specialty glass, chilled
Rim glass with powdered cocoa (optional)
Pour ingredients into blender
2 oz. Dr. McGillicuddy's Vanilla Liqueur
1 oz. orange juice
2 scoops vanilla ice cream
Blend ingredients (with ice optional)
Orange slice garnish

DR. VANILLA PEANUT BUTTER CUP
House specialty glass, chilled
Rim glass with powdered cocoa (optional)
Pour ingredients into blender
2 oz. Dr. McGillicuddy's Vanilla Liqueur
1 tbsp. peanut butter
1 oz. half & half cream
2 scoops chocolate ice cream
Blend ingredients (with ice optional)
Graham cracker garnish

DR. VANILLA WAFER
Rocks glass, ice
Build in glass
1 3/4 oz. Dr. McGillicuddy's Vanilla Liqueur
3/4 oz. DeKuyper Buttershots Schnapps
1/2 oz. half & half cream

DRUNKEN MONKEY
Large house specialty glass, ice
Pour ingredients into iced mixing glass
3/4 oz. Appleton Estate V/X Jamaica Rum
3/4 oz. Mount Gay Eclipse Rum
3/4 oz. Cruzan Coconut Rum
3/4 oz. Midori Melon Liqueur
3/4 oz. Crème de Banana
1 1/2 oz. orange juice
1 1/2 oz. pineapple juice
Shake and strain
Float 3/4 oz. St. James Extra Old Rhum
Lime, lemon and orange wedge garnish

DRY ARROYO
Champagne glass, chilled
Pour ingredients into iced mixing glass
3/4 oz. Tia Maria
3/4 oz. Chambord Liqueur
3/4 oz. orange juice
3/4 oz. sweet 'n' sour
Shake and strain
Fill with Champagne
Orange twist garnish

DRY CREEK
Rocks glass, ice
Build in glass
2 oz. Pike Creek Canadian Whisky
3/4 oz. NapaSaki Saké
Lemon twist garnish

DUBONNET COCKTAIL
Cocktail glass, chilled
Pour ingredients into iced mixing glass
1 1/2 oz. Gin
1 1/2 oz. Dubonnet Rouge
Stir and strain
Lemon twist garnish

VINCENT VAN GOGH® VODKA

Ultra-premium VINCENT VAN GOGH VODKA is handcrafted at the renowned Dirkswager Distillery in the historic district of Schiedam, Holland. Created according to an archival family recipe, Vincent Vodka is a delightfully aromatic, character-laden spirit.

Vincent Vodka is skillfully crafted in extremely small batches under the scrutiny of master distiller John DeLange. The vodka is distilled from a proprietary blend of premium grains and purified water.

Vincent Vodka is elegant and flavorful. It has an expansive bouquet with notes of herbs, charcoal and grain. It has a silky texture, medium-weight body and a palate brimming with the taste of sweet grain. The vodka finishes warm and flavorful. Altogether an outstanding experience.

The distillery also produces VINCENT CITROEN and VINCENT ORANJE VODKAS. The Citroen has a light, appealing bouquet and a vibrant palate of tree-ripened citrus. Made from Spanish Valencia oranges and Mediterranean blood oranges, Vincent Oranje has a floral bouquet and sensational orange taste.

New to the line-up is VINCENT WILD APPEL VODKA, an amazingly delicious spirit infused with organic, tree-ripened apples. The first of its type, it must be tasted to be fully appreciated.

While a chilled cocktail glass and lemon twist are ideal, Vincent Vodkas enjoys scores of applications behind the bar.

DUBONNET FUZZY
Bucket glass, ice
Build in glass
2 oz. Dubonnet Rouge
3/4 oz. Disaronno Amaretto Liqueur
1 1/4 oz. pineapple juice
Pineapple wedge garnish

DUCK FART
Presentation shot glass, chilled
Layer ingredients
1/3 fill Kahlúa Coffee Liqueur
1/3 fill Baileys Irish Cream
1/3 fill Crown Royal

DUDLEY DOES RIGHT
House specialty glass, ice
Pour ingredients into iced mixing glass
1 3/4 oz. Forty Creek Canadian Whisky
1/2 oz. Rémy Red
1 1/2 oz. sweet 'n' sour
Shake and strain
Fill with Squirt
Lemon wheel garnish

DUKE OF EARL
Coffee mug, heated
Build in glass
1 1/4 oz. X.O. Café Coffee Liqueur
3/4 oz. Bacardi Select Rum
1/2 oz. Disaronno Amaretto Liqueur
1/2 fill hot coffee
1/2 fill frothed milk
Sprinkle shaved chocolate

DU MONDE
Champagne glass, chilled
Build in glass
1 3/4 oz. Villa Massa Limoncello
Fill with Champagne
Lemon twist garnish

DUNHAM GOOD
Presentation shot glass, chilled
Build in glass
1 1/4 oz. Goldschläger
1/2 oz. Disaronno Amaretto Liqueur

DUSTY ROSE
Presentation shot glass, chilled
Build in glass
1 oz. Chambord Liqueur
1 oz. Baileys Irish Cream

DUTCH COFFEE
Coffee mug, heated
Build in glass
1 oz. Vandermint Liqueur
Near fill with hot coffee
Whipped cream garnish

DUTCH VELVET
Cocktail glass, chilled
Pour ingredients into iced mixing glass
1 oz. Vandermint Liqueur
3/4 oz. Crème de Banana
2 oz. half & half cream
Shake and strain
Sprinkle shaved chocolate

DYING NAZI FROM HELL
Presentation shot glass, chilled
Build in glass
1/3 fill Jägermeister Liqueur
1/3 fill Baileys Irish Cream
1/3 fill Stolichnaya Russian Vodka

EARL OF GREY
Tea cup or coffee mug, heated
Build in glass
1 1/4 oz. Dewar's White Label Scotch
    Whisky
Fill with Earl Grey tea
Lemon wedge garnish

EAST INDIA
Cocktail glass, chilled
Pour ingredients into iced mixing glass
1 1/2 oz. Brandy
3/4 oz. Cointreau Liqueur
2-3 dashes Angostura Bitters
2 oz. pineapple juice
Shake and strain
Lemon twist garnish

EAST RIVER
Champagne glass, chilled
Pour ingredients into iced mixing glass
1 1/2 oz. Chambord Liqueur
2 1/2 oz. orange juice
Shake and strain
Fill with Champagne
Orange twist garnish

EAU de GIN
Cocktail glass, chilled
Pour ingredients into iced mixing glass
1/2 oz. NapaSaki Saké
1/2 oz. Rose's Lime Juice
1 1/2 oz. Bafferts Gin
Stir and strain

ECSTASY SHOOTER
Rocks glass, chilled
Pour ingredients into iced mixing glass
1 oz. Chambord Liqueur
1/2 oz. Artic Vodka & Strawberry Liqueur
1 oz. pineapple juice
1/2 oz. cranberry juice
Shake and strain

ED SULLIVAN
House specialty glass, chilled
Pour ingredients into blender
1 1/4 oz. Bacardi Light Rum
3/4 oz. Disaronno Amaretto Liqueur
1/2 cup strawberries
1/2 oz. half & half cream
2 oz. sweet 'n' sour
Blend with ice
Fill with Champagne
Strawberry garnish

EIFFEL VIEW
Champagne glass, chilled
Pour ingredients into iced mixing glass
1 oz. Vincent Van Gogh Citroen Vodka
1 oz. Vincent Van Gogh Oranje Vodka
1/4 oz. grenadine
1 1/2 oz. sweet 'n' sour
Shake and strain
Fill with Champagne
Orange slice garnish

EL CAJON SUNRISE
Bucket glass, ice
Build in glass
1 oz. Herradura Reposado Tequila
Near fill with orange juice
Float 3/4 oz. Briottet Crème de Cassis

EL CONQUISTADOR
House specialty glass, chilled
Pour ingredients into blender
1 oz. Sauza Conmemorativo Añejo Tequila
1 oz. Sauza Hornitos Tequila
1/2 oz. DeKuyper Raspberry Pucker
3/4 oz. DeKuyper Triple Sec
3/4 oz. Rose's Lime Juice
1/2 oz. grenadine
2 oz. sweet 'n' sour
2 oz. pineapple juice
Blend with ice
Lime wedge garnish

EL DIABLO
Bucket glass, ice
Build in glass
1 1/2 oz. El Jimador Reposado Tequila
3/4 oz. Briottet Crème de Cassis
1/2 oz. fresh lime juice
Fill with ginger ale
Lime wedge garnish

ELECTRICAL STORM
Presentation shot glass, chilled
Layer ingredients
1/4 fill Baileys Irish Cream
1/4 fill Rumple Minze Schnapps
1/4 fill Goldschläger
1/4 fill Jägermeister Liqueur

EXTASE® XO LIQUEUR

Extase XO Liqueur is a masterpiece with two artists. It is the result of a collaborative effort between legendary cognac maker A. Hardy and one of France's premier liqueur producers, Lejay-Lagoute. All marriages should work so well.

Extase XO is handcrafted in Dijon, France, at the firm of Lejay-Lagoute, a 160-year-old company renowned for their luscious fruit liqueurs, and home to France's oldest operating alembic stills. The liqueur's principal flavoring is derived from orange peels grown on Curaçao in the Dutch West Indies. The brandy selected as its foundation is the supremely elegant A. Hardy X.O. Fine Champagne Cognac, an *assemblage* of Grande Champagne and Petite Champagne brandies with an average age of 25 years.

This *liqueur d'orange* is a rare and genuine pleasure. It has a burnished honey and bronze hue, and a satiny textured, medium-weight body. Extase XO is highly aromatic, endowed with an alluring bouquet of mixed citrus. It makes a personal statement immediately, bathing the palate with an array of delectable flavors. The liqueur is expertly balanced, such that the taste of tangy orange and aged cognac appears simultaneously. The flavors mingle agreeably and persist well into the long and relaxed finish.

Extase XO Liqueur is an indulgence best presented in a heated snifter, or in an elegant, top-notch cocktail.

ELECTRIC JAM
House specialty glass, ice
Pour ingredients into iced mixing glass
1 1/4 oz. Rain Vodka
1/2 oz. Blue Curaçao
2 oz. sweet 'n' sour
Shake and strain
Fill with club soda
Lemon wedge garnish

ELECTRIC LEMONADE
aka **Adios Mother**
House specialty glass, ice
Pour ingredients into iced mixing glass
1/2 oz. Pearl Vodka
1/2 oz. Tanqueray № Ten Gin
1/2 oz. Bacardi Limón Rum
1/2 oz. Mandarine Napoléon Liqueur
2 oz. sweet 'n' sour
Shake and strain
Fill with Seven-Up

ELECTRIC WATERMELON (1)
House specialty glass, ice
Pour ingredients into iced mixing glass
1/2 oz. Midori Melon Liqueur
1/2 oz. Zone Melon Italian Vodka
1/2 oz. Light Rum
1/2 oz. DeKuyper Watermelon Pucker
1/2 oz. grenadine
2 oz. orange juice
Shake and strain
Fill with Seven-Up

ELECTRIC WATERMELON (2)
Bucket glass, ice
Build in glass
3/4 oz. Southern Comfort Liqueur
3/4 oz. Midori Melon Liqueur
Near fill with orange juice
Float 3/4 oz. DeKuyper Raspberry Pucker

ELECTRODE OVERLOAD
Coffee mug, heated
Build in glass
3/4 oz. Cruzan Estate Diamond Rum
1/2 oz. Godiva Chocolate Liqueur
1/2 oz. DeKuyper Peppermint Schnapps
Near fill with hot coffee
Whipped cream garnish
Drizzle 1/2 oz. Godiva Chocolate Liqueur

ELIXIR OF LOVE
House specialty glass, ice
Pour ingredients into iced mixing glass
2 oz. Disaronno Amaretto Liqueur
2 oz. White Crème de Cacao
1 oz. Bacardi Light Rum
2 oz. half & half cream
Shake and strain

EL PRESIDENTÉ COCKTAIL (1)
Cocktail glass, chilled
Pour ingredients into iced mixing glass
1 1/2 oz. Light Rum
1/2 oz. Dry Vermouth
1/2 oz. Sweet Vermouth
1/2 oz. Cointreau Liqueur
1/4 oz. grenadine
1/4 oz. fresh lemon juice
Stir and strain
Lime wedge garnish

EL PRESIDENTÉ COCKTAIL (2)
Cocktail glass, chilled
Pour ingredients into iced mixing glass
1 1/2 oz. Bacardi Light Rum
1/2 oz. fresh lime juice
1/2 oz. pineapple juice
1/2 oz. grenadine
Shake and strain
Lime wedge garnish

EL PRESIDENTÉ COCKTAIL (3)
Cocktail glass, chilled
Pour ingredients into iced mixing glass
1/2 oz. Dry Vermouth
2 dashes Angostura Bitters
3/4 oz. Mount Gay Eclipse Rum
2 1/4 oz. Bacardi Light Rum
Stir and strain
Lime wedge garnish

EL TORO
Bucket glass, ice
Build in glass
1 1/4 oz. Sauza Conmemorativo
    Añejo Tequila
3/4 oz. Giori Lemoncillo Liqueur
Near fill with lemonade
Splash Seven-Up
Lime wheel garnish

EMBOLISM
Presentation shot glass, chilled
Build in glass
1/2 fill Baileys Irish Cream
1/2 fill DeKuyper Raspberry Pucker

EMERALD ICE
House specialty glass, chilled
Pour ingredients into blender
3/4 oz. Hot Damn Cinnamon Schnapps
3/4 oz. Green Crème de Menthe
1 1/2 oz. half & half cream
2 scoops vanilla ice cream
Blend ingredients (with ice optional)

EMERALD ISLE
Cappuccino cup, heated
Build in glass
3/4 oz. Celtic Crossing Irish Liqueur
3/4 oz. Baileys Irish Cream
3/4 oz. Knappogue Castle Irish Whiskey
1/4 oz. Kahlúa Coffee Liqueur
Near fill with hot espresso coffee
Top with frothed milk
Sprinkle shaved chocolate

EMPIRE STATE SLAMMER
Rocks glass, chilled
Pour ingredients into iced mixing glass
1 1/4 oz. Canadian Club Whisky
1/2 oz. Crème de Banana
1/2 oz. Sloe Gin
3 oz. orange juice
Shake and strain

ENCINADA HILL CLIMBER
Bucket glass, ice
Build in glass
1 1/4 oz. Sauza Conmemorativo
    Añejo Tequila
1/2 oz. fresh lime juice
Fill with grapefruit juice

ENGLISH MULE
Beer or ale glass, ice
Build in glass
1 1/2 oz. Gin
3 oz. green ginger beer
2 1/2 oz. orange juice
Fill with club soda
Preserved ginger garnish (optional)

E PLURIBUS UNUM
House specialty glass, chilled
Pour ingredients into blender
3/4 oz. Frangelico Liqueur
3/4 oz. Chambord Liqueur
3/4 oz. Kahlúa Coffee Liqueur
2 scoops chocolate ice cream
Blend ingredients (with ice optional)
Sprinkle shaved white chocolate

ERIE CANAL
Rocks glass, ice
Build in glass
1 1/2 oz. Knappogue Castle Irish Whiskey
1/2 oz. Celtic Crossing Irish Liqueur
1/2 oz. Baileys Irish Cream

ESTES FIZZ
Champagne glass, chilled
Build in glass
2-3 strawberries
1 1/2 oz. orange juice
Fill with Champagne
Strawberry garnish

PLYMOUTH® GIN

PLYMOUTH GIN could well be called the gin that launched 1000 ships. The landmark brand has a long, storied history with the British Royal Navy. Produced within walking distance of the famed naval base at Plymouth, the gin is still the daily issue to officers in the British Royal Navy.

Plymouth Gin continues to be made where it originated over 200 years ago, at England's oldest, continuously operating distillery, the historic Black Friars Distillery of Coates & Co. Distilled in a large copper alembic still, this distinguished gin is exceedingly dry and highly aromatic.

Back in America after a 20 year absence, Plymouth Gin has an expansive, citrus and juniper bouquet, and a full, silky smooth body. It immediately fills the mouth with the flavors of juniper, coriander, orange and lemon. The 82.4 proof gin finishes long, dry and brimming with flavor.

It's little wonder why the BBC consistently names Plymouth as England's finest gin.

It should be noted in 1896, the first published recipe for the martini called for the use of Plymouth gin. It remains an ideal brand to choose when creating a signature martini. Its bold, assertive character is also perfectly suited for any type of gin-based assignment.

E.T.
Presentation shot glass, chilled
Build in glass
1/3 fill Midori Melon Liqueur
1/3 fill Baileys Irish Cream
1/3 fill Stolichnaya Russian Vodka

EVE'S APPLE
House specialty glass, chilled
Pour ingredients into blender
1 oz. DeKuyper Pucker Sour Apple
1/2 oz. Hot Damn Cinnamon Schnapps
1/2 oz. Blue Curaçao
1/2 oz. Rose's Lime Juice
1 1/2 oz. apple juice
2 scoops vanilla ice cream
Blend ingredients (with ice optional)
Apple wedge garnish

EVE'S PEACH
Cocktail glass, chilled
Pour ingredients into iced mixing glass
1 1/2 oz. Sauza Conmemorativo
 Añejo Tequila
1/2 oz. DeKuyper Peach Pucker
1 oz. sweet 'n' sour
1 oz. orange juice
Shake and strain
Peach wedge garnish

EXPRESS MAIL DROP
House specialty glass, chilled
Pour ingredients into iced mixing glass
1 1/4 oz. Disaronno Amaretto Liqueur
1/2 oz. Chambord Liqueur
2 1/2 oz. orange juice
Shake and strain
Fill with Champagne

EYE TO EYE
Rocks glass, chilled
Pour ingredients into iced mixing glass
1 oz. Baileys Irish Cream
1 oz. Jameson Irish Whiskey
Shake and strain

FACE ERASER
Bucket glass, crushed ice
Build in glass
1 oz. Luksusowa Polish Vodka
1 oz. Kahlúa Coffee Liqueur
Fill with Seven-Up

FAHRENHEIT 5000
Presentation shot glass, chilled
Build in glass
Cover bottom of glass with Tabasco Sauce
1 oz. Hot Damn Cinnamon Schnapps
1 oz. Absolut Peppar Vodka

FAT CAT FIZZ
Bucket glass, ice
Build in glass
1 oz. Dubonnet Rouge
1 oz. Chambord Liqueur
Fill with Seven-Up
Lemon wedge garnish

FATMANCILLO
Cocktail glass, chilled
Pour ingredients into iced mixing glass
1 oz. Giori Lemoncillo Cream Liqueur
3/4 oz. Frangelico Liqueur
3/4 oz. Kahlúa Coffee Liqueur
Shake and strain
Sprinkle shaved chocolate

FEDERAL EXPRESS
House specialty glass, chilled
Pour ingredients into iced mixing glass
1 1/4 oz. Disaronno Amaretto Liqueur
1/2 oz. Chambord Liqueur
2 1/2 oz. sweet 'n' sour
Shake and strain
Fill with Champagne
Lemon twist garnish

FEDORA
Cocktail glass, chilled
Pour ingredients into iced mixing glass
3/4 oz. Christian Brothers Brandy
3/4 oz. Jim Beam White Label Bourbon
3/4 oz. Myers's Jamaican Rum
1/2 oz. Cointreau Liqueur
1 oz. sweet 'n' sour
Shake and strain

'57 CHEVY
Bucket glass, ice
Pour ingredients into iced mixing glass
1/2 oz. Southern Comfort Liqueur
1/2 oz. Disaronno Amaretto Liqueur
1/2 oz. Vodka
1/2 oz. Light Rum
1/2 oz. Crème de Noyaux
1 1/2 oz. sweet 'n' sour
1 1/2 oz. pineapple juice
Shake and strain

'57 T-BIRD WITH ARIZONA PLATES
Bucket glass, ice
Build in glass
1/2 oz. Pearl Vodka
1/2 oz. Disaronno Amaretto Liqueur
1/2 oz. Midori Melon Liqueur
1/2 oz. DeKuyper Peach Pucker
1/2 oz. DeKuyper Triple Sec
1/2 oz. grenadine
1 oz. orange juice
1 oz. cranberry juice
Lemon wedge garnish

'57 T-BIRD WITH FLORIDA PLATES
Bucket glass, ice
Build in glass
1/2 oz. Stolichnaya Russian Vodka
1/2 oz. Disaronno Amaretto Liqueur
1/2 oz. Grand Marnier Liqueur
Fill with orange juice

'57 T-BIRD WITH HAWAIIAN PLATES
Bucket glass, ice
Build in glass
1/2 oz. Stolichnaya Russian Vodka
1/2 oz. Disaronno Amaretto Liqueur
1/2 oz. Grand Marnier Liqueur
Fill with pineapple juice

FINLANDIA LIME LIGHT
Cocktail glass, chilled
Pour ingredients into iced mixing glass
1 3/4 oz. Finlandia Vodka
3/4 oz. Midori Melon Liqueur
2 oz. grapefruit juice
Shake and strain
Lime wheel garnish

FIRE AND ICE (1)
House specialty glass, chilled
Pour ingredients into blender
3/4 oz. Hot Damn Cinnamon Schnapps
3/4 oz. White Crème de Cacao
1 1/2 oz. half & half cream
2 scoops vanilla ice cream
Blend ingredients (with ice optional)

FIRE AND ICE (2)
Rocks glass, chilled
Build in glass
1 oz. Rumple Minze Schnapps
1 oz. Hot Damn Cinnamon Schnapps

BRUSHING UP ON YOUR PRODUCT KNOWLEDGE

1. What is the main botanical or flavoring agent in gin?
2. Chambord Royale Liqueur has the rich flavor of what fruit?
3. What is another name for quinine?
4. What does the term "straight-up" mean?
5. Baileys Irish Cream is made from chocolate, coffee, cream and what distilled spirit?
6. What liqueur has the initials D.O.M. on its label?
7. Other than color, what is the principle difference between Blue Curaçao and triple sec?
8. Laird's is the leading brand name of this type of spirit.
9. If you saw the designation "X.X.O." on a label, what would you be looking at?
10. What is Marc?
11. This dry, aromatic eau de vie is distilled from the fermented mash of William, Bartlett and Anjou pears.
12. What do the initials V.S.O.P. stand for?
13. This Swedish vodka is infused with the delicate flavor of black currants.
14. What two ingredients combine with Campari to make a negroni?
15. This brand of pastis has been made in Marseilles, France, since the 1930's.

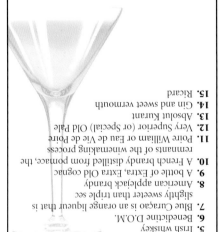

Answers

1. Juniper berries
2. French black raspberries
3. Tonic water
4. A drink served "straight-up" is first prepared in an iced mixing glass and then strained into a chilled cocktail glass
5. Irish whiskey
6. Benedictine D.O.M.
7. Blue Curaçao is an orange liqueur that is slightly sweeter than triple sec
8. American applejack brandy
9. A bottle of Extra, Extra Old cognac
10. A French brandy distilled from pomace, the remnants of the winemaking process
11. Poire William or Eau de Vie de Poire
12. Very Superior (or Special) Old Pale
13. Absolut Kurant
14. Gin and sweet vermouth
15. Ricard

FIREBALL
aka **Jaw Breaker**
Presentation shot glass, chilled
Build in glass
Fill with Cinnamon Schnapps
2-3 dashes Tabasco Sauce

FIRECRACKER
Bucket glass, ice
Build in glass
1 1/2 oz. Bacardi Spiced Rum
1/2 oz. Bacardi 151° Rum
1/2 oz. grenadine
Fill with orange juice

FIRE IN THE HOLE
Presentation shot glass, chilled
Build in glass
1 1/2 oz. Ouzo
3 dashes Tabasco Sauce

FIRE-IT-UP
Rocks glass, ice
Build in glass
1 1/2 oz. Fireball Cinnamon Canadian Whisky
3/4 oz. Kahlúa Coffee Liqueur

FIRST AID KIT
Bucket glass, ice
Build in glass
1 1/4 oz. Sauza Tres Generaciones Plata Tequila
1/2 fill grapefruit juice
1/2 fill cranberry juice

FITZGERALD COCKTAIL
Cocktail glass, chilled
Pour ingredients into iced mixing glass
1 1/2 oz. Bafferts Gin
1/2 oz. simple syrup
1 1/2 oz. fresh lemon juice
3 dashes Angostura Bitters
Shake and strain
Lemon twist garnish

FIVE DOLLAR MARGARET
Rocks glass, chilled
Pour ingredients into iced mixing glass
1 oz. Chambord Liqueur
1 oz. Kahlúa Coffee Liqueur
1 oz. Disaronno Amaretto Liqueur
1 oz. half & half cream
Shake and strain

FLAMING ARMADILLO
Rocks glass, chilled
Pour ingredients into iced mixing glass
3/4 oz. Kahlúa Coffee Liqueur
3/4 oz. Disaronno Amaretto Liqueur
3/4 oz. Grand Marnier Liqueur
3/4 oz. Bacardi Select Rum
Stir and strain

FLAMING BLUE BLASTER
Rocks glass, ice
Pour ingredients into iced mixing glass
1 oz. Wild Turkey 101° Bourbon
3/4 oz. DeKuyper Peppermint Schnapps
3/4 oz. Blue Curaçao
1/4 oz. Foursquare Spiced Rum
Shake and strain

FLAMING BLUE JEANS
aka **Flaming Blue Jesus**
Rocks glass, ice
Pour ingredients into iced mixing glass
1 oz. Southern Comfort Liqueur
3/4 oz. DeKuyper Peppermint Schnapps
3/4 oz. DeKuyper Raspberry Pucker
1/4 oz. 151 proof Rum
Shake and strain

FLAMINGO (1)
Bucket glass, ice
Build in glass
1 1/2 oz. Bacardi Spiced Rum
3/4 oz. grenadine
1/2 fill orange juice
Near fill with lemonade
Float 3/4 oz. Gosling's Black Seal Rum
Lemon wedge garnish

FLAMINGO (2)
House specialty glass, ice
Pour ingredients into iced mixing glass
1 1/2 oz. Bacardi Select Rum
1/2 oz. grenadine
2 oz. sweetened lime juice
2 oz. pineapple juice
Shake and strain
Float 3/4 oz. Pusser's British Navy Rum
Lime wedge garnish

FLOATING HEART
Champagne glass, chilled
Pour ingredients into iced mixing glass
2 oz. Alizé Red Passion
1 oz. Alizé de France
1 oz. pineapple juice
1 oz. sweet 'n' sour
Shake and strain
1 1/2 oz. Champagne
Orange twist garnish

FLORIDA
Bucket glass, ice
Pour ingredients into iced mixing glass
1 1/2 oz. Light Rum
1/2 oz. Rose's Lime Juice
1/2 oz. pineapple juice
2 oz. grapefruit juice
Shake and strain
Near fill with club soda
Float 3/4 oz. Matusalem Gran Reserva Rum
Mint sprig garnish (optional)

FLORIDA T-BACK
Bucket glass, ice
Pour ingredients into iced mixing glass
1 oz. Appleton Estate V/X Jamaica Rum
1 oz. Mount Gay Eclipse Rum
1 oz. Cruzan Coconut Rum
1/2 oz. grenadine
1/2 oz. Rose's Lime Juice
1 1/2 oz. pineapple juice
1 1/2 oz. orange juice
Shake and strain
Pineapple wedge and cherry garnish

FOGCUTTER
House specialty glass, ice
Pour ingredients into iced mixing glass
3/4 oz. Brandy
1/2 oz. Light Rum
1/2 oz. Gin
1 1/2 oz. orange juice
1 1/2 oz. sweet 'n' sour
Shake and strain
Float 3/4 oz. Oloroso Sherry
Lemon wedge garnish

FOGCUTTER, ROYAL NAVY
House specialty glass, ice
Pour ingredients into iced mixing glass
1 1/2 oz. Pusser's British Navy Rum
1/2 oz. Brandy
1/2 oz. Gin
1/2 oz. orgeat syrup
1 oz. orange juice
1 oz. sweet 'n' sour
Shake and strain
Float 3/4 oz. Dry Sherry
Lemon wedge garnish

FOGHORN
Highball glass, ice
Build in glass
1 1/4 oz. Gin
1/2 oz. Rose's Lime Juice
Fill with ginger ale

GLENFARCLAS® SINGLE MALT SCOTCH WHISKY

The Highlands is the largest of the Scotch-producing appellations, and the heart of the region is called the Speyside, home of the majority of Scotland's preeminent distilleries. Single malts from the Speyside are noted for their sophistication, elegance, and impressive complexity. One of the most respected and venerable distillers of Speyside malt whiskies is GLENFARCLAS.

In operation since 1836, the Glenfarclas is one of the few distilleries still under private ownership. The modernized distillery houses six, large alembic stills. The soft spring water used in the whisky comes from the forested hills above the distillery. Glenfarclas now ages nearly all of its highly sought after whiskies in oloroso sherry casks.

The award-winning line of malt whiskies is spearheaded by the highly acclaimed GLENFARCLAS 17-YEAR SINGLE MALT. It has a tempting floral, nutty and sherry-laced bouquet. Its palate is a deliciously complex affair of fresh fruit, malt, oak and sherry with wisps of smoke on the long, lingering finish. It is a magnificently satisfying dram.

The distillery produces several other widely acclaimed whiskies, including Glenfarclas 21-year and 25-year-old single malts, and the cask strength "105" (120 proof), the strongest single malt whisky issued by any Scotch distillery.

FOOL'S GOLD
Rocks glass, chilled
Pour ingredients into iced mixing glass
3/4 oz. Fireball Cinnamon
    Canadian Whisky
3/4 oz. Goldschläger
3/4 oz. Foursquare Spiced Rum
3/4 oz. sweet 'n' sour
Shake and strain

FOREIGN LEGION
Cappuccino cup, heated
Build in glass
1/2 oz. Christian Brothers Brandy
1/2 oz. B & B Liqueur
1/2 oz. Frangelico Liqueur
1/2 oz. Disaronno Amaretto Liqueur
Near fill with hot espresso coffee
Top with frothed milk
Sprinkle shaved chocolate

FOREVER AMBER
Brandy snifter, heated
Build in glass
1 1/2 oz. Tuaca
1/2 oz. Brandy

FORTRESS OF SINGAPORE
Cocktail glass, chilled
Pour ingredients into iced mixing glass
1 3/4 oz. Old Raj Dry Gin
1 1/2 oz. Vincent Van Gogh Citroen Vodka
1/2 oz. Courvoisier V.S.O.P. Cognac
1/3 oz. Canton Ginger Liqueur
Stir and strain
Lemon twist garnish

.44 MAGNUM
Bucket glass, ice
Pour ingredients into iced mixing glass
1/2 oz. Bacardi Light Rum
1/2 oz. Bacardi Select Rum
1/2 oz. Myers's Jamaican Rum
1/2 oz. Van Hoo Belgium Vodka
1/2 oz. DeKuyper Triple Sec
3/4 oz. pineapple juice
1 1/2 oz. sweet 'n' sour
Shake and strain
Fill with Seven-Up

FOUR WISE MEN
Presentation shot glass, chilled
Build in glass
1/2 oz. Jack Daniel's Tennessee Whiskey
1/2 oz. Jim Beam White Label Bourbon
1/2 oz. Jose Cuervo Especial Tequila
1/2 oz. Don Bacardi Gold Rum

FRAMBOISE KISS
Brandy snifter, heated
Build in glass
1 1/2 oz. Otard XO Cognac
1/2 oz. Chambord Liqueur

FRANGELICO FREEZE
House specialty glass, chilled
Pour ingredients into blender
3/4 oz. Frangelico Liqueur
1/2 oz. Godiva Chocolate Liqueur
1/2 oz. Kahlúa Coffee Liqueur
2 scoops vanilla ice cream
Blend ingredients (with ice optional)
Vanilla wafer garnish

FRAPPÉ
Cocktail or champagne saucer, chilled
Build in glass
Fill to a mound with crushed ice
2 oz. requested liqueur
Short straw

FRAPPÉ, APRICOT BRANDY
Cocktail or champagne saucer, chilled
Build in glass
Fill to a mound with crushed ice
1 oz. Brandy
1/2 oz. Apricot Brandy
1/2 oz. Crème de Noyaux
Short straw

FRAPPÉ, BANANA RUM
Cocktail or champagne saucer, chilled
Build in glass
Fill to a mound with crushed ice
1 1/4 oz. Bacardi Light Rum
3/4 oz. Crème de Banana
1/2 oz. orange juice
Short straw

FRAPPÉ, COFFEE MARNIER
Cocktail or champagne saucer, chilled
Build in glass
Fill to a mound with crushed ice
1 oz. Kahlúa Coffee Liqueur
1 oz. Grand Marnier Liqueur
Splash orange juice
Short straw

FRAPPÉ, DERBY MINT
Cocktail or champagne saucer, chilled
Build in glass
Fill to a mound with crushed ice
1/2 oz. DeKuyper Peppermint Schnapps
2 oz. Jack Daniel's Single Barrel Whiskey
Short straw

FRAPPÉ, DOCTOR CHOCOLATE MINT
Cocktail or champagne saucer, chilled
Build in glass
Fill to a mound with crushed ice
1 1/2 oz. Dr. McGillicuddy's
    Mentholmint Schnapps
Drizzle 1 1/2 oz. Hershey's chocolate syrup
Cherry garnish
Short straw

FRAPPÉ, LAGNIAPPE
Rocks glass, chilled
Build in glass
1/2 peach
Fill to a mound with crushed ice
1 1/2 oz. Bourbon
Note: The 'lagniappe' or 'bonus',
    is the bourbon-soaked peach

FRAPPÉ, LEMON
Cocktail or champagne saucer, chilled
Build in glass
Fill to a mound with crushed ice
1 oz. Tuaca
3/4 oz. Giori Lemoncillo Liqueur
1 1/2 oz. sweet 'n' sour
Short straw

FRAPPÉ, MOCHA
Cocktail or champagne saucer, chilled
Build in glass
Fill to a mound with crushed ice
1 oz. Kahlúa Coffee Liqueur
1/2 oz. White Crème de Menthe
1/2 oz. White Crème de Cacao
1/2 oz. Cointreau Liqueur
Short straw

FRAPPÉ, MULATTA
Cocktail or champagne saucer, chilled
Build in glass
Fill to a mound with crushed ice
1 1/4 oz. Bacardi Gold Rum
3/4 oz. Dark Crème de Cacao
1/4 oz. Rose's Lime Juice
1/4 oz. fresh lime juice
Lime wedge garnish

FRAPPÉ, PARISIAN
Cocktail or champagne saucer, chilled
Build in glass
Fill to a mound with crushed ice
1 oz. Yellow Chartreuse
1 oz. V.S. Cognac
Short straw

CELTIC CROSSING®
IRISH LIQUEUR

CELTIC CROSSING is a guaranteed crowd pleaser. Made in Bailieboro, Ireland, this ideally balanced liqueur is made from a recipe first devised over 150 years ago. It is skillfully crafted from a blend of barrel-aged Irish whiskies and cognac, then sweetened with a touch of honey. The real question surrounding Celtic Crossing is how did it get so much flavor without sporting a hefty body and syrupy consistency?

Clearly someone knows the answer, but they're not talking. What is known about this liqueur is that it has an exceptionally light body and a velvety smooth texture. Its wafting, assertive bouquet is laced with the aromas of honey, vanilla and toasted oak.

Celtic Crossing's most laudable quality is its sumptuous palate, which features the flavors of honey, spice and a dram-sized taste of whiskey. The finish is delectably long and flavorful.

Celtic Crossing is best appreciated sipped neat, or with a single cube of ice. It does, however, enjoy numerous applications behind the bar. It is a marvelous addition to specialty coffees, cappuccinos, and cocoas. It also blends extremely well with a wide range of whiskies and liqueurs.

Celtic Crossing is a creative marvel.

FRAPPÉ, SAMBUCA MOCHA
Cocktail or champagne saucer, chilled
Build in glass
Fill to a mound with crushed ice
1 oz. Kahlúa Coffee Liqueur
1 oz. Sambuca Romano
3 Roasted coffee beans
Short straw

FRAPPÉ, TRICONTINENTAL
Cocktail or champagne saucer, chilled
Build in glass
Fill to a mound with crushed ice
1 1/2 oz. Bacardi Gold Rum
1/2 oz. grenadine
1/2 oz. Dark Crème de Cacao
Short straw

FREDDY FUDPUCKER
aka **Cactus Banger, Charlie Goodleg**
Bucket glass, ice
Build in glass
1 1/4 oz. Tequila
Near fill with orange juice
Float 3/4 oz. Galliano Liqueur

FREDDY KRUGER
Presentation shot glass, chilled
Layer ingredients
1/3 fill Sambuca
1/3 fill Jägermeister Liqueur
1/3 fill Stolichnaya Russian Vodka

FRENCH CONNECTION
Brandy snifter, heated
Build in glass
1 oz. V.S. Cognac
1 oz. Grand Marnier Liqueur

FRENCH CONSULATE
House specialty glass, chilled
Pour ingredients into iced mixing glass
3/4 oz. B & B Liqueur
3/4 oz. Brandy
1/2 oz. Cointreau Liqueur
1/2 oz. orange juice
2 oz. sweet 'n' sour
Shake and strain
Fill with Champagne
Lemon twist garnish

FRENCH CRUSH
Bucket glass, ice
Build in glass
1 oz. Cointreau Liqueur
3/4 oz. White Crème de Cacao
1/2 oz. half & half cream
Fill with orange juice
Orange slice garnish

FRENCH DREAM
Brandy snifter, ice
Build in glass
1 oz. Baileys Irish Cream
3/4 oz. Chambord Liqueur
3/4 oz. Tia Maria

FRENCH HARVEST
Brandy snifter, heated
Build in glass
1 1/2 oz. Hardy Noces d'Or Cognac
1/2 oz. Extase XO Liqueur
Lemon twist garnish

FRENCH KISS
Coffee mug, heated
Build in glass
3/4 oz. Kahlúa Coffee Liqueur
3/4 oz. Disaronno Amaretto Liqueur
Near fill with hot chocolate
Whipped cream garnish
Dust powdered cocoa

FRENCH MAID'S CAFÉ
Coffee mug, heated
Build in glass
1/2 oz. Kahlúa Coffee Liqueur
1/2 oz. Grand Marnier Liqueur
1/2 oz. Brandy
Near fill with hot coffee
Whipped cream garnish
Sprinkle shaved chocolate

FRENCH MANDARINE
Brandy snifter, heated
Build in glass
1 1/2 oz. Armagnac
3/4 oz. Mandarine Napoléon Liqueur

FRENCH MOUNTIE
Cocktail glass, chilled
Pour ingredients into iced mixing glass
2 oz. Gooderham & Worts
   Canadian Whisky
3/4 oz. Alizé V.S.O.P. Cognac
1 oz. fresh lemon juice
Shake and strain
Lemon wheel garnish

FRENCH 95
Champagne glass, chilled
Pour ingredients into iced mixing glass
1 oz. Bourbon
2 oz. sweet 'n' sour
Shake and strain
Fill with Champagne
Lemon twist garnish

FRENCH 75 (1)
Champagne glass, chilled
Pour ingredients into iced mixing glass
1 oz. Gin
2 oz. sweet 'n' sour
Shake and strain
Fill with Champagne
Lemon twist garnish

FRENCH 75 (2)
aka **French 125**
Champagne glass, chilled
Pour ingredients into iced mixing glass
1 oz. V.S. Cognac
2 oz. sweet 'n' sour
Shake and strain
Fill with Champagne
Lemon twist garnish

FRENCH SWEETHEART
Bucket glass, ice
Build in glass
1 1/2 oz. Cointreau Liqueur
2 oz. orange juice
Fill with club soda
Orange slice garnish

FRENCH TICKLER
Presentation shot glass, chilled
Build in glass
1 1/4 oz. Goldschläger
3/4 oz. Grand Marnier Liqueur

FRENCH TOAST ROYALE
Brandy snifter, heated
Build in glass
1 oz. Courvoisier V.S.O.P. Cognac
1 oz. Chambord Liqueur

FRENCH TWIST
Brandy snifter, heated
Build in glass
1 oz. Courvoisier V.S.O.P. Cognac
1 oz. Mandarine Napoléon Liqueur

FRESH SQUEEZED BAT JUICE
Highball glass, ice
Build in glass
1 1/4 oz. Forty Creek Canadian Whisky
Fill with blood orange juice

FREUDIAN SLIP
Champagne glass, chilled
Pour ingredients into iced mixing glass
1 oz. Brandy
3/4 oz. Grand Marnier Liqueur
1 1/2 oz. sweet 'n' sour
Shake and strain
Fill with Champagne
Orange twist garnish

CASA NOBLE®
REPOSADO TEQUILA

Casa Noble 100% Agave Tequilas are crafted using traditional methods. While artisan in nature, they are highly sophisticated spirits worthy of *grand cru* status.

The agaves used for Casa Noble Tequilas are slow baked in stone ovens and then spontaneously fermented. The natural yeast lends an intriguing flavor to the finished spirit. All of Casa Noble's tequilas are triple-distilled in alembic stills.

CASA NOBLE REPOSADO strikes a true balance between the fresh, spirited character of a silver tequila, and the mellow refinement of an añejo. It is aged just long enough for its character to soften, while leaving the inherent quality of the agave unaffected by the tannins in the wood.

The distillery also produces CASA NOBLE CRYSTAL, a superb, blanco tequila with a sleek body and engaging bouquet. The palate features a balanced offering of floral and spice, and the finish is long and relaxed. CASA NOBLE GOLD is aged in oak for 2 months to soften its character and add light notes of vanilla in the bouquet and palate.

CASA NOBLE AÑEJO LIMITED RESERVE is an elegant, añejo tequila extended aged in French White Oak casks rather than ex-bourbon barrels. Made in limited quantities, the Casa Noble Añejo has a silky texture, a spicy palate, and a slightly sweet, smoky finish.

FRIAR TUCK
Rocks glass, ice
Build in glass
1 1/2 oz. Pike Creek Canadian Whisky
3/4 oz. Frangelico Liqueur

FROSTBITE
House specialty glass, chilled
Pour ingredients into blender
1 1/2 oz. Yukon Jack Liqueur
1/4 oz. DeKuyper Peppermint Schnapps
2 1/2 oz. sweet 'n' sour
Blend with ice

FROSTED COKE
Beer mug or house specialty glass, ice
Build in glass
1 1/2 oz. Pearl Vodka
1/2 oz. Kahlúa Coffee Liqueur
1/2 oz. Dark Crème de Cacao
3/4 oz. half & half cream
Fill with cola

FROSTED PEACH BREEZE
House specialty glass, chilled
Pour ingredients into blender
1 oz. DeKuyper Peachtree Schnapps
3/4 oz. Zone Peach Italian Vodka
2 oz. cranberry juice
2 oz. grapefruit juice
Blend with ice

FROSTED STRAWBERRY TEA
House specialty glass, chilled
Pour ingredients into blender
4 oz. English Breakfast tea
2 tbsp. sugar
1/2 cup frozen strawberries
2 oz. sweet 'n' sour
Blend with ice
Strawberry garnish

FROSTY NAVEL
House specialty glass, chilled
Pour ingredients into blender
1 oz. DeKuyper Peachtree Schnapps
1 1/2 oz. orange juice
1 1/2 oz. half & half cream
2 scoops vanilla ice cream
Blend ingredients (with ice optional)
Vanilla wafer garnish

FROZEN CAPPUCCINO
House specialty glass, chilled
Rim glass with cinnamon (optional)
Pour ingredients into blender
3/4 oz. Baileys Irish Cream
3/4 oz. Kahlúa Coffee Liqueur
3/4 oz. Frangelico Liqueur
2 scoops vanilla ice cream
Blend ingredients (with ice optional)

FROZEN DEVOTION
House specialty glass, chilled
Pour ingredients into blender
1 1/4 oz. Cruzan Estate Diamond Rum
3/4 oz. Disaronno Amaretto Liqueur
3 oz. strawberry puree
2 scoops vanilla ice cream
Blend ingredients (with ice optional)
Strawberry garnish

FROZEN MONK
House specialty glass, chilled
Pour ingredients into blender
3/4 oz. Frangelico Liqueur
3/4 oz. Kahlúa Coffee Liqueur
3/4 oz. Dark Crème de Cacao
2 scoops vanilla ice cream
Blend ingredients (with ice optional)

FROZEN ROSE
House specialty glass, chilled
Pour ingredients into blender
1 1/4 oz. Tequila Rose Cream Liqueur
1 oz. Hussong's Reposado Tequila
1/2 oz. Hiram Walker Triple Sec
Blend with ice
Lime wedge and strawberry (rose) garnish

FRUIT BURST
House specialty glass, ice
Pour ingredients into iced mixing glass
1 3/4 oz. Giori Lemoncillo Cream Liqueur
3/4 oz. Stolichnaya Russian Vodka
3/4 oz. Razzmatazz Raspberry Liqueur
1 oz. orange juice
1 oz. cranberry juice
1 oz. pineapple juice
Shake and strain
Pineapple wedge garnish

FRUIT STRIPE
House specialty glass, chilled
Object is to create a 2-layer drink
1—Pour ingredients into blender
   1 oz. Bacardi Light Rum
   1/2 cup strawberries
   2 oz. sweet 'n' sour
Blend with ice
Pour first drink into glass 1/2 full
2—Pour ingredients into blender
   1 oz. Bacardi Light Rum
   2 oz. coconut cream syrup
   3 oz. pineapple juice
Blend with ice
Pour second drink on top of first drink
Whipped cream garnish
Drizzle 3/4 oz. Cockspur V.S.O.R. Rum

FRUITY TUTTI
Rocks glass, ice
Pour ingredients into iced mixing glass
1 oz. DeKuyper Peachtree Schnapps
1/2 oz. Chambord Liqueur
1/2 oz. Midori Melon Liqueur
Splash cranberry juice
Shake and strain
Lime wedge garnish

F-16
aka **B-53**
Presentation shot glass, chilled
Layer ingredients
1/3 fill Kahlúa Coffee Liqueur
1/3 fill Frangelico Liqueur
1/3 fill Baileys Irish Cream

FULL MOON
Brandy snifter, heated
Build in glass
1 oz. Grand Marnier Liqueur
1 oz. Disaronno Amaretto Liqueur

FU MANCHU
Cocktail glass, chilled
Pour ingredients into iced mixing glass
1 1/2 oz. Gold Rum
1/2 oz. Hiram Walker Triple Sec
1/2 oz. White Crème de Menthe
1/2 oz. Rose's Lime Juice
1 dash simple syrup
Stir and strain
Orange twist garnish

FUN IN THE SUN
Rocks glass, ice
Build in glass
1 3/4 oz. Knappogue Castle Irish Whiskey
3/4 oz. Kahlúa Coffee Liqueur
1/2 oz. Chambord Liqueur

FUNKY MONKEY
House specialty glass, ice
Pour ingredients into iced mixing glass
1 1/4 oz. Bacardi Light Rum
1 oz. Cruzan Coconut Rum
3/4 oz. Cruzan Banana Rum
3/4 oz. apple-grape juice concentrate
2 oz. pineapple juice
Shake and strain
Pineapple wedge and cherry garnish

FUZZY DICK
Coffee mug, heated
Build in glass
3/4 oz. Grand Marnier Liqueur
3/4 oz. Kahlúa Coffee Liqueur
Near fill with hot coffee
Whipped cream garnish
Dust powdered cocoa

THE JEWEL OF RUSSIA®
CLASSIC VODKA

Some people are looking for a spirit to slap them around a little and make their heart skip a beat. Others are looking for a somewhat more refined and sophisticated experience. It is those people who will most appreciate a slow dance with luxurious THE JEWEL OF RUSSIA CLASSIC VODKA.

The spirit is skillfully crafted in a traditional Russian style, from a blend of premium rye, hardy winter wheat and artesian spring water. The fermented mash is distilled in continuous stills, then repeatedly filtered through high absorption screens.

The Jewel of Russia Classic Vodka is appropriately named. It has a pristine clarity, a satiny texture and a rounded, medium-weight body. Even at room temperature the vodka barely generates any heat on the palate, then makes its presence known by completely filling the mouth with crisp, spicy flavors. The finish is warm and lingering.

As magnificent as The Jewel of Russia Classic Vodka is, the distillery has done it one better. Presented in a beautiful, hand-painted bottle, THE JEWEL OF RUSSIA ULTRA VODKA is imbued with a slightly more flavorful palate and subjected to a more strenuous filtration regimen. Minor differences aside, both of The Jewel of Russia Vodkas are classy, museum-quality spirits.

FUZZY MUSSY
Coffee mug, heated
Build in glass
1 oz. Frangelico Liqueur
1/2 oz. Baileys Irish Cream
1/2 oz. Grand Marnier Liqueur
Near fill with hot coffee
Whipped cream garnish
Dust powdered cocoa

FUZZY NAVEL
Highball glass, ice
Build in glass
1 1/4 oz. DeKuyper Peachtree Schnapps
Fill with orange juice

FUZZY WUZZIE
Cocktail glass, chilled
Pour ingredients into iced mixing glass
1 3/4 oz. Original Cristall Russian Vodka
1/2 oz. DeKuyper Peachtree Schnapps
1/2 oz. Rose's Lime Juice
1/2 oz. orange juice
Stir and strain
Peeled kiwi slice garnish

GALLIANO STINGER
Rocks glass, ice
Build in glass
1 1/2 oz. Galliano Liqueur
1/2 oz. White Crème de Menthe

GANGBUSTER (serves two)
2 house specialty glasses, ice
Pour ingredients into iced mixing glass
1 1/2 oz. Bacardi Light Rum
1 oz. Mount Gay Eclipse Rum
1 1/2 oz. guava nectar
1 1/2 oz. pineapple juice
1 1/2 oz. sweet 'n' sour
Shake and strain
Float 1/2 oz. Bacardi Select Rum and
    1/2 oz. Bacardi 151° Rum
Lime, lemon and orange wedge garnish

GANG GREEN
House specialty glass, ice
Pour ingredients into iced mixing glass
1 1/2 oz. Bacardi Light Rum
1 oz. Midori Melon Liqueur
1/2 oz. Bacardi Spiced Rum
3/4 oz. Blue Curaçao
2 oz. orange juice
2 oz. sweet 'n' sour
Shake and strain
Pineapple wedge and cherry garnish

GATOR JUICE

Bucket glass, ice
Build in glass
1 1/4 oz. Southern Comfort Liqueur
1/4 oz. Rose's Lime Juice
Near fill with orange juice
Float 3/4 oz. Blue Curaçao

GAUGUIN

House specialty glass, chilled
Pour ingredients into blender
2 oz. Bacardi Limón Rum
1 oz. passion fruit syrup
1 1/2 oz. sweet 'n' sour
1 1/2 oz. sweetened lime juice
Blend with ice
Lime, lemon and orange wedge garnish

G-BOY

Rocks glass, chilled
Pour ingredients into iced mixing glass
3/4 oz. Grand Marnier Liqueur
3/4 oz. Baileys Irish Cream
3/4 oz. Frangelico Liqueur
Shake and strain

GENTLEMAN'S BOILERMAKER

Brandy snifter, heated
Build in glass
1 oz. Armagnac
1 oz. Tawny Port

GEORGIA PEACH (1)

Highball glass, ice
Build in glass
1 1/4 oz. DeKuyper Peach Pucker
Fill with cranberry juice

GEORGIA PEACH (2)

House specialty glass, chilled
Pour Ingredients into iced mixing glass
1 1/2 oz. DeKuyper Peachtree Schnapps
1/2 oz. grenadine
2 oz. sweet 'n' sour
Shake and strain
Peach wedge and cherry garnish

GEORGIA'S OWN

House specialty glass, chilled
Pour ingredients into blender
3 oz. Peach Nectar
1 1/2 oz. orange juice
3/4 oz. sweet 'n' sour
Blend with ice
Fill with club soda

GEORGIA TURNOVER

Coffee mug, heated
Build in glass
1 1/2 oz. DeKuyper Peachtree Schnapps
1 1/2 oz. cranberry juice
Fill with hot apple cider

GERMAN CHOCOLATE CAKE

Cocktail glass, chilled
Pour ingredients into iced mixing glass
1/2 oz. Baileys Irish Cream
1/2 oz. Kahlúa Coffee Liqueur
1/2 oz. Frangelico Liqueur
1 1/2 oz. half & half cream
Shake and strain

GIBSON

Cocktail glass, chilled
Pour ingredients into iced mixing glass
8 drops Dry Vermouth
1 1/2 oz. Gin
Stir and strain
Cocktail onions garnish

GIBSON, DRY

Cocktail glass, chilled
Pour ingredients into iced mixing glass
4 drops Dry Vermouth
1 1/2 oz. Gin
Stir and strain
Cocktail onions garnish

GIBSON, EXTRA DRY

Cocktail glass, chilled
Pour ingredients into iced mixing glass
1 drop Dry Vermouth (optional)
1 1/2 oz. Gin
Stir and strain
Cocktail onions garnish

GIBSON, VODKA

Cocktail glass, chilled
Pour ingredients into iced mixing glass
8 drops Dry Vermouth
1 1/2 oz. Vodka
Stir and strain
Cocktail onions garnish
Note: Use less dry vermouth to make
a **Dry Vodka Gibson**, use little or no
dry vermouth to make an **Extra Dry
Vodka Gibson**

GIMLET

Cocktail glass, chilled
Pour ingredients into iced mixing glass
1 1/2 oz. Gin
1/2 oz. Rose's Lime Juice
Stir and strain
Lime wedge garnish

BRIOTTET®
CRÈME DE CASSIS DE DIJON

Crème de cassis originated in the centuries old town of Dijon, the capital of Burgundy and the gastronomic center of France, famous for its wines, mustard and wild black currants. These luscious, claret-colored berries provide the principle flavoring for renowned BRIOTTET CRÈME DE CASSIS DE DIJON.

The Edmond Briottet Company has produced this remarkably elegant liqueur since 1836, and it may soon become the standard by which other crème de cassis are measured. Briottet uses only Noir de Bourgogne currants grown within the commune of Dijon, considered to be the finest black currants in the world. The fruit macerates in premium grape spirits for a minimum of 2 months before being sweetened, filtered and bottled at 40 proof.

Briottet Crème de Cassis de Dijon can best be described as succulent. It has the deep, rich color of a vintage port, and a lush, velvety smooth body. The liqueur's bouquet is a delectable array of citrus, nuts and sun-drenched fruit. Its concentrated palate is that of fresh fruit, both semi-sweet and naturally tart. The flavors persist throughout the impressively long finish.

The incomparable Briottet Crème de Cassis de Dijon has numerous applications behind the bar. Perhaps its most unforgettable roles are in the venerable cocktails Kir, Kir Royale and Vermouth Cassis.

GIMLET, CHER'S
Cocktail glass, chilled
Pour ingredients into iced mixing glass
1 3/4 oz. Cascade Mountain Gin
1/2 oz. Gran Gala Orange Liqueur
1/2 oz. fresh lime juice
1/2 oz. Rose's Lime Juice
Shake and strain
Lime wedge garnish

GIMLET, COBBLER'S
Cocktail glass, chilled
Pour ingredients into iced mixing glass
1/2 oz. Rose's Lime Juice
1/2 oz. Giori Lemoncillo Liqueur
1 3/4 oz. Damrak Amsterdam Gin
Shake and strain
Lime wheel and lemon twist garnish

GIMLET, MARTINIQUE (1)
Cocktail glass, chilled
Pour ingredients into iced mixing glass
1 3/4 oz. St. James Extra Old Rhum
3/4 oz. Cointreau Liqueur
1/2 oz. fresh lime juice
1/2 oz. sweet 'n' sour
Shake and strain
Lime wedge garnish

GIMLET, MARTINIQUE (2)
Cocktail glass, chilled
Pour ingredients into iced mixing glass
1 oz. J. Bally Rhum Vieux 12-Year
1 oz. Dillon Dark Rhum
3/4 oz. Citrónge Orange Liqueur
1/2 oz. fresh lime juice
1/2 oz. sweet 'n' sour
Shake and strain
Lime wedge garnish

GIMLET, PYRAT
Cocktail glass, chilled
Pour ingredients into iced mixing glass
1 1/2 oz. Pyrat X.O. Reserve Rum
1/2 oz. Rose's Lime Juice
1/4 oz. fresh lime juice
1/4 oz. Citrónge Orange Liqueur
Stir and strain
Lime wedge garnish

GIMLET, RASPBERRY
Cocktail glass, chilled
Pour ingredients into iced mixing glass
1 1/2 oz. Original Cristall Russian Vodka
3/4 oz. Chambord Liqueur
1/2 oz. fresh lime juice
1/2 oz. Rose's Lime Juice
Stir and strain
Lime wedge garnish

GIMLET, SAPPHIRE
Cocktail glass, chilled
Pour ingredients into iced mixing glass
1 3/4 oz. Bombay Sapphire London Dry Gin
1/2 oz. Gran Gala Orange Liqueur
1/2 oz. fresh lime juice
1/2 oz. sweet 'n' sour
Shake and strain
Lime wedge garnish

GIMLET, SOHO
Cocktail glass, chilled
Pour ingredients into iced mixing glass
1 3/4 oz. Beefeater London Dry Gin
1/2 oz. Gran Gala Orange Liqueur
1/2 oz. fresh lime juice
1/2 oz. sweet 'n' sour
Shake and strain
Lime wedge garnish

GIMLET, TUACA
Cocktail glass, chilled
Pour ingredients into iced mixing glass
1 1/2 oz. Vodka
3/4 oz. Tuaca
1/2 oz. Rose's Lime Juice
Stir and strain
Lime wedge garnish

GIMLET, VODKA
Cocktail glass, chilled
Pour ingredients into iced mixing glass
1 1/2 oz. Vodka
1/2 oz. Rose's Lime Juice
Stir and strain
Lime wedge garnish

GIMLET, WHALER
Cocktail glass, chilled
Pour ingredients into iced mixing glass
1 1/2 oz. Whaler's Hawaiian Vanilla Rum
3/4 oz. Tuaca
1/2 oz. Rose's Lime Juice
Stir and strain
Lime wedge garnish

GIN ALEXANDER
aka **Plain Alexander**
Cocktail glass, chilled
Pour ingredients into iced mixing glass
3/4 oz. Gin
3/4 oz. White Crème de Cacao
2 oz. half & half cream
Shake and strain
Sprinkle nutmeg

GIN AND IT
Cocktail glass, chilled
Pour ingredients into iced mixing glass
1/2 oz. Sweet Vermouth
1 1/2 oz. Gin
Stir and strain

GIN & SIN
Cocktail glass, chilled
Pour ingredients into iced mixing glass
1 1/2 oz. Bombay Sapphire London Dry Gin
1/4 oz. grenadine
3/4 oz. Extase XO Liqueur
3/4 oz. orange juice
3/4 oz. sweet 'n' sour
Shake and strain
Lemon wheel garnish

GINGER BEER SHANDY
Beer glass, chilled
Build in glass
9 oz. Amber Ale
Fill with Ginger Beer

GINGERBREAD MAN
Rocks glass, chilled
Build in glass
3/4 oz. Goldschläger
3/4 oz. Baileys Irish Cream
3/4 oz. DeKuyper Buttershots Schnapps

GINGER SNAP
Bucket glass, ice
Build in glass
1 1/2 oz. Foursquare Spiced Rum
Fill with ginger ale

GIN RICKEY
Highball glass, ice
Build in glass
1 1/4 oz. Gin
Fill with club soda
Lime wedge garnish

GIRL SCOUT COOKIE
Cocktail glass, chilled
Pour ingredients into iced mixing glass
3/4 oz. Peppermint Schnapps
3/4 oz. Kahlúa Coffee Liqueur
1 1/2 oz. half & half cream
Shake and strain
Cookie garnish

GLACIER BREEZE
Bucket glass, ice
Build in glass
1 1/2 oz. Finlandia Vodka
3/4 oz. cranberry juice
3/4 oz. apple juice
Fill with orange juice

SEA WYNDE®
POT STILL RUM

If you're in the market for a rare and singular rum, the likes of which hasn't been seen in more than three decades, then look no further than ultra-premium SEA WYNDE POT STILL RUM, a Caribbean rum crafted in a traditional style made famous by British Royal Navy.

The majority of rums are produced in column stills, which is an economical method of producing large quantities of relatively light-bodied spirits. As the name implies, the rums used to create Sea Wynde are distilled in pot stills, a significantly more laborious and expensive process. This robust, flavorful and aromatic rum would suggest that the investment is well worth it.

The Sea Wynde blend is comprised of five remarkable, yet very different pure pot still rums. They are distilled in Jamaica and Guyana, aged in oak barrels between 5 to 11 years.

There may not be a more eminently satisfying rum than Sea Wynde. It is in all respects near perfection. Sea Wynde has a marvelous, full body, a generous bouquet and a palate bursting at the seams with the flavors of vanilla, honey, fruit, and roasted coffee. Its long, warm and sultry finish is reminiscent of an aged malt whisky.

While this is an ideal rum to serve straight-up or over ice, it is also substantial enough to feature in cocktails.

GLASNOST
Bucket glass, ice
Pour ingredients into iced mixing glass
1 oz. Stolichnaya Russian Vodka
1 oz. Chambord Liqueur
2 oz. sweet 'n' sour
2 oz. orange juice
Shake and strain
Orange slice and cherry garnish

GLASS TOWER
House specialty glass, ice
Build in glass
1 oz. Bacardi Light Rum
1 oz. Zone Peach Italian Vodka
1 oz. DeKuyper Peachtree Schnapps
1 oz. DeKuyper Triple Sec
1/2 oz. Sambuca
Fill with Seven-Up

GLENDA
Champagne flute, chilled
Build in glass
3/4 oz. DeKuyper Peachtree Schnapps
3/4 oz. Grand Marnier Liqueur
Fill with Champagne
Lemon twist garnish

GLOOMRAISER
Cocktail glass, chilled
Pour ingredients into iced mixing glass
1 1/2 oz. Gin
1/4 oz. Dry Vermouth
2 dashes Pernod
2 dashes grenadine
Stir and strain
Cherry garnish (optional)

GOAL POST
Presentation shot glass, chilled
Layer ingredients
1/2 fill White Crème de Menthe
1/2 fill Tequila

GODCHILD
Rocks glass, ice
Build in glass
1 1/2 oz. Vodka
3/4 oz. Disaronno Amaretto Liqueur
1/2 oz. half & half cream

GODFATHER
Rocks glass, ice
Build in glass
1 1/2 oz. Scotch Whisky
3/4 oz. Disaronno Amaretto Liqueur

GODMOTHER
Rocks glass, ice
Build in glass
1 1/2 oz. Vodka
3/4 oz. Disaronno Amaretto Liqueur

GOLD AND LAGER
Beer glass, chilled
Build in glass
1 1/4 oz. Goldschläger
Fill with Pilsner

GOLD AND RICHES
Brandy snifter, heated
Build in glass
1 1/2 oz. Kelt XO Tour du Monde Cognac
1/2 oz. Godiva Chocolate Liqueur
1/2 oz. Grand Marnier 100th Anniversary
Serve with underliner, add 3 gold-covered
    chocolate coins

GOLDEN CADILLAC
Cocktail glass, chilled
Pour ingredients into iced mixing glass
3/4 oz. White Crème de Cacao
3/4 oz. Galliano Liqueur
2 oz. half & half cream
Shake and strain

GOLDEN DRAGON
House specialty glass, ice
Pour ingredients into iced mixing glass
1 1/2 oz. Bacardi 8 Reserva Rum
1/2 oz. Vya California Sweet Vermouth
1 oz. orgeat syrup
1 1/2 oz. coconut cream syrup
1 1/2 oz. half & half cream
Shake and strain
Dust ground cinnamon

GOLDEN DREAM
Cocktail glass, chilled
Pour ingredients into iced mixing glass
3/4 oz. Galliano Liqueur
3/4 oz. Triple Sec
3/4 oz. orange juice
1 1/2 oz. half & half cream
Shake and strain

GOLDEN DREAM WITH DOUBLE
   BUMPERS
House specialty glass, chilled
Pour ingredients into iced mixing glass
3/4 oz. Galliano Liqueur
3/4 oz. Hiram Walker Triple Sec
3/4 oz. Brandy
3/4 oz. B & B Liqueur
3/4 oz. orange juice
2 oz. half & half cream
Shake and strain

GOLDEN FIZZ
Bucket glass, ice
Pour ingredients into iced mixing glass
1 1/4 oz. Gin
1/2 oz. simple syrup
1 1/2 oz. sweet 'n' sour
1 1/2 oz. half & half cream
1 egg yolk (optional)
Shake and strain
Splash club soda

GOLDEN MAX
Brandy snifter, heated
Build in glass
1 1/2 oz. Rémy Martin V.S. Cognac
3/4 oz. Cointreau Liqueur

GOLDEN NAIL
Highball glass, ice
Build in glass
1 1/4 oz. Drambuie Liqueur
Fill with grapefruit juice

GOLDEN PEACH
Bucket glass, ice
Pour ingredients into iced mixing glass
1 3/4 oz. Jameson Irish Whiskey
3/4 oz. DeKuyper Peachtree Schnapps
1 1/2 oz. orange juice
1 1/2 oz. sweet 'n' sour
Shake and strain
Orange slice garnish

GOLDEN RAM
House specialty glass, chilled
Pour ingredients into blender
1 oz. Southern Comfort Liqueur
1/2 oz. Galliano Liqueur
1/2 oz. Disaronno Amaretto Liqueur
1/2 oz. DeKuyper Peach Pucker
3 oz. orange juice
Blend with ice

GOLDEN SCREW
aka **Italian Screw**
Highball glass, ice
Build in glass
1 1/4 oz. Galliano Liqueur
Fill with orange juice

GOLD FURNACE
Presentation shot glass, chilled
Build in glass
1 1/2 oz. Goldschläger
2 dashes Tabasco Sauce

HARDY® NOCES D'OR COGNAC

The esteemed cognac house of A. Hardy was founded in 1863, and within a decade became one of the preeminent brandy distillers in Europe. Their sales were helped in no small measure by Czar Nicholas II, who regularly served Hardy Cognac de l'Alliance at all royal functions, formal or not.

Despite its rapid rise in popularity, A. Hardy began bottling their extraordinary brandies for the first time shortly after World War II. While the limelight shines brightly on all of the Hardy cognacs, it is the legendary HARDY NOCES D'OR COGNAC that deservedly draws much of the attention.

Introduced in 1946 to commemorate the 50th wedding anniversary of Armand Hardy, handcrafted Noces d'Or is a *Tres Ancienne Grande Champagne* cognac, meaning it is a blend of very old brandies, all of which were double-distilled entirely from grapes grown in the Grande Champagne district of Cognac. The vintage, barrel-matured brandies used in its blend average in age an extraordinary 50 years.

Hardy Noces d'Or Cognac is a magnificent brandy. It has a lustrous, deep copper color and a firm, lightweight body. The expansive bouquet features an array of savory aromas, including ripe fruit, spice, honey, and toasted oak. The brandy has a remarkably lush, sophisticated palate and a warm, lingering finish.

GOLD RUSH (1)
Cocktail glass, chilled
Rim glass with salt (optional)
Pour ingredients into iced mixing glass
1 1/2 oz. Jose Cuervo Especial Tequila
1/2 oz. Grand Marnier Liqueur
1/2 oz. Rose's Lime Juice
Stir and strain
Lime wedge garnish

GOLD RUSH (2)
Presentation shot glass, chilled
Build in glass
3/4 oz. Goldschläger
3/4 oz. Gold Tequila

GOLD RUSH (3)
Cocktail glass, chilled
Pour ingredients into iced mixing glass
1 1/2 oz. Sauza Hornitos Tequila
3/4 oz. Licor 43 (Cuarenta y Tres)
1/2 oz. Rose's Lime Juice
Stir and strain
Lime wedge garnish

GOOD & PLENTY
Rocks glass, ice
Build in glass
1 1/2 oz. Kahlúa Coffee Liqueur
1/2 oz. Anisette

GOOM BAY SMASH (1)
House specialty glass, chilled
Pour ingredients into blender
1 1/4 oz. Bacardi Gold Rum
1 1/4 oz. Malibu Rum
3/4 oz. Crème de Banana
2 oz. pineapple juice
2 oz. orange juice
Blend with ice
Banana slice garnish

GOOM BAY SMASH (2)
House specialty glass, chilled
Pour ingredients into blender
1 1/4 oz. Gosling's Black Seal Rum
1 1/4 oz. Cruzan Coconut Rum
3/4 oz. Crème de Banana
2 oz. pineapple juice
2 oz. orange juice
Blend with ice
Banana slice garnish

GOOSE DOWN
Cocktail glass, chilled
Pour ingredients into iced mixing glass
1 1/2 oz. Grey Goose Vodka
1 oz. Giori Lemoncillo Cream Liqueur
Shake and strain
Lemon twist garnish

GORILLA MILK
House specialty glass, chilled
Pour ingredients into blender
1 oz. Bacardi Light Rum
3/4 oz. Kahlúa Coffee Liqueur
3/4 oz. Baileys Irish Cream
3/4 oz. Crème de Banana
1 oz. half & half cream
1 scoop vanilla ice cream
Blend ingredients (with ice optional)
Pineapple wedge and banana slice garnish

GORKY PARK COOLER (1)
House specialty glass, ice
Pour ingredients into iced mixing glass
1 1/4 oz. Jewel of Russia
　　Wild Bilberry Infusion
3/4 oz. Cruzan Coconut Rum
3/4 oz. Jewel of Russia Classic Vodka
1 oz. sweet 'n' sour
2 oz. pineapple juice
Shake and strain
Pineapple wedge garnish

GORKY PARK COOLER (2)
House specialty glass, chilled
Pour ingredients into blender
1 1/2 oz. Stolichnaya Razberi Russian Vodka
1/2 oz. Captain Morgan Spiced Rum
1/2 oz. Cruzan Coconut Rum
4 oz. pineapple juice
Blend with ice
Pineapple wedge garnish

GOTHAM LEMONADE
Bucket glass, ice
Build in glass
1 1/2 oz. Jewel of Russia
　　Wild Bilberry Infusion
1/2 oz. DJ Dotson Triple Sec
1 oz. cranberry juice
Fill with lemonade
Lemon wheel garnish

GRAN BLISS
Champagne glass, chilled
Build in glass
3/4 oz. Gran Gala Orange Liqueur
1/2 oz. DeKuyper Peachtree Schnapps
Fill with Champagne
Lemon twist garnish

GRAND ALLIANCE
Sherry glass, chilled
Build in glass
1/2 fill Disaronno Amaretto Liqueur
1/2 fill Champagne

GRAN BOMBAY
Cocktail glass, chilled
Pour ingredients into iced mixing glass
1 oz. Bombay Sapphire London Dry Gin
3/4 oz. Gran Gala Orange Liqueur
1 oz. sweet 'n' sour
Shake and strain
Orange twist garnish

GRAN CAPPUCCINO
Cappuccino cup, heated
Build in glass
3/4 oz. Gran Gala Orange Liqueur
1/2 oz. V.S. Cognac
1/2 oz. Kahlúa Coffee Liqueur
Near fill with hot espresso coffee
Top with frothed milk
Sprinkle shaved chocolate

GRAND BALL
Rocks glass, ice
Build in glass
2 oz. Pike Creek Canadian Whisky
3/4 oz. Grand Marnier 100th Anniversary

GRANDFATHER
Tankard or pilsner glass, chilled
Build in glass
1/3 fill Guinness Stout
1/3 fill Bass
1/3 fill Harp

GRAND MARSHALL SOUR
Cocktail glass, chilled
Pour ingredients into iced mixing glass
1 oz. Jack Daniel's Single Barrel Whiskey
1/2 oz. Grand Marnier 100th Anniversary
1 1/2 oz. sweet 'n' sour
Shake and strain
Orange and starfruit slice garnish

GRAND ORANGE BLOSSOM
Cocktail glass, chilled
Pour ingredients into iced mixing glass
1 1/4 oz. Stolichnaya Ohranj Russian Vodka
3/4 oz. Grand Marnier Liqueur
1/2 oz. orange juice
1/4 oz. sugar syrup
Shake and strain
Orange slice garnish

GRAND SIDECAR
Brandy snifter, ice
Rim glass with sugar (optional)
Pour ingredients into iced mixing glass
1 1/4 oz. Brandy
3/4 oz. Grand Marnier Liqueur
1 1/2 oz. sweet 'n' sour
Shake and strain

MIDORI® MELON LIQUEUR

MIDORI MELON LIQUEUR burst into the American limelight in the early 1980s and the brand can now be found on nearly every back bar in the country. In fact, its popularity continues to grow as steadily increasing numbers of contemporary drinks incorporate it into their recipes.

This indispensable liqueur is produced in Japan by the famed spirits company, Suntory. Midori is made from a base of neutral spirits and proprietary flavors, the most readily identifiable of which is honeydew melon. Its lustrous, emerald green color is intriguing, and has certainly played a role in the liqueur's meteoric success.

Midori has a moderately assertive bouquet with the engaging aromas of melon, banana and strawberry. Its soft, supple body immediately coats the mouth with the fresh fruit flavors of honeydew, ripe cantaloupe and bananas. The medium-weight body and slightly sweet palate make it ideal for use in mixed drinks. The liqueur has good persistence of flavor.

Midori's ascendancy into "must have" status can be attributed to its one-of-a-kind flavor, vivid color and moderate 21% abv (42 proof), all of which contribute to its exceptionally high mixability quotient. Add to that a distinctively shaped, textured bottle and you've got a modern classic.

GRAN SONORAN SUNSET
Highball glass, ice
Build in glass
1 1/4 oz. El Tesoro Añejo Tequila
1 1/4 oz. fresh lime juice
1/2 oz. cranberry juice
Float 3/4 oz. Gran Gala Orange Liqueur
Lime wheel garnish

GRAPE NEHI
Rocks glass, ice
Pour ingredients into iced mixing glass
1 1/2 oz. Van Hoo Belgium Vodka
1/2 oz. DeKuyper Grape Pucker
1 1/2 oz. sweet 'n' sour
Shake and strain

GRAPES OF WRATH
Cocktail glass, chilled
Pour ingredients into iced mixing glass
2 oz. Belvedere Polish Vodka
1/2 oz. white grape juice
Stir and strain
Grape bunch garnish

GRASSHOPPER
Cocktail glass, chilled
Pour ingredients into iced mixing glass
3/4 oz. White Crème de Cacao
3/4 oz. Green Crème de Menthe
2 oz. half & half cream
Shake and strain

GREAT LAKES TRAPPER
Coffee mug, heated
Build in glass
3/4 oz. Brandy
3/4 oz. White Crème de Menthe
Near fill with hot chocolate
Whipped cream garnish
Sprinkle nutmeg

GREEK COFFEE
Coffee mug, heated
Build in glass
3/4 oz. Metaxa 5 Star Brandy
3/4 oz. Ouzo
Fill with hot coffee

GREEN HORNET
Rocks glass, ice
Build in glass
1 1/2 oz. Brandy
1/2 oz. Green Crème de Menthe

GREEN LIZARD
Presentation shot glass, chilled
Layer ingredients
1/2 fill Green Chartreuse
1/2 fill 151 proof Rum

GREEN MINT FLOAT
Rocks glass, ice
Build in glass
1 3/4 oz. Knappogue Castle Irish Whiskey
1 oz. Green Crème de Menthe
1 oz. half & half cream
Cherry garnish

GREEN MONSTER
Bucket glass, ice
Build in glass
1 oz. KéKé Beach Cream Liqueur
1/2 oz. Bacardi Light Rum
3/4 oz. Midori Melon Liqueur
Near fill with orange juice
Splash pineapple juice

GREEN REEF
Bucket glass, ice
Build in glass
3/4 oz. Bacardi Light Rum
3/4 oz. Midori Melon Liqueur
1/2 oz. White Crème de Cacao
Near fill with pineapple juice
Float 3/4 oz. Cruzan Pineapple Rum
Pineapple wedge and cherry garnish

GREEN RUSSIAN
Rocks glass, ice
Build in glass
1 1/2 oz. Jewel of Russia Classic Vodka
1/2 oz. Midori Melon Liqueur

GREEN SNEAKERS
Bucket glass, ice
Pour ingredients into iced mixing glass
1 oz. Luksusowa Polish Vodka
1/2 oz. Midori Melon Liqueur
1/2 oz. DeKuyper Pucker Sour Apple
1/2 oz. DeKuyper Triple Sec
2 oz. orange juice
Shake and strain

GREEN SPIDER
Rocks glass, ice
Build in glass
1 1/2 oz. Vincent Van Gogh Vodka
1/2 oz. Green Crème de Menthe

GREYHOUND
Highball glass, ice
Build in glass
1 1/4 oz. Vodka
Fill with grapefruit juice
Note: May be requested made with Gin

GRIFFEN, THE
Champagne glass, chilled
Build in glass
1 oz. Pineau des Charentes
Fill with Champagne
Frozen grapes garnish

GROUND ZERO
Bucket glass, ice
Build in glass
1 1/4 oz. Cruzan Pineapple Rum
3/4 oz. Midori Melon Liqueur
Fill with pineapple juice
Pineapple wedge and cherry garnish

GUAVA COOLER
Bucket glass, ice
Pour ingredients into iced mixing glass
1 1/2 oz. Light Rum
1/2 oz. DeKuyper Raspberry Pucker
1 1/2 oz. guava nectar
1/2 oz. simple syrup
1 oz. sweet 'n' sour
1 oz. pineapple juice
Shake and strain

GUAVA MARTINIQUE
House specialty glass, ice
Pour ingredients into iced mixing glass
1 1/2 oz. Rhum Barbancourt 3-Star Rum
1/2 oz. Chambord Liqueur
1/2 oz. Godiva Chocolate Liqueur
1 1/2 oz. guava nectar
1 1/2 oz. pineapple juice
1 1/2 oz. sweet 'n' sour
Shake and strain
Float 3/4 oz. St. James Extra Old Rhum
Orange slice and cherry garnish

GULF BREEZE
Bucket glass, ice
Build in glass
1 1/4 oz. Cascade Mountain Gin
1/2 fill grapefruit juice
1/2 fill cranberry juice

GULF STREAM SCREAM
House specialty glass, ice
Pour ingredients into iced mixing glass
1 oz. Bacardi Light Rum
1 oz. Midori Melon Liqueur
1/2 oz. DeKuyper Peachtree Schnapps
2 oz. pineapple juice
2 oz. orange juice
Shake and strain
Float 3/4 oz. Mount Gay Eclipse Rum
Orange slice and cherry garnish

GREY GOOSE® VODKA

France is widely recognized for incomparable wines, brandies, and cheese, but it has never cracked the charts with a world class light spirit. That all changed with the 1997 release of ultra-premium GREY GOOSE VODKA. The brand hit the market with a splash, and within months, the vodka was earning medals at international competitions and ranked among the world's elite.

Grey Goose Vodka is made at the H. Mounier Distillery in the heart of Cognac. It is distilled in small batches in copper alembic stills from a blend of rye, barley, wheat, and corn. This pure grain vodka is produced with limestone-filtered water drawn from the famous Genté Springs located in the Champagne region of Provence. The spirit is rigorously filtered and bottled at 80 proof.

A moment alone with Grey Goose Vodka will reveal why it has caught on big with consumers. The vodka has pristine clarity and a supple, medium-weight body. The bouquet is semi-sweet and inviting. Grey Goose enters the mouth without a trace of excess heat and features a skillfully crafted, grainy-sweet palate. The finish is crisp, clean and eminently smooth.

The vibrant citrus essence in GREY GOOSE L'ORANGE is a brilliant complement to the personality of the vodka. Its flavorful finish is best captured in a chilled cocktail glass.

GULF TIDE
Highball glass, ice
Build in glass
1 1/4 oz. Gin
1/2 fill orange juice
1/2 fill cranberry juice

GULLET PLEASER
Presentation shot glass, chilled
Build in glass
1/3 fill DeKuyper Peach Pucker
1/3 fill Stolichnaya Limonnaya
    Russian Vodka
1/3 fill cranberry-grapefruit juice

GUMBY
Bucket glass, chilled
Pour ingredients into iced mixing glass
1 1/4 oz. Belvedere Polish Vodka
3/4 oz. Midori Melon Liqueur
3/4 oz. sweet 'n' sour
Shake and strain
Fill with Seven-Up
Cherry garnish

GYPSY
Cocktail glass, chilled
Pour ingredients into iced mixing glass
1 1/2 oz. Ketel One Dutch Vodka
1/2 oz. B & B Liqueur
2-3 dashes Angostura Bitters
Stir and strain
Lemon twist garnish

HABANA LIBRE
House specialty glass, ice
Build in glass
1 1/2 oz. Matusalem Light Dry Rum
1/2 oz. fresh lime juice
1/4 oz. grenadine
Near fill with cola
Float 3/4 oz. Bacardi 151° Rum
Lime wedge and mint sprig garnish

HABANOS HAVANA
Cocktail glass, chilled
Pour ingredients into iced mixing glass
1 3/4 oz. Matusalem Golden Dry Rum
3/4 oz. Cointreau Liqueur
1 1/2 oz. sweetened lime juice
Shake and strain
Lime wedge garnish

HAIRY SUNRISE

Bucket glass, ice
Build in glass
3/4 oz. Sauza Tres Generaciones
   Plata Tequila
3/4 oz. Van Hoo Belgium Vodka
1/2 oz. DeKuyper Triple Sec
Near fill with orange juice
Float 3/4 oz. DeKuyper Raspberry Pucker
Lime wheel garnish

HALEKULANI SUNSET

House specialty glass, ice
Pour ingredients into iced mixing glass
1 1/2 oz. Bacardi Light Rum
3/4 oz. Blue Curaçao
1/2 oz. grenadine
3 oz. guava nectar
1 1/2 oz. sweet 'n' sour
Shake and strain
Float 3/4 oz. Gosling's Black Seal Rum
Pineapple wedge and cherry garnish

HALF & HALF (1)

Cocktail glass, chilled
Pour ingredients into iced mixing glass
1 1/2 oz. Dry Vermouth
1 1/2 oz. Sweet Vermouth
Stir and strain
Lemon twist garnish

HALF & HALF (2)

Beer glass, chilled
Build in glass
1/2 fill Bitter Ale
1/2 fill Pilsner

HANGIN' ON A STICK

Rocks glass, chilled
Pour ingredients into iced mixing glass
1 oz. Jose Cuervo Especial Tequila
3/4 oz. Cointreau Liqueur
1/2 oz. cranberry juice
1/2 oz. pineapple juice
3/4 oz. orange juice
Shake and strain

HAPPY HOUR

Bucket glass, ice
Build in glass
1 1/2 oz. Doorly's XO Barbados Rum
3/4 oz. Mandarine Napoléon Liqueur
Fill with papaya juice

HAPPY JACKS

Presentation shot glass, chilled
Build in glass
1/2 fill Jack Daniel's Tennessee Whiskey
1/2 fill Laird's Applejack Brandy

HARBOR LIGHTS

Presentation shot glass, chilled
Layer ingredients
1/3 fill Kahlúa Coffee Liqueur
1/3 fill Tequila
1/3 fill 151 proof Rum

HARVARD

Cocktail glass, chilled
Pour ingredients into iced mixing glass
1 3/4 oz. Brandy
3/4 oz. Sweet Vermouth
2 dashes Angostura Bitters
1/4 oz. simple syrup
Stir and strain
Lemon twist garnish

HARVEST GROG

Coffee mug, heated
Build in glass
1 oz. Laird's Applejack Brandy
1 oz. Chambord Liqueur
2 dashes cinnamon
3 cloves
6 oz. apple cider
Cinnamon stick garnish
*Heat mix of apple cider and spices in small
   sauce pan for 5 minutes. Remove cloves,
   pour mixture into glass with Applejack
   and Chambord.*

HARVEY WALLBANGER

Bucket glass, ice
Build in glass
1 1/4 oz. Vodka
Near fill with orange juice
Float 3/4 oz. Galliano Liqueur

HASTA LA VISTA, BABY

Highball glass, chilled
Pour ingredients into iced mixing glass
1/2 oz. Jose Cuervo Especial Tequila
1/2 oz. Absolut Peppar Vodka
1/2 oz. DeKuyper Peachtree Schnapps
1/4 oz. DeKuyper Triple Sec
1/4 oz. Crème de Noyaux
1/4 oz. B & B Liqueur
1/2 oz. Rose's Lime Juice
3/4 oz. pineapple juice
3/4 oz. orange juice
Shake and strain

HAVANA

Cocktail glass, chilled
Pour ingredients into iced mixing glass
1/2 oz. Dry Sherry
1 3/4 oz. Gold Rum
1 dash Angostura Bitters
1 1/2 oz. sweet 'n' sour
Shake and strain
Orange twist garnish

MAKER'S MARK® BOURBON

As the country's first small batch whiskey, MAKER'S MARK is generally credited with bourbon's phenomenal resurgence. By the late 1970s, the distinctive, red wax-dipped bottle had secured its place on top shelves across the country and had become known as the brand to pour for those with discriminating taste. Today, Maker's Mark continues to be one of the most recognizable whiskies in the world.

After seven generations, Maker's Mark has developed a large and loyal following, especially in the brand's home state of Kentucky. It is one of only a small number of bourbons to include wheat instead of rye in its mash bill.

Maker's Mark Bourbon has a soft, supple body and a marvelous bouquet of honey, vanilla, spices and fruit. The color is rich with the red hue of aged wood. The palate is loaded with the flavors of caramel, butter and notes of toasty oak. The whiskey has a relaxed and slightly smoky finish.

Here's a world-class whiskey that doesn't cost a week's paycheck. While its captivating array of flavors and aromas come alive with a splash of spring water, there are no limits to its creative potential.

This is an ideal bourbon to feature in a signature Manhattan, mint julep or muddled old fashion. It's a "must have" for any great bourbon bar.

HAVANA CLUB
Cocktail glass, chilled
Pour ingredients into iced mixing glass
1/2 oz. Sweet Vermouth
1 3/4 oz. Gold Rum
1 dash Angostura Bitters
Stir and strain
Cherry garnish

HAVANA COCKTAIL
Cocktail glass, chilled
Pour ingredients into iced mixing glass
1 3/4 oz. Matusalem Golden Dry Rum
1/2 oz. fresh lemon juice
1 1/2 oz. pineapple juice
Shake and strain
Cherry garnish

HAVANA SIDECAR (1)
Cocktail glass, chilled
Rim glass with sugar (optional)
Pour ingredients into iced mixing glass
1 1/2 oz. Matusalem Golden Dry Rum
3/4 oz. Cointreau Liqueur
1 1/2 oz. sweet 'n' sour
Shake and strain
Lime wedge garnish

HAVANA SIDECAR (2)
Cocktail glass, chilled
Rim glass with sugar (optional)
Pour ingredients into iced mixing glass
1 1/2 oz. Bacardi 8 Reserva Rum
3/4 oz. Cointreau Liqueur
3/4 oz. sweet 'n' sour
Shake and strain
Lemon wedge garnish

HAWAIIAN HURRICANE
House specialty glass, ice
Pour ingredients into iced mixing glass
1/2 oz. Bacardi Light Rum
1/2 oz. Bacardi Gold Rum
1/2 oz. Myers's Jamaican Rum
1/2 oz. Tequila
1/2 oz. Vodka
2 oz. pineapple juice
2 oz. papaya juice
Shake and strain
Float 3/4 oz. 151 proof Rum
Orange slice and cherry garnish

HAWAIIAN PUNCH (1)
Bucket glass, ice
Pour ingredients into iced mixing glass
1 oz. Jewel of Russia Wild Bilberry Infusion
1/2 oz. Disaronno Amaretto Liqueur
1/2 oz. Southern Comfort Liqueur
1/2 oz. Sloe Gin
2 oz. pineapple juice
Shake and strain
Splash Seven-Up (optional)

HAWAIIAN PUNCH (2)
Bucket glass, ice
Build in glass
3/4 oz. Southern Comfort Liqueur
3/4 oz. Disaronno Amaretto Liqueur
3/4 oz. Crème de Noyaux
1 1/2 oz. pineapple juice
1 1/2 oz. orange juice

HAWAIIAN SHOOTER
Rocks glass, chilled
Pour ingredients into iced mixing glass
1 1/4 oz. Southern Comfort Liqueur
3/4 oz. Crème de Noyaux
1/2 oz. pineapple juice
Shake and strain

HAWAIIAN SUNBURN
Bucket glass, ice
Build in glass
1 1/4 oz. Hussong's Reposado Tequila
1/2 oz. Gran Gala Orange Liqueur
Near fill with cranberry juice
Splash pineapple juice

HEARTBREAK
Bucket glass, ice
Build in glass
1 1/4 oz. Canadian Club Whisky
Near fill with cranberry juice
Float 3/4 oz. Brandy

HEATHER BLUSH
Champagne glass, chilled
Build in glass
1 1/4 oz. Dewar's White Label
   Scotch Whisky
1 oz. Chambord Liqueur
Fill with Champagne

HEAT WAVE
Bucket glass, ice
Build in glass
1 oz. Mount Gay Eclipse Rum
1/2 oz. DeKuyper Peachtree Schnapps
Near fill with pineapple juice
Float 3/4 oz. Appleton Estate
   V/X Jamaica Rum
Lime wedge garnish

HEAVENLY TODDY
Coffee mug, heated
Build in glass
2 oz. Christian Brothers Brandy
2 tsp. honey
2 oz. fresh lemon juice
Fill with hot water
Lemon twist garnish

HEAVYWEIGHT SAILOR
Cocktail glass, chilled
Pour ingredients into iced mixing glass
1 1/4 oz. Pyrat Pistol Rum
1/2 oz. Tia Maria
1/2 oz. Rose's Lime Juice
1 3/4 oz. sweet 'n' sour
Shake and strain
Lime wedge garnish

HELENE
Brandy snifter (ice optional)
Build in glass
1 1/2 oz. Poire William (Eau de Vie de Poire)
1/2 oz. Godiva Chocolate Liqueur

HELL ON ICE
Bucket glass, ice
Build in glass
1 oz. Foursquare Spiced Rum
1 oz. Jim Beam Black Label Bourbon
1/2 oz. Fireball Cinnamon Canadian Whisky
Fill with orange juice

HEMINGWAY
aka **Death in the Afternoon**
Champagne glass, chilled
Build in glass
1 1/2 oz. Pernod
Fill with Champagne

HEMINGWAY'S FLAMBÉ COFFEE
Coffee mug, heated
Build in glass
1 oz. Frangelico Liqueur
1/2 oz. Sambuca Romano
1/2 oz. Brandy
Near fill with hot coffee
Whipped cream garnish
Sprinkle nutmeg

HIGHBALL
Highball glass, ice
Build in glass
1 1/4 oz. Bourbon
Fill with ginger ale

GRAND MARNIER®
150ᵀᴴ ANNIVERSARY

The liqueur that may very well be the pinnacle of sophistication is GRAND MARNIER 150ᵀᴴ ANNIVERSARY. Introduced in 1977 to commemorate the 150th anniversary of Marnier-Lapostolle, this magnificent liqueur is the company's crowning achievement.

In 1827, the Lapostolle family built a distillery in France to produce liqueurs. More than 50 years later, the firm perfected a cognac-based liqueur flavored with the peels of bitter Haitian oranges. The liqueur was given the name Grand Marnier and debuted in 1880.

Grand Marnier 150th Anniversary is skillfully crafted at the Marnier-Lapostolle distillery on a base of Grande Champagne cognacs ranging in age up to 50 years. The liqueur is then aged in Limousin oak barrels at the Marnier-Lapostolle cellars.

The 150th Anniversary has a burnished amber hue and a delicate, silky smooth body. The wafting bouquet is lavishly endowed with the aromas of well-aged cognac and citrus. The liqueur has a sensationally full and rich palate prominently featuring the flavor of cognac with vibrant orange notes. The finish is delectably long and warming.

In 1927, GRAND MARNIER 100ᵀᴴ ANNIVERSARY was released to celebrate the company's centenary. This world class liqueur is made on a base of cognacs ranging in age up to 25 years.

HIGHLAND COCKTAIL
aka **Highland Fling**
Cocktail glass, chilled
Pour ingredients into iced mixing glass
1 1/2 oz. Scotch Whisky
1/2 oz. Sweet Vermouth
2-3 dashes Angostura Bitters
Stir and strain
Lemon twist garnish

HIGHLAND GOLFER
Bucket glass, ice
Build in glass
1 1/4 oz. Scotch Whisky
1/2 oz. Hiram Walker Triple Sec
1/2 oz. Green Crème de Menthe
Fill with apple cider

HIGHLAND HIGHBALL
Highball glass, ice
Build in glass
1 1/4 oz. Dewar's White Label
   Scotch Whisky
Fill with ginger ale
Lemon twist garnish

HIMBEERSAFT
Highball glass, ice
Build in glass
3 oz. raspberry syrup
Fill with club soda
Mint sprig garnish

HOLE-IN-ONE
Presentation shot glass, chilled
Build in glass
1 1/4 oz. Midori Melon Liqueur
3/4 oz. Laird's Applejack Brandy
4 drops half & half cream

HOLLAND'S OPUS
Cocktail glass, chilled
Pour ingredients into iced mixing glass
2 oz. Van Gogh Gin
1/2 oz. Chambord Liqueur
1 3/4 oz. sweet 'n' sour
Shake and strain
Lemon twist garnish

HOLLYWOOD
Highball glass, ice
Build in glass
3/4 oz. Jewel of Russia
   Wild Bilberry Infusion
3/4 oz. Chambord Liqueur
Fill with pineapple juice

HOLY HAND GRENADE
Rocks glass, chilled
Build in glass
1 1/4 oz. Chambord Liqueur
3/4 oz. Kurant Vodka
1 1/2 oz. lemonade

HONEY BEE
Cocktail glass, chilled
Pour ingredients into iced mixing glass
1 oz. Myers's Jamaican Rum
1/2 oz. honey
1 1/2 oz. sweet 'n' sour
Shake and strain

HONEYBUNCH PUNCH
House specialty glass, ice
Pour ingredients into iced mixing glass
1 1/2 oz. Cruzan Estate Diamond Rum
1/2 oz. Mandarine Napoléon Liqueur
1/2 oz. Rose's Lime Juice
2-3 dashes Angostura Bitters
1/4 oz. grenadine
1/2 oz. orange juice
1/2 oz. pineapple juice
Shake and strain
Orange slice and cherry garnish

HONEYDEW
Bucket glass, ice
Pour ingredients into iced mixing glass
1 1/2 oz. Midori Melon Liqueur
3 oz. lemonade
Shake and strain
Fill with Champagne

HONEYMOON
aka **Farmer's Daughter**
Cocktail glass, chilled
Pour ingredients into iced mixing glass
1 1/4 oz. Laird's Applejack Brandy
1/2 oz. B & B Liqueur
1/2 oz. DJ Dotson Triple Sec
1 3/4 oz. sweet 'n' sour
Shake and strain

HONEY RUM TODDY
Coffee mug, heated
Build in glass
2 oz. Bacardi Gold Rum
2 tbsp. honey
1 tbsp. fresh lime juice
A thin slice of lime
Fill with boiling water
Lemon wedge and cinnamon stick garnish

HOOCHIE KÉKÉ MAMA
Bucket glass, ice
Build in glass
1 oz. KéKé Beach Cream Liqueur
1 oz. Finlandia Vodka
3/4 oz. Kahlúa Coffee Liqueur
1/2 fill with cola
1/2 fill with half & half cream

HORSE'S NECK WITH A KICK
Highball glass, ice
Build in glass
1 1/4 oz. Bourbon
Fill with ginger ale
Long lemon peel spiral garnish
  (a 'horse's neck')

HOT APPLE PIE
Coffee mug, heated
Build in glass
1 oz. Tuaca
Near fill with hot apple cider
Whipped cream garnish
Sprinkle nutmeg

HOT APPLE ROSE
Coffee mug, heated
Build in glass
1 1/4 oz. Tequila Rose Cream Liqueur
Near fill with hot apple cider
Whipped cream and cinnamon stick garnish

HOT BUTTERED RUM
Coffee mug, heated
Build in glass
1 1/2 oz. Appleton Estate V/X Jamaica Rum
1/2 oz. simple syrup
2 pinches nutmeg
Fill with hot water
Float pat of butter
Cinnamon stick garnish

HOT CHAMBORD DREAM
Coffee mug, heated
Build in glass
3/4 oz. Dark Crème de Cacao
3/4 oz. Chambord Liqueur
Near fill with hot espresso coffee
Top with frothed milk
Sprinkle shaved chocolate

HOT HONEY POT
Cocktail glass, chilled
Pour ingredients into iced mixing glass
1 oz. Fireball Cinnamon Canadian Whisky
1/2 oz. honey
1 1/2 oz. sweet 'n' sour
Shake and strain

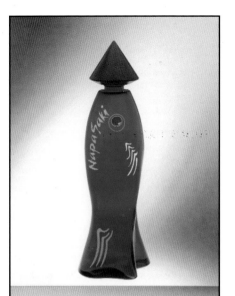

NAPASAKI® SAKÉ

NAPASAKI is an American made, super-premium saké that will likely change how many people view this traditionally Japanese beverage and appreciate all of its creative possibilities.

NapaSaki is a handcrafted *Junmai-Ginjo* type of saké, meaning that it is an entirely natural product, containing only polished rice, water, yeast and *koji*, an enzyme that converts the rice's starches into glucose. It is bottled at 15% abv.

The ultra-premium *Akitakomachi* rice used to make NapaSaki is organically grown in the fertile soil of California. The rice is polished to 58% of the original kernel size. While a costly and laborious process, it yields the finest, lightest and most aromatic saké.

The all-important *koji* is cultivated in a traditional, time-honored manner and the mother yeast strain used to precipitate fermentation is a closely guarded secret. NapaSaki is filtered 8 times, pasteurized twice and aged for 6 months.

NapaSaki is a luscious and captivating saké, one that will tempt aficionados and newcomers alike. It is crystal clear with a soft, delicate body. The saké's bouquet is subtle, yet clean and fresh. The palate is as refreshing as a light, dry white wine on a hot day.

NapaSaki is at its best when served slightly chilled. It is, however, also sensational as a featured performer in a variety of cocktails.

HOT IRISH DREAM
Coffee mug, heated
Build in glass
1 oz. Ballylarkin Irish Liqueur
1/2 oz. Baileys Irish Cream
1/2 oz. Frangelico Liqueur
Near fill with coffee
Whipped cream garnish
Drizzle 1/2 oz. Chambord Liqueur

HOT MILK PUNCH
Coffee mug, heated
Build in glass
1 1/2 oz. W.L. Weller Bourbon
1/2 oz. simple syrup
Fill with hot milk
Sprinkle nutmeg

HOT MULLED WINE
Punch bowl or decanter
Pour ingredients into saucepan
36 oz. Dry Red Wine
1/2 cup sugar
12 oz. cranberry juice
1/4 cup mulling spices
Simmer for 30 minutes
Makes 8-10 servings

HOT RUM COW
Coffee mug, heated
Build in glass
1 3/4 oz. Bacardi Gold Rum
1 tsp. powdered sugar
1 dash Angostura Bitters
2 dashes vanilla extract
2 pinches nutmeg
Fill with hot milk

HOT TIMES
Presentation shot glass
Build in glass
1/4 fill DeKuyper Pucker Sour Apple
1/4 fill Hot Damn Cinnamon Schnapps
1/4 fill Light Rum
1/4 fill hot apple cider

HOT TODDY
Coffee mug, heated
Build in glass
1 1/2 oz. Brandy
1 tsp. sugar
Fill with hot water
Lemon twist garnish
Note: May be requested made
    with Bourbon

HOT TROPICO MAMA
Cocktail glass, chilled
Pour ingredients into iced mixing glass
3/4 oz. Tropico
3/4 oz. Crème de Banana
3/4 oz. Hiram Walker Triple Sec
1 1/4 oz. orange juice
1 1/4 oz. half & half cream
Shake and strain
Sprinkle shaved chocolate

HOUNDSTOOTH
Rocks glass, ice
Build in glass
1 1/2 oz. Vincent Van Gogh Vodka
1/2 oz. White Crème de Cacao
1/2 oz. Blackberry Brandy

HOURGLASS
Cocktail glass, chilled
Pour ingredients into iced mixing glass
1 1/4 oz. Knappogue Castle Irish Whiskey
1 oz. orange juice
1 oz. cranberry juice
Shake and strain
Lime wheel garnish

HULA SKIRT
Brandy snifter, ice
Pour ingredients into iced mixing glass
1 oz. Extase XO Liqueur
1 oz. Cruzan Estate Single Barrel Rum
3/4 oz. pineapple juice
3/4 oz. fresh lime juice
Shake and strain
Lime wedge garnish

HUMMER
House specialty glass, chilled
Pour ingredients into blender
3/4 oz. Bacardi Gold Rum
3/4 oz. Kahlúa Coffee Liqueur
3/4 oz. Dark Crème de Cacao
2 scoops vanilla ice cream
Blend ingredients (with ice optional)
Float 3/4 oz. Mount Gay Eclipse Rum
Oreo cookie garnish

HUNKER PUNKER
Cocktail glass, chilled
Pour ingredients into iced mixing glass
2 oz. Damrak Amsterdam Gin
3/4 oz. Cointreau Liqueur
3/4 oz. fresh lime juice
Shake and strain
Lime wedge garnish

HUNTER'S COFFEE
Coffee mug, heated
Build in glass
3/4 oz. Tia Maria
3/4 oz. Cointreau Liqueur
Near fill with hot coffee
Whipped cream garnish
Drizzle 1/2 oz. Tia Maria

HURRICANE (1)
House specialty glass, ice
Pour ingredients into iced mixing glass
1 1/2 oz. Light Rum
1 1/2 oz. Gold Rum
1/2 oz. Rose's Lime Juice
1/2 oz. simple syrup
1/2 oz. grenadine
2 oz. orange juice
2 oz. pineapple juice
Shake and strain
Lime, lemon and orange wedge garnish

HURRICANE (2)
House specialty glass, ice
Pour ingredients into iced mixing glass
1 1/2 oz. Light Rum
1 1/2 oz. Gold Rum
1/2 oz. simple syrup
1 1/2 oz. passion fruit juice or nectar
1 1/2 oz. fresh lime juice
1 1/2 oz. pineapple juice
Shake and strain
Float 3/4 oz. Overproof Rum
Lime, lemon and orange wedge garnish

IACOCCA
Cappuccino cup, heated
Build in glass
3/4 oz. Kahlúa Coffee Liqueur
1/2 oz. Grand Marnier Liqueur
1/2 oz. Baileys Irish Cream
Near fill with hot espresso coffee
Top with frothed milk
Drizzle 1 oz. Frangelico Liqueur
Sprinkle shaved chocolate

ICEBERG (1)
Rocks glass, ice
Build in glass
1 1/2 oz. Original Cristall Russian Vodka
3/4 oz. DeKuyper Peppermint Schnapps

ICEBERG (2)
Rocks glass, ice
Build in glass
1 1/2 oz. Brilliant Vodka
3/4 oz. Pernod

CREAM DRINKS

Cream drinks are like liquid desserts. These cocktails have excellent appeal and are low in alcoholic potency. They are most often served in restaurants and lounges after dinner or later at night.

The base ingredient in almost all of these drinks is half & half cream. It is preferred over milk, which is too thin for use in these drinks, and whole cream, which is too sweet and heavy. For a creative variation, substitute several scoops of ice cream for the half & half in these recipes. The results are drinks that turn out like adult milkshakes— thick, rich and loaded with great taste.

Cream drinks will be ordered and prepared in one of three ways. The classic style of service is straight-up, requiring the drink to be prepared in an iced mixing set or cocktail shaker and served in a chilled cocktail glass.

These drinks are also often requested served on-the-rocks, in which case it is prepared in a mixing set or cocktail shaker and presented in an iced snifter or house specialty glass.

Third, cream cocktails can be prepared blended or "frozen." The drink is then prepared in a commercial grade or home-style blender with an amount of ice almost equal to the liquid ingredients. If ice cream is substituted for half & half, the ice can be omitted.

These delicious, milkshake-like creations look sensational, especially when presented in house specialty glassware. They require a glass with a capacity of around 14 to 18 ounces. Inside a beautiful glass they look like elegant desserts.

ICE CHOCOLATE
Rocks glass, chilled
Build in glass
1 oz. Rumple Minze Schnapps
1 oz. Godiva Chocolate Liqueur

ICE CREAM BELLINI
House specialty glass, chilled
Pour ingredients into blender
2 scoops peach ice cream
4-5 frozen peach slices
5 oz. ginger ale
Blend ingredients (with ice optional)
Fill with Champagne
Peach wedge garnish

ICED TEA, AFTERBURNER
House specialty glass, ice
Pour ingredients into iced mixing glass
1/2 oz. Gin
1/2 oz. Vodka
1/2 oz. Rum
1/2 oz. Tequila
1/2 oz. Triple Sec
2 oz. sweet 'n' sour
2 oz. cola
Shake and strain
Float 3/4 oz. 151 proof Rum

ICED TEA, ALASKAN
House specialty glass, ice
Pour ingredients into iced mixing glass
1/2 oz. Gin
1/2 oz. Vodka
1/2 oz. Light Rum
1/2 oz. Blue Curaçao
4 oz. sweet 'n' sour
Shake and strain
Fill with Seven-Up
Lemon wedge garnish

ICED TEA, BIMINI
House specialty glass, ice
Pour ingredients into iced mixing glass
1/2 oz. Gin
1/2 oz. Vodka
1/2 oz. Light Rum
1/2 oz. Tequila
1/2 oz. Blue Curaçao
2 oz. orange juice
2 oz. pineapple juice
1 1/2 oz. sweet 'n' sour
2 oz. cola
Shake and strain
Lemon wedge garnish

ICED TEA, BLUE KANGAROO
House specialty glass, ice
Pour ingredients into iced mixing glass
1/2 oz. Gin
1/2 oz. Vodka
1/2 oz. Light Rum
1/2 oz. Tequila
1/2 oz. Blue Curaçao
2 oz. sweet 'n' sour
Shake and strain
1/2 fill Seven-Up
1/2 fill club soda
Lemon wedge garnish

ICED TEA, CALIFORNIA
House specialty glass, ice
Pour ingredients into iced mixing glass
1/2 oz. Gin
1/2 oz. Vodka
1/2 oz. Light Rum
1/2 oz. Tequila
1/2 oz. Triple Sec
1 oz. cola
2 oz. sweet 'n' sour
2 oz. grapefruit juice
Shake and strain
Lemon wedge garnish

ICED TEA, DIRTY ASHTRAY
House specialty glass, ice
Pour ingredients into iced mixing glass
1/2 oz. Gin
1/2 oz. Vodka
1/2 oz. Light Rum
1/2 oz. Tequila
1/2 oz. Blue Curaçao
1/2 oz. grenadine
1 1/2 oz. pineapple juice
2 oz. sweet 'n' sour
Shake and strain
Lemon wedge garnish

ICED TEA, FLORIDA
House specialty glass, ice
Pour ingredients into iced mixing glass
1/2 oz. Gin
1/2 oz. Vodka
1/2 oz. Light Rum
1/2 oz. Tequila
1/2 oz. Triple Sec
1 oz. cola
2 oz. sweet 'n' sour
2 oz. orange juice
Shake and strain
Lemon wedge garnish

ICED TEA, GREEN TEA
aka **Green Dinosaur**
House specialty glass, ice
Pour ingredients into iced mixing glass
1/2 oz. Gin
1/2 oz. Vodka
1/2 oz. Rum
1/2 oz. Tequila
1/2 oz. Hiram Walker Triple Sec
1 1/2 oz. sweet 'n' sour
1 1/2 oz. cranberry juice
Shake and strain
Float 1 oz. Midori Melon Liqueur
Lemon wedge garnish

ICED TEA, HAVANA
House specialty glass, ice
Pour ingredients into iced mixing glass
1/2 oz. Christian Brothers Brandy
1/2 oz. Matusalem Golden Dry Rum
1/2 oz. Matusalem Light Dry Rum
1/2 oz. DJ Dotson Triple Sec
1 1/2 oz. orange juice
1 1/2 oz. sweet 'n' sour
1 1/2 oz. cola
Shake and strain
Lemon wedge garnish

ICED TEA, HAWAIIAN
House specialty glass, ice
Pour ingredients into iced mixing glass
1/2 oz. Gin
1/2 oz. Vodka
1/2 oz. Light Rum
1/2 oz. Tequila
1/2 oz. Triple Sec
1 oz. cola
2 oz. sweet 'n' sour
2 oz. pineapple juice
Shake and strain
Lemon wedge garnish

ICED TEA, ITALIAN
House specialty glass, ice
Pour ingredients into iced mixing glass
1/2 oz. Gin
1/2 oz. Vodka
1/2 oz. Light Rum
1/2 oz. Triple Sec
2 oz. sweet 'n' sour
2 oz. cola
Shake and strain
Float 3/4 oz. Disaronno Amaretto Liqueur
Lemon wedge garnish

HERRADURA®
REPOSADO TEQUILA

Founded in 1870, HERRADURA TEQUILA is one of the preeminent brands of tequila. Every stage of its production takes place on the Herradura estate in Amatitán, and it is among only a few distilleries that have always only produced 100% agave tequila. Originally imported by Bing Crosby and Phil Harris in the 1950s, Herradura was the first brand of 100% agave tequila available in the United States.

Herradura crafts its tequila using many of the same techniques perfected more than a century ago. Mature, estate-grown blue agaves are baked in clay ovens, then slowly fermented with wild, naturally occurring yeasts. Herradura tequilas are double-distilled in large, stainless steel, alembic stills and aged in both American and French oak barrels. HERRADURA BLANCO is an aromatic tequila with spicy, peppery and citrus flavors. HERRADURA REPOSADO is aged in oak barrels for 11 months. It has a generous, floral and dried fruit bouquet, and a lavish, vanilla and oak laced palate.

The luxurious, 2-year-old HERRADURA AÑEJO is richly colored and loaded with the aromas and flavors of pepper, ripe apples and toasted oak. Ultra-premium HERRADURA SELECCIÓN SUPREMA is a 4-year-old añejo brimming with sophistication and character, similar in nature to an aged brandy.

ICED TEA, JESSE'S SHOCKING
House specialty glass, ice
Pour ingredients into iced mixing glass
1/2 oz. Ketel One Citroen Dutch Vodka
1/2 oz. Bacardi Limón Rum
1/2 oz. Tropico
1/2 oz. Chambord Liqueur
1/2 oz. Cointreau Liqueur
2 oz. sweet 'n' sour
2 oz. Seven-Up
Shake and strain
Lemon wedge garnish

ICED TEA, LONG BEACH
House specialty glass, ice
Pour ingredients into iced mixing glass
1/2 oz. Gin
1/2 oz. Vodka
1/2 oz. Light Rum
1/2 oz. Tequila
1/2 oz. Triple Sec
1 oz. cola
2 oz. cranberry juice
2 oz. sweet 'n' sour
Shake and strain
Lemon wedge garnish

ICED TEA, LONG ISLAND
aka **Texas Iced Tea**
House specialty glass, ice
Pour ingredients into iced mixing glass
1/2 oz. Gin
1/2 oz. Vodka
1/2 oz. Light Rum
1/2 oz. Tequila
1/2 oz. Triple Sec
2 oz. sweet 'n' sour
2 oz. cola
Shake and strain
Lemon wedge garnish

ICED TEA, MANHATTAN
House specialty glass, ice
Pour ingredients into iced mixing glass
1/2 oz. Gin
1/2 oz. Vodka
1/2 oz. Light Rum
1/2 oz. Tequila
2 oz. cola
2 oz. sweet 'n' sour
Shake and strain
Float 3/4 oz. Bourbon
Lemon wedge garnish

ICED TEA, RASPBERRY
aka **Grateful Dead, Purple Haze**
House specialty glass, ice
Pour ingredients into iced mixing glass
1/2 oz. Gin
1/2 oz. Vodka
1/2 oz. Light Rum
1/2 oz. Tequila
1/2 oz. Triple Sec
2 oz. sweet 'n' sour
2 oz. cola
Shake and strain
Float 3/4 oz. Chambord Liqueur
Lemon wedge garnish

ICED TEA, STRAWBERRY
House specialty glass, ice
Pour ingredients into iced mixing glass
1/2 oz. Gin
1/2 oz. Vodka
1/2 oz. Rum
1/2 oz. Tequila
1/2 oz. Triple Sec
2 oz. sweet 'n' sour
2 oz. strawberry puree
Shake and strain
Splash cola
Lemon wedge garnish

ICED TEA, TAHITI
House specialty glass, ice
Pour ingredients into iced mixing glass
1/2 oz. Gin
1/2 oz. Vodka
1/2 oz. Rum
1/2 oz. Tequila
1/2 oz. Triple Sec
1 oz. sweet 'n' sour
1 1/2 oz. orange juice
1 1/2 oz. pineapple juice
Shake and strain
Lemon wedge garnish

ICED TEA, TERMINAL
aka **Terminal Tea**
House specialty glass, ice
Pour ingredients into iced mixing glass
1/2 oz. Jose Cuervo Especial Tequila
1/2 oz. Smirnoff Vodka
1/2 oz. Tanqueray Gin
1/2 oz. Bacardi Light Rum
1/2 oz. Grand Marnier Liqueur
2 oz. sweet 'n' sour
2 oz. cola
Shake and strain
Lemon wedge garnish

ICED TEA, TEXAS
House specialty glass, ice
Pour ingredients into iced mixing glass
3/4 oz. Light Rum
3/4 oz. Vodka
1/2 oz. Gin
1/2 oz. Grand Marnier Liqueur
2 oz. cranberry juice
1 1/2 oz. pineapple juice
1 1/2 oz. orange juice
Shake and strain

ICED TEA, TROPICAL
House specialty glass, ice
Pour ingredients into iced mixing glass
1/2 oz. Gin
1/2 oz. Vodka
1/2 oz. Rum
1/2 oz. Tequila
1/2 oz. Triple Sec
1/2 oz. grenadine
1 oz. sweet 'n' sour
1 oz. pineapple juice
1 oz. cranberry juice
Shake and strain
Lemon wedge garnish

ICE PICK ICED TEA
Bucket glass, ice
Build in glass
1 1/4 oz. Vincent Van Gogh Citroen Vodka
Fill with lemon-flavored, iced tea
Lemon wedge garnish

IDEAL COCKTAIL
Cocktail glass, chilled
Pour ingredients into iced mixing glass
1 1/2 oz. Damrak Amsterdam Gin
1/2 oz. Vya California Dry Vermouth
1 dash simple syrup
1 oz. grapefruit juice
Shake and strain

IL DUCE
House specialty glass, chilled
Pour ingredients into blender
Rim glass with cinnamon and sugar
   (optional)
1/2 oz. Baileys Irish Cream
1/2 oz. Frangelico Liqueur
1/2 oz. Kahlúa Coffee Liqueur
1/2 oz. half & half cream
3 oz. espresso coffee
2 scoops vanilla ice cream
Blend ingredients (with ice optional)
Whipped cream garnish
Dust powdered cocoa

ORIGINAL® POLISH VODKA

There has long been a debate about whether vodka originated in Poland or Russia. Proponents for each side contend that this most famous of spirits was born in their homeland in the early part of the 16th century. From an intellectual perspective, the matter will likely never be resolved. On a more personal level, however, sampling super-premium ORIGINAL POLISH VODKA may tip the scales of public opinion in Poland's favor.

Produced at the Polmos Bielsko-Biala Distillery, Original Polish Vodka is made entirely from rye using only the heart of the grain. The heads and tails of the grain shaft are discarded prior to distillation. The rye is meticulously cleaned, fermented, then distilled six times in column stills with mineral-free, artesian well water. The final distillation continues until the vodka conforms to the exact taste profile. Prior to bottling, the vodka is subjected to a complex filtration process designed to render it essentially pure.

Original Polish Vodka is crystal clear with a lightweight, satiny smooth body. The vodka is remarkably aromatic with an engaging bouquet of caramel and sweet grain. It immediately upon entry, fills the mouth with a flourish of delectably spicy, sweet flavors, before gradually tapering off in a luxurious finish.

Original Polish Vodka is sensational and makes a very persuasive case as to the origins of the species.

IMPERIAL DUO
Champagne glass, chilled
Pour ingredients into iced mixing glass
1 1/2 oz. Rémy Martin V.S. Cognac
3/4 oz. Chambord Liqueur
1/4 oz. Godiva Chocolate Liqueur
2 oz. sweet 'n' sour
Shake and strain
Lemon twist garnish

IMPERIAL FUZZ
Champagne glass, chilled
Build in glass
1 1/2 oz. DeKuyper Peachtree Schnapps
2 oz. orange juice
Fill with Champagne
Orange slice and cherry garnish

IMPERIAL SIDECAR
Cocktail, chilled or brandy snifter, ice
Pour ingredients into iced mixing glass
1 1/4 oz. Brandy
3/4 oz. Gran Gala Orange Liqueur
1 1/2 oz. sweet 'n' sour
Shake and strain
Orange twist

INDEPENDENCE SWIZZLE
House specialty glass, crushed ice
Build in glass
1 1/2 oz. Appleton Estate V/X Jamaica Rum
3 dashes Angostura Bitters
1/4 oz. honey
1/2 oz. simple syrup
1 oz. fresh lime juice
Swizzle thoroughly with spoon
until glass frosts
Lime wedge garnish

INFUSION, ALIEN SECRETION
Large covered jar
Steep in jar
Fill 1/2 full with pineapples,
    peeled and sliced
Fill 1/2 full with Midori Melon Liqueur
    (1/2 - 1 1/2 liters)
Fill with Malibu Rum (1/2 - 1 1/2 liters)
Taste test after 3-4 days

INFUSION, ASTRAL APRICOT
Large covered jar
Steep in jar
Fill 1/2 full with apricots, pitted and halved
Add 4 cinnamon sticks
Add 2 vanilla beans
Fill with Vodka (1/2 - 2 liters)
Float 2 naval orange slices
Taste test after 4-5 days

INFUSION, BARRIER REEF

Large covered jar
Steep in jar
Fill 1/2 full with pineapples,
  peeled and sliced
Fill 1/4 full with cantaloupe,
  peeled and sliced
Fill 1/4 full with honey dew melon,
  peeled and sliced
Add 3 cups maraschino cherries
Fill with Light Rum (1/2 - 2 liters)
Taste test after 2-3 days

INFUSION, BEACH

Large covered jar
Steep in jar
Fill 1/2 full with pineapples,
  peeled and sliced
Fill 1/2 full with cranberries, fresh or frozen
Add Peach Schnapps (5 - 10 oz.)
Fill 1/2 full with Vodka (1/2 - 1 liter)
Fill with Midori Melon Liqueur
  (1/2 - 1 liter)
Taste test after 3-4 days

INFUSION, BEEFEATER
BLOODY CAESAR

Large covered jar
Steep in jar
Fill 1/2 full with sun-dried tomatoes
Fill 1/3 full with celery, cut into stalks
Add clam juice (5-10 oz.)
Add 3 tbsp. seasoned salt
Add 4 oz. Tabasco Sauce
Add Bloody Mary mix (8 - 16 oz.)
Fill with Beefeater London Dry Gin
  (1/2 - 1 liter)
Float lime wheels (3-4 limes)
Taste test after 3-4 days

INFUSION, BEEFEATER DELI

Large covered jar
Steep in jar
Fill 1/3 full with sun-dried tomatoes
Fill 1/3 full with large olives
Add 6 oz. sliced garlic
Add 6 oz. whole dill
Add 4 large red onions, peeled and sliced
Fill with Beefeater London Dry Gin
  (1/2 - 1 liter)
Taste test after 3-4 days

INFUSION, BRAZILIAN DAIQUIRI

Large covered jar
Steep in jar
Fill with pineapples, peeled and sliced
Add 3 vanilla beans
Add 1 cup brown sugar
Fill 1/3 full with Bacardi Light Rum
  (1/2 - 1 liter)
Fill 1/3 full with Bacardi Gold Rum
  (1/2 - 1 liter)
Fill with Bacardi Select Rum (1/2 - 1 liter)
Taste test after 4-5 days

INFUSION, CHERRY BOMB

Large covered jar
Steep in jar
Fill with maraschino cherries
  (1/2 - 1 gallon)
Add 3 vanilla beans
Fill with Light Rum (1 - 3 liters)
Taste test after 3-4 days

INFUSION, COSMIC COCONUT

Large covered jar
Steep in jar
Fill with pineapples, peeled and sliced
Add 8 oz. grated coconut
Fill with Vodka (1/2 - 3 liters)
Float sliced navel oranges (3-6 oranges)
Taste test after 3-4 days

INFUSION, ICE
BLUE MARGARITA

Large covered jar
Steep in jar
Fill 1/3 full with lemons, sliced
Fill 1/6 full with limes, sliced
Fill 1/6 full with oranges, sliced
Fill with Tequila (1 liter)
Fill with Midori Melon Liqueur (1 liter)
Add 10 oz. Blue Curaçao
Taste test after 2-3 days
Note: Mix equal parts of infusion with
  sweet 'n' sour, shake and serve

INFUSION, LEMONEATER

Large covered jar
Steep in jar
Fill 1/3 full with lemons, sliced
Fill 1/3 full with limes, sliced
Fill 1/3 full with oranges, sliced
Add 6 oz. simple syrup
Add 16 oz. Hiram Walker Triple Sec
Fill with Gin (2-3 liters)
Taste test after 3-4 days

DEKUYPER®
PUCKER® SOUR APPLE

If you're still capable of cranking out a smile, then you still have enough life in you to enjoy PUCKER DEKUYPER SOUR APPLE. Everything about this product screams of fun, from the lighthearted packaging to its spry, low-proof character. DeKuyper has concocted a hit.

Pucker Sour Apple is one of a line of similarly constructed sweet 'n' sour schnapps that are balanced with surgical precision to be just this side of tart. In fact they are delightfully tart, anymore so and the effect would be dashed. The tartness works, especially when it is used as a principal flavoring agent in cocktails.

The liqueur has a light, delicate body and a cheerful apple green hue, two qualities ideal for drink making. Sipped neat, the liqueur will bring about a pucker, but when mixed, the tangy tartness acts as a counterbalance. The sour apple flavor seems true enough and persists for a remarkably long time.

DeKuyper Pucker Sour Apple burst into the spotlight when it debuted in the Appletini, and has never looked back. You can now find it in uptown cocktails and downtown shooters all over the planet.

What this Pucker hasn't found yet is its creative limitations.

INFUSION, LEMONTREE MARGARITA
Large covered jar
Steep in jar
Fill 1/4 full with lemons, sliced
Fill 1/4 full with limes, sliced
Fill 1/4 full with oranges, sliced
Add 16 oz. Hiram Walker Triple Sec
Add 6 oz. simple syrup
Fill with Sauza Blanco Tequila (1-2 liters)
Taste test after 3-4 days
Note: Mix equal parts of infusion with
    sweet 'n' sour, shake and serve

INFUSION, LIME LIGHTS
Large covered jar
Steep in jar
Fill 1/2 full with kiwis, peeled and sliced
Fill 1/2 full with limes, sliced
Fill with Vodka (1-3 liters)
Taste test after 2-3 days

INFUSION, LIME-TEQUILA
Large covered jar
Steep in jar
Fill 1/3 full with limes, sliced
Fill 1/3 full with oranges, sliced
Add 6 oz. simple syrup
Fill with Sauza Blanco Tequila (1-2 liters)
Taste test after 2-3 days

INFUSION, LUMBERJACK
Large covered jar
Steep in jar
Fill with apples, cored and sliced
Add 4 vanilla beans
Add 12 cloves
Fill with Canadian Club Whisky (1-3 liters)
Taste test after 3-4 days

INFUSION, MARS MANGO
Large covered jar
Steep in jar
Fill 3/4 full with mangos, peeled and cubed
Fill 1/4 full with limes, sliced
Fill with Vodka (1-3 liters)
Taste test after 1-2 days
Note: See **Mango Bloody Mary** for
    serving suggestions

INFUSION, PEPPER-TEQUILA
aka **Sonoran Spittoon** Infusion
Large covered jar
Steep in jar
Fill 1/4 full with red bell peppers, sliced
Fill 1/4 full with green bell peppers, sliced
Fill 1/4 full with yellow bell peppers, sliced
Add 4-6 jalapeño peppers
Add 1 serrano chili
Fill with Gold Tequila (1-2 liters)
Taste test after 2-3 days

INFUSION, PINEAPPLE PURPLE PASSION

Large covered jar
Steep in jar
Fill with pineapples, peeled and sliced
Add 10 oz. Blue Curaçao
Add 10 oz. grenadine
Fill with Vodka (1-3 liters)
Taste test after 3-4 days

INFUSION, PLANETARY PINEAPPLE

Large covered jar
Steep in jar
Fill 3/4 full with pineapples,
  peeled and sliced
Add 2 pints raspberries, washed
Fill with Vodka (1-3 liters)
Taste test after 6-7 days

INFUSION, POOL WATER

Large covered jar
Steep in jar
Fill 3/4 full with pineapples,
  peeled and sliced
Fill 1/4 full with oranges, sliced
Add 10 oz. Peach Schnapps
Fill with Midori Melon Liqueur (1-2 liters)
Taste test after 3-4 days

INFUSION, ROXBURY PINEAPPLE

Large covered jar
Steep in jar
Fill with pineapples, peeled and sliced
Add 1 cup sugar
Fill with Vodka (1-3 liters)
Taste test after 2-3 days

INFUSION, SICILIAN MARTINI

Large covered jar
Steep in jar
16-24 garlic cloves, peeled, crushed and
  wrapped in cheese cloth
Add 10 oz. Dry Vermouth
Fill with Vodka (1-3 liters)
Taste test after 24 hours
Note: See **Sicilian Martini (1)** for
  serving suggestions

INFUSION, SKY BLUE

Large covered jar
Steep in jar
Fill with lemons, washed and sliced
Add 1 cup sugar
Fill 1/2 full with Blue Curaçao (1/2 -1 liter)
Taste test after 2-3 days

INFUSION, SONORAN SPITTOON

Large covered jar
Steep in jar
Fill 1/3 full with green bell peppers, sliced
Fill 1/3 full with red bell peppers, sliced
Fill 1/3 full with yellow bell peppers, sliced
Add 8 jalapeño peppers, washed and lanced
Add 4 serrano chilis, washed
Fill with Gold Tequila (1-3 liters)
Taste test after 3-4 days
Note: Remove serrano chilis after desired
  spiciness is achieved

INFUSION, SPICE SATELLITE

Large covered jar
Steep in jar
Fill with hard apples, cored and sliced
Add 5 cinnamon sticks
Add raisins (1/2 - 1 lb.)
Fill with Vodka (1-3 liters)
Taste test after 6-7 days

INFUSION, SUMMER SHADES MARGARITA

Large covered jar
Steep in jar
Fill 1/5 full with pineapples,
  peeled and sliced
Fill 1/5 full with cantaloupe,
  peeled and sliced
Fill 1/5 full with strawberries
Fill 1/5 full with peaches, pitted and sliced
Fill 1/2 full with Sauza Gold Tequila
  (1/2 - 1 liter)
Fill 1/2 full with Midori Melon Liqueur
  (1/2 - 1 liter)
Add 10 oz. Blue Curaçao
Taste test after 4-5 days
Note: Mix equal parts of infusion with
  sweet 'n' sour, shake and serve

INFUSION, VENUS VANILLA

Large covered jar
Steep in jar
Fill 1/2 full with peaches, pitted and sliced
Fill 1/2 full with nectarines, pitted and sliced
Add 2 vanilla beans
Fill with Vodka (1-3 liters)
Taste test after 4-5 days

INFUSION, VODKA CROCODILE

Large covered jar
Steep in jar
Fill 3/4 full with lemons, sliced
Add 1 liter Midori Melon Liqueur
Fill with Vodka (1-3 liters)
Taste test after 2-3 days

CANADIAN CLUB® WHISKY

In 1884, Hiram Walker first exported his 6-year-old Canadian blended whisky across the Detroit River into the United States. It quickly became the brand of choice by the gentlemen members of exclusive hotels, taverns and men's clubs, earning it the name CANADIAN CLUB WHISKY. For more than a century it has been the best-selling brand of Canadian whisky in the world.

Canadian Club is comprised of a blend of continuous-distilled whiskies. While its exact composition is a closely guarded secret, the blend is made up principally of corn whisky, and lesser proportions of rye, malted rye and malted barley whiskies. These whiskies are blended prior to aging, allowing the elements to thoroughly integrate during their stay in oak.

Canadian Club Whisky has a dry, rounded body and a creamy, pronounced bouquet laced with the aromas of grain, toffee and toasted oak. The whisky lilts over the palate without a trace of bitterness, leaving behind the lip-smacking flavors of caramel, butter, orange zest and notes of cereal. The whisky finishes long and relaxed.

Canadian whisky enthusiasts will also greatly appreciate the 8-year-old, "double matured" CANADIAN CLUB SHERRY CASK WHISKY and the superpremium CANADIAN CLUB CLASSIC 12-YEAR-OLD WHISKY.

INOCULATION
Presentation shot glass, chilled
Layer ingredients
3/4 fill Dr. McGillicuddy's Mentholmint Schnapps
1/4 fill Brandy

INTERNATIONAL AFFAIR
Coffee mug, heated
Build in glass
1/2 oz. Grand Marnier Liqueur
1/2 oz. Baileys Irish Cream
1/2 oz. Laird's 12-Year Apple Brandy
Near fill with hot coffee
Whipped cream garnish
Dust powdered cocoa

INTERNATIONAL CAPPUCCINO
Cappuccino cup, heated
Build in glass
1/2 oz. Kahlúa Coffee Liqueur
1/2 oz. Disaronno Amaretto Liqueur
1/2 oz. Vandermint Liqueur
1/2 oz. Baileys Irish Cream
Near fill with hot espresso coffee
Top with frothed milk
Sprinkle shaved chocolate

INTERNATIONAL DREAM
Presentation shot glass, chilled
Build in glass
1/4 fill Kahlúa Coffee Liqueur
1/4 fill Godiva Chocolate Liqueur
1/4 fill Oro di Mazzetti Grappa Liqueur
1/4 fill Fireball Cinnamon Canadian Whisky

INTERNATIONAL STINGER
Rocks glass, ice
Build in glass
1 1/2 oz. Metaxa 5 Star Brandy
3/4 oz. Galliano Liqueur

INTERNATIONAL VELVET CAFÉ
Cappuccino cup, heated
Build in glass
3/4 oz. Gran Gala Orange Liqueur
3/4 oz. Kahlúa Coffee Liqueur
1/2 oz. Baileys Irish Cream
Near fill with hot espresso coffee
Top with frothed milk
Sprinkle shaved chocolate

IN THE RED
Bucket glass, ice
Build in glass
1 1/2 oz. Sauza Conmemorativo Añejo Tequila
1/2 oz. Rose's Lime Juice
Near fill with cranberry juice
Float 1/2 oz. grenadine

INVERTED NAIL
Sherry glass, chilled
Layer ingredients
1/2 fill Drambuie Liqueur
1/2 fill Glenfiddich Single Malt

I.R.A.
Presentation shot glass, chilled
Layer ingredients
1/4 fill Kahlúa Coffee Liqueur
1/4 fill DeKuyper Buttershots Schnapps
1/4 fill Baileys Irish Cream
1/4 fill Irish Whiskey

IRISH ALEXANDER (1)
Cocktail glass, chilled
Pour ingredients into iced mixing glass
1 oz. Irish Mist
3/4 oz. White Crème de Cacao
2 oz. half & half cream
Shake and strain
Sprinkle nutmeg

IRISH ALEXANDER (2)
Cocktail glass, chilled
Pour ingredients into iced mixing glass
1 1/2 oz. Jameson Irish Whiskey
3/4 oz. Dark Crème de Cacao
3/4 oz. DeKuyper Triple Sec
1 1/2 oz. half & half cream
Shake and strain
Sprinkle nutmeg

IRISH AMERICAN
Tankard or pilsner glass, chilled
Build in glass
1/2 fill Guinness Stout
1/2 fill Budweiser

IRISH BOGGLE
Coffee mug, heated
Build in glass
1 oz. Knappogue Castle Irish Whiskey
1 oz. Celtic Crossing Irish Liqueur
1/2 oz. Kahlúa Coffee Liqueur
Near fill with hot coffee
Top with whipped cream
Dust powdered cocoa

IRISH BROGUE
Rocks glass, ice
Build in glass
1 1/2 oz. Jameson Irish Whiskey
3/4 oz. Irish Mist

IRISH CAR BOMB
Shot glass and tankard or
    pilsner glass, chilled
Build in shot glass
1 oz. Baileys Irish Cream
1 oz. Jameson Irish Whiskey
Build in tankard or pilsner glass
3/4 fill Guinness Stout
Drop shot glass of Baileys and
    Jameson into Guinness

IRISH CHOCOLATE KISS
Cocktail glass, chilled
Pour ingredients into iced mixing glass
2 oz. Stolichnaya Russian Vodka
3/4 oz. Baileys Irish Cream
1/2 oz. Green Crème de Menthe
1/2 oz. White Crème de Cacao
Shake and strain
Orange slice garnish

IRISH-CHOCO-ORANGE
Cocktail glass, chilled
Pour ingredients into iced mixing glass
1 1/2 oz. Knappogue Castle Irish Whiskey
3/4 oz. Godiva Chocolate Liqueur
3/4 oz. Gran Gala Orange Liqueur
3/4 oz. Baileys Irish Cream
Shake and strain
Shaved chocolate garnish

IRISH COFFEE
Coffee mug, heated
Build in glass
1 1/4 oz. Irish Whiskey
1/2 oz. simple syrup
Near fill with hot coffee
Top with frothed milk or
    whipped cream garnish

IRISH COFFEE ROYALE (1)
Coffee mug, heated
Build in glass
1 1/4 oz. Irish Whiskey
1 oz. Kahlúa Coffee Liqueur
1/2 oz. simple syrup
Near fill with hot coffee
Top with frothed milk or
    whipped cream garnish

IRISH COFFEE ROYALE (2)
Coffee mug, heated
Build in glass
1 1/4 oz. Irish Whiskey
3/4 oz. Baileys Irish Cream
1/2 oz. Irish Mist
Near fill with hot coffee
Top with frothed milk or
    whipped cream garnish

VAN GOGH® GIN

If you're going to name an ultra-premium Dutch gin after someone, it might as well be the country's most celebrated son, Vincent Van Gogh. Fortunately, VAN GOGH GIN is indeed a masterpiece and all is right with the world.

Introduced in 1999, the brand originated at the renowned Dirkswager Distillery—makers of Leyden and Vincent Vodkas—in the historic district of Schiedam, Holland. Van Gogh Gin is created from 10 herbs and botanicals, which are steeped in neutral grain spirits and individually distilled in earthenware pots. These infusions are then blended together and double-distilled in small batches in column stills.

The crucial third distillation occurs in a copper, coal-fired alembic still designed specifically for producing gin. It allows for the various flavors and spirits to become fully integrated.

Award-winning Van Gogh Gin has a full, seamlessly textured body and a fresh bouquet of citrus, berries and pine. The gin glides over the palate filling the mouth with a wave of herbal and fruit flavors that persist long into the lingering finish.

Van Gogh is a sensational gin, and it might be at its best served in a chilled cocktail glass. But don't stop there, it is an ideal headliner in a martini or other such attraction.

IRISH DISH
Cocktail glass, chilled
Pour ingredients into iced mixing glass
2 oz. Glenfarclas Single Highland Malt
　　Scotch Whisky
3/4 oz. Drambuie Liqueur
Stir and strain
Lemon twist garnish

IRISH FLOAT
Beer mug, chilled
Pour ingredients into blender
1 oz. Baileys Irish Cream
1 oz. Root Beer Schnapps
2 scoops vanilla ice cream
Blend ingredients (with ice optional)
Fill with root beer

IRISH HEADLOCK
Rocks glass, chilled
Pour ingredients into iced mixing glass
1/2 oz. Baileys Irish Cream
1/2 oz. Irish Whiskey
1/2 oz. Disaronno Amaretto Liqueur
1/2 oz. Brandy
Shake and strain

IRISH MARIA
Rocks glass, ice
Build in glass
1 oz. Tia Maria
1 oz. Baileys Irish Cream

IRISH RASPBERRY
House specialty glass, chilled
Pour ingredients into blender
1 1/4 oz. Jameson Irish Whiskey
3/4 oz. Chambord Liqueur
3/4 oz. Baileys Irish Cream
1/2 oz. half & half cream
1 scoop vanilla ice cream
Blend ingredients (with ice optional)
Whipped cream and berries garnish
Drizzle 3/4 oz. Kahlúa Coffee Liqueur

IRISH SHILLELAGH
Cocktail glass, chilled
Pour ingredients into iced mixing glass
1 1/2 oz. Irish Whiskey
1/2 oz. Sloe Gin
1/2 oz. Light Rum
1 oz. sweet 'n' sour
Shake and strain
Lemon wedge garnish

IRISH STINGER
Rocks glass, ice
Build in glass
3/4 oz. Irish Whiskey
3/4 oz. Irish Mist
1/2 oz. Peppermint Schnapps

IRISH TEA
Coffee mug, heated
Build in glass
1 oz. Irish Mist
1/2 oz. Irish Whiskey
Fill with hot tea
Lemon wedge garnish

IRISH WISH
Cocktail glass, chilled
Pour ingredients into iced mixing glass
1 3/4 oz. Jameson Irish Whiskey
1/2 oz. Vya California Sweet Vermouth
1/2 oz. Giori Lemoncillo Liqueur
Stir and strain
Lemon twist garnish

ISLA de PIÑOS
House specialty glass, ice
Pour ingredients into iced mixing glass
1 1/2 oz. Matusalem Light Dry Rum
1 1/2 oz. grapefruit juice
1/2 oz. simple syrup
1/2 oz. grenadine
Shake and strain
Grapefruit slice garnish

ISLAND DITTY
Cocktail glass, chilled
Pour ingredients into iced mixing glass
2 oz. Matusalem Gran Reserva Rum
1/2 oz. Rose's Lime Juice
1/2 oz. fresh lime juice
Shake and strain
Lime wedge garnish

ISLAND DREAM
Cocktail glass, chilled
Pour ingredients into iced mixing glass
2 oz. Cruzan Estate Single Barrel Rum
1 oz. Giori Lemoncillo Cream Liqueur
Shake and strain

ISLAND FEVER
Cocktail glass, chilled
Pour ingredients into iced mixing glass
1 1/2 oz. Cruzan Estate Single Barrel Rum
1/2 oz. fresh lime juice
1 1/2 oz. sweet 'n' sour
Shake and strain
Lime wedge garnish

ISLAND FLOWER
Cocktail glass, chilled
Pour ingredients into iced mixing glass
2 1/2 oz. Cruzan Estate Single Barrel Rum
1/2 oz. Blue Curaçao
2 dashes Rose's Lime Juice
1/2 oz. fresh lime juice
Stir and strain
Lime wheel garnish

ISLAND SUNSET
House specialty glass, ice
Pour ingredients into iced mixing glass
1 oz. Absolut Vodka
1 oz. Malibu Rum
1/2 oz. Blue Curaçao
1 oz. pineapple juice
1 oz. orange juice
Shake and strain
Near fill with Seven-Up
Float 3/4 oz. Razzmatazz Raspberry Liqueur
Lime wedge and orange slice garnish

ISLEÑA
House specialty glass, ice
Build in glass
1 1/2 oz. Bacardi Light Rum
1 1/2 oz. pineapple juice
Near fill with Perrier Sparkling Water
Float 1/2 oz. grenadine
Raspberries garnish

ISLE OF PINES
Highball glass, ice
Build in glass
1 1/2 oz. Light Rum
Fill with grapefruit juice

ITALIAN COFFEE
Coffee mug, heated
Build in glass
3/4 oz. Sambuca
3/4 oz. Disaronno Amaretto Liqueur
Near fill with hot coffee
Whipped cream garnish

ITALIAN PUNCH
Bucket glass, ice
Build in glass
1 oz. Disaronno Amaretto Liqueur
1 oz. Bacardi Limón Rum
Fill with cranberry juice

ITALIAN STALLION
Rocks glass, ice
Build in glass
1 1/2 oz. Scotch Whisky
3/4 oz. Galliano Liqueur

ITALIAN STINGER
Rocks glass, ice
Build in glass
1 1/2 oz. Brandy
3/4 oz. Galliano Liqueur

MANDARINE NAPOLÉON® LIQUEUR

When Chinese tangerines were first introduced in Europe at the end of the 18th century, the fruit quickly became the favorite of Napoleon Bonaparte and the imperial court. The Emperor even went so far as to eat tangerine peels soaked in cognac. This eventually sparked the creation of MANDARINE NAPOLÉON LIQUEUR.

Produced in Brussels since 1892, Mandarine Napoléon Liqueur is made from fresh tangerines—*mandarine* in French—grown exclusively in Sicily. The peels are macerated in fine spirits for several weeks. The infused alcohol is then redistilled three times with a secret mix of botanicals before being aged in oak barrels for a minimum of 3 years. To make the final liqueur, these spirits are sweetened and blended with well-aged cognac.

Mandarine Napoléon is a sensational liqueur. It has a lustrous amber/orange color and a generous bouquet of citrus and floral aromas. The liqueur has a full, rich body and a refined palate featuring the flavors of tangerine, vanilla and brandy. The finish is warm and lingering.

The Fourcroy Distillery also makes the limited edition MANDARINE IMPÉRIALE X.O., which is aged in French oak casks for 8 to 10 years. Its smooth, luxurious palate makes a marvelous companion for the evening.

ITALIAN SUNRISE (1)
House specialty glass, ice
Build in glass
1 1/4 oz. Disaronno Amaretto Liqueur
1 oz. Bacardi Gold Rum
Near fill with orange juice

ITALIAN SUNRISE (2)
Bucket glass, ice
Build in glass
1 1/4 oz. Disaronno Amaretto Liqueur
Near fill with orange juice
Float 3/4 oz. Briottet Crème de Cassis

ITALIAN SURFER
Rocks glass, chilled
Pour ingredients into iced mixing glass
3/4 oz. Malibu Rum
3/4 oz. Disaronno Amaretto Liqueur
1 oz. pineapple juice
1 oz. cranberry juice
Shake and strain

ITALIAN VALIUM
Rocks glass, ice
Build in glass
1 1/2 oz. Gin
3/4 oz. Disaronno Amaretto Liqueur

ITHMUS BUFFALO MILK
House specialty glass, chilled
Pour ingredients into blender
1 1/2 oz. Bacardi Select Rum
1 1/2 oz. Cruzan Estate Light Rum
3/4 oz. Kahlúa Coffee Liqueur
3/4 oz. Cruzan Banana Rum
1 peeled, ripe banana
1 1/2 oz. milk
3/4 oz. chocolate syrup
Blend with ice
Whipped cream garnish
Sprinkle nutmeg

JACKALOPE
House specialty glass, ice
Pour ingredients into iced mixing glass
1 3/4 oz. Mount Gay Eclipse Rum
3/4 oz. Kahlúa Coffee Liqueur
3/4 oz. Disaronno Amaretto Liqueur
3/4 oz. Dark Crème de Cacao
3 oz. pineapple juice
Shake and strain
Float 3/4 oz. Appleton Estate
   V/X Jamaica Rum
Orange slice garnish

JACKARITA
Cocktail glass, chilled
Pour ingredients into iced mixing glass
1 1/4 oz. Jack Daniel's Tennessee Whiskey
3/4 oz. Gran Gala Orange Liqueur
1 3/4 oz. sweet 'n' sour
Lime wedge garnish
Shake and strain

JACK BENNY
Rocks glass, ice
Build in glass
1 1/2 oz. Jack Daniel's Tennessee Whiskey
1/2 oz. Baileys Irish Cream
1/2 oz. Kahlúa Coffee Liqueur

JACKIE SPECIAL
House specialty glass, ice
Pour ingredients into iced mixing glass
1/2 oz. Absolut Vodka
1/2 oz. Malibu Rum
1/2 oz. Southern Comfort Liqueur
1/2 oz. Disaronno Amaretto Liqueur
1 1/2 oz. pineapple juice
1 1/2 oz. orange juice
Shake and strain
Float 3/4 oz. Razzmatazz Raspberry Liqueur
Orange slice and cherry garnish

JACK ROSE COCKTAIL
Cocktail glass, chilled
Pour ingredients into iced mixing glass
1 oz. Laird's Applejack Brandy
1 1/2 oz. sweet 'n' sour
1/2 oz. grenadine
Shake and strain

JACK TAIL
Bucket glass, ice
Pour ingredients into iced mixing glass
1 1/2 oz. Jack Daniel's Tennessee Whiskey
1/2 oz. grenadine
1 1/2 oz. pineapple juice
2 oz. sweet 'n' sour
Shake and strain
Orange slice garnish

JACQUELINE
Cocktail glass, chilled
Pour ingredients into iced mixing glass
2 oz. Bacardi 8 Reserva Rum
3/4 oz. Grand Marnier 100th Anniversary
1/2 oz. Rose's Lime Juice
1 oz. fresh lime juice
Stir and strain
Lime wedge garnish

JADE
Cocktail glass, chilled
Pour ingredients into iced mixing glass
1 1/2 oz. Bacardi Light Rum
1/2 oz. DJ Dotson Triple Sec
1/2 oz. Green Crème de Menthe
1/2 oz. Rose's Lime Juice
Stir and strain
Lime wedge garnish

JÄGERITA
Rocks glass, chilled
Pour ingredients into iced mixing glass
1/2 oz. Jägermeister Liqueur
1/2 oz. Jose Cuervo Especial Tequila
1/2 oz. Cointreau Liqueur
3/4 oz. fresh lime juice
Shake and strain
Lime wedge garnish

JÄGER MONSTER
Bucket glass, ice
Build in glass
1 1/4 oz. Jägermeister Liqueur
1/2 oz. Disaronno Amaretto Liqueur
Near fill with orange juice
Float 3/4 oz. Razzmatazz Raspberry Liqueur

JÄGER MY WORM
Presentation shot glass, chilled
Build in glass
1/2 fill Jägermeister Liqueur
1/2 fill Tequila

JAMAICA JUICE
House specialty glass, chilled
Pour ingredients into blender
1 1/2 oz. Appleton Special Jamaica Rum
1 oz. pineapple juice
1 oz. orange juice
1 oz. cranberry juice
2 oz. coconut cream syrup
Blend with ice
Float 3/4 oz. Appleton Estate
    V/X Jamaica Rum
Pineapple wedge and cherry garnish

JAMAICA ME CRAZY (1)
Bucket glass, ice
Build in glass
1 1/2 oz. Appleton Estate V/X Jamaica Rum
3/4 oz. Tia Maria
Fill with pineapple juice
Orange slice garnish

CHAMPAGNE DRINKS

Champagne has a nearly universal appeal. No other product enjoys its reputation for outstanding quality. It is also the one wine that may be appropriately served any time of day, at any meal and with about any type of food.

Champagne drinks are light, effervescent and delicious. Eye appeal alone qualifies them as bona fide works of art. It's their luscious flavor, though, that makes them masterpieces.

With the advent of the reusable bottle-stopper that keeps champagne carbonated overnight, you can pour champagne by the glass without being concerned that the unused portion will go flat and be wasted.

Not surprisingly, many of the famous champagne drink recipes have their origins in France. The French 75 is a classic example. Created during World War I by American army officers, it is made with gin, sweet 'n' sour and champagne. Substitute bourbon to make a French 95. The cognac-based version is a French 125.

Champagne is an incomparable mixer. It marries with about every type of fruit juice or puree imaginable. Best known is the 1920's creation, the mimosa, the combination of orange juice and champagne. Since its inception, others have followed, including the belini (peach puree), poinsettia (cranberry juice), Puccini (tangerine juice), moon walk (grapefruit juice), pizzetti (orange and grapefruit juice), Jersey Jack (apple juice), bikini (passion fruit syrup), ruddy mimosa (orange and cranberry juice), and champagne Hawaiian (pineapple juice).

The classic Ritz fizz was created at the Ritz-Carlton Hotel in Boston, and is made with Disaronno Amaretto, Blue Curaçao, sweet 'n' sour, and champagne. For a light change of pace, consider sampling the Caribbean champagne, which is made with light rum, crème de banana, and a fill of champagne.

JAMAICA ME CRAZY (2)
House specialty glass, chilled
Pour ingredients into blender
1 1/2 oz. Appleton Estate V/X Jamaica Rum
3/4 oz. Blue Curaçao
2 oz. coconut cream syrup
2 oz. pineapple juice
2 oz. orange juice
Blend with ice
Pineapple wedge and cherry garnish

JAMAICAN BARBADOS BOMBER
Rocks glass, chilled
1 3/4 oz. Appleton Estate V/X Jamaica Rum
1 3/4 oz. Mount Gay Eclipse Rum
3/4 oz. DeKuyper Triple Sec
1/2 oz. Rose's Lime Juice
Stir and strain
Lime wedge garnish

JAMAICAN COFFEE
Coffee mug, heated
Build in glass
1 1/4 oz. Appleton Estate V/X Jamaica Rum
3/4 oz. Tia Maria
Near fill with hot coffee
Whipped cream garnish
Sprinkle shaved chocolate

JAMAICAN CRAWLER
Bucket glass, ice
Pour ingredients into iced mixing glass
1 1/2 oz. Appleton Estate V/X Jamaica Rum
1 1/2 oz. Midori Melon Liqueur
1/2 oz. grenadine
3 oz. pineapple juice
Shake and strain

JAMAICAN DUST
Presentation shot glass, chilled
Build in glass
1/3 fill Myers's Jamaican Rum
1/3 fill Tia Maria
1/3 fill pineapple juice

JAMAICAN FEVER
House specialty glass, ice
Pour ingredients into iced mixing glass
1 1/2 oz. Appleton Special Jamaica Rum
3/4 oz. Brandy
3/4 oz. mango syrup
1 1/2 oz. guava nectar
1 1/2 oz. pineapple juice
Shake and strain
Float 3/4 oz. Appleton Estate
    V/X Jamaica Rum
Pineapple wedge and cherry garnish

JAMAICAN HOLIDAY
Presentation shot glass, chilled
Build in glass
1/3 fill Myers's Jamaican Rum
1/3 fill Tia Maria
1/3 fill Crème de Banana

JAMAICAN PLANTER'S PUNCH
House specialty glass, chilled
Pour ingredients into blender
1 1/2 oz. Appleton Special Jamaica Rum
1 oz. simple syrup
2 oz. fresh lime juice
2 oz. pineapple juice
3 large, peeled and cored
pineapple slices
Blend with ice
Float 3/4 oz. Appleton Estate
   V/X Jamaica Rum
Pineapple wedge and cherry garnish

JAMAICAN ROSE
Cocktail glass, chilled
Pour ingredients into iced mixing glass
1 1/2 oz. Tequila Rose Cream Liqueur
3/4 oz. Appleton Special Jamaica Rum
3/4 oz. Godiva Chocolate Liqueur
1 1/2 oz. half & half cream
Shake and strain
Sprinkle shaved chocolate

JAMAICAN RUM COW
House specialty glass, chilled
Pour ingredients into blender
1 1/2 oz. Appleton Special Jamaica Rum
3/4 oz. Kahlúa Coffee Liqueur
1/2 oz. chocolate syrup
2 dashes Angostura Bitters
2 oz. milk
2 scoops chocolate ice cream
Blend ingredients (with ice optional)
Float 3/4 oz. Appleton Estate
   V/X Jamaica Rum
Pineapple wedge and cherry garnish

JAMAICAN SHAKE
House specialty glass, chilled
Pour ingredients into blender
1 1/4 oz. Appleton Estate V/X Jamaica Rum
3/4 oz. Tia Maria
3/4 oz. Disaronno Amaretto Liqueur
1 tsp. vanilla extract
2 scoops vanilla ice cream
Blend ingredients (with ice optional)
Whipped cream garnish
Sprinkle shaved chocolate

JAMAICAN SPICE
Bucket glass, ice
Build in glass
1 oz. Appleton Estate V/X Jamaica Rum
1 oz. Captain Morgan Spiced Rum
1/2 oz. Hot Damn Cinnamon Schnapps
Near fill with ginger ale
Float 3/4 oz. Crème de Banana

JAMAICAN TENNIS BEADS
Bucket glass, ice
Pour ingredients into iced mixing glass
1 oz. Appleton Estate V/X Jamaica Rum
3/4 oz. Bacardi Light Rum
3/4 oz. Midori Melon Liqueur
3/4 oz. Crème de Banana
1/2 oz. half & half cream
1 oz. pineapple juice
Shake and strain
Float 3/4 oz. Gosling's Black Seal Rum

JAMAICAN TEN SPEED
Rocks glass, chilled
Pour ingredients into iced mixing glass
1 1/4 oz. Cruzan Banana Rum
3/4 oz. Midori Melon Liqueur
3/4 oz. pineapple juice
3/4 oz. cranberry juice
Shake and strain

JAMBA JUICE
Bucket glass, ice
Pour ingredients into iced mixing glass
3/4 oz. Bacardi Spiced Rum
3/4 oz. Mount Gay Eclipse Rum
1 oz. cranberry juice
1 oz. orange juice
1 oz. pineapple juice
Shake and strain
Float 3/4 oz. Appleton Estate
   V/X Jamaica Rum
Orange slice and cherry garnish

JAMESON CANNES-STYLE
Cocktail glass, chilled
Pour ingredients into iced mixing glass
1 3/4 oz. Jameson Irish Whiskey
1 oz. Crème de Banana
3/4 oz. orange juice
3/4 oz. half & half cream
Shake and strain
Speared banana slice and cherry garnish

JANE'S MILK
Presentation shot glass, chilled
Build in glass
1 oz. Cruzan Banana Rum
1 oz. Baileys Irish Cream

DRAMBUIE® LIQUEUR

If you could pick your family, a good choice would be the Mackinnons of the Isle of Skye. They are the family that makes the world renowned DRAMBUIE LIQUEUR.

Legend has it that its recipe was brought to Scotland in 1745 by Prince Charles Stuart—better known as Bonnie Prince Charlie. After his army's defeat at the Battle of Culloden Moor, Bonnie Prince Charlie took refuge in Strathaird on the Isle of Skye at the home of Captain John Mackinnon. In gratitude the Prince gave his protector the recipe for present day Drambuie.

The Mackinnons introduced the liqueur to the world in 1906. Scottish Gaelic for "the drink that satisfies," Drambuie is made in Scotland to this day, from a base of well aged, single malt and grain whiskies. The blend is then infused with herbs, spices and heather honey, and is bottled at 80 proof.

Ultra-premium Drambuie has a striking amber hue and medium-weight, satiny textured body. The liqueur has an intriguing bouquet laced with the prominent aromas of anise, dried herbs and the slightly smoky scent of whisky. The palate is an elegant offering of spice, honey and a satisfying taste of whisky. The finish is especially long and flavorful.

Drambuie is a classic liqueur with unlimited creative possibilities.

JAPANESE COCKTAIL
Cocktail glass, chilled
Pour ingredients into iced mixing glass
1 1/2 oz. Brandy
1/2 oz. orgeat syrup
2 dashes Angostura Bitters
Stir and strain
Lemon twist garnish

JARDINERA
House specialty glass, chilled
Pour ingredients into blender
2 oz. Sauza Tres Generaciones Plata Tequila
3/4 oz. Whaler's Hawaiian Vanille Rum
2 oz. coconut cream syrup
2 oz. limeade
1/2 cup pineapple cubes
Blend with ice
Coconut flakes and
   shaved chocolate garnish

JAR JUICE
Mason jar, ice
Build in glass
1 oz. Chambord Liqueur
1 oz. Pearl Vodka
1/2 fill orange juice
1/2 fill pineapple juice

JAUNDICE JUICE
Highball glass, ice
Build in glass
1 1/4 oz. Jim Beam White Label Bourbon
Fill with lemonade

JEALOUSY
House specialty glass, ice
Pour ingredients into iced mixing glass
1 oz. Midori Melon Liqueur
1 oz. Blue Curaçao
3/4 oz. Wild Turkey 101° Bourbon
3/4 oz. Bacardi Light Rum
3/4 oz. Tanqueray Gin
3/4 oz. Rose's Lime Juice
1 oz. pineapple juice
1 oz. sweet 'n' sour
Shake and strain
Fill with ginger ale
Lemon wedge garnish

JELLY BEAN
Presentation shot glass, chilled
Layer ingredients
1/2 fill Anisette
1/2 fill Blackberry Brandy

JELLY FISH

Presentation shot glass, chilled
Layer ingredients
1/3 fill White Crème de Cacao
1/3 fill Disaronno Amaretto Liqueur
1/3 fill Baileys Irish Cream
3 drops grenadine in center

JENNY WALLBANGER

Bucket glass, ice
Build in glass
1 oz. Vodka
1/2 fill orange juice
Near fill with half & half cream
Float 3/4 oz. Galliano Liqueur

JERSEY DEVIL

Cocktail glass, chilled
Pour ingredients into iced mixing glass
1 1/2 oz. Laird's Applejack Brandy
1 oz. Cointreau Liqueur
1/2 oz. simple syrup
1/2 oz. cranberry juice
1/2 oz. Rose's Lime Juice
Stir and strain

JERSEY LILLY

Wine glass, chilled
Pour ingredients into iced mixing glass
5 oz. carbonated apple juice
2 dashes non-alcoholic bitters
1/4 tsp. sugar
Stir and strain
Orange slice and cherry garnish

JERSEY ROOT BEER

aka **Italian Root Beer**
Highball glass, ice
Build in glass
1 1/4 oz. Galliano Liqueur
Fill with cola

JET FUEL (1)

Bucket glass, ice
Build in glass
1/2 oz. Bacardi 151° Rum
1/2 oz. Malibu Rum
1/2 oz. Gosling's Black Seal Rum
1/2 oz. Royal Oak Extra Old Rum
Near fill with pineapple juice
Float 1/2 oz. grenadine
Orange slice garnish

JET FUEL (2)

Presentation shot glass, chilled
Build in glass
1/4 fill Jägermeister Liqueur
1/4 fill Wild Turkey 101° Bourbon
1/4 fill DeKuyper Peppermint Schnapps
1/4 fill 151 proof Rum

JEWEL

Bucket glass, ice
Pour ingredients into iced mixing glass
2 oz. Jameson Irish Whiskey
3/4 oz. DeKuyper Peachtree Schnapps
1/2 oz. Blue Curaçao
2 oz. pineapple juice
Shake and strain
Orange slice garnish

JEWEL OF RUSSIA

Champagne glass, chilled
Pour ingredients into iced mixing glass
1 3/4 oz. Jewel of Russia
   Wild Bilberry Infusion
1/2 oz. Chambord Liqueur
3/4 oz. orange juice
1 oz. sweet 'n' sour
Stir and strain
Fill with Champagne
Strawberry garnish

JEWELS AND GOLD

Cocktail glass, chilled
Pour ingredients into iced mixing glass
1 3/4 oz. Jewel of Russia Classic Vodka
3/4 oz. Oro di Mazzetti Grappa Liqueur
Stir and strain
Lemon twist garnish

JOE CANOE

aka **Jonkanov**
Bucket glass, ice
Build in glass
1 oz. Light Rum
Near fill with orange juice
Float 3/4 oz. Galliano Liqueur

JOGGER

Bucket glass, ice
Build in glass
1/2 oz. Rose's Lime Juice
Fill with club soda
1 packet of artificial sweetener (optional)
Lime wedge garnish

JOHN WAYNE

Cocktail glass, chilled
Pour ingredients into iced mixing glass
2 oz. Maker's Mark Bourbon
1/2 oz. Disaronno Amaretto Liqueur
2-3 dashes Angostura Bitters
1/4 oz. orange juice
Shake and strain
Orange slice garnish

MATUSALEM®
GRAN RESERVA RUM

Ron Matusalem originated in Santiago, Cuba in 1872. By the turn of the century, the distillery was producing a range of rums, including a light, dry rum and an overproof. The distillery was one of a few in the Caribbean to mature their rum using the famed Solera aging system. With the fall of Cuba in 1960, the Alvarez family relocated Ron Matusalem to Florida, where the firm remains to this day.

Introduced in 1997, RON MATUSALEM GRAN RESERVA is a luxurious rum, comprised of rums produced by several West Indies distillers. It is built around a core "blender rum," which is Solera aged about 15 years and is comprised of rums between 8 and 32 years old.

Several younger rums, ranging in age between 3 to 4 years, are added to the core blend to capitalize on their exuberance. The result is a sublime marriage of the two generations.

Matusalem Gran Reserva has a satiny texture and generous bouquet of vanilla, caramel, plums and molasses. The rum has a layered palate of toasty, bakery shelf flavors. The finish is long and satisfying.

Sipping the Matusalem Gran Reserva neat is a marvelous experience for aficionados and novices alike. It also excels when featured in cocktails.

JOKE JUICE
Cocktail glass, chilled
Pour ingredients into iced mixing glass
1 1/4 oz. Southern Comfort Liqueur
1/2 oz. DeKuyper Triple Sec
1/2 oz. Rose's Lime Juice
1/2 oz. sweet 'n' sour
Shake and strain

JOLLY RANCHER (1)
Rocks glass, chilled
Pour ingredients into iced mixing glass
1/2 oz. Dewar's White Label Scotch Whisky
1/2 oz. DeKuyper Peach Pucker
1/2 oz. Midori Melon Liqueur
3/4 oz. Absolut Vodka
Shake and strain
Splash Seven-Up

JOLLY RANCHER (2)
Rocks glass, chilled
Pour ingredients into iced mixing glass
3/4 oz. Midori Melon Liqueur
1/2 oz. Disaronno Amaretto Liqueur
1/2 oz. Absolut Citron Vodka
1/2 oz. sweet 'n' sour
1/2 oz. pineapple juice
Shake and strain

JOLLY RANCHER (3)
Rocks glass, chilled
Pour ingredients into iced mixing glass
1/2 oz. DeKuyper Pucker Sour Apple
1/2 oz. Midori Melon Liqueur
3/4 oz. sweet 'n' sour
1/4 oz. pineapple juice
Shake and strain

JU JU BEE
Rocks glass, chilled
Pour ingredients into iced mixing glass
3/4 oz. Midori Melon Liqueur
3/4 oz. Zone Melon Italian Vodka
1/2 oz. Malibu Rum
Splash cranberry juice
Splash Seven-Up
Shake and strain

JULIA
House specialty glass, chilled
Pour ingredients into blender
1 oz. Bacardi Light Rum
1 oz. Disaronno Amaretto Liqueur
1 oz. Angostura Caribbean Rum Cream
1/2 cup strawberries
1 oz. sweet 'n' sour
2 scoops vanilla ice cream
Blend ingredients (with ice optional)
Float 3/4 oz. Gosling's Black Seal Rum
Strawberry garnish

JULIO'S BUTTERSCOTCH
House specialty glass, chilled
Pour ingredients into blender
1/2 oz. Kahlúa Coffee Liqueur
1/2 oz. Baileys Irish Cream
1/2 oz. DeKuyper Buttershots Schnapps
2 scoops vanilla ice cream
Blend ingredients (with ice optional)

JUMBY BAY PUNCH
Cocktail glass, chilled
Pour ingredients into iced mixing glass
1 1/2 oz. Amber Rum
1 oz. fresh lime juice
1 oz. simple syrup
3 dashes Angostura Bitters
Stir and strain
Sprinkle nutmeg
Orange slice and cherry garnish

JUMPER CABLES
Coffee mug or glass, heated
Build in glass
3/4 oz. Cruzan Coconut Rum
1/2 oz. Baileys Irish Cream
1/2 oz. Disaronno Amaretto Liqueur
Near fill with hot coffee
Top with frothed milk
Dust powdered cocoa

JUMP ME
Bucket glass, ice
Build in glass
1 1/2 oz. Bacardi Select Rum
1 oz. Mount Gay Eclipse Rum
2-3 dashes Angostura Bitters
1 oz. fresh lime juice
Near fill with pineapple juice
Float 3/4 oz. Gosling's Black Seal Rum

JUNGLE CREAM
Brandy snifter, ice
Build in glass
1 1/2 oz. Cruzan Estate Single Barrel Rum
3/4 oz. Tia Maria
3/4 oz. Cruzan Rum Cream

JUNGLE JUICE
Bucket glass, ice
Build in glass
1 oz. Damrak Amsterdam Gin
1 oz. Blavod Black Vodka
1/2 fill orange juice
1/2 fill grapefruit juice

JUNGLE MILK
Coffee mug, heated
Build in glass
3/4 oz. Baileys Irish Cream
3/4 oz. Crème de Banana
Near fill with hot chocolate
Whipped cream garnish
Sprinkle shaved chocolate

KAHLÚA CLUB
Highball glass, ice
Build in glass
1 1/4 oz. Kahlúa Coffee Liqueur
Fill with club soda

KAHLÚA MINT
Cocktail glass, chilled
Pour ingredients into iced mixing glass
1 oz. Kahlúa Coffee Liqueur
1/2 oz. White Crème de Menthe
1 1/2 oz. half & half cream
Shake and strain

KAMIKAZE
Cocktail glass, chilled
Pour ingredients into iced mixing glass
1 1/2 oz. Vodka
1/2 oz. Triple Sec
1/2 oz. Rose's Lime Juice
Stir and strain
Lime wedge garnish

KAMIKAZE, APPLE
Cocktail glass, chilled
Pour ingredients into iced mixing glass
1 oz. Brilliant Vodka
1 oz. DeKuyper Pucker Sour Apple
1/2 oz. DeKuyper Triple Sec
1/2 oz. Rose's Lime Juice
Stir and strain
Lime wedge garnish

KAMIKAZE, BLOODY
Cocktail glass, chilled
Pour ingredients into iced mixing glass
1 1/4 oz. Luksusowa Polish Vodka
1/2 oz. Southern Comfort Liqueur
1/2 oz. Rose's Lime Juice
Stir and strain
Splash Hot Damn Cinnamon Schnapps
Lime wedge garnish

KAMIKAZE, BLUE
aka **Devine Wind**
Cocktail glass, chilled
Pour ingredients into iced mixing glass
1 1/2 oz. Original Polish Vodka
1/2 oz. Blue Curaçao
1/2 oz. Rose's Lime Juice
Stir and strain
Lime wedge garnish

JÄGERMEISTER® LIQUEUR

The mere mention of JÄGERMEISTER LIQUEUR is enough to raise a knowing smile to the face of any seasoned imbiber. The popular elixir has become a classic rite of passage and can be found behind nearly every bar on the planet.

The Mast family founded the Mast-Jägermeister Company in 1878 in Wolfenbüttel, Germany. Jägermeister in German means "master of the hunt." The herbal liqueur was first bottled and widely marketed in 1935, just prior to the beginning of World War II.

Jägermeister is comprised of a sophisticated blend of 56 roots, herbs and spices from around the world. It contains gentian roots, valerian, ginseng and chamomile blossoms. The list of botanicals also includes citrus peels, anise, licorice, poppy seeds, saffron, ginger, rhubarb roots and juniper berries.

The various botanicals are individually macerated in neutral spirits for up to 6 weeks. They are then filtered and matured in charred oak barrels for a minimum of one year prior to blending. The liqueur is bottled at 70 proof.

Jägermeister has a reddish brown hue and a wafting bouquet loaded with spice and peppery aromas. The liqueur immediately fills the mouth with a montage of flavors ranging from bittersweet to spicy hot. The finish is long and spectacular.

Jägermeister is a singular sensation not to be missed. It's at its best served chilled.

KAMIKAZE, CASCADE MOUNTAIN
Cocktail glass, chilled
Pour ingredients into iced mixing glass
1 3/4 oz. Cascade Mountain Gin
1/2 oz. Cointreau Liqueur
1/4 oz. Rose's Lime Juice
3/4 oz. sweet 'n' sour
Shake and strain
Lime wedge garnish

KAMIKAZE, CITRON
aka **Citron Kami**
Cocktail glass, chilled
Pour ingredients into iced mixing glass
1 1/2 oz. Absolut Citron Vodka
1/2 oz. DJ Dotson Triple Sec
1/2 oz. Rose's Lime Juice
Stir and strain
Lime wheel garnish

KAMIKAZE, CRANBERRY
Cocktail glass, chilled
Pour ingredients into iced mixing glass
1 1/2 oz. Vodka
1/2 oz. Hiram Walker Triple Sec
1/2 oz. Rose's Lime Juice
1/2 oz. cranberry juice
Stir and strain
Lime wedge garnish

KAMIKAZE, FRENCH
Cocktail glass, chilled
Pour ingredients into iced mixing glass
1 1/2 oz. Grey Goose Vodka
1/2 oz. Grand Marnier 100th Anniversary
3/4 oz. fresh lime juice
Stir and strain
Lime wedge garnish

KAMIKAZE, FUZZY
Cocktail glass, chilled
Pour ingredients into iced mixing glass
1 1/4 oz. Ketel One Dutch Vodka
3/4 oz. DeKuyper Peach Pucker
3/4 oz. Rose's Lime Juice
Stir and strain
Lime wedge garnish

KAMIKAZE, ITALIAN
Cocktail glass, chilled
Pour ingredients into iced mixing glass
1 1/4 oz. Vodka
3/4 oz. Villa Massa Limoncello
3/4 oz. Gran Gala Orange Liqueur
1/2 oz. Rose's Lime Juice
Stir and strain
Lime wedge garnish

KAMIKAZE, KOKONUT (1)
Cocktail glass, chilled
Pour ingredients into iced mixing glass
2 oz. Cruzan Coconut Rum
1 oz. pineapple juice
1/2 oz. sweet 'n' sour
Stir and strain
Lime wedge garnish

KAMIKAZE, KOKONUT (2)
Cocktail glass, chilled
Pour ingredients into iced mixing glass
2 oz. Malibu Rum
1 oz. pineapple juice
1/2 oz. sweet 'n' sour
Stir and strain
Lime wedge garnish

KAMIKAZE, MELON
aka **Melon Kami**
Cocktail glass, chilled
Pour ingredients into iced mixing glass
1 oz. Belvedere Polish Vodka
1 oz. Midori Melon Liqueur
1/2 oz. Rose's Lime Juice
Stir and strain
Lime wedge garnish

KAMIKAZE, PURPLE (1)
aka **Purple Kami**
Cocktail glass, chilled
Pour ingredients into iced mixing glass
1 1/2 oz. Vodka
1/2 oz. Chambord Liqueur
1/2 oz. Grand Marnier 100th Anniversary
1/2 oz. Rose's Lime Juice
Stir and strain
Lime wedge garnish

KAMIKAZE, PURPLE (2)
aka **Purple Kami**
Cocktail glass, chilled
Pour ingredients into iced mixing glass
3/4 oz. Vodka
3/4 oz. Chambord Liqueur
3/4 oz. cranberry juice
1/2 oz. Rose's Lime Juice
Stir and strain
Lime wheel garnish

KAMIKAZE, RADIOACTIVE
Cocktail glass, chilled
Pour ingredients into iced mixing glass
1/2 oz. Bacardi Light Rum
1/2 oz. Cruzan Coconut Rum
1/2 oz. Bacardi 151° Rum
1/2 oz. Blue Curaçao
1 oz. Rose's Lime Juice
1/2 oz. grenadine
Stir and strain
Lime wedge garnish

KAMIKAZE, RASPBERRY
Cocktail glass, chilled
Pour ingredients into iced mixing glass
1 1/2 oz. Original Polish Vodka
1/2 oz. Chambord Liqueur
1/2 oz. Cointreau Liqueur
1/2 oz. fresh lime juice
Stir and strain
Lime wedge garnish

KAMIKAZE, SOUTHERN COMFORT
Cocktail glass, chilled
Pour ingredients into iced mixing glass
1 1/2 oz. Southern Comfort Liqueur
1/2 oz. DJ Dotson Triple Sec
1/2 oz. Rose's Lime Juice
Stir and strain
Lime wedge garnish

KAPALUA BUTTERFLY
House specialty glass, chilled
Pour ingredients into blender
1 1/4 oz. Mount Gay Eclipse Rum
1 1/4 oz. Bacardi Gold Rum
1/2 oz. grenadine
1 1/2 oz. sweet 'n' sour
1 1/2 oz. pineapple juice
1 1/2 oz. coconut cream syrup
2 oz. orange juice
Blend with ice
Pineapple wedge and orange slice garnish

KATINKA
Cocktail glass, chilled
Pour ingredients into iced mixing glass
1 1/2 oz. Jewel of Russia Classic Vodka
1/2 oz. Apricot Brandy
1/2 oz. Rose's Lime Juice
Stir and strain
Mint sprig garnish (optional)

KÉKÉ KICKER
Bucket glass, ice
Build in glass
1 1/4 oz. KéKé Beach Cream Liqueur
1/2 oz. Jose Cuervo Especial Tequila
1/2 oz. Kahlúa Coffee Liqueur
Fill with orange juice

KÉ LARGO
Presentation shot glass, chilled
Build in glass
1/2 fill KéKé Beach Cream Liqueur
1/2 fill Midori Melon Liqueur

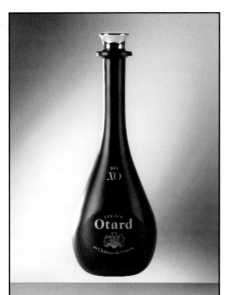

OTARD® XO COGNAC

The renowned cognac house of Otard is best described as the smallest of the large producers and largest of the boutique brands. Nobleman Baron Otard de la Grange founded the company in 1795 on the south bank of the River Charente in the town of Cognac. The firm does not own a vineyard or operate a distillery. Instead, it purchases young brandies from small, independent distillers, ages and blends them into highly acclaimed and sought after cognacs. Among its world-class line-up is the inimitable OTARD XO FINE CHAMPAGNE COGNAC.

This extraordinary brandy is an assemblage of brandies distilled in the Grande Champagne, Petite Champagne and Borderies regions of Cognac. The brandies are aged in both Limousin and Traçais French oak barrels and assembled by the firm's master blender. The Otard XO is an impressively mature and sophisticated brandy, containing cognacs in excess of 35 years old.

This luxurious and skillfully crafted cognac is a celebration for the senses. It has a radiant copper hue with brilliant orange highlights and a lightweight, velvety textured body. The captivating bouquet is laced with aromas of butter, plums and mushrooms. The brandy bathes the palate with waves of caramel, fruit, spice and chocolate flavors. The finish lingers like a savored memory.

KENTUCKY SHUFFLE
Cocktail glass, chilled
Pour ingredients into iced mixing glass
2 oz. Knob Creek Small Batch Bourbon
3/4 oz. Grand Marnier 100th Anniversary
1/2 oz. fresh lime juice
Stir and strain

KENTUCKY SWAMP WATER
Bucket glass, ice
Build in glass
1 1/2 oz. Jim Beam Black Label Bourbon
1/2 oz. Blue Curaçao
1/2 oz. fresh lime juice
Fill with orange juice
Lime wedge garnish

KEOKI COFFEE
Coffee mug, heated
Build in glass
1/2 oz. Brandy
1/2 oz. Kahlúa Coffee Liqueur
1/2 oz. Dark Crème de Cacao
Near fill with hot coffee
Whipped cream garnish
Dust powdered cocoa

KEOKI SHOOTER
Presentation shot glass, chilled
Build in glass
1/4 fill Kahlúa Coffee Liqueur
1/4 fill Dark Crème de Cacao
1/4 fill Brandy
Near fill with hot coffee
Whipped cream garnish
Dust powdered cocoa

KEY ISLA MORADA
House specialty glass, chilled
Pour ingredients into blender
1 oz. Conch Republic Light Rum
3/4 oz. Cruzan Coconut Rum
3/4 oz. Cruzan Pineapple Rum
Peeled, ripe banana
1 tsp. vanilla extract
3/4 oz. half & half cream
2 oz. sweet 'n' sour
Blend with ice
Float 3/4 oz. Conch Republic Dark Rum
Lime wedge and orange slice garnish

KEY LARGO
House specialty glass, ice
Pour ingredients into iced mixing glass
1 1/2 oz. Conch Republic Light Rum
3/4 oz. Cruzan Coconut Rum
3/4 oz. Disaronno Amaretto Liqueur
Shake and strain
Near fill with club soda
Float 3/4 oz. Conch Republic Dark Rum
Lime wedge and orange slice garnish

KEY LIME COOLER
Cocktail glass, chilled
Pour ingredients into iced mixing glass
1 oz. Licor 43 (Cuarenta y Tres)
1/2 oz. fresh lime juice
1 oz. half & half cream
Shake and strain
Lime wheel garnish

KEY LIME PIE (1)
Rocks glass, chilled
Pour ingredients into iced mixing glass
1 1/4 oz. Licor 43 (Cuarenta y Tres)
3/4 oz. fresh lime juice
1 1/4 oz. half & half cream
Shake and strain

KEY LIME PIE (2)
House specialty glass, ice
Pour ingredients into iced mixing glass
1 1/2 oz. Dr. McGillicuddy's Vanilla Liqueur
1/2 oz. fresh lime juice
3/4 oz. half & half cream
Shake and strain
Fill with Seven-Up

KEY WEST
House specialty glass, ice
Pour ingredients into iced mixing glass
1 1/2 oz. Conch Republic Light Rum
1 1/2 oz. Conch Republic
Durdy White Rum
1/2 oz. Crème de Banana
1/2 oz. DeKuyper Raspberry Pucker
2 oz. sweet 'n' sour
2 oz. orange juice
Shake and strain
Near fill with Seven-Up
Float 3/4 oz. Conch Republic Dark Rum
Orange slice and cherry garnish

KIDDY COCKTAIL
Cocktail glass, chilled
Pour ingredients into iced mixing glass
1 oz. grenadine
2 oz. sweet 'n' sour
Shake and strain
Cherry garnish

KILLER KOOLAID
Cocktail glass, chilled
Pour ingredients into iced mixing glass
1 oz. Southern Comfort Liqueur
1 oz. Midori Melon Liqueur
3/4 oz. Crème de Noyaux
1 oz. cranberry juice
Shake and strain

KILLER WHALE
House specialty glass, ice
Pour ingredients into iced mixing glass
1 1/4 oz. Bacardi Gold Rum
1 1/4 oz. Mount Gay Eclipse Rum
1/2 oz. DeKuyper Raspberry Pucker
1/2 fill cranberry juice
1/2 fill orange juice
Shake and strain
Near fill with Seven-Up
Float 3/4 oz. Grand Marnier Liqueur
Orange slice garnish

KING ALFONSE
aka **King Alphonso**
Cordial or sherry glass, chilled
Layer ingredients
3/4 fill Dark Crème de Cacao
1/4 fill half & half cream

KING MIDAS
Bucket glass, ice
Build in glass
1 1/4 oz. Canadian Club Whisky
3/4 oz. Oro di Mazzetti Grappa Liqueur
Fill with Seven-Up
Lime wedge garnish

KING'S CUP
Cocktail glass, chilled
Pour ingredients into iced mixing glass
1 oz. Galliano Liqueur
1/2 oz. Disaronno Amaretto Liqueur
1 1/2 oz. half & half cream
Shake and strain

KIR
Wine glass, chilled
Build in glass
Near fill with White Wine
Float 3/4 oz. Briottet Crème de Cassis
Lemon twist garnish

KIR ROYALE
Champagne glass, chilled
Build in glass
Near fill with Champagne
Float 3/4 oz. Briottet Crème de Cassis
Lemon twist garnish

JACK DANIEL'S® SINGLE BARREL TENNESSEE WHISKEY

Considered one of the *grand cru* American whiskies, Jack Daniel's Tennessee Whiskey has been produced in Lynchburg, Tennessee since 1866. Jack Daniel founded the distillery when he was just 16 years old, already having owned a whiskey still for the previous 3 years. Now Jack Daniel's Tennessee Whiskey can be found behind nearly every bar in the world.

JACK DANIEL'S SINGLE BARREL TENNESSEE WHISKEY is handcrafted straight from the cask, exactly as Jack Daniel intended it. This is the real thing. Master distiller Jimmy Bedford carefully selects barrels of whiskey that have attained maturity, and display the aroma and full flavor that has become the brand's trademark. The whiskey is hand-bottled one barrel at a time, with each label marked with the rick and barrel number, as well as the date of bottling. Jack Daniel's Single Barrel is bottled at 94 proof.

Since no two barrels of whiskey are identical, each bottle of Jack Daniel's Single Barrel is a slice of whiskey immortality. It's the whiskey once reserved for the master distiller and Jack Daniel himself. It has a disarming bouquet, rich with the aromas of oak, sweet corn and roasted pepper. It has a supple, wonderfully round palate, and a memorable, long lasting finish.

KISS OF THE ISLANDS
House specialty glass, ice
Pour ingredients into iced mixing glass
1 1/2 oz. Gosling's Black Seal Rum
1 1/2 oz. Mount Gay Eclipse Rum
1 oz. Crème de Banana
3/4 oz. Blue Curaçao
1 oz. coconut cream syrup
1 1/2 oz. pineapple juice
1 1/2 oz. orange juice
Shake and strain
Float 3/4 oz. Appleton Estate
    V/X Jamaica Rum
Orange slice and cherry garnish

KIWI
Highball glass, ice
Build in glass
3/4 oz. Razzmatazz Raspberry Liqueur
3/4 oz. Cruzan Banana Rum
Fill with orange juice

KLONDIKE
aka **Star Cocktail**
Cocktail glass, chilled
Pour ingredients into iced mixing glass
1 1/2 oz. Laird's Applejack Brandy
1/2 oz. Dry Vermouth
3 dashes Angostura Bitters
1/4 oz. simple syrup (optional)
Stir and strain
Lemon twist garnish

KNICKERBOCKER
Bucket glass, ice
Pour ingredients into iced mixing glass
1 1/2 oz. Bacardi Limón Rum
1 oz. Mount Gay Eclipse Rum
1/2 oz. grenadine
3/4 oz. pineapple juice
1 oz. orange juice
1 oz. sweet 'n' sour
Shake and strain
Float 3/4 oz. Gosling's Black Seal Rum
Orange slice and cherry garnish

KNICKERBOCKER KNOCKER
House specialty glass, ice
Pour ingredients into iced mixing glass
3/4 oz. Midori Melon Liqueur
3/4 oz. DeKuyper Peachtree Schnapps
3/4 oz. sweet 'n' sour
1 1/2 oz. orange juice
1 1/2 oz. cranberry juice
Shake and strain
Float 3/4 oz. Crème de Banana
Orange slice and cherry garnish

KNICKERBOCKER
KNEE KNOCKER
House specialty glass, chilled
Pour ingredients into blender
1 1/2 oz. Chopin Polish Vodka
3/4 oz. Briottet Crème de Cassis
1/2 oz. fresh lime juice
1 scoop raspberry sherbet
1 scoop pineapple sherbet
Blend ingredients (with ice optional)
Berries garnish

KNICKERBOCKER
SPECIAL COCKTAIL
Cocktail glass, chilled
Pour ingredients into iced mixing glass
1 1/2 oz. Bacardi Limón Rum
1/2 oz. Cointreau Liqueur
1/2 oz. Chambord Liqueur
3/4 oz. orange juice
1 oz. sweet 'n' sour
Shake and strain
Orange slice garnish

KNICKER KNOCKER
Bucket glass, ice
Pour ingredients into iced mixing glass
3/4 oz. Southern Comfort Liqueur
3/4 oz. Captain Morgan Spiced Rum
3/4 oz. Vodka
1 oz. orange juice
1 oz. sweet 'n' sour
2 oz. cranberry juice
Shake and strain
Orange slice and cherry garnish

KNOB CREEK
Rocks glass, ice
Build in glass
2 oz. Knob Creek Small Batch Bourbon
3/4 oz. branch (spring) water

KNOCKOUT
Cocktail glass, chilled
Pour ingredients into iced mixing glass
3/4 oz. Gin
3/4 oz. Pernod
3/4 oz. Dry Vermouth
1/4 oz. White Crème de Menthe
Stir and strain
Lemon twist garnish

KOALA BEAR (1)
House specialty glass, chilled
Pour ingredients into blender
1 oz. Crème de Banana
1 oz. Dark Crème de Cacao
2 scoops vanilla ice cream
Blend ingredients (with ice optional)
Whipped cream garnish
Sprinkle nutmeg

KOALA BEAR (2)
Pilsner glass, chilled 16 oz.
Build in glass
1/2 fill Foster's Lager
1/2 fill Guinness Stout

KOALA FLOAT
House specialty glass, chilled
Pour ingredients into blender
1 oz. Kahlúa Coffee Liqueur
1 oz. Baileys Irish Cream
2 oz. coconut cream syrup
3 oz. pineapple juice
Blend with ice
Pineapple wedge and cherry garnish

KOOL AID (1)
Bucket glass, ice
Build in glass
3/4 oz. Jewel of Russia Berry Infusion
3/4 oz. Midori Melon Liqueur
3/4 oz. Disaronno Amaretto Liqueur
2 oz. cranberry juice

KOOL AID (2)
Bucket glass, ice
Build in glass
3/4 oz. Midori Melon Liqueur
3/4 oz. Disaronno Amaretto Liqueur
3/4 oz. Southern Comfort Liqueur
3/4 oz. Vodka
1/4 oz. grenadine
2 oz. cranberry juice

KOOLO
Rocks glass (ice optional)
Build in glass
1 1/4 oz. Baileys Irish Cream
1 oz. DeKuyper Buttershots Schnapps
Splash Crown Royal

KRAKOW WITCH
Rocks glass, ice
Build in glass
1 3/4 oz. Zubrówka Bison Brand Vodka
1/2 oz. Liquore Strega
Lemon twist garnish

GIORI® LEMONCILLO LIQUEUR

Leave it to the Italians, one of the oldest societies on Earth, to devise something so luscious as lemon liqueur, or *lemoncillo*. Light and refreshing, lemoncillo has conquered the Continent and can be found in virtually every café, bistro and *ristorante* throughout Europe. Now one of the leading brands, GIORI LEMONCILLO LIQUEUR, has arrived on our shores, and from around the country there can be heard the cry, "It's about time!"

Giori Lemoncillo is made in Trentino, Italy, from handpicked Sorrento lemons. On the day of harvest, the tree-ripened fruit is washed and peeled. The lemon peels are then immediately immersed in spirits distilled from molasses. This cold infusion process takes place in stainless steel containers. Then the peels are removed and the infused-alcohol is filtered, sweetened and bottled at 60 proof.

Giori Lemoncillo Liqueur is a marvelous taste sensation. It has the appearance of freshly squeezed lemonade and a lively, medium-weight body. The liqueur has an abundant bouquet brimming with robust citrus aromas. Its lemon-infused palate is a balanced affair, semi-sweet and naturally tangy. The finish is crisp, flavorful and of medium duration.

This succulent liqueur is extremely versatile behind the bar and can be featured in cocktails, frappés and numerous specialty drinks.

KURANT AFFAIR
Rocks glass, chilled
Pour ingredients into iced mixing glass
1 1/4 oz. Absolut Kurant Vodka
1 1/4 oz. orange juice
1 1/4 oz. cranberry juice
Shake and strain

KUWAITI COOLER
Bucket glass, ice
Pour ingredients into iced mixing glass
1 oz. Midori Melon Liqueur
1 oz. DeKuyper Pucker Sour Apple
2 oz. sweet 'n' sour
Shake and strain
Fill with club soda

LA BAMBA
House specialty glass, ice
Pour ingredients into iced mixing glass
1 1/4 oz. Sauza Conmemorativo
    Añejo Tequila
3/4 oz. Cointreau Liqueur
1 1/2 oz. pineapple juice
1 1/2 oz. orange juice
Shake and strain
Float 3/4 oz. Razzmatazz Raspberry Liqueur

LADY MADONNA
Brandy snifter, ice
Build in glass
1 1/2 oz. Dubonnet Rouge
1 1/2 oz. Dry Vermouth
Lemon twist

LA FRESCA
Bucket glass, ice
Rim glass with salt (optional)
Build in glass
2 oz. Sauza Hornitos Tequila
Fill with Squirt
Lime wedge garnish

LAGER AND BLACK
Beer glass, chilled
Build in glass
1 1/2 oz. black currant juice
Fill with draft lager

LAGER AND LIME
Beer glass, chilled
Build in glass
3/4 oz. Rose's Lime Juice
Fill with draft lager

LAKE STREET LEMONADE
Bucket glass, ice
Build in glass
1 1/2 oz. Luksusowa Polish Vodka
1/2 oz. Disaronno Amaretto Liqueur
Fill with lemonade
Lemon wedge garnish

LA MOSCA
aka **Sambuca con Mosca**
Sherry glass, chilled
Build in glass
2 1/2 oz. Sambuca
Coffee beans (3) garnish

LANDSLIDE
Presentation shot glass, chilled
Layer ingredients
1/3 fill Crème de Banana
1/3 fill Baileys Irish Cream
1/3 fill Grand Marnier Liqueur

L.A.P.D.
Presentation shot glass, chilled
Build in glass
Rim glass with salt (optional)
1 oz. Sauza Hornitos Tequila
1/2 oz. Blue Curaçao
1/4 oz. Razzmatazz Raspberry Liqueur

LARCHMONT (1)
Cocktail glass, chilled
Pour ingredients into iced mixing glass
1 1/2 oz. Bacardi 8 Reserva Rum
3/4 oz. Grand Marnier Liqueur
1/2 oz. Rose's Lime Juice
Stir and strain
Orange twist garnish

LARCHMONT (2)
Cocktail glass, chilled
Pour ingredients into iced mixing glass
1 1/2 oz. Pyrat Cask 23 Rum
3/4 oz. Grand Marnier Liqueur
1/2 oz. Rose's Lime Juice
Stir and strain
Orange twist garnish

LARCHMONT (3)
Cocktail glass, chilled
Pour ingredients into iced mixing glass
1 1/2 oz. Cruzan Estate Single Barrel Rum
3/4 oz. Grand Marnier Liqueur
1/2 oz. Rose's Lime Juice
Stir and strain
Orange twist garnish

LASTING PASSION
House specialty glass, chilled
Pour ingredients into blender
1 1/2 oz. Royal Oak Extra Old Rum
3/4 oz. Forres Park Overproof Rum
3/4 oz. Rose's Lime Juice
2 oz. coconut cream syrup
2 oz. pineapple juice
2 1/2 oz. passion fruit juice
Blend with ice
Float 3/4 oz. Rhum Barbancourt
    3-Star Rum
Pineapple wedge and orange slice garnish

LATE-NITE LEMON DROP
Cocktail glass, chilled
Rim glass with sugar (optional)
Pour ingredients into iced mixing glass
1 1/2 oz. Blavod Black Vodka
3/4 oz. Villa Massa Limoncello
3/4 oz. fresh lemon juice
Shake and strain
Lemon twist garnish

LATIN LOVE
House specialty glass, chilled
Rim glass with grenadine and shaved
    coconut
Pour ingredients into blender
1 oz. Cruzan Coconut Rum
1 oz. Cruzan Banana Rum
1 oz. raspberry juice
1 oz. coconut cream syrup
3 oz. pineapple juice
Blend with ice
Pineapple wedge and cherry garnish

LATIN LOVER (1)
House specialty glass, ice
Pour ingredients into iced mixing glass
1 1/2 oz. Pyrat Pistol Rum
1/2 oz. Crème de Banana
1/2 oz. grenadine
2 oz. orange juice
2 oz. pineapple juice
Shake and strain
Float 3/4 oz. Pyrat X.O. Reserve Rum
Lemon twist garnish

LATIN LOVER (2)
House specialty glass, chilled
Pour ingredients into blender
1 oz. Cruzan Estate Dark Rum
1 oz. Cruzan Banana Rum
3/4 oz. Chambord Liqueur
1 oz. raspberry syrup
1 1/2 oz. coconut cream syrup
3 oz. pineapple juice
Blend with ice
Pineapple wedge and cherry garnish

TESTING YOUR PRODUCT I.Q.

1. What is the difference between lagers and ales?
2. This renowned German liqueur is made from 56 herbs, roots, fruit and gentian.
3. The House of Burrough has produced this London Dry Gin since the early 1800's.
4. This premium whiskey is considered the first of the small batch bourbons.
5. Produced in limited quantity, this 100% agave añejo was issued to commemorate Herradura's 125th anniversary.
6. What gives red wine its color?
7. What is brandy?
8. Brewed with bottom-fermenting yeasts, it is the most widely produced type of beer in America.
9. What spirit can be distilled from potatoes, rice, beets, grapes or grain?
10. What is the alcohol-base of Drambuie?
11. What is the primary difference between Chivas Regal and Glenfiddich whiskies?
12. What is rum distilled from?
13. This Italian anise-flavored liqueur is made from wild elderbush berries.
14. What is tequila distilled from?
15. Is schnapps a liquor or liqueur?

Answers

1. Lagers are brewed with bottom-fermenting yeasts; ales are brewed using top-fermenting yeasts
2. Jägermeister
3. Beefeater London Dry Gin
4. Maker's Mark Bourbon
5. Herradura Selección Suprema Tequila
6. When making red wine, the grape skins are left in contact with the juice after the grapes have been pressed. Within the skins are pigments that give the grapes their color. These pigments, in turn, give color to the resulting wine.
7. Brandy is a spirit distilled from the fermented mash of grapes or fruit
8. Lager
9. Vodka
10. Drambuie is made from single Highland malt and straight grain whiskies
11. Chivas Regal is a blended Scotch whisky and Glenfiddich is a Highland single malt Scotch whisky
12. Rum is distilled from sugar cane, molasses or fermented sugar cane sap
13. Sambuca
14. Tequila is distilled from the Weber Blue Agave
15. Schnapps is a liqueur

LAUGHING BACARDI COW

House specialty glass, chilled
Pour ingredients into blender
1 1/2 oz. Bacardi Limón Rum
1/2 oz. Cointreau Liqueur
1/2 oz. fresh lime juice
1/2 oz. cranberry juice
2 scoops vanilla ice cream
Blend ingredients (with ice optional)
Orange twist garnish

LEAF

Cocktail or house specialty glass, chilled
Pour ingredients into iced mixing glass
1 oz. Midori Melon Liqueur
1/2 oz. Light Rum
1 1/2 oz. half & half cream
Shake and Strain

LEANING TOWER

House specialty glass, ice
Pour ingredients into iced mixing glass
1 oz. Captain Morgan Spiced Rum
1 oz. Crème de Banana
1 oz. coconut cream syrup
2 oz. orange juice
2 oz. pineapple juice
Shake and strain
Float 3/4 oz. Razzmatazz Raspberry Liqueur
Orange slice and cherry garnish

LEAVE US ALONE

Coffee mug, heated
Build in glass
3/4 oz. Courvoisier V.S.O.P. Cognac
3/4 oz. Extase XO Liqueur
1/2 oz. Godiva Chocolate Liqueur
Near fill with hot coffee
Whipped cream garnish

LE BISTRO

Cappuccino cup, heated
Build in glass
3/4 oz. B & B Liqueur
3/4 oz. Brandy
Near fill with hot espresso coffee
Top with frothed milk
Sprinkle shaved chocolate

LEFT BANK

Rocks glass, ice
Build in glass
1 1/4 oz. Baileys Irish Cream
1 1/4 oz. Chambord Liqueur

LEISURE SUIT
House specialty glass, ice
Pour ingredients into iced mixing glass
1 oz. Galliano Liqueur
1 oz. Crème de Banana
2 oz. pineapple juice
2 oz. orange juice
2 oz. cranberry juice
Shake and strain

LEMON DROP (1)
Cocktail glass, chilled
Rim glass with sugar (optional)
Pour ingredients into iced mixing glass
1 1/2 oz. Stolichnaya Russian Vodka
1/2 oz. Cointreau Liqueur
1/2 oz. fresh lemon juice
Shake and strain
Lemon twist garnish

LEMON DROP (2)
Bucket glass, ice
Pour ingredients into iced mixing glass
1 1/4 oz. Vincent Van Gogh Citroen Vodka
2 oz. sweet 'n' sour
Shake and strain
1/2 fill club soda
1/2 fill Seven-Up

LEMON DROP (3)
Cocktail glass, chilled
Pour ingredients into iced mixing glass
1 oz. Vodka
3/4 oz. Hiram Walker Triple Sec
1/4 oz. Rose's Lime Juice
1 oz. sweet 'n' sour
Shake and strain
Splash Seven-Up

LEMONGRAD
Highball glass, ice
Build in glass
1 1/4 oz. Stolichnaya Limonnaya
    Russian Vodka
Fill with cranberry juice

LEMON HEAVEN
Cocktail glass, chilled
Pour ingredients into iced mixing glass
1 3/4 oz. Giori Lemoncillo Cream Liqueur
1 oz. Giori Lemoncillo Liqueur
3/4 oz. Cruzan Orange Rum
1 oz. half & half cream
Shake and strain
Lemon wheel garnish

LEMON HEIGHTS
Rocks glass, ice
Build in glass
1 1/2 oz. Cristall Lemon Twist
    Russian Vodka
1/2 oz. Giori Lemoncillo Liqueur
1/2 oz. Giori Lemoncillo Cream Liqueur
Lemon twist garnish

LEMON LAVENDER
Cocktail glass, chilled
Pour ingredients into iced mixing glass
1 3/4 oz. Cristall Lemon Twist
    Russian Vodka
1/2 oz. Blue Curaçao
1/2 oz. Rose's Lime Juice
1/2 oz. cranberry juice
Stir and strain

LEMON NOG
Coffee mug or glass, heated
Build in glass
1 3/4 oz. Giori Lemoncillo Cream Liqueur
3/4 oz. Kahlúa Coffee Liqueur
3/4 oz. Disaronno Amaretto Liqueur
Near fill with hot coffee
Float 1 scoop vanilla ice cream
Drizzle chocolate syrup

LEMON PARFAIT
House specialty glass, chilled
Pour ingredients into blender
1 1/4 oz. Tequila
3/4 oz. Giori Lemoncillo Liqueur
1/2 oz. fresh lemon juice
1 1/2 oz. orange juice
1 1/2 oz. lemonade
Blend with ice

LEMON SPORTSMAN
Bucket glass, ice
Build in glass
1 oz. Stolichnaya Russian Vodka
Near fill with lemonade
Float 3/4 oz. Stolichnaya Limonnaya
    Russian Vodka

LEMON SQUEEZE
Bucket glass, ice
Build in glass
1 oz. Giori Lemoncillo Liqueur
1 oz. Bacardi Limón Rum
Fill with lemonade
Lemon wedge garnish

LEMON TART
Rocks glass, ice
Build in glass
2 oz. Belvedere Polish Vodka
1/2 oz. Villa Massa Limoncello
Lemon wedge garnish

BRILLIANT® VODKA

At first, the thought of an ultra-premium vodka hailing from the Highlands of Scotland might sound a wee bit peculiar. To the contrary, BRILLIANT VODKA is a skillfully crafted spirit made from high quality ingredients in a country that is home to many of the world's greatest whisky distilleries. In fact, the name Scotland on the label is an excellent indication of things to come.

This award-winning, wheat-based vodka is distilled five times in column stills, then quadruple-filtered, the final stage of which is conducted over a screen of cut diamonds. One of the major issues for any vodka is the quality and taste of the water used in production. Brilliant is made from the same renowned spring water that has made the Highlands the single malt Mecca of the world.

Brilliant is a gem of a vodka. It has crystal clarity and a clean, fresh bouquet laced with a hint of lemon. The lightweight body lilts over the palate without a trace of excess or harshness. Its soft, well-rounded palate presents an array of subtle floral and citrus flavors. The finish is cool, crisp and refreshing.

Brilliant Vodka is extremely smooth and begs to be presented straight-up in a chilled cocktail glass. Because its palate is close to being neutral, the vodka also makes an ideal base for a wide range of cocktails.

LEMON TOP
Beer glass, chilled
Build in glass
3/4 fill draft lager
1/4 fill Seven-Up

LEMON TREE TANTALIZER
House specialty glass, chilled
Pour ingredients into blender
1 1/2 oz. Stolichnaya Limonnaya
　　Russian Vodka
2 scoops lemon sorbet
Blend ingredients (with ice optional)
Lemon wedge garnish

LENA COCKTAIL
Cocktail glass, chilled
Pour ingredients into iced mixing glass
1/4 oz. Vya California Sweet Vermouth
1/4 oz. Vya California Dry Vermouth
1/4 oz. Campari Aperitivo
1 1/2 oz. Knob Creek Small Batch Bourbon
Stir and strain
Lemon twist and cherry garnish

LEPRECHAUN
Highball glass, ice
Build in glass
3/4 oz. DeKuyper Peachtree Schnapps
3/4 oz. Blue Curaçao
Fill with orange juice

LETHAL INJECTION
Bucket glass, ice
Pour ingredients into iced mixing glass
1 1/4 oz. Bacardi Light Rum
3/4 oz. Mount Gay Eclipse Rum
3/4 oz. Cruzan Coconut Rum
1/2 oz. Crème de Noyaux
1 1/2 oz. orange juice
1 1/2 oz. pineapple juice
Shake and strain
Float 3/4 oz. Gosling's Black Seal Rum
Pineapple wedge and cherry garnish

LET US ALONE
Cocktail glass, chilled
Pour ingredients into iced mixing glass
1 oz. Ballylarkin Irish Liqueur
3/4 oz. Brandy
1/2 oz. Mandarine Napoléon Liqueur
1 1/2 oz. sweet 'n' sour
Shake and strain
Orange twist garnish

LIAM'S PASSION
House specialty glass, chilled
Pour ingredients into blender
2 oz. Myers's Jamaican Rum
2 oz. coconut cream syrup
2 oz. pineapple juice
2 oz. passion fruit juice
Blend with ice

LICKETY-SPLIT
Bucket glass, ice
Build in glass
1 1/4 oz. Casa Noble Reposado Tequila
1/2 oz. Gran Gala Orange Liqueur
Fill with cranberry juice

LIFESAVER (1)
House specialty glass, ice
Pour ingredients into iced mixing glass
1 oz. Mount Gay Eclipse Rum
1 oz. Bacardi Select Rum
2 oz. orange juice
2 oz. sweet 'n' sour
Shake and strain
Float 3/4 oz. Grand Marnier Liqueur
Orange slice and cherry garnish

LIFESAVER (2)
Bucket glass, ice
Build in glass
1 1/2 oz. Malibu Rum
1 oz. DeKuyper Buttershots Schnapps
Near fill with pineapple juice
Float 3/4 oz. Razzmatazz Raspberry Liqueur
Orange slice and cherry garnish (optional)

LIGHTHOUSE
Rocks glass, ice
Build in glass
1/2 oz. Tequila
1/2 oz. Kahlúa Coffee Liqueur
1/2 oz. Peppermint Schnapps
1/2 oz. 151 proof Rum

LILLET CHAMPAGNE ROYALE
Champagne glass, chilled
Build in glass
2 oz. Lillet Blonde
1/2 oz. Briottet Crème de Cassis
Fill with Champagne
Lemon twist

LIMERICK
Bucket glass, ice
Pour ingredients into iced mixing glass
1 1/2 oz. Finlandia Vodka
3/4 oz. Celtic Crossing Irish Liqueur
3/4 oz. Midori Melon Liqueur
1/2 oz. Rose's Lime Juice
1 1/2 oz. sweet 'n' sour
Shake and strain
Lemon wedge garnish

LIMÓN FITZGERALD
Cocktail glass, chilled
Pour ingredients into iced mixing glass
1 1/2 oz. Bacardi Limón Rum
1/2 oz. Villa Massa Limoncello
4 dashes Angostura Bitters
1 oz. sweet 'n' sour
Stir and strain
Lemon wheel garnish

LIMÓN ORANGE BREEZE
House specialty glass, ice
Pour ingredients into iced mixing glass
1 1/2 oz. Bacardi Limón Rum
1/2 oz. Cointreau Liqueur
2 oz. orange juice
2 oz. cranberry juice
Shake and strain
Orange twist garnish

LIMÓN RUNNER
House specialty glass, ice
Pour ingredients into iced mixing glass
1 1/2 oz. Bacardi Limón Rum
1/2 oz. Crème de Banana
1/2 oz. grenadine
2 oz. orange juice
2 oz. pineapple juice
Shake and strain
Lemon twist garnish

LIQUID GOLD
Brandy snifter, ice
Build in glass
1 1/2 oz. Herradura Reposado Tequila
1 oz. Kahlúa Coffee Liqueur
3/4 oz. Gran Gala Orange Liqueur
3/4 oz. Baileys Irish Cream
Shaved chocolate garnish

SAUZA® TRES GENERACIONES® PLATA TEQUILA

The newest member of Sauza's ultra-premium line-up is SAUZA TRES GENERACIONES PLATA, a satiny smooth, 100% blue agave silver tequila. It is triple-distilled in an alembic still and bottled within 24 hours of distillation. Since the tequila isn't aged in oak, its inherent attributes are readily apparent and most extraordinary. The result is an extremely pure, refined spirit.

Tres Generaciones Plata is a marvelous example of just how skillful the craftsmen at Sauza's La Perseverancia are. The tequila has brilliant clarity and a sleek, lightweight body. It is exceptionally aromatic, far more pronounced than most silver tequilas. The bouquet offers up the captivating aromas of citrus and spice. The tequila lilts over the palate without a trace of heat or harshness, then slowly builds in intensity revealing layers of spicy, peppery flavor. The finish is relaxed, lingering and quite flavorful.

Sauza's ultra-premium silver deserves to be served neat in a snifter. Sipping Tres Generaciones Plata reinforces why so many are enamored with silver tequila. It is fresh and lively, yet every bit as sophisticated as a fine European eau-de-vie. On the other hand, don't miss out on the opportunity to use the Plata in an uptown margarita.

LIZARD BITCH
House specialty glass, ice
Pour ingredients into iced mixing glass
1 oz. Ketel One Dutch Vodka
1 oz. Midori Melon Liqueur
1/2 oz. Southern Comfort Liqueur
1 oz. sweet 'n' sour
1 oz. cranberry juice
1 oz. pineapple juice
Shake and strain
Lime wedge garnish

LOBOTOMY
Champagne glass, chilled
Pour ingredients into iced mixing glass
3/4 oz. Disaronno Amaretto Liqueur
3/4 oz. Chambord Liqueur
3/4 oz. pineapple juice
Shake and strain
Fill with Champagne

LOCH LOMOND (1)
Cocktail glass, chilled
Pour ingredients into iced mixing glass
1 1/2 oz. Scotch Whisky
2 dashes simple syrup
1 dash Angostura Bitters
Stir and strain
Lemon twist garnish

LOCH LOMOND (2)
House specialty glass, ice
Pour ingredients into iced mixing glass
1 1/4 oz. Dewar's White Label
   Scotch Whisky
1/2 oz. DeKuyper Peachtree Schnapps
1/2 oz. Blue Curaçao
1/2 oz. fresh lemon juice
2 1/2 oz. grapefruit juice
Shake and strain
Star fruit (carambola) garnish

LOCKHART ZOO
House specialty glass, ice
Pour ingredients into iced mixing glass
3/4 oz. Pearl Vodka
3/4 oz. Cascade Mountain Gin
3/4 oz. Farias Silver Tequila
3 oz. cranberry juice
Shake and strain
Fill with draft beer

LOCO EN LA CABEZA (1)

House Specialty glass, ice
Pour ingredients into iced mixing glass
1 1/2 oz. Sauza Conmemorativo
  Añejo Tequila
1/2 oz. Grand Marnier Liqueur
1/2 oz. Razzmatazz Raspberry Liqueur
1 1/2 oz. orange juice
1/2 oz. Rose's Lime Juice
Shake and strain
Lime wedge garnish

LOCO EN LA CABEZA (2)

House Specialty glass, ice
Pour ingredients into iced mixing glass
1 1/2 oz. Tequila
1/2 oz. Hiram Walker Triple Sec
1 1/2 oz. orange juice
1/2 oz. Rose's Lime Juice
1/2 oz. grenadine
Shake and strain
Lime wedge garnish

LONDON GOLD

Cocktail glass, chilled
Pour ingredients into iced mixing glass
2 oz. Bafferts Gin
1 oz. Oro di Mazzetti Grappa Liqueur
3/4 oz. Cointreau Liqueur
Shake and strain
Orange slice garnish

LONDON LEMONADE

Cocktail glass, chilled
Pour ingredients into iced mixing glass
1 3/4 oz. Bombay Sapphire London Dry Gin
1 oz. fresh lemon juice
1/2 oz. Rose's Lime Juice
1/2 oz. Cointreau Liqueur
Stir and strain
Lemon twist garnish

LONDON REDHEAD

Cocktail glass, chilled
Pour ingredients into iced mixing glass
3/4 oz. Bafferts Gin
3/4 oz. Dubonnet Rouge
3/4 oz. Dubonnet Blanc
2-3 dashes Angostura Bitters
1 1/2 oz. orange juice
Shake and strain

LONDON NIGHTCLUB

Highball glass, ice
Build in glass
1 1/4 oz. Old Raj Dry Gin
Near fill with club soda
Float 3/4 oz. Rose's Lime Juice
Lime wedge garnish

LOOKING FOR TROUBLE

House specialty glass, ice
Pour ingredients into iced mixing glass
1/2 oz. Bafferts Gin
1/2 oz. Van Hoo Belgium Vodka
1/2 oz. Cruzan Estate Diamond Rum
1/2 oz. El Jimador Añejo Tequila
1/2 oz. Forty Creek Canadian Whisky
1/2 oz. DeKuyper Triple Sec
1/2 oz. grenadine
1 oz. sweet 'n' sour
1 oz. pineapple juice
1 oz. cranberry juice
Shake and strain
Lemon wedge garnish

LOOKOUT POINT

Cocktail glass, chilled
Pour ingredients into iced mixing glass
1 1/2 oz. Sea Wynde Pot Still Rum
3/4 oz. Chambord Liqueur
3/4 oz. sweet 'n' sour
Shake and strain
Lime wedge garnish

LOST LOVERS

House specialty glass, chilled
Pour ingredients into blender
3/4 oz. Bacardi Light Rum
3/4 oz. Bacardi Spiced Rum
3/4 oz. Mount Gay Eclipse Rum
3/4 oz. Crème de Banana
1 oz. coconut cream syrup
2 oz. orange juice
2 oz. pineapple juice
Blend with ice
Float 3/4 oz. Chambord Liqueur
Orange slice and cherry garnish

LOUISIANA SHOOTER

Presentation shot glass, chilled
Build in glass
1 1/2 oz. Absolut Peppar Vodka
1/4 tsp. horseradish
3 dashes Tabasco Sauce
1 small raw oyster

LOUNGE LIZARD

House specialty glass, ice
Build in glass
1 oz. Bacardi Gold Rum
1 oz. Bacardi Spiced Rum
1/2 oz. Disaronno Amaretto Liqueur
Fill with cola
Lime wedge garnish

GRAN GALA®
TRIPLE ORANGE LIQUEUR

The Stock Distillery has been producing world class brandies in Italy for over a century. While renowned throughout Europe, the firm has greatly enhanced its presence in the U.S. market with the introduction of award-winning GRAN GALA TRIPLE ORANGE LIQUEUR.

This lively liqueur is made from a blend of premium triple oranges and mature, barrel-aged, Italian brandy. The craftsmen at Stock imbued the liqueur with a fetching bronze color and supple, medium-weight body. Its expansive bouquet is loaded with the aroma of fresh oranges and delicate notes of almonds and brandy. The lush, semi-sweet palate is an offering of zesty orange and lemon flavors, and sumptuous Italian brandy. The liqueur sports a warm, flavorful finish.

The natural inclination is to serve Gran Gala in a heated snifter or on-the-rocks. While certainly a popular way to enjoy it, the liqueur enjoys many uses behind the bar.

The most noteworthy application is as a modifier in a specialty margarita, where its brandy-base and exuberant orange flavor make it an ideal substitute for triple sec.

Some popular Gran Gala recipes include the Sea Breeze Margarita, Italian Martini and the Opulent Coffee.

LOUVRE ME ALONE
Cappuccino cup, heated
Build in glass
1/2 oz. Grand Marnier Liqueur
1/2 oz. V.S. Cognac
1/2 oz. Tia Maria
Near fill with hot espresso coffee
Top with frothed milk
Sprinkle shaved chocolate

LOVE CANAL
Bucket glass, ice
Build in glass
1 3/4 oz. Sauza Hornitos Tequila
3/4 oz. Disaronno Amaretto Liqueur
Near fill with lemonade
Splash Squirt
Lemon wedge garnish

LOVE POTION #9
House specialty glass, chilled
Pour ingredients into blender
1 oz. Bacardi Gold Rum
1 oz. Mount Gay Eclipse Rum
2 oz. strawberry puree
1 1/2 oz. coconut cream syrup
3 oz. pineapple juice
Blend with ice
Whipped cream garnish
Drizzle 1/2 oz. Bacardi Select Rum and
    1/2 oz. St. James Extra Old Rhum

LOVER'S LANE
Cocktail glass, chilled
Pour ingredients into iced mixing glass
1 3/4 oz. Matusalem Gran Reserva Rum
3/4 oz. Extase XO Liqueur
1/2 oz. fresh lime juice
1 1/2 oz. sweet 'n' sour
Shake and strain
Lime wedge garnish

LUAU
Bucket glass, ice
Build in glass
1 oz. Malibu Rum
1 oz. Midori Melon Liqueur
Fill with pineapple juice
Orange slice and cherry garnish

LUNCH BOX
Rocks glass, chilled
Build in glass
1 oz. Disaronno Amaretto Liqueur
1 oz. orange juice
3-4 oz. Draft Beer

LYNCHBURG LEMONADE
Bucket glass, ice
Pour ingredients into iced mixing glass
1 oz. Jack Daniel's Tennessee Whiskey
3/4 oz. Hiram Walker Triple Sec
1 1/2 oz. sweet 'n' sour
Shake and strain
Fill with Seven-Up

MACINTOSH PRESS
Highball glass, ice
Build in glass
1 1/4 oz. DeKuyper Pucker Sour Apple
1/2 fill ginger ale
1/2 fill club soda

MACKENZIE GOLD
Highball glass, ice
Build in glass
1 1/2 oz. Yukon Jack Liqueur
Fill with grapefruit juice

MADAME BUTTERFLY
Cocktail glass, chilled
Pour ingredients into iced mixing glass
2 oz. Brilliant Vodka
1/4 oz. NapaSaki Saké
1/4 oz. Otard XO Cognac
Stir and strain
Lemon twist garnish

MADAME MANDARINE
Cocktail glass, chilled
Pour ingredients into iced mixing glass
1 1/2 oz. Grey Goose Vodka
1/2 oz. Mandarine Napoléon Liqueur
1/2 oz. Oro di Mazzetti Grappa Liqueur
Shake and strain
Orange twist garnish

MADE IN THE SHADE
Cocktail glass, chilled
Pour ingredients into iced mixing glass
2 1/4 oz. Original Polish Vodka
3/4 oz. Extase XO Liqueur
Stir and strain
Orange twist garnish

MAD HATTER
Coffee mug, heated
Build in glass
3/4 oz. Doorly's XO Barbados Rum
3/4 oz. Foursquare Spiced Rum
Near fill with hot chocolate
Whipped cream garnish
Sprinkle shaved chocolate

MADONNA'S BRASSIERE
Presentation shot glass, chilled
Build in glass
1/4 fill Absolut Vodka
1/4 fill DeKuyper Raspberry Pucker
1/4 fill DeKuyper Watermelon Pucker
1/4 fill Baileys Irish Cream

MADRAS
Highball glass, ice
Build in glass
1 1/4 oz. Vodka
1/2 fill orange juice
1/2 fill cranberry juice

MADTOWN MILKSHAKE
House specialty glass, chilled
Pour ingredients into blender
1 oz. Baileys Irish Cream
1 oz. Chambord Liqueur
3/4 oz. Frangelico Liqueur
1/2 oz. half & half cream
2 scoops vanilla ice cream
Blend ingredients (with ice optional)
Whipped cream garnish
Sprinkle shaved chocolate

MAGIC POTION
House specialty glass, ice
Pour ingredients into iced mixing glass
1 3/4 oz. Bafferts Gin
3/4 oz. Alizé Red Passion
1/2 oz. DJ Dotson Triple Sec
1 oz. fresh lime juice
1 oz. sweet 'n' sour
Shake and strain
Top with club soda
Lime wedge garnish

MAHOGANY GOLD
Sherry glass, chilled
Layer in glass
1/2 fill Oro di Mazzetti Grappa Liqueur
1/2 fill Glenfarclas Single Highland Malt
    Scotch Whisky

MAIDEN'S PRAYER
Cocktail glass, chilled
Pour ingredients into iced mixing glass
1 1/2 oz. Van Gogh Gin
1/2 oz. Cointreau Liqueur
1 dash orange juice
1 dash Angostura Bitters
1 oz. sweet 'n' sour
Shake and strain

KNAPPOGUE CASTLE®
PURE POT STILL IRISH
WHISKEY~1951

This exquisite whiskey is the last
remaining link to a past generation.
KNAPPOGUE CASTLE PURE POT
STILL IRISH WHISKEY 1951 is the
oldest, most exclusive and highly sought
after Irish whiskey in the world. It is so
limited in supply that only 300 bottles
are released for sale each year.

The rare, pure pot still whiskey was
triple-distilled in 1951 at the famous B.
Daly Distillery in Tullamore, County
Offaly. After distillation, it was placed in
sherry casks to mature. The distillery
closed several years later.

In the mid-1960s, American Mark E.
Andrews purchased the remaining casks
of whiskey and wisely left the majority of
it untouched. Working closely with a
whiskey expert, they continued to
monitor the progress of the whiskey,
until 1987 when they determined that
after 36 years of aging it had reached
optimum maturity.

After more than three decades in
wood, the Knappogue (pronounced
nah-POG) Castle 1951 has acquired a
delectable bouquet of fruit and toasted
oak, a spicy, malt, and sherried palate,
and a prolonged, flavor-packed finish.
Retailing at $600 per bottle, the '51
should be doled out in mere drams and
only to those people that you genuinely
like. Grab it while you can.

MAI TAI (1)
House specialty glass, ice
Pour ingredients into iced mixing glass
1 3/4 oz. Light Rum
1/2 oz. Crème de Noyaux
1/2 oz. Triple Sec
2 oz. sweet 'n' sour
Shake and strain
Orange slice and cherry garnish

MAI TAI (2)
House specialty glass, ice
Pour ingredients into iced mixing glass
2 1/2 oz. Light Rum
1 oz. Gold Rum
1 oz. Triple Sec
3/4 oz. grenadine
3/4 oz. orgeat syrup
1 oz. fresh lime juice
1 3/4 oz. sweet 'n' sour
Shake and strain
Float 3/4 oz. Overproof Rum
Pineapple wedge and cherry garnish

MAI TAI (3)
House specialty glass, ice
Pour ingredients into iced mixing glass
1 oz. Overproof Rum
1 oz. Gold Rum
1 oz. Light Rum
3/4 oz. Orange Curaçao
1/2 oz. grenadine
1 1/2 oz. orange juice
1 3/4 oz. fresh lime juice
Shake and strain
Lime wedge, orange slice and
   mint sprig garnish

MAI TAI, MOBAY
House specialty glass, ice
Pour ingredients into iced mixing glass
1 oz. Appleton Estate V/X Jamaica Rum
1 oz. Mount Gay Eclipse Rum
1 oz. DJ Dotson Triple Sec
1 oz. orgeat syrup
3/4 oz. grenadine
1 3/4 oz. sweet 'n' sour
1 3/4 oz. sweetened lime juice
Shake and strain
Mint sprig garnish

MALIBU BEACH
Bucket glass, ice
Build in glass
1 1/2 oz. Malibu Rum
3/4 oz. Myers's Jamaican Rum
Fill with papaya juice

MALIBU FIZZ
Bucket glass, ice
Build in glass
1 oz. Malibu Rum
3/4 oz. Midori Melon Liqueur
Near fill with ginger ale
Float 3/4 oz. Baileys Irish Cream

MALIBU RUNNER
Bucket glass, ice
Build in glass
1 oz. Malibu Rum
3/4 oz. Disaronno Amaretto Liqueur
Near fill with pineapple juice
Float 3/4 oz. Razzmatazz Raspberry Liqueur

MALIBU SLIDE
Bucket glass, ice
Build in glass
1 1/2 oz. Malibu Rum
1/2 oz. Kahlúa Coffee Liqueur
1/2 oz. Irish Cream
2 oz. pineapple juice
2 oz. milk

MALIBU SUNSET
Bucket glass, ice
Build in glass
1 1/2 oz. Malibu Rum
1/2 oz. DeKuyper Peach Pucker
Near fill with orange juice
Float 3/4 oz. Razzmatazz Raspberry Liqueur

MAMA CITRON
Rocks glass, ice
Build in glass
1 1/2 oz. Absolut Citron Vodka
1/2 oz. Disaronno Amaretto Liqueur

MAMIE'S SISTER
Highball glass, ice
Build in glass
1 1/4 oz. Gin
Fill with ginger ale
Lemon wedge garnish

MAMIE'S SOUTHERN SISTER
Highball glass, ice
Build in glass
1 1/4 oz. Bourbon
Fill with ginger ale
Lemon wedge garnish

MAMIE TAYLOR
Highball glass, ice
Build in glass
1 1/4 oz. Scotch Whisky
Fill with ginger ale
Lemon wedge garnish

MANDARINE DREAM
House specialty glass, ice
Pour ingredients into iced mixing glass
2 oz. Mandarine Napoléon Liqueur
3/4 oz. Chambord Liqueur
1 1/2 oz. sweet 'n' sour
1 1/2 oz. orange juice
Shake and strain
Orange slice garnish

MANGO-A-GOGO
Cocktail glass, chilled
Pour ingredients into blender
1 3/4 oz. Original Polish Vodka
1/4 oz. Rose's Lime Juice
1 scoop mango sorbet
Blend ingredients (with ice optional)
Mango cube garnish

MANGO IN THE WYNDE
House specialty glass, chilled
Pour ingredients into blender
1 1/2 oz. Sea Wynde Pot Still Rum
2 scoops mango sorbet
Blend ingredients (with ice optional)
Mango cube garnish

MANGO MINGLE
House specialty glass, ice
Pour ingredients into blender
3/4 oz. Cruzan Estate Diamond Rum
1/2 oz. Whaler's Hawaiian Vanille Rum
2 oz. peach puree
2 oz. mango cubes
Blend with ice
Float 3/4 oz. Appleton Estate
   V/X Jamaica Rum
Mango cube and cherry garnish

MANGO MONSOON
Highball glass, ice
Build in glass
1 1/4 oz. Rain Vodka
1 oz. mango juice
Fill with pineapple juice

MANHATTAN
Cocktail glass, chilled
Pour ingredients into iced mixing glass
1/2 oz. Sweet Vermouth
1 dash Angostura Bitters (optional)
1 1/2 oz. Bourbon
Stir and strain
Cherry garnish

CASCADE MOUNTAIN® GIN

Bendistillery was founded by Jim Bendis in Bend, Oregon, a city completely surrounded by glorious stands of juniper trees. It is perfectly evident that these magnificent, berry-bearing trees were the creative inspiration behind CASCADE MOUNTAIN GIN.

Bendis and his family handpick the berries used to flavor this superb, micro-distilled spirit. In addition to juniper, Bendis uses a proprietary mix of botanicals indigenous to the Northwest. The botanicals are mixed in small 250-gallon batches with neutral grain spirits from the distillery's copper alembic still. It is bottled at 95 proof.

This is gin the way it used to be made. It has a lightweight body and a delicate, fruit-laced bouquet. The gin generates a slight sizzle on the tongue, which is soon replaced by a wave of delicious herbal and juniper flavors. The finish of Cascade Mountain Gin is surgically clean.

Bendistillery CRATER LAKE VODKA is a hand-made, small batch spirit, alembic-distilled from American grain and water from the Cascade Mountains. The vodka is filtered ten times through lava and charcoal—one gallon at a time—then aged briefly in oak barrels. The result is a sensational vodka of incomparable quality. CRATER LAKE HAZELNUT ESPRESSO VODKA is made with premium espresso beans and hazelnuts.

MANHATTAN, AFFINITY
aka **Affinity Cocktail, Perfect Rob Roy**
Cocktail glass, chilled
Pour ingredients into iced mixing glass
1/2 oz. Dry Vermouth
1/2 oz. Sweet Vermouth
2 dashes Angostura Bitters
1 1/2 oz. Scotch Whisky
Stir and strain
Lemon twist garnish

MANHATTAN, ALGONQUIN
Cocktail glass, chilled
Pour ingredients into iced mixing glass
1/4 oz. Dry Vermouth
1/4 oz. pineapple juice
3 dashes Angostura Bitters
1 1/2 oz. Jim Beam Black Label Bourbon
Stir and strain
Orange slice and cherry garnish

MANHATTAN BEACH
House specialty glass, ice
Pour ingredients into iced mixing glass
1 1/4 oz. Matusalem Light Dry Rum
1 1/4 oz. Matusalem Golden Dry Rum
3/4 oz. Disaronno Amaretto Liqueur
1/2 oz. grenadine
3 oz. pineapple juice
Shake and strain
Float 3/4 oz. Matusalem Classic Black Rum
Lime, lemon and orange wedge garnish

MANHATTAN, BENEDICTINE
Cocktail glass, chilled
Pour ingredients into iced mixing glass
1/4 oz. Dry Vermouth
1 1/2 oz. Benedictine
Stir and strain
Lemon twist or cherry garnish

MANHATTAN, BIG APPLE
Cocktail glass, chilled
Pour ingredients into iced mixing glass
1/2 oz. Sweet Vermouth
1 1/2 oz. Laird's Applejack Brandy
Stir and strain
Orange twist garnish

MANHATTAN, BISCAYNE
Cocktail glass, chilled
Pour ingredients into iced mixing glass
1/2 oz. Sweet Vermouth
3 dashes B & B Liqueur
1/2 oz. DeKuyper Triple Sec
1 1/2 oz. Jim Beam White Label Bourbon
Stir and strain
Lemon twist or cherry garnish

MANHATTAN, BLOOD AND SAND
Cocktail glass, chilled
Pour ingredients into iced mixing glass
1 3/4 oz. Brandy
1/2 oz. Chambord Liqueur
1/2 oz. Sweet Vermouth
1/2 oz. orange juice
Stir and strain
Orange slice garnish

MANHATTAN, BLUE GRASS BLUES
Cocktail glass, chilled
Pour ingredients into iced mixing glass
1/2 oz. Dry Vermouth
3 dashes Angostura Bitters
1/4 oz. Blue Curaçao
1 1/2 oz. Wild Turkey 101° Bourbon
Stir and strain
Lemon twist or cherry garnish

MANHATTAN, BOULEVARD
Cocktail glass, chilled
Pour ingredients into iced mixing glass
1/4 oz. Dry Vermouth
1/4 oz. Grand Marnier Liqueur
3 dashes orange bitters
1 1/2 oz. Knob Creek Small Batch Bourbon
Stir and strain
Orange slice and cherry garnish

MANHATTAN, BRANDY
aka **Delmonico**
Cocktail glass, chilled
Pour ingredients into iced mixing glass
1/2 oz. Sweet Vermouth
2-3 dashes Angostura Bitters
1 1/2 oz. Brandy
Stir and strain
Cherry garnish

MANHATTAN, CHERBOURG
Cocktail glass, chilled
Pour ingredients into iced mixing glass
1/2 oz. Vya California Dry Vermouth
1/2 oz. Vya California Sweet Vermouth
1/4 oz. fresh lemon juice
3 dashes Angostura Bitters
1 3/4 oz. Evan Williams Single Barrel
    Vintage Bourbon
Stir and strain
Orange slice and cherry garnish

MANHATTAN, CONTINENTAL PERFECT
Cocktail glass, chilled
Pour ingredients into iced mixing glass
3/4 oz. Vya California Dry Vermouth
3/4 oz. Vya California Sweet Vermouth
3 dashes Angostura Bitters
1 1/2 oz. Knob Creek Small Batch Bourbon
Stir and strain
Orange slice garnish

MANHATTAN, CUBAN
Cocktail glass, chilled
Pour ingredients into iced mixing glass
3/4 oz. Sweet Vermouth
2-3 dashes Angostura Bitters
1 3/4 oz. Matusalem Light Dry Rum
Stir and strain
Cherry garnish

MANHATTAN, CUBAN MEDIUM
Cocktail glass, chilled
Pour ingredients into iced mixing glass
1/2 oz. Sweet Vermouth
1/2 oz. Dry Vermouth
2-3 dashes Angostura Bitters
1 3/4 oz. Matusalem Light Dry Rum
Stir and strain
Cherry garnish

MANHATTAN, DANISH
Cocktail glass, chilled
Pour ingredients into iced mixing glass
1/4 oz. Peter Heering Cherry Heering
1/4 oz. Kirschwasser
1 1/2 oz. W.L. Weller Bourbon
Stir and strain
Lemon twist or cherry garnish

MANHATTAN, DIJON
Cocktail glass, chilled
Pour ingredients into iced mixing glass
1/2 oz. Dry Vermouth
1/2 oz. Briottet Crème de Cassis
1 1/2 oz. Jim Beam White Label Bourbon
Stir and strain
Lemon twist or cherry garnish

MANHATTAN, DRY
Cocktail glass, chilled
Pour ingredients into iced mixing glass
1/4 oz. Dry Vermouth
1 dash Angostura Bitters (optional)
1 1/2 oz. Bourbon
Stir and strain
Lemon twist garnish

BAK'S ZUBRÓWKA®
BISON BRAND VODKA

Long revered by enthusiasts and aficionados, ZUBRÓWKA is a traditional Polish vodka flavored with buffalo grass. For years this spectacular spirit was trapped behind the Iron Curtain and unavailable in America. Hopes for its importation rose with the end of the Cold War, only to be dashed when a trace element in the grass—coumarin—resulted in the vodka being banned in America.

Well, worry not, and welcome the long awaited arrival of BAK'S ZUBRÓWKA BISON BRAND VODKA. Produced at the Polmos Poznan Distillery, the vodka is triple-distilled in column stills from potatoes and artesian well water. It is then infused with the essential oils of the buffalo grass before being filtered through charcoal and oak chips. It is bottled at 82 proof.

Bak's Zubrówka is free of coumarin and is a dead ringer for the original infused version. The bottle even contains a long, slender blade of buffalo grass. The vodka has a pale, yellow hue, lightweight body and a generous bouquet of fresh, grassy aromas. The palate is loaded with spicy, sweet flavors that gradually fade into a warm and relaxed finish.

The buffalo grass in the Zubrówka is said to give one vitality and strength. Others say it has aphrodisiac properties. Whatever the motivation, Zubrówka is an experience not to be missed.

MANHATTAN, DRY BRANDY
Cocktail glass, chilled
Pour ingredients into iced mixing glass
1/4 oz. Dry Vermouth
1 dash Angostura Bitters (optional)
1 1/2 oz. Brandy
Stir and strain
Lemon twist garnish

MANHATTAN, DUBONNET
Cocktail glass, chilled
Pour ingredients into iced mixing glass
1/4 oz. Vya California Dry Vermouth
3/4 oz. Dubonnet Rouge
3 dashes Angostura Bitters
1 3/4 oz. Jim Beam White Label Bourbon
Stir and strain
Lemon twist or cherry garnish

MANHATTAN, GALLIANO
Cocktail glass, chilled
Pour ingredients into iced mixing glass
1/4 oz. Galliano Liqueur
1 1/2 oz. Jim Beam White Label Bourbon
Stir and strain
Lemon twist or cherry garnish

MANHATTAN GLITZ
Cocktail glass, chilled
Pour ingredients into iced mixing glass
3/4 oz. Oro di Mazzetti Grappa Liqueur
2 oz. Jack Daniel's Single Barrel Whiskey
Stir and strain
Lemon twist garnish

MANHATTAN, IRISH
aka **Paddy**
Cocktail glass, chilled
Pour ingredients into iced mixing glass
1/2 oz. Sweet Vermouth
3 dashes Angostura Bitters
1 1/2 oz. Irish Whiskey
Stir and strain
Lemon twist or cherry garnish

MANHATTAN, ITALIAN
Cocktail glass, chilled
Pour ingredients into iced mixing glass
1/4 oz. maraschino cherry juice
1/2 oz. Disaronno Amaretto Liqueur
1 1/2 oz. Maker's Mark Bourbon
Stir and strain
Orange slice and cherry garnish

MANHATTAN, JACK'S BEST
Cocktail glass, chilled
Pour ingredients into iced mixing glass
1/4 oz. Vya California Sweet Vermouth
3 dashes orange bitters
2 oz. Jack Daniel's Single Barrel Whiskey
Stir and strain
Orange slice and cherry garnish

MANHATTAN, LAFAYETTE
Cocktail glass, chilled
Pour ingredients into iced mixing glass
3/4 oz. Dubonnet Rouge
3 dashes Angostura Bitters
2 oz. Maker's Mark Bourbon
Stir and strain
Lemon twist or cherry garnish

MANHATTAN, LATIN
Cocktail glass, chilled
Pour ingredients into iced mixing glass
1/4 oz. Sweet Vermouth
1/4 oz. Dry Vermouth
2 dashes Angostura Bitters (optional)
1 3/4 oz. Matusalem Light Dry Rum
Stir and strain
Lemon twist garnish

MANHATTAN, LORETTO
Cocktail glass, chilled
Pour ingredients into iced mixing glass
1/2 oz. Vya California Sweet Vermouth
3 dashes Amer Picon
1/4 oz. B & B Liqueur
1 1/2 oz. Maker's Mark Bourbon
Stir and strain
Lemon twist or cherry garnish

MANHATTAN, MAPLE LEAF
Cocktail glass, chilled
Pour ingredients into iced mixing glass
1/2 oz. Sweet Vermouth
1/4 oz. maraschino cherry juice
1 1/2 oz. Canadian Whisky
Stir and strain
Cherry garnish

MANHATTAN, MARIANNE
Cocktail glass, chilled
Pour ingredients into iced mixing glass
1/4 oz. Dry Vermouth
1/2 oz. Byrrh
3 dashes Angostura Bitters
1 1/2 oz. Jim Beam Black Label Bourbon
Stir and strain
Lemon twist or cherry garnish

MANHATTAN, MAZATLAN
Cocktail glass, chilled
Pour ingredients into iced mixing glass
1/2 oz. Dubonnet Rouge
1/2 oz. fresh lime juice
1/4 oz. maraschino cherry juice
2 oz. Maker's Mark Bourbon
Stir and strain
Cherry garnish

MANHATTAN, METS
Cocktail glass, chilled
Pour ingredients into iced mixing glass
1/2 oz. Dry Vermouth
1/4 oz. Fraise Liqueur
1 1/2 oz. Canadian Whisky
Stir and strain
Lemon twist or cherry garnish

MANHATTAN, MOON
OVER MANHATTAN
Cocktail glass, chilled
Pour ingredients into iced mixing glass
1/4 oz. cranberry juice
1/2 oz. Disaronno Amaretto Liqueur
1 3/4 oz. Crown Royal
Stir and strain
Cherry garnish

MANHATTAN, NAPOLEON
Cocktail glass, chilled
Pour ingredients into iced mixing glass
1/2 oz. Vya California Sweet Vermouth
2 oz. Courvoisier V.S.O.P. Cognac
Stir and strain
Orange twist garnish

MANHATTAN, NEW ORLEANS
Cocktail glass, chilled
Pour ingredients into iced mixing glass
Swirl 1/2 oz. Frangelico Liqueur,
    discard excess
1/2 oz. Sweet Vermouth
1 1/2 oz. W.L. Weller Bourbon
Stir and strain
Cherry garnish

MANHATTAN, PAPARAZZI
Cocktail glass, chilled
Pour ingredients into iced mixing glass
1/2 oz. Sweet Vermouth
1/4 oz. Fernet Branca
3 dashes Pernod
1 1/2 oz. Wild Turkey 101° Bourbon
Stir and strain
Orange slice and cherry garnish

AN INTRODUCTION TO OPENING CHAMPAGNE

Champagne is bottled at a pressure of 90 p.s.i., which is sufficient force to turn the cork into a potentially dangerous projectile in an instant. Safely opening a bottle of champagne requires mastering some technique.

To that end, the following are points to remember when opening a bottle of champagne and some tips regarding the proper service of the wine:

- Champagne should be served thoroughly chilled, which is why it is most often served in an iced wine bucket. Opening a bottle of warm or only slightly chilled champagne is very messy.

- Place a towel or cloth napkin over the bottle when loosening the wire cage over the cork. It is not necessary to completely remove the wire enclosure before opening the bottle.

- Keep a firm grip on the cork during the entire procedure. Make sure that the bottle is aimed away from anyone nearby, which includes you.

- Loosen the cork by holding on to it tightly with one hand and turning the bottle with the other.

- Slowly work the cork loose until it eases out of the bottle. Do not let it make a popping sound, which may cause the champagne to gush out of the bottle.

- Always wipe the brim and bottle before serving. The champagne bottle should be held at the very bottom such that the label is always facing the guest(s).

- Whenever possible, serve champagne in chilled glassware. Chilling champagne glasses is best accomplished by storing them in refrigeration.

MANHATTAN, PARK PARADISE
Cocktail glass, chilled
Pour ingredients into iced mixing glass
1/2 oz. Sweet Vermouth
3 dashes Angostura Bitters
3 dashes Maraschino Liqueur
1 1/2 oz. Canadian Whisky
Stir and strain
Lemon twist or cherry garnish

MANHATTAN, PERFECT
aka **Medium Manhattan**
Cocktail glass, chilled
Pour ingredients into iced mixing glass
1/4 oz. Dry Vermouth
1/4 oz. Sweet Vermouth
1 dash Angostura Bitters (optional)
1 1/2 oz. Bourbon
Stir and strain
Lemon twist garnish

MANHATTAN, PERFECT BRANDY
Cocktail glass, chilled
Pour ingredients into iced mixing glass
1/4 oz. Dry Vermouth
1/4 oz. Sweet Vermouth
1 dash Angostura Bitters (optional)
1 1/2 oz. Brandy
Stir and strain
Lemon twist garnish

MANHATTAN, PERFECT SOUTHERN COMFORT
Cocktail glass, chilled
Pour ingredients into iced mixing glass
1/4 oz. Dry Vermouth
1/4 oz. Sweet Vermouth
1 1/2 oz. Southern Comfort Liqueur
Stir and strain
Lemon twist garnish

MANHATTAN, POOR TIM
Cocktail glass, chilled
Pour ingredients into iced mixing glass
1/2 oz. Vya California Dry Vermouth
1/2 oz. Chambord Liqueur
1 1/2 oz. Gentleman Jack
   Tennessee Whiskey
Stir and strain
Lemon twist or cherry garnish

MANHATTAN, PREAKNESS
Cocktail glass, chilled
Pour ingredients into iced mixing glass
1/2 oz. Sweet Vermouth
3 dashes Angostura Bitters
3/4 oz. B & B Liqueur
1 1/2 oz. Knob Creek Small Batch Bourbon
Stir and strain
Lemon twist garnish

MANHATTAN, PROHIBITION
Cocktail glass, chilled
Pour ingredients into iced mixing glass
1 oz. Sweet Vermouth
3 dashes orange bitters
1 oz. Rye Whiskey
Stir and strain
Lemon twist garnish

MANHATTAN, QUEBEC
Cocktail glass, chilled
Pour ingredients into iced mixing glass
1/2 oz. Dry Vermouth
3 dashes Amer Picon
3 dashes Maraschino Liqueur
1 1/2 oz. Canadian Whisky
Stir and strain
Lemon twist garnish

MANHATTAN, RASPBERRY
Cocktail glass, chilled
Pour ingredients into iced mixing glass
1/2 oz. Vya California Dry Vermouth
1/2 oz. Chambord Liqueur
1 1/2 oz. Maker's Mark Bourbon
Stir and strain
Lemon twist garnish

MANHATTAN, ROMAN
Cocktail glass, chilled
Pour ingredients into iced mixing glass
1/2 oz. Sweet Vermouth
1/4 oz. Sambuca Romano
1 1/2 oz. Canadian Whisky
Stir and strain
Lemon twist or cherry garnish

MANHATTAN, ROSE
Cocktail glass, chilled
Pour ingredients into iced mixing glass
1/2 oz. Dry Vermouth
1/2 oz. Briottet Crème de Cassis
1/4 oz. fresh lemon juice
1 1/2 oz. Knob Creek Small Batch Bourbon
Stir and strain
Lemon twist or cherry garnish

MANHATTAN, ROSEBUD
Cocktail glass, chilled
Pour ingredients into iced mixing glass
1/2 oz. Rémy Red
1 1/2 oz. Jim Beam White Label Bourbon
Stir and strain
Lemon twist garnish

MANHATTAN, ST. MORITZ
aka **Sidney Manhattan**
Cocktail glass, chilled
Pour ingredients into iced mixing glass
1/4 oz. Dry Vermouth
1/4 oz. Green Chartreuse
3 dashes orange bitters
1 1/2 oz. Jim Beam Black Label Bourbon
Stir and strain
Lemon twist garnish

MANHATTAN, SATIN
Cocktail glass, chilled
Pour ingredients into iced mixing glass
1/2 oz. Vya California Sweet Vermouth
1/2 oz. Grand Marnier Liqueur
1 1/2 oz. Gentleman Jack Tennessee Whiskey
Stir and strain
Lemon twist garnish

MANHATTAN, SHAMROCK
Cocktail glass, chilled
Pour ingredients into iced mixing glass
1/2 oz. Sweet Vermouth
3 dashes Angostura Bitters
1/2 oz. Green Crème de Menthe
1 1/2 oz. Jim Beam White Label Bourbon
Stir and strain
Lemon twist garnish

MANHATTAN, SHEEPSHEAD BAY
Cocktail glass, chilled
Pour ingredients into iced mixing glass
1/4 oz. Sweet Vermouth
1/4 oz. B & B Liqueur
3 dashes Angostura Bitters
1 1/2 oz. Knob Creek Small Batch Bourbon
Stir and strain
Lemon twist or cherry garnish

MANHATTAN, SMOKY
Cocktail glass, chilled
Swirl and coat inside of glass
1/2 oz. Maker's Mark Bourbon
Pour ingredients into iced mixing glass
1/2 oz. Vya California Dry Vermouth
1 1/2 oz. Ketel One Dutch Vodka
Stir and strain
Lemon twist garnish

MANHATTAN, SOUTHERN COMFORT
Cocktail glass, chilled
Pour ingredients into iced mixing glass
1/4 oz. Dry Vermouth
1 1/2 oz. Southern Comfort Liqueur
Stir and strain
Cherry garnish

DEKUYPER®
PEACHTREE® SCHNAPPS

When DEKUYPER PEACHTREE
SCHNAPPS was introduced in the early
1980s, it immediately shot to the top of
the charts like a bullet. Drinks like the
Fuzzy Navel, Silk Panties and Sex on the
Beach became all the rage, making
Peachtree Schnapps indispensable
behind the bar. Today it remains a "must
have" brand.

Peach schnapps is produced by
distilling a blend of pure grain, neutral
spirits and natural peach flavoring.
While the quality of the grain spirits is a
factor, what really differentiates one
brand from another is the peach
flavoring. DeKuyper Peachtree Schnapps
is made from a blend of different peach
varieties, some selected for their
bouquet, others for their taste.

The art and science of making high
quality schnapps came together in
DeKuyper Peachtree. It has a satiny,
light/medium body and a robust
bouquet of freshly sliced peaches.
The fresh fruit experience continues
on the palate, where the flavor of peach
is predominant. The finish is long
and flavorful.

DeKuyper Peachtree Schnapps has
become something of a modern classic,
the brand synonymous with the peach
schnapps category. The delicious drinks
it can create are almost limitless.

MANHATTAN, SPICED
APPLE BRANDY
Cocktail glass, chilled
Pour ingredients into iced mixing glass
1/2 oz. Vya California Dry Vermouth
1/2 oz. Celtic Crossing Irish Liqueur
1 1/2 oz. Laird's 12-Year Apple Brandy
Stir and strain
Cherry garnish

MANHATTAN,
TENNESSEE BLUSH
Cocktail glass, chilled
Pour ingredients into iced mixing glass
1/2 oz. Alizé Red Passion
2 oz. Jack Daniel's Single Barrel Whiskey
Stir and strain
Lemon twist and cherry garnish

MANHATTAN, TIVOLI
Cocktail glass, chilled
Pour ingredients into iced mixing glass
1/2 oz. Vya California Sweet Vermouth
1/2 oz. Aquavit
3 dashes Campari Aperitivo
1 1/2 oz. Maker's Mark Bourbon
Stir and strain
Orange slice and cherry garnish

MANHATTAN, TWIN PEAKS
Cocktail glass, chilled
Pour ingredients into iced mixing glass
1/2 oz. Dubonnet Rouge
1/4 oz. Cointreau Liqueur
1 1/2 oz. Gentleman Jack
    Tennessee Whiskey
Stir and strain
Lemon twist or cherry garnish

MANHATTAN, VINTAGE (1)
Cocktail glass, chilled
Pour ingredients into iced mixing glass
1 oz. Dubonnet Rouge
2-3 dashes Angostura Bitters
2 1/2 oz. Evan Williams Single Barrel
    Vintage Bourbon
Stir and strain
Cherry garnish

MANHATTAN, VINTAGE (2)
Cocktail glass, chilled
Pour ingredients into iced mixing glass
1/2 oz. Ballylarkin Irish Liqueur
2 oz. Evan Williams Single Barrel
    Vintage Bourbon
Stir and strain
Lemon twist garnish

MANHATTAN, WALDORF
Cocktail glass, chilled
Pour ingredients into iced mixing glass
1/2 oz. Sweet Vermouth
1/4 oz. Pernod
3 dashes Angostura Bitters
1 1/2 oz. Jim Beam White Label Bourbon
Stir and strain
Orange slice and cherry garnish

MANHATTAN, WESTCHESTER
Cocktail glass, chilled
Pour ingredients into iced mixing glass
1/4 oz. Vya California Dry Vermouth
1/4 oz. Rose's Lime Juice
3 dashes Angostura Bitters
1 1/2 oz. Knob Creek Small Batch Bourbon
Stir and strain
Lemon twist or cherry garnish

MARASCHINO RUM MIST
House specialty glass, ice
Build in glass
1 1/2 oz. Bacardi Gold Rum
1 1/2 oz. maraschino cherry juice
1 oz. Rose's Lime Juice
Fill with club soda
Orange slice and cherry garnish

MARGARITA, AGAVE JUICE
House specialty glass, ice
Rim glass with salt (optional)
Pour ingredients into iced mixing glass
1 1/4 oz. Sauza Hornitos Tequila
1/2 oz. DeKuyper Triple Sec
1/2 oz. Rose's Lime Juice
1-2 dashes Angostura Bitters
1/2 oz. grenadine
1 oz. orange juice
1 oz. sweet 'n' sour
Shake and strain
Lime wedge garnish

MARGARITA AZUL
House specialty glass, ice
Rim glass with salt (optional)
Pour ingredients into iced mixing glass
1 1/4 oz. Sauza Hornitos Tequila
1/2 oz. Disaronno Amaretto Liqueur
1/2 oz. Blue Curaçao
1/4 oz. fresh lime juice
1 1/2 oz. sweet 'n' sour
Shake and strain
Lime wedge garnish

MARGARITA, ANITA
House specialty glass, ice
Rim glass with salt (optional)
Pour ingredients into iced mixing glass
1 1/4 oz. Farias Reposado Tequila
1/2 oz. Mandarine Napoléon Liqueur
1/2 oz. Rose's Lime Juice
1 1/2 oz. sweet 'n' sour
1 oz. cranberry juice
Shake and strain
Lime wedge garnish

MARGARITA, BAHAMA MAMA
House specialty glass, ice
Rim glass with sugar (optional)
Pour ingredients into iced mixing glass
1 oz. Sauza Conmemorativo Añejo Tequila
1 oz. Malibu Rum
1/2 oz. DJ Dotson Triple Sec
1/2 oz. Rose's Lime Juice
1 1/2 oz. pineapple juice
1 1/2 oz. sweet 'n' sour
Shake and strain
Pineapple wedge and cherry garnish

MARGARITA, BAJA
aka **Damiana Margarita**
Cocktail glass, chilled
Rim glass with salt (optional)
Pour ingredients into iced mixing glass
1 1/4 oz. Sauza Gold Tequila
3/4 oz. Damiana Liqueur
1 1/2 oz. sweet 'n' sour
Shake and strain
Lime wedge garnish

MARGARITA, BLACK FOREST
aka **Black Cherry Margarita**
House specialty glass, ice
Rim glass with salt (optional)
Pour ingredients into iced mixing glass
1 1/4 oz. El Jimador Reposado Tequila
3/4 oz. Cherry Schnapps
1/2 oz. Rose's Lime Juice
2 oz. sweet 'n' sour
2 oz. orange juice
Shake and strain
Lime wedge garnish

MARGARITA, BLACK GOLD
House specialty glass, ice
Rim glass with salt (optional)
Pour ingredients into iced mixing glass
1 oz. Sauza Conmemorativo Añejo Tequila
1 oz. Lime-infused Sauza Blanco Tequila
3/4 oz. Chambord Liqueur
1/4 oz. Rose's Lime Juice
1 1/4 oz. sweet 'n' sour
Shake and strain
Lime wedge garnish

CRUZAN® COCONUT RUM

When it comes to mixology, flavor rules supreme. This adage bodes well for the Caribbean rum giant Cruzan, who in 1996 and 1997, launched a line of five, fabulously flavorful rums. The quintet includes CRUZAN COCONUT RUM, CRUZAN BANANA RUM, CRUZAN PINEAPPLE RUM, CRUZAN ORANGE RUM, and the dry and tangy CRUZAN JUNKANU CITRUS RUM.

These light, savory rums are made from a blend of triple-distilled rums aged in oak bourbon barrels between 2 and 3 years. After aging, it is filtered through activated charcoal to remove impurities and any color it obtained while maturing in the barrel. Natural flavorings are added to create the finished product.

To put it simply, each of these rums is delicious. They have light to medium bodies and bouquets that lead with the aroma of their namesake flavor. Because they are relatively low in alcohol at 27.5% abv (55 proof), the fresh fruit flavors stay on the palate for a considerably long time.

The taste of the Cruzan premium light rum can easily be perceived, a taste that complements the featured fruit or coconut flavor.

The rum quintet is ideally suited for drink making. Everything about them screams of fun. Clearly it's why they were created.

MARGARITA, BLOODY
House specialty glass, ice
Rim glass with salt and pepper (optional)
Pour ingredients into iced mixing glass
1 1/4 oz. Silver Tequila
3/4 oz. Hiram Walker Triple Sec
1/2 oz. Rose's Lime Juice
1/4 oz. jalapeño pepper juice
1-2 dashes Tabasco Sauce
2 oz. Sangrita Mix
Shake and strain
Sprinkle ground habanero chile
 (use sparingly)
Lime wedge garnish
Note: See **Sangrita Mix**

MARGARITA, BLUE
aka **Midnight Margarita**
House specialty glass, ice
Rim glass with salt (optional)
Pour ingredients into iced mixing glass
1 1/4 oz. Sauza Blanco Tequila
3/4 oz. Blue Curaçao
1/2 oz. Rose's Lime Juice
1 1/2 oz. sweet 'n' sour
Shake and strain
Lime wedge garnish

MARGARITA, BLUE
MAESTRO GRAN
House specialty glass, ice
Rim glass with salt (optional)
Pour ingredients into iced mixing glass
1 1/2 oz. Mezcal del Maestro Añejo
1/2 oz. Grand Marnier Liqueur
3/4 oz. Blue Curaçao
1/4 oz. Rose's Lime Juice
1 1/2 oz. sweet 'n' sour
Shake and strain
Lime wedge garnish

MARGARITA, BLUE MOON
House specialty glass, chilled
Rim glass with salt (optional)
Pour ingredients into blender
1 1/4 oz. Sauza Conmemorativo
 Añejo Tequila
3/4 oz. Blue Curaçao
1/2 oz. Rose's Lime Juice
1 1/2 oz. sweet 'n' sour
1-2 scoops lemon sorbet
Blend ingredients (with ice optional)
Lime wedge garnish

MARGARITA BRITANNIA (1)
Cocktail glass, chilled
Pour ingredients into iced mixing glass
3/4 oz. Silver Tequila
3/4 oz. Gin
1/2 oz. Triple Sec
1 1/2 oz. sweet 'n' sour
Shake and strain
Lime wedge garnish

MARGARITA BRITANNIA (2)
Cocktail glass, chilled
Pour ingredients into iced mixing glass
3/4 oz. Sauza Tres Generaciones
   Plata Tequila
3/4 oz. Beefeater London Dry Gin
1/2 oz. Grand Marnier Liqueur
1 1/2 oz. sweet 'n' sour
Shake and strain
Lime wedge garnish

MARGARITA, CADILLAC
House specialty glass, ice
Rim glass with salt (optional)
Pour ingredients into iced mixing glass
1 1/4 oz. Jose Cuervo 1800 Tequila
3/4 oz. Grand Marnier Liqueur
1/2 oz. Rose's Lime Juice
1 1/2 oz. sweet 'n' sour
Shake and strain
Lime wedge garnish

MARGARITA, CAJUN
Cocktail glass, chilled
Rim glass with salt and pepper (optional)
Pour ingredients into iced mixing glass
1 1/4 oz. Pepper-infused Silver Tequila
1-2 dashes Tabasco Sauce
1-2 dashes jalapeño pepper juice
2 oz. sweet 'n' sour
Shake and strain
Small jalapeño peppers garnish

MARGARITA, CAMINO REAL
House specialty glass, ice
Rim glass with salt (optional)
Pour ingredients into iced mixing glass
1 1/4 oz. El Tesoro Silver Tequila
3/4 oz. Cruzan Banana Rum
1/2 oz. Rose's Lime Juice
1 oz. orange juice
1 oz. sweet 'n' sour
Shake and strain
Lime wedge garnish

MARGARITA, CANTINA WINE
House specialty glass, ice
Rim glass with salt (optional)
Build in glass
2 oz. Dry White Wine
1 oz. Triple Sec
1/4 oz. Rose's Lime Juice
2 oz. sweet 'n' sour
Fill with club soda
Lime wedge garnish

MARGARITA, CAPTAIN
House specialty glass, ice
Rim glass with salt (optional)
Pour ingredients into iced mixing glass
1 1/4 oz. Captain Morgan Spiced Rum
1/2 oz. DJ Dotson Triple Sec
1/2 oz. Rose's Lime Juice
2 oz. sweet 'n' sour
Shake and strain
Lime wedge garnish

MARGARITA, CARIBBEAN
aka **Caribbean 'Rita**
House specialty glass, ice
Rim glass with pink lemonade mix
   (optional)
Pour ingredients into iced mixing glass
1 oz. Herradura Silver Tequila
1 oz. Appleton Estate V/X Jamaica Rum
1/2 oz. DJ Dotson Triple Sec
1/2 oz. Rose's Lime Juice
1 1/2 oz. orange juice
1 1/2 oz. sweet 'n' sour
Shake and strain
Pineapple wedge and cherry garnish

MARGARITA, CATALINA
House specialty glass, ice
Rim glass with sugar (optional)
Pour ingredients into iced mixing glass
1 1/4 oz. Gold Tequila
1/2 oz. Blue Curaçao
1/2 oz. DeKuyper Peachtree Schnapps
1/4 oz. Rose's Lime Juice
2 oz. sweet 'n' sour
Shake and strain
Lime wedge garnish

MARGARITA, CHAMPAGNE
Champagne glass, chilled
Rim glass with Cointreau and sugar
   (optional)
Pour ingredients into iced mixing glass
1 oz. Casa Noble Gold Tequila
1/2 oz. Cointreau Liqueur
1/2 oz. Rose's Lime Juice
1/2 oz. orange juice
Shake and strain
Fill with Champagne
Lemon twist garnish

CHRISTIAN BROTHERS®
BRANDY

CHRISTIAN BROTHERS BRANDY is one of the oldest and best-selling American spirits. Their winery and adjacent distillery comprise a huge, state of the art complex located in the fertile San Joaquin Valley, California. Despite all of the technological innovations the Christian Brothers have built into their facility, little has changed in their artisan approach to making brandy.

In 1882, the religious order of the Christian Brothers began distilling brandy from California grapes. Their commitment was and remains to create singularly light, flavorful brandies using locally grown grape varietals.

The Christian Brothers selected the Thompson Seedless grape as the principal variety, because they possess the highly sought after qualities of high acidity, balanced flavor and low alcohol output. They distill their brandies in huge, copper alembic stills, as well as extremely efficient patent stills. Prior to blending, the brandies are aged in American white oak bourbon barrels a minimum of 3 to 6 years.

The Christian Brothers Brandy has a tempting, fruity bouquet and a soft, supple texture. The full body is imbued with layers of well-balanced fruit flavors. Its finish is warm and lingering.

Superb also is the CHRISTIAN BROTHERS XO RARE RESERVE, a 10-year-old blend containing a high percentage of pot-distilled brandies.

MARGARITA, CHAPALA
House specialty glass, ice
Rim glass with salt (optional)
Pour ingredients into iced mixing glass
1 1/4 oz. Herradura Reposado Tequila
1/2 oz. Cointreau Liqueur
1/2 oz. orange juice
1/2 oz. Rose's Lime Juice
1/4 oz. grenadine
1-2 dashes of orange flower water
1 1/2 oz. sweet 'n' sour
Shake and strain
Lime wedge garnish

MARGARITA, CILLO ITALIAN
Cocktail glass, chilled
Rim glass with salt (optional)
Pour ingredients into iced mixing glass
1 1/4 oz. El Jimador Añejo Tequila
1 oz. Giori Lemoncillo Liqueur
3/4 oz. Cointreau Liqueur
1/2 oz. Rose's Lime Juice
1/2 oz. cranberry juice
2 oz. sweet 'n' sour
Shake and strain
Lime wedge garnish

MARGARITA CLASSICO
Cocktail glass, chilled
Rim glass with salt (optional)
Pour ingredients into iced mixing glass
1 1/4 oz. Silver Tequila
1/2 oz. Triple Sec
1/4 oz. Rose's Lime Juice (optional)
1/4 oz. orange juice (optional)
1 1/2 oz. sweet 'n' sour
Shake and strain
Lime wedge garnish

MARGARITA, CONGA
Cocktail glass, chilled
Pour ingredients into iced mixing glass
1 oz. Cruzan Banana Rum
1 oz. Cruzan Pineapple Rum
3/4 oz. Citrónge Orange Liqueur
1/2 oz. Rose's Lime Juice
1 1/2 oz. sweet 'n' sour
Shake and strain
Lime wedge garnish

MARGARITA, COYOTE (1)

House specialty glass, ice
Rim glass with salt and pepper (optional)
Pour ingredients into iced mixing glass
1 1/4 oz. Farias Silver Tequila
1/2 oz. DeKuyper Triple Sec
1/2 oz. Rose's Lime Juice
1/4 oz. jalapeño pepper juice
1 oz. cranberry juice
1 1/2 oz. sweet 'n' sour
Shake and strain
Lime wedge garnish

MARGARITA, COYOTE (2)

House specialty glass, ice
Rim glass with salt and pepper (optional)
Pour ingredients into iced mixing glass
1 1/2 oz. Sauza Conmemorativo
   Añejo Tequila
1/2 oz. DeKuyper Triple Sec
1/2 oz. Rose's Lime Juice
1 1/2 oz. prickly pear juice
1 1/2 oz. sweet 'n' sour
Shake and strain
Lime wedge garnish

MARGARITA, CRANBERRY (1)

House specialty glass, chilled
Rim glass with salt (optional)
Pour ingredients into blender
1 1/2 oz. Sauza Blanco Tequila
1/2 oz. Mandarine Napoléon Liqueur
3/4 oz. Rose's Lime Juice
3/4 oz. sweet 'n' sour
2 oz. cranberry juice
2 oz. strawberry puree
Blend with ice
Lime wedge garnish

MARGARITA, CRANBERRY (2)

House specialty glass, chilled
Rim glass with sugar (optional)
Pour ingredients into blender
1 1/2 oz. Sauza Blanco Tequila
1/2 oz. DJ Dotson Triple Sec
1/4 cup jellied cranberry sauce
1 1/2 oz. sweet 'n' sour
Blend with ice
Fresh strawberry garnish

MARGARITA, DAMRAK 'RITA

House specialty glass, ice
Rim glass with salt (optional)
Pour ingredients into iced mixing glass
2 oz. Damrak Amsterdam Gin
1/2 oz. Cointreau Liqueur
1/4 oz. orange juice
1 1/2 oz. fresh lime juice
Shake and strain
Lime wedge garnish

MARGARITA, DC 3

House specialty glass, ice
Rim glass with salt (optional)
Pour ingredients into iced mixing glass
3/4 oz. Sauza Conmemorativo
   Añejo Tequila
3/4 oz. Sauza Hornitos Tequila
1/2 oz. Cointreau Liqueur
1/2 oz. Rose's Lime Juice
1 oz. lemon/lime soda
1 1/4 oz. sweet 'n' sour
Shake and strain
Float 3/4 oz. Sauza Tres Generaciones
   Añejo Tequila
Lime wedge garnish

MARGARITA de FRUTA
aka **Fruit Margarita**

House specialty glass, chilled
Rim glass with sugar (optional)
Pour ingredients into blender
1 1/4 oz. Silver Tequila
1/2 oz. Triple Sec
1/2 oz. Rose's Lime Juice
1/2 cup requested fruit
1 dash orange juice (optional)
1 1/2 oz. sweet 'n' sour
Blend with ice
Fresh fruit garnish
Note: Fruit choices include apple, apricot,
   banana, kiwi, melon, peach, pomegranate,
   raspberry, strawberry and watermelon

MARGARITA de MEXICO

Cocktail glass, chilled
Rim glass with salt (optional)
Pour ingredients into iced mixing glass
1 oz. Silver Tequila
1 oz. Controy Licor de Naranjas
1 oz. fresh lime juice
Shake and strain
Lime wedge garnish

MARGARITA, DIABLO
aka **Red Hot Margarita**

House specialty glass, ice
Rim glass with cinnamon and sugar
   (optional)
Pour ingredients into iced mixing glass
1 1/4 oz. El Jimador Reposado Tequila
3/4 oz. Hot Damn Cinnamon Schnapps
1/2 oz. Rose's Lime Juice
1 1/2 oz. orange juice
1 1/2 oz. sweet 'n' sour
Shake and strain
Lime wedge garnish

SOUTHERN COMFORT®
LIQUEUR

SOUTHERN COMFORT is the first and best-known liqueur crafted in the United States. The origin of this distinguished liqueur was in New Orleans, where in 1874 a barman named M. W. Herron created the concoction and named it Cuffs and Buttons, an upscale reference to white tie and tails. He later moved to St. Louis where he renamed his potion Southern Comfort.

While this great American classic is now made in Louisville, Kentucky, the recipe is still a closely guarded, proprietary secret. The makers have let it be known that it is crafted from a base of pure grain neutral spirits and is flavored with peach liqueur, fresh peach and citrus extracts. After the infusion process is complete, the liqueur is filtered and bottled at 80 proof.

It is interesting to note that to this day many people think of Southern Comfort as a bourbon. This widely held misconception is easily understood. Southern Comfort has a marvelous, whiskey quality to its character. The liqueur is pleasingly aromatic with floral and citrus notes. Its medium-weight body is flawlessly textured, and the palate features the amazingly delicious flavors of fresh peaches, oranges and vanilla.

Southern Comfort is an extremely versatile liqueur and an absolute "must have" product.

MARGARITA, EL CIEN
Cocktail glass, chilled
Rim glass with salt (optional)
Pour ingredients into iced mixing glass
1 1/2 oz. Herradura Seleccion
    Suprema Tequila
1 oz. El Tesoro Paradiso Añejo Tequila
3/4 oz. Cointreau Liqueur
1/2 oz. fresh lime juice
1/2 oz. fresh lemon juice
1/2 oz. orange juice
1 1/2 oz. sweet 'n' sour
Shake and strain
Float 3/4 oz. Grand Marnier
    150th Anniversary
Lime wedge garnish

MARGARITA, EL CONQUISTADOR
House specialty glass, ice
Rim glass with salt (optional)
Pour ingredients into iced mixing glass
3/4 oz. Sauza Conmemorativo
    Añejo Tequila
3/4 oz. Sauza Hornitos Tequila
1/2 oz. Chambord Liqueur
1/2 oz. Mandarine Napoléon Liqueur
1/2 oz. Rose's Lime Juice
1 1/2 oz. sweet 'n' sour
1 1/2 oz. pineapple juice
Shake and strain
Lime wedge garnish

MARGARITA, ELEGANTÉ
House specialty glass, ice
Rim glass with salt (optional)
Pour ingredients into iced mixing glass
3/4 oz. Sauza Conmemorativo
    Añejo Tequila
3/4 oz. Sauza Hornitos Tequila
1/2 oz. Cointreau Liqueur
1/2 oz. Rose's Lime Juice
1 1/2 oz. sweet 'n' sour
Shake and strain
Lime wedge garnish

MARGARITA, EMERALD ISLE
Cocktail glass, chilled
Rim glass with salt (optional)
Pour ingredients into iced mixing glass
1 1/4 oz. Hussong's Añejo Tequila
3/4 oz. Ballylarkin Irish Liqueur
1/2 oz. Rose's Lime Juice
1/2 oz. orange juice
1 1/2 oz. sweet 'n' sour
Shake and strain
Lime wedge garnish

MARGARITA, FLORIDITA
aka **Floridita 'Rita**
House specialty glass, ice
Rim glass with pink lemonade mix
   (optional)
Pour ingredients into iced mixing glass
1 1/4 oz. Sauza Hornitos Tequila
1/2 oz. DeKuyper Triple Sec
1/4 oz. Rose's Lime Juice
1/2 oz. cranberry juice
1 1/2 oz. grapefruit juice
1 1/2 oz. sweet 'n' sour
Shake and strain
Lime wedge garnish

MARGARITA FRAMBOISE
House specialty glass, ice
Rim glass with salt and sugar (optional)
Pour ingredients into iced mixing glass
1 1/2 oz. El Tesoro Paradiso Añejo Tequila
3/4 oz. Bonny Doon Framboise Wine
1/4 oz. Cointreau Liqueur
1/4 oz. Grand Marnier 100th Anniversary
1/4 oz. orange juice
1/2 oz. fresh lime juice
2 oz. sweet 'n' sour
Shake and strain
Float red raspberries
Lime wheel garnish

MARGARITA, FRENCH/RUSSIAN
House specialty glass, ice
Rim glass with salt (optional)
Pour ingredients into iced mixing glass
1 1/4 oz. Stolichnaya Ohranj Russian Vodka
1/2 oz. Grand Marnier Liqueur
1/4 oz. orange juice
1/2 oz. Rose's Lime Juice
1 1/2 oz. sweet 'n' sour
Shake and strain
Orange twist garnish

MARGARITA, GEORGIA
House specialty glass, ice
Rim glass with sugar (optional)
Pour ingredients into iced mixing glass
1 1/4 oz. El Tesoro Silver Tequila
3/4 oz. DeKuyper Peachtree Schnapps
1/2 oz. Rose's Lime Juice
1 1/2 oz. sweet 'n' sour
Shake and strain
Lime wedge garnish

MARGARITA, GEORGIA PEACH
House specialty glass, ice
Rim glass with sugar (optional)
Pour ingredients into iced mixing glass
1 1/4 oz. Sauza Conmemorativo
   Añejo Tequila
1/2 oz. DeKuyper Peachtree Schnapps
1/2 oz. DeKuyper Triple Sec
1/2 oz. Rose's Lime Juice
1 1/2 oz. orange juice
1 1/2 oz. sweet 'n' sour
Shake and strain
Orange slice garnish

MARGARITA, GUAYMAS
House specialty glass, ice
Rim glass with salt (optional)
Pour ingredients into iced mixing glass
1 1/4 oz. Sauza Tres Generaciones
   Añejo Tequila
3/4 oz. Cointreau Liqueur
1/2 oz. Rose's Lime Juice
1 1/2 oz. sweet 'n' sour
Shake and strain
Lime wedge garnish

MARGARITA, HAWAIIAN
aka **Giggling Margarita**
House specialty glass, chilled
Rim glass with sugar (optional)
Pour ingredients into blender
1 1/4 oz. Sauza Blanco Tequila
1/2 oz. Disaronno Amaretto Liqueur
1/2 oz. Blue Curaçao
3-4 slices of cored pineapple
2 oz. sweet 'n' sour
Blend with ice
Lime and pineapple wedge garnish

MARGARITA, HERBA BUENA
aka **Margarita Mojito**
House specialty glass, chilled
Rim glass with salt (optional)
Muddle 5-6 mint leaves with
   1/2 oz. simple syrup then add ice
Pour ingredients into iced mixing glass
1 1/4 oz. Sauza Conmemorativo
   Añejo Tequila
1/2 oz. Hiram Walker Triple Sec
1/2 oz. Rose's Lime Juice
2 oz. lemon/lime soda
2 oz. sweet 'n' sour
Shake and strain
Lime wedge and mint sprig garnish

FINLANDIA® VODKA

Spirits had been distilled in Finland for over 400 years when the country enacted Prohibition. The ban mirrored what was happening in the United States at the time, and ended in 1932, at which point the state assumed control over the production of spirits. Thus began the storied existence of highly acclaimed FINLANDIA VODKA.

The vodka was originally produced at the historic Rajamäki Distillery, just outside of Helsinki, that had been producing vodka since 1888. In 1970, production moved to the state of the art facilities of the Koskenkorva Distillery.

Finlandia Vodka is distilled entirely from premium, 6-row barley and glacier-fed spring water. It is triple-distilled in continuous column stills, where it is rectified to 96% alcohol by volume, then diluted with the same glacial spring water to its bottle strength of 80 proof.

Finlandia is an exemplary neutral vodka possessing a silky texture, medium-weight body and a prominent bouquet of grain and dried herbs. It glides over the palate without a trace of harshness, filling the mouth with warmth before it slips away in a clean, crisp finish.

The distillery also produces two flavored vodkas, FINLANDIA ARCTIC CRANBERRY and FINLANDIA ARCTIC PINEAPPLE.

MARGARITA, HONEYDEW THIS
House specialty glass, chilled
Rim glass with sugar (optional)
Pour ingredients into blender
1 1/4 oz. Sauza Gold Tequila
1/2 oz. Rose's Lime Juice
1/2 cup diced honeydew melon
2 oz. sweet 'n' sour
Blend with ice
Honeydew slice garnish

MARGARITA, HORNI (1)
House specialty glass, ice
Rim glass with salt (optional)
Pour ingredients into iced mixing glass
1 1/2 oz. Sauza Hornitos Tequila
1/2 oz. Cointreau Liqueur
1/4 oz. Rose's Lime Juice
2 oz. fresh lime juice
2 oz. sweet 'n' sour
Shake and strain
Lime wedge garnish

MARGARITA, HORNI (2)
House specialty glass, ice
Rim glass with salt (optional)
Pour ingredients into iced mixing glass
1 1/4 oz. Sauza Hornitos Tequila
3/4 oz. DeKuyper Triple Sec
1/2 oz. Rose's Lime Juice
1/2 oz. cranberry juice
1 3/4 oz. sweet 'n' sour
Shake and strain
Lime wedge garnish

MARGARITA, ICE CREAM
House specialty glass, chilled
Pour ingredients into blender
1 1/4 oz. Hussong's Añejo Tequila
3/4 oz. Crème de Banana
1/2 oz. DJ Dotson Triple Sec
2 oz. sweet 'n' sour
1-2 scoops vanilla ice cream
Blend ingredients (with ice optional)
Orange slice and cherry garnish

MARGARITA, ITALIAN
House specialty glass, ice
Rim glass with sugar (optional)
Pour ingredients into iced mixing glass
1 1/4 oz. Gold Tequila
3/4 oz. Disaronno Amaretto Liqueur
1/2 oz. Hiram Walker Triple Sec
1/2 oz. orange juice
2 oz. sweet 'n' sour
Shake and strain
Lime wedge, orange slice and cherry garnish

MARGARITA, JALAPEÑO
aka **Jalapeñorita**
House specialty glass, ice
Rim glass with salt and pepper (optional)
Pour ingredients into iced mixing glass
1 1/4 oz. El Jimador Reposado Tequila
3/4 oz. Grand Marnier Liqueur
1/2 tsp. Tabasco Jalapeño Sauce
2 oz. sweet 'n' sour
Shake and strain
Lime wedge garnish

MARGARITA, JAMAICAN
Cocktail glass, chilled
Pour ingredients into iced mixing glass
1 1/4 oz. Appleton Estate V/X Jamaica Rum
3/4 oz. Cointreau Liqueur
1/2 oz. Rose's Lime Juice
1/2 oz. orange juice
1 1/2 oz. sweet 'n' sour
Shake and strain
Lime wedge garnish

MARGARITA, KAMIKAZE
aka **Kami 'Rita**
House specialty glass, ice
Rim glass with salt (optional)
Pour ingredients into iced mixing glass
1 oz. Sauza Hornitos Tequila
1 oz. Absolut Citron Vodka
1/2 oz. Cointreau Liqueur
1/2 oz. Rose's Lime Juice
1 1/2 oz. sweet 'n' sour
Shake and strain
Lime wedge garnish

MARGARITA, KENTUCKY
Cocktail glass, chilled
Pour ingredients into iced mixing glass
1 1/4 oz. Maker's Mark Bourbon
1/2 oz. Grand Marnier Liqueur
1/4 oz. fresh lime juice
1 1/2 oz. sweet 'n' sour
Shake and strain
Lime wedge garnish

MARGARITA, KEY LIME
Cocktail glass, chilled
Rim glass with salt (optional)
Pour ingredients into iced mixing glass
1 1/4 oz. Lime-infused Sauza Blanco Tequila
1/2 oz. DeKuyper Triple Sec
1/4 oz. Rose's Lime Juice
1 1/2 oz. sweet 'n' sour
Shake and strain
Lime wedge garnish

MARGARITA, LA BAMBA
House specialty glass, ice
Rim glass with sugar (optional)
Pour ingredients into iced mixing glass
1 1/4 oz. Sauza Conmemorativo
   Añejo Tequila
1/2 oz. Cointreau Liqueur
1/4 oz. grenadine
1 1/2 oz. pineapple juice
1 1/2 oz. orange juice
Shake and strain
Lemon wedge garnish

MARGARITA LA PERSEVERANCIA
Cocktail glass, chilled
Rim glass with salt (optional)
Pour ingredients into iced mixing glass
1 1/4 oz. Sauza Tres Generaciones
   Añejo Tequila
3/4 oz. Cointreau Liqueur
1 1/2 oz. sweet 'n' sour
Shake and strain
Lime wedge garnish

MARGARITA LA REYNA DEL PLAYA
House specialty glass, ice
Rim glass with salt (optional)
Pour ingredients into iced mixing glass
1 1/2 oz. Jose Cuervo Reserva
   de la Familia Tequila
3/4 oz. Lillet Blonde
1/2 oz. Midori Melon Liqueur
1/4 oz. pineapple juice
1/4 oz. orange juice
2 oz. sweet 'n' sour
Shake and strain
Lime wedge and orange slice garnish

MARGARITA, LIMONITA
House specialty glass, ice
Rim glass with salt (optional)
Pour ingredients into iced mixing glass
1 1/4 oz. Stolichnaya Limonnaya
   Russian Vodka
1/2 oz. Cointreau Liqueur
1/2 oz. Rose's Lime Juice
3/4 oz. cranberry juice
2 oz. sweet 'n' sour
Shake and strain
Lemon wedge garnish

EL JIMADOR® TEQUILA

In 1995, Mexico was in the throes of a prolonged economic slump. The folks at Herradura wanted to make a tequila that the people could afford and fully appreciate. So they created the brand, EL JIMADOR, and it now ranks among the best selling tequilas in Mexico.

The tequilas of Herradura and El Jimador share many similarities. Both brands are made on the Herradura estate from the same estate-grown blue agaves. They both undergo the same methods of fermentation, distillation and aging, although each process takes longer for Herradura Tequila.

The principle difference between the two brands is that Herradura is a 100% agave tequila, whereas El Jimador is a *mixto*, meaning that it contains 51% agave. Originally made entirely of agave, the change in formula was designed to make El Jimador more affordable.

The three versions of El Jimador Tequilas still retain a great deal of the Herradura "house style." EL JIMADOR SILVER TEQUILA is unaged, aromatic and loaded with spicy, energetic flavors. EL JIMADOR REPOSADO strikes a true balance between the fresh, spirited character of the silver tequila, and the mellow refinement of the añejo.

Ultra-premium EL JIMADOR AÑEJO is a superb, limited edition, 100% agave tequila aged in oak barrels for a minimum of one year.

MARGARITA, LUNA AZUL
House specialty glass, ice
Rim glass with salt (optional)
Pour ingredients into iced mixing glass
1 1/4 oz. Casa Noble Reposado Tequila
3/4 oz. Blue Curaçao
1/2 oz. Cointreau Liqueur
1/2 oz. Rose's Lime Juice
1 1/2 oz. sweet 'n' sour
Shake and strain
Lime wedge garnish

MARGARITA, MAD RUSSIAN
House specialty glass, ice
Rim glass with salt (optional)
Pour ingredients into iced mixing glass
1 1/4 oz. Sauza Gold Tequila
3/4 oz. Blue Curaçao
1/2 oz. Grand Marnier Liqueur
1/2 oz. cranberry juice
2 oz. sweet 'n' sour
Shake and strain
Lime wedge garnish

MARGARITA, MALTA'S GRAPPARITA
House specialty glass, ice
Rim glass with salt (optional)
Pour ingredients into iced mixing glass
1 1/4 oz. Grappa
3/4 oz. Hiram Walker Triple Sec
1/2 oz. Rose's Lime Juice
1/2 oz. orange juice
2 oz. sweet 'n' sour
Shake and strain
Lime wedge garnish

MARGARITA, MANGO
aka **Mangorita**
House specialty glass, chilled
Rim glass with salt (optional)
Pour ingredients into blender
1 1/4 oz. Sauza Gold Tequila
1/2 cup mango cubes
1/2 oz. Rose's Lime Juice
2 oz. sweet 'n' sour
Blend with ice
Lime wedge garnish

MARGARITA MARTINI
Cocktail glass, chilled
Rim glass with salt (optional)
Pour ingredients into iced mixing glass
1 1/4 oz. Sauza Tres Generaciones
    Añejo Tequila
1/4 oz. Cointreau Liqueur
1/4 oz. Rose's Lime Juice
1/4 oz. sweet 'n' sour
Shake and strain
Lime wedge garnish

MARGARITA MAS FINO
House specialty glass, ice
Rim glass with salt (optional)
Pour ingredients into iced mixing glass
3/4 oz. El Tesoro Añejo Tequila
3/4 oz. El Tesoro Silver Tequila
3/4 oz. Cointreau Liqueur
1/2 oz. orange juice
1/2 oz. Rose's Lime Juice
1 1/2 oz. sweet 'n' sour
Shake and strain
Lime wedge garnish

MARGARITA, MAUI (1)
House specialty glass, chilled
Rim glass with salt (optional)
Pour ingredients into blender
1 1/4 oz. Sauza Gold Tequila
1/2 oz. Hiram Walker Triple Sec
1/2 oz. Rose's Lime Juice
1 1/2 oz. orange juice
2 oz. sweet 'n' sour
Blend with ice
Lime wedge garnish

MARGARITA, MAUI (2)
House specialty glass, ice
Rim glass with salt (optional)
Pour ingredients into iced mixing glass
1 1/4 oz. Sauza Gold Tequila
3/4 oz. Grand Marnier Liqueur
1/2 oz. pineapple juice
1 1/2 oz. sweet 'n' sour
Shake and strain
Lime wedge garnish

MARGARITA, MAXIMILIAN
House specialty glass, ice
Rim glass with salt (optional)
Pour ingredients into iced mixing glass
1 1/4 oz. Chinaco Añejo Tequila
3/4 oz. Cointreau Liqueur
1/2 oz. Rose's Lime Juice
1/4 oz. orange juice
1 1/2 oz. sweet 'n' sour
Shake and strain
Lime wedge garnish

MARGARITA, MELTDOWN
House specialty glass, chilled
Rim glass with salt (optional)
Pour ingredients into blender
1 1/4 oz. Sauza Blanco Tequila
1/2 oz. Grand Marnier Liqueur
1/2 oz. Rose's Lime Juice
1/2 oz. cranberry juice
1 1/2 oz. pureed raspberries
2 oz. sweet 'n' sour
Blend with ice
Float 3/4 oz. Chambord Liqueur
Lime wedge garnish

MARGARITA, MEZCAL
House specialty glass, ice
Rim glass with salt (optional)
Pour ingredients into iced mixing glass
1 1/4 oz. Añejo Mezcal
1/2 oz. Brandy
2-3 dashes Peychaud bitters
1/2 oz. simple syrup
2 oz. sweet 'n' sour
Shake and strain
Lime wedge garnish

MARGARITA, MIDNIGHT MADNESS
House specialty glass, chilled
Rim glass with salt (optional)
Object is to create a 2-layer drink
1—*Pour ingredients into blender*
   3/4 oz. Sauza Gold Tequila
   3/4 oz. Blue Curaçao
   1/2 oz. Rose's Lime Juice
   1 1/2 oz. sweet 'n' sour
Blend with ice
Pour first drink into glass 1/2 full
2—*Pour ingredients into blender*
   3/4 oz. Sauza Gold Tequila
   3/4 oz. Chambord Liqueur
   1 oz. cranberry juice
   1 oz. sweet 'n' sour
Blend with ice
Pour second drink on top of first drink
Lime wedge garnish

MARGARITA, MIDORI
aka **Melon Margarita, Green Iguana**
Cocktail glass, chilled
Rim glass with salt (optional)
Pour ingredients into iced mixing glass
1 oz. Sauza Hornitos Tequila
1 oz. Midori Melon Liqueur
1 1/2 oz. sweet 'n' sour
Shake and strain
Lime wedge garnish

ROCKS DRINKS

The Rocks category is a popular type of mixed drinks. They are perhaps best illustrated by the venerable black Russian, a classic concoction made from a base of vodka flavored with Kahlúa presented in an iced 7 ounce glass.

Rocks drinks are normally prepared with a liquor base of 1 1/2 to 2 ounces of liquor topped with a 1/2 to 3/4 ounce portion of liqueur. The key to their enduring popularity is the synergy created by marrying a liquor with a complementary liqueur. Excellent examples include the rusty nail (Drambuie and Scotch), the brave bull (tequila and Kahlúa), the Boss (bourbon and Disaronno Amaretto).

Nearly all of these drinks are built directly into an iced 7 ounce glass. The liquor portion is always poured first, followed by the liqueur. Being the denser, heavier product, the liqueur will settle through the layer of liquor, making any further mixing unnecessary.

Some of the drink recipes in this category—namely the gimlet, kamikaze and stinger—may be requested served straight-up. Other liquor and liqueur combinations are served neat, in which case the ingredients are poured directly into the service glass without ice.

In some instances, cognacs, brandies and liqueurs, such as Grand Marnier or Extase XO, are requested served neat in a heated snifter. This is accomplished by filling the glass with hot water, allowing it to sit for a minute, then emptying the glass out prior to making the drink. The heated snifter will help the brandy release its bouquet. Before serving, place a cocktail napkin over the mouth of the glass to help keep it warm and to retain the bouquet until the drink is served.

MARGARITA, MIMOSA
aka **Mimosarita**
Tulip champagne glass, chilled
Pour ingredients into iced mixing glass
1 1/2 oz. Sauza Gold Tequila
1/2 oz. Hiram Walker Triple Sec
1/4 oz. Rose's Lime Juice
1 oz. orange juice
1 oz. sweet 'n' sour
Shake and strain
Fill with champagne
Orange twist garnish

MARGARITA, MONTEGO
Cocktail glass, chilled
Pour ingredients into iced mixing glass
1 1/2 oz. Appleton Estate V/X Jamaica Rum
3/4 oz. Citrónge Orange Liqueur
1/2 oz. Rose's Lime Juice
1/2 oz. orange juice
1 1/2 oz. sweet 'n' sour
Shake and strain
Lime and lemon wedge garnish

MARGARITA, MOSCOW
House specialty glass, ice
Rim glass with salt (optional)
Pour ingredients into iced mixing glass
1 1/2 oz. Smirnoff Vodka
1/2 oz. Hiram Walker Triple Sec
1/2 oz. Rose's Lime Juice
2 oz. sweet 'n' sour
Shake and strain
Lime wedge garnish

MARGARITA, MOUNT FUGI
House specialty glass, ice
Rim glass with salt (optional)
Pour ingredients into iced mixing glass
2 oz. NapaSaki Saké
1/2 oz. DeKuyper Triple Sec
2 oz. sweet 'n' sour
Shake and strain
Lemon wheel garnish

MARGARITA, MY BABY GRAND
Cocktail glass, chilled
Rim glass with salt (optional)
Pour ingredients into iced mixing glass
2 oz. Casa Noble Reposado Tequila
3/4 oz. Grand Marnier Liqueur
1/2 oz. Rose's Lime Juice
1/2 oz. fresh lime juice
Stir and strain
Lime wedge garnish

MARGARITA, NEON WATERMELON

House specialty glass, chilled
Rim glass with sugar (optional)
Pour ingredients into blender
1 1/4 oz. Sauza Blanco Tequila
1 oz. Midori Melon Liqueur
1/2 oz. DeKuyper Triple Sec
1/2 cup frozen seedless watermelon cubes
3 oz. sweet 'n' sour
Blend with ice
Watermelon slice garnish

MARGARITA, NORMANDY

aka **Apple Margarita**
House specialty glass, chilled
Rim glass with cinnamon and sugar
Pour ingredients into blender
1 oz. Sauza Blanco Tequila
1 oz. Calvados Apple Brandy
1/2 oz. Mandarine Napoléon Liqueur
1/2 oz. apple juice or cider
1/2 oz. apple sauce (optional)
1 1/2 oz. sweet 'n' sour
Blend with ice
Apple wedge garnish

MARGARITA, ORANGITA

House specialty glass, ice
Rim glass with sugar (optional)
Pour ingredients into iced mixing glass
1 1/4 oz. Sauza Gold Tequila
1/2 oz. Hiram Walker Triple Sec
1/4 oz. Rose's Lime Juice
1/2 oz. sweet 'n' sour
1 1/2 oz. orange juice
Shake and strain
Lime wedge garnish

MARGARITA, ORIGINAL ™

aka **Margarita Sames' Margarita**
Cocktail glass, chilled
Rim glass with salt
Pour ingredients into iced mixing glass
1 1/2 oz. Silver Tequila
3/4 oz. Cointreau Liqueur
3/4 oz. fresh lime juice
Shake and strain
Lime wedge garnish

MARGARITA, OSCARITA

House specialty glass, ice
Rim glass with sugar (optional)
Pour ingredients into iced mixing glass
1 1/4 oz. Sauza Gold Tequila
3/4 oz. Cointreau Liqueur
1/4 oz. Disaronno Amaretto Liqueur
1 1/2 oz. orange juice
1 1/2 oz. sweet 'n' sour
Shake and strain
Lime wedge garnish

MARGARITA, PASSION

House specialty glass, chilled
Rim glass with salt (optional)
Pour ingredients into iced mixing glass
1 1/2 oz. Alizé de France
1 oz. Sauza Tres Generaciones Añejo Tequila
1/2 oz. Cointreau Liqueur
1 1/2 oz. sweet 'n' sour
1 1/2 oz. cranberry juice
Shake and strain
Lime wedge garnish

MARGARITA, PEAR

aka **Pearita**
House specialty glass, chilled
Rim glass with salt (optional)
Pour ingredients into blender
1 1/2 oz. Sauza Blanco Tequila
1/2 oz. Hiram Walker Triple Sec
1 whole canned Bartlett pear
1/2 oz. Rose's Lime Juice
1 1/2 oz. sweet 'n' sour
Blend with ice
Lime wheel garnish

MARGARITA PICANTE

House specialty glass, ice
Rim glass with salt and pepper (optional)
Pour ingredients into iced mixing glass
3/4 oz. Sauza Hornitos Tequila
3/4 oz. Absolut Peppar Vodka
1/2 oz. DeKuyper Triple Sec
1-2 dashes Tabasco Sauce
2 pinches black pepper
4-6 drops jalapeño pepper juice
2 oz. sweet 'n' sour
Shake and strain
Small jalapeño peppers garnish

MARGARITA, PICOSITA

House specialty glass, ice
Rim glass with salt and pepper (optional)
Pour ingredients into iced mixing glass
3/4 oz. Hussong's Reposado Tequila
3/4 oz. Pepper-infused Silver Tequila
1/2 oz. DeKuyper Triple Sec
1/2 oz. Rose's Lime Juice
1/2 oz. orange juice
1 3/4 oz. sweet 'n' sour
Shake and strain
Lime wedge and small
    jalapeño pepper garnish

KÉKÉ BEACH®
KEY LIME CREAM LIQUEUR

Few products have enjoyed the international success that Baileys Irish Cream has. Scores of other cream-based liqueurs have come and gone, with most attempting to replicate Baileys now famous chocolate, whiskey and fresh dairy cream formula. Instead of mirroring something that had already been perfected, the creators of KÉKÉ BEACH KEY LIME CREAM LIQUEUR set off in an entirely different direction altogether. Fortunately for us, they did.

Their objective was to capture the flavor of a popular dessert, namely the key lime pie, in a cream liqueur. You'll know with your first sip that they hit the mark spot on.

KéKé Beach is virtually a key lime pie in a glass. It is made from a base of pure grain, neutral spirits with a blend of cream and natural flavorings, the exact composition of which is a proprietary secret.

The liqueur has an exotic lime green color and a creamy bouquet of citrus, vanilla and spice. KéKé Beach has a surprisingly lightweight body that immediately delivers on the promise of key lime pie, down to the tantalizing hint of graham cracker.

KéKé Beach is a natural behind the bar, and in the hands of a skilled mixologist, it's a slam dunk.

MARGARITA, PINEAPPLE
aka **Piñarita**
Cocktail or house specialty glass, chilled
Pour ingredients into blender
1 1/4 oz. Sauza Blanco Tequila
3/4 oz. Hiram Walker Triple Sec
1/2 cup pineapple cubes
1 1/2 oz. pineapple juice
Blend with ice
Lime wedge garnish

MARGARITA, PINK
House specialty glass, ice
Rim glass with salt (optional)
Pour ingredients into iced mixing glass
1 1/4 oz. Silver Tequila
3/4 oz. Triple Sec
1/2 oz. Rose's Lime Juice
1/2 oz. grenadine
1 1/2 oz. sweet 'n' sour
Shake and strain
Lime wedge garnish

MARGARITA, PINK CADILLAC
House specialty glass, ice
Rim glass with salt (optional)
Pour ingredients into iced mixing glass
1 1/4 oz. Jose Cuervo 1800 Tequila
1/2 oz. Cointreau Liqueur
1/2 oz. Rose's Lime Juice
1/2 oz. cranberry juice
1 1/2 oz. sweet 'n' sour
Shake and strain
Lime wedge garnish

MARGARITA, PRESIDENTÉ
House specialty glass, ice
Rim glass with salt (optional)
Pour ingredients into iced mixing glass
1 oz. Sauza Tres Generaciones Añejo Tequila
1 oz. Presidenté Brandy
3/4 oz. Cointreau Liqueur
1/4 oz. orange juice
1/2 oz. Rose's Lime Juice
2 oz. sweet 'n' sour
Shake and strain
Lime wedge and orange slice garnish

MARGARITA, PRICKLY PEAR (1)
House specialty glass, chilled
Rim glass with salt (optional)
Pour ingredients into blender
1 1/4 oz. Sauza Blanco Tequila
1/2 oz. DeKuyper Triple Sec
1/2 oz. Rose's Lime Juice
1/4 oz. grenadine
3/4 oz. prickly pear juice
1 1/2 oz. sweet 'n' sour
Blend with ice
Lime wedge garnish

MARGARITA, PRICKLY PEAR (2)

House specialty glass, chilled
Rim glass with salt (optional)
Pour ingredients into blender
1 1/4 oz. Sauza Blanco Tequila
1/2 oz. Hiram Walker Triple Sec
3/4 oz. Rose's Lime Juice
1 1/2 oz. prickly pear juice
2 oz. sweet 'n' sour
Blend with ice
Lime wheel garnish

MARGARITA, PRICKLY PINEAPPLE

Cocktail glass, chilled
Rim glass with salt (optional)
Pour ingredients into iced mixing glass
1 1/4 oz. Sauza Conmemorativo
  Añejo Tequila
1/2 oz. Grand Marnier Liqueur
1/2 oz. prickly pear syrup
3/4 oz. pineapple juice
1 1/2 oz. sweet 'n' sour
Shake and strain
Lime wedge garnish

MARGARITA PRIMERO CLASE

House specialty glass, ice
Rim glass with salt (optional)
Pour ingredients into iced mixing glass
1 1/4 oz. El Tesoro Añejo Tequila
3/4 oz. Cointreau Liqueur
1/2 oz. Rose's Lime Juice
1 1/2 oz. sweet 'n' sour
Shake and strain
Lime wedge garnish

MARGARITA PUNCH

Punch Bowl (256 oz.), quarter-full with ice
Pour ingredients into punch bowl
2 liters Sauza Gold Tequila
1.5 (750ml) bottles of chilled champagne
20 oz. Hiram Walker Triple Sec
10 oz. Rose's Lime Juice
10 oz. orange juice
5 oz. fresh lime juice
18 oz. ginger ale
45 oz. sweet 'n' sour
Stir thoroughly
Lime, lemon and orange slice garnish

MARGARITA, PURPLE (1)

aka **Purple Gecko, Purple Haze Margarita**
House specialty glass, ice
Rim glass with salt (optional)
Pour ingredients into iced mixing glass
1 1/4 oz. Reposado Tequila
1/2 oz. Blue Curaçao
1/2 oz. Chambord Liqueur
1/2 oz. Rose's Lime Juice
1 oz. cranberry juice
1 1/2 oz. sweet 'n' sour
Shake and strain
Lime wedge garnish

MARGARITA, PURPLE (2)

House specialty glass, ice
Rim glass with salt (optional)
Pour ingredients into iced mixing glass
1 1/4 oz. El Jimador Reposado Tequila
3/4 oz. Razzmatazz Raspberry Liqueur
1/2 oz. Rémy Red
1/2 oz. Rose's Lime Juice
1 oz. Welch's 100% Grape Juice
1 1/2 oz. sweet 'n' sour
Shake and strain
Lime wedge garnish

MARGARITA, RASPBERRY

House specialty glass, chilled
Rim glass with sugar (optional)
Pour ingredients into blender
1 1/2 oz. Sauza Gold Tequila
3/4 oz. DJ Dotson Triple Sec
1 1/2 oz. raspberry puree
1 1/2 oz. orange juice
1 1/2 oz. sweet 'n' sour
Blend with ice
Lime wedge and orange slice garnish

MARGARITA, RASPBERRY TORTE

House specialty glass, chilled
Rim glass with sugar (optional)
Object is to create a 3-layer drink
1—Pour ingredients into blender
  1 1/2 oz. Sauza Blanco Tequila
  1/2 oz. Hiram Walker Triple Sec
  2 oz. sweet 'n' sour
Blend with ice
Pour blended drink into glass 1/2 full
2—Add in glass
  2 oz. raspberry puree
3—Slowly fill glass with blended drink to create a third layer
Lime wedge and orange slice garnish

SIGNATORY® SINGLE MALT SCOTCH WHISKY

Stocking a balanced selection of single malt Scotches can be a formidable assignment. While carrying 100 different whiskies is bound to satisfy every request, most operators, however, opt instead to offer their clientele a balanced, more discriminating selection, one that best represents the varieties of styles of each Scotch-producing region.

Thus the need for SIGNATORY REGIONALS, an unrivaled set of 6 independently bottled single malt whiskies, each of which best captures and preserves the malt heritage of their birthplace. Founded in Edinburgh, Signatory has ascended into one of the preeminent private bottlers of rare malts. The whiskies featured in the Regionals collection were crafted by the finest distillers in Scotland and further aged by Signatory.

The one detail missing from these exceptional whiskies is a heavy price tag. Without the identity of the distiller on the label, the whiskies are priced at a fraction of other comparable single malts. It may be one of the last spectacular values.

The Signatory Regionals are a guided tour of the best and brightest whiskies Scotland has to offer. It includes the Highlands, Orkney Islands, Isle of Mull, Islay, Campbeltown and the Lowlands.

These incomparable single malts are guaranteed to exceed the expectations of Scotch connoisseurs and aficionados alike.

MARGARITA, RED CACTUS
House specialty glass, chilled
Rim glass with sugar (optional)
Pour ingredients into blender
1 1/4 oz. Sauza Gold Tequila
1/2 oz. DeKuyper Triple Sec
1/2 oz. Chambord Liqueur
1/2 oz. Rose's Lime Juice
1/2 cup frozen raspberries
1 1/2 oz. sweet 'n' sour
Blend with ice
Lime wedge garnish

MARGARITA, RIO GRANDE
House specialty glass, ice
Rim glass with salt (optional)
Pour ingredients into iced mixing glass
3/4 oz. Sauza Hornitos Tequila
3/4 oz. Tia Maria
3/4 oz. Frangelico Liqueur
1 1/2 oz. orange juice
1 1/2 oz. sweet 'n' sour
Shake and strain
Lime wedge garnish

MARGARITA, RIVER SPEY
Cocktail glass, chilled
Rim glass with salt (optional)
Pour ingredients into iced mixing glass
1 1/4 oz. Scotch Whisky
1/2 oz. Cointreau Liqueur
1 1/2 oz. sweet 'n' sour
Shake and strain
Lime wedge garnish

MARGARITA, ROCKY POINT
Cocktail glass, chilled
Rim glass with salt (optional)
Pour ingredients into iced mixing glass
1 1/4 oz. Jose Cuervo Especial Tequila
3/4 oz. Tropico
3/4 oz. Damiana Liqueur
1/2 oz. fresh lime juice
1 1/2 oz. sweet 'n' sour
Shake and strain
Lime wedge garnish

MARGARITA, ROSARITA
House specialty glass, ice
Rim glass with salt (optional)
Pour ingredients into iced mixing glass
1 1/4 oz. Sauza Conmemorativo
    Añejo Tequila
3/4 oz. Grand Marnier Liqueur
1/2 oz. cranberry juice
1/2 oz. Rose's Lime Juice
1 1/2 oz. sweet 'n' sour
Shake and strain
Lime wedge garnish

MARGARITA, ROSE

House specialty glass, chilled
Rim glass with sugar (optional)
Pour ingredients into blender
2 oz. Tequila Rose Cream Liqueur
1 oz. Gran Gala Orange Liqueur
1/2 oz. Rose's Lime Juice
2 oz. sweet 'n' sour
2 oz. frozen strawberries
Blend with ice
Lime wedge garnish

MARGARITA, SAKÉ

Cocktail glass, chilled
Rim glass with salt (optional)
Pour ingredients into iced mixing glass
1 1/4 oz. NapaSaki Saké
3/4 oz. Grand Marnier Liqueur
1/2 oz. Rose's Lime Juice
2 oz. sweet 'n' sour
Shake and strain
Lime wheel garnish

MARGARITA, SANGRITA

aka **Sangria 'Rita**
House specialty glass, ice
Rim glass with sugar (optional)
Pour ingredients into iced mixing glass
1 oz. Sauza Blanco Tequila
2 oz. Dry Red Wine
1/2 oz. DeKuyper Triple Sec
1/2 oz. DeKuyper Peachtree Schnapps
1/2 oz. Rose's Lime Juice
2 oz. sweet 'n' sour
Shake and strain
Lime, lemon and orange slice garnish

MARGARITA, SANTA RITA

House specialty glass, ice
Rim glass with salt (optional)
Pour ingredients into iced mixing glass
1 1/4 oz. Herradura Reposado Tequila
1/2 oz. Chambord Liqueur
1/2 oz. DeKuyper Peachtree Schnapps
2 oz. sweet 'n' sour
Shake and strain
Lime wedge garnish

MARGARITA, SANTIAGO

House specialty glass, ice
Rim glass with pink lemonade mix
   (optional)
Pour ingredients into iced mixing glass
1 1/4 oz. Herradura Silver Tequila
3/4 oz. Midori Melon Liqueur
1/2 oz. Mandarine Napoléon Liqueur
1/2 oz. Rose's Lime Juice
1/4 oz. grenadine
1 1/2 oz. grapefruit juice
2 oz. sweet 'n' sour
Shake and strain
Orange slice garnish

MARGARITA, SAUZA PURE

House specialty glass, ice
Rim glass with salt (optional)
Pour ingredients into iced mixing glass
1 1/2 oz. Sauza Hornitos Tequila
3/4 oz. Hiram Walker Triple Sec
1 1/2 oz. fresh lime juice
Shake and strain
Lime wedge garnish

MARGARITA, SEA BREEZE

House specialty glass, chilled
Rim glass with salt (optional)
Pour ingredients into iced mixing glass
1 3/4 oz. Sauza Conmemorativo
   Añejo Tequila
3/4 oz. Gran Gala Orange Liqueur
1/2 oz. Rose's Lime Juice
1 oz. sweet 'n' sour
1 oz. cranberry juice
2 oz. grapefruit juice
Shake and strain
Lime wedge garnish

MARGARITA, SEÑORITA

House specialty glass, ice
Rim glass with salt (optional)
Pour ingredients into iced mixing glass
1 1/4 oz. Herradura Reposado Tequila
1/2 oz. Cointreau Liqueur
1/4 oz. Rose's Lime Juice
1/4 oz. fresh lime juice
1 1/2 oz. sweet 'n' sour
Shake and strain
Float 3/4 oz. Herradura Reposado Tequila
Lime wedge garnish

VYA™ PREFERRED CALIFORNIA SWEET VERMOUTH

Don't fall into the trap of thinking that any brand of vermouth will do. The difference between a great vermouth and one that's merely adequate is enormous. Winemaker Andrew Quady of Madera, California, looked to produce a pair of premium vermouths in a style more in keeping with today's tastes. In 1998, after several years of development, Quady introduced VYA PREFERRED CALIFORNIA SWEET VERMOUTH.

The vermouth is made from a blend of Orange Muscat, French Colombard and Valdepenas varietal wines that are infused with herbs, spices, flowers, and citrus. Its beautiful tawny hue is enhanced with the addition of port. It has a lush body and a tantalizing semi-sweet bouquet. The palate is a savory array of spicy and tangy citrus flavors. It is fortified to 16% abv.

VYA PREFERRED CALIFORNIA EXTRA DRY VERMOUTH is crisp, light and equally sensational. It is made from a blend of French Colombard and Orange Muscat white wines that are infused with highly aromatic herbs, flowers and plants, and fortified to 18% abv. The vermouth has a complex floral and fruity bouquet and a dry, mouth-filling palate laced with spice and citrus.

Armed with Vya Vermouths, your martinis and Manhattans will become the tingling combination of wine and spirit they were originally intended to be.

MARGARITA, SHOOTAH
aka **Shootah 'Rita**
Presentation shot glass, chilled
Rim glass with salt (optional)
Pour ingredients into iced mixing glass
1 oz. Sauza Hornitos Tequila
1/2 oz. DeKuyper Triple Sec
1/4 oz. sweet 'n' sour
1/4 oz. fresh lime juice
Shake and strain
Lime wedge garnish

MARGARITA, SONORAN
House specialty glass, ice
Rim glass with salt (optional)
Pour ingredients into iced mixing glass
1 1/4 oz. Sauza Tres Generaciones
    Añejo Tequila
3/4 oz. Grand Marnier Liqueur
1/2 oz. Rose's Lime Juice
1 1/2 oz. sweet 'n' sour
Shake and strain
Lime wedge garnish

MARGARITA, SONORAN SPITTOON
Cocktail glass, chilled
Rim glass with salt and pepper (optional)
Pour ingredients into iced mixing glass
1 1/4 oz. Pepper-infused Silver Tequila
1/2 oz. Triple Sec
1/2 oz. Rose's Lime Juice
1 1/2 oz. sweet 'n' sour
Shake and strain
Lime wedge and small
    jalapeño pepper garnish

MARGARITA, SPANISH
aka **Gold Rush Margarita**
House specialty glass, ice
Rim glass with salt (optional)
Pour ingredients into iced mixing glass
1 1/2 oz. Herradura Reposado Tequila
3/4 oz. Licor 43 (Cuarenta y Tres)
1/2 oz. Rose's Lime Juice
1 1/2 oz. sweet 'n' sour
Shake and strain
Lime wedge garnish

MARGARITA SPLASH
House specialty glass, ice
Rim glass with salt (optional)
Pour ingredients into iced mixing glass
1 1/4 oz. Sauza Blanco Tequila
1/2 oz. Hiram Walker Triple Sec
1 1/2 oz. fresh lime juice
1 1/2 oz. sweet 'n' sour
Shake and strain
Fill with club soda
Lime wedge garnish

MARGARITA, STRAWBERRY LOVER'S

House specialty glass, chilled
Rim glass with sugar (optional)
Pour ingredients into blender
1 oz. Sauza Blanco Tequila
1 oz. Stolichnaya Strasberi Russian Vodka
1/2 oz. Mandarine Napoléon Liqueur
1/3 cup fresh or frozen strawberries
2 oz. sweet 'n' sour
Blend with ice
Strawberry garnish

MARGARITA, SUNNY

House specialty glass, chilled
Rim glass with salt (optional)
Pour ingredients into blender
1 1/4 oz. Sauza Gold Tequila
3/4 oz. DJ Dotson Triple Sec
1/2 oz. Rose's Lime Juice
2 oz. sweet 'n' sour
2 scoops orange sorbet
Blend ingredients (with ice optional)
Lime wedge garnish

MARGARITA, TEA-ARITA-IT

House specialty glass, ice
Rim glass with salt (optional)
Pour ingredients into iced mixing glass
1 1/4 oz. Sauza Blanco Tequila
1/2 oz. DeKuyper Triple Sec
1/2 oz. Rose's Lime Juice
2 oz. iced tea
2 oz. sweet 'n' sour
Shake and strain
Lime and lemon wedge garnish

MARGARITA, TEAL

House specialty glass, ice
Rim glass with salt (optional)
Pour ingredients into iced mixing glass
1 1/4 oz. Sauza Hornitos Tequila
1/2 oz. Grand Marnier Liqueur
1/2 oz. Blue Curaçao
1/2 oz. cranberry juice
1 1/2 oz. sweet 'n' sour
Shake and strain
Lime wedge garnish

MARGARITA, TRES COMPADRES

House specialty glass, ice
Rim glass with salt (optional)
Pour ingredients into iced mixing glass
1 1/4 oz. Sauza Conmemorativo
   Añejo Tequila
1/2 oz. Cointreau Liqueur
1/2 oz. Chambord Liqueur
1/2 oz. Rose's Lime Juice
3/4 oz. fresh lime juice
3/4 oz. orange juice
3/4 oz. grapefruit juice
Shake and strain
Lime wedge garnish

MARGARITA, TRIPLE GOLD

House specialty glass, ice
Rim glass with salt (optional)
Pour ingredients into iced mixing glass
1 1/2 oz. Sauza Tres Generaciones
   Añejo Tequila
1/2 oz. Cointreau Liqueur
1 1/2 oz. sweet 'n' sour
Shake and strain
Float 3/4 oz. Goldschläger
Lime wedge garnish

MARGARITA, TUACA

Cocktail glass, chilled
Rim glass with sugar (optional)
Pour ingredients into iced mixing glass
1 oz. Farias Silver Tequila
1 oz. Tuaca
1 1/2 oz. sweet 'n' sour
Splash lemon/lime soda (optional)
Shake and strain
Lime wedge garnish

MARGARITA, TWO-TONED

House specialty glass, 3/4 fill with ice
Rim glass with salt (optional)
Pour ingredients into iced mixing glass
1 1/2 oz. Sauza Hornitos Tequila
3/4 oz. DeKuyper Triple Sec
1/2 oz. Rose's Lime Juice
1 1/2 oz. orange juice
2 oz. sweet 'n' sour
Shake, strain and fill glass 3/4 full
Pour remaining contents into blender
Add 1 oz. Chambord or
   Midori Melon Liqueur
*Blend with ice and pour blended drink
   on top of iced margarita*
Lime wedge garnish

VAN HOO® VODKA

While VAN HOO VODKA was introduced in 1996, its origins can be traced to the beginning of the 19th century in Eeklo, Belgium. It was then that the Van Hoorebeke family began distilling a spirit called jenever—an early relative of gin. The first step in the production of jenever was the distillation of high quality, neutral grain spirits, which eventually gave birth to award-winning Van Hoo Vodka.

The vodka is produced at the Van Hoorebeke Distillery, world renowned for making Mandarine Napoléon Liqueur. It is the oldest distillery in Belgium, having been rebuilt in 1815 after the original building was destroyed in the battle of Waterloo.

Van Hoo Vodka is distilled entirely from grain and soft, spring water. The first distillation takes place in an alembic still and results in a full-bodied spirit with a robust, flavorful character. The vodka is then triple-distilled in a column still, a process that dramatically lightens its body and temperament. Lastly, the vodka is repeatedly filtered through charcoal to eliminate any trace congeners or impurities.

Van Hoo is a superb vodka with a medium-weight body and fetching bouquet of citrus, cocoa and grain. The semi-sweet palate is endowed with light, delicate floral flavors and notes of quinine and lemon. The finish is warm and long lasting.

MARGARITA, ULTIMATE SHOT
aka **Ultimate 'Rita Shot**
Presentation shot glass, chilled
Rim glass with salt (optional)
Pour ingredients into iced mixing glass
3/4 oz. Sauza Tres Generaciones
   Añejo Tequila
3/4 oz. Cointreau Liqueur
1/4 oz. sweet 'n' sour
1/4 oz. fresh lime juice
Shake and strain
Lime wedge garnish

MARGARITA, VINTNER'S
House specialty glass, ice
Rim glass with salt (optional)
Pour ingredients into iced mixing glass
3 oz. Dry White Wine
1/2 oz. Triple Sec
1/2 oz. Rose's Lime Juice
1/2 oz. orange juice
2 oz. sweet 'n' sour
Shake and strain
Lime wedge and orange slice garnish

MARGARITA, VIRGIN (1)
Cocktail glass, chilled
Rim glass with salt (optional)
Pour ingredients into iced mixing glass
2 oz. sweet 'n' sour
1/2 oz. DJ Dotson Triple Sec
1 oz. orange juice
3/4 oz. Rose's Lime Juice
Shake and strain
Lime wedge garnish

MARGARITA, VIRGIN (2)
House specialty glass, ice
Pour ingredients into iced mixing glass
1 oz. DJ Dotson Triple Sec
2 oz. sweet 'n' sour
1/2 oz. Rose's Lime Juice
1/2 oz. orange juice
Shake and strain
Lime wedge garnish

MARGARITA, WATERMELON
House specialty glass, chilled
Rim glass with sugar (optional)
Pour ingredients into blender
1 1/4 oz. Sauza Blanco Tequila
3/4 oz. DeKuyper Triple Sec
3/4 oz. DeKuyper Watermelon Pucker
1/2 cup frozen seedless watermelon cubes
3 oz. sweet 'n' sour
Blend with ice
Watermelon slice garnish

MARGARITA, ZINFUL

House specialty glass, ice
Rim glass with salt (optional)
Pour ingredients into iced mixing glass
1 1/4 oz. Sauza Gold Tequila
3 oz. White Zinfandel
1/2 oz. Chambord Liqueur
1 oz. sweet 'n' sour
1/2 oz. Rose's Lime Juice
1 1/2 oz. orange juice
Shake and strain
Lime wedge and orange slice garnish

MARGARITA, Z-RATED

House specialty glass, ice
Rim glass with salt (optional)
Pour ingredients into iced mixing glass
1/2 oz. Zafarrancho Silver Tequila
1/2 oz. Zafarrancho Gold Tequila
1/2 oz. Cointreau Liqueur
1/2 oz. Rose's Lime Juice
1/2 oz. orange juice
1 1/2 oz. sweet 'n' sour
Shake and strain
Float 3/4 oz. Zafarrancho Reposado Tequila
Lime wedge garnish

MARGO MOORE

Bucket glass, ice
Build in glass
1 1/2 oz. Brandy
3/4 oz. Light Rum
1/2 oz. Blue Curaçao
Fill with bitter lemon soda

MARIACHI LOCO

Bucket glass, ice
Pour ingredients into iced mixing glass
1 1/4 oz. Alizé de France
3/4 oz. Sauza Tres Generaciones
   Añejo Tequila
1/4 oz. Rose's Lime Juice
1 1/2 oz. sweet 'n' sour
2 oz. cranberry juice
Shake and strain
Lime wedge garnish

MARIA SANGRITA

House specialty glass, ice
Rim glass with salt (optional)
Build in glass
1 1/2 oz. Tequila
1/2 oz. fresh lime juice
2 pinches each, salt and black pepper
1/2 tsp. grated red onion
Fill with Sangrita Mix
Lime wedge garnish
Note: See **Sangrita Mix**

MARITIME SUNRISE

Bucket glass, ice
Build in glass
2 oz. Original Cristall Russian Vodka
4 oz. grapefruit juice
1 oz. cranberry juice
Float 3/4 oz. Chambord Liqueur

MARQUIS

Rocks glass, ice
Build in glass
3/4 oz. B & B Liqueur
3/4 oz. Kahlúa Coffee Liqueur
1/4 oz. Mandarine Napoléon Liqueur
1/2 oz. half & half cream

MARSEILLES STOCKINGS

Brandy snifter, heated
Build in glass
1 1/2 oz. Courvoisier V.S.O.P. Cognac
3/4 oz. Extase XO Liqueur

MARTINI

Cocktail glass, chilled
Pour ingredients into iced mixing glass
6 drops Dry Vermouth
1 1/2 oz. Gin
Stir and strain
Olives or lemon twist garnish

MARTINI, ABSOLUT MANDRIN

Cocktail glass, chilled
Pour ingredients into iced mixing glass
1/4 oz. Cointreau Liqueur
2 1/4 oz. Absolut Mandrin Vodka
Stir and strain
Orange twist garnish

MARTINI, ALEXANDER NEVSKY

Cocktail glass, chilled
Pour ingredients into iced mixing glass
1/4 oz. Chambord Liqueur
1 oz. Bombay Sapphire London Dry Gin
1 oz. Stolichnaya Razberi Russian Vodka
Stir and strain
Raspberries garnish

MARTINI, ALL AMERICAN (1)

Cocktail glass, chilled
Pour ingredients into iced mixing glass
1/4 oz. Jack Daniel's Single Barrel Whiskey
1/4 oz. Vya California Dry Vermouth
1 1/2 oz. Cascade Mountain Gin
Stir and strain
Lemon twist garnish

BALLYLARKIN®
IRISH LIQUEUR

The success of BALLYLARKIN has been centuries in the making. The liqueur was originally created by the Augustinian monks at the Ballylarkin Abbey in the heart of Ireland. When King Henry VIII ordered the dissolution of all monasteries in Ireland and England, the monks disbanded, the Abbey was laid to ruin and the liqueur disappeared.

Nearly 250 years later, descendents of the man to whom the secret recipe was entrusted opened a small distillery in County Kilkenny. There in 1777, he recreated the ancestral liqueur, Ballylarkin. While the distillery has undergone several incarnations, it is once again producing the ancient liqueur.

Produced under the strict supervision of the Irish government, Ballylarkin is a marvelous medley of citrus and vanilla flavorings, blended on a base of premium Irish malt whiskies and pure cane spirits. The liqueur has a golden/amber hue, a delicate, lightweight body and an abundant bouquet with herbal notes. The well-balanced palate features essences of honey, spice, and citrus. Perhaps its best feature is the warm, relaxed and flavor-filled finish.

While ideally sampled neat or over ice, Ballylarkin is also a versatile performer behind the bar. It marries beautifully with whiskies, brandies and a large number of liqueurs.

MARTINI, ALL AMERICAN (2)
Cocktail glass, chilled
Pour ingredients into iced mixing glass
1/2 oz. Vya California Sweet Vermouth
1/2 oz. Vya California Dry Vermouth
1 3/4 oz. Cascade Mountain Gin
Stir and strain
Lemon twist garnish

MARTINI, AMADORA
Cocktail glass, chilled
Pour ingredients into iced mixing glass
1/4 oz. Tawny Port
1 1/2 oz. Bafferts Gin
Stir and strain
Lemon twist garnish

MARTINI, AMBER SKIES
Cocktail glass, chilled
Rim glass with finely crushed almonds (optional)
Pour ingredients into iced mixing glass
1/2 oz. Disaronno Amaretto Liqueur
1/4 oz. Frangelico Liqueur
1 1/2 oz. Brilliant Vodka
Stir and strain
Lemon twist garnish

MARTINI, APPLETINI (1)
Cocktail glass, chilled
Pour ingredients into iced mixing glass
2 1/2 oz. Vodka
3/4 oz. DeKuyper Pucker Sour Apple
Stir and strain
Green apple wedge garnish

MARTINI, APPLETINI (2)
Cocktail glass, chilled
Pour ingredients into iced mixing glass
2 1/2 oz. VOX Vodka
3/4 oz. DeKuyper Pucker Sour Apple
1/2 oz. sweet 'n' sour
Shake and strain
Green apple wedge garnish

MARTINI, APPLETINI (3)
Cocktail glass, chilled
Rim glass with apple-flavored sugar (optional)
Pour ingredients into iced mixing glass
1 3/4 oz. VOX Vodka
1 oz. DeKuyper Pucker Sour Apple
3/4 oz. sweet 'n' sour
Shake and strain
Green apple wedge garnish

MARTINI, BALD HEAD

Cocktail glass, chilled
Pour ingredients into iced mixing glass
1/4 oz. Dry Vermouth
1/4 oz. Sweet Vermouth
1/4 oz. Pernod
1 1/2 oz. Gin
Stir and strain
Lemon twist garnish

MARTINI, BECCO

Cocktail glass, chilled
Pour ingredients into iced mixing glass
1 1/2 oz. Stolichnaya Ohranj Russian Vodka
1/2 oz. Campari Aperitivo
1/2 oz. Vya California Sweet Vermouth
Stir and strain
Orange peel

MARTINI, BEL-AIR

Cocktail glass, chilled
Pour ingredients into iced mixing glass
1/2 oz. Sherry
2 oz. Belvedere Polish Vodka
Stir and strain
Lemon twist garnish

MARTINI, BELVEDERE STARTINI™

Cocktail glass, chilled
Pour ingredients into iced mixing glass
1 1/2 oz. lemonade
1/8 oz. Chambord Liqueur
1/4 oz. Grand Marnier Liqueur
1 1/2 oz. Belvedere Polish Vodka
Shake and strain
Starfruit garnish

MARTINI, BENTLEY

Cocktail glass, chilled
Pour ingredients into iced mixing glass
1/2 oz. Dry Vermouth
1/2 oz. Sweet Vermouth
1/4 oz. B & B Liqueur
1 1/2 oz. Old Raj Dry Gin
Stir and strain
Lemon twist garnish

MARTINI, BITCHIN'

Cocktail glass, chilled
Pour ingredients into iced mixing glass
1/2 oz. Dry Vermouth
2 dashes White Crème de Menthe
2 dashes Pernod
1 1/2 oz. Gin
Stir and strain
Lemon twist garnish

MARTINI, BLACK (1)

Cocktail glass, chilled
Pour ingredients into iced mixing glass
1/2 oz. Chambord Liqueur
1 1/2 oz. Stolichnaya Russian Vodka
Stir and strain
Lemon twist garnish

MARTINI, BLACK (2)

Cocktail glass, chilled
Pour ingredients into iced mixing glass
1/2 oz. Briottet Crème de Cassis
1 1/2 oz. Absolut Vodka
Stir and strain
Lemon twist garnish

MARTINI, BLACK (3)

Cocktail glass, chilled
Pour ingredients into iced mixing glass
1/2 oz. Quady Elysium Wine
1/2 oz. Quady Essensia Wine
1 3/4 oz. Absolut Vodka
Stir and strain
Orange slice garnish

MARTINI, BLACK APPLE

Cocktail glass, chilled
Pour ingredients into iced mixing glass
3/4 oz. DeKuyper Pucker Sour Apple
1 3/4 oz. Blavod Black Vodka
1/2 oz. sweet 'n' sour
Shake and strain
Green apple wedge garnish

MARTINI, BLACK DEVIL

Cocktail glass, chilled
Pour ingredients into iced mixing glass
1/4 oz. Dry Vermouth
2 oz. Cruzan Estate Light Rum
Stir and strain
Black olives garnish

MARTINI, BLACK TIE (1)

Cocktail glass, chilled
Pour ingredients into iced mixing glass
1/4 oz. Dry Vermouth
2 oz. Appleton Estate Extra Jamaica Rum
Stir and strain
Black olives garnish

MARTINI, BLACK TIE (2)

Cocktail glass, chilled
Pour ingredients into iced mixing glass
2 dashes Campari Aperitivo
1/4 oz. Dewar's White Label Scotch Whisky
1 1/2 oz. Original Polish Vodka
Stir and strain
Cocktail onions and black olive garnish

KNOB CREEK®
SMALL BATCH™ BOURBON

KNOB CREEK KENTUCKY STRAIGHT BOURBON is bourbon the way it used to be. Fortunately, great taste is timeless, which is why Jim Beam included Knob Creek as a charter member of the Original Small Batch Bourbon Collection, an unparalleled set of four distinctively different styles of bourbon.

Knob Creek Bourbon is distilled in small batches and aged for a minimum of 9 years in new white oak barrels. These barrels are first seared over a low flame to bring out the natural sugars in the wood, and then "flash-fired" to create a deep char. Underneath the charcoal is a rich layer of red caramelized wood that touches every aspect of the bourbon.

A few moments alone with Knob Creek are all it takes to grasp why the whiskey is both critically acclaimed and universally popular. It has a bouquet laden with bakery fresh aromas and a semi-sweet palate found no where else on Earth.

The collection also includes BOOKER'S which is aged 6- to 8-years and bottled unfiltered and uncut at about 126 proof. Booker's is a tremendous, traditional bourbon. BASIL HAYDEN'S is an 8-year-old bourbon made with a higher percentage of rye and barley malt for a more flavorful, peppery whiskey. BAKER'S BOURBON is an accessible 7-year-old whiskey with the character of a well-aged brandy.

MARTINI, BLEU
Cocktail glass, chilled
Pour ingredients into iced mixing glass
1/2 oz. Dry Vermouth
1 1/2 oz. Luksusowa Polish Vodka
Stir and strain
Olives stuffed with bleu cheese

MARTINI, BLOOD ORANGE
Cocktail glass, chilled
Pour ingredients into iced mixing glass
1/2 oz. Campari Aperitivo
1 1/2 oz. Stolichnaya Ohranj Russian Vodka
Stir and strain
Lemon twist garnish

MARTINI, BLOOD SHOT
Cocktail glass, chilled
Pour ingredients into iced mixing glass
1/4 oz. Absolut Peppar Vodka
1/2 oz. Campari Aperitivo
1 1/2 oz. Stolichnaya Russian Vodka
Stir and strain
Chili peppers garnish

MARTINI, BLUE MOON (1)
Cocktail glass, chilled
Pour ingredients into iced mixing glass
1/4 oz. Blue Curaçao
3/4 oz. Bombay Sapphire London Dry Gin
3/4 oz. Stolichnaya Russian Vodka
Stir and strain
Lemon twist garnish

MARTINI, BLUE MOON (2)
Cocktail glass, chilled
Pour ingredients into iced mixing glass
1/2 oz. Blue Curaçao
1 1/2 oz. Beefeater London Dry Gin
Stir and strain
Lemon twist garnish

MARTINI, BLUE PACIFIC
Cocktail glass, chilled
Pour ingredients into iced mixing glass
1/4 oz. Dry Vermouth
1/4 oz. Blue Curaçao
1 oz. Plymouth Dry Gin
1 oz. Original Polish Vodka
Stir and strain
Lemon twist garnish

MARTINI BLUES
Cocktail glass, chilled
Pour ingredients into iced mixing glass
1/2 oz. Blue Curaçao
1 oz. Plymouth Dry Gin
1 oz. Original Cristall Russian Vodka
Stir and strain
Lemon twist garnish

MARTINI, BLUE SHOCK
Cocktail glass, chilled
Pour ingredients into iced mixing glass
1 1/2 oz. Crown Royal
1/2 oz. Disaronno Amaretto Liqueur
1/2 oz. Blue Curaçao
3/4 oz. sweet 'n' sour
3/4 oz. cranberry juice
1/2 oz. Seven-Up
Stir and strain
Orange slice and cherry garnish

MARTINI, BOOTLEGGER
Cocktail glass, chilled
Pour ingredients into iced mixing glass
1/4 oz. Dry Vermouth
1/2 oz. Southern Comfort Liqueur
1 1/2 oz. Cascade Mountain Gin
Stir and strain
Lemon twist garnish

MARTINI, BOSTON
Cocktail glass, chilled
Pour ingredients into iced mixing glass
3 dashes Dry Vermouth
2 oz. Cascade Mountain Gin
Stir and strain
Anchovy-wrapped or
    almond-stuffed olives garnish

MARTINI, BRAZEN
Cocktail glass, chilled
Pour ingredients into iced mixing glass
1/4 oz. Briottet Crème de Cassis
2 1/2 oz. Zubrówka Bison Brand Vodka
Stir and strain
Kumquat garnish

MARTINI, BRONX
Cocktail glass, chilled
Pour ingredients into iced mixing glass
1/4 oz. Dry Vermouth
1/4 oz. Sweet Vermouth
1/4 oz. orange juice
1 1/2 oz. Gin
Stir and strain
Lemon twist garnish

MARTINI, BUBBLEGUM
Cocktail glass, chilled
Pour ingredients into iced mixing glass
1/4 oz. Chambord Liqueur
1/4 oz. Rose's Lime Juice
2 oz. Cascade Mountain Gin
Shake and strain
Lime wedge garnish

MARTINI, BUCKEYE
Cocktail glass, chilled
Pour ingredients into iced mixing glass
3 dashes Dry Vermouth
2 oz. Bafferts Gin
Stir and strain
Black olive garnish

MARTINI, CAJUN (1)
Cocktail glass, chilled
Pour ingredients into iced mixing glass
1/4 oz. Dry Vermouth
1/4 oz. Sweet Vermouth
3/4 oz. Gin
3/4 oz. jalapeño-steeped Gin
Stir and strain
Small jalapeño peppers garnish

MARTINI, CAJUN (2)
Cocktail glass, chilled
Pour ingredients into iced mixing glass
1/4 oz. Dry Vermouth
1/4 oz. Absolut Peppar Vodka
2-3 dashes Tabasco Sauce
2 oz. Bafferts Gin
Stir and strain
Cooked crawfish garnish
Note: Steep crawfish in Absolut Peppar
    prior to cooking

MARTINI, CAJUN KING
Cocktail glass, chilled
Pour ingredients into iced mixing glass
2 dashes Dry Vermouth
1/2 oz. Absolut Citron Vodka
1 1/2 oz. Absolut Peppar Vodka
Stir and strain
Small jalapeño peppers garnish

MARTINI, CARIBBEAN
Cocktail glass, chilled
Pour ingredients into iced mixing glass
1/2 oz. fresh lemon juice
1 oz. Bacardi Limón Rum
2 1/2 Alizé de France
Stir and strain
Lemon twist garnish

MARTINI, CELTIC
Cocktail glass, chilled
Pour ingredients into iced mixing glass
1 1/2 oz. Stolichnaya Limonnaya
    Russian Vodka
1 1/2 oz. Celtic Crossing Irish Liqueur
Stir and strain
Lemon twist garnish

DRINKS FOR THE BUSINESS CROWD

Happy Hour has evolved into an entrenched social institution. When 5:00 p.m. rolls around, most people are looking to gain some separation from work and begin enjoying what remains of the day. Here's a short list of offerings to tempt the captains of industry.

- **Martinis** — In the kingdom of Cocktails, the martini still reigns supreme. It has prompted a wave of new and intriguing variations that rival the appeal of the original. Consider substituting dry vermouth in your specialty martinis with Dubonnet, Lillet, port, or Saké. Splash in a liqueur or two to add a blast of flavor and an attractive hue. And why limit your martinis to just gin or vodka? Try adding a healthy dose of tequila, cognac or Scotch. The crowning touch is an equally fitting garnish. Popular options include garlic- or bleu cheese-stuffed olives, orange peels, fresh strawberries, and peeled shrimp.

- **Manhattans** — The popular resurgence of bourbon has prompted a renewed interest in this most classic of whiskey cocktails. One creative twist is to substitute another type of aperitif for the vermouth. Another variation includes adding a splash or two of a liqueur such as Chambord, Frangelico, Grand Marnier or Benedictine.

- **Cosmopolitans** — A derivative of the kamikaze, the popular appeal of the cosmopolitan made it a contemporary standard bearer. For those who refuse to leave well enough alone there's the Limón cosmopolitan, made with the citrus-infused Bacardi Limón Rum. Consider using Stolichnaya Limonnaya as the power train in your cosmopolitan, or substitute Absolut Kurant for Citron to make the metropolitan.

MARTINI, CHOCOLATE
Cocktail glass, chilled
Pour ingredients into iced mixing glass
1/2 oz. Godiva Chocolate Liqueur
1 1/2 oz. Vincent Van Gogh Vodka
Stir and strain
Lemon twist garnish

MARTINI, CHOCOLATE CRANBERRY
Cocktail glass, chilled
Pour ingredients into iced mixing glass
1/2 oz. cranberry juice
3/4 oz. Godiva Chocolate Liqueur
2 oz. Luksusowa Polish Vodka
Stir and strain
Orange slice garnish

MARTINI, CITRUS
Cocktail glass, chilled
Pour ingredients into iced mixing glass
3/4 oz. DeKuyper Peach Pucker
1/2 oz. lemonade
2 oz. Absolut Citron Vodka
Stir and strain
Lemon wedge garnish

MARTINI, COPPER ILLUSION
Cocktail glass, chilled
Pour ingredients into iced mixing glass
1/2 oz. Cointreau Liqueur
1/2 oz. Campari Aperitivo
1 1/2 oz. Beefeater London Dry Gin
Stir and strain
Lemon twist garnish

MARTINI, COZUMEL
Cocktail glass, chilled
Pour ingredients into iced mixing glass
1/4 oz. fresh lime juice
1/4 oz. Grand Marnier 100th Anniversary
2 1/2 oz. El Tesoro Silver Tequila
Stir and strain
Lemon twist garnish

MARTINI, CRÈME BRÛLÉE (1)
Cocktail glass, chilled
Rim glass with brown sugar (optional)
Pour ingredients into iced mixing glass
1/4 oz. Frangelico Liqueur
1/4 oz. Cointreau Liqueur
1 oz. Crème Anglaise
2 oz. Grey Goose Vodka
Shake and strain
Vanilla stick swizzle

MARTINI, CRÈME BRÛLÉE (2)
Cocktail glass, chilled
Rim glass with brown sugar (optional)
Pour ingredients into iced mixing glass
1/4 oz. half & half cream
1/2 oz. Cointreau Liqueur
1/2 oz. Frangelico Liqueur
1 oz. Stolichnaya Vanil Russian Vodka
Shake and strain
Orange slice garnish

MARTINI, CRÈME BRÛLÉE (3)
Cocktail glass, chilled
Paint inside of glass with ribbons of
    caramel syrup
Pour ingredients into iced mixing glass
1/4 oz. half & half cream
1/4 oz. Chambord Liqueur
1/2 oz. DeKuyper Buttershots Schnapps
2 oz. Stolichnaya Vanil Russian Vodka
Stir and strain
Orange slice garnish

MARTINI, CREOLE
Cocktail glass, chilled
Pour ingredients into iced mixing glass
1/4 oz. Dry Vermouth
2 oz. Absolut Peppar Vodka
Stir and strain
Pepperoncini garnish

MARTINI, CUPID'S BOW
Cocktail glass, chilled
Pour ingredients into iced mixing glass
1/2 oz. Dry Vermouth
1/2 oz. Dubonnet Blanc
1 1/2 oz. Damrak Amsterdam Gin
Stir and strain
Lemon twist and cherry garnish

MARTINI, DARK CRYSTAL
Cocktail glass, chilled
Pour ingredients into iced mixing glass
1/2 oz. Courvoisier V.S.O.P. Cognac
1 1/2 oz. Stolichnaya Russian Vodka
Stir and strain
Lemon twist garnish

MARTINI, DIAMOND
Cocktail glass, chilled
Rim glass with sugar (optional)
Pour ingredients into iced mixing glass
1 oz. Alizé V.S.O.P. Cognac
1 oz. Brilliant Vodka
1/4 oz. fresh lemon juice
1 oz. pineapple juice
Stir and strain
Lemon wheel garnish

MARTINI, DIRTY (1)
Cocktail glass, chilled
Pour ingredients into iced mixing glass
2 dashes Dry Vermouth
1 1/2 oz. Vodka
1/4 oz. olive juice (brine)
Stir and strain
Olives garnish

MARTINI, DIRTY (2)
Cocktail glass, chilled
Pour ingredients into iced mixing glass
1/2 oz. Dirty Olive Vodka
1 1/2 oz. Dirty Olive Gin
Stir and strain
Olive garnish

MARTINI, DIRTY CITRUS
Cocktail glass, chilled
Pour ingredients into iced mixing glass
2 oz. Dirty Olive Vodka
1 oz. Absolut Citron Vodka
Shake vigorously and strain
Lemon twist garnish

MARTINI, DIRTY GIN TWIST
Cocktail glass, chilled
Pour ingredients into iced mixing glass
2 oz. Dirty Olive Gin
1 oz. Stolichnaya Limonnaya Russian Vodka
Shake vigorously and strain
Lemon twist garnish

MARTINI, DIRTY OLIVE GIN
Cocktail glass, chilled
Pour ingredients into iced mixing glass
2 1/2 oz. Dirty Olive Gin
Shake vigorously and strain
Olive garnish

MARTINI, DIRTY OLIVE VODKA
Cocktail glass, chilled
Pour ingredients into iced mixing glass
2 1/2 oz. Dirty Olive Vodka
Shake vigorously and strain
Olive garnish

MARTINI, 008
Champagne or cocktail glass, chilled
Pour ingredients into iced mixing glass
1/4 oz. Dubonnet Blanc
1 oz. Brilliant Vodka
1 oz. Beefeater London Dry Gin
Shake and strain
Lemon twist garnish

LOT NO. 40®
CANADIAN WHISKY

THE CANADIAN WHISKY GUILD is a remarkable collection of three, small batch whiskies created by Corby Distilleries to celebrate the country's long and prestigious whisky making heritage. Master distiller Michael Booth crafted each individual whisky to represent a distinctive style. One of the members of this top-shelf collection is the vivacious LOT NO. 40 CANADIAN WHISKY.

The whisky is made entirely from prairie rye and malted rye, and distilled in small batches in copper alembic stills. Lot No. 40 is a rare, unblended, single pot still whisky. It is diluted to an alcohol strength of 63% before being aged in re-charred American oak, ex-bourbon barrels. The whisky is aged a minimum of 8 years before being bottled at a strength of 86 proof.

Lot No. 40 has an assertiveness that is rarely seen from Canadian whisky. It has an enthralling bouquet loaded with spice, toffee and honey. The whisky is energetic and immediately fills the mouth with warmth and the savory flavors of vanilla, fruit and baking spices. For such a powerful, muscular whisky, it is remarkably well balanced and thoroughly enjoyable. The finish is extremely long and flavorful.

Without question, Lot No. 40 is a whisky to be savored neat or with a few splashes of spring water.

MARTINI, 007
Champagne or cocktail glass, chilled
Pour ingredients into iced mixing glass
1/4 oz. Lillet Blonde
1 oz. Vodka
1 oz. Gin
Shake and strain
Lemon twist garnish

MARTINI, DRAGON'S BREATH
Cocktail glass, chilled
Pour ingredients into iced mixing glass
1/4 oz. Vya California Dry Vermouth
1/2 oz. Cointreau Liqueur
1/2 oz. blood orange juice
2 oz. Bombay Sapphire London Dry Gin
Stir and strain
Lemon wheel garnish

MARTINI, DRY
Cocktail glass, chilled
Pour ingredients into iced mixing glass
2 drops Dry Vermouth
1 1/2 oz. Gin
Stir and strain
Olives or lemon twist garnish

MARTINI, DRY RAIN
Cocktail glass, chilled
Pour ingredients into iced mixing glass
2 drops Vya California Dry Vermouth
1/4 oz. Mandarine Napoléon Liqueur
1 oz. Old Raj Dry Gin
1 oz. Rain Vodka
Stir and strain
Olives or lemon twist garnish

MARTINI, DRY VODKA
Cocktail glass, chilled
Pour ingredients into iced mixing glass
4 drops Dry Vermouth
1 1/2 oz. Vodka
Stir and strain
Olives or lemon twist garnish

MARTINI, DUTCH (1)
Cocktail glass, chilled
Pour ingredients into iced mixing glass
1/4 oz. Dubonnet Blanc
2 oz. Damrak Amsterdam Gin
Stir and strain
Lemon twist garnish

MARTINI, DUTCH (2)
Cocktail glass, chilled
Pour ingredients into iced mixing glass
1/4 oz. Dry Vermouth
1 1/2 oz. Genever Gin
Stir and strain
Lemon twist garnish

MARTINI, ELEPHANT'S EAR
Cocktail glass, chilled
Pour ingredients into iced mixing glass
1/2 oz. Vya California Dry Vermouth
1/2 oz. Dubonnet Blanc
1 1/2 oz. Old Raj Dry Gin
Stir and strain
Lemon twist garnish

MARTINI, ELISA'S MARTINI OF LOVE
Cocktail glass, chilled
Pour ingredients into iced mixing glass
1/2 oz. Baileys Irish Cream
1/2 oz. Frangelico Liqueur
1/2 oz. Godiva Chocolate Liqueur
1 1/4 oz. Grey Goose Vodka
Stir and strain
Hershey Kiss (unwrapped) garnish

MARTINI, EL PRESIDENTÉ
Cocktail glass, chilled
Pour ingredients into iced mixing glass
1/2 oz. Dry Vermouth
1/2 oz. Sweet Vermouth
1/2 oz. Cointreau Liqueur
2 dashes grenadine
1 1/2 oz. Bacardi Light Rum
Stir and strain
Lemon twist garnish

MARTINI, EMERALD
Cocktail glass, chilled
Pour ingredients into iced mixing glass
1/2 oz. Midori Melon Liqueur
1 1/2 oz. Bacardi Limón Rum
Stir and strain
Lemon twist garnish

MARTINI, ESPRESSO
Cocktail glass, chilled
Pour ingredients into iced mixing glass
1/2 oz. Tia Maria
1/2 oz. Kahlúa Coffee Liqueur
1 oz. espresso coffee
2 oz. Vincent Van Gogh Vodka
Stir and strain

MARTINI, EVERGLADES
Cocktail glass, chilled
Pour ingredients into iced mixing glass
1/4 oz. Dry Vermouth
1/4 oz. Extase XO Liqueur
2 oz. Tanqueray № Ten Gin
Stir and strain
Lemon twist garnish

MARTINI, EXTRA DRY
Cocktail glass, chilled
Pour ingredients into iced mixing glass
1 drop Dry Vermouth (optional)
1 1/2 oz. Gin
Stir and strain
Olives or lemon twist garnish

MARTINI, EXTRA DRY VODKA
Cocktail glass, chilled
Pour ingredients into iced mixing glass
1 drop Dry Vermouth (optional)
1 1/2 oz. Vodka
Stir and strain
Olives or lemon twist garnish

MARTINI, FANTINO
Cocktail glass, chilled
Pour ingredients into iced mixing glass
2 dashes Campari Aperitivo
1/2 oz. Giori Lemoncillo Liqueur
2 oz. Luksusowa Polish Vodka
Stir and strain
Lemon twist garnish

MARTINI, F.D.R.
Cocktail glass, chilled
Pour ingredients into iced mixing glass
1/2 oz. Dry Vermouth
1/4 oz. olive juice (brine)
2 oz. Gin
Stir and strain
Twist lemon peel, rub glass
    with peel, discard.
Olive garnish

MARTINI, FIDEL'S
Cocktail glass, chilled
Pour ingredients into iced mixing glass
1/2 oz. Cruzan Banana Rum
1 1/2 oz. Stolichnaya Russian Vodka
Stir and strain
Banana slice garnish

MARTINI, FINO
Cocktail glass, chilled
Pour ingredients into iced mixing glass
1/2 oz. Fino Sherry
2 oz. Gin
Stir and strain
Lemon twist garnish

DEKUYPER®
TRIPLE SEC LIQUEUR

Depending on the particular survey you consult, the margarita is either the first or second most frequently requested cocktail in the United States. While tequila is certainly the driving force behind the margarita's enormous popularity, the drink would be nothing more than a tequila sour were it not modified by triple sec. One of the best selling brands in the world is DEKUYPER TRIPLE SEC.

The liqueur originated in Holland and is flavored principally from orange peels grown on the Dutch West-Indies island of Curaçao. The flavor of these slightly bitter oranges is offset by the addition of sweet, aromatic Valencia oranges. The peels are steeped in neutral spirits, then redistilled to bring the total number of distillations to three.

DeKuyper Triple Sec is crystal clear with a light body and delicate citrus bouquet. The liqueur is silky smooth with a light, semi-sweet orange palate. It finishes without a trace of harshness. All of these qualities make it a highly mixable liqueur.

In fact, DeKuyper Triple Sec was created for use in drinks such as the margarita, kamikaze, sidecar and Long Island iced tea. Its low cost and low alcohol content (48 proof) are added benefits.

MARTINI, FLIRTINI (1)
Champagne glass, chilled
Muddle 4 raspberries in bottom of glass
Pour ingredients into iced mixing glass
1 oz. VOX Vodka
1/2 oz. Cointreau Liqueur
1/2 oz. Rose's Lime Juice
1/2 oz. cranberry juice
1/2 oz. pineapple juice
Shake and strain
Fill with Champagne
Mint sprig garnish

MARTINI, FLIRTINI (2)
Champagne glass, chilled
Pour ingredients into iced mixing glass
1 oz. Stolichnaya Razberi Vodka
2 oz. pineapple juice
Shake and strain
Fill with Champagne

MARTINI, FOURTH DEGREE
Cocktail glass, chilled
Pour ingredients into iced mixing glass
1/2 oz. Alizé de France
1/2 oz. Dubonnet Blanc
1 3/4 oz. Beefeater London Dry Gin
Stir and strain
Lemon twist garnish

MARTINI, FRENCH (1)
Cocktail glass, chilled
Pour ingredients into iced mixing glass
1/4 oz. Dry Vermouth
3/4 oz. Grand Marnier Liqueur
1 3/4 oz. Grey Goose Vodka
Stir and strain
Lemon twist garnish

MARTINI, FRENCH (2)
Cocktail glass, chilled
Pour ingredients into iced mixing glass
1/2 oz. Chambord Liqueur
1 oz. pineapple juice
2 oz. Grey Goose Vodka
Stir and strain
Orange twist garnish

MARTINI, FRENCH (3)
aka **Golden Drop**
Cocktail glass, chilled
Pour ingredients into iced mixing glass
1/4 oz. Scotch Whisky
1/4 oz. Dry Vermouth (optional)
1 1/2 oz. Gin
Stir and strain
Lemon twist garnish

MARTINI, FRIAR PAUL
Cocktail glass, chilled
Pour ingredients into iced mixing glass
4 drops Vya California Dry Vermouth
1 1/2 oz. Plymouth Dry Gin
Stir and strain
Cocktail onions garnish

MARTINI, FULL MOON (1)
Cocktail glass, chilled
Pour ingredients into iced mixing glass
3/4 oz. Grand Marnier Liqueur
3/4 oz. Disaronno Amaretto Liqueur
3/4 oz. Stolichnaya Russian Vodka
Stir and strain
Lemon twist garnish

MARTINI, FULL MOON (2)
Cocktail glass, chilled
Pour ingredients into iced mixing glass
3/4 oz. Gran Gala Orange Liqueur
3/4 oz. Disaronno Amaretto Liqueur
Stir and strain
Lemon twist garnish

MARTINI, FULL NELSON
Cocktail glass, chilled
Pour ingredients into iced mixing glass
4 drops Dry Vermouth
1 1/2 oz. Plymouth Dry Gin
Stir and strain
Cocktail onion and green olives garnish

MARTINI, GODIVA MINT
Cocktail glass, chilled
Pour ingredients into iced mixing glass
3/4 oz. Godiva Chocolate Liqueur
3/4 oz. White Crème de Menthe
1 3/4 oz. Stolichnaya Russian Vodka
Stir and strain
Peppermint stick garnish

MARTINI, GOLDEN GIRL
Cocktail glass, chilled
Pour ingredients into iced mixing glass
3/4 oz. Dry Sherry
2 dashes Angostura Bitters
2 dashes orange bitters
1 1/2 oz. Tanqueray Gin
Stir and strain
Lemon twist garnish

MARTINI, GOTHAM
Cocktail glass, chilled
Pour ingredients into iced mixing glass
1/4 oz. Opal Nera Black Sambuca
1/4 oz. Briottet Crème de Cassis
2 oz. Blavod Black Vodka
Stir and strain
Lemon twist garnish

MARTINI, GREEN APPLE
Cocktail glass, chilled
Rim glass with sugar
Pour ingredients into iced mixing glass
1 1/2 oz. Vincent Van Gogh
   Wild Appel Vodka
1 1/2 oz. DeKuyper Pucker Sour Apple
Splash sweet 'n' sour
Shake and strain
Apple wedge garnish

MARTINI, GREEN LANTERN
Cocktail glass, chilled
Pour ingredients into iced mixing glass
1/2 oz. Midori Melon Liqueur
1/4 oz. Rose's Lime Juice
1/4 oz. sweet 'n' sour
2 oz. Finlandia Vodka
Stir and strain
Lemon twist garnish

MARTINI, GUMMIE BARE
Cocktail glass, chilled
Pour ingredients into iced mixing glass
1 oz. Midori Melon Liqueur
1 1/2 oz. Zone Peach Italian Vodka
1/2 oz. cranberry juice
1/2 oz. sweet 'n' sour
Shake and strain
Gummie Bears (3) garnish

MARTINI, HALF NELSON
Cocktail glass, chilled
Pour ingredients into iced mixing glass
1 drop Dry Vermouth (optional)
1 1/2 oz. Plymouth Dry Gin
Stir and strain
Green olives garnish

MARTINI, HARPER'S
Cocktail glass, chilled
Pour ingredients into iced mixing glass
3/4 oz. Dubonnet Rouge
1/4 oz. Chambord Liqueur
2 oz. Stolichnaya Persik Russian Vodka
Stir and strain
Orange slice garnish

MARTINI, HAVANA
Cocktail glass, chilled
Pour ingredients into iced mixing glass
1/2 oz. Vintage Tawny Port
1 1/2 oz. Bacardi 8 Reserva Rum
Stir and strain
Cherry garnish

OLD RAJ® DRY GIN

The Scottish firm of Cadenhead's is famous for procuring vast holdings of rare spirits from distillers around the world, extending their aging and then bottling the spirits unadulterated, typically at cask strength. While best known for their collection of rare and old malt whiskies and Caribbean rums, Cadenhead's is now also exporting to the United States a genuinely singular spirit, OLD RAJ DRY GIN.

Scour the Earth if you must, but you'll find no other dry gin like Old Raj. This distinctive gin is made with alembic-distilled, pure grain neutral spirits. Its all-important botanical blend contains saffron, a rare and expensive spice derived from the crocus flower that endows the gin with an intriguing pale yellow tint. The blend also contains juniper berries, coriander, angelica root, lemon and orange peels, orris root, cassia bark and almond powder.

Old Raj Dry Gin is delightfully fragrant, charged with the aromas of citrus, juniper and spice. Its broad, satiny textured body delivers an amazing array of fresh, crisp citrus flavors. The finish is exceptional—long, dry and flavorful.

Cadenhead's produces Old Raj Dry Gin at a lip-tingling, 110 proof (55% abv). While the spirit was bred for a chilled cocktail glass, it also adds marvelous pizzazz to any gin-based libation.

MARTINI, HAWAIIAN
Cocktail glass, chilled
Pour ingredients into iced mixing glass
1/4 oz. Dry Vermouth
1/4 oz. Sweet Vermouth
1/4 oz. pineapple juice
1 1/2 oz. Zone Melon Italian Vodka
Stir and strain
Pimento-stuffed green olive garnish

MARTINI, HENNESSY
Cocktail glass, chilled
Pour ingredients into iced mixing glass
1/4 oz. fresh lemon juice
2 oz. Hennessy V.S. Cognac
Stir and strain
Lemon twist garnish

MARTINI, HOT
Cocktail glass, chilled
Pour ingredients into iced mixing glass
1/4 oz. Dry Vermouth
1/4 oz. pickled jalapeño juice
1/4 oz. fresh lime juice
2 oz. Stolichnaya Russian Vodka
Stir and strain
Jalapeño-stuffed olive garnish

MARTINI, HOT MARTI
Cocktail glass, chilled
Pour ingredients into iced mixing glass
1/2 oz. Dry Vermouth
1/4 oz. pickled jalapeño juice
1/4 oz. fresh lime juice
2 oz. Rain Vodka
Stir and strain
Cocktail onions garnish

MARTINI, ICEBERG
Cocktail glass, chilled
Pour ingredients into iced mixing glass
1/4 oz. White Crème de Menthe
2 oz. Damrak Amsterdam Gin
Stir and strain
Mint sprig garnish

MARTINI, IMPERIAL
Cocktail glass, chilled
Pour ingredients into iced mixing glass
3 dashes Dry Vermouth
3 dashes Angostura Bitters
1/4 oz.Chambord Liqueur
1 1/2 oz. Van Gogh Gin
Stir and strain
Lemon twist garnish

MARTINI, INFUSED
Cocktail glass, chilled
Pour ingredients into iced mixing glass
1/4 oz. Dry Vermouth
1/4 oz. Sweet Vermouth
3/4 oz. Bafferts Gin
3/4 oz. Lemoneater Infused Gin
Stir and strain
Lemon twist garnish

MARTINI, IRISH
Cocktail glass, chilled
Rim glass with cinnamon and sugar
  (optional)
Pour ingredients into iced mixing glass
3/4 oz. Celtic Crossing Irish Liqueur
3/4 oz. Baileys Irish Cream
1 3/4 oz. Knappogue Castle Irish Whiskey
Stir and strain
Orange slice garnish

MARTINI, ITALIAN (1)
Cocktail glass, chilled
Pour ingredients into iced mixing glass
1/2 oz. Gran Gala Orange Liqueur
1 1/4 oz. Villa Massa Limoncello
1 1/4 oz. Mezzaluna Italian Vodka
Stir and strain
Lemon wedge garnish

MARTINI, ITALIAN (2)
Cocktail glass, chilled
Pour ingredients into iced mixing glass
1/2 oz. Marsala Wine
2 oz. Gin
Stir and strain
Lemon twist garnish

MARTINI, JACKSON
Cocktail glass, chilled
Pour ingredients into iced mixing glass
1/2 oz. Dubonnet Blanc
3 dashes Angostura Bitters
2 oz. Tanqueray № Ten Gin
Stir and strain
Lemon twist garnish

MARTINI, JADED
Cocktail glass, chilled
Pour ingredients into iced mixing glass
1/4 oz. Giori Lemoncillo Liqueur
1/4 oz. Midori Melon Liqueur
1 3/4 oz. Beefeater London Dry Gin
Stir and strain
Orange twist garnish

MARTINI, JALISCO
Cocktail glass, chilled
Pour ingredients into iced mixing glass
1/4 oz. Grand Marnier Liqueur
1 1/2 oz. Chili-infused Tequila
Stir and strain
Chili peppers garnish

MARTINI, JOURNALIST
Cocktail glass, chilled
Pour ingredients into iced mixing glass
1/4 oz. Dry Vermouth
1/4 oz. Southern Comfort Liqueur
1/4 oz. DeKuyper Triple Sec
2 dashes Angostura Bitters
2 dashes fresh lemon juice
1 1/2 oz. Damrak Amsterdam Gin
Stir and strain
Lemon twist garnish

MARTINI, KÉKÉ V
Cocktail glass, chilled
Pour ingredients into iced mixing glass
1/2 oz. KéKé Beach Cream Liqueur
2 oz. Pearl Vodka
Shake and strain
Lime wedge garnish

MARTINI, KENTUCKY
Cocktail glass, chilled
Pour ingredients into iced mixing glass
1/2 oz. Disaronno Amaretto Liqueur
1 1/2 oz. Maker's Mark Bourbon
Stir and strain
Lemon twist garnish

MARTINI, KETEL ONE
Cocktail glass, chilled
Pour ingredients into iced mixing glass
1/4 oz. Tomolive juice (optional)
2 1/2 oz. Ketel One Dutch Vodka
Stir and strain
Tomolive (3) garnish

MARTINI, KEY LIME PIE
Cocktail glass, chilled
Rim glass with lime juice and
  crushed graham crackers
Pour ingredients into iced mixing glass
3/4 oz. Midori Melon Liqueur
1/4 oz. Rose's Lime Juice
1/4 oz. half & half cream
1 1/4 oz. Stolichnaya Limonnaya
  Russian Vodka
1 1/4 oz. Stolichnaya Vanil Russian Vodka
Shake and strain

THE JEWEL OF RUSSIA®
WILD BILBERRY INFUSION

It is safe to say that THE JEWEL OF RUSSIA WILD BILBERRY INFUSION is unlike any other product currently available in the U.S. This traditional Russian spirit is a contemporary classic in the making and something that must be sampled to fully appreciate.

The Jewel of Russia Wild Bilberry Infusion, and its sibling, THE JEWEL OF RUSSIA BERRY INFUSION, are each made according to a distillation technique devised 300 years ago. The fresh wild cranberries and bilberries used in the two infusions are handpicked and crushed in a vat. Super-premium Jewel of Russia Vodka is then steeped in the mash of fresh fruit for an extended period of time. As a result, the vodka is infused with a lavish fruit flavor and aroma.

Each Jewel of Russia Infusion is remarkable. Each has a lustrous, red color and satiny, lightweight bodies. Their palates are similar and brimming with the luscious flavors of berries and a hint of chocolate. The flavors persist throughout the lingering finish.

Blindfolded, one would be hard pressed to identify them as vodkas. The infusions are relatively low in alcohol (40 and 44 proof), so there's no excessive heat or biting edge. They are ideally served chilled, or featured in a bevy of cocktails.

MARTINI, LEMONEATER
Cocktail glass, chilled
Pour ingredients into iced mixing glass
1/2 oz. Villa Massa Limoncello
1 1/2 oz. Lemon-infused Beefeater
    London Dry Gin
Stir and strain
Lemon twist garnish

MARTINI, LEMON GROVE
Cocktail glass, chilled
Pour ingredients into iced mixing glass
2 dashes Grand Marnier Liqueur
2 dashes fresh lemon juice
1 1/2 oz. Absolut Citron Vodka
Stir and strain
Lemon twist garnish

MARTINI, LOBSTER
Cocktail glass, chilled
Pour ingredients into iced mixing glass
1/4 oz. Vya California Dry Vermouth
2 oz. Old Raj Dry Gin
Stir and strain
Lobster claw meat garnish

MARTINI, LONDON DRY
Cocktail glass, chilled
Pour ingredients into iced mixing glass
1/4 oz. Vya California Dry Vermouth
2 oz. Bafferts Gin
Stir and strain
Lemon twist and olive garnish

MARTINI, LOS ALTOS
Cocktail glass, chilled
Pour ingredients into iced mixing glass
2 dashes Chardonnay
2 oz. El Tesoro Silver Tequila
Stir and strain
Lemon twist garnish

MARTINI, LOUISIANA RAIN
Cocktail glass, chilled
Pour ingredients into iced mixing glass
1/4 oz. Dry Vermouth
2 oz. Rain Vodka
3-4 dashes Louisiana Gold Pepper Sauce
Stir and strain
Red peppers (2) garnish

MARTINI, MANDARINE
Cocktail glass, chilled
Pour ingredients into iced mixing glass
1 3/4 oz. Ketel One Dutch Vodka
1 3/4 oz. Mandarine Napoléon Liqueur
Stir and strain
Orange slice garnish

MARTINI, MARGUERITE
Cocktail glass, chilled
Pour ingredients into iced mixing glass
1/4 oz. Dry Vermouth
3 dashes orange bitters
1 3/4 oz. Van Gogh Gin
Stir and strain
Orange twist garnish

MARTINI, MARITIME
Cocktail glass, chilled
Pour ingredients into iced mixing glass
1/2 oz. Cherry-infused Light Rum
1 1/2 oz. Pineapple-infused Vodka
Stir and strain
Orange slice and cherry garnish

MARTINI, MARSEILLES
Cocktail glass, chilled
Pour ingredients into iced mixing glass
1/2 oz. Dry Vermouth
3 dashes Dubonnet Blanc
1 1/2 oz. Bafferts Gin
Stir and strain
Lemon twist garnish

MARTINI, MARTINIQUE
Cocktail glass, chilled
Pour ingredients into iced mixing glass
Powdered sugar rim
1/2 oz. fresh lime juice
3/4 oz. sugar cane syrup
1 1/2 oz. St. James Extra Old Rhum
Stir and strain
Lime wedge garnish

MARTINI, MAYFLOWER
Cocktail glass, chilled
Pour ingredients into iced mixing glass
2 1/4 oz. Plymouth Dry Gin
1/2 oz. Harvey's Bristol Cream Sherry
1/2 oz. Courvoisier V.S.O.P. Cognac
Stir and strain
Orange twist garnish

MARTINI, MEDICI
Cocktail glass, chilled
Pour ingredients into iced mixing glass
1/2 oz. Grappa
2 dashes Chambord Liqueur
2 oz. Luksusowa Polish Vodka
Stir and strain
Lemon twist garnish

MARTINI, METROPOLIS
Cocktail glass, chilled
Pour ingredients into iced mixing glass
1/2 oz. Chambord Liqueur
1 1/2 oz. VOX Vodka
Stir and strain
Splash Champagne
Lemon twist garnish

MARTINI, MIDNIGHT (1)
Cocktail glass, chilled
Pour ingredients into iced mixing glass
2-3 dashes Dry Vermouth
2 1/2 oz. Blavod Black Vodka
Stir and strain
Lemon twist garnish

MARTINI, MIDNIGHT (2)
Cocktail glass, chilled
Pour ingredients into iced mixing glass
1/2 oz. cranberry juice
1/2 oz. Chambord Liqueur
1 1/2 oz. Original Polish Vodka
Stir and strain
Lemon twist garnish

MARTINI, MIDNIGHT (3)
Cocktail glass, chilled
Pour ingredients into iced mixing glass
3/4 oz. Opal Nera Black Sambuca
2 oz. Ketel One Dutch Vodka
Stir and strain
Coffee beans (3) garnish

MARTINI, MIGHTY
Cocktail glass, chilled
Pour ingredients into iced mixing glass
1/4 oz. Vya California Dry Vermouth
2 1/2 oz. Zubrówka Bison Brand Vodka
Stir and strain
Olive garnish

MARTINI, MIKHAIL'S
Cocktail glass, chilled
Pour ingredients into iced mixing glass
1/2 oz. Stolichnaya Vanil Russian Vodka
1 1/2 oz. Stolichnaya Ohranj Russian Vodka
Stir and strain
Orange twist garnish

MARTINI, MONASTERY
Cocktail glass, chilled
Pour ingredients into iced mixing glass
1/2 oz. B & B Liqueur
1 1/2 oz. Grey Goose Vodka
Stir and strain
Lemon twist garnish

DEKUYPER®
RASPBERRY PUCKER®

Here's a liqueur begging to join the party! DEKUYPER RASPBERRY PUCKER is an unpretentious product created with fun in mind. You don't have to look further than its packaging to realize that good times are just around the corner.

Raspberry Pucker is one of a line of similarly concocted sweet 'n' sour schnapps. What differentiates the Pucker line of schnapps from the rest of the field is that they are brimming with tart and zesty flavor, just enough tangy zing to make them something special.

Raspberry Pucker has a subtle, enticing fruit bouquet. On the palate it is exceptionally light without being excessively sweet. The real treat comes when the flavor kicks in.

Those of us who spent much of our childhood with stained fingers from feasting on wild raspberries can attest that this Pucker liqueur has all of the tang and tart of fresh sun-ripened raspberries.

It makes a great variation of the cosmopolitan and is a welcome addition in a margarita. Blend it with ice cream, use it to doctor a martini, or mix it in a specialty daiquiri.

Have fun with it. That's why they named it Raspberry Pucker rather than Framboise DeKuyper.

MARTINI, MORO
Cocktail glass, chilled
Pour ingredients into iced mixing glass
1/2 oz. Vya California Dry Vermouth
2 1/4 oz. Ketel One Dutch Vodka
3/4 oz. blood orange juice
Stir and strain
Blood orange slice garnish

MARTINI, MOSCOW CHILL
Cocktail glass, chilled
Pour ingredients into iced mixing glass
3/4 oz. Godiva Chocolate Liqueur
3/4 oz. Extase XO Liqueur
2 oz. Stolichnaya Russian Vodka
Stir and strain
Orange slice garnish

MARTINI, MUSCOVY
Cocktail glass, chilled
Pour ingredients into iced mixing glass
1 oz. Stolichnaya Zinamon Russian Vodka
1 oz. Stolichnaya Ohranj Russian Vodka
1/2 oz. DeKuyper Triple Sec
1/2 oz. orange juice
1 pinch cinnamon
Stir and strain
Orange twist garnish

MARTINI, MYSTICAL
Cocktail glass, chilled
Pour ingredients into iced mixing glass
1/4 oz. Blonde Lillet
1 1/2 oz. Encantado Mezcal
Stir and strain
Lemon twist garnish

MARTINI, NAPOLEON
Cocktail glass, chilled
Pour ingredients into iced mixing glass
1/2 oz. Dubonnet Rouge
1/2 oz. Grand Marnier Liqueur
1 1/2 oz. Van Gogh Gin
Stir and strain
Lemon twist garnish

MARTINI, NEW BOND
Cocktail glass, chilled or rocks glass, ice
Pour ingredients into iced mixing glass
1/2 oz. Blonde Lillet
2 oz. Jewel of Russia Classic Vodka
Shake and strain
Lemon twist garnish

MARTINI, NEWBURY

Cocktail glass, chilled
Pour ingredients into iced mixing glass
1/2 oz. Sweet Vermouth
2 dashes Triple Sec
1 1/2 oz. Gin
Stir and strain
Lemon and orange twist garnish

MARTINI, NITELIFE

Cocktail glass, chilled
Pour ingredients into iced mixing glass
3/4 oz. Chambord Liqueur
1 1/4 oz. Stolichnaya Ohranj Russian Vodka
1 oz. cranberry juice
3/4 oz. Seven-Up
Stir and strain
Lime wedge garnish

MARTINI, NUTCRACKER

Cocktail glass, chilled
Pour ingredients into iced mixing glass
2 dashes Frangelico Liqueur
1 1/2 oz. Chopin Polish Vodka
Stir and strain
Lemon twist garnish

MARTINI, NUTTINI

Cocktail glass, chilled
Pour ingredients into iced mixing glass
3/4 oz. Frangelico Liqueur
3/4 oz. Disaronno Amaretto Liqueur
2 oz. Stolichnaya Russian Vodka
Stir and strain
Orange twist garnish

MARTINI, ORANGE GROVE

Cocktail glass, chilled
Pour ingredients into iced mixing glass
1/2 oz. Cointreau Liqueur
2 dashes orange juice
2 dashes Angostura Bitters
1 1/2 oz. Stolichnaya Ohranj Russian Vodka
Stir and strain
Orange twist garnish

MARTINI, PAISLEY

Cocktail glass, chilled
Pour ingredients into iced mixing glass
1/2 oz. Dewar's White Label Scotch Whisky
1/2 oz. Vya California Dry Vermouth
2 oz. Bombay Sapphire London Dry Gin
Stir and strain
Lemon twist garnish

MARTINI, PALM ISLAND

Cocktail glass, chilled
Pour ingredients into iced mixing glass
1/4 oz. White Crème de Cacao
1/2 oz. Dry Vermouth
1 1/2 oz. Gin
Stir and strain
Lemon twist garnish

MARTINI, PASSION

Cocktail glass, chilled
Pour ingredients into iced mixing glass
1 oz. sweet 'n' sour
3/4 oz. Chambord Liqueur
2 oz. Absolut Mandrin Vodka
Stir and strain
Raspberry garnish

MARTINI, PEAR

Cocktail glass, chilled
Pour ingredients into iced mixing glass
3/4 oz. Poire William (Eau de Vie de Poire)
2 oz. Belvedere Polish Vodka
Stir and strain
Pear slice garnish

MARTINI, PEARL JAM

Cocktail glass, chilled
Pour ingredients into iced mixing glass
1 tsp. strawberry jelly
2 1/2 oz. Pearl Vodka
Shake and strain
Strawberry garnish

MARTINI, PERFECT

aka **Perfect Cocktail**
Cocktail glass, chilled
Pour ingredients into iced mixing glass
1/4 oz. Sweet Vermouth
1/4 oz. Dry Vermouth
1 dash Angostura Bitters (**optional**)
1 3/4 oz. Gin
Stir and strain
Lemon twist garnish

MARTINI, PIÑA

Cocktail glass, chilled
Pour ingredients into iced mixing glass
3/4 oz. pineapple juice
1 oz. Cruzan Pineapple Rum
1 1/2 oz. Pearl Vodka
Stir and strain
Small pineapple wedge

FARIAS® REPOSADO TEQUILA

The Farias family has enjoyed international fame and success before. In 1889, patriarch Heraclio Farias debuted the first machine for manufacturing cigars at the World's Fair exhibition in Paris. It was about the same time that the family in Mexico began distilling FARIAS 100% AGAVE TEQUILAS.

These premium, silky smooth tequilas are distilled from mature blue agaves grown in Jalisco. After harvesting, the agaves are taken to the Industrializadora de Agave Distillery located in the town of Tepatitlan. There, the agaves are baked in stone ovens, fermented and double-distilled in copper alembic stills.

Unaged FARIAS SILVER TEQUILA is crystal clear with a light, fresh bouquet and a slightly sweet, peppery palate. The FARIAS REPOSADO is aged for 9 months in American white oak barrels, about 3 to 6 months longer than most comparable reposados. The tequila has a pale, yellow color and an enticing, herbal bouquet. The palate is delectable, rich with the flavors of caramel, citrus and hints of toasted oak.

Elegant FARIAS AÑEJO TEQUILA is aged for 2 years in ex-bourbon barrels. The extended aging has influenced every aspect of its refined character, rendering the tequila exceptionally smooth, flavorful and delightfully complex.

Farias is packaged in an eye-catching, barrel-shaped bottle, one that will be difficult to miss sitting on your back bar.

MARTINI, POINSETTIA
Cocktail glass, chilled
Pour ingredients into iced mixing glass
1/4 oz. Chambord Liqueur
1/4 oz. pineapple juice
1 1/2 oz. Luksusowa Polish Vodka
Stir and strain
Lemon twist garnish

MARTINI, PRINCETON
Cocktail glass, chilled
Pour ingredients into iced mixing glass
1/2 oz. Dry Vermouth
1/2 oz. fresh lime juice
2 oz. Bombay Sapphire London Dry Gin
Stir and strain
Lemon twist garnish

MARTINI, PYRAT
Cocktail glass, chilled
Pour ingredients into iced mixing glass
1/2 oz. Godiva Chocolate Liqueur
1 3/4 oz. Pyrat Cask 23 Rum
Stir and strain
Lemon twist garnish

MARTINI, RASPBERRY
Cocktail glass, chilled
Pour ingredients into iced mixing glass
1/2 oz. Briottet Crème de Framboise
1 1/2 oz. Old Raj Dry Gin
Stir and strain
Raspberry garnish

MARTINI, RAVING RHINO
Cocktail glass, chilled
Pour ingredients into iced mixing glass
1/4 oz. jalapeño juice
3-4 dashes Tabasco Sauce
2 1/2 oz. Absolut Peppar Vodka
Stir and strain
Speared jalapeño garnish

MARTINI, RED RAIN
Cocktail glass, chilled
Pour ingredients into iced mixing glass
3/4 oz. Rémy Red
2 oz. Rain Vodka
Stir and strain
Orange slice and cherry garnish

MARTINI, RIVERS
Cocktail glass, chilled
Pour ingredients into iced mixing glass
1/4 oz. Cointreau Liqueur
1 3/4 oz. Plymouth Dry Gin
Stir and strain
Anchovy-stuffed olives garnish

MARTINI, RIVIERA
Cocktail glass, chilled
Pour ingredients into iced mixing glass
1/2 oz. Sweet Vermouth
2-3 dashes orange flower water
2-3 dashes Angostura Bitters
2 1/4 oz. Old Raj Dry Gin
Stir and strain
Lemon twist garnish

MARTINI, ROLLS ROYCE
Cocktail glass, chilled
Pour ingredients into iced mixing glass
1/2 oz. Vya California Dry Vermouth
1/2 oz. Vya California Sweet Vermouth
1/2 oz. B & B Liqueur
1 3/4 oz. Bombay Sapphire London Dry Gin
Stir and strain
Lemon twist garnish

MARTINI, ROMANA
Cocktail glass, chilled
Pour ingredients into iced mixing glass
1/4 oz. Dry Vermouth
3 dashes Campari Aperitivo
1 1/2 oz. Gin
Stir and strain
Lemon twist garnish

MARTINI, ROSALIND RUSSELL
Cocktail glass, chilled
Pour ingredients into iced mixing glass
1/4 oz. Aquavit
1 1/2 oz. Brilliant Vodka
Stir and strain
Lemon twist garnish

MARTINI, ROSEBUD
Cocktail glass, chilled
Pour ingredients into iced mixing glass
1/4 oz. Campari Aperitivo
2 oz. VOX Vodka
Stir and strain
Lemon twist garnish

MARTINI, RUSSIAN TEA ROOM
Cocktail glass, chilled
Pour ingredients into iced mixing glass
1/4 oz. Dry Vermouth
1/4 oz. Sweet Vermouth
2 oz. Jewel of Russia Classic Vodka
Stir and strain
Black olive garnish

MARTINI, SAKÉ
Cocktail glass, chilled
Pour ingredients into iced mixing glass
1/2 oz. Saké
1 1/2 oz. Gin
Stir and strain
Olive garnish

MARTINI, SAKÉTINI
Cocktail glass, chilled
Pour ingredients into iced mixing glass
1/2 oz. Blue Curaçao
1 3/4 oz. Bombay Sapphire London Dry Gin
1 3/4 oz. NapaSaki Saké
Stir and strain
Lemon twist garnish

MARTINI, SAN FRANCISCO
Cocktail glass, chilled
Pour ingredients into iced mixing glass
1/4 oz. Tawny Port
1 3/4 oz. Beefeater London Dry Gin
2 dashes Angostura Bitters
Stir and strain
Lemon twist garnish

MARTINI, SAPPHIRE SIN
Cocktail glass, chilled
Pour ingredients into iced mixing glass
1/4 oz. Vya California Dry Vermouth
3/4 oz. Absolut Citron Vodka
2 oz. Bombay Sapphire London Dry Gin
Stir and strain
Lemon twist garnish

MARTINI, SHADE TREE
Cocktail glass, chilled
Pour ingredients into iced mixing glass
1/2 oz. lemonade
3/4 oz. Giori Lemoncillo Liqueur
1 1/2 oz. Original Polish Vodka
Stir and strain
Lemon wedge garnish

MARTINI, SHAGGED
Cocktail glass, chilled
Pour ingredients into iced mixing glass
1/4 oz. Sweet Vermouth
1/4 oz. Extase XO Liqueur
1 3/4 oz. Beefeater London Dry Gin
Stir and strain
Orange twist garnish

MARTINI, SICILIAN (1)
Cocktail glass, chilled
Pour ingredients into iced mixing glass
1/4 oz. Dry Vermouth
2 oz. Garlic-infused Vodka
Stir and strain
Garlic-stuffed olive garnish
Note: See **Sicilian Martini Infusion**

MARTINI, SICILIAN (2)
Cocktail glass, chilled
Pour ingredients into iced mixing glass
1/2 oz. Opal Nera Black Sambuca
1 1/2 oz. Vodka
Stir and strain
Lemon twist garnish

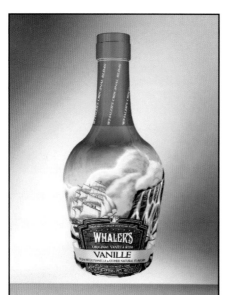

WHALER'S® ORIGINAL VANILLE RUM

WHALER'S ORIGINAL VANILLE RUM isn't likely to be shelved at a tablecloth restaurant or a highbrow haunt. One look at this Hawaiian rum and you know it was created for places where the bar hops and people appreciate a good time.

These enticing spirits originated on the island of Maui, Hawaii. The rums are distilled in continuous stills using molasses from locally grown sugar cane. Whaler's Original Vanille (Van-ee) is a dark, highly aromatic rum infused with natural vanilla flavors. The rum has a creamy texture and delicious palate absolutely brimming with vanilla and hints of cocoa. Little wonder why it is the featured act in many popular drinks.

WHALER'S GREAT WHITE is a silver rum with a sleek, lightweight body and a lively palate. WHALER'S HAWAIIAN SPICED RUM has a wafting bouquet and a palate saturated with the warm flavors of vanilla, caramel and spice that reach a crescendo during the lingering finish.

The dean of the group is WHALER'S RARE RESERVE DARK RUM, an elegant, aged rum with a deep amber hue, subtle yet beckoning bouquet and a deliciously wholesome palate. New to the team is WHALER'S KILLER COCONUT, a vibrant silver rum loaded with the fresh flavor of coconut.

Whaler's Hawaiian Rums are a bona fide good time waiting to happen.

MARTINI, SMOKED (1)
Cocktail glass, chilled
Pour ingredients into iced mixing glass
1/4 oz. Dry Vermouth
1 1/2 oz. Tanqueray Gin
Stir and strain
Lemon twist garnish
Note: Prior to pouring drink, light
   match, blow it out, and let smoke
   fill the inside of glass

MARTINI, SMOKED (2)
Cocktail glass, chilled
Pour ingredients into iced mixing glass
3/4 oz. Rhum Barbancourt 3-Star Rum
1 1/2 oz. Gin
Stir and strain
Lemon twist garnish

MARTINI, SNICKERTINI
Cocktail glass, chilled
Rim glass with powdered cocoa (optional)
Pour ingredients into iced mixing glass
3/4 oz. Frangelico Liqueur
3/4 oz. Godiva Chocolate Liqueur
1 1/2 oz. Ketel One Dutch Vodka
Shake and strain
Orange slice garnish

MARTINI, SPANISH
Cocktail glass, chilled
Pour ingredients into iced mixing glass
1/2 oz. Dry Sack Sherry
1 1/2 oz. Gin
Stir and strain
Lemon twist garnish

MARTINI, STARLIGHT
Cocktail glass, chilled
Pour ingredients into iced mixing glass
3/4 oz. Opal Nera Black Sambuca
2 oz. Brilliant Vodka
Stir and strain
Lemon twist garnish

MARTINI, STAR'S
Cocktail glass, chilled
Pour ingredients into iced mixing glass
1/4 oz. El Tesoro Silver Tequila
1 3/4 oz. Van Gogh Gin
Stir and strain
Lemon wedge garnish

MARTINI, STAR'S JEWEL
Cocktail glass, chilled
Pour ingredients into iced mixing glass
1/4 oz. Absolut Peppar Vodka
1 1/2 oz. Bombay Sapphire London Dry Gin
Stir and strain
Lemon twist garnish

MARTINI, STRAWBERRY (1)

Cocktail glass, chilled
Pour ingredients into iced mixing glass
1 1/2 oz. Artic Vodka & Strawberry Liqueur
1 oz. Vodka
Stir and strain
Strawberry garnish

MARTINI, STRAWBERRY (2)

Cocktail glass, chilled
Pour ingredients into iced mixing glass
1/2 oz. Chambraise or Fraise
1 1/2 oz. Old Raj Dry Gin
Stir and strain
Strawberry garnish

MARTINI, TARTINI (1)

Cocktail glass, chilled
Pour ingredients into iced mixing glass
1/2 oz. Sambuca
2 oz. Grey Goose Vodka
Stir and strain
Float 3/4 oz. Kahlúa Coffee Liqueur
Coffee beans (3) garnish

MARTINI, TARTINI (2)

Cocktail glass, chilled
Pour ingredients into iced mixing glass
1/2 oz. Chambord Liqueur
1/2 oz. cranberry juice
1/2 oz. sweet 'n' sour
1 1/2 oz. Jewel of Russia Classic Vodka
Stir and strain
Lime wedge garnish

MARTINI THYME

Cocktail glass, chilled
Pour ingredients into iced mixing glass
1/2 oz. Green Chartreuse
2 oz. Gin
Stir and strain
Thyme sprig garnish

MARTINI, TIRAMISU

Cocktail glass, chilled
Rim glass with powdered cocoa (optional)
Pour ingredients into iced mixing glass
1 1/2 oz. Stolichnaya Vanil Russian Vodka
1/2 oz. Kahlúa Coffee Liqueur
1/2 oz. Godiva White Chocolate Liqueur
1/4 oz. Disaronno Amaretto Liqueur
Stir and strain
Sprinkle shaved chocolate

MARTINI, TOASTED NUTS

Cocktail glass, chilled
Rim glass with powdered cocoa (optional)
Pour ingredients into iced mixing glass
3/4 oz. Godiva Chocolate Liqueur
3/4 oz. Disaronno Amaretto Liqueur
1 3/4 oz. VOX Vodka
Stir and strain

MARTINI, TOPAZ

Cocktail glass, chilled
Pour ingredients into iced mixing glass
1/4 oz. Dark Crème de Cacao
1/4 oz. Frangelico Liqueur
1 1/2 oz. Brilliant Vodka
Stir and strain
Coffee beans (3) garnish

MARTINI, TROPICAL

Cocktail glass, chilled
Pour ingredients into iced mixing glass
1/2 oz. Godiva Chocolate Liqueur
1 oz. Malibu Rum
2 1/2 Alizé de France
Stir and strain
Lemon twist garnish

MARTINI, TY-WON-ON

Cocktail glass, chilled
Pour ingredients into iced mixing glass
1/2 oz. Chambord Liqueur
3/4 oz. NapaSaki Saké
1 3/4 oz. Zubrówka Bison Brand Vodka
Stir and strain
Lemon twist garnish

MARTINI, VODKA

aka **Kangaroo**
Cocktail glass, chilled
Pour ingredients into iced mixing glass
8 drops Dry Vermouth
1 1/2 oz. Vodka
Stir and strain
Olives or lemon twist garnish

MARTINI, VIRGIN ISLAND

Cocktail glass, chilled
Pour ingredients into iced mixing glass
2 1/4 oz. Plymouth Dry Gin
3/4 oz. Cruzan Orange Rum
Stir and strain
Orange slice garnish

DJ DOTSON® TRIPLE SEC

Triple sec is an absolutely indispensable product behind the bar. It's integral to such cocktails as the kamikaze, margarita, Long Island iced tea and the Lynchburg lemonade, just to name a few. Its clarity makes triple sec a versatile player in a large number of drinks In many instances, however, what mixologists are looking for from a triple sec is to add an orange dimension to a cocktail, not necessarily more alcohol. Thus the need for DJ DOTSON TRIPLE SEC.

DJ Dotson Triple Sec would be widely considered as an excellent liqueur, except for the fact that it is entirely alcohol-free, which is a rare quality for a triple sec. What DJ Dotson does have is a vibrant, sweet and sour orange flavor that shines in cocktails of all shapes and sizes. Here's a product whose time has arrived with a low price to boot.

DJ Dotson Triple Sec is perfectly clear and has a lightweight, velvety smooth body. It is highly aromatic with a wafting bouquet of freshly peeled oranges and lemon zest. The triple sec is well balanced, far from cloying or syrupy. To the contrary, it has a realistic citrus pucker and a palate loaded with a brilliant orange flavor. The finish is crisp and clean.

DJ Dotson Triple Sec can be found behind increasingly more bars, and in drinks, both with and without alcohol.

MARTINI, WATERMELON
Cocktail glass, chilled
Pour ingredients into iced mixing glass
1/2 oz. DeKuyper Watermelon Pucker
1/2 oz. watermelon juice
1 1/2 oz. Stolichnaya Limonnaya
    Russian Vodka
Stir and strain
Small watermelon wedge garnish

MARTINI, WILLY NILLY
Cocktail glass, chilled
Pour ingredients into iced mixing glass
1/2 oz. blood orange juice
3/4 oz. Alizé de France
1 1/2 oz. Grey Goose Vodka
Stir and strain
Blood orange slice garnish

MARTINI, YELLOW RATTLER
Cocktail glass, chilled
Pour ingredients into iced mixing glass
1/2 oz. Dry Vermouth
2-3 dashes orange bitters
2 oz. Bombay Sapphire London Dry Gin
Stir and strain
Lemon twist garnish

MARTINI, ZORBATINI
Cocktail glass, chilled
Pour ingredients into iced mixing glass
1/2 oz. Metaxa Ouzo
2 oz. Vodka
Stir and strain
Green olives garnish

MARZ BAR
Rocks glass, chilled
Pour ingredients into iced mixing glass
3/4 oz. Pearl Vodka
3/4 oz. Godiva Chocolate Liqueur
3/4 oz. Disaronno Amaretto Liqueur
1/2 oz. half & half cream (optional)
Shake and strain

MASSAPPEAL
Cocktail glass, chilled
Pour ingredients into iced mixing glass
2 oz. Villa Massa Limoncello
1/2 oz. Artic Vodka & Peach Liqueur
1 oz. orange juice
1/2 oz. half & half cream
Shake and strain
Sprinkle nutmeg

MAUI BREEZER
House specialty glass, chilled
Pour ingredients into blender
1 1/2 oz. Disaronno Amaretto Liqueur
1/2 oz. Hiram Walker Triple Sec
1/2 oz. Brandy
1 oz. sweet 'n' sour
2 oz. orange juice
2 oz. guava juice
Blend with ice
Fresh fruit garnish

MAUI WOWIE
Cocktail glass, chilled
Pour ingredients into iced mixing glass
3/4 oz. Matusalem Light Dry Rum
3/4 oz. Cruzan Coconut Rum
3/4 oz. Midori Melon Liqueur
1 oz. pineapple juice
1 oz. orange juice
Shake and strain
Float 3/4 oz. Gosling's Black Seal Rum
Orange slice garnish

MAXIM'S A LONDRES
Champagne glass, chilled
Pour ingredients into iced mixing glass
1 1/2 oz. Brandy
1/2 oz. Cointreau Liqueur
1/2 oz. orange juice
Shake and strain
Fill with Champagne
Orange twist garnish

MCGILLICUDDY'S CREAM SODA
Bucket glass, ice
Build in glass
1 3/4 oz. Dr. McGillicuddy's Vanilla Liqueur
Fill with cola

MEADOWLARK LEMON
Cocktail glass, chilled
Pour ingredients into iced mixing glass
1 1/2 oz. Stolichnaya Russian Vodka
3/4 oz. Cointreau Liqueur
1/2 oz. fresh lemon juice
Stir and strain
Lemon wedge garnish

MEADOW SNOW
House specialty glass, chilled
Pour ingredients into blender
2 oz. Cascade Mountain Gin
3/4 oz. Midori Melon Liqueur
1 1/2 oz. sweet 'n' sour
Blend with ice
Cantaloupe cube garnish

MEDITERRANEAN FREEZE
House specialty glass, chilled
Pour ingredients into blender
1 oz. Rain Vodka
3/4 oz. Midori Melon Liqueur
1/2 oz. DeKuyper Peachtree Schnapps
2 oz. sweet 'n' sour
3 oz. orange juice
Blend with ice
Orange slice and cherry garnish

MEISTER-BATION
House specialty glass, chilled
Pour ingredients into blender
1 1/4 oz. Jägermeister Liqueur
3/4 oz. Crème de Banana
2 oz. half & half cream
2 oz. coconut cream syrup
Blend with ice
Pineapple wedge garnish

MELLONAIRE
House specialty glass, chilled
Pour ingredients into iced mixing glass
1 3/4 oz. Cruzan Banana Rum
1 oz. Midori Melon Liqueur
1/2 oz. DeKuyper Triple Sec
2 oz. sweet 'n' sour
Shake and strain

MELLOW DRAMATIC
Presentation shot glass, chilled
Build in glass
1/3 fill Chambord Liqueur
1/3 fill White Crème de Cacao
1/3 fill Baileys Irish Cream

MELON BALL (1)
Highball glass, ice
Build in glass
1 1/4 oz. Midori Melon Liqueur
1/2 oz. Vodka
Fill with orange juice

MELON BALL (2)
Rocks glass, chilled
Pour ingredients into iced mixing glass
1 1/2 oz. Midori Melon Liqueur
1/2 oz. Vodka
1/2 oz. orange juice
1/2 oz. pineapple juice
Shake and strain

PEARL® VODKA

The Pearl Vodka Distillery is located off in the majestic mountains of Western Canada. Surrounded by large fields of wheat and perennially crisp air, the medium-sized facility has been able to accomplish a great deal, namely to produce a spirit that captures the essence of its idyllic setting. The spirit is award-winning PEARL VODKA and there's a little slice of pristine wilderness in every sip.

Master distiller R.R. Strothers distills Pearl Vodka in small batches with soft, Canadian winter wheat and spring water drawn from the leeward side of the Rockies. The wheat is an especially vibrant strain lauded for its quality and consistency. The rigorous distillation process requires two pounds of wheat to yield 750ml of finished vodka. In total, Pearl is distilled 5 times and subjected to repeated purification. The vodka has no additives or flavor enhancers, and is bottled at 80 proof.

Pearl Vodka is bracing and refreshing, created where brisk is a way of life. The vodka is perfectly clear and outfitted with a sleek, medium-weight body. Its rousing bouquet is redolent with the soft, creamy aromas. The slightly sweet palate expands in the mouth quickly, then slowly fades away into a relaxed finish.

Pearl Vodka is tailor-made for the nearest dry martini.

MELON BALL COOLER
House specialty glass, ice
Pour ingredients into iced mixing glass
1 1/2 oz. Midori Melon Liqueur
3/4 oz. Luksusowa Polish Vodka
1 oz. pineapple juice
1 oz. orange juice
Shake and strain
Fill with ginger ale

MELON BREEZE
Highball glass, ice
Build in glass
1 oz. Midori Melon Liqueur
1/2 oz. Ketel One Dutch Vodka
1/2 fill cranberry juice
1/2 fill pineapple juice

MELON GRIND
Bucket glass, ice
Build in glass
1 1/2 oz. Zone Melon Italian Vodka
3/4 oz. Midori Melon Liqueur
1/2 oz. Light Rum
Fill with pineapple juice

MELON MOOSE
Bucket glass, ice
Build in glass
3/4 oz. Bacardi Light Rum
3/4 oz. Midori Melon Liqueur
Near fill with pineapple juice
Float 1 oz. Appleton Estate
    V/X Jamaica Rum

MELON SCOOP
House specialty glass, chilled
Pour ingredients into blender
1 3/4 oz. Mount Gay Eclipse Rum
1 1/2 oz. Midori Melon Liqueur
3/4 oz. Kahlúa Coffee Liqueur
1/2 oz. grenadine
1 oz. sweet 'n' sour
2 scoops vanilla ice cream
Blend ingredients (with ice optional)
Float 3/4 oz. Matusalem Classic Black Rum
Orange slice and cherry garnish

MEL'S CHOCOLATE
BUTTERSCOTCH SHAKE
House specialty glass, chilled
Pour ingredients into blender
1 1/2 oz. Kahlúa Coffee Liqueur
3/4 oz. Appleton Estate V/X Jamaica Rum
2 oz. butterscotch topping
1 oz. chocolate syrup
4 oz. whole milk
2 scoops vanilla ice cream
Blend ingredients (with ice optional)
Whipped cream garnish
Sprinkle shaved chocolate

MEL'S CHOC/PB/NANA SHAKE

House specialty glass, chilled
Pour ingredients into blender
1 1/2 oz. Kahlúa Coffee Liqueur
3/4 oz. Appleton Estate V/X Jamaica Rum
1 peeled, ripe banana
1 oz. chocolate syrup
2 tbsp. creamy peanut butter
4 oz. whole milk
2 scoops vanilla ice cream
Blend ingredients (with ice optional)
Whipped cream garnish
Sprinkle shaved chocolate

MÉNAGE À TROIS

Bucket glass, ice
Build in glass
1 1/2 oz. Brandy
1 1/2 oz. Kahlúa Coffee Liqueur
1 oz. cream
3 oz. club soda

MERRY WIDOW (1)

Cocktail glass, chilled
Pour ingredients into iced mixing glass
1 1/2 oz. Dubonnet Rouge
1/2 oz. Dry Vermouth
1 dash Angostura Bitters
2 dashes Pernod
2 dashes B & B Liqueur
Stir and strain
Lemon twist garnish

MERRY WIDOW (2)

Bucket glass, ice
Pour ingredients into iced mixing glass
1 1/2 oz. Gin
1 oz. orange juice
1 oz. sweet 'n' sour
Shake and strain
Fill with club soda

METRO COCKTAIL

Champagne glass, chilled
Pour ingredients into iced mixing glass
1 oz. Jewel of Russia Classic Vodka
1 oz. Jewel of Russia Berry Infusion
1/4 oz. Cointreau Liqueur
1/4 oz. fresh lime juice
1/2 oz. cranberry juice
Shake and strain
Fill with Champagne
Lemon twist garnish

MEXICAN BLACKJACK

Rocks glass, chilled
Pour ingredients into iced mixing glass
1/2 oz. Jose Cuervo Especial Tequila
1/2 oz. Black Velvet Canadian
1/2 oz. Jack Daniel's Tennessee Whiskey
1/2 oz. DeKuyper Triple Sec
Shake and strain

MEXICAN BULLFROG

Highball glass, ice
Build in glass
1 1/4 oz. Tequila
Fill with lemonade
Lime wheel garnish

MEXICAN COCOA

Coffee mug, heated
Build in glass
3/4 oz. Kahlúa Coffee Liqueur
3/4 oz. Brandy
Near fill with hot chocolate
Whipped cream garnish
Sprinkle nutmeg

MEXICAN COFFEE

Coffee mug, heated
Build in glass
3/4 oz. Tequila
3/4 oz. Kahlúa Coffee Liqueur
Near fill with hot coffee
Whipped cream garnish (optional)

MEXICAN FLAG

Cordial or sherry glass, chilled
Layer ingredients
1/3 fill grenadine
1/3 fill Green Crème de Menthe
1/3 fill 151 proof Rum

MEXICAN GRASSHOPPER

Cocktail glass, chilled
Pour ingredients into iced mixing glass
1/2 oz. White Crème de Cacao
1/2 oz. Green Crème de Menthe
1/2 oz. Kahlúa Coffee Liqueur
2 oz. half & half cream
Shake and strain

MEXICAN ITCH

Presentation shot glass, chilled
Rim glass with salt (optional)
Build in glass
1/3 fill El Tesoro Añejo Tequila
1/3 fill Grand Marnier Liqueur
1/3 fill lime juice
Lime wedge garnish

COURVOISIER®
V.S.O.P. COGNAC

Courvoisier began creating brandies during the reign of Napoleon Bonaparte and soon became the emperor's favorite. This famous house of cognac owns no vineyards, rather they acquire young brandies from over 400 private distillers. The firm's cellar master then oversees their maturation and eventual assemblage into cognac. At any one point, Courvoisier has roughly 45,000 barrels of brandy aging and adds another 3,000 every year.

Famed COURVOISIER V.S.O.P. is a Fine Champagne cognac, meaning it is made from a blend of brandies from the prized Grande Champagne and Petite Champagne districts of Cognac. The brandies used in its blend are matured a minimum of 8 years in Limousin oak, with most aged for 12 years.

Courvoisier V.S.O.P. is a classically structured cognac. It has a soft, round body and an assertive bouquet brimming with fruity and floral notes. The brandy has a seamlessly smooth entry and a layered palate of chocolate, citrus and nuts. The finish is fruity, spicy and of medium duration.

The brandy is best presented neat in a snifter, allowing several minutes to fully aerate before enjoying. Courvoisier V.S.O.P. is also marvelous when featured in such classic cocktails as the Manhattan, sidecar and stinger.

MEXICAN MELON
House specialty glass, ice
Rim glass with sugar (optional)
Pour ingredients into iced mixing glass
1 oz. Herradura Reposado Tequila
1 oz. Midori Melon Liqueur
1/2 oz. Chambord Liqueur
1/2 oz. fresh lime juice
1 oz. orange juice
2 oz. sweet 'n' sour
Shake and strain
Lime wedge garnish

MEXICAN MONK
Coffee mug, heated
Build in glass
1 oz. Kahlúa Coffee Liqueur
1 oz. Frangelico Liqueur
1/2 oz. Dark Crème de Cacao
Near fill with hot coffee
Whipped cream garnish
Dust powdered cocoa

MEXICAN NAZI KILLER
aka **Albright of Tucson**
Presentation shot glass, chilled
Layer ingredients
1/3 fill Jägermeister Liqueur
1/3 fill Rumple Minze Schnapps
1/3 fill Tequila

MEXICAN RUNNER
House specialty glass, chilled
Pour ingredients into blender
3/4 oz. Hussong's Reposado Tequila
3/4 oz. Cruzan Estate Diamond Rum
1/2 oz. Razzmatazz Raspberry Liqueur
1/2 oz. Cruzan Banana Rum
1/2 oz. grenadine
1/2 oz. fresh lime juice
1 oz. sweet 'n' sour
2 oz. limeade
Blend with ice
Lime wheel garnish

MEXICAN SIESTA
Rocks glass, chilled
Rim glass with salt (optional)
Pour ingredients into iced mixing glass
3/4 oz. Sauza Conmemorativo
    Añejo Tequila
3/4 oz. Grand Marnier Liqueur
1 1/4 oz. sweet 'n' sour
Shake and strain
Lime wedge garnish

MIAMI ICE
House specialty glass, ice
Pour ingredients into iced mixing glass
1/2 oz. Van Gogh Gin
1/2 oz. Vincent Van Gogh Vodka
1/2 oz. Cruzan Estate Light Rum
1/2 oz. DeKuyper Peach Pucker
1 oz. orange juice
1 oz. sweet 'n' sour
Shake and strain
Splash Seven-Up

MIAMI VICE (1)
House specialty glass, chilled
Pour ingredients into blender
1 1/4 oz. Ypioca Cachaça
3/4 oz. Blue Curaçao
1 1/2 oz. sweet 'n' sour
Blend with ice
Lime wedge garnish

MIAMI VICE (2)
Bucket glass, ice
Build in glass
1/2 oz. chocolate syrup
2 oz. root beer
2 oz. half & half cream
Fill with cola

MICHELADA, SAUZA
Pilsner or pint glass, ice
Rim glass with salt (optional)
Build in glass
1 1/4 oz. Sauza Hornitos Tequila
1/2 oz. Rose's Lime Juice
6-7 oz. Corona Beer
Serve with bottle of Corona
Lime wedge garnish

MIDNIGHT EXPRESS (1)
Cocktail glass, chilled
Pour ingredients into iced mixing glass
1 3/4 oz. Bacardi 8 Reserva Rum
3/4 oz. Cointreau Liqueur
1/2 oz. fresh lime juice
1/2 oz. sweet 'n' sour
Shake and strain
Lime wedge garnish

MIDNIGHT EXPRESS (2)
Cocktail glass, chilled
Pour ingredients into iced mixing glass
1 3/4 oz. Angostura 1824
    Limited Reserve Rum
3/4 oz. Cointreau Liqueur
1/2 oz. fresh lime juice
1/2 oz. sweet 'n' sour
Shake and strain
Lime wedge garnish

MIDNIGHT EXPRESS (3)
Cocktail glass, chilled
Pour ingredients into iced mixing glass
1 3/4 oz. Rhum Barbancourt 5-Star Rum
3/4 oz. Cointreau Liqueur
1/2 oz. fresh lime juice
1/2 oz. sweet 'n' sour
Shake and strain
Lime wedge garnish

MIDNIGHT LACE
Coffee mug, heated
Build in glass
1 1/2 oz. B & B Liqueur
1/2 oz. Hiram Walker Triple Sec
1 sugar cube
Near fill with hot coffee
Lemon twist garnish
Whipped cream garnish (optional)

MIDNIGHT OIL
Tankard or pilsner glass, chilled
Build in glass
2 1/2 oz. Tawny Port
Fill with Guinness Stout

MIDNIGHT ORCHID
Cocktail glass, chilled
Pour ingredients into iced mixing glass
1 oz. Rain Vodka
3/4 oz. Razzmatazz Raspberry Liqueur
3/4 oz. cranberry juice
2 oz. pineapple juice
Shake and strain

MIDORABLE
Cocktail glass, chilled
Pour ingredients into iced mixing glass
1 oz. Midori Melon Liqueur
3/4 oz. Crème de Banana
1/2 oz. fresh lime juice
1 oz. sweet 'n' sour
Shake and strain

MIDORI CANUCK
Rocks glass, ice
Build in glass
1 oz. Vodka
1 oz. Midori Melon Liqueur
1/2 oz. Canadian Club Whisky

MIDORI COOLER
Bucket glass, ice
Build in glass
1 oz. Midori Melon Liqueur
1/2 oz. DeKuyper Peach Pucker
1/2 oz. DeKuyper Raspberry Pucker
Fill with pineapple juice

LICOR 43®
(CUARENTA Y TRES)

LICOR 43 is a fascinating product with an equally fascinating heritage. Better known as CUARENTA Y TRES in its homeland of Spain, it is conjectured that its origin dates back to ancient times and the seafaring Phoenicians. The earliest version of the present day liqueur, however, can be traced back to the 16th century, with the mastering of distillation and the discovery of vanilla in Mexico by the Spanish Conquistadors.

Today the Diego Zamora Company makes Licor 43 in Cartegena, Spain. This delectable liqueur is made from a base of premium Spanish brandy with an infusion of berries, citrus fruit and fragrant herbs. The "43" in the liqueur's name refers to the number of ingredients used in its proprietary recipe. It is bottled at 62 proof.

Licor 43 is wildly popular in Spain and is continuing to find its niche behind American bars. The liqueur has a lustrous golden hue with brilliant amber highlights and a richly textured, medium-weight body. It is endowed with a generous bouquet of butterscotch, oranges and vanilla. Licor 43 presents a sweet, lively palate of citrus, herbs and vanilla, which persist well into the warm and flavorful finish.

Savory Licor 43 is a versatile player behind the bar. The liqueur adds a wonderful vanilla and light citrus essence to mixed drinks.

MIDORI DRIVER
Highball glass, ice
Build in glass
1 1/4 oz. Midori Melon Liqueur
Near fill with orange juice
Splash club soda

MIDORI STINGER
Rocks glass, ice
Build in glass
1 oz. Midori Melon Liqueur
1 oz. Brandy
1/2 oz. White Crème de Menthe

MIDWAY MANHATTAN
House specialty glass, ice
Pour ingredients into iced mixing glass
1 1/4 oz. Bacardi Gold Rum
1 1/4 oz. Mount Gay Eclipse Rum
3/4 oz. Disaronno Amaretto Liqueur
3/4 oz. Tia Maria
2 oz. orange juice
2 oz. sweet 'n' sour
Shake and strain
Orange slice and cherry garnish

MIDWAY RAT (1)
Rocks glass, chilled
Pour ingredients into iced mixing glass
1/2 oz. Bacardi Light Rum
1/2 oz. Disaronno Amaretto Liqueur
1/2 oz. Tia Maria
1/2 oz. pineapple juice
Shake and strain

MIDWAY RAT (2)
Bucket glass, ice
Build in glass
1 oz. Bacardi Light Rum
3/4 oz. Disaronno Amaretto Liqueur
3/4 oz. Tia Maria
3 oz. pineapple juice
Orange slice and cherry garnish

MIGHTY BULL SHOOTER
Presentation shot glass, chilled
Layer ingredients
1/2 fill Kahlúa Coffee Liqueur
1/2 fill Sauza Tres Generaciones
   Plata Tequila

MIGHTY KONG
Rocks glass, chilled
Build in glass
3/4 oz. Cruzan Banana Rum
3/4 oz. Kahlúa Coffee Liqueur
3/4 oz. Baileys Irish Cream

MIKHAIL COCKTAIL

House specialty glass, ice
Pour ingredients into iced mixing glass
3/4 oz. Stolichnaya Russian Vodka
3/4 oz. Chambord Liqueur
1 oz. orange juice
1 1/2 oz. sweet 'n' sour
Shake and strain
Fill with Champagne
Lemon wedge garnish

MILK OF AMNESIA

Presentation shot glass, chilled
Build in glass
1/2 fill Jägermeister Liqueur
1/2 fill Baileys Irish Cream

MILLIONAIRE COCKTAIL

Cocktail glass, chilled
Pour ingredients into iced mixing glass
1 1/2 oz. W.L. Weller Bourbon
1/2 oz. DeKuyper Triple Sec
1/2 oz. grenadine
1 oz. sweet 'n' sour
1 egg white (optional)
Shake and strain

MILLIONAIRE'S COFFEE

Coffee mug, heated
Build in glass
1/2 oz. Kahlúa Coffee Liqueur
1/2 oz. Baileys Irish Cream
1/2 oz. Grand Marnier Liqueur
Near fill with hot coffee
Whipped cream garnish
Drizzle 1/2 oz. Frangelico Liqueur

MILWAUKEE RIVER

Presentation shot glass, chilled
Layer ingredients
1/3 fill Kahlúa Coffee Liqueur
1/3 fill Blue Curaçao
1/3 fill Baileys Irish Cream

MIMOSA

aka **Buck's Fizz**
Champagne glass, chilled
Build in glass
1/2 fill orange juice
1/2 fill Champagne
Orange slice garnish

MINCEMEAT MOCHA

Coffee mug, heated
Build in glass
1 1/2 oz. Bacardi Gold Rum
3/4 oz. Tuaca
1 oz. Hershey's chocolate syrup
Near fill with hot coffee
Whipped cream garnish
Drizzle 1/2 oz. Apple Schnapps

MIND BENDER

Rocks glass, ice
Build in glass
1 1/2 oz. Absolut Kurant Vodka
3/4 oz. Chambord Liqueur
Splash club soda

MIND ERASER (1)

Rocks glass, crushed ice
Build in glass
3/4 oz. VOX Vodka
3/4 oz. Kahlúa Coffee Liqueur
3/4 oz. Rumple Minze Schnapps

MIND ERASER (2)

Highball glass, ice
Build in glass
1 1/2 oz. Vodka
1 1/2 oz. Kahlúa Coffee Liqueur
Fill with club soda

MINI BEER

Presentation shot glass, chilled
Build in glass
1 oz. Licor 43 (Cuarenta y Tres)
Whipped cream garnish

MINISKIRT LIMBO

Bucket glass, ice
Build in glass
1 3/4 oz. KéKé Beach Cream Liqueur
3/4 oz. Cruzan Orange Rum
1/2 fill with orange juice
1/2 fill with half & half cream

MINNEHAHA

Bucket glass, ice
Pour ingredients into iced mixing glass
1 1/2 oz. Gin
1/2 oz. Dry Vermouth
1/2 oz. Sweet Vermouth
1/2 oz. Pernod
1/2 oz. orange juice
Shake and strain

EVAN WILLIAMS® SINGLE BARREL 1992 VINTAGE BOURBON

There is something intrinsically special about a vintage-dated product, a slice of life that cannot be duplicated. It offers a precise snapshot of the conditions and circumstances surrounding everything that went into the making of the product inside. Such is the case with EVAN WILLIAMS SINGLE BARREL 1992 VINTAGE BOURBON, a spectacular American whiskey garnering critical acclaim.

Made in Bardstown, Kentucky, it is the seventh consecutive year that Heaven Hill has issued the vintage-dated bourbon, the previous six vintages having sold out within a few months of release.

This issue of Evan Williams Bourbon was distilled and barreled in the autumn of 1992. After resting for 10 years in charred white oak, the whiskey is drawn from the barrel, reduced to 86.6 proof and bottled unblended.

The bourbon is an extravaganza for the senses. It's dark, bold and full of personality. The bouquet is a lavish affair of caramel, honey and oak. On the palate, the bourbon offers up layers of zesty, bakery fresh flavors. The finish is equally tantalizing, quite long and loaded with vibrant and slightly spicy flavors.

As truly fabulous as this bourbon is, perhaps its most laudable quality is its remarkably reasonable price. So go ahead and pour it freely, your guests will be glad you did.

MINT FREEZE
House specialty glass, chilled
Pour ingredients into blender
1 3/4 oz. Jameson Irish Whiskey
3/4 oz. Green Crème de Menthe
2 scoops vanilla ice cream
Blend ingredients (with ice optional)
Whipped cream garnish
Drizzle 3/4 oz. Kahlúa Coffee Liqueur

MINT JULEP
Collins or chimney glass, frosted
Build in glass
3-4 mint sprigs
3 oz. Bourbon
1/2 oz. simple syrup
Muddle contents
Add crushed ice
Mint leaf garnish

MINT JULEP, GENTLEMAN'S
Rocks glass
Build in glass
3-4 mint sprigs
3 oz. Gentleman Jack Tennessee Whiskey
1/2 oz. Villa Massa Limoncello
Muddle contents
Add crushed ice
Mint leaf garnish

MINT JULEP, KENTUCKY
Bucket glass
Build in glass
1/2 oz. fresh lime juice
1/2 oz. simple syrup
3-4 mint sprigs
2 lime wedges
Muddle contents
Add ice
2 oz. Evan Williams Single Barrel
    Vintage Bourbon
2-3 splashes club soda
Lime wedge and mint sprig garnish

MINT JULEP, ON THE MARK
Collins or chimney glass, chilled
Build in glass
3-4 mint sprigs
3 oz. Maker's Mark Bourbon
1/2 oz. Alizé Red Passion
Muddle contents
Add crushed ice
Mint leaf garnish

MINT JULEP, PINEAPPLE
Collins or chimney glass, frosted
Build in glass
Muddle 3 mint sprigs
3 oz. Jack Daniel's Tennessee Whiskey
1/2 oz. simple syrup
1/2 oz. Green Crème de Menthe
2 oz. pineapple juice
Stir ingredients
Fill with crushed ice
Mint leaf garnish

MISS UBE DARN
House specialty glass, ice
Pour ingredients into iced mixing glass
1 oz. Stolichnaya Russian Vodka
1 oz. Chambord Liqueur
2 oz. sweet 'n' sour
2 oz. orange juice
Shake and strain

MIST
Rocks glass, crushed ice
Build in glass
1 1/2 oz. requested liquor

MOBAY RUNNER
Bucket glass, ice
Build in glass
1 oz. Appleton Estate V/X Jamaica Rum
1 oz. Mount Gay Eclipse Rum
1 oz. Cruzan Coconut Rum
Fill with papaya juice
Orange slice garnish

MOCHA JAMOCHA
Coffee mug, heated
Build in glass
3/4 oz. Appleton Estate V/X Jamaica Rum
1/2 oz. Cruzan Rum Cream
1/2 oz. Tia Maria
1/2 oz. Dark Crème de Cacao
Near fill with hot coffee
Whipped cream garnish
Dust powdered cocoa

MOCHA MY EYE
House specialty glass, chilled
Pour ingredients into blender
1 oz. Kahlúa Coffee Liqueur
1 oz. Vodka
3/4 oz. Nestle's chocolate syrup
2 tbsp. vanilla yogurt
2 scoops vanilla ice cream
Blend ingredients (with ice optional)
Whipped cream and
   chocolate-covered pretzel garnish
Sprinkle shaved chocolate

MOJITO (1)
Bucket glass
Build in glass
3/4 oz. fresh lime juice
1/2 oz. simple syrup
3-4 mint sprigs
2 lime wedges
Muddle contents
Add ice
2 oz. Light Rum
2-3 splashes club soda
Lime wedge and mint sprig garnish

MOJITO (2)
Bucket glass
Build in glass
1 oz. fresh lime juice
2 lime wedges
2-3 dashes Angostura Bitters
4 mint leaves
1 1/2 tbsp. superfine sugar
Muddle contents
Add ice
2 oz. Light Rum
2-3 splashes club soda
Lime wedge and mint sprig garnish

MOJITO, MASSA
Bucket glass
Build in glass
1 oz. fresh lemon juice
1/2 oz. simple syrup
3-4 mint sprigs
Muddle contents
Add ice
2 oz. Villa Massa Limoncello
2-3 splashes club soda
Lime wedge and mint sprig garnish

MOJITO, MY KENTUCKY
House specialty glass, ice
Pour ingredients into mixing glass
1/2 oz. simple syrup
5-6 mint sprigs
Muddle contents
Add ice
1 1/4 oz. Evan Williams
   Black Label Bourbon
1/2 oz. Cointreau
1/2 oz. Rose's Lime Juice
1 1/2 oz. sweet 'n' sour
1 1/2 oz. iced tea
Shake and strain
Orange slice and mint sprig garnish

MIXOLOGY BAR EXAM

1. Which vermouth is used to make a Southern Comfort Manhattan?
2. What two mixers are used to prepare a "Presbyterian?"
3. Unless instructed otherwise, a "splash" refers to what product?
4. What liqueur is floated on top of a tall screwdriver to turn it into a Harvey Wallbanger?
5. What is the name for a vodka gimlet made with triple sec?
6. What name is a martini given when garnished with a cocktail onion?
7. What is the difference between a wine spritzer and a wine cooler?
8. What is a frappé?
9. What is the purpose for heating a snifter before serving a brandy neat?
10. What is the more common name for a double old fashion glass?
11. What is the difference between a madras and a seabreeze?
12. How many ounces are in a liter?
13. What is the difference between a "split" and "half-bottle" of wine?
14. What does the term "neat" mean?

Answers

1. A Southern Comfort Manhattan is made with dry vermouth
2. A Presbyterian is made with ginger ale and club soda
3. A splash always means water unless otherwise instructed
4. A float of Galliano turns a screwdriver into a Harvey Wallbanger
5. A vodka gimlet made with triple sec is a kamikaze
6. A gibson is a martini garnished with a cocktail onion
7. A spritzer is made with equal parts of wine and club soda and a cooler is made with equal parts of wine and Seven-Up
8. A frappé is a recipe or liqueur served over crushed ice
9. A heated snifter causes brandy to hasten the release of its bouquet
10. Bucket glass
11. A madras is made with vodka, orange juice and cranberry, and a seabreeze is made with vodka, grapefruit and cranberry juice
12. A liter is 33.8 ounces
13. A split of wine contains 187ml, 6.35 ounces, or one-quarter of a wine bottle; a half-bottle of wine contains 375ml or 12.7 ounces
14. The term neat means to serve a product undiluted and usually at room temperature; with no ice

MOJITO, WAYWARD WIND
Bucket glass
Build in glass
1 oz. fresh lime juice
1/2 oz. Rose's Lime Juice
2 lime wedges
2-3 dashes Angostura Bitters
4 mint leaves
1 1/2 tbsp. brown sugar
Muddle contents
Add ice
2 oz. Sea Wynde Pot Still Rum
2-3 splashes club soda
Lime wedge and mint sprig garnish

MOLOTOV'S COCKTAIL
Rocks glass, ice
Build in glass
2 1/4 oz. Vodka
1/2 oz. Dr. McGillicuddy's
    Mentholmint Schnapps

MONKEY BITE
Rocks glass, chilled
Build in glass
3/4 oz. Cruzan Banana Rum
3/4 oz. Malibu Rum
3/4 oz. pineapple juice

MONKEY GLAND
Cocktail glass, chilled
Pour ingredients into iced mixing glass
1 1/2 oz. Gin
1/2 oz. Pernod
1/2 oz. grenadine
1 oz. orange juice
Shake and strain

MONKEY JUICE
Rocks glass, ice
Build in glass
1 3/4 oz. Royal Oak Extra Old Rum
3/4 oz. Angostura Caribbean Rum Cream
3/4 oz. Crème de Banana

MONK'S COFFEE
Coffee mug, heated
Build in glass
1 1/4 oz. B & B Liqueur
3/4 oz. Grand Marnier Liqueur
Near fill with hot coffee
Whipped cream garnish
Dust powdered cocoa

MONSOON
Rocks glass, chilled
Build in glass
1/2 oz. Rain Vodka
1/2 oz. Kahlúa Coffee Liqueur
1/2 oz. Disaronno Amaretto Liqueur
1/2 oz. Baileys Irish Cream
1/2 oz. Frangelico Liqueur

MONSTER APPEASER
Rocks glass, chilled
Pour ingredients into iced mixing glass
1/2 oz. Luksusowa Polish Vodka
1/2 oz. Midori Melon Liqueur
1/2 oz. Blue Curaçao
1/2 oz. Disaronno Amaretto Liqueur
1/2 oz. Crown Royal
1 1/2 oz. orange juice
Shake and strain

MONTE CRISTO SHOOTER
Presentation shot glass
Build in glass
1/3 fill Grand Marnier Liqueur
1/3 fill Kahlúa Coffee Liqueur
Near fill with hot coffee
Whipped cream garnish

MONTEGO BAY (1)
Coffee mug, heated
Build in glass
3/4 oz. Tia Maria
3/4 oz. Appleton Special Jamaica Rum
3/4 oz. Cruzan Banana Rum
Near fill with hot coffee
Whipped cream garnish
Sprinkle shaved chocolate

MONTEGO BAY (2)
House specialty glass, ice
Pour ingredients into iced mixing glass
2 oz. sweet 'n' sour
2 oz. orange juice
1/2 oz. Rose's Lime Juice
1/2 oz. grenadine
1 egg yolk (optional)
Shake and strain
Fill with club soda
Lime wedge garnish

MONTMARTE
Champagne glass, chilled
Pour ingredients into iced mixing glass
1 1/2 oz. Brandy
1/2 oz. Benedictine
2-3 dashes Angostura Bitters
1/2 oz. sweet 'n' sour
Shake and strain
Fill with Champagne
Lemon twist garnish

MOOSEBERRY
House specialty glass, ice
Pour ingredients into iced mixing glass
3/4 oz. Jewel of Russia Classic Vodka
3/4 oz. Jewel of Russia
    Wild Bilberry Infusion
3/4 oz. Disaronno Amaretto Liqueur
2 oz. cranberry juice
2 oz. sweet 'n' sour
Shake and strain
Float 3/4 oz. Grand Marnier Liqueur

MOOSE MILK
Highball glass, ice
Build in glass
1 1/4 oz. Kahlúa Coffee Liqueur
Fill with milk

MOP IN A BUCKET
Bucket glass, ice
Build in glass
1 oz. Myers's Jamaican Rum
1/2 fill orange juice
1/2 fill pineapple juice

MORNING SUN
House specialty glass, chilled
Pour ingredients into blender
1 1/2 oz. Beefeater London Dry Gin
2 oz. grapefruit juice
2 oz. orange juice
1/4 oz. maraschino cherry juice
2-3 dashes Angostura Bitters
Blend with ice
Whipped cream garnish
Dust powdered cocoa

MOSCOW MULE
Highball glass, ice
Build in glass
1 1/4 oz. Vodka
Fill with Ginger Beer
Lime wedge garnish

MOTHER
Rocks glass, ice
Build in glass
1 1/2 oz. Brandy
1/2 oz. Kahlúa Coffee Liqueur

MOTHER LODE
Rocks glass, ice
Build in glass
1 1/2 oz. Canadian Club Whisky
1/2 oz. DeKuyper Peppermint Schnapps

PIKE CREEK®
CANADIAN WHISKY

THE CANADIAN WHISKY GUILD is a remarkable collection of three, small batch whiskies created by Corby Distilleries to celebrate the country's long and prestigious whisky making heritage. Master distiller Michael Booth crafted each individual whisky to represent a distinctive style. One of the members of this incomparable collection is the double-barreled PIKE CREEK CANADIAN WHISKY.

Like fellow Guild member, Lot No. 40, Pike Creek is a departure in style from other Canadian whiskies. It is made from a blend of column-distilled, grain whiskies that have been aged in re-charred white oak barrels for a minimum of 10 years. Pike Creek is then further matured for about 6 weeks in 550-liter port pipes, oak barrels that were previously used to age Cockburn port.

Pike Creek has an attractive pale amber hue with lustrous red highlights derived from the port wine. The whisky has a light to medium body, satiny texture and an abundant bouquet of sweet grain and ripe fruit. It is an extremely flavorful spirit with a palate of toffee, vanilla and the savory overtones of Cockburn port. The long lasting finish is warm and delectable.

Pike Creek Canadian Whisky compares most favorably with the famed wood-finished whiskies of Scotland, Ireland and the U.S. It is bottled at 80 proof.

MOTHER MASON'S DELIGHT
House specialty glass, chilled
Pour ingredients into blender
3/4 oz. Disaronno Amaretto Liqueur
3/4 oz. Dark Crème de Cacao
1/2 cup strawberries
1/2 oz. half & half cream
2 oz. sweet 'n' sour
Blend with ice
Strawberry garnish

MOULIN ROUGE
Brandy snifter, heated
Build in glass
1 1/2 oz. Briottet Crème de Cassis
1/2 oz. Courvoisier V.S.O.P. Cognac
1/2 oz. Dry Sherry
1-2 dashes Angostura Bitters
Lemon twist garnish

MOUNTAIN RETREAT
Cocktail glass, chilled
Pour ingredients into iced mixing glass
1 oz. Cascade Mountain Gin
1/2 oz. honey
1 1/2 oz. sweet 'n' sour
1/2 oz. fresh lemon juice
Shake and strain

MOUNT GAY CAFÉ
Cocktail glass, chilled
Sugar rim (optional)
Pour ingredients into iced mixing glass
1 1/4 oz. Mount Gay Eclipse Rum
1 oz. Tia Maria
3/4 oz. Grand Marnier Liqueur
1 oz. cold coffee
Shake and strain
Top with frothed milk
Dust powdered cocoa

MR. MURPHY
Rocks glass, ice
Build in glass
1 1/2 oz. Irish Mist
3/4 oz. Baileys Irish Cream

MRS. BAILEYS' BUSH
Rocks glass, ice
Build in glass
1 oz. Bushmill's Irish Whiskey
1 oz. Baileys Irish Cream

MRS. BAILEYS' FAVOR
Cappuccino cup, heated
Build in glass
1/2 oz. Irish Whiskey
1/2 oz. Baileys Irish Cream
1/2 oz. Frangelico Liqueur
Near fill with hot espresso coffee
Top with frothed milk
Sprinkle shaved chocolate

MUD PUDDLE
Cocktail glass, chilled
Pour ingredients into iced mixing glass
1 3/4 oz. Rain Vodka
3/4 oz. Godiva Chocolate Liqueur
1/2 oz. Frangelico Liqueur
1/2 oz. Baileys Irish Cream
Shake and strain
Sprinkle shaved chocolate

MUDSLIDE (1)
Bucket glass, ice
Build in glass
1 1/2 oz. Vodka
1/2 oz. Kahlúa Coffee Liqueur
1/2 oz. Baileys Irish Cream
Fill with cola

MUDSLIDE (2)
Rocks glass, ice
Build in glass
3/4 oz. Vodka
3/4 oz. Kahlúa Coffee Liqueur
3/4 oz. Baileys Irish Cream

MULTIPLE ORGASM
Rocks glass, chilled
Pour ingredients into iced mixing glass
1 1/2 oz. Tia Maria
3/4 oz. Disaronno Amaretto Liqueur
1/2 oz. half & half cream
Shake and strain

MYSTIC RUNNER
House specialty glass, chilled
Pour ingredients into blender
3/4 oz. Sauza Tres Generaciones
    Plata Tequila
3/4 oz. Cruzan Coconut Rum
3/4 oz. Cruzan Banana Rum
1/2 oz. Rose's Lime Juice
2 oz. strawberry puree
2 oz. sweet 'n' sour
Blend with ice

NÁCIONAL
Cocktail glass, chilled
Pour ingredients into iced mixing glass
1 1/2 oz. Bacardi Gold Rum
3/4 oz. Apricot Liqueur
3/4 oz. fresh lime juice
3/4 oz. pineapple juice
Shake and strain
Lime wedge garnish

NAKED PRETZEL
Bucket glass, ice
Build in glass
3/4 oz. Van Hoo Belgium Vodka
1 oz. Midori Melon Liqueur
1/2 oz. Briottet Crème de Cassis
Fill with pineapple juice

NATIVE SUN
Cocktail glass, chilled
Pour ingredients into iced mixing glass
1 1/2 oz. Sauza Conmemorativo
    Añejo Tequila
1 oz. Disaronno Amaretto Liqueur
1/2 oz. Rose's Lime Juice
1/2 oz. orange Juice
1/2 oz. cranberry juice
Shake and strain
Orange slice garnish

NAVAL COMMISSION
House specialty glass, ice
Pour ingredients into iced mixing glass
1 1/2 oz. Pusser's British Navy Rum
3/4 oz. Matusalem Light Dry Rum
3/4 oz. Matusalem Red Flame Rum
1/2 oz. Rose's Lime Juice
1/2 oz. grenadine
1 1/2 oz. orange juice
1 1/2 oz. pineapple juice
Shake and strain
Lime, lemon and orange wedge garnish

NAVY GROG
Bucket glass, ice
Pour ingredients into iced mixing glass
1 1/2 oz. Myers's Jamaican Rum
3/4 oz. Light Rum
3/4 oz. Cadenhead's Green Label
    Demerara 151° Rum
1 1/2 oz. orange juice
1 1/2 oz. pineapple juice
1/2 oz. Rose's Lime Juice
Shake and strain

RAIN® VODKA

First introduced in 1996, RAIN VODKA is a skillfully crafted "New World" spirit made at the historic Buffalo Trace Distillery in Frankfort, Kentucky, by the same good folks who distill Blanton's Single Barrel Bourbon.

This exceptionally pure spirit is the first super-premium vodka made from organic strains of yeast and organically grown white corn. The grain is completely free of artificial fertilizers, insecticides and pesticides. The vodka is distilled with pure Kentucky limestone water drawn from underground springs. This famous water is at the heart of every great bourbon.

Rain Vodka is quadruple-distilled in three different column stills. The master distiller uses only the heart of each distillation, discarding the first and last portion of the run as too weak and too harsh, respectively. The vodka then undergoes a rigorous filtration process. It is filtered through activated charcoal and diamond dust in small batches to ensure absolute purity.

Award-winning Rain Vodka has a seamlessly smooth texture and a subtle, delicate bouquet of fruit and toffee. The lightweight body generates a moderate amount of heat in the mouth, while its palate is laced with fresh citrus flavors. The vodka has a clean, crisp finish.

There likely isn't a vodka-based cocktail devised by man that Rain couldn't make that much better.

NAVY GROG, MODERN
House specialty glass, chilled
Pour ingredients into blender
2 oz. Pusser's British Navy Rum
1/2 oz. fresh lime juice
1/4 oz. Falernum (sugar cane liqueur)
1 oz. orange juice
1 oz. pineapple juice
1 oz. guava nectar
Blend with ice
Orange slice garnish

NAVY GROG, NOR'EASTER
Coffee mug, heated
Build in glass
1 oz. Gosling's Black Seal Rum
1 oz. Pusser's British Navy Rum
1/2 oz. Cointreau Liqueur
1/2 oz. Tia Maria
1/2 oz. Disaronno Amaretto Liqueur
1 tsp. brown sugar
1 pinch cinnamon
Near fill with hot coffee
Whipped cream garnish
Drizzle 3/4 oz. Baileys Irish Cream
Sprinkle shaved chocolate

NAVY GROG, ORIGINAL
Coffee mug, heated
Build in glass
2 oz. Gold Rum
1 oz. Brandy
1 oz. fresh lemon juice
1 sugar cube
1 cinnamon stick
6 cloves
1 slice lemon
Fill with hot water
Lemon wedge garnish

NEGRONI
Cocktail glass, chilled
Pour ingredients into iced mixing glass
3/4 oz. Gin
3/4 oz. Campari Aperitivo
3/4 oz. Sweet Vermouth
Stir and strain
Lemon twist garnish

NEGRONI, UPTOWN
Cocktail glass, chilled
Pour ingredients into iced mixing glass
1/2 oz. Vya California Sweet Vermouth
1/2 oz. Campari Aperitivo
1 1/2 oz. Bombay Sapphire London Dry Gin
Stir and strain
Lemon twist garnish

NELSON'S BLOOD (1)
Rocks glass, ice
Build in glass
2 oz. Pusser's British Navy Rum
1/2 oz. fresh lime juice
2 oz. Ginger Beer
Lime wedge garnish

NELSON'S BLOOD (2)
Bucket glass, ice
Build in glass
2 oz. Pusser's British Navy Rum
1/2 fill with cranberry juice
1/2 fill pineapple juice
Lime wedge garnish

NELSON'S BLOOD (3)
Champagne glass, chilled
Build in glass
1 1/2 oz. Tawny Port
Fill with Champagne
Orange twist garnish

NEON TWISTER
House specialty glass, ice
Pour ingredients into iced mixing glass
1/2 oz. Bacardi Light Rum
1/2 oz. Midori Melon Liqueur
1/2 oz. DeKuyper Peach Pucker
1 1/2 oz. sweet 'n' sour
1 1/2 oz. orange juice
1 1/2 oz. pineapple juice
Shake and strain
Orange slice and cherry garnish

NEUTRON BOMB
Presentation shot glass, chilled
Layer ingredients
1/3 fill Kahlúa Coffee Liqueur
1/3 fill Baileys Irish Cream
1/3 fill DeKuyper Buttershots Schnapps

NEVADA PETE COCKTAIL
Cocktail glass, chilled
Pour ingredients into iced mixing glass
1 3/4 oz. Royal Oak Extra Old Rum
3/4 oz. Citrónge Orange Liqueur
1/2 oz. Rose's Lime Juice
1 oz. grapefruit juice
1 oz. sweet 'n' sour
Shake and strain
Lime wedge garnish

NEW ENGLAND
SUMMER SPRITZER
House specialty glass, ice
Build in glass
1 3/4 oz. Bacardi Limón Rum
3 oz. White Zinfandel
3 oz. cranberry juice
Lemon wedge garnish

NEW ORLEANS BUCK
House specialty glass, ice
Pour ingredients into iced mixing glass
1 3/4 oz. Bacardi Limón Rum
1 oz. orange juice
1 oz. sweet 'n' sour
Shake and strain
Fill with ginger ale
Lemon wedge garnish

NEW ORLEANS FIZZ
House specialty glass, ice
Pour ingredients into iced mixing glass
1 oz. Gin
1 oz. sweet 'n' sour
2 oz. half & half cream
1 egg white (optional)
Shake and strain
Splash club soda
Orange slice and cherry garnish

NEW ORLEANS JAZZ TIME
Champagne glass, chilled
Pour ingredients into iced mixing glass
1 1/2 oz. Bacardi Light Rum
1/2 oz. DeKuyper Peachtree Schnapps
1/2 oz. orange juice
1/2 oz. Rose's Lime Juice
Shake and strain
Fill with Champagne
Orange twist garnish

NEW YORK NUT
Rocks glass, chilled
Pour ingredients into iced mixing glass
1/2 oz. Disaronno Amaretto Liqueur
1/2 oz. Frangelico Liqueur
1/2 oz. Whaler's Hawaiian Vanille Rum
1/2 oz. VOX Vodka
1/2 oz. Tia Maria
1 oz. half & half cream
Shake and strain

NICOLAS
House specialty glass, ice
Pour ingredients into iced mixing glass
2 oz. orange juice
2 oz. sweet 'n' sour
2 oz. grapefruit juice
1/2 oz. grenadine
1 egg white (optional)
Shake and strain
Fill with club soda

TEQUILA ROSE®
STRAWBERRY
CREAM LIQUEUR

The TEQUILA ROSE story is a simple one to tell. It came, it saw and it conquered. Seriously, how else would you describe the liqueur's meteoric rise to stardom? When Tequila Rose debuted in 1997, there was nothing on the market remotely similar to it, and since it has hit the scene, the brand hasn't looked back.

Tequila Rose Liqueur is a blend of cream, tequila and natural strawberry flavorings. To call marrying these flavors together innovative would be an understatement. But as throngs of devotees will attest, the combination works.

Tequila Rose has a true-to-Crayola pink hue. While not necessarily the most rugged color they could have chosen, it may well be the only pink product behind the bar. The plump bouquet is that of strawberries and cream, which also best describes the palate. To fully appreciate how its flavors fully integrate, Tequila Rose should be sampled well chilled, either straight-up or on-the-rocks.

The liqueur may be at its best when playing a featured role in a cocktail or mixed libation. Tequila Rose is great when mixed over ice with a fruit flavored liqueur, or blended with strawberry ice cream and presented as a liquid dessert. It also works beautifully with coffee and chocolate.

NINA'S COFFEE
Coffee mug, heated
Build in glass
3/4 oz. Tuaca
3/4 oz. Disaronno Amaretto Liqueur
Near fill with hot coffee
Whipped cream garnish
Drizzle grenadine and
    Green Crème de Menthe

NINJA
Presentation shot glass, chilled
Build in glass
1/3 fill Dark Crème de Cacao
1/3 fill Midori Melon Liqueur
1/3 fill Frangelico Liqueur

NOBLE HOLIDAY
Rocks glass, ice
Build in glass
1 1/2 oz. Casa Noble Reposado Tequila
3/4 oz. Kahlúa Coffee Liqueur

NOBLE NYMPH
Cocktail glass, chilled
Pour ingredients into iced mixing glass
1 oz. Old Raj Dry Gin
1/2 oz. Mandarine Napoléon Liqueur
1/2 oz. fresh lime juice
1/2 oz. fresh lemon juice
Shake and strain
Orange slice garnish

N'ORLEANS CHILLER
House specialty glass, ice
Pour ingredients into iced mixing glass
1 1/2 oz. Bacardi Limón Rum
1 1/2 oz. Cruzan Orange Rum
1 oz. orange juice
1 oz. sweet 'n' sour
2 oz. iced herbal tea
Shake and strain
Orange slice garnish

NORTHERN LIGHTS (1)
Coffee mug, heated
Build in glass
1 oz. Yukon Jack Liqueur
3/4 oz. Grand Marnier Liqueur
Fill with hot coffee

NORTHERN LIGHTS (2)
Highball glass, ice
Build in glass
1 oz. Yukon Jack Liqueur
1/2 oz. DeKuyper Peachtree Schnapps
1/2 fill cranberry juice
1/2 fill orange juice

NOSFERATU
Cocktail glass, chilled
Pour ingredients into iced mixing glass
2 oz. Blavod Black Vodka
3/4 oz. Dr. McGillycuddy's
   Mentholmint Schnapps
3/4 oz. Godiva Chocolate Liqueur
Stir and strain
Lemon twist garnish

NOSFERATU'S SHOOTER
Presentation shot glass, chilled
Layer in glass
1/3 fill Godiva Chocolate Liqueur
1/3 fill Dr. McGillycuddy's
   Mentholmint Schnapps
1/3 fill Blavod Black Vodka

NO TELL MOTEL
Presentation shot glass, chilled
Layer ingredients
1/2 fill Dr. McGillicuddy's
   Mentholmint Schnapps
1/2 fill Jack Daniel's Tennessee Whiskey

NUCKIN FUTS
House specialty glass, chilled
Pour ingredients into blender
1 oz. Disaronno Amaretto Liqueur
3/4 oz. Kahlúa Coffee Liqueur
3/4 oz. DeKuyper Cherry Pucker
2 oz. chocolate milk
2 scoops vanilla ice cream
Blend ingredients (with ice optional)
Splash Dr. Pepper
Pineapple wedge garnish

NUN OUT OF HABIT
Brandy snifter, ice
Build in glass
1 1/2 oz. Courvoisier V.S.O.P. Cognac
3/4 oz. Baileys Irish Cream
3/4 oz. Godiva Chocolate Liqueur

NUT CREAM COFFEE
Coffee mug, heated
Build in glass
1/2 oz. Baileys Irish Cream
1/2 oz. Frangelico Liqueur
1/2 oz. Irish Whiskey
Near fill with hot coffee
Whipped cream garnish
Sprinkle nutmeg

NUT 'N' HOLLI
Rocks glass, chilled
Pour ingredients into iced mixing glass
1/2 oz. Irish Mist
1/2 oz. Disaronno Amaretto Liqueur
1/2 oz. Baileys Irish Cream
1/2 oz. Frangelico Liqueur
Shake and strain

NUT 'N' HONEY
Rocks glass, chilled
Pour ingredients into iced mixing glass
1/2 oz. Vodka
1/2 oz. Frangelico Liqueur
1/2 oz. Baileys Irish Cream
1/2 oz. Kahlúa Coffee Liqueur
1/2 oz. Tuaca
Shake and strain

NUTTY PROFESSOR
Rocks glass, ice
Build in glass
1 1/2 oz. Sauza Conmemorativo
   Añejo Tequila
1/2 oz. Disaronno Amaretto Liqueur
1/2 oz. Kahlúa Coffee Liqueur

NUTS & BERRIES
Cocktail glass, chilled
Pour ingredients into iced mixing glass
1 1/2 oz. Frangelico Liqueur
1 1/2 oz. Raspberry Liqueur
Shake and strain

NUTS TO YOU
Cocktail glass, chilled
Pour ingredients into iced mixing glass
3/4 oz. White Crème de Cacao
3/4 oz. Frangelico Liqueur
2 oz. half & half cream
Shake and strain

NUTTY IRISHMAN
Rocks glass, ice
Build in glass
1 1/2 oz. Baileys Irish Cream
1/2 oz. Frangelico Liqueur

NUTTY MEXICAN
Rocks glass, ice
Build in glass
1 oz. Frangelico Liqueur
1 oz. Kahlúa Coffee Liqueur
3/4 oz. El Tesoro Silver Tequila
3/4 oz. Baileys Irish Cream

HUSSONG'S®
100% AGAVE TEQUILA

Juan Hussong opened a cantina in Ensenada, Mexico in 1892. The small tavern soon became a regular stop for the stagecoach and a popular watering hole for thirsty riders. It was around that time that Hussong erected an alembic still in the back of the cantina and began distilling an agave spirit, known then as mezcal wine. More than a century later, the award-winning brand is known simply as HUSSONG'S 100% AGAVE TEQUILA.

Marketed in cork-finished, stoneware jugs, Hussong's tequila is made according to traditional methods at the González González Distillery in Guadalajara. The agaves are slow baked in stone ovens, and double-distilled in alembic stills. Each bottle of tequila carries its own registration number and Ricardo Hussong's signature.

HUSSONG'S 100% AGAVE REPOSADO TEQUILA is aged a minimum of 6 months in American oak barrels. It has a medium-weight body and a prominent bouquet of spice and a hint of smoke. The palate is loaded with the flavors of white pepper, oak, citrus and caramel.

New to the line is HUSSONG'S 100% AGAVE AÑEJO TEQUILA. This silky añejo rolls over the palate like a fond memory. It is exceptionally smooth and flavorful, and provides a lot of tequila for the buck.

NYMPHOMANIAC (1)
Bucket glass, chilled
Build in glass
1 1/4 oz. Bacardi Limón Rum
3/4 oz. Midori Melon Liqueur
1 oz. sweet 'n' sour
1 oz. Seven-Up

NYMPHOMANIAC (2)
Presentation shot glass, chilled
Build in glass
1 oz. Captain Morgan Spiced Rum
1/2 oz. DeKuyper Peachtree Schnapps
1/2 oz. Malibu Rum

OATMEAL COOKIE (1)
Rocks glass, chilled
Pour ingredients into iced mixing glass
1/2 oz. Goldschläger
1/2 oz. Frangelico Liqueur
1/2 oz. Baileys Irish Cream
1/2 oz. Disaronno Amaretto Liqueur
1/2 oz. half & half cream (optional)
Shake and strain

OATMEAL COOKIE (2)
Rocks glass, chilled
Pour ingredients into iced mixing glass
1/2 oz. Goldschläger
1/2 oz. Jägermeister Liqueur
1/2 oz. Baileys Irish Cream
1/2 oz. DeKuyper Buttershots Schnapps
1/2 oz. half & half cream (optional)
Shake and strain

O'BRAIN FREEZE
House specialty glass, chilled
Pour ingredients into blender
1 1/2 oz. Ballylarkin Irish Liqueur
1/2 oz. Frangelico Liqueur
1/2 oz. Kahlúa Coffee Liqueur
2 scoops vanilla ice cream
Blend ingredients (with ice optional)

OCEAN BREEZE
Bucket glass, ice
Build in glass
1 1/2 oz. Vodka
1/2 oz. Midori Melon Liqueur
Fill with lemonade

OCHO RIOS
Champagne glass, chilled
Pour ingredients into iced mixing glass
3/4 oz. Light Rum
3/4 oz. Cruzan Banana Rum
2-3 dashes orange bitters
Shake and strain
Fill with Champagne
Lemon twist garnish

OCTUPUS INK
Cocktail glass, chilled
Pour ingredients into iced mixing glass
1 1/2 oz. Blavod Black Vodka
3/4 oz. Blue Curaçao
1 oz. cranberry juice
Stir and strain
Lime wedge garnish

OFFENBURG FLIP
House specialty glass, chilled
Pour ingredients into blender
3/4 oz. Cruzan Coconut Rum
3/4 oz. Cruzan Banana Rum
1/2 oz. Rose's Lime Juice
1/2 oz. fresh lemon juice
1 peeled, ripe banana
1 egg yolk (optional)
2 oz. orange juice
Blend with ice
Float 3/4 oz. St. James Extra Old Rhum
Banana slice and cherry garnish

OLD FASHION
Rocks or old fashion glass
Build in glass
3 dashes Angostura Bitters
1/2 oz. simple syrup
Add ice
1 1/2 oz. Bourbon
Splash club soda
Orange slice and cherry garnish
Note: Old Fashions may be made with
   any requested dark liquor

OLD FASHION, APPLE
Rocks or old fashion glass, ice
Build in glass
3 dashes Angostura Bitters
1/2 oz. simple syrup
2 1/2 oz. Laird's Applejack Brandy
Splash club soda
Orange slice and cherry garnish

OLD FASHION, EVAN'S
Rocks or old fashion glass
Build in glass
3 dashes Angostura Bitters
1/2 oz. simple syrup
1 orange slice
5 fresh raspberries
Muddle contents
2 1/2 oz. Evan Williams Single Barrel
   Vintage Bourbon
Add ice
Splash club soda

OLD FASHION, KNOB CREEK
Rocks or old fashion glass
Build in glass
3 dashes Angostura Bitters
1/2 oz. simple syrup
1 peeled peach slice
Muddle contents
2 1/2 oz. Knob Creek Small Batch Bourbon
Add ice
Splash club soda

OLD FASHION, MUDDLED
Rocks or old fashion glass
Build in glass
3 dashes Angostura Bitters
1/2 oz. simple syrup
1 orange slice and cherry
Muddle contents
1 1/2 oz. Bourbon
Add ice
Splash club soda

OLD FLAME
Cocktail glass, chilled
Pour ingredients into iced mixing glass
1 oz. Bombay Sapphire London Dry Gin
1/2 oz. Vya California Sweet Vermouth
1/2 oz. Campari Aperitivo
1 oz. orange juice
1 oz. simple syrup
Shake and strain
Orange zest garnish

110 DEGREES IN THE SHADE
Beer glass, ice
Build in glass
1 1/4 oz. Jalapeño-infused Vodka
Fill with Modelo Especial Mexican Beer
Lime wedge and jalapeño slice garnish

OPERA COCKTAIL
Cocktail glass, chilled
Pour ingredients into iced mixing glass
1 1/2 oz. Gin
1/2 oz. Dubonnet Rouge
1/2 oz. Maraschino Liqueur
Stir and strain
Orange twist garnish

OPULENT COFFEE
Coffee mug, heated
Build in glass
3/4 oz. Gran Gala Orange Liqueur
1/2 oz. Kahlúa Coffee Liqueur
1/2 oz. Baileys Irish Cream
1/2 oz. Frangelico Liqueur
Near fill with hot coffee
Whipped cream garnish

DAMRAK® AMSTERDAM GIN

Founded in 1575, the Lucas Bols Company of Amsterdam is one of the oldest spirits companies in Europe. From the onset, the distillery has made a juniper-infused grain spirit called jenever. Bols became the spirits purveyor to the Dutch East India Company, which also secured the company a steady source of spices and herbs from Indonesia, Ceylon, Malaya and the Spice Islands. These exotic flavorings would eventually give birth to DAMRAK AMSTERDAM GIN.

Introduced in 2001, this ultra-premium spirit is crafted from a proprietary recipe dating back to the early 1700s. It combines 17 fruits, berries, herbs and spices, each individually distilled to lock in the flavor and fragrance. The spirit base of the gin is made from grain and malt, which after it has been infused with botanicals, undergoes a total of 5 distillations. The gin is bottled at 83.6 proof.

In every respect, Damrak Amsterdam Gin is absolutely superb. It has pristine clarity and a lightweight, silky smooth body. The generous bouquet is a captivating array of floral, citrus and herbal aromas. Initially, the flavor of luscious juniper berries is most prevalent on the palate, followed by a surge of the tart, zesty flavors of the botanical mix. The gin has a crisp and flavorful finish.

Damrak Amsterdam Gin makes a marvelous martini, but is also ideally suited for any gin-based assignment.

ORANGE BLOSSOM (1)
Cocktail glass, chilled
Rim glass with sugar (optional)
Pour ingredients into iced mixing glass
1 oz. Gin
1/2 oz. simple syrup
1 1/2 oz. orange juice
Shake and strain

ORANGE BLOSSOM (2)
aka **Left-Handed Screwdriver**
Highball glass, ice
Build in glass
1 1/4 oz. Gin
Fill with orange juice

ORANGE CHILLER
Highball glass, ice
Build in glass
1 1/4 oz. requested liquor
1/2 fill orange juice
1/2 fill cranberry juice

ORANGE CRANBERRY TODDY
Coffee mug, heated
Pour into saucepan
1 oz. Grand Marnier Liqueur
1 oz. Chambord Liqueur
1/2 tsp. fine granulated sugar
2 oz. cranberry juice
4 oz. orange juice
1 cinnamon stick
1 clove
Simmer and pour into heated mug
Orange slice garnish

ORANGE DELIGHT
Cocktail glass, chilled
Pour ingredients into iced mixing glass
1 3/4 oz. Belvedere Polish Vodka
3/4 oz. Extase XO Liqueur
2-3 dashes Angostura Bitters
Stir and strain
Orange twist garnish

ORANGE DREAM
Cocktail glass, chilled
Pour ingredients into iced mixing glass
1 1/2 oz. Pearl Vodka
3/4 oz. Dr. McGillycuddy's Vanilla Liqueur
1/2 oz. Mandarine Napoléon Liqueur
1/2 oz. orange juice
1/2 oz. half & half cream
Shake and strain
Orange slice garnish

ORANGE FRAPPÉ
House specialty glass, chilled
Pour ingredients into blender
1 3/4 oz. Gran Gala Orange Liqueur
3/4 oz. Dark Crème de Cacao
1/2 oz. Rain Vodka
1 oz. sweet 'n' sour
1 3/4 oz. orange juice
2 scoops vanilla ice cream
Blend ingredients (with ice optional)
Whipped cream garnish
Drizzle 3/4 oz. Disaronno Amaretto Liqueur

ORANGE JULIUS
Presentation shot glass, chilled
Build in glass
1/4 fill Vodka
1/4 fill Disaronno Amaretto Liqueur
1/4 fill orange juice
1/4 fill Draft Beer

ORANGE-U-GLAD-2-C-ME
Cocktail glass, chilled
Pour ingredients into iced mixing glass
1 1/2 oz. W.L. Weller Bourbon
1/2 oz. Rémy Red
1 1/2 oz. sweet 'n' sour
Shake and strain
Orange twist garnish

ORCHARD HAZE
Coffee mug, heated
Build in glass
3/4 oz. DeKuyper Pucker Sour Apple
1/2 oz. Hot Damn Cinnamon Schnapps
1/2 oz. Light Rum
Near fill with hot apple cider
Whipped cream garnish
Sprinkle nutmeg

ORGASM (1)
Bucket glass, ice
Build in glass
1/2 oz. Kahlúa Coffee Liqueur
1/2 oz. Disaronno Amaretto Liqueur
1/2 oz. Baileys Irish Cream
1/2 fill half & half cream
1/2 fill club soda

ORGASM (2)
Presentation shot glass, chilled
Layer ingredients
1/2 fill DeKuyper Peppermint Schnapps
1/2 fill Baileys Irish Cream

ORIGINAL MONK
Cocktail glass, chilled
Pour ingredients into iced mixing glass
1 3/4 oz. Original Cristall Russian Vodka
1/2 oz. Hardy Noces d'Or Cognac
1/2 oz. Benedictine
Stir and strain
Orange twist garnish

ORIGINAL SIN
Coffee mug, heated
Build in glass
1 1/2 oz. Vincent Van Gogh
   Wild Appel Vodka
Near fill with hot apple cider
Whipped cream and cinnamon stick garnish

ORSINI
House specialty glass, chilled
Pour ingredients into blender
1 oz. Gin
3/4 oz. Triple Sec
1 oz. half & half cream
2 oz. sweet 'n' sour
2 oz. orange juice
Blend with ice

OSMOSIS
Bucket glass, ice
Build in glass
1 1/4 oz. Sauza Conmemorativo
   Añejo Tequila
1/2 fill lemonade
1/2 fill Squirt
Float 3/4 oz. Midori Melon Liqueur
Lime wedge garnish

OTTER WATER
House specialty glass, ice
Build in glass
3/4 oz. Bacardi Light Rum
3/4 oz. Bacardi Gold Rum
3/4 oz. Mount Gay Eclipse Rum
1/2 oz. Chambord Liqueur
1 oz. orange juice
1 oz. pineapple juice
Near fill with Seven-Up
Float 3/4 oz. Cockspur V.S.O.R. Rum
Orange slice garnish

OUTRIGGER
Cocktail Glass, chilled
Pour ingredients into iced mixing glass
1 oz. Cruzan Junkanu Citrus Rum
1/2 oz. Disaronno Amaretto Liqueur
1 1/2 oz. cranberry juice
1 1/2 oz. pineapple juice
Shake and strain
Float 3/4 oz. Cruzan Estate Diamond Rum
Orange slice and cherry garnish

DEKUYPER®
PEPPERMINT SCHNAPPS

Despite having originated in Europe, peppermint schnapps has become an American institution. It can be found behind nearly every bar in the country and with good reason. It is a bracing, refreshing liqueur, and DEKUYPER PEPPERMINT SCHNAPPS is one of the best examples of just how refreshing schnapps can be.

Peppermint schnapps is a colorless, mint-flavored liqueur with approximately half the sugar content and twice the alcohol of crème de menthe. It is produced from a base of multiple-distilled neutral spirits and pure oil of peppermint.

The mark of a great schnapps is a light, rounded body, a dry, clean palate and a crisp, refreshing finish. Add to that a reasonable price and moderate alcohol content (60 proof) and you've just described DeKuyper Peppermint Schnapps.

Traditionally, schnapps is consumed as a shot, so it's advisable to keep one bottle in the cooler. This will allow you to serve the peppermint schnapps icy cold without having to dilute it.

Today, peppermint schnapps enjoys scores of applications behind the bar, including such mainstream recipes as the Snowshoe, Peppermint Pattie, Smiles for Miles, and many more.

OYSTER SHOOTER
Rocks glass, chilled
Build in glass
2 dashes Tabasco Sauce
1/2 tsp. horseradish
3 oz. Draft Beer
1 raw oyster

PACIFIC RIM
House specialty glass, chilled
Pour ingredients into iced mixing glass
1/2 oz. Midori Melon Liqueur
1/2 oz. DeKuyper Peachtree Schnapps
1/2 oz. sweet 'n' sour
1 1/2 oz. orange juice
1 1/2 oz. cranberry juice
Shake and strain
Fill with Champagne
Lemon twist garnish

PADDY
Cocktail glass, chilled
Pour ingredients into iced mixing glass
1 dash Angostura Bitters (optional)
1/2 oz. Sweet Vermouth
1 1/2 oz. Irish Whiskey
Stir and strain
Cherry garnish

PADDY O'ROCCO
Bucket glass, ice
Build in glass
1 1/2 oz. Irish Mist
1/2 oz. half & half cream (optional)
Near fill with orange juice
Float 3/4 oz. Disaronno Amaretto Liqueur

PAIN IN THE BUTT
House specialty glass, chilled
1—Pour ingredients into blender
   3/4 oz. Crème de Banana
   3/4 oz. Blackberry Brandy
   3/4 oz. Bacardi Select Rum
   1/2 oz. Bacardi 151° Rum
   1/2 oz. grenadine
   3/4 oz. Rose's Lime Juice
Blend with ice
Pour first drink into glass 1/2 full
2—Pour ingredients into blender
   1 1/4 oz. Mount Gay Eclipse Rum
   3/4 oz. Chambord Liqueur
   1/2 cup strawberries
   1/2 oz. Rose's Lime Juice
   2 1/2 oz. sweet 'n' sour
Blend with ice
Pour second drink on top of first drink
Pineapple wedge and cherry garnish

PAINKILLER
House specialty glass, ice
Build in glass
2 oz. Pusser's British Navy Rum
1 oz. orange juice
1 oz. coconut cream syrup
4 oz. pineapple juice
Stir ingredients
Orange slice and cherry garnish
Sprinkle nutmeg

PALACE GUARD
Cocktail glass, chilled
Pour ingredients into iced mixing glass
1 1/2 oz. Old Raj Dry Gin
1/4 oz. Vya California Dry Vermouth
1/4 oz. B & B Liqueur
Stir and strain
Lemon twist garnish

PANAMA JACK
Bucket glass, ice
Build in glass
1 1/2 oz. Yukon Jack Liqueur
1/2 fill pineapple juice
Near fill with cranberry juice
Splash club soda

PANAMA RED
Rocks glass, chilled
Pour ingredients into iced mixing glass
1 oz. Jose Cuervo Especial Tequila
3/4 oz. DeKuyper Triple Sec
1/2 oz. grenadine
1 1/4 oz. sweet 'n' sour
Shake and strain

PANTHER
Rocks glass, ice
Pour ingredients into iced mixing glass
1 1/2 oz. Tequila
3/4 oz. sweet 'n' sour
Shake and strain

PAPA DOBLES
House specialty glass, chilled
Pour ingredients into blender
1 3/4 oz. Bacardi Light Rum
3/4 oz. maraschino cherry juice
1 1/4 oz. fresh lime juice
1 1/4 oz. grapefruit juice
Blend with ice
Float 1 oz. Mount Gay Eclipse Rum
Lime wedge and cherry garnish

PARANOIA
Bucket glass, ice
Build in glass
1 oz. Cruzan Coconut Rum
1 oz. Disaronno Amaretto Liqueur
1/2 fill orange juice
Near fill with pineapple juice
Float 3/4 oz. Gosling's Black Seal Rum
Orange slice garnish

PARFAIT
House specialty glass, chilled
Pour ingredients into blender
1 1/2 oz. requested liqueur
2 scoops vanilla ice cream
Blend ingredients (with ice optional)
Whipped cream garnish

PARIS BURNING
Brandy snifter, heated
Build in glass
1 oz. V.S. Cognac
1 oz. Chambord Liqueur

PARPLE THUNDER
Bucket glass, ice
Pour ingredients into iced mixing glass
1 oz. Bacardi Select Rum
1 oz. Bacardi Light Rum
1/2 oz. Hiram Walker Triple Sec
1 1/2 oz. grape juice
1 1/2 oz. cranberry juice
Shake and strain
Splash club soda

PARSON'S PARTICULAR
Wine glass, ice
Pour ingredients into iced mixing glass
3 oz. orange juice
1 1/2 oz. sweet 'n' sour
1 egg yolk (optional)
1/2 oz. grenadine
Shake and strain
Orange slice and cherry garnish

PASSION ALEXANDER
Cocktail glass, chilled
Pour ingredients into iced mixing glass
3/4 oz. Opal Nera Black Sambuca
3/4 oz. White Crème de Cacao
1 1/2 oz. half & half cream
Shake and strain

- If a glass breaks within close proximity to the ice bin, all of the ice in the bin must be immediately removed and replaced. This is an absolute rule of safety behind every bar. It is impossible to see and remove pieces of broken glass from ice cubes.

- The traditional method of determining the proper serving portion for any size brandy snifter is to tip the glass onto its side on a hard, level surface. Proceed to pour in the requested product until the fluid reaches the inside rim of the glass. When you upright the snifter it will contain the proper portion for its capacity.

- Creating a well-prepared blended drink is as much art as science. There are two key things to making consistently great "frozen" drinks.

  First, there should be about equal amounts of ice and liquid ingredients in the blender canister at the onset. Using too much ice in relation to the fluid will result in the drink being too thick. On the contrary, not using enough ice yields a thin, watery drink.

  Secondly, check out the drink's consistency before pouring it into the glass. If it's too thin and liquefied, add a small amount of ice into the canister and blend for another 10 seconds. If the cocktail is too thick and undrinkable, add some more mixer to it and reblend for a few moments.

- Because blended drinks often contain as much ice as reciped ingredients, they are less alcoholically potent than the same drink served straight up or on the rocks.

PASSIONATE FRUIT
Bucket glass, ice
Pour ingredients into iced mixing glass
1 oz. Alizé Red Passion
1 oz. Stolichnaya Ohranj Russian Vodka
1/2 oz. DeKuyper Peach Pucker
1 oz. lemonade
Shake and strain
Lemon wedge garnish

PASSIONATE POINT
House specialty glass, ice
Pour ingredients into iced mixing glass
1 3/4 oz. Mount Gay Eclipse Rum
3/4 oz. Grand Marnier Liqueur
3/4 oz. DeKuyper Peachtree Schnapps
2 oz. orange juice
2 oz. cranberry juice
Shake and strain
Float 3/4 oz. Mount Gay Extra Old

PASSIONATE SCREW
Bucket glass, ice
Pour ingredients into iced mixing glass
1 1/4 oz. Bacardi Limón Rum
1 oz. Cruzan Pineapple Rum
1 oz. Chambord Liqueur
1/2 oz. grenadine
2 oz. orange juice
2 oz. sweet 'n' sour
Shake and strain
Orange slice and cherry garnish

PASSIONATE SUNSET
House specialty glass, ice
Pour ingredients into iced mixing glass
1 1/2 oz. Alizé de France
1 oz. Hussong's Reposado Tequila
1/2 oz. grenadine
1 oz. orange juice
1 oz. grapefruit juice
1 oz. sweet 'n' sour
Shake and strain
Float 3/4 oz. Grand Marnier Liqueur
Orange slice garnish

PASSION PUNCH
Bucket glass, ice
Pour ingredients into iced mixing glass
2 oz. Alizé de France
2 oz. orange juice
2 oz. pineapple juice
1/2 oz. grenadine
2-3 dashes Angostura Bitters
Shake and strain
Orange slice garnish

PASSION POTION
House specialty glass, ice
Pour ingredients into iced mixing glass
3/4 oz. Gin
3/4 oz. Vodka
3/4 oz. Light Rum
1/2 oz. grenadine
2 1/2 oz. orange juice
2 1/2 oz. pineapple juice
Shake and strain
Splash Seven-Up

PASSION ROYALÉ
Champagne glass, chilled
Pour ingredients into iced mixing glass
1 1/2 oz. Alizé V.S.O.P. Cognac
2 oz. sweet 'n' sour
Shake and strain
Fill with Champagne
Lemon twist garnish

PAZZO GRAND SPANISH COFFEE
Coffee mug, heated
Build in glass
1 oz. X.O. Café Coffee Liqueur
1 oz. Courvoisier V.S. Cognac
3/4 oz. Citrónge Orange Liqueur
1/2 oz. Bacardi 151° Rum
2 pinches cinnamon
1 1/2 oz. espresso
Fill with hot coffee
Whipped cream garnish
Dust powdered cocoa

PEACH BLASTER
Highball glass, ice
Build in glass
1 1/4 oz. DeKuyper Peachtree Schnapps
Fill cranberry juice

PEACH BOMB
Presentation shot glass, chilled
Build in glass
1/4 fill Vodka
1/4 fill DeKuyper Peach Pucker
1/4 fill orange juice
1/4 fill cranberry juice

PEACH BREEZE
Highball glass, ice
Build in glass
1 oz. DeKuyper Peach Pucker
1/2 oz. Vodka
1/2 fill cranberry juice
1/2 fill grapefruit juice

PEACH COBBLER
Cocktail glass, chilled
Pour ingredients into iced mixing glass
1 oz. Farias Reposado Tequila
3/4 oz. Peachtree Schnapps
3/4 oz. Foursquare Spiced Rum
3/4 oz. Whaler's Hawaiian Vanille Rum
1 1/2 oz. sweet 'n' sour
Shake and strain
Lemon twist garnish

PEACHES AND DREAMS
House specialty glass, ice
Pour ingredients into iced mixing glass
1 3/4 oz. Knappogue Castle Irish Whiskey
3/4 oz. DeKuyper Peachtree Schnapps
3/4 oz. Whaler's Hawaiian Vanille Rum
1 1/2 oz. orange juice
1 1/2 oz. half & half cream
Shake and strain
Orange slice garnish

PEACHES 'N' BERRIES
Rocks glass, ice
Build in glass
1 1/2 oz. Tequila Rose Cream Liqueur
1 oz. Peachtree Schnapps
Splash half & half cream

PEACH FUZZ
Rocks glass, chilled
Pour ingredients into iced mixing glass
1 1/4 oz. Vodka
3/4 oz. DeKuyper Peachtree Schnapps
1/2 oz. orange juice
1/2 oz. cranberry juice
Shake and strain

PEACHIE KEEN
House specialty glass, chilled
Pour ingredients into blender
1 oz. DeKuyper Peachtree Schnapps
1 oz. Galliano Liqueur
1/2 oz. half & half cream
2 scoops vanilla ice cream
Blend ingredients (with ice optional)

PEACHY CONGO COOLER
Bucket glass, ice
Build in glass
1 1/2 oz. Zone Peach Italian Vodka
3/4 oz. half & half cream
Near fill with orange juice
Float 3/4 oz. Crème de Banana
Peach wedge garnish

LUKSUSOWA®
POLISH POTATO VODKA

When Pablo Picasso was asked what three things astonished him the most, his answer was, "the blues, cubism and Polish vodka." The brand he was referring to was LUKSUSOWA POLISH POTATO VODKA. A few sips into your first sampling of this crisp and refined vodka and you'll understand why Picasso was astonished.

Luksusowa Vodka is made entirely from potatoes grown in the Baltic region of northern Poland. Distilling potatoes is an expensive proposition. Ten bushels of potatoes are required to produce the same amount of vodka as derived from one bushel of grain. Produced by the Polmos Poznan Distillery, the vodka is triple-distilled in column stills with mineral-free, artesian well water, then filtered through charcoal and oak chips to render it pure.

Luksusowa in Polish means "luxurious," which is an appropriate description of the vodka. It is crystal clear with a richly textured, medium-weight body. The vodka has a compact bouquet of herbs and caramel. Its palate is initially a touch sweet, then slowly tapers off into a pleasantly dry, long lasting finish.

Luksusowa also produces two delectable flavored vodkas. LUKSUSOWA WILD BERRY VODKA is brimming with the luscious flavors of blackberries, raspberries, blueberries, cranberries and wild cherries. The LUKSUSOWA CITRUS VODKA is lightly flavored with lemons.

PEARL DIVER
Rocks glass, chilled
Pour ingredients into iced mixing glass
1 oz. Pearl Vodka
1/2 oz. DeKuyper Pucker Sour Apple
1/4 oz. Galliano Liqueur
1/2 oz. grapefruit juice
Shake and strain

PEARL HARBOR
Highball glass, ice
Build in glass
1 1/2 oz. Midori Melon Liqueur
1/2 oz. Vodka
Fill with pineapple juice

PECKERHEAD
Rocks glass, chilled
Pour ingredients into iced mixing glass
3/4 oz. Yukon Jack Liqueur
3/4 oz. Disaronno Amaretto Liqueur
3/4 oz. pineapple juice
Shake and strain

PEPPERMINT COOLER
Highball glass, ice
Build in glass
1 1/2 oz. Peppermint Schnapps
Fill with Seven-Up

PEPPERMINT PATTIE
Cocktail glass, chilled
Pour ingredients into iced mixing glass
3/4 oz. White Crème de Cacao
3/4 oz. Peppermint Schnapps
2 oz. half & half cream
Shake and strain

PERFECT FIT
Bucket glass, ice
Build in glass
1 1/4 oz. Farias Silver Tequila
1/2 fill grapefruit juice
1/2 fill orange juice

PERFECT 10
Cocktail glass, chilled
Pour ingredients into iced mixing glass
2 oz. Tanqueray № Ten Gin
1/2 oz. Villa Massa Limoncello
1/2 oz. fresh lime juice
Stir and strain
Lemon twist garnish

PERIODISTA (1)
Cocktail glass, chilled
Pour ingredients into iced mixing glass
1 1/4 oz. Light Rum
3/4 oz. Cointreau Liqueur
1/2 oz. Apricot Brandy
1/2 oz. simple syrup
1 oz. fresh lime juice
Shake and strain
Lime wedge garnish

PERIODISTA (2)
Cocktail glass chilled
Pour ingredients into iced mixing glass
1 1/4 oz. Gosling's Black Seal Rum
3/4 oz. Cointreau Liqueur
1/2 oz. Apricot Brandy
1/2 oz. simple syrup
1 oz. fresh lime juice
Shake and strain
Lime wedge garnish

PERSUADER
Highball glass, ice
Build in glass
3/4 oz. Disaronno Amaretto Liqueur
3/4 oz. Brandy
Fill with orange juice

PETER PRESCRIPTION
Coffee mug, heated
Build in glass
1 1/4 oz. Appleton Estate V/X Jamaica Rum
1/2 oz. Tia Maria
1/2 oz. Grand Marnier Liqueur
1/2 oz. Chambord Liqueur
Near fill with hot coffee
Whipped cream garnish
Sprinkle shaved chocolate

PHILIPPI CREEK
Coffee mug, heated
Build in glass
1 oz. Sambuca
1 oz. V.S. Cognac
4 oz. hot espresso coffee
Splash half & half cream
Lemon twist garnish

PILGRIM
House specialty glass, chilled
Pour ingredients into blender
1 1/2 oz. Bacardi Light Rum
1/2 oz. grenadine
4 oz. cranberry juice
1 scoop orange sherbet
Blend ingredients (with ice optional)

PILGRIM'S PRIDE
House specialty glass, chilled
Pour ingredients into blender
1 1/2 oz. Bacardi Light Rum
1 oz. Cruzan Orange Rum
1/2 oz. grenadine
3 oz. cranberry juice
2 scoops orange sherbet
Blend ingredients (with ice optional)
Float 3/4 oz. Bacardi Select Rum
Orange slice garnish

PILLOWTALK
Brandy snifter, heated
Build in glass
1 1/2 oz. Benrinnes '89 Signatory
    Scotch Whisky
1/2 oz. Ballylarkin Irish Liqueur

PIMM'S CUP
Collins or bucket glass, ice
Build in glass
1 1/2 oz. Pimm's Cup No. 1
Fill with Seven-Up
Lemon twist and cucumber slice garnish

PIÑA COLADA
House specialty glass, chilled
Pour ingredients into blender
1 oz. Light Rum
1/2 oz. half & half cream (optional)
2 oz. coconut cream syrup
3 oz. pineapple juice
Blend with ice
Pineapple wedge and cherry garnish

PIÑA COLADA, ACAPULCO
House specialty glass, chilled
Pour ingredients into blender
1 oz. El Jimador Reposado Tequila
1/2 oz. Rose's Lime Juice
2 oz. coconut cream syrup
3 oz. pineapple juice
Blend with ice
Pineapple wedge and cherry garnish

PIÑA COLADA, AMARETTO
aka **Italian Colada**
House specialty glass, chilled
Pour ingredients into blender
1 oz. Disaronno Amaretto Liqueur
1 oz. Bacardi Light Rum
1/2 oz. half & half cream (optional)
2 oz. coconut cream syrup
3 oz. pineapple juice
Blend with ice
Pineapple wedge and cherry garnish

FOURSQUARE® SPICED RUM

Rum dates back to the 1630s on the island of Barbados. Since then, Barbadian rum has flourished on the world market, thanks in large part to the continuing efforts of R.L. Seale & Company. The latest stroke of creative genius from this premiere distiller is super-premium FOURSQUARE SPICED RUM.

The award-winning spirit is made at the Seales' Foursquare Rum Distillery. It is one of the most technologically advanced distilleries in the Caribbean. Foursquare Spiced Rum is a blend of molasses-based Bajan rums, barrel-aged a minimum of 2 years. The rum is steeped with a reciped mix of ground nutmeg, cinnamon and vanilla, then filtered and bottled at 70 proof.

Foursquare Spiced Rum is a carnival for the senses. It has a lightweight body and an enticing bouquet saturated with citrus and baking spice aromas that persist long into the lively finish.

R.L. Seale makes two other ultra-classy rums. DOORLY'S XO BARBADOS RUM is a superior blend of barrel-aged, Bajan rums that undergo a second maturation in Oloroso sherry oak casks. The sherry influence shines throughout this exceptional rum. Doorly's XO is a rare treat not to be missed. Also highly recommended is R.L. SEALE 10-YEAR-OLD BARBADOS RUM, a luxurious spirit with a tasting age much older than tens years.

PIÑA COLADA, AUSSIE
aka **Flying Kangaroo**
House specialty glass, chilled
Pour ingredients into blender
1 oz. Bacardi Light Rum
1/2 oz. Galliano Liqueur
1/2 oz. Vodka
1/2 oz. orange juice
2 oz. coconut cream syrup
3 oz. pineapple juice
1/2 oz. half & half cream (optional)
Blend with ice
Pineapple wedge and cherry garnish

PIÑA COLADA, BAHAMA
House specialty glass, chilled
Pour ingredients into blender
1 1/4 oz. Midori Melon Liqueur
1 oz. Crème de Banana
1 oz. orange juice
2 oz. coconut cream syrup
2 oz. pineapple juice
1/2 oz. half & half cream (optional)
Blend with ice
Pineapple wedge and cherry garnish

PIÑA COLADA, BELLEVUE
House specialty glass, chilled
Pour ingredients into blender
1 1/2 oz. Matusalem Golden Dry Rum
3/4 oz. Citrónge Orange Liqueur
1/2 oz. Rose's Lime Juice
2 oz. coconut cream syrup
3 oz. pineapple juice
Blend with ice
Float 3/4 oz. Matusalem Classic Black Rum
Pineapple wedge and cherry garnish

PIÑA COLADA, BERMUDA
House specialty glass, chilled
Pour ingredients into blender
2 3/4 oz. Gosling's Black Seal Rum
2 oz. coconut cream syrup
3 oz. pineapple juice
Blend with ice
Pineapple wedge and cherry garnish

PIÑA COLADA, BLACK PEARL
House specialty glass, chilled
Pour ingredients into blender
1 1/4 oz. Mount Gay Eclipse Rum
1 oz. Bacardi Gold Rum
3/4 oz. Tia Maria
2 oz. coconut cream syrup
3 oz. pineapple juice
Blend with ice
Float 3/4 oz. Gosling's Black Seal Rum
Pineapple wedge and cherry garnish

PIÑA COLADA, BRAZILIAN
House specialty glass, chilled
Pour ingredients into blender
1 oz. Bacardi Light Rum
1 oz. Ypióca Cachaça
1/2 cup cored, peeled pineapple
2 oz. coconut cream syrup
3 oz. pineapple juice
Blend with ice
Pineapple wedge and cherry garnish

PIÑA COLADA, CACTUS
aka **Cactus Colada**
House specialty glass, chilled
Pour ingredients into blender
1 1/4 oz. Hussong's Reposado Tequila
3/4 oz. Midori Melon Liqueur
1/2 oz. grenadine
1 oz. orange juice
1 oz. pineapple juice
2 oz. coconut cream syrup
Blend with ice
Pineapple wedge and cherry garnish

PIÑA COLADA, CANNE BAY
House specialty glass, chilled
Pour ingredients into blender
1 1/2 oz. Cruzan Coconut Rum
1 1/2 oz. Cruzan Pineapple Rum
1/2 oz. Roses's Lime Juice
1/2 oz. fresh lemon juice
2 oz. coconut cream syrup
3 oz. pineapple juice
Blend with ice
Pineapple wedge and cherry garnish

PIÑA COLADA, CHOCO
House specialty glass, chilled
Pour ingredients into blender
3/4 oz. Bacardi Spiced Rum
3/4 oz. Bacardi Gold Rum
3/4 oz. Mount Gay Eclipse Rum
3/4 oz. Kahlúa Coffee Liqueur
3/4 oz. chocolate syrup
1 3/4 oz. coconut cream syrup
2 oz. pineapple juice
2 scoops vanilla ice cream
Blend ingredients (with ice optional)
Float 3/4 oz. Matusalem Classic Black Rum
Pineapple wedge and cherry garnish

PIÑA COLADA, CHOCOLATE
House specialty glass, chilled
Pour ingredients into blender
1 1/2 oz. Bacardi Gold Rum
1 oz. chocolate syrup
2 oz. coconut cream syrup
3 oz. pineapple juice
2 scoops chocolate ice cream
Blend ingredients (with ice optional)
Float 3/4 oz. Bacardi Select Rum
Pineapple wedge and cherry garnish

PIÑA COLADA, LT. KIJE'S
House specialty glass, chilled
Pour ingredients into blender
1 1/2 oz. Jewel of Russia
   Wild Bilberry Infusion
1/2 oz. Cruzan Banana Rum
1/2 small ripe banana
1/2 cup strawberries
1 oz. coconut cream syrup
3 oz. pineapple juice
Blend with ice
Pineapple wedge garnish

PIÑA COLADA, EMERALD ISLE
House specialty glass, chilled
Pour ingredients into blender
1 3/4 oz. Mount Gay Eclipse Rum
1 oz. Cruzan Coconut Rum
1 oz. Blue Curaçao
2 oz. coconut cream syrup
4 oz. pineapple juice
1 scoop vanilla ice cream
Blend ingredients (with ice optional)
Float 3/4 oz. Gosling's Black Seal Rum
Pineapple wedge and cherry garnish

PIÑA COLADA, FRENCH
House specialty glass, chilled
Pour ingredients into blender
1 3/4 oz. St. James Extra Old Rhum
3/4 oz. Cognac
3/4 oz. Briottet Crème de Cassis
1/2 oz. half & half cream
1 oz. coconut cream syrup
1 1/2 oz. orange juice
2 oz. pineapple juice
Blend with ice
Pineapple wedge and cherry garnish

PIÑA COLADA, FRUIT (BASIC)
House specialty glass, chilled
Pour ingredients into blender
1 1/2 oz. Light Rum
1/2 cup requested fruit
2 oz. coconut cream syrup
3 oz. pineapple juice
Blend with ice
Fresh fruit garnish

GIORI® LEMONCILLO CREAM LIQUEUR

Innovation is a grand and wonderful thing. In addition to being delicious and extremely versatile, GIORI LEMONCILLO CREAM LIQUEUR is an innovative product literally in a class by itself. Considering the vast popularity of cream liqueurs, and how fond Americans are of lemon-flavored anything, this Italian thoroughbred is on the fast track to success.

Giori Lemoncillo Cream Liqueur is made in Trentino, Italy, from succulent Sorrento lemons that are handpicked, washed and peeled on the day they are harvested. The lemon peels are immediately placed in stainless steel containers in cold temperatures and steeped in molasses-distilled spirits. The lemon-infused alcohol is then filtered, sweetened and combined with cream. It is bottled at 34 proof.

Giori Lemoncillo Cream Liqueur is a genuine pleasure to drink. It has an attractive, yellowish-white hue, a velvety smooth texture and a delicate, lightweight body. The liqueur is graced with a lightly scented bouquet of citrus and dairy fresh cream. The semi-sweet palate is ideally balanced such that the flavor of lemon is readily perceived within the cream. The finish is clean and enjoyable.

This delectable liqueur is a mixologist's dream come true.

PIÑA COLADA, GOLDEN BACARDI

House specialty glass, chilled
Pour ingredients into blender
1 1/2 oz. Bacardi Gold Rum
3/4 oz. Bacardi Light Rum
1/2 oz. half & half cream
1 1/2 oz. orange juice
2 oz. coconut cream syrup
2 oz. pineapple juice
Blend with ice
Float 3/4 oz. Galliano Liqueur
Pineapple wedge and cherry garnish

PIÑA COLADA, HAWAIIAN LION

House specialty glass, chilled
Pour ingredients into blender
1 1/2 oz. Mount Gay Eclipse Rum
1 oz. Chambord Liqueur
1/2 cup raspberries
2 oz. coconut cream syrup
3 oz. pineapple juice
Blend with ice
Float 3/4 oz. Kahlúa Coffee Liqueur
Pineapple wedge and cherry garnish

PIÑA COLADA, HOLIDAY ISLE

House specialty glass, chilled
Pour ingredients into blender
1 1/4 oz. Bacardi 151° Rum
3/4 oz. Grand Marnier Liqueur
2 scoops French vanilla ice cream
Blend ingredients (with ice optional)
Float 3/4 oz. Mount Gay Extra Old Rum
Pineapple wedge and cherry garnish

PIÑA COLADA, ITALIAN

House specialty glass, chilled
Pour ingredients into blender
1 1/2 oz. Bacardi Gold Rum
3/4 oz. Mount Gay Eclipse Rum
1/2 oz. half & half cream
2 oz. coconut cream syrup
3 oz. pineapple juice
Blend with ice
Float 3/4 oz. Disaronno Amaretto Liqueur
Pineapple wedge and cherry garnish

PIÑA COLADA, KAHLÚA
aka **Kahlúa Colada**
House specialty glass, chilled
Pour ingredients into blender
1 1/2 oz. Bacardi Light Rum
3/4 oz. Kahlúa Coffee Liqueur
1/2 oz. half & half cream
2 oz. coconut cream syrup
3 oz. pineapple juice
1 scoop vanilla ice cream
Blend ingredients (with ice optional)
Float 1 oz. Kahlúa Coffee Liqueur
Pineapple wedge and cherry garnish

PIÑA COLADA, KÉKÉ COLADA

House specialty glass, chilled
Pour ingredients into blender
1 1/2 oz. KéKé Beach Cream Liqueur
1 1/2 oz. Rum
2 oz. coconut cream syrup
3 oz. pineapple juice
Blend with ice
Pineapple wedge and cherry garnish

PIÑA COLADA, KINGSTON

House specialty glass, chilled
Pour ingredients into blender
1 3/4 oz. Appleton Estate V/X Jamaica Rum
3/4 oz. Cointreau Liqueur
1 1/2 oz. orange juice
1 1/2 oz. pineapple juice
2 oz. coconut cream syrup
Blend with ice
Float 3/4 oz. Tia Maria
Pineapple wedge and orange slice garnish

PIÑA COLADA, KOKOMO JOE

House specialty glass, chilled
Pour ingredients into blender
3/4 oz. Bacardi Light Rum
3/4 oz. Bacardi Gold Rum
3/4 oz. Mount Gay Eclipse Rum
3/4 oz. Crème de Banana
1 oz. orange juice
2 oz. coconut cream syrup
3 oz. pineapple juice
Blend with ice
Pineapple wedge and banana slice garnish

PIÑA COLADA, LEMONADA (1)

House specialty glass, chilled
Pour ingredients into blender
1 1/2 oz. Bacardi Limón Rum
1 1/4 oz. Lemoncello Lemon Liqueur
1 oz. Mount Gay Eclipse Rum
2 oz. cranberry juice
2 oz. coconut cream syrup
2 oz. pineapple juice
Blend with ice
Pineapple wedge and cherry garnish

PIÑA COLADA, LEMONADA (2)

House specialty glass, chilled
Pour ingredients into blender
1 3/4 oz. Whaler's Hawaiian Vanille Rum
1 oz. Giori Lemoncillo Liqueur
3/4 oz. Disaronno Amaretto Liqueur
1 scoop vanilla ice cream
2 oz. coconut cream syrup
3 oz. pineapple juice
Blend ingredients (with ice optional)
Pineapple wedge and cherry garnish

PIÑA COLADA, LIQUEUR-FLAVORED

House specialty glass, chilled
Pour ingredients into blender
1 oz. Light Rum
1 oz. requested liqueur
2 oz. coconut cream syrup
3 oz. pineapple juice
1/2 oz. half & half cream (optional)
Blend with ice
Pineapple wedge and cherry garnish

PIÑA COLADA, MALIBU ORANGE

House specialty glass, chilled
Pour ingredients into blender
1 1/2 oz. Malibu Rum
1 oz. Hiram Walker Triple Sec
1 oz. orange juice
2 oz. coconut cream syrup
2 oz. pineapple juice
Blend with ice
Pineapple wedge and cherry garnish

PIÑA COLADA, MIDORI

aka **Green Eyes**
House specialty glass, chilled
Pour ingredients into blender
1 1/2 oz. Midori Melon Liqueur
1 1/2 oz. Bacardi Limón Rum
1/2 oz. half & half cream
2 oz. coconut cream syrup
3 oz. pineapple juice
Blend with ice
Pineapple wedge and cherry garnish

PIÑA COLADA, MONKALADA

Large house specialty glass, chilled
Pour ingredients into blender
1 oz. Appleton Estate V/X Jamaica Rum
1 oz. Mount Gay Eclipse Rum
1 oz. Cruzan Banana Run
2 oz. coconut cream syrup
2 oz. pineapple juice
2 scoops vanilla ice cream
Blend ingredients (with ice optional)
Float 1/2 oz. Appleton Estate
    V/X Jamaica Rum and 1/2 oz. Tia Maria
Pineapple wedge and cherry garnish

PIÑA COLADA, PORT ROYAL

House specialty glass, chilled
Pour ingredients into blender
1 3/4 oz. Appleton Special Jamaica Rum
1 oz. Chambord Liqueur
1 1/2 oz. strawberry juice
1 1/2 oz. orange juice
1 1/2 oz. pineapple juice
2 oz. coconut cream syrup
Blend with ice
Float 1 oz. Tia Maria
Pineapple wedge and strawberry garnish

ALIZÉ® V.S.O.P. COGNAC

Sometimes you have to open the window of opportunity yourself, other times it's thrown open for you. Preceded by mega-superstar Alizé de France, the arrival of ALIZÉ V.S.O.P. COGNAC into the United States has generated considerable interest. As you'll see, however, there's more than just a name connection going on. There are ample reasons why Alizé V.S.O.P. Cognac and its younger brother are enjoying success.

Alizé brandies are distilled by the Jean Paul and Marie Claude Lafragette families at the L&L Cognac House in the heart of the town of Cognac. The cognacs are made from an *assemblage* of *eaux-de-vie* from the Grande Champagne, Petite Champagne, Borderies, Fin Bois and Bon Bois districts of the region. A variety of grapes are used in the blend and the brandies are alembic distilled in strict adherence to traditional distillation techniques. The cognac is matured in French Limousin oak barrels.

Alizé V.S.O.P. Cognac has a copper hue with rich amber highlights, a round, supple body, and a wafting bouquet of fruit, caramel and baking spices. Distilling on the lees has given this brandy some extra zing on the palate and an array of lively oaky and spicy flavors. The finish is warm and lingering.

ALIZÉ V.S. COGNAC is youthful with a floral bouquet, a semi-sweet, fruity palate and solid finish.

PIÑA COLADA, PUSSER'S ISLAND
House specialty glass, chilled
Pour ingredients into blender
1 3/4 oz. Pusser's British Navy Rum
3/4 oz. Sloe Gin
2 oz. coconut cream syrup
3 1/2 oz. pineapple juice
Blend with ice
Pineapple wedge and cherry garnish

PIÑA COLADA, RÉMY COLADA
House specialty glass, chilled
Pour ingredients into blender
1 oz. Rémy Martin V.S. Cognac
1 oz. Mount Gay Eclipse Rum
2 oz. coconut cream syrup
4 oz. pineapple juice
Blend with ice
Pineapple wedge and cherry garnish

PIÑA COLADA, SPANISH
House specialty glass, chilled
Pour ingredients into blender
1 1/4 oz. Licor 43 (Cuarenta y Tres)
1 1/4 oz. Gold Rum
2 oz. coconut cream syrup
3 oz. pineapple juice
Blend with ice
Pineapple wedge and cherry garnish

PIÑA COLADA, STRAMARETTO
House specialty glass, chilled
Pour ingredients into blender
1 oz. Bacardi Gold Rum
1 oz. Disaronno Amaretto Liqueur
1/2 cup strawberries
1/2 oz. half & half cream
2 oz. coconut cream syrup
3 oz. pineapple juice
Blend with ice
Float 3/4 oz. Bacardi Select Rum
Pineapple wedge and strawberry garnish

PIÑA COLADA, STRAWBERRY BANANA
House specialty glass, chilled
Pour ingredients into blender
1 3/4 oz. Gosling's Black Seal Rum
1 oz. Cruzan Banana Rum
3/4 oz. Kahlúa Coffee Liqueur
1 peeled, ripe banana
1 1/2 oz. coconut cream syrup
2 oz. pureed strawberries
2 oz. pineapple juice
Blend with ice
Pineapple wedge and cherry garnish
Whipped cream garnish (optional)

PIÑA COLADA, TOASTED ALMOND
House specialty glass, chilled
Pour ingredients into blender
1 1/4 oz. Bacardi Gold Rum
3/4 oz. Kahlúa Coffee Liqueur
3/4 oz. Disaronno Amaretto Liqueur
1/2 oz. half & half cream
2 oz. coconut cream syrup
3 oz. pineapple juice
Blend with ice
Float 1/2 oz. Kahlúa Coffee Liqueur and
   1/2 oz. Disaronno Amaretto Liqueur
Pineapple wedge and cherry garnish

PIÑA COLADA, TROPICAL MOON
House specialty glass, chilled
Pour ingredients into blender
1 1/2 oz. Bacardi Light Rum
3/4 oz. Disaronno Amaretto Liqueur
3/4 oz. Blue Curaçao
2 oz. coconut cream syrup
3 oz. pineapple juice
2 scoops chocolate ice cream
Blend ingredients (with ice optional)
Float 3/4 oz. Appleton Estate
   V/X Jamaica Rum
Pineapple wedge and cherry garnish

PIÑA COLADA, TROPICAL SPLASHES
House specialty glass, chilled
Pour ingredients into blender
1 oz. Mount Gay Eclipse Rum
2 oz. coconut cream syrup
3 oz. pineapple juice
1 scoop vanilla ice cream
Blend ingredients (with ice optional)
Float 1 oz. Appleton Estate
   V/X Jamaica Rum
Pineapple wedge and cherry garnish

PINEAPPLE FIZZ
Cocktail glass, chilled
Pour ingredients into iced mixing glass
1 3/4 oz. Bacardi Select Rum
3/4 oz. fresh lemon juice
1 3/4 oz. pineapple juice
Shake and strain
Orange slice garnish

PINEAPPLE SMOOCH
Cocktail glass, chilled
Pour ingredients into iced mixing glass
1 1/2 oz. Alizé de France
3/4 oz. Cointreau Liqueur
2-3 dashes Angostura Bitters
2 oz. pineapple juice
Shake and strain
Orange twist garnish

PINK BABY
Cocktail glass, chilled
Pour ingredients into iced mixing glass
1 1/2 oz. Absolut Citron Vodka
1/2 oz. Cherry Marnier
1/2 oz. fresh lemon juice
Stir and strain
Lemon twist garnish

PINK CADILLAC
Champagne glass, chilled
Pour ingredients into blender
1 oz. Chambord Liqueur
1/2 oz. sweet 'n' sour
1/2 cup strawberry puree
Blend with ice
Fill with Champagne
Strawberry garnish

PINK COCONUT
Bucket glass, ice
Build in glass
1 3/4 oz. Cruzan Coconut Rum
1 oz. Chambord Liqueur
1 1/2 oz. pineapple juice
1 1/2 oz. orange juice
Lime wedge garnish

PINK CREOLE
Cocktail glass, chilled
Pour ingredients into iced mixing glass
1 1/4 oz. Bacardi Select Rum
3/4 oz. Chambord Liqueur
1 oz. orange juice
1 oz. pineapple juice
1 oz. sweet 'n' sour
Shake and strain
Orange slice garnish

PINK FLAMINGO
House specialty glass, ice
Pour ingredients into iced mixing glass
1 1/2 oz. DeKuyper Raspberry Pucker
2 oz. cranberry juice
2 oz. sweet 'n' sour
Shake and strain
Splash club soda

PINK GATOR
Bucket glass, ice
Build in glass
1 1/4 oz. Bacardi Select Rum
1/2 fill orange juice
Near fill with pineapple juice
Float 3/4 oz. Razzmatazz Raspberry Liqueur

RÉMY® RED

Launched in 1999, RÉMY RED is a cognac-based liqueur made by one of the preeminent cognac houses, Rémy Martin. Its style is an engaging blend of tradition and contemporary living. In fact, it makes a lively cocktail in itself, just chill over ice and let the rave reviews pour forth.

Rémy Red is made in the heart of the Cognac region of France from a blend of Rémy Martin Fine Champagne Cognac and the juice of freshly picked red currants, apricots and peaches. The naturally derived flavors of South American guarana and Chinese ginseng are then added to the mix. The firm infuses this lively blend with aged, Rémy Martin Fine Champagne cognac.

Rémy Red has an exotic appearance. It is opaque with a brilliant, lustrous, red-orange color. The generous bouquet is that of freshly squeezed juice, predominantly apricot and currant, plus a hint of the underlying cognac. The liqueur has a full, luscious body, and a slightly tart palate in which no one juice flavor predominates. The cognac is the decisive element in the blend, balancing out the natural sweetness in the juice.

Thank goodness for innovation. Rémy Red is a true-blue friend behind the bar. It adds a splash of personality to a wide range of cocktails, often just the thing to tip the scales of fate.

PINK GIN
Cocktail glass, chilled
Pour ingredients into iced mixing glass
2 oz. Plymouth Dry Gin
3-4 dashes Angostura Bitters
Stir and strain
Splash water or club soda (optional)

PINK HIGHLITER
House specialty glass, ice
Pour ingredients into iced mixing glass
1 3/4 oz. Sauza Hornitos Tequila
3/4 oz. Light Rum
3/4 oz. Cruzan Banana Rum
2 oz. cranberry juice
2 oz. pineapple juice
Shake and strain
Orange slice and cherry garnish

PINK LADY (1)
Cocktail glass, chilled
Pour ingredients into iced mixing glass
1 oz. Gin
1/2 oz. grenadine
1 1/2 oz. half & half cream
Shake and strain

PINK LADY (2)
Cocktail glass, chilled
Pour ingredients into iced mixing glass
1 oz. Laird's Applejack Brandy
1 oz. Gin
1/2 oz. grenadine
1 1/2 oz. sweet 'n' sour
1 egg white (optional)
Shake and strain

PINK LEMONADE (1)
Rocks glass, chilled
Pour ingredients into iced mixing glass
1 1/2 oz. Vodka
1/2 oz. grapefruit juice
1/2 oz. cranberry juice
1/2 oz. sweet 'n' sour
Shake and strain

PINK LEMONADE (2)
House specialty glass, ice
Pour ingredients into iced mixing glass
1 1/4 oz. Bacardi Limón Rum
1 1/4 oz. Stolichnaya Limonnaya
    Russian Vodka
1/2 oz. grenadine
3 oz. lemonade
2 oz. cranberry juice
Shake and strain
Splash Seven-Up
Orange slice and cherry garnish

PINK MOMENT
Cocktail glass, chilled
Pour ingredients into iced mixing glass
1 1/2 oz. Artic Vodka & Peach Liqueur
1/2 oz. Alizé Red Passion
1/2 oz. DeKuyper Peachtree Schnapps
1/2 oz. orange juice
1/2 oz. cranberry juice
1/2 oz. lemonade
Shake and strain
Whipped cream and peach wedge garnish

PINK PANTHER (1)
Tankard or pilsner glass, chilled
Build in glass
1/2 fill Guinness Stout
1/2 fill Raspberry-Flavored Ale

PINK PANTHER (2)
Champagne glass, chilled
Pour ingredients into iced mixing glass
1 1/4 oz. Disaronno Amaretto Liqueur
1/4 oz. grenadine
1 oz. orange juice
1 1/2 oz. cranberry juice
Shake and strain
Fill with Champagne
Orange slice garnish

PINK PARADISE
House specialty glass, ice
Pour ingredients into iced mixing glass
1 oz. Appleton Estate V/X Jamaica Rum
1 oz. Mount Gay Eclipse Rum
1 oz. Disaronno Amaretto Liqueur
1 1/2 oz. pineapple juice
3 oz. cranberry juice
Shake and strain
Pineapple wedge and cherry garnish

PINK PASSION
House specialty glass, ice
Build in glass
1 oz. Captain Morgan Spiced Rum
1 oz. Malibu Rum
1/2 oz. grenadine
2 oz. orange juice
2 oz. pineapple juice
Orange slice and cherry garnish

PINK SLIPPER
House specialty glass, chilled
Pour ingredients into blender
1 1/2 oz. Bacardi Light Rum
3/4 oz. Matusalem Golden Dry Rum
1 1/2 oz. coconut cream syrup
3 oz. pink lemonade concentrate
Blend with ice
Whipped cream garnish
Drizzle 3/4 oz. Chambord Liqueur

PINK SQUIRREL
Cocktail glass, chilled
Pour ingredients into iced mixing glass
3/4 oz. White Crème de Cacao
3/4 oz. Crème de Noyaux
2 oz. half & half cream
Shake and strain

PINK SUNSET
Bucket glass, ice
Build in glass
1 1/4 oz. Vodka
3/4 oz. Mandarine Napoléon Liqueur
1/2 oz. fresh lemon juice
1 1/2 oz. grapefruit juice
1 1/2 oz. cranberry juice
Kiwi slice garnish

PIRANHA
House specialty glass, ice
Pour ingredients into iced mixing glass
3/4 oz. Light Rum
3/4 oz. Gold Rum
3/4 oz. Malibu Rum
1 oz. grapefruit juice
1 oz. cranberry juice
1 oz. pineapple juice
Shake and strain
Orange slice and cherry garnish

PIRANHA CLUB INITIATION
Bucket glass, ice
Build in glass
1 1/2 oz. Bacardi 151° Rum
3/4 oz. Blue Curaçao
1/2 oz. DeKuyper Peachtree Schnapps
1 1/2 oz. sweet 'n' sour
Near fill with orange juice
Float 3/4 oz. Bacardi Select Rum

PIRANHA PUNCH
Punch Bowl, ice
Build in bowl
26 oz. Matusalem Classic Black Rum
12 oz. Matusalem Red Flame Rum
12 oz. fresh lime juice
12 oz. strawberry syrup
32 oz. orange juice
32 oz. pineapple juice
32 oz. mango or peach nectar
Thoroughly stir ingredients
Lime, lemon and orange wedge garnish

DR. MCGILLICUDDY'S®
MENTHOLMINT SCHNAPPS

Ever since DR. MCGILLICUDDY'S
MENTHOLMINT SCHNAPPS debuted
in the United States 20 years ago, it has
developed a significant cult following.
One sip of the good doctor's elixir and
you'll know its vast popularity is justly
deserved.

There is nothing even remotely close
in personality to Dr. McGillicuddy's
Mentholmint Schnapps. Uniquely
different than other mint-flavored
schnapps, this Canadian-born liqueur is
made from a base of neutral grain spirits
and flavored with menthol crystals that
form during the distillation process.
These crystals create a cool, refreshing
taste sensation quite unlike any other
mint schnapps.

Dr. McGillicuddy's Mentholmint
Schnapps is crystal clear with a medium-
weight body and a soft, supple texture.
The bouquet immediately fills the glass
with the spicy aroma of peppermint.
Whatever heat may have been generated
by the alcohol on the palate is quickly
doused by frigid waves of menthol-mint
flavor. The liqueur has an exceptionally
long, flavorful finish.

Drinking Dr. McGillicuddy's
Mentholmint Schnapps is a bracing, yet
thoroughly enjoyable experience. The
liqueur is also extremely useful behind
the bar, capable of adding a wonderfully
refreshing dimension to mixed drinks.

PIRATE LOVE
House specialty glass, chilled
Pour ingredients into blender
1 1/2 oz. Pyrat Pistol Rum
3/4 oz. Tia Maria
3/4 oz. Disaronno Amaretto Liqueur
1 tsp. vanilla extract
2 scoops vanilla ice cream
Blend ingredients (with ice optional)
Whipped cream garnish
Sprinkle shaved chocolate

PIRATE'S HICCUP
Bucket glass, ice
Build in glass
1 1/2 oz. Whaler's Hawaiian Vanille Rum
3/4 oz. Kahlúa Coffee Liqueur
1/2 fill cola
1/2 fill half & half cream

PISCO SOUR
Sour glass, chilled
Rim glass with sugar (optional)
Pour ingredients into iced mixing glass
3 dashes Angostura Bitters
1 1/4 oz. Pisco Brandy
2 oz. sweet 'n' sour
Shake and strain
Orange slice and cherry garnish

PISTACHIO MINT ICE CREAM
House specialty glass, chilled
Pour ingredients into blender
3/4 oz. Frangelico Liqueur
3/4 oz. Green Crème de Menthe
3/4 oz. Kahlúa Coffee Liqueur
2 scoops vanilla ice cream
Blend ingredients (with ice optional)
Mint leaf garnish

PITLESS SHOT
Presentation shot glass, chilled
Build in glass
1/3 fill DeKuyper Peach Pucker
1/3 fill Vodka
1/3 fill orange juice

PIZZETTI
Champagne glass, chilled
Build in glass
1/4 fill orange juice
1/4 fill grapefruit juice
Fill with Champagne

PLANTER'S PUNCH (1)

House specialty glass, ice
Pour ingredients into iced mixing glass
1 1/2 oz. Dark Jamaican Rum
1/2 oz. grenadine
2 dashes Angostura Bitters
1 1/2 oz. sweet 'n' sour
1 1/2 oz. orange juice
Shake and strain
Orange slice and cherry garnish

PLANTER'S PUNCH (2)

House specialty glass, ice
Pour ingredients into iced mixing glass
1 1/2 oz. Appleton Estate V/X Jamaica Rum
1 oz. Bacardi Light Rum
3/4 oz. Hiram Walker Triple Sec
2-3 dashes Angostura Bitters
1/2 oz. grenadine
1/2 oz. Rose's Lime Juice
2 oz. orange juice
2 oz. pineapple juice
Shake and strain
Lime, lemon and orange wedge garnish

PLANTER'S PUNCH (3)

House specialty glass, ice
Pour ingredients into iced mixing glass
1 1/2 oz. Appleton Estate V/X Jamaica Rum
1 1/4 oz. Bacardi Select Rum
3/4 oz. Orange Curaçao or Triple Sec
2-3 dashes Angostura Bitters
3/4 oz. fresh lime juice
1/2 oz. grenadine
1 1/2 oz. orange juice
1 1/2 oz. pineapple juice
Shake and strain
Float 3/4 oz. Matusalem Classic Black Rum
Lime, lemon and orange wedge garnish

PLANTER'S RUM PUNCH

House specialty glass, ice
Pour ingredients into iced mixing glass
2 oz. Pyrat X.O. Reserve Rum
1 oz. simple syrup
3 dashes Angostura Bitters
3/4 oz. fresh lime juice
2 oz. fresh water
Shake and strain
Sprinkle nutmeg
Lemon wedge garnish

PLATA V.I.P. COCKTAIL

Bucket glass, ice
Build in glass
1 1/2 oz. Sauza Tres Generaciones
    Plata Tequila
Fill with Squirt
Orange wedge garnish

PLYMOUTH ROCKS

Bucket glass, ice
Build in glass
1 1/2 oz. Bacardi Light Rum
1/2 fill grape juice
1/2 fill club soda
Lime wedge garnish

POIREISSE

Champagne glass, chilled
Build in glass
3/4 oz. Poire William (Eau de Vie de Poire)
3/4 oz. Godiva Chocolate Liqueur
Fill with Champagne

POM POM

Wine glass, ice
Pour ingredients into iced mixing glass
1 1/2 oz. sweet 'n' sour
4 1/2 oz. lemonade
1 egg white (optional)
1/2 oz. grenadine
Shake and strain
Fill with club soda
Lemon wedge garnish

POPE ON VACATION

Rocks glass, chilled
Pour ingredients into iced mixing glass
1/2 oz. Frangelico Liqueur
1/2 oz. Malibu Rum
1/2 oz. Myers's Jamaican Rum
1/2 oz. Chambord Liqueur
3/4 oz. orange juice
3/4 oz. sweet 'n' sour
Shake and strain

POPPYCOCK ROCK

Presentation shot glass, chilled
Layer ingredients
1/3 fill Kahlúa Coffee Liqueur
1/3 fill Dr. McGillicuddy's
    Mentholmint Schnapps
1/3 fill Razzmatazz Raspberry Liqueur

PORT AND LEMON

Wine glass, chilled
Build in glass
2 oz. Tawny Port
Fill with Seven-Up

PORT IN A STORM

Wine glass or house specialty glass, ice
Pour ingredients into iced mixing glass
2 oz. Tawny Port
3/4 oz. Brandy
4 oz. Dry Red Wine
Stir and strain
Mint sprig garnish

DECIPHERING CAPPUCCINO SPEAK

Years ago, if you ordered a cup of coffee "regular," you'd get it served with cream and sugar. Now, ask for a cup of regular coffee and you'll get coffee laced with caffeine. So if you're not completely up on your "café lingo," here's a short course to get you up to speed.

- **Americano** — espresso diluted with more hot water
- **Breve** — espresso highly diluted with steamed half & half and little foam
- **Café Au Lait** — 1/3 part espresso and 2/3 parts steamed milk served in large cups
- **Caffè Correcto** — espresso "corrected" with a splash of grappa or cognac
- **Caffè Latte** — espresso highly diluted with steamed milk and little foam
- **Caffè Macchiato** — espresso with a little steamed milk
- **Caffè Mocha** — espresso with cocoa and steamed milk
- **Caffè Ristretto** — espresso made using less water
- **Cappuccino** — espresso served with a layer of frothed milk
- **Cappuccino Chiaro** — light cappuccino made with less espresso
- **Cappuccino Scuro** — dark cappuccino made with more espresso
- **Dry** — latte or cappuccino made with more froth than steamed milk
- **Espresso** — a coffee dense in body with a light brown head
- **Half-Caf** — equal parts of caffeinated and decaffeinated coffee
- **Latte Macchiato** — steamed milk "stained" with espresso
- **Mochaccino** — cappuccino made with frothed chocolate milk or cocoa
- **Red Eye** — a cup of regular coffee with espresso mixed in
- **Skinny** — a cappuccino or latte made with steamed skim milk

PORT O' CALL
Bucket glass, ice
Build in glass
1 1/2 oz. Tawny Port
Near fill with cranberry juice
Splash orange juice

POT O' GOLD
Presentation shot glass, chilled
Build in glass
1/2 fill Goldschläger
1/2 fill Baileys Irish Cream

POUSSE CAFÉ (1)
Cordial or sherry glass, chilled
Layer ingredients
1/5 fill grenadine
1/5 fill Green Crème de Menthe
1/5 fill Triple Sec
1/5 fill Sloe Gin
1/5 fill Brandy

POUSSE CAFÉ (2)
Cordial or sherry glass, chilled
Layer ingredients
1/6 fill grenadine
1/6 fill Yellow Chartreuse
1/6 fill White Crème de Menthe
1/6 fill Apricot Brandy
1/6 fill Green Chartreuse
1/6 fill Brandy

POUSSE CAFÉ (3)
Cordial or sherry glass, chilled
Layer ingredients
1/7 fill grenadine
1/7 fill Kahlúa Coffee Liqueur
1/7 fill White Crème de Menthe
1/7 fill Blue Curaçao
1/7 fill Galliano Liqueur
1/7 fill Green Chartreuse
1/7 fill Brandy

POUSSE CAFÉ, FOUR-WAY
Cordial or sherry glass, chilled
Layer ingredients
1/4 fill Kahlúa Coffee Liqueur
1/4 fill White Crème de Menthe
1/4 fill Galliano Liqueur
1/4 fill Baileys Irish Cream

POUSSE CAFÉ, TUACA
Cordial or sherry glass, chilled
Layer ingredients
1/4 fill grenadine
1/4 fill White Crème de Menthe
1/4 fill Midori Melon Liqueur
1/4 fill Tuaca

PRAIRIE FIRE

Presentation shot glass, chilled
Build in glass
1 1/4 oz. Gold Tequila
5 dashes Tabasco Sauce

PRAIRIE OYSTER (1)

Rocks glass
Build in glass
1 1/2 oz. Brandy (optional)
1 egg yolk (optional)
2 dashes wine vinegar
1 tsp. Worcestershire sauce
2 dashes Tabasco Sauce
1/2 tsp. salt
2 oz. tomato juice
Stir gently, do not break egg yolk

PRAIRIE OYSTER (2)

Rocks glass, chilled
Build in glass
1 1/2 oz. Chili-infused Vodka
3 dashes Tabasco Sauce
1 tsp. oyster sauce
1 raw oyster

PRESBYTERIAN

Highball glass, ice
Build in glass
1 1/4 oz. requested liquor
1/2 fill ginger ale
1/2 fill club soda

PRESIDENTÉ

Cocktail glass, chilled
Pour ingredients into iced mixing glass
1 1/2 oz. Light Rum
1/2 oz. Dry Vermouth
1/2 oz. Sweet Vermouth
1/2 oz. Cointreau Liqueur
2 dashes grenadine
Stir and strain
Lemon twist garnish

PRESIDENTIAL JUICE

Rocks glass, ice
Build in glass
1 3/4 oz. Sauza Hornitos Tequila
3/4 oz. Kahlúa Coffee Liqueur
3/4 oz. Baileys Irish Cream

PRESUMPTION COCKTAIL

Cocktail glass, chilled
Pour ingredients into iced mixing glass
1 1/4 oz. Cascade Mountain Gin
1/2 oz. Grand Marnier Liqueur
3/4 oz. fresh lime juice
3/4 oz. sweet 'n' sour
Shake and strain
Orange slice garnish

PRIMAL SHOOTER

Presentation shot glass, chilled
Layer ingredients
1/2 fill X.O. Café Coffee Liqueur
1/2 fill Bacardi Light Rum

PRIMO BACIO

Champagne glass, chilled
Pour ingredients into iced mixing glass
1 oz. Vodka
1 oz. Tropico
1/2 oz. Chambord Liqueur
1 oz. orange juice
Shake and strain
Fill with Champagne
Orange twist garnish

PRINCESS MARGARET

House specialty glass, chilled
Pour ingredients into blender
Rim glass with grenadine and sugar
   (optional)
1 1/2 oz. sweet 'n' sour
1 1/2 oz. orange juice
3 dashes raspberry syrup
6 strawberries
1 pineapple slice
Blend with ice
Strawberry garnish

PROVINCE TOWN

House specialty glass, ice
Pour ingredients into iced mixing glass
1 oz. Absolut Vodka
1/2 oz. Absolut Citron Vodka
2 oz. grapefruit juice
2 oz. cranberry juice
Shake and strain
Fill with club soda
Lemon wedge garnish

PUCCINI

Champagne glass, chilled
Build in glass
1/2 fill tangerine juice
1/2 fill Champagne

PUCKER-UP

Presentation shot glass, chilled
Build in glass
1/3 fill Cruzan Rum Cream
1/3 fill DeKuyper Raspberry Pucker
1/3 fill Cruzan Estate Diamond Rum

DIRTY OLIVE® VODKA

DIRTY OLIVE VODKA is an ingenious product worthy of its "Hot New Brands" status. With the rebirth of the "Cocktail Nation," martinis and Bloody Marys have naturally come to the forefront.

One variation of the martini that has over the years fostered something of a cult following is the Dirty Martini, formulated by adding a healthy dose of olive juice to a martini.

The creators of Dirty Olive Vodka and Dirty Olive Gin decided to remove any of the guesswork by infusing both premium vodka and gin with equally premium olive juice.

Both the Dirty Olive Vodka and Dirty Olive Gin are triple-distilled, pure grain spirits. They are infused with Spanish, green olive juice, making the product salty, savory and olivey. Because of the strong character of the vodka, it must be shaken vigorously when used in a cocktail. This will get it cold, icy and ready for take-off. The shaking recommendation is twenty-five times.

Dirty Olive Vodka is at its best when served in the Dirty Bloody Mary. This drink is a "must-have" for Sunday brunch, tail-gate parties, or weekend football gatherings.

Maybe it's time to uncork an adventure, and these two singular spirits are just the ticket. Grab a bottle and get dirty without being accused of being in bad taste.

PULLMAN PORTER
House specialty glass, chilled
Pour ingredients into blender
1 1/2 oz. Vodka
1/2 oz. grenadine
1 oz. lemonade concentrate
2 scoops raspberry sorbet
Blend ingredients (with ice optional)
Berries garnish

PURPLE DEATH
Pilsner glass, chilled 16 oz.
Build in glass
3/4 fill Bass Ale
1 oz. Chambord Liqueur
Top with Blackthorn Cider

PURPLE FLIRT
Rocks glass, chilled
Pour ingredients into iced mixing glass
1 oz. Gosling's Black Seal Rum
1/4 oz. Blue Curaçao
1/2 oz. sweet 'n' sour
1/4 oz. grenadine
1 oz. pineapple juice
Shake and strain
Orange slice and cherry garnish

PURPLE HOOTER (1)
Cocktail glass, chilled
Pour ingredients into iced mixing glass
1 oz. Vodka
1/2 oz. Hiram Walker Triple Sec
1/2 oz. Chambord Liqueur
1/4 oz. Rose's Lime Juice
Shake and strain
Lime wedge garnish

PURPLE HOOTER (2)
Rocks glass, chilled
Pour ingredients into iced mixing glass
1 oz. Absolut Vodka
1 oz. Chambord Liqueur
1 oz. sweet 'n' sour
Shake and strain
Splash Seven-Up

PURPLE MATADOR
Sherry glass, chilled
Pour ingredients into iced mixing glass
1 1/2 oz. Disaronno Amaretto Liqueur
1/2 oz. Chambord Liqueur
1/2 oz. pineapple juice
Shake and strain

PURPLE PASSION
Bucket glass, ice
Build in glass
1 oz. DeKuyper Peach Pucker
1/3 fill orange juice
1/3 fill cranberry juice
Near fill with pineapple juice
Float 3/4 oz. Razzmatazz Raspberry Liqueur

PURPLE PEOPLE BEEFEATER
House specialty glass, chilled
Pour ingredients into blender
1 3/4 oz. Beefeater London Dry Gin
1 oz. Razzmatazz Raspberry Liqueur
1/2 oz. Rose's Lime Juice
1 1/2 oz. sweet 'n' sour
2 oz. cranberry juice
Blend with ice
Lime wedge garnish

PURPLE PIRANHA
House specialty glass, ice
Pour ingredients into iced mixing glass
3/4 oz. Bacardi Light Rum
3/4 oz. Bacardi Gold Rum
3/4 oz. Mount Gay Eclipse Rum
1 oz. Blue Curaçao
1 oz. cranberry juice
1 3/4 oz. sweet 'n' sour
Shake and strain
Float 3/4 oz. Bacardi 151° Rum
Orange slice and cherry garnish

PUSSER'S DAILY RATION
House specialty glass, ice
Pour ingredients into iced mixing glass
2 oz. Pusser's British Navy Rum
1/2 oz. fresh lime juice
2 oz. sweet 'n' sour
Shake and strain
Fill with lemon/lime soda
Lime wedge garnish

PUSSER'S PAIN KILLER
House specialty glass, chilled
Pour ingredients into blender
2 oz. Pusser's British Navy Rum
1 oz. coconut cream syrup
1 oz. orange juice
4 oz. pineapple juice
Blend with ice
Sprinkle nutmeg

PUSSER'S STALEMATE
Coffee mug, heated
Build in glass
1 1/2 oz. Pusser's British Navy Rum
1/2 oz. X.O. Café Coffee Liqueur
1/2 oz. Dark Crème de Cacao
Near fill with hot chocolate
Whipped cream garnish
Sprinkle shaved chocolate

PUTTING ON THE RITZ
Cocktail glass, chilled
Pour ingredients into iced mixing glass
1 oz. Sauza Hornitos Tequila
1/2 oz. DeKuyper Peachtree Schnapps
3/4 oz. cranberry juice
1 1/2 oz. sweet 'n' sour
Shake and strain
Lemon twist garnish

QUAALUDE
Rocks glass, chilled
Pour ingredients into iced mixing glass
1/2 oz. Vodka
1/2 oz. Frangelico Liqueur
1/2 oz. Kahlúa Coffee Liqueur
1/2 oz. Dark Crème de Cacao
1/2 oz. half & half cream
Shake and strain

QUAALUDE, ALASKAN
Rocks glass, ice
Build in glass
1 1/2 oz. Vodka
1/2 oz. White Crème de Cacao
1/2 oz. Frangelico Liqueur

QUAALUDE, IRANIAN
Rocks glass, chilled
Pour ingredients into iced mixing glass
1/2 oz. Vodka
1/2 oz. Kahlúa Coffee Liqueur
1/2 oz. Baileys Irish Cream
1/2 oz. Disaronno Amaretto Liqueur
1/2 oz. Frangelico Liqueur
Shake and strain

QUAALUDE, IRISH
Presentation shot glass, chilled
Build in glass
1/2 oz. Vodka
1/2 oz. Baileys Irish Cream
1/2 oz. Frangelico Liqueur
1/2 oz. Dark Crème de Cacao

CRUZAN® ESTATE DIAMOND RUM

Once an indulgence only available in the Virgin Islands, CRUZAN ESTATE DIAMOND RUM is among the fastest growing spirits in the country. For those looking for a fabulous rum at an amazingly low price (SRP $17 US), this Cruzan is just the ticket.

Cruzan Estate Diamond is a blend of triple-distilled rums produced in a five-column continuous still and aged in American oak bourbon barrels for 5 to 10 years. After reaching maturity, the rum is blended in small batches to assure consistency and maintain the highest quality control. It is then lightly filtered through activated charcoal to remove impurities and particulate.

Cruzan Estate Diamond Rum has an orange-amber hue and a medium-weight body. The expansive bouquet immediately fills the glass with the toasty aromas of vanilla, chocolate, spice and oak. The rum enters the mouth softly, without a trace of heat, and bathes the palate with the rich, delectable flavors of coffee, cocoa, caramel, and vanilla. The finish is dry, warm and relatively long.

This is a rum that should be appreciated neat, or on-the-rocks before playing with it in a cocktail, although it is highly versatile and excellent when mixed. Cruzan Estate Diamond Rum is skillfully crafted and a pleasure to drink.

QUAALUDE, RUSSIAN
Rocks glass, chilled
Build in glass
1/2 oz. Stolichnaya Russian Vodka
1/2 oz. Frangelico Liqueur
1/2 oz. Kahlúa Coffee Liqueur
1/2 oz. Baileys Irish Cream

QUARTER DECK
aka **QuarterMaster**
Rocks glass, ice
Build in glass
1 oz. Appleton Estate V/X Jamaica Rum
1 oz. Mount Gay Eclipse Rum
3/4 oz. Sherry
1 dash Rose's Lime Juice
Lime wedge garnish

RABID DOG
Beer mug, chilled
Build in glass
3/4 oz. Wild Turkey 101° Bourbon
3/4 oz. Disaronno Amaretto Liqueur
Fill with Draft Beer

RAINBOW HOLIDAY CUP
House specialty glass, ice
Build in glass
1 1/2 oz. Light Rum
1/4 oz. Hot Damn Cinnamon Schnapps
2 dashes bitters
2 dashes grenadine
4 oz. orange juice
Fill with club soda
Orange slice and cinnamon stick garnish

RAINBOW INTERNATIONAL COCKTAIL
Cocktail glass, chilled
Pour ingredients into iced mixing glass
1/2 oz. Dry Sack Sherry
2-3 dashes Angostura Bitters
2 1/2 oz. Gentleman Jack
    Tennessee Whiskey
Stir and strain
Orange twist garnish

RAINBOW SHOOTER (1)
Presentation shot glass, chilled
Layer ingredients
1/3 fill Crème de Noyaux
1/3 fill Midori Melon Liqueur
1/3 fill White Crème de Menthe

RAINBOW SHOOTER (2)
Rocks glass, chilled
Build in glass
3/4 oz. Malibu Rum
3/4 oz. Midori Melon Liqueur
3/4 oz. Crème de Noyaux

RAIN MAN
House specialty glass, ice
Pour ingredients into iced mixing glass
1 1/4 oz. Bacardi Select Rum
3/4 oz. Midori Melon Liqueur
4 oz. orange juice
Shake and strain
Orange slice garnish

RAMOS FIZZ
House specialty glass, ice
Pour ingredients into iced mixing glass
1 oz. Gin
1 oz. sweet 'n' sour
3 oz. half & half cream
1 egg white (optional)
1/2 oz. simple syrup
2 dashes orange flower water
Shake and strain
Splash club soda
Orange twist garnish

RANCHO VALENCIA RUM PUNCH
Wine goblet, ice
Pour ingredients into iced mixing glass
1 oz. Bacardi Light Rum
1 oz. Mount Gay Eclipse Rum
2-3 dashes Angostura Bitters
1 1/2 oz. pineapple juice
1 1/2 oz. orange juice
Shake and strain
Float 3/4 oz. Appleton Estate
   V/X Jamaica Rum
Lime, lemon and orange wedge garnish

RANDY BRANDY EGG NOG
House specialty glass, ice
Pour ingredients into iced mixing glass
1 1/2 oz. Christian Brothers Brandy
1 oz. Whaler's Hawaiian Vanille Rum
1 tsp. sugar
1 egg (optional)
4 oz. half & half cream
Shake and strain
Sprinkle nutmeg

RASPBERRY BANANA SPLIT
House specialty glass, chilled
Object is to create a 3-layer drink
1—Pour ingredients into blender
   1 oz. Kahlúa Coffee Liqueur
   1 scoop vanilla ice cream
Blend ingredients (with ice optional)
Pour first drink into glass 1/3 full
2—Pour ingredients into blender
   1 oz. Crème de Banana
   1 scoop vanilla ice cream
Blend ingredients (with ice optional)
Pour second drink into glass 1/3 full
3—Pour ingredients into blender
   1 oz. Chambord Liqueur
   1 scoop vanilla ice cream
Blend ingredients (with ice optional)
Pour third drink into glass 1/3 full
Whipped cream garnish

RASPBERRY CREAM
House specialty glass, chilled
Pour ingredients into blender
1 oz. Bacardi Light Rum
3/4 oz. White Crème de Cacao
1/2 oz. Chambord Liqueur
1 1/2 oz. raspberry yogurt
1 1/2 oz. half & half cream
2 scoops raspberry ice cream
Blend ingredients (with ice optional)
Whipped cream garnish
Drizzle 3/4 oz. Chambord Liqueur

RASPBERRY KISS
House specialty glass, ice
Pour ingredients into iced mixing glass
6 oz. cran-raspberry drink (Ocean Spray)
1 oz. orange juice
1/2 oz. Rose's Lime Juice
Shake and strain
Fill with club soda

RASPBERRY SOUR
House specialty glass, ice
Pour ingredients into iced mixing glass
1 3/4 oz. Jameson Irish Whiskey
3/4 oz. Grand Marnier Liqueur
1 oz. orange juice
2 oz. sweet 'n' sour
Shake and strain
Whipped cream garnish
Drizzle 3/4 oz. Chambord Liqueur

DEKUYPER® RAZZMATAZZ® RASPBERRY LIQUEUR

In Europe, raspberries have long been associated with royalty, the berries of kings, so to speak. In fact, the raspberry liqueurs made on the Continent—where they're referred to as Framboise—are regal, luxurious and quite sophisticated. Here in the U.S., however, the raspberry belongs to the people and while it is one of the most popular flavors in the country, we just want to have fun. Enter DEKUYPER RAZZMATAZZ, a savory raspberry liqueur born and bred for the nightlife.

DeKuyper Razzmatazz is made on a base of pure grain, neutral spirits that are liberally infused with natural raspberry flavorings. It is remarkably similar in character to Framboise, the chief difference being that Razzmatazz has a slightly lighter body than most of its European counterparts.

The liqueur has a deep, true-raspberry color and a lively, fresh fruit bouquet. Razzmatazz is well balanced between sweet and sour and is loaded with raspberry flavor.

Here's a product with no creative boundaries. DeKuyper Razzmatazz is featured in everything from martinis, margaritas and daiquiris to coffee, hot cocoa and ice cream drinks. So have fun with it and give your drinks some pizzazz with Razzmatazz.

RASPBERRY SWEET TART
Rocks glass, chilled
Pour ingredients into iced mixing glass
1 oz. Chambord Liqueur
1 oz. DeKuyper Triple Sec
1 oz. Rose's Lime Juice
Stir and strain
Lime wedge garnish

RASPBERRY TORTE
Cordial or sherry glass, chilled
Layer ingredients
1/2 fill Chambord Liqueur
1/2 fill Vodka

RASTA MAN
Presentation shot glass, chilled
Layer ingredients
1/3 fill Tia Maria
1/3 fill Godiva Chocolate Liqueur
1/3 fill Baileys Irish Cream

RASTA SPLEEF
Bucket glass, ice
Build in glass
1 1/2 oz. Myers's Jamaican Rum
2 oz. orange juice
Fill with pineapple juice

RAZORBACK HOGCALLER
Rocks glass, ice
Build in glass
1 1/2 oz. Bacardi 151° Rum
1/2 oz. Green Chartreuse

RAZTINI
Rocks glass, chilled
Pour ingredients into iced mixing glass
1 1/2 oz. Chambord Liqueur
1/2 oz. Vincent Van Gogh Vodka
1/2 oz. Mandarine Napoléon Liqueur
1 oz. sweet 'n' sour
Shake and strain

RAZZLE DAZZLE
Highball glass, ice
Build in glass
1 1/4 oz. Razzmatazz Raspberry Liqueur
Near fill with cranberry juice
Splash club soda

RAZZLE DAZZLE ROSE
Cocktail glass, chilled
Pour ingredients into iced mixing glass
1 1/2 oz. Luksusowa Polish Vodka
1/2 oz. Razzmatazz Raspberry Liqueur
1/2 oz. raspberry puree
1 1/2 oz. sweet 'n' sour
Shake and strain
Raspberry garnish

RAZZMATAZZ
Rocks glass, ice
Build in glass
1 oz. Disaronno Amaretto Liqueur
1 oz. Razzmatazz Raspberry Liqueur

RAZZPUTENEE
Presentation shot glass, chilled
Build in glass
Rim glass with salt (optional)
1 oz. Farias Silver Tequila
1/2 oz. Razzmatazz Raspberry Liqueur
1/4 oz. cranberry juice

RECESSION DEPRESSION
Cocktail glass, chilled
Pour ingredients into iced mixing glass
1 1/2 oz. Absolut Citron Vodka
1/2 oz. Cointreau Liqueur
1/2 oz. fresh lemon juice
3 dashes Rose's Lime Juice
Stir and strain
Lime wedge garnish

RECONSIDER
Cocktail glass, chilled
Pour ingredients into iced mixing glass
1 1/2 oz. Casa Noble Gold Tequila
3/4 oz. Cointreau Liqueur
1/2 oz. Rose's Lime Juice
Stir and strain
Lime wedge garnish

RED BEER
aka **Tom Boy**
Beer glass or mug, chilled
Build in glass
Near fill with Draft Beer
2 oz. Bloody Mary mix or tomato juice

RED BEER SHOOTER
Presentation shot glass, chilled
Build in glass
3 dashes Tabasco Sauce
1/2 fill Draft Beer
1/2 fill Bloody Mary mix

RED DEATH
Presentation shot glass, chilled
Build in glass
1/2 oz. Stolichnaya Russian Vodka
1/2 oz. Hot Damn Cinnamon Schnapps
1/2 oz. Yukon Jack Liqueur
1/2 oz. 151 proof Rum

RED DEVIL
Rocks glass, chilled
Pour ingredients into iced mixing glass
1/2 oz. Disaronno Amaretto Liqueur
1/2 oz. Southern Comfort Liqueur
1/2 oz. Sloe Gin
1/2 oz. Vodka
1/2 oz. Hiram Walker Triple Sec
Splash Rose's Lime Juice
Splash cranberry juice
Shake and strain

RED ECLIPSE
Bucket glass, ice
Build in glass
2 oz. Rémy Red
Near fill with orange juice
Float 3/4 oz. Chambord Liqueur
Orange slice garnish

RED LION
Cocktail glass, chilled
Rim glass with sugar (optional)
Pour ingredients into iced mixing glass
1 oz. Gin
3/4 oz. Grand Marnier Liqueur
1 oz. sweet 'n' sour
1 oz. orange juice
Shake and strain

RED RUSSIAN
Rocks glass, ice
Build in glass
1 1/2 oz. Vodka
3/4 oz. Cherry Heering

RED SKY
House specialty glass, chilled
Pour ingredients into blender
1 1/2 oz. Vodka
1 3/4 oz. Rémy Red
2 oz. cranberry juice
2 scoops vanilla ice cream
Blend ingredients (with ice optional)
Pineapple wedge garnish

RED TAIL DRAGON
House specialty glass, ice
Pour ingredients into iced mixing glass
1 oz. Midori Melon Liqueur
1/2 oz. Gin
1/2 oz. Rum
3/4 oz. grenadine
2 oz. sweet 'n' sour
Shake and strain
Lime wedge garnish

DEWAR'S® WHITE LABEL SCOTCH WHISKY

DEWAR'S WHITE LABEL SCOTCH WHISKY is the preeminent blended whisky in the world. The origins of this most famous brand began in Perth, Scotland. In 1846, John Dewar opened a business as a wine and spirits merchant. After years of patient experimentation, he perfected a recipe for a blended Scotch whisky that became so popular its success prompted him to be the first to market his whisky in bottles.

Long the best selling Scotch whisky in the United States, Dewar's White Label is a skillfully crafted blend of malt and straight grain whiskies. At the core of its blend are the renowned malts of their Highland distilleries, most notably Aberfeldy, Lochnagar and Glen Ord. It is bottled at 80 proof.

Dewar's White Label has a rich amber hue and flawlessly textured body. The wafting bouquet is peppery, fruity and lightly peated. The whisky comes alive on the palate featuring a balanced offering of mildly smoky, semi-sweet grain flavor. It has a somewhat long and peaty finish.

The firm also produces DEWAR'S SPECIAL RESERVE, an extraordinary blend of individually aged, 12-year-old single malt whiskies distilled in different regions of Scotland. After blending, the whisky is further matured in oak barrels to allow the blend to "marry." It is bottled at 86 proof.

RED ZIPPER
Bucket glass, ice
Build in glass
3/4 oz. Galliano Liqueur
3/4 oz. Vodka
Fill with cranberry juice

REGGAE SUNSPLASH
House specialty glass, ice
Build in glass
1 1/4 oz. Absolut Citron Vodka
1/2 oz. Malibu Rum
1/2 oz. Briottet Crème de Cassis
1/2 oz. grenadine
2 oz. orange juice
Fill with club soda

REGGAE WALKER
House specialty glass, chilled
Pour ingredients into blender
1 1/4 oz. DeKuyper Peachtree Schnapps
3 oz. pineapple juice
Blend with ice
Float 3/4 oz. Tia Maria
Pineapple wedge and cherry garnish

RELEASE VALVE
Highball glass, ice
Build in glass
3/4 oz. Vodka
3/4 oz. Light Rum
Near fill with pineapple juice
Float 3/4 oz. Razzmatazz Raspberry Liqueur

RÉMY RED PUNCH
Bucket glass, ice
Build in glass
1 1/2 oz. Rémy Red
1 1/2 oz. Mount Gay Eclipse Rum
Fill with pineapple juice
Pineapple wedge garnish

RÉMY RED SUNRISE
Bucket glass, ice
Build in glass
1 1/2 oz. Rémy Red
Near fill with orange juice
Float 1 oz. Rémy Red

RENDEZVOUS MUUMUU
Bucket glass, ice
Pour ingredients into iced mixing glass
1 1/2 oz. Cruzan Estate Diamond Rum
3/4 oz. Cruzan Estate Light Rum
1/2 oz. grenadine
1/2 oz. Rose's Lime Juice
1 oz. pineapple juice
1 1/2 oz. sweet 'n' sour
Shake and strain
Lime wedge garnish

RENDEZVOUS PUNCH
Coffee mug, heated
Build in glass
3/4 oz. Royal Oak Extra Old Rum
3/4 oz. Chambord Liqueur
Fill with hot spiced apple cider
Cinnamon stick garnish

RESERVA COCKTAIL
Cocktail glass, chilled
Rim glass with sugar
Pour ingredients into iced mixing glass
2 oz. Bacardi 8 Reserva Rum
3/4 oz. Cointreau Liqueur
1/2 oz. fresh lime juice
1 oz. sweet 'n' sour
Shake and strain
Lime wedge garnish

RESTORATION
Bucket glass, ice
Pour ingredients into iced mixing glass
4 oz. Dry Red Wine
3/4 oz. Christian Brothers Brandy
3/4 oz. Chambord Liqueur
1 1/2 oz. sweet 'n' sour
Shake and strain
Lemon twist garnish

REVEREND CRAIG
Bucket glass, ice
Pour ingredients into iced mixing glass
1 1/2 oz. Jim Beam White Label Bourbon
1 1/2 oz. sweet 'n' sour
Shake and strain
Fill with Draft Beer

REVERSE RUSSIAN
Sherry glass, chilled
Layer ingredients
1/2 fill Kahlúa Coffee Liqueur
1/2 fill Vodka

R. F. & E.
Rocks glass, chilled
Pour ingredients into iced mixing glass
1/2 oz. Bacardi Light Rum
1/2 oz. Bacardi Select Rum
1/2 oz. Malibu Rum
1/2 oz. Captain Morgan Spiced Rum
1/2 oz. Myers's Jamaican Rum
1/4 oz. grenadine
1 oz. sweet 'n' sour
1 oz. pineapple juice
Shake and strain

RHETT BUTLER
Bucket glass, ice
Pour ingredients into iced mixing glass
1 oz. Southern Comfort Liqueur
1/2 oz. DeKuyper Triple Sec
1 1/2 oz. sweet 'n' sour
1/2 oz. Rose's Lime Juice
Shake and strain
Fill with club soda
Lime wedge garnish

RHODODENDRON
House specialty glass, chilled
Pour ingredients into blender
1 1/2 oz. Bacardi Light Rum
3/4 oz. Crème de Noyaux
1/2 oz. fresh lemon juice
1/2 oz. fresh lime juice
1/2 oz. simple syrup
2 oz. pineapple juice
Blend with ice
Float 3/4 oz. Gosling's Black Seal Rum
Lime wedge garnish

RHUMBA ESCAPADES
House specialty glass, chilled
Pour ingredients into blender
1 1/4 oz. Bacardi Light Rum
3/4 oz. Mount Gay Eclipse Rum
3/4 oz. Crème de Banana
1/2 oz. grenadine
1 1/2 oz. pineapple juice
1 peeled, ripe banana
1 scoop vanilla ice cream
Blend ingredients (with ice optional)
Whipped cream garnish

RHUM BARBANCOURT FREEZE
House specialty glass, chilled
Pour ingredients into blender
1 3/4 oz. Rhum Barbancourt 3-Star Rum
1 oz. Blue Curaçao
1 oz. grapefruit juice
1 oz. sweet 'n' sour
2 oz. orange juice
Blend with ice
Float 3/4 oz. Rhum Barbancourt
    5-Star Rum
Lime, lemon and orange wedge garnish

RICKEY
Highball glass, ice
Build in glass
1 1/4 oz. requested light liquor
Fill with club soda
Lime wedge garnish

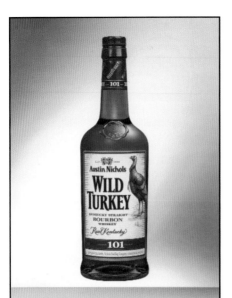

WILD TURKEY®
101° BOURBON WHISKEY

The Ripy family established what would become the Wild Turkey distillery in Lawrenceburg, Kentucky in 1855. Forty years later, the distillery's bourbon was selected out of 400 brands to represent Kentucky at the World's Fair. By the 1940s, the 101° proof whiskey would become known throughout the world as WILD TURKEY BOURBON.

Now one of the top-selling brands of whiskey, Wild Turkey 101° is distilled from corn, rye and barley malt before being aged a minimum of 8 years in heavily charred oak barrels. Its alluring bouquet is saturated with the aromas of fruit, honey and oak. The elevated alcohol content is lip tingling, but the bourbon quickly fills the mouth with the robust flavors of caramel, honey, vanilla and raisins. The finish is warm, long and flavorful.

The famous distillery also crafts several other, award-winning whiskies. The limited release WILD TURKEY RARE BREED is a sumptuous, amazingly smooth bourbon bottled undiluted, unfiltered and at barrel-proof. The WILD TURKEY KENTUCKY SPIRIT is an unforgettable, single barrel bourbon experience. It is unblended and marketed at 101 proof. The most recent addition is WILD TURKEY RUSSELL RESERVE, an exceptionally delicious, small batch bourbon aged for 10 years and bottled at the distillery's trademark 101 proof.

RIGOR MORTIS
Rocks glass, chilled
Pour ingredients into iced mixing glass
1 1/2 oz. Absolut Vodka
3/4 oz. Disaronno Amaretto Liqueur
1 oz. pineapple juice
1 oz. orange juice
Shake and strain

RIN TIN GIN TONIC
Bucket glass, ice
Build in glass
1 3/4 oz. Beefeater London Dry Gin
1/2 oz. Giori Lemoncillo Liqueur
Fill with tonic water
Lemon twist garnish

RIO RITA
Cocktail glass, chilled
Pour ingredients into iced mixing glass
1 1/2 oz. Ypioca Cachaça
1/2 oz. simple syrup
2 oz. sweet 'n' sour
Shake and strain
Lime wheel garnish

RITZ AMERICANA
Champagne glass, chilled
Pour ingredients into iced mixing glass
1 1/4 oz. Jim Beam Black Label Bourbon
2-3 dashes Angostura Bitters
1 1/2 oz. sweet 'n' sour
Shake and strain
Fill with Champagne
Peach wedge garnish

RITZ FIZZ
House specialty glass, ice
Pour ingredients into iced mixing glass
1 oz. Disaronno Amaretto Liqueur
1/2 oz. Blue Curaçao
1 1/2 oz. sweet 'n' sour
Shake and strain
Fill with Champagne
Lemon twist garnish

RITZ PICK-ME-UP
Champagne glass, chilled
Pour ingredients into iced mixing glass
1 oz. V.S. Cognac
1 oz. Cointreau Liqueur
2 oz. orange juice
Shake and strain
Fill with Champagne

RIVER MADNESS
Bucket glass, ice
Build in glass
1 1/4 oz. Farias Reposado Tequila
2 oz. limeade
Fill with club soda
Lime wedge garnish

RIVER SEINE CAPPUCCINO
Cappuccino cup, heated
Build in glass
1 oz. Kahlúa Coffee Liqueur
3/4 oz. V.S. Cognac
Near fill with hot espresso coffee
Top with frothed milk
Sprinkle shaved chocolate

RIVIERA DAYS
Rocks glass, ice
Build in glass
3/4 oz. Bacardi Light Rum
3/4 oz. Cointreau Liqueur
3/4 oz. Chambord Liqueur
Lemon wedge garnish

RIVIERA NIGHTS
Rocks glass, ice
Build in glass
3/4 oz. Bacardi Gold Rum
3/4 oz. Bacardi Select Rum
3/4 oz. Citrónge Orange Liqueur
3/4 oz. Chambord Liqueur
Lemon wedge garnish

ROASTED TOASTED ALMOND
Cocktail glass, chilled
Pour ingredients into iced mixing glass
1/2 oz. Disaronno Amaretto Liqueur
1/2 oz. Kahlúa Coffee Liqueur
1/2 oz. Vodka
2 oz. half & half cream
Shake and strain

ROB ROY
Cocktail glass, chilled
Pour ingredients into iced mixing glass
1/2 oz. Sweet Vermouth
2-3 dashes Angostura Bitters (optional)
1 1/2 oz. Scotch Whisky
Stir and strain
Cherry garnish

ROB ROY, DRY
Cocktail glass, chilled
Pour ingredients into iced mixing glass
1/4 oz. Dry Vermouth
2-3 dashes Angostura Bitters (optional)
1 1/2 oz. Scotch Whisky
Stir and strain
Lemon twist garnish

ROB ROY, HIGHLAND FLING
Cocktail glass, chilled
Pour ingredients into iced mixing glass
1/2 oz. Vya California Sweet Vermouth
2-3 dashes Angostura Bitters
2 oz. Dewar's White Label Scotch Whisky
Stir and strain
Cherry garnish

ROB ROY, OH JOY
Cocktail glass, chilled
Pour ingredients into iced mixing glass
1/2 oz. Dubonnet Rouge
1/2 oz. Tawny Port
1 1/2 oz. Aberlour a'bunadh
    Single Speyside Malt
Stir and strain
Cherry garnish

ROB ROY, PERFECT
aka **Affinity Cocktail, Affinity Manhattan**
Cocktail glass, chilled
Pour ingredients into iced mixing glass
1/4 oz. Dry Vermouth
1/4 oz. Sweet Vermouth
2-3 dashes Angostura Bitters (optional)
1 1/2 oz. Scotch Whisky
Stir and strain
Lemon twist garnish

ROCK-A-FELLOW'S FANCY
Brandy snifter, ice
Build in glass
1 3/4 oz. Matusalem Gran Reserva Rum
1/2 oz. Grand Marnier Liqueur
1/2 oz. Kahlúa Coffee Liqueur

ROCKET
Bucket glass, ice
Build in glass
1 1/2 oz. Yukon Jack Liqueur
Near fill with lemonade
Float 3/4 oz. 151 proof Rum

ROCK LOBSTER
House specialty glass, chilled
Pour ingredients into blender
1 oz. Malibu Rum
1/2 oz. Crème de Banana
1/2 oz. Myers's Jamaican Rum
1/2 oz. grenadine
1 1/2 oz. orange juice
1 1/2 oz. pineapple juice
Blend with ice
Float 3/4 oz. Myers's Jamaican Rum
Orange slice and cherry garnish

ZONE® PEACH VODKA

Ultra-premium ZONE PEACH VODKA is exactly the vodka you want to take to your next soirée. The brand was created for those occasions where substance is a more valuable commodity than impact. With their perfect balance of vodka and wide variety of true-to-fruit flavors, Zone Vodkas have zeroed in on a growing niche, namely those people looking to entertain with a spirit that's a little lower in proof plus enjoyable to drink.

Zone Vodkas are skillfully crafted in the beautiful city of Padova located in northeastern Italy. They are column-distilled entirely from locally grown wheat and soft, purified water. One of the secrets behind the brand's success is the brilliant natural flavoring infused into each vodka before it is filtered and bottled.

These vodkas are definitely loaded with Italian charm. Zone Peach is brilliantly clear with a trim, nicely shaped body. Its wafting bouquet of fresh peaches sets the stage for the vodka's vibrant, slightly sweet palate. The vodka has a lingering, relaxed finish.

The other flavors featured in the Zone quintet include melon (cantaloupe), tangerine, lemon, and banana. It is an ideal line-up of performers for behind the bar. The packaging is Euro-contemporary with lightly frosted glass, colorful label, and wood and cork closure.

ROCK 'N' BOCK
Pilsner glass, chilled
Build in glass
1/2 fill Rolling Rock
1/2 fill Shiner Double Bock

RODÉO DRIVER
Bucket glass, ice
Pour ingredients into iced mixing glass
1 1/2 oz. Casa Noble Reposado Tequila
3/4 oz. Mandarine Napoléon Liqueur
1 oz. pineapple juice
1 1/2 oz. sweet 'n' sour
Shake and strain
Fill with club soda
Orange slice garnish

ROLLS ROYCE
Cocktail glass, chilled
Pour ingredients into iced mixing glass
1 oz. Gin
1 oz. Benedictine
1/2 oz. Dry Vermouth
1/2 oz. Sweet Vermouth
Stir and strain
Lemon twist garnish

ROOM SERVICE AT THE RITZ
Champagne glass, chilled
Pour ingredients into iced mixing glass
1 oz. Courvoisier V.S.O.P. Cognac
3/4 oz. Grand Marnier Liqueur
1 1/2 oz. sweet 'n' sour
Shake and strain
Fill with Champagne
Lemon twist garnish

ROOT BEER
Bucket glass, ice
Build in glass
1 oz. Kahlúa Coffee Liqueur
3/4 oz. Galliano Liqueur
3/4 oz. Vodka
Fill with cola

ROOT BEER FLOAT
Bucket glass, ice
Build in glass
1 oz. Kahlúa Coffee Liqueur
3/4 oz. Galliano Liqueur
1/2 oz. Vodka (optional)
1/2 fill cola
1/2 fill half & half cream

ROOT BEER TOOTER
Highball glass, ice
Build in glass
3/4 oz. Root Beer Schnapps
3/4 oz. Vodka
3/4 oz. half & half cream
Fill with cola

ROOT CANAL
House specialty glass, ice
Pour ingredients into iced mixing glass
1/2 oz. Light Rum
1/2 oz. Gin
1/2 oz. Vodka
1/2 fill orange juice
Near fill with pineapple juice
Shake and strain
Float 1/2 oz. Myers's Jamaican Rum and
   1/2 oz. Razzmatazz Raspberry Liqueur

ROSE BEAM
Sherry glass, chilled
Layer ingredients
1/3 fill Tequila Rose Cream Liqueur
1/3 fill Kahlúa Coffee Liqueur
1/3 fill Crème de Banana

ROSEBUD
House specialty glass, chilled
Pour ingredients into blender
2 oz. Tequila Rose Cream Liqueur
1 1/2 oz. Godiva White Chocolate Liqueur
2 scoops vanilla ice cream
Blend with ice
Strawberry garnish

ROSE PETAL
House specialty glass, chilled
Pour ingredients into blender
1 oz. Disaronno Amaretto Liqueur
1/2 oz. Baileys Irish Cream
1/2 oz. grenadine
2 oz. strawberry puree
1 scoop vanilla ice cream
Blend ingredients (with ice optional)
Whipped cream garnish (optional)

ROSY PIPPIN
Wine glass, ice
Pour ingredients into iced mixing glass
4 1/2 oz. apple juice
1/2 oz. grenadine
1/2 oz. sweet 'n' sour
Shake and strain
Fill with ginger ale
Apple wedge garnish

ROXANNE
Rocks glass, chilled
Pour ingredients into iced mixing glass
3/4 oz. Absolut Vodka
3/4 oz. DeKuyper Peachtree Schnapps
1/2 oz. Disaronno Amaretto Liqueur
1/2 oz. orange juice
1/2 oz. cranberry juice
Shake and strain

ROYAL BAY BREEZE
Cocktail glass, chilled
Pour ingredients into iced mixing glass
1 1/2 oz. Pearl Vodka
3/4 oz. Chambord Liqueur
1 1/2 oz. pineapple juice
1 1/2 oz. cranberry Juice
Shake and strain

ROYAL CANADIAN
Presentation shot glass, chilled
Build in glass
1/3 fill Kahlúa Coffee Liqueur
1/3 fill Disaronno Amaretto Liqueur
1/3 fill Crown Royal

ROYAL FIZZ
House specialty glass, ice
Pour ingredients into iced mixing glass
1 oz. Gin
2 oz. half & half cream
1 egg (optional)
1 oz. sweet 'n' sour
1/2 oz. simple syrup
Shake and strain
Splash club soda

ROYAL FLUSH
aka **Chicago Sports Jim**
Rocks glass, chilled
Pour ingredients into iced mixing glass
1/2 oz. Crown Royal
1/2 oz. DeKuyper Peachtree Schnapps
1/2 oz. Chambord Liqueur
1/2 oz. pineapple juice
1/2 oz. sweet 'n' sour
Shake and strain

ROYAL GODIVA
Highball glass, ice
Build in glass
3/4 oz. Godiva Chocolate Liqueur
3/4 oz. Razzmatazz Raspberry Liqueur
Fill with club soda

ROYAL STREET COFFEE
Coffee mug, heated
Build in glass
3/4 oz. Disaronno Amaretto Liqueur
3/4 oz. Kahlúa Coffee Liqueur
1/2 tsp. nutmeg
Near fill with hot coffee
Whipped cream garnish (optional)

ROY ROGERS
Collins or bucket glass, ice
Build in glass
Near fill with cola
Float 1 oz. grenadine
Cherry garnish

MIXOLOGY TRIVIA
The Who, What and Where of Mixology

1. What is a mist?

2. How many liters is a magnum?

3. What does the mixology instruction "over and up" mean?

4. What is a "bourbon and branch?"

5. What is "seasoned" ice?

6. What is the continental term for a liquor served on-the-rocks?

7. What type of bitters is used to make the New Orleans classic, the sazerac?

8. What will club soda poured into an empty glass reveal about the glass?

9. What is the difference between a Kir and a Kir Royale?

10. How is a sweet Manhattan prepared?

11. What drink requires the use of a muddler?

12. What are the two most frequently used fortified wines behind a bar?

13. What name is given to the combination of peach puree and champagne?

14. How is a red beer prepared?

15. How is Bloody Mary mix converted into Bloody Bull mix?

Answers

1. A mist is a liquor served over crushed ice

2. A magnum is equal to two wine bottles, 1.5 liters, or 50.4 fluid ounces

3. The mixology instruction "over and up" means that the drink is to be prepared in a mixing glass over ice and then strained straight-up

4. Bourbon and branch is a highball made with bourbon and spring water

5. Seasoned ice refers to the ice remaining in a person's glass after finishing a drink. Often customers will request that their next drink be built upon the "seasoned ice."

6. Over, as in "Scotch, over."

7. Peychaud Bitters, an anise-flavored bitters

8. The carbon dioxide present within the club soda will form a stream of bubbles on the glass wherever it is oily or dirty

9. A Kir is made with white wine and crème de cassis, and the Kir Royale is a mix of champagne and crème de cassis

10. A sweet Manhattan is prepared with an additional 1/4 ounce of maraschino cherry juice

11. A muddler is similar to a pestle and is used to "muddle" the fruit in an old fashion

12. Dry and sweet vermouth

13. The belini

14. A red beer is made by adding a splash of tomato juice

15. Adding beef bouillon to Bloody Mary mix turn it into bloody bull mix

RUBY RED
Bucket glass, ice
Build in glass
1 1/2 oz. Absolut Citron Vodka
Fill with ruby red grapefruit juice

RUDDY MIMOSA
Champagne glass, chilled
Build in glass
3 oz. Champagne
1 1/2 oz. orange juice
1 1/2 oz. cranberry juice
1/2 oz. DeKuyper Peachtree Schnapps

RUE DE LA PAIX
Champagne glass, chilled
Pour ingredients into iced mixing glass
1 oz. Chambord Liqueur
1 oz. Courvoisier V.S.O.P. Cognac
Stir and strain
Fill with Champagne
Lemon twist garnish

RUM ALEXANDER
aka **Panama**
House specialty glass, chilled
Pour ingredients into blender
1 1/4 oz. Bacardi Light Rum
1 oz. White Crème de Cacao
1 oz. half & half cream
2 scoops vanilla ice cream
Blend ingredients (with ice optional)
Whipped cream garnish
Sprinkle nutmeg

RUM AND BLACK
Rocks glass, chilled
1 3/4 oz. Dillon Dark Rhum
3/4 oz. black currant juice or syrup

RUMBA
Bucket glass, ice
Pour ingredients into iced mixing glass
1 1/2 oz. Myers's Jamaican Rum
3/4 oz. Light Rum
3/4 oz. Gin
1/2 oz. grenadine
1/2 oz. Rose's Lime Juice
1 1/2 oz. sweet 'n' sour
Shake and strain

RUMBALL
Brandy snifter, heated
1 3/4 oz. Pyrat Pistol Rum
3/4 oz. Godiva Chocolate Liqueur

RUM FIX

Bucket glass, ice
Build in glass
2 1/2 oz. Light Rum
2 1/2 oz. sweet 'n' sour
Fill with water
Lemon wedge garnish

RUM MILK PUNCH

Bucket glass, ice
Pour ingredients into iced mixing glass
1 tsp. powdered sugar
2 oz. Light Rum
4 oz. milk
Shake and strain
Sprinkle nutmeg

RUM MINT JULEP

House specialty glass
Build in glass
3-4 mint sprigs
1/2 oz. simple syrup
2 oz. water
Muddle contents
2 1/2 oz. Light Rum
Add crushed ice
Mint sprig garnish

RUM OLD-FASHIONED

Bucket glass
Build in glass
1/2 oz. simple syrup
2-3 dashes Angostura Bitters
1-2 splashes club soda
Orange slice and cherry
Muddle contents
Add ice
2 oz. Light Rum
1/2 oz. 151 proof Rum
Lime wedge garnish

RUMPLEMEISTER

aka **Screaming Nazi**
Presentation shot glass, chilled
Build in glass
1 oz. Rumple Minze Schnapps
1 oz. Jägermeister Liqueur

RUM PUNCH

Bucket glass, ice
Pour ingredients into iced mixing glass
1 1/2 oz. Overproof Rum (strong)
1/2 oz. fresh lemon juice (sour)
2-3 dashes Angostura Bitters (bitters)
1 oz. grenadine (sweet)
2 oz. fresh fruit juice (weak)
Shake and strain
Sprinkle nutmeg
Pineapple wedge and cherry garnish
Note: An island favorite— The traditional
 way to remember this recipe: 1 of sour,
 2 of sweet, 3 of strong, and 4 of weak,
 5 drops of bitters and nutmeg spice,
 serve well chilled and lots of ice.

RUM RUNNER (1)

House specialty glass, ice
Pour ingredients into iced mixing glass
3/4 oz. Bacardi Light Rum
3/4 oz. Appleton Estate V/X Jamaica Rum
3/4 oz. Crème de Banana
3/4 oz. Blackberry Brandy
2 oz. orange juice
2 oz. sweet 'n' sour
Shake and strain
Float 3/4 oz. Matusalem Classic Black Rum
Orange slice garnish

RUM RUNNER (2)

House specialty glass, ice
Pour ingredients into iced mixing glass
1 1/4 oz. Bacardi Select Rum
1 1/4 oz. Mount Gay Eclipse Rum
3/4 oz. Blackberry Brandy
3/4 oz. Crème de Banana
1 1/2 oz. orange juice
1 1/2 oz. sweet 'n' sour
Shake and strain
Orange slice garnish

RUMSCAPES

House specialty glass, ice
Build in glass
1 1/4 oz. Bacardi Gold Rum
1 1/4 oz. Mount Gay Eclipse Rum
3/4 oz. Chambord Liqueur
3/4 oz. Crème de Banana
Fill with ginger ale
Lime wedge garnish

RUM SCREW

Highball glass, ice
Build in glass
1 1/4 oz. Light Rum
Fill with orange juice

VILLA MASSA®
LIMONCELLO

Limoncello has long been one of the favorite types of liqueurs served throughout Europe. Originally called *rasoli* in Italian, this classic lemon liqueur was often made at home according to a family recipe passed from one generation to the next. Such was the beginning of VILLA MASSA LIMONCELLO, now the premium category leader worldwide.

Villa Massa Limoncello is a semi-sweet liqueur made on a base of pure grain neutral spirits infused with succulent Sorrento lemons. The lemons grown in Sorrento are renowned for being sweet, aromatic and thick skinned. The peels contain an abundance of essential oils that imbue the liqueur with its singularly luscious flavor.

Villa Massa Limoncello has a true lemon color and an impressively light body. Its generous bouquet is rich with the aroma of freshly squeezed lemons laced with floral notes. The palate of the liqueur is skillfully balanced between the natural astringency and exuberance of the lemon juice and the tangy bitterness of the peel. The resulting flavor is delicious and refreshing. The limoncello finishes crisp and clean.

This light lemon liqueur, 60 proof, is particularly amenable to being mixed, adding a zesty pizzazz to cocktails and scores of other libations.

RUM SWIZZLE
House specialty glass, crushed ice
Build in glass
2 1/2 oz. Gosling's Black Seal Rum
3/4 oz. fresh lime juice
1/2 oz. simple syrup
2-3 dashes Angostura Bitters
2 oz. club soda
Orange slice and cherry garnish

RUM TODDY
Coffee mug, heated
Build in glass
2 oz. Gold Rum
1/2 oz. simple syrup
Fill with hot water
Lemon wedge garnish

RUN, SKIP AND GO NAKED
House specialty glass, ice
Pour ingredients into iced mixing glass
1/2 oz. Brandy
1/2 oz. Light Rum
1/2 oz. Gin
1/2 oz. Triple Sec
1 1/2 oz. sweet 'n' sour
Shake and strain
Fill with Draft Beer

RUSSIAN' ABOUT
Cocktail glass, chilled
Pour ingredients into iced mixing glass
1 1/2 oz. Stolichnaya Russian Vodka
1/2 oz. Baileys Irish Cream
1/2 oz. Tia Maria
1/2 oz. Frangelico Liqueur
Shake and strain

RUSSIAN BEAR
Cocktail glass, chilled
Pour ingredients into iced mixing glass
1 oz. Kahlúa Coffee Liqueur
1/2 oz. Vodka
1 1/2 oz. half & half cream
Shake and strain

RUSSIAN NIGHTS
Champagne glass, chilled
Pour ingredients into iced mixing glass
1 1/2 oz. Stolichnaya Limonnaya
   Russian Vodka
1 1/2 oz. orange juice
1 1/2 oz. cranberry juice
Shake and strain
Fill with Champagne
Lemon wheel garnish

RUSSIAN POLAR BEAR
House specialty glass, ice
Pour ingredients into iced mixing glass
1 1/4 oz. Stolichnaya Russian Vodka
3/4 oz. Baileys Irish Cream
3/4 oz. Kahlúa Coffee Liqueur
1/2 oz. DeKuyper Peppermint Schnapps
2 oz. milk
Shake and strain
Fill with cola
Orange slice and cherry garnish

RUSSIAN SUNRISE
Bucket glass, ice
Build in glass
1 oz. Vodka
Near fill with orange juice
Float 1/2 oz. grenadine

RUSTY NAIL®
aka **Scotch Plaid**
Rocks glass, ice
Build in glass
1 1/2 oz. Scotch Whisky
3/4 oz. Drambuie Liqueur

RUSTY NICKEL
Presentation shot glass, chilled
Build in glass
Fill with Bacardi Light Rum
3 dashes Tabasco Sauce

SACRIFICE FLY
Coffee mug, heated
Build in glass
1/2 oz. Christian Brothers Brandy
1/2 oz. DeKuyper Buttershots Schnapps
1/2 oz. Godiva Chocolate Liqueur
Near fill with hot chocolate
Whipped cream garnish
Sprinkle shaved chocolate

SAGINAW SNOOZE
Coffee mug, heated
Build in glass
3 oz. cranberry juice
3 oz. apple juice
1 tsp. honey
Heat and serve
Lemon wheel and cinnamon stick garnish

SAIL OF THE CENTURY
Cocktail glass, chilled
Pour ingredients into iced mixing glass
1 3/4 oz. Sea Wynde Pot Still Rum
3/4 oz. Grand Marnier 100th Anniversary
1/2 oz. fresh lime juice
Shake and strain
Lime wedge garnish

SAINT MORITZ
Cordial or sherry glass, chilled
Layer ingredients
3/4 fill Chambord Liqueur
1/4 fill half & half cream

ST. PATRICK'S DAY
Cocktail glass, chilled
Pour ingredients into iced mixing glass
1 1/2 oz. Jameson Irish Whiskey
3/4 oz. Blue Curaçao
1/2 oz. DeKuyper Peachtree Schnapps
1 oz. orange juice
Shake and strain
Orange slice garnish

ST. PETERSBURG SUNDAE
House specialty glass, chilled
Pour ingredients into blender
1 1/4 oz. Stolichnaya Vanil Russian Vodka
3/4 oz. Disaronno Amaretto Liqueur
1 oz. milk
2 scoops chocolate ice cream
Blend ingredients (with ice optional)
Whipped cream garnish
Drizzle 1/2 oz. Kahlúa Coffee Liqueur
Sprinkle chopped roasted almonds

ST. TROPEZ
Bucket glass, ice
Build in glass
2 oz. Dubonnet Rouge
1 1/2 oz. orange juice
1 1/2 oz. cranberry juice
Orange slice garnish

SAKÉ PASSION
Cocktail glass, chilled
Pour ingredients into iced mixing glass
1 1/2 oz. Canadian Club Whisky
1/2 oz. Alizé Red Passion
1/2 oz. NapaSaki Saké
1 1/2 oz. sweet 'n' sour
Shake and strain

SAKÉ PASSION CLUB
House specialty glass, ice
Pour ingredients into iced mixing glass
1 1/2 oz. Canadian Club Whisky
1/2 oz. Alizé Red Passion
1/2 oz. NapaSaki Saké
1 1/2 oz. sweet 'n' sour
Shake and strain
Fill with club soda

SAKÉ-RAMA
Brandy snifter, ice
Build in glass
1 3/4 oz. Casa Noble Gold Tequila
1 3/4 oz. Saké

GOODERHAM & WORTS®
CANADIAN WHISKY

THE CANADIAN WHISKY GUILD is a remarkable collection of three, small batch whiskies created by Corby Distilleries to celebrate the country's long and prestigious whisky making heritage. Master distiller Michael Booth crafted each individual whisky to represent a distinctive style. One of the members of this unrivaled collection is the classically structured GOODERHAM & WORTS CANADIAN WHISKY.

The whisky is named in honor of the Gooderham & Worts Distillery. Founded in Toronto in 1832, it was Canada's first licensed distillery and among the first in Canada to age their whiskies in wood.

To re-create the complexity and near-perfect balance of the original Gooderham & Worts whisky, Corby relied on tasting notes written by the master distiller dating back to the early 1930s. The whisky is made in small batches from a blend of double-distilled rye, barley, malt, and wheat whiskies. The various spirits are well aged prior to blending and the finished whisky is filtered through charcoal.

There are only a handful of whiskies that are as mellow and flavorful as this re-creation of Gooderham & Worts whisky. It is a sophisticated spirit with an enticing bouquet and complex array of robust, delicious flavors. The whisky has a sublime, satisfying finish. It is bottled at a spry 90 proof.

SALTY BULL
Highball glass, ice
Rim glass with salt
Build in glass
1 1/4 oz. Tequila
Fill with grapefruit juice

SALTY DOG
Highball glass, ice
Rim glass with salt
Build in glass
1 1/4 oz. Vodka
Fill with grapefruit juice
Note: May be requested made with gin

SALTY DOGITRON
Highball glass, ice
Rim glass with salt
Build in glass
1 1/2 oz. Absolut Citron Vodka
1 dash grenadine
Fill with grapefruit juice

SAMMY JÄGER
Presentation shot glass, chilled
Build in glass
1/2 fill Sambuca
1/2 fill Jägermeister Liqueur

SAN ANDREAS FAULT
Coffee mug, heated
Build in glass
1 oz. Bacardi Select Rum
3/4 oz. Cruzan Banana Rum
3/4 oz. Godiva Chocolate Liqueur
Near fill with hot coffee
Whipped cream garnish
Dust powdered cocoa

SAND BLASTER
House specialty glass, ice
Build in glass
1 1/2 oz. Jägermeister Liqueur
3/4 oz. Bacardi Light Rum
Fill with cola
Lime wedge garnish

SANDY BEACH BAY
Champagne glass, chilled
Rim glass with sugar
Pour ingredients into iced mixing glass
1 oz. Whaler's Hawaiian Vanille Rum
2 oz. Chambord Liqueur
Shake and strain
Fill with Champagne
Pineapple wedge garnish

SAN FRANCISCO
House specialty glass, ice
Pour ingredients into iced mixing glass
1 1/2 oz. orange juice
1 1/2 oz. pineapple juice
1 1/2 oz. sweet 'n' sour
1 1/2 oz. grapefruit juice
1/2 oz. grenadine
1 egg white (optional)
Shake and strain
Fill with club soda
Fresh fruit garnish

SANGRIA
Wine glass or goblet, ice
Build in glass
4 oz. Dry Red Wine
3/4 oz. DeKuyper Peachtree Schnapps
3/4 oz. grenadine
3/4 oz. Rose's Lime Juice
1 1/2 oz. orange juice
1 1/2 oz. sweet 'n' sour
Lime, lemon, and orange wheel garnish

SANGRIA, MARGARITA
Pitcher (64 oz.), quarter-full with ice
Build in pitcher
20 oz. Dry Red Wine
12 oz. Sauza Gold Tequila
5 oz. DeKuyper Peachtree Schnapps
2 oz. Rose's Lime Juice
1 oz. grenadine
4 oz. orange juice
4 oz. sweet 'n' sour
Stir thoroughly
Float lime, lemon and orange wheels
Serve over ice (Serves 6-8)

SANGRIA, NEW WORLD PUNCH
(serves two)
Wine goblet or house specialty glass, ice
Pour ingredients into iced mixing glass
5 oz. Dry Red Wine
3/4 oz. DeKuyper Peachtree Schnapps
3 oz. Champagne, Brut
3/4 oz. cranberry juice
3/4 oz. grenadine
3/4 oz. Rose's Lime Juice
1 oz. orange juice
1 1/2 oz. sweet 'n' sour
Shake and strain
Float 3/4 oz. Briottet Crème de Cassis
Lime, lemon and orange wheel garnish

SANGRIA PUNCH, BERRY NEW
Pitcher (64 oz.), quarter-full with ice
Build in pitcher
750 ml Dry Red Wine
2 1/2 oz. DeKuyper Peachtree Schnapps
16 oz. cran-raspberry juice
3 oz. raspberry puree, sweetened
3 oz. strawberry puree, sweetened
1 1/2 oz. grapefruit juice
1 1/2 oz. orange juice
2 oz. sweet 'n' sour
Stir thoroughly
Refrigerate for 2-3 hours
Serve over ice (Serves 6-8)
Lime, lemon and orange wheel garnish

SANGRITA MIX
aka **Sangrita Camino Real**
Pitcher (64 oz.), 1/4 fill with ice
Build in pitcher
1 cup tomato juice
1 cup orange juice
4 oz. grenadine
4 oz. fresh lime juice
5 oz. Worcestershire sauce
1/2 tsp. black pepper
1 tsp. salt
12 dashes Tabasco Sauce
1 tsp. red onion, grated
1 pinch allspice
Stir thoroughly
Serve over ice (Serves 6-8)

SANTA CLAUS IS COMING
Presentation shot glass, chilled
Layer ingredients
1/2 oz. Rumple Minze Schnapps
1/2 oz. Hot Damn Cinnamon Schnapps
1/2 oz. Midori Melon Liqueur
Whipped cream garnish
Sprinkle nutmeg

SANTIAGO (1)
House specialty glass, ice
Pour ingredients into iced mixing glass
1 1/4 oz. Bacardi Select Rum
1 1/4 oz. Mount Gay Eclipse Rum
3/4 oz. Cointreau Liqueur
1/2 oz. Rose's Lime Juice
2 oz. sweet 'n' sour
2 dashes Angostura Bitters
Shake and strain
Fill with Champagne
Lime wedge garnish

BEEFEATER®
LONDON DRY GIN

First produced in 1820 by pharmacist James Burrough, BEEFEATER LONDON DRY GIN is still made according to the same family-held recipe using time-honored production techniques. Burrough named the spirit after the Yeomen of the Guard at the Tower of London, who are commonly known as Beefeaters.

The flavoring agents—called botanicals—used to make Beefeater Gin are steeped in the neutral spirits for a full 24 hours before being redistilled in an alembic still. The botanicals used include juniper berries, coriander, angelica root, licorice, cassia bark, dried Seville orange peels and Spanish lemon peels.

Beefeater Gin has a lavish, thoroughly engaging bouquet, one laced with floral, spice and juniper. Its lightweight body is crisp and exceptionally dry. The gin immediately fills the mouth with layers of delicious flavors, notably citrus, juniper, lavender and spice. The persistence of flavors is remarkably long. The gin is bottled at a lip-tingly 47% abv (94 proof).

Beefeater definitely deserves its reputation as the driest of the elite London dry gins, making it a natural choice to feature in martinis and gimlets. But rest assured, this is a spirit that knows no creative limits.

SANTIAGO (2)
House specialty glass, ice
Pour ingredients into iced mixing glass
1 1/2 oz. Bacardi Light Rum
3/4 oz. Cockspur V.S.O.R. Rum
3/4 oz. Hiram Walker Triple Sec
2-3 dashes Angostura Bitters
1/2 oz. Rose's Lime Juice
1 1/2 oz. sweet 'n' sour
Shake and strain
Orange slice garnish

SAOCO
Highball glass, ice
Build in glass
1 3/4 oz. Light Rum
Fill with coconut milk

SASSAFRAS SUNSET
House specialty glass, ice
Pour ingredients into iced mixing glass
1 1/4 oz. Bacardi Gold Rum
1 oz. St. James Extra Old Rhum
3/4 oz. Hiram Walker Triple Sec
1 oz. orange juice
1 1/2 oz. cranberry juice
1 1/2 oz. sweet 'n' sour
Shake and strain
Fill with club soda
Orange slice and cherry garnish

SATIN PILLOW
Rocks glass, chilled
Build in glass
1/2 oz. Tia Maria
1/2 oz. Frangelico Liqueur
1/2 oz. DeKuyper Triple Sec
1/2 oz. Razzmatazz Raspberry Liqueur

SAUZA SUNRISE
Bucket glass, ice
Build in glass
1 1/4 oz. Sauza Conmemorativo
  Añejo Tequila
Near fill with orange juice
Float 1/4 oz. grenadine
Orange slice and cherry garnish

SAUZA THREESOME
Cocktail glass, chilled
Pour ingredients into iced mixing glass
1 1/2 oz. Sauza Tres Generaciones
  Añejo Tequila
1 oz. Hiram Walker Triple Sec
Shake and strain
Lime wedges (3) garnish

SAVANNAH

Cocktail glass, chilled
Pour ingredients into iced mixing glass
1 1/2 oz. Gin
1 oz. orange juice
1 egg white (optional)
1 dash White Crème de Cacao
Shake and strain

SAVOY CHAMPAGNE COCKTAIL

Champagne glass, chilled
Build in glass
Sugar cube soaked with
   1/4 oz. Angostura Bitters
1/2 oz. Grand Marnier Liqueur
1/2 oz. V.S. Cognac
Fill with Champagne
Lemon twist garnish

SAX WITH BILL

Cocktail glass, chilled
Pour ingredients into iced mixing glass
1 1/2 oz. Cascade Mountain Gin
1/2 oz. simple syrup
1 oz. orange juice
3 dashes Angostura Bitters
Shake and strain
Lemon twist garnish

SAY HEY MARSEILLES

Coffee mug, heated
Build in glass
1 oz. Kahlúa Coffee Liqueur
1 oz. Chambord Liqueur
1/2 oz. Frangelico Liqueur
3/4 oz. half & half cream
Near fill with hot coffee
Whipped cream garnish
Sprinkle shaved chocolate

SAZERAC

Rocks glass or brandy snifter
Build in glass
Swirl 1/2 oz. Pernod in glass, discard excess
2 dashes Angostura Bitters
2 dashes Peychaud bitters
Add ice
2 oz. Rye Whiskey
Lemon twist garnish

SCARLETT O'HARA

Highball glass, ice
Build in glass
1 1/2 oz. Southern Comfort Liqueur
1/2 oz. Rose's Lime Juice
Fill with cranberry juice

SCORPION

House Specialty glass, ice
Pour ingredients into iced mixing glass
1 1/4 oz. Light Rum
1 1/4 oz. Gold Rum
1 oz. White Wine
3/4 oz. Gin
3/4 oz. Brandy
3/4 oz. Crème de Noyaux
1/2 oz. Rose's Lime Juice
1 1/2 oz. orange juice
1 1/2 oz. sweet 'n' sour
Shake and strain
Pineapple wedge and cherry garnish

SCOTCH BOUNTY

House specialty glass, ice
Pour ingredients into iced mixing glass
1 1/2 oz. Dewar's White Label
   Scotch Whisky
1 oz. Malibu Rum
1/2 oz. White Crème de Cacao
1/2 oz. grenadine
1 oz. sweet 'n' sour
2 oz. orange juice
Shake and strain
Orange slice and cherry garnish

SCOTCH COFFEE

Coffee mug, heated
Build in glass
3/4 oz. Scotch Whisky
3/4 oz. Drambuie Liqueur
Fill with hot coffee

SCOTTISH DREAMS

Brandy snifter, heated
Build in glass
1 1/2 oz. Abelour a'Bunadh Single Malt
   Scotch Whisky
1/2 oz. Drambuie Liqueur
Lemon twist garnish

SCOTTISH TAN

Rocks glass, ice
Build in glass
1 1/2 oz. Glenfarclas Single Highland Malt
   Scotch Whisky
3/4 oz. Kahlúa Coffee Liqueur
3/4 oz. Baileys Irish Cream

SCREAMING FUZZY NAVEL

Highball glass, ice
Build in glass
1 oz. DeKuyper Peachtree Schnapps
1/2 oz. Vodka
Fill with orange juice

DEKUYPER® HOT DAMN!®
CINNAMON SCHNAPPS

They weren't kidding when they named DEKUYPER HOT DAMN! CINNAMON SCHNAPPS. Furthermore, the exclamation mark in the middle of its name is warranted. It's fascinating how many BTUs a spicy cinnamon schnapps can generate, and on behalf of mixologists around the world, bravo DeKuyper for boldly going where no man has gone before.

It would have been easy for the good people at DeKuyper to be conservative and create a cinnamon schnapps identical to the rest. But instead of mild and somewhat spicy, they imbued DeKuyper Hot Damn! Schnapps with a lip-tingling personality and enough exuberance to shine in a wide variety of mixed drinks.

DeKuyper Hot Damn! is a smooth textured, light-bodied cinnamon schnapps with a warm, prominent bouquet. The spicy heat begins to fill the mouth immediately and somewhat sizzles as it glides over the palate. As the heat subsides, it is replaced with semi-sweet waves of cinnamon flavor that persist for an impressively long time.

This cinnamon schnapps has an ideal disposition for drink making, perfect for shooters and ice cream drinks, or mixing with hot cocoa, coffee or cappuccinos.

SCREAMING HAWAIIAN
House specialty glass, ice
Pour ingredients into iced mixing glass
1/2 oz. Vodka
1/2 oz. Midori Melon Liqueur
1/2 oz. Malibu Rum
Splash pineapple juice
Splash Seven-Up
Splash grenadine
Shake and strain
Orange slice and cherry garnish

SCREAMING GOOD TIMES
House specialty glass, chilled
Pour ingredients into blender
1 1/2 oz. Bacardi Gold Rum
3/4 oz. Bacardi Limón Rum
3/4 oz. Midori Melon Liqueur
2 scoops vanilla ice cream
Blend ingredients (with ice optional)
Whipped cream garnish

SCREAMING ORGASM
House specialty glass, ice
Build in glass
1/2 oz. Vodka
1/2 oz. Kahlúa Coffee Liqueur
1/2 oz. Disaronno Amaretto Liqueur
1/2 oz. Baileys Irish Cream
1/2 fill half & half cream
1/2 fill club soda

SCREAMING WEEBIES
House specialty glass, ice
Pour ingredients into iced mixing glass
1 oz. Matusalem Light Dry Rum
1/2 oz. Cruzan Coconut Rum
1/2 oz. Midori Melon Liqueur
1/2 oz. grenadine
2 oz. pineapple juice
2 oz. Seven-Up
Shake and strain
Orange slice and cherry garnish

SCREWDRIVER
Highball glass, ice
Build in glass
1 1/4 oz. Vodka
Fill with orange juice

SCURVEY ABATOR
Cocktail glass, chilled
Pour ingredients into iced mixing glass
1 1/2 oz. Plymouth Dry Gin
1/2 oz. Extase XO Liqueur
1/2 oz. orange juice
1/2 oz. fresh lime juice
1/2 oz. sweet 'n' sour
Shake and strain
Orange slice garnish

SEABREEZE
Highball glass, ice
Build in glass
1 1/4 oz. Vodka
1/2 fill grapefruit juice
1/2 fill cranberry juice

SEA DEW
Brandy snifter, heated
Build in glass
1 3/4 oz. Sea Wynde Pot Still Rum
3/4 oz. Mandarine Napoléon Liqueur

SEA SIDE LIBERTY
House specialty glass, chilled
Pour ingredients into blender
1 oz. Mount Gay Eclipse Rum
1 oz. Cruzan Coconut Rum
3/4 oz. X.O. Café Coffee Liqueur
1/2 oz. half & half cream
1 oz. coconut cream syrup
3 oz. pineapple juice
Blend with ice
Pineapple wedge and cherry garnish

SEATTLE'S 6.3
Cocktail glass, chilled
Pour ingredients into iced mixing glass
2 oz. Tanqueray Gin
1/4 oz. fresh lemon juice
1/4 oz. cranberry juice
1/2 oz. fresh lime juice
1/2 oz. simple syrup
Stir and strain
Orange slice garnish

SEA WATER
House specialty glass, ice
Pour ingredients into iced mixing glass
1 1/4 oz. Sauza Conmemorativo
   Añejo Tequila
3/4 oz. Blue Curaçao
1 1/2 oz. orange juice
2 1/2 oz. sweet 'n' sour
Shake and strain
Lime wedge garnish

SEPARATOR (1)
Cordial or sherry glass, chilled
Layer ingredients
1/3 fill Kahlúa Coffee Liqueur
1/3 fill half & half cream
1/3 fill Brandy

SEPARATOR (2)
Rocks glass, ice
Build in glass
1 oz. Brandy
1 oz. Kahlúa Coffee Liqueur
1/2 oz. half & half cream

SEVEN & SEVEN
Highball glass, ice
Build in glass
1 1/4 oz. Seagram's 7 Whisky
Fill with Seven-Up

SEVEN OF HEARTS
Bucket glass, ice
Build in glass
2 oz. Rémy Red
Fill with Seven-Up

1701 FOG
Cocktail glass, chilled
Pour ingredients into iced mixing glass
1 1/4 oz. Smirnoff Vodka
1 1/4 oz. Chambord Liqueur
1 1/4 oz. sweet 'n' sour
Stir and strain

SEVENTH AVENUE
Cocktail or house specialty glass, chilled
Pour ingredients into iced mixing glass
3/4 oz. Disaronno Amaretto Liqueur
3/4 oz. Godiva Chocolate Liqueur
3/4 oz. Drambuie Liqueur
1 1/2 oz. half & half cream
Shake and strain

SEVENTH HEAVEN
Highball glass, ice
Build in glass
1 oz. Seagram's 7 Whisky
1/2 oz. Disaronno Amaretto Liqueur
Fill with orange juice

SEVEN TWENTY-SEVEN (727)
Rocks glass, ice
Build in glass
3/4 oz. Stolichnaya Russian Vodka
3/4 oz. Kahlúa Coffee Liqueur
3/4 oz. Baileys Irish Cream
3/4 oz. Grand Marnier Liqueur

SEX AT THE BEACH
Rocks glass, chilled
Pour ingredients into iced mixing glass
1/2 oz. Vodka
1/2 oz. DeKuyper Peachtree Schnapps
1/2 oz. DeKuyper Pucker Sour Apple
1/2 oz. Grand Marnier Liqueur
1/2 oz. Southern Comfort Liqueur
1/2 oz. cranberry juice
1/2 oz. orange juice
1/2 oz. half & half cream
Shake and strain

BLAVOD® BLACK VODKA

Imported from England, triple-distilled BLAVOD BLACK VODKA is a well-structured, neutral grain vodka with one remarkable distinguishing feature, it doesn't look at all like vodka. Blavod has cast off its transparency, opting for a cloak of darkness. It is virtually opaque with an intriguing blackberry hue with a violet tint. It is unlike any other vodka in the world.

Blavod Black Vodka is the brainchild of Mark Dorman of Blavod Black Vodka plc of London. The vodka has a semi-sweet, herbal bouquet, and a lush, full body. The vodka fills the mouth with an electric warmth not dissimilar to grappa, then finishes on a dime.

Without a doubt, Blavod's most extraordinary characteristic is its dramatic appearance. The outrageous color comes from black catechu, an exotic herb from Burma.

In the hands of an accomplished mixologist, Blavod is a dream come true. It makes a spectacular martini, and adds an eerie quality to a cosmopolitan. The blackish vodka turns screwdrivers green and cape codders irresistible.

Blindfolded, most enthusiasts would be hard pressed to distinguish Blavod Vodka from other well-known imports. But who drinks with their eyes shut? Grab a bottle and let the magic work for you.

SEX IN THE COAL REGION
Bucket glass, ice
Build in glass
1 oz. Vodka
1/2 oz. DeKuyper Raspberry Pucker
1/2 oz. Blackberry Brandy
Splash Seven-Up
Splash club soda
Near fill with Draft Beer
Float 3/4 oz. Malibu Rum

SEX IN THE TROPICS
House specialty glass, ice
Pour ingredients into iced mixing glass
1 1/2 oz. Alizé Red Passion
1 1/2 oz. Malibu Rum
2 oz. pineapple juice
2 oz. sweet 'n' sour
Shake and strain
Pineapple wedge garnish

SEX IN THE WOODS
House specialty glass, chilled
Pour ingredients into blender
1 1/2 oz. Vodka
3/4 oz. Disaronno Amaretto Liqueur
1/2 oz. Tia Maria
2 1/2 oz. pineapple juice
Blend with ice

SEX ON A BLACK SAND BEACH
Rocks glass, ice
Build in glass
1/2 oz. Blavod Black Vodka
1/2 oz. Chambord Liqueur
1/2 oz. Licor 43 (Cuarenta y Tres)
Fill with pineapple juice

SEX ON THE BEACH (1)
Highball glass, ice
Build in glass
1/2 oz. Vodka
1/2 oz. Chambord Liqueur
1/2 oz. Tia Maria
Fill with pineapple juice

SEX ON THE BEACH (2)
Highball glass, ice
Build in glass
3/4 oz. Midori Melon Liqueur
3/4 oz. Chambord Liqueur
Fill with pineapple juice

SEX ON THE BEACH (3)
Rocks glass, chilled
Pour ingredients into iced mixing glass
1 oz. Southern Comfort Liqueur
3/4 oz. Chambord Liqueur
1 oz. pineapple juice
1 oz. orange juice
Shake and strain

SEX ON THE BEACH (4)
Rocks glass, chilled
Pour ingredients into iced mixing glass
3/4 oz. Vodka
3/4 oz. Chambord Liqueur
1/2 oz. DeKuyper Peachtree Schnapps
3/4 oz. sweet 'n' sour
3/4 oz. orange juice
Shake and strain

SEX ON THE BEACH (5)
Rocks glass, chilled
Pour ingredients into iced mixing glass
1 1/2 oz. Midori Melon Liqueur
3/4 oz. Chambord Liqueur
1/2 oz. DeKuyper Peachtree Schnapps
1 oz. sweet 'n' sour
Shake and strain

SEX ON THE BEACH ON A CLOUDY DAY
Rocks glass, ice
Build in glass
1 oz. Malibu Rum
1/2 oz. Disaronno Amaretto Liqueur
1/2 oz. Baileys Irish Cream
1 oz. pineapple juice

SEXUAL CHOCOLATE
Rocks glass, chilled
Build in glass
3/4 oz. Jägermeister Liqueur
3/4 oz. Baileys Irish Cream
3/4 oz. Kahlúa Coffee Liqueur
3/4 oz. Dark Crème de Cacao

SEX WITH AN ALLIGATOR (1)
Cocktail glass, chilled
Pour ingredients into iced mixing glass
1 1/2 oz. Midori Melon Liqueur
1/2 oz. Chambord Liqueur
1/2 oz. Jägermeister Liqueur
1 1/2 oz. sweet 'n' sour
Shake and strain

SEX WITH AN ALLIGATOR (2)
Cocktail glass, chilled
Pour ingredients into iced mixing glass
1 1/2 oz. DeKuyper Pucker Sour Apple
1/2 oz. Razzmatazz Raspberry Liqueur
1/2 oz. Vodka
1/2 oz. Jägermeister Liqueur
1/2 oz. Rose's Lime Juice
1 1/2 oz. sweet 'n' sour
Shake and strain

SHANDY GAFF
Large beer glass or mug, chilled
Build in glass
1/2 fill Draft Deer
1/2 fill ginger ale

SHARK ATTACK
Bucket glass, ice
Build in glass
1 1/4 oz. Bacardi Light Rum
Near fill with lemonade
Float 3/4 oz. Blue Curaçao
Orange slice garnish

SHARK BITE
Bucket glass, ice
Build in glass
1 oz. Appleton Estate V/X Jamaica Rum
Near fill with orange juice
Float 3/4 oz. grenadine
Orange slice garnish
Note: Immerse orange slice
to resemble shark's fin

SHARK'S TOOTH
House specialty glass, chilled
Pour ingredients into blender
1 1/2 oz. Bacardi Light Rum
1 oz. Blue Curaçao
3/4 oz. White Crème de Cacao
2 scoops vanilla ice cream
Blend ingredients (with ice optional)
Whipped cream garnish
Drizzle 1/2 oz. grenadine

SHEILABERRY
House specialty glass, chilled
Pour ingredients into blender
1/2 oz. Gin
1/2 oz. Vodka
1/2 oz. Rum
1/2 oz. Tequila
1/2 oz. Triple Sec
2 oz. sweet 'n' sour
2 oz. strawberries, frozen
Blend with ice
Splash cola
Lemon wedge garnish

SHERRY'S BLOSSOM
Cocktail glass, chilled
Pour ingredients into iced mixing glass
1 1/2 oz. Vodka
1/2 oz. Doorly's XO Barbados Rum
1/2 oz. Extase XO Liqueur
1/4 oz. Rose's Lime Juice
Stir and strain
Orange twist garnish

SHILLELAGH
House specialty glass, ice
Build in glass
2 oz. Light Rum
1 oz. Green Crème de Menthe
1 oz. fresh lime juice
1/2 oz. Rose's Lime Juice
Green cherry garnish

GOSLING'S®
BLACK SEAL RUM

GOSLING'S BLACK SEAL RUM is the national spirit of Bermuda. In the spring of 1806, English wine and spirits merchant James Gosling arrived in St George's, Bermuda, where he and his family decided to set up shop. To this day, Gosling Brothers remains the oldest surviving business in Bermuda.

Gosling's Black Seal Rum originated in 1860. The Gosling brothers experimented with different blends of barrel-aged Caribbean rum until they created a masterpiece, which they initially named the "Old Rum." During World War I, the company began filling champagne bottles reclaimed from the British Officer's mess. The corks were secured in place with the use of black sealing wax. It soon became known as the "Black Seal" brand.

Gosling's Black Seal Rum has a dark amber/brown color and a compact bouquet of coffee, sugar cane, caramel and toasted oak. Its palate is a medley of roasted and spicy flavors that completely fill the mouth before slipping away in a warm, lingering finish.

It is understandable why Gosling's Black Seal Rum is the best selling spirit in Bermuda. While a pleasure to drink neat, it is a delight to mix in cocktails, and is the core of such classics as the Dark'n Stormy and Rum Swizzle.

SHIP WRECK
Bucket glass, ice
Build in glass
1 oz. Malibu Rum
1 oz. Sauza Tres Generaciones Añejo Tequila
Fill with pineapple juice
Pineapple wedge and cherry garnish

SHIRLEY TEMPLE
Collins or bucket glass, ice
Build in glass
Near fill with Seven-Up
Float 1 oz. grenadine
Cherry garnish

SHORE BOAT
Coffee mug, heated
Build in glass
1 oz. Pusser's British Navy Rum
3/4 oz. Appleton Estate V/X Jamaica Rum
3/4 oz. Angostura Caribbean Rum Cream
1/2 oz. Kahlúa Coffee Liqueur
Near fill with hot coffee
Whipped cream garnish

SHORE BREEZE
Bucket glass, ice
Build in glass
1 1/2 oz. Bacardi Light Rum
2-3 dashes Angostura Bitters
2 oz. cranberry juice
2 oz. pineapple juice
Float 3/4 oz. Mount Gay Eclipse Rum

SHOT IN THE DARK
Presentation shot glass
Build in glass
1/3 fill Yukon Jack Liqueur
1/3 fill Grand Marnier Liqueur
1/3 fill hot coffee

SHOT THRU THE HEART
Rocks glass, chilled
Build in glass
3/4 oz. Bacardi Select Rum
3/4 oz. Kahlúa Coffee Liqueur
3/4 oz. Baileys Irish Cream
3/4 oz. Grand Marnier Liqueur

SIBERIAN
Rocks glass, ice
Build in glass
1 1/2 oz. Vodka
1/2 oz. Brandy
1/2 oz. Kahlúa Coffee Liqueur

SICILIAN KISS
Rocks glass, ice
Build in glass
1 oz. Disaronno Amaretto Liqueur
1 oz. Southern Comfort Liqueur

SICILIAN SUNRISE
Bucket glass, ice
Build in glass
1 oz. Casa Noble Reposado Tequila
Near fill with Orange Pelligrino
Float 1 oz. cranberry juice

SIDECAR (1)
Cocktail glass, chilled
Rim glass with sugar (optional)
Pour ingredients into iced mixing glass
1 oz. V.S. Cognac
1/2 oz. Cointreau Liqueur
1 1/2 oz. sweet 'n' sour
Shake and strain

SIDECAR (2)
Cocktail glass, chilled
Rim glass with sugar (optional)
Pour ingredients into iced mixing glass
1 oz. Brandy
1/2 oz. Triple Sec
1 1/2 oz. sweet 'n' sour
Shake and strain

SIDECAR IN BOMBAY
Cocktail glass, chilled
Rim glass with sugar (optional)
Pour ingredients into iced mixing glass
1 3/4 oz. Bombay Sapphire London Dry Gin
3/4 oz. Grand Marnier 100th Anniversary
3/4 oz. fresh lemon juice
Shake and strain

SIDECAR, IRISH
Cocktail glass, chilled
Rim glass with sugar (optional)
Pour ingredients into iced mixing glass
1 1/2 oz. Knappogue Castle Irish Whiskey
3/4 oz. Cointreau Liqueur
2 oz. sweet 'n' sour
Shake and strain

SIDECAR ROYALE
Cocktail glass, chilled
Rim glass with sugar (optional)
Pour ingredients into iced mixing glass
1 oz. V.S. Cognac
1/2 oz. Cointreau Liqueur
1/2 oz. Benedictine
1 1/2 oz. sweet 'n' sour
Shake and strain

SIDE SHOT
Rocks glass, chilled
Pour ingredients into iced mixing glass
1 1/4 oz. Absolut Kurant Vodka
1 1/2 oz. cranberry juice
Shake and strain

SILKEN VEIL
Brandy snifter, ice
Build in glass
1 1/2 oz. Vodka
1 1/2 oz. Dubonnet Rouge
Lemon twist garnish

SILK PANTIES (1)
aka **Pink Silk Panties, Woo-Woo**
Highball glass, ice
Build in glass
1 oz. DeKuyper Peachtree Schnapps
1/2 oz. Vodka
Fill with cranberry juice

SILK PANTIES (2)
Rocks glass, ice
Build in glass
1 1/2 oz. Vodka
1/2 oz. DeKuyper Peachtree Schnapps

SILK TIE
House specialty glass, ice
Pour ingredients into iced mixing glass
2 oz. Jameson Irish Whiskey
1 oz. Dewar's White Label Scotch Whisky
1/2 oz. Rose's Lime Juice
1 oz. orange juice
2 3/4 oz. sweet 'n' sour
Shake and strain
Lime wheel garnish

SILVER BULLET
Rocks glass, ice
Build in glass
1 1/2 oz. Tequila
1/2 oz. White Crème de Menthe

SILVER CLOUD
House specialty glass, chilled
Pour ingredients into iced mixing glass
1/2 oz. Kahlúa Coffee Liqueur
1/2 oz. Disaronno Amaretto Liqueur
1/2 oz. Dark Crème de Cacao
1/2 oz. Vodka
1 1/2 oz. half & half cream
Shake and strain

CORDIAL AND SHOOTER DRINKS

This diverse body of drink recipes ranges from the elegant and sophisticated to the radically bizarre. Shooters and cordials are anything but one-dimensional. If one recipe can be credited for launching the popularity of these drinks, it's the "B-52."

When appropriate, shooters should be served in chilled glasses. This will help keep the ingredients at their proper serving temperature and improve the drink's presentation.

Pousse Cafés are layered cordial drinks with three or more stripes, which requires using liqueurs with different specific gravities. The layering effect is similar to the way oil will float on vinegar.

To accomplish this, care must be taken to prevent the various products from mixing in the glass. The ingredients should be poured in the order specified in the recipe, since the ingredients are listed from heaviest to lightest.

The easiest and fastest way to create these layers is to use the back of a bar spoon to slow the pour of the liqueur. The spoon is held just above the level of the first liqueur poured into the glass, and the next ingredient is poured slowly and carefully over the sloped back of the spoon. Each layer is poured using this same technique.

The same effect for a two-layer drink can be obtained by first tilting the glass so that the bottom layer is almost touching the inside rim. The second product is then slowly and gently poured onto the glass surface between the first liqueur and the rim. While pouring the second layer, the glass should be carefully brought upright.

SILVER FIZZ
House specialty glass, chilled
Pour ingredients into iced mixing glass
1 oz. Gin
2 oz. half & half cream
1 egg white (optional)
1 oz. sweet 'n' sour
1/2 oz. simple syrup
Shake and strain
Splash club soda

SILVER SHADOW
Coffee mug, heated
Build in glass
1 1/4 oz. Disaronno Amaretto Liqueur
Fill with English Breakfast tea
Lemon wedge garnish

SILVER SPIDER
Rocks glass, chilled
Pour ingredients into iced mixing glass
1/2 oz. Vodka
1/2 oz. Light Rum
1/2 oz. Triple Sec
1/2 oz. White Crème de Menthe
Stir and strain

SIMPLY CRIMSON
Cocktail glass, chilled
Pour ingredients into iced mixing glass
1 1/2 oz. Cointreau Liqueur
4 dashes Angostura Bitters
1 1/2 oz. cranberry juice
Stir and strain
Splash club soda
Orange slice and cherry garnish

SINGAPORE SLING (1)
House specialty glass, ice
Pour ingredients into iced mixing glass
1 oz. Gin
1/2 oz. grenadine
1 1/2 oz. sweet 'n' sour
Shake and strain
Near fill with club soda
Float 3/4 oz. Cherry Brandy
Orange slice and cherry garnish

SINGAPORE SLING (2)
House specialty glass, ice
Pour ingredients into iced mixing glass
1 oz. Gin
1/2 oz. Cointreau Liqueur
1/2 oz. Benedictine
1/2 oz. Cherry Brandy
2 dashes Angostura Bitters
1/2 oz. fresh lime juice
2 oz. pineapple juice
Shake and strain
Orange slice and cherry garnish

SIN IN HAWAII
Cocktail glass, chilled
Pour ingredients into iced mixing glass
1 1/2 oz. Vincent Van Gogh
    Wild Appel Vodka
1 oz. pineapple juice
1 oz. cran-apple juice
Shake and strain
Apple wedge garnish

SKINNY DIPPING
House specialty glass, ice
Build in glass
3/4 oz. Vodka
3/4 oz. DeKuyper Peachtree Schnapps
3/4 oz. Disaronno Amaretto Liqueur
1/2 fill cranberry juice
1/2 fill orange juice

SKIP AND GO NAKED
Bucket glass, ice
Pour ingredients into iced mixing glass
1 1/2 oz. Gin
1/2 oz. grenadine
1 1/2 oz. sweet 'n' sour
Shake and strain
Fill with Draft Beer

SKY HIGH
House specialty glass, chilled
Pour ingredients into blender
1 oz. Finlandia Vodka
1/2 oz. Baileys Irish Cream
1/2 oz. Frangelico Liqueur
1/2 oz. Grand Marnier Liqueur
2 oz. milk
Blend with ice
Whipped cream garnish
Drizzle 1/2 oz. Kahlúa Coffee Liqueur

SKYSCRAPER
Highball glass, ice
Build in glass
1 1/4 oz. Jim Beam White Label Bourbon
1/2 oz. Rose's Lime Juice
2 dashes Angostura Bitters
Fill with cranberry juice
Cucumber garnish (optional)

SLAM DUNK
Bucket glass, ice
Build in glass
1 1/2 oz. Southern Comfort Liqueur
1/2 fill cranberry juice
1/2 fill orange juice

SLEIGH RIDE
Coffee mug, heated
Build in glass
1 1/4 oz. Gooderham & Worts
    Canadian Whisky
3/4 oz. Whaler's Hawaiian Vanille Rum
1/2 oz. Fireball Cinnamon Canadian Whisky
1/2 fill warm cranberry juice
1/2 fill warm apple cider
Cinnamon stick garnish

SLIPPED DISK
House specialty glass, chilled
Pour ingredients into blender
1 1/4 oz. Bacardi Gold Rum
1 oz. Bacardi Spiced Rum
3/4 oz. Disaronno Amaretto Liqueur
3/4 oz. Grand Marnier Liqueur
1/2 oz. cranberry juice
1/2 oz. orange juice
1/2 oz. grenadine
1/2 oz. sweet 'n' sour
1 oz. coconut cream syrup
1 oz. pineapple juice
Blend with ice
Pineapple wedge and cherry garnish

SLIPPERY BANANA
Presentation shot glass, chilled
Layer ingredients
1/3 fill Kahlúa Coffee Liqueur
1/3 fill Crème de Banana
1/3 fill Baileys Irish Cream

SLIPPERY DICK
Rocks glass, chilled
Build in glass
1 oz. DeKuyper Peppermint Schnapps
1 oz. DeKuyper Buttershots Schnapps

SLIPPERY GREEK
Presentation shot glass, chilled
Layer ingredients
1/3 fill Ouzo
2/3 fill Baileys Irish Cream

SLIPPERY NIPPLE
Presentation shot glass, chilled
Layer ingredients
1/2 fill Sambuca
1/2 fill Baileys Irish Cream

SLOE COMFORTABLE SCREW
Highball glass, ice
Build in glass
3/4 oz. Sloe Gin
Near fill with orange juice
Float 3/4 oz. Southern Comfort Liqueur

DEKUYPER®
WATERMELON PUCKER®

If someone doesn't have a good time with DEKUYPER WATERMELON PUCKER behind the bar, check their pulse and call a medic! It's an unpretentious, great tasting product that's chaffing at the bit to have some fun.

Watermelon Pucker is one of a line of similarly concocted sweet 'n' sour schnapps. What differentiates the DeKuyper Puckers line of schnapps from the rest of the field is that they are brimming with tart and zesty flavor, just enough zing to make them something special.

There is simply nothing else behind the bar to compare with this spry, watermelon liqueur. It has a feathery light body, a pink watermelon hue and a fresh fruit bouquet. Its tangy, watermelon flavor persists on the palate for an impressively long time and is completely free of any cloying sweetness.

There are scores of creative applications for low-proof Watermelon Pucker. It is a popular addition in specialty drinks, everything from signature cosmopolitans, margaritas, and martinis, to specialty coladas, daiquiris and gimlets.

Like all of DeKuyper's other flavored Puckers, they're a fun addition to have on your team.

SLOE COMFORTABLE SCREW
UP AGAINST THE WALL
Bucket glass, ice
Build in glass
1/2 oz. Sloe Gin
1/2 oz. Southern Comfort Liqueur
Near fill with orange juice
Float 3/4 oz. Galliano Liqueur

SLOE GIN FIZZ
Bucket glass, ice
Pour ingredients into iced mixing glass
1 1/2 oz. Sloe Gin
2 oz. sweet 'n' sour
Shake and strain
Fill with club soda

SLOE POKE
Highball glass, ice
Build in glass
1 1/4 oz. Sloe Gin
Fill with cola

SLOE SCREW
aka **Cobra**
Highball glass, ice
Build in glass
1 1/4 oz. Sloe Gin
Fill with orange juice

SLOPPY JOE'S COCKTAIL
Cocktail glass, chilled
Pour ingredients into iced mixing glass
1 1/2 oz. Bacardi Light Rum
1/2 oz. Dry Vermouth
1/4 oz. Hiram Walker Triple Sec
1/4 oz. grenadine
1/2 oz. fresh lime juice
Shake and strain
Lime wedge garnish

SLOW TROPICO CRUISE
Bucket glass, ice
Build in glass
1 1/4 oz. Tropico
3/4 oz. Sloe Gin
1 1/2 oz. pineapple juice
1 1/2 oz. orange juice
Orange slice garnish

SMILES FOR MILES
Rocks glass, ice
Build in glass
3/4 oz. Canadian Club Whisky
3/4 oz. Disaronno Amaretto Liqueur
3/4 oz. DeKuyper Peppermint Schnapps

SMITH & KERNS
Brandy snifter, ice
Build in glass
1 1/2 oz. Kahlúa Coffee Liqueur
1/2 fill half & half cream
1/2 fill club soda

SMITH & WESSON
Brandy snifter, ice
Build in glass
1 1/2 oz. Kahlúa Coffee Liqueur
1/2 fill half & half cream
1/2 fill cola

SMOOTH DRIVER
Highball glass, ice
Build in glass
1 oz. Vodka
Near fill with orange juice
Float 3/4 oz. Cointreau Liqueur

SMOOTH GENTLEMAN
Bucket glass, ice
Build in glass
1 1/4 oz. Gentleman Jack Tennessee Whiskey
1/2 oz. Disaronno Amaretto Liqueur
Fill with cranberry juice
Orange slice and cherry garnish

SMOOTH SCREW
House specialty glass, chilled
Pour ingredients into blender
3/4 oz. Appleton Estate V/X Jamaica Rum
3/4 oz. Mount Gay Eclipse Rum
3/4 oz. Tia Maria
1 1/2 oz. pineapple juice
1 1/2 oz. orange juice
Blend with ice
Float 3/4 oz. Cockspur V.S.O.R. Rum

SMOOTHY
Rocks glass, ice
Build in glass
1 1/2 oz. W.L. Weller Bourbon
1/2 oz. White Crème de Menthe

SMURF PISS
Rocks glass, chilled
Pour ingredients into iced mixing glass
1/2 oz. Light Rum
1/2 oz. Blueberry Schnapps
1/2 oz. Blue Curaçao
1 oz. sweet 'n' sour
1 oz. Seven-Up
Shake and strain

SNAKE BITE (1)
Rocks glass, ice
Build in glass
1 1/2 oz. Yukon Jack Liqueur
1/2 oz. Rose's Lime Juice
Lime wedge garnish

SNAKE BITE (2)
Beer glass, chilled
Build in glass
1/2 fill Draft Ale
1/2 fill apple cider (hard)

SNAKE BITE (3)
Presentation shot glass, chilled
Layer ingredients
1/2 fill White Crème de Cacao
1/2 fill Southern Comfort Liqueur

SNEAK & PEAK COCKTAIL
Cocktail glass, chilled
Pour ingredients into iced mixing glass
1 1/4 oz. Bacardi Limón Rum
1 oz. Stolichnaya Razberi Russian Vodka
1/2 oz. Chambord Liqueur
1 oz. Seven-Up
1 oz. sweet 'n' sour
Shake and strain
Lemon twist and raspberry garnish

SNEAKY PEACH
House specialty glass, chilled
Pour ingredients into blender
1 1/2 oz. DeKuyper Peachtree Schnapps
3/4 oz. grenadine
1 oz. sweet 'n' sour
2 oz. orange juice
2 oz. coconut cream syrup
Blend with ice

SNO-CAP
House specialty glass, chilled
Pour ingredients into blender
1 oz. Finlandia Vodka
1 oz. Baileys Irish Cream
1/2 oz. Kahlúa Coffee Liqueur
2 oz. espresso coffee
2 oz. coffee
2 scoops chocolate ice cream
Blend ingredients (with ice optional)
Whipped cream garnish
Drizzle 1/2 oz. Kahlúa Coffee Liqueur

SNOWBALL
Cocktail glass, chilled
Pour ingredients into iced mixing glass
1 oz. Gin
1/2 oz. Anisette
1 1/2 oz. half & half cream
Shake and strain

ORO di MAZZETTI®

If anyone was going to perfect a grappa-based liqueur, it undoubtedly had to be Italian Mazzetti d'Altavilla. They are the oldest and most prestigious grappa producer in the Piedmont region and the second oldest producer in all of Italy. ORO DI MAZZETTI is an ultra-premium grappa liqueur imbued with more than its fair share of pleasant surprises.

The base of this modern marvel is grappa made from moscato grapes. After the grapes have been pressed during the winemaking process, the remnants in the press—the skins, stalks and pips—are collected, fermented and double-distilled in copper pot stills. To make this highly innovative liqueur, Mazzetti d'Altavilla sweetens their moscato grappa and adds 23-carat gold micro-flecks. The gold is added for its purported healing properties.

Good luck finding a more compelling liqueur than Oro di Mazzetti. The liqueur is crystal clear and has a feathery, lightweight body. The bouquet offers a fetching array of spicy and herbal aromas. Its palate is quite delicious and features the fresh flavors of sage, rose and elderflower.

The tiny gold flecks add a fascinating quality to the liqueur, and when swirled, the flurry stays suspended for an extended amount of time. Overall, Oro di Mazzetti is a splendid elixir.

SNOWSHOE (1)
Rocks glass, ice
Build in glass
1 1/2 oz. Wild Turkey 80° Bourbon
1/2 oz. DeKuyper Peppermint Schnapps

SNOWSHOE (2)
Rocks glass, ice
Build in glass
1 1/2 oz. Wild Turkey 80° Bourbon
3/4 oz. Dr. McGillicuddy's
    Mentholmint Schnapps

SOCIALITE
Rocks glass, ice
Build in glass
1 1/2 oz. Original Cristall Russian Vodka
3/4 oz. Godiva Chocolate Liqueur
1/2 oz. half & half cream
Reception stick candy garnish

SOCIALITE PRIZE FIGHT
House specialty glass, chilled
Pour ingredients into blender
2 oz. Doorly's XO Barbados Rum
2 oz. coconut cream syrup
1 oz. mango fruit juice
2 oz. pineapple juice
Blend with ice
Pineapple wedge garnish

SOMBRERO
aka **Kahlúa & Cream, Muddy River**
Brandy snifter, ice
Build in glass
1 1/2 oz. Kahlúa Coffee Liqueur
1/2 oz. half & half cream

SOMOSA BAY
House specialty glass, ice
Pour ingredients into iced mixing glass
1 oz. Absolut Vodka
1/2 oz. Grand Marnier Liqueur
1/2 oz. Chambord Liqueur
1 oz. orange juice
1/4 oz. Angostura lime juice
2 oz. sweet 'n' sour
Shake and strain
Lime wedge and orange slice garnish

SON OF A PEACH
House specialty glass, ice
Pour ingredients into iced mixing glass
1 1/2 oz. Artic Vodka & Peach Liqueur
1 oz. sweet 'n' sour
2 oz. pineapple juice
3 oz. orange juice
Shake and strain
Orange slice and cherry garnish

SONOMA CHILLER
Wine glass, ice
Build in glass
1 3/4 oz. Chopin Polish Vodka
1/2 oz. fresh lemon juice
Fill with Chardonnay Wine

SONOMA NOUVEAU
Wine glass, ice
Build in glass
5 oz. alcohol-free Dry White Wine
Near fill with club soda
Float 3/4 oz. cranberry juice
Lemon twist garnish

SONORAN SUNRISE
Bucket glass, ice
Build in glass
3/4 oz. Sauza Hornitos Tequila
3/4 oz. Sauza Conmemorativo
   Añejo Tequila
1/2 oz. Gran Gala Orange Liqueur
Near fill with orange juice
Float 1/2 oz. grenadine
Lime wheel garnish

SONORAN SUNSET
Highball glass, ice
Build in glass
1 1/4 oz. El Tesoro Añejo Tequila
1/2 oz. Grand Marnier 100th Anniversary
1/2 oz. cranberry juice
1 1/2 oz. fresh lime juice
Lime wheel garnish

SOUR
Cocktail glass, chilled
Pour ingredients into iced mixing glass
1 oz. requested liquor/liqueur
2 oz. sweet 'n' sour
Shake and strain
Orange slice and cherry garnish

SOUR MELON PATCH
Cocktail glass, chilled
Pour ingredients into iced mixing glass
1 3/4 oz. Jameson Irish Whiskey
3/4 oz. Midori Melon Liqueur
3/4 oz. fresh lime juice
1 1/2 oz. orange juice
1 1/2 oz. pineapple juice
Shake and strain
Lemon wheel garnish

SOUR MINT
Brandy snifter, ice
Pour ingredients into iced mixing glass
1 oz. Light Rum
1/2 oz. Peppermint Schnapps
2 oz. sweet 'n' sour
Shake and strain

SOUR, SPARKLING
SWEET APPLE
House specialty glass, ice
Pour ingredients into iced mixing glass
1 1/4 oz. Canadian Club Whisky
3/4 oz. DeKuyper Pucker Sour Apple
2 oz. sweet 'n' sour
Shake and strain
Splash Seven-Up
Lemon wedge garnish

SOUTH BEACH TWIST
House specialty glass, ice
Pour ingredients into iced mixing glass
1 1/4 oz. Giori Lemoncillo Liqueur
3/4 oz. Giori Lemoncillo Cream Liqueur
1/2 oz. Finlandia Vodka
1/2 oz. Gran Gala Orange Liqueur
Shake and strain
Orange slice garnish

SOUTHERN BELLE
Rocks glass, chilled
Build in glass
2-3 mint sprigs
1/2 oz. simple syrup
1/2 oz. sweet 'n' sour
Muddle contents
Add ice
Fill with ginger ale
Mint sprig garnish

SOUTHERN SUICIDE
Rocks glass, chilled
Pour ingredients into iced mixing glass
3/4 oz. Jack Daniel's Tennessee Whiskey
3/4 oz. Southern Comfort Liqueur
1/2 oz. orange juice
1/4 oz. Seven-Up
1/4 oz. grenadine
Shake and strain

SOUTH OF FRANCE
House specialty glass, chilled
Pour ingredients into blender
1 1/2 oz. Bacardi Light Rum
1 oz. B & B Liqueur
1 1/2 oz. coconut cream syrup
2 1/2 oz. pineapple juice
Blend with ice
Pineapple wedge and cherry garnish

LAIRD'S® APPLEJACK APPLE BRANDY

Crafted by the country's oldest distiller, LAIRD'S APPLEJACK is a venerable American brandy as old as the Republic itself. The company's founder, Robert Laird, fought in the American Revolution under the command of General George Washington. Soldiers of the beleaguered Continental Army were fed and given Applejack while camped near the Laird family's inn in Colt's Neck, New Jersey.

Laird's Applejack is made from tree-ripened apples grown in Shenandoah Valley orchards. The apples are naturally fermented in large, 20,000-gallon oak vats. No cultures, yeasts, starters, sugars or blending agents are used, making Laird's Applejack an impressively pure spirit. The fermented mash is double-distilled in pot stills, then blended with 65% neutral grain spirits prior to being aged a minimum of 4 years in American white oak barrels.

Laird's Applejack has a smooth, light to medium-weight body and a beckoning bouquet of peeled apples and a hint of toasted oak. The brandy's palate leads off with the delightfully tart flavor of apple cider, followed by notes of toffee, caramel, and oak. The finish is warming and of medium duration.

This apple brandy is more spirited and exuberant than its French counterpart, Calvados, which brings to mind the phrase, *viva la différence!*

SOUTH-OF-THE-BORDER MANGO MASH

House specialty glass, chilled
Pour ingredients into blender
1 3/4 oz. El Jimador Reposado Tequila
3/4 oz. Gran Gala Orange Liqueur
1 oz. pineapple juice
2 oz. coconut cream syrup
3 oz. mango puree
Blend with ice
Orange slice garnish

SOVEREIGNTY

Cappuccino cup, heated
Build in glass
1 oz. Chambord Liqueur
1/2 oz. Tia Maria
1/2 oz. White Crème de Cacao
Near fill with hot espresso coffee
Top with frothed milk
Sprinkle shaved chocolate

SOYER-AU-CHAMPAGNE

House specialty glass, chilled
Pour ingredients into iced mixing glass
1/2 oz. Brandy
1/2 oz. Blue Curaçao
1/2 oz. grenadine
1 tbsp. vanilla ice cream
Shake and strain
Fill with Champagne
Strawberry garnish

SPANISH FLY

Bucket glass, ice
Pour ingredients into iced mixing glass
1 1/4 oz. Vodka
2 oz. sweet 'n' sour
2 oz. pineapple juice
Shake and strain
Float 3/4 oz. Blue Curaçao

SPATS COLUMBO

House specialty glass, ice
Build in glass
1 1/2 oz. Bacardi Light Rum
1 oz. Midori Melon Liqueur
2 oz. orange juice
2 oz. pineapple juice
Float 3/4 oz. Sloe Gin
Pineapple wedge and cherry garnish

SPEARMINT ICED TEA

Bucket glass, ice
Build in glass
1 1/4 oz. Spearmint Schnapps
Fill with iced herbal tea
Lemon wedge garnish

SPERM BANK
Presentation shot glass, chilled
Layer ingredients
1/3 fill Baileys Irish Cream
1/3 fill White Crème de Cacao
1/3 fill Disaronno Amaretto Liqueur
1 drop grenadine in center with straw

SPIDER CIDER
Bucket glass, ice
Build in glass
1 oz. DeKuyper Pucker Sour Apple
1 oz. Vodka
1/2 fill cranberry juice
1/2 fill orange juice

SPLENDID GIN
Cocktail glass, chilled
Pour ingredients into iced mixing glass
1 1/2 oz. Tanqueray Nº Ten Gin
3/4 oz. Dubonnet Rouge
3/4 oz. Villa Massa Limoncello
Shake and strain
Lemon twist garnish

SPILT MILK (1)
House specialty glass, ice
Pour ingredients into iced mixing glass
1 oz. Baileys Irish Cream
1/2 oz. Canadian Club Whisky
1/2 oz. Bacardi Light Rum
1/2 oz. Crème de Noyaux
1 1/2 oz. half & half cream
Shake and strain

SPILT MILK (2)
Rocks glass, chilled
Build in glass
1 1/2 oz. Baileys Irish Cream
1/2 oz. Crown Royal
1/2 oz. Disaronno Amaretto Liqueur
Splash half & half cream

SPIRIT OF ERIE COFFEE
Coffee mug or glass, heated
Build in glass
1 1/4 oz. Knappogue Castle Irish Whiskey
3/4 oz. Cruzan Coconut Rum
Near fill with hot coffee
Whipped cream garnish
Drizzle 1/2 oz. Celtic Crossing Irish Liqueur

SPRING BREAK
Bucket glass, ice
Build in glass
1 3/4 oz. Malibu Rum
1/2 fill cranberry juice
1/2 fill Seven-Up

SPRITZER
Wine glass or goblet, ice
Build in glass
1/2 fill White Wine
1/2 fill club soda
Lime or lemon wedge garnish
Note: May be requested made with Red or
   Rosé Wine

SPUTNIK
Champagne glass, chilled
Rim glass with grenadine and sugar
   (optional)
Pour ingredients into iced mixing glass
1 oz. Stolichnaya Ohranj Russian Vodka
1 oz. orange juice
1/4 oz. grenadine
Stir and strain
Fill with Champagne
Lemon twist garnish

SPY'S DEMISE
House specialty glass, ice
Pour ingredients into iced mixing glass
3/4 oz. Vodka
3/4 oz. Gin
3/4 oz. Sloe Gin
1/2 oz. Light Rum
1/2 oz. grenadine
1 oz. sweet 'n' sour
Shake and strain
Fill with Seven-Up

STARBOARD TACK
House specialty glass, ice
Build in glass
1 1/2 oz. Mount Gay Eclipse Rum
1 oz. Mount Gay Special Reserve Rum
1/2 fill cranberry juice
Near fill with orange juice
Float 3/4 oz. Mount Gay Extra Old Rum
Orange slice and cherry garnish

STARBURST
House specialty glass, chilled
Pour ingredients into blender
1 1/2 oz. Bacardi Select Rum
1 1/2 oz. Bacardi Limón Rum
1 oz. Rose's lime juice
2 oz. pureed strawberries
3 oz. orange juice
Blend with ice
Strawberry garnish

STAR GAZER
Rocks glass, ice
Build in glass
1 1/2 oz. El Jimador Reposado Tequila
3/4 oz. Kahlúa Coffee Liqueur
3/4 oz. Mandarine Napoléon Liqueur

ARTIC® VODKA & MELON LIQUEUR

After almost 100 years, the Illva Saronno Distillery of Saronno, Italy has learned a thing or two about capturing the essential flavors of fruit and infusing them with distilled spirits. They are, after all, the makers of classic Disaronno Amaretto. Illva Saronno is also now becoming known for a line of flavorful, contemporary spirits, an ensemble led by ARTIC VODKA & MELON LIQUEUR.

These are products whose time has come. Also included in the line-up are ARTIC VODKA & PEACH LIQUEUR and ARTIC VODKA & STRAWBERRY LIQUEUR. The vodka used in these products is a high quality, pure grain neutral spirit. It is then blended with a liqueur made from a mixture of the fresh fruit flavorings.

Artic Vodka & Melon Liqueur is rainwater clear with a supple, light to medium-weight body. While subtle, the bouquet is marked by the aroma of fresh cantaloupe. The vodka does generate some heat on the palate, but that is quickly replaced by a wave of semi-sweet melon flavors. This Artic expedition has a fairly long, flavorful finish.

In addition to their light, pleasing flavors, these "New Age" spirits are relatively low in alcohol (50 proof), making them fashionably hip and well suited for use in cocktails.

STARLIGHT
Cocktail glass, chilled
Pour ingredients into iced mixing glass
2 oz. Vodka
1/2 oz. Opal Nera Black Sambuca
Stir and strain
Lemon twist garnish

STARS & STRIPES
Sherry glass, chilled
Layer ingredients
1/3 fill Blue Curaçao
1/3 fill grenadine
1/3 fill half & half cream

STARS AT NIGHT
Presentation shot glass, chilled
Layer ingredients
1/2 fill Goldschläger
1/2 fill Jägermeister Liqueur

STEALTH BOMBER (1)
House specialty glass, ice
Pour ingredients into iced mixing glass
1 1/4 oz. Matusalem Light Dry Rum
1 1/4 oz. Matusalem Golden Dry Rum
3/4 oz. Blue Curaçao
1 1/2 oz. grapefruit juice
1 1/2 oz. cranberry juice
Shake and strain
Float 1 oz. Matusalem Classic Black Rum

STEALTH BOMBER (2)
Bucket glass, ice
Pour ingredients into iced mixing glass
1 1/4 oz. Myer's Jamaican Rum
1/2 oz. DeKuyper Triple Sec
1 1/2 oz. grapefruit juice
1 1/2 oz. cranberry juice
Shake and strain
Splash club soda (optional)

STEEPLECHASE
House specialty glass, ice
Pour ingredients into iced mixing glass
1 1/2 oz. W.L. Weller Bourbon
1/2 oz. Hiram Walker Triple Sec
1/4 oz. Blackberry Brandy
2 dashes Angostura Bitters
2 oz. orange juice
Shake and strain
Mint sprigs (2) garnish

STEEPLE JACK
Bucket glass, ice
Pour ingredients into iced mixing glass
1 1/2 oz. Laird's Applejack Brandy
1/2 oz. Rose's Lime Juice
2 1/2 oz. apple juice
Shake and strain
Fill with club soda
Lime wedge garnish

STIFF DICK
Rocks glass, chilled
Build in glass
1 oz. Baileys Irish Cream
1 oz. DeKuyper Buttershots Schnapps

STILETTO
House specialty glass, ice
Pour ingredients into iced mixing glass
1 oz. Disaronno Amaretto Liqueur
3/4 oz. Crème de Banana
1/2 fill orange juice
1/2 fill pineapple juice
Shake and strain

STINGER
Rocks glass, ice
Build in glass
1 1/2 oz. Brandy
3/4 oz. White Crème de Menthe

STOCK MARKET ZOO
Bucket glass, ice
Pour ingredients into iced mixing glass
1/2 oz. Farias Silver Tequila
1/2 oz. Damrak Amsterdam Gin
1/2 oz. Foursquare Spiced Rum
1/2 oz. Jim Beam Black Label Bourbon
1/2 oz. grenadine
1 oz. orange juice
2 oz. pineapple juice
Shake and strain

STOLICHNAYA LEMONADE
House specialty glass, ice
Build in glass
1 1/4 oz. Stolichnaya Limonnaya
    Russian Vodka
1/2 oz. Grand Marnier Liqueur
1/2 fill sweet 'n' sour
1/2 fill lemon-lime soda
Lemon wheel garnish

STONE SOUR
Cocktail glass, chilled
Pour ingredients into iced mixing glass
1 oz. requested liquor/liqueur
1 oz. sweet 'n' sour
1 oz. orange juice
Shake and strain
Orange slice and cherry garnish

STORM-A-LONG BAY
House specialty glass, chilled
Pour ingredients into blender
1 1/2 oz. Matusalem Classic Black Rum
3/4 oz. Chambord Liqueur
1 oz. cranberry juice
2 oz. pineapple juice
2 scoops vanilla ice cream
Blend ingredients (with ice optional)
Whipped cream garnish

STRAIGHT SHOOTER
Presentation shot glass, chilled
Build in glass
1/3 fill Midori Melon Liqueur
1/3 fill Vodka
1/3 fill orange juice

STRAWBERRIES 'N' CREAM
aka **Wimbleton**
House specialty glass, chilled
Pour ingredients into blender
1 1/2 oz. Strawberry Schnapps
1/2 oz. simple syrup
1/2 cup strawberries
1 oz. sweet 'n' sour
2 oz. half & half cream
Blend with ice
Strawberry garnish

STRAWBERRY ALEXANDRA
House specialty glass, chilled
Pour ingredients into blender
1 oz. Brandy
1 oz. White Crème de Cacao
3 oz. strawberry puree
2 scoops vanilla ice cream
Blend ingredients (with ice optional)
Whipped cream garnish
Sprinkle shaved chocolate

STRAWBERRY BANANA SPLIT
House specialty glass, chilled
Pour ingredients into blender
1 1/4 oz. Royal Oak Extra Old Rum
3/4 oz. Crème de Banana
1/2 cup strawberries
1 oz. half & half cream
1/2 tsp. vanilla
2 scoops vanilla ice cream
Blend ingredients (with ice optional)
Whipped cream and banana slice garnish

DR. MCGILLICUDDY'S®
VANILLA LIQUEUR

Put the name Dr. McGillicuddy's on a bottle of schnapps and you can presume that you're in for a rare treat. If you rely on a great recipe and make it with great ingredients, you'll end up with a great schnapps. The creators of Dr. McGillicuddy's have taken it a step further than that by adding something unexpected. DR. MCGILLICUDDY'S VANILLA LIQUEUR is no exception.

The liqueur is made in Canada from a base of high-quality neutral grain spirits steeped with whole vanilla beans. Although it seems like it should be a straightforward proposition, this schnapps has a few surprises up its sleeve.

The first surprise is just how light and delicious Dr. McGillicuddy's Vanilla Liqueur is. It has a crystal clear appearance and a sleek, lightweight body. The next unexpected attribute is its precisely honed balance. The liqueur barely registers on the sweetness meter, so there's absolutely nothing cloying about it.

The final surprise is the subtle pairing of chocolate with the vanilla in the bouquet and palate. The two flavors merge naturally and give this schnapps more dimension than one would expect.

Dr. McGillicuddy's Vanilla Liqueur is superb chilled and served as a shot or over ice. It also makes an excellent ingredient in many cocktails.

STRAWBERRY NUT
House specialty glass, chilled
Pour ingredients into blender
1 1/4 oz. Frangelico Liqueur
1/2 oz. half & half cream
1/2 cup strawberries
2 scoops macadamia ice cream
Blend ingredients (with ice optional)
Whipped cream garnish
Dust powdered cocoa

STRAWBERRY QUICKIE
Rocks glass, chilled
Pour ingredients into iced mixing glass
1 1/4 oz. Tequila Rose Cream Liqueur
1 oz. DeKuyper Buttershots Schnapps
3/4 oz. Baileys Irish Cream
Shake and strain

STRAWBERRY ROSE
House specialty glass, ice
Pour ingredients into iced mixing glass
1 1/2 oz. Tequila Rose Cream Liqueur
1 oz. White Crème de Cacao
2 oz. half & half cream
Shake and strain
Strawberry garnish

STRAWBERRY SHAKE
House specialty glass, chilled
Pour ingredients into blender
1 1/2 oz. Disaronno Amaretto Liqueur
1/2 cup strawberries
1 1/2 oz. half & half cream
2 scoops vanilla ice cream
Blend ingredients (with ice optional)
Strawberry garnish

STRAWBERRY SMASH
House specialty glass, chilled
Pour ingredients into blender
1 oz. Bacardi Gold Rum
1 oz. Chambord Liqueur
1/2 oz. Bacardi 151° Rum
1/2 cup strawberries
1 ripe banana
1 oz. orange juice
2 oz. sweet 'n' sour
Blend with ice
Strawberry garnish

STRAW HOUSE HUMMER
House specialty glass, chilled
Pour ingredients into blender
1 1/4 oz. Bacardi Light Rum
3/4 oz. Crème de Banana
3/4 oz. Disaronno Amaretto Liqueur
1 peeled, ripe banana
1 oz. orange juice
1 oz. sweet 'n' sour
Blend with ice
Whipped cream and banana slice garnish
Drizzle 3/4 oz. Dillon Dark Rhum

STRUMMER HUMMER
House specialty glass, chilled
Pour ingredients into blender
3/4 oz. Light Rum
3/4 oz. Cruzan Banana Rum
3/4 oz. Disaronno Amaretto Liqueur
1 ripe banana
Blend with ice
Banana slice garnish

STUBB'S AYERS ROCK
House specialty glass, ice
Pour ingredients into iced mixing glass
1 1/2 oz. Stubb's Queensland Rum
2 oz. sweet 'n' sour
3 oz. cranberry juice
Shake and strain

SUFFERING BASTARD
House specialty glass, ice
Pour ingredients into iced mixing glass
1 1/2 oz. St. James Extra Old Rhum
3/4 oz. Bacardi Light Rum
3/4 oz. Crème de Noyaux
3/4 oz. Cointreau Liqueur
1/2 oz. simple syrup
1 1/2 oz. fresh lime juice
Shake and strain
Cucumber peel garnish

SUGAR BABY
Rocks glass, chilled
Pour ingredients into iced mixing glass
3/4 oz. Kahlúa Coffee Liqueur
3/4 oz. DeKuyper Buttershots Schnapps
3/4 oz. Dr. McGillicuddy's Vanilla Liqueur
3/4 oz. Baileys Irish Cream
Shake and strain

SUGAR DADDY
Rocks glass, ice
Build in glass
1 1/2 oz. Courvoisier V.S.O.P. Cognac
1 1/2 oz. Kahlúa Coffee Liqueur
Orange twist garnish

SUISSESSE
House specialty glass, ice
Pour ingredients into iced mixing glass
1 oz. Pernod
2 oz. sweet 'n' sour
Shake and strain
Fill with club soda

SUMMER BREEZE
Highball glass, ice
Build in glass
1 1/4 oz. Rum
1/2 fill grapefruit juice
1/2 fill cranberry juice

SUMMERCILLO
Bucket glass, ice
Build in glass
1 1/2 oz. Giori Lemoncillo Liqueur
3/4 oz. Giori Lemoncillo Cream Liqueur
3/4 oz. Zone Peach Italian Vodka
1 3/4 oz. orange juice
1 3/4 oz. pineapple juice
Orange slice garnish

SUMMER HUMMER
Cocktail glass, chilled
Pour ingredients into iced mixing glass
1 3/4 oz. Tanqueray Nº Ten Gin
1/2 oz. Chambord Liqueur
1 3/4 oz. sweet 'n' sour
Shake and strain
Lime wedge garnish

SUMMER IN THE PARK
Champagne glass, chilled
Pour ingredients into iced mixing glass
2 oz. Alizé de France
1 oz. cranberry juice
1 oz. sweet 'n' sour
Shake and strain
Fill with Champagne
Orange twist garnish

SUMMER LEMONADE
Bucket glass, ice
Build in glass
1 1/2 oz. Stolichnaya Limonnaya
    Russian Vodka
1/2 oz. Blue Curaçao
1/2 fill lemonade
1/2 fill Seven-Up

SUMMER MEMORIES
Cocktail glass, chilled
Pour ingredients into iced mixing glass
2 oz. Original Polish Vodka
1/2 oz. fresh watermelon juice
Stir and strain
Watermelon cube garnish

W.L. WELLER® SPECIAL RESERVE BOURBON

William LaRue Weller originated the W.L. Weller Bourbon brand in 1849. Weller Bourbon now has the good fortune of being made at the Buffalo Trace Distillery located in Franklin County, Kentucky.

W.L. WELLER SPECIAL RESERVE BOURBON is only one of a few Kentucky whiskies distilled with a mash bill containing wheat instead of rye. The result is a softer, milder whiskey with a big, full body. This Weller classic comes out of the still at low proof, a technique designed to accentuate the sweet flavors in the whiskey.

The 7-year-old Weller Special Reserve, 90 proof, is indeed something special. The bourbon has a spicy, semi-sweet bouquet with caramel and honey aromas. Its medium-weight body is supple and well rounded, and on the palate, the whiskey is rich with the flavors of butterscotch, fruit, spice and vanilla. The flavors persist well into the long, warming finish.

W. L. WELLER 19-YEAR-OLD BOURBON is a glorious whiskey featuring a palate stuffed full of fruity, oaky flavors and a long, robust finish. The distillery also makes W.L. WELLER CENTENNIAL, a highly acclaimed, 10-year-old bourbon, OLD WELLER ANTIQUE, an immense semi-sweet bourbon aged for 7 years and bottled at 107 proof, and the long awaited arrival of W.L. WELLER 12-YEAR-OLD BOURBON, a spry, brilliant whiskey bottled at 90 proof.

SUMMER SLAMMER
House specialty glass, ice
Pour ingredients into iced mixing glass
1/2 oz. Galliano Liqueur
1/2 oz. Crème de Banana
1/2 oz. Myers's Jamaican Rum
1/2 oz. sweet 'n' sour
1/2 oz. grenadine
1 1/2 oz. orange juice
1 1/2 oz. pineapple juice
Shake and strain
Cherry garnish

SUMMER TONIC
House specialty glass, chilled
Rim glass with lemon flavored salt (optional)
Pour ingredients into blender
2 oz. Tanqueray No. Ten Gin
3/4 oz. Giori Lemoncillo Liqueur
3/4 oz. Giori Lemoncillo Cream Liqueur
3/4 oz. sweet 'n' sour
Blend with ice
Float 3/4 oz. Briottet Crème de Cassis
Lemon wheel garnish

SUNBURNT SEÑORITA
Cocktail glass, chilled
Pour ingredients into iced mixing glass
1 1/4 oz. El Tesoro Añejo Tequila
1 oz. fresh lime juice
3/4 oz. watermelon juice
Shake and strain
Lime wedge garnish

SUNDAY BRUNCH PUNCH COCKTAIL
Cocktail glass, chilled
Pour ingredients into iced mixing glass
2 oz. Tanqueray No. Ten Gin
1/2 oz. Mandarine Napoléon Liqueur
1 oz. orange juice
3 dashes Angostura Bitters
Shake and strain
Orange twist garnish

SUNFLOWER
Cocktail glass, chilled
Pour ingredients into iced mixing glass
2 oz. Vincent Van Gogh Vodka
1/2 oz. Grand Marnier Liqueur
3/4 oz. orange juice
Stir and strain
Orange slice garnish

SUNGLOW
Cocktail glass, chilled
Pour ingredients into iced mixing glass
2 oz. Original Cristall Russian Vodka
1/2 oz. Kelt XO Tour du Monde Cognac
3-4 drops orange flower water
Stir and strain
Orange twist garnish

SUNKNEE DELITE
Bucket glass, ice
Pour ingredients into iced mixing glass
1 1/2 oz. Canadian Club Whisky
3/4 oz. Giori Lemoncillo Liqueur
2 oz. sweet 'n' sour
Shake and strain
Fill with Squirt
Lemon wheel garnish

SUN SEEKER
House specialty glass, ice
Build in glass
1 1/4 oz. Bacardi Select Rum
1 oz. Mount Gay Eclipse Rum
1 oz. Crème de Banana
2 oz. pineapple juice
2 oz. orange juice
Splash Seven-Up
Orange slice and cherry garnish

SUNRISE
Bucket glass, ice
Build in glass
1 1/2 oz. Bacardi Select Rum
1/2 oz. DeKuyper Triple Sec
1/2 oz. orange juice
Near fill with grapefruit juice
Float 1/2 oz. grenadine

SUNSTROKE
Cocktail glass, chilled
Pour ingredients into iced mixing glass
1 oz. Absolut Vodka
1/2 oz. Grand Marnier Liqueur
2 oz. grapefruit juice
Shake and strain

SUNTAN TEASER
Rocks glass, chilled
Pour ingredients into iced mixing glass
1 1/2 oz. Malibu Rum
1/2 oz. Cruzan Banana Rum
1/4 oz. DeKuyper Triple Sec
1/4 oz. Captain Morgan Spiced Rum
1/2 oz. pineapple juice
1 dash grenadine
Shake and strain

SURFERS ON ACID
Rocks glass, chilled
Pour ingredients into iced mixing glass
3/4 oz. Malibu Rum
3/4 oz. Jägermeister Liqueur
1 1/2 oz. pineapple juice
Shake and strain

SURF SIDER (1)
Cocktail glass, chilled
Pour ingredients into iced mixing glass
1 1/4 oz. Gosling's Black Seal Rum
3/4 oz. Blue Curaçao
3/4 oz. Grand Marnier Liqueur
1/2 oz. Rose's Lime Juice
1 1/4 oz. pineapple juice
Shake and strain
Lime wedge garnish

SURF SIDER (2)
Bucket glass, ice
Build in glass
1 1/4 oz. Malibu Rum
1/2 oz. Rose's Lime Juice
Near fill with cranberry juice
Splash club soda

SUSIE TAYLOR
Highball glass, ice
Build in glass
1 1/4 oz. Light Rum
Fill with ginger ale
Lemon wedge garnish

SWAMP WATER
Mason jar, ice
Build in glass
1 1/2 oz. Green Chartreuse
Fill with grapefruit juice

SWAMP WATER STINGER
House specialty glass, ice
Pour ingredients into iced mixing glass
1 1/2 oz. Van Hoo Belgium Vodka
3/4 oz. Southern Comfort Liqueur
1/2 oz. DeKuyper Peachtree Schnapps
1/2 oz. Blue Curaçao
1/2 oz. pineapple juice
1/2 oz. cranberry juice
1 oz. orange juice
Shake and strain

SWEATY BETTY
House specialty glass, chilled
Pour ingredients into blender
1 oz. Yukon Jack Liqueur
1 oz. Dr. McGillicuddy's
   Mentholmint Schnapps
2 1/2 oz. sweet 'n' sour
Blend with ice
Lemon wedge garnish

QUESTIONS FOR THE SEASONED PRO

1. The majority of the world's vodkas are distilled from what product?
2. In what city was the first Bacardi distillery located?
3. How does the pear get into the bottle of Poire William?
4. What ingredient in Sambuca, Ouzo and Pernod turns them cloudy when in contact with ice?
5. This blended Caribbean rum was standard issue for sailors of the British Royal Navy.
6. What whisky was introduced in 1939 to commemorate the visit of King George and Queen Elizabeth to Canada?
7. Legend has it that this Italian liqueur was formulated as a love potion by a coven of witches?
8. Bonnie Prince Charles brought the recipe for what liqueur to Scotland in 1745?
9. Drier and more potent than anisette, this anise liqueur is made in Greece and Cyprus.
10. What American liquor was the first to be marketed in a square-shaped bottle?
11. What fortified wine is most closely associated with Solera aging?
12. This liqueur is made from black currants grown the Burgundy region of France.
13. What was America's first proprietary liqueur?
14. What is the principal difference between a brandy and an eau de vie?

Answers

1. The majority of vodkas are distilled from corn
2. Santiago, Cuba
3. Bottles are attached to the branches of pear trees such that the budding fruit grows inside the bottles
4. Oil of anise
5. Pusser's British Navy Rum
6. Crown Royal Canadian Whisky
7. Liquore Strega
8. Drambuie
9. Ouzo
10. Jack Daniel's Tennessee Whiskey
11. Sherry
12. Crème de Cassis
13. Southern Comfort
14. Brandies are invariably aged in wood; eaux de vie are either left unaged or aged in glass vessels so they retain their clarity.

SWEET (IRISH) DREAMS
Brandy snifter, ice
Pour ingredients into iced mixing glass
1 oz. Knappogue Castle Irish Whiskey
1 oz. Baileys Irish Cream
1 oz. Celtic Crossing Irish Liqueur
Shake and strain

SWEET 'N' SOUR STONE SOUR
Collins or bucket glass, ice
Pour ingredients into iced mixing glass
1 1/4 oz. Tanqueray № Ten Gin
1 1/2 oz. sweet 'n' sour
3/4 oz. orange juice
3/4 oz. grapefruit juice
Shake and strain
Fill with Seven-Up
Lime wedge, orange slice and cherry garnish

SWEET RED KISS
Cocktail glass, chilled
Rim glass with sugar (optional)
Pour ingredients into iced mixing glass
1 1/2 oz. Dubonnet Rouge
3/4 oz. Chambord Liqueur
3/4 oz. Absolut Kurant Vodka
1/2 oz. orange juice
1/2 oz. of pineapple juice
1/2 oz. cranberry juice
Shake and strain
Orange slice garnish

SWEET TART (1)
House specialty glass, chilled
Pour ingredients into blender
2 oz. Rain Vodka
1/4 oz. Rose's Lime Juice
2 oz. cranberry juice
2 oz. pineapple juice
Blend with ice
Lime wheel garnish

SWEET TART (2)
Bucket glass, ice
Pour ingredients into iced mixing glass
1 1/4 oz. VOX Vodka
3/4 oz. Chambord Liqueur
1/4 oz. simple syrup (optional)
3 oz. sweet 'n' sour
Shake and strain
Fill with Seven-Up

SWEET TART (3)
Rocks glass, chilled
Pour ingredients into iced mixing glass
3/4 oz. Chambord Liqueur
3/4 oz. Disaronno Amaretto Liqueur
1 1/2 oz. sweet 'n' sour
Shake and strain

SWIMMING NAKED AT SUNSET
Bucket glass, ice
Build in glass
1 1/2 oz. Bacardi Select Rum
1/2 oz. Grand Marnier Liqueur
1/2 oz. orange juice
1/4 oz. grenadine
3 oz. grapefruit juice

TAHITIAN APPLE
Highball glass, ice
Build in glass
1 1/4 oz. Light Rum
Fill with apple juice

TAJ MAJAL
Cocktail glass, chilled
Pour ingredients into iced mixing glass
2 oz. Original Polish Vodka
1/4 oz. Old Raj Dry Gin
1/4 oz. Vya California Dry Vermouth
Stir and strain
Lemon twist garnish

TAKE THE 'A' TRAIN
House specialty glass, ice
Pour ingredients into iced mixing glass
1 1/4 oz. Absolut Citron Vodka
1/2 oz. Absolut Vodka
2 oz. grapefruit juice
2 oz. cranberry juice
Shake and strain
Fill with club soda
Lemon wedge garnish

TAKE THE PRIZE
Cocktail glass, chilled
Pour ingredients into iced mixing glass
1 1/2 oz. Casa Noble Gold Tequila
3/4 oz. Chambord Liqueur
1 1/2 oz. sweet 'n' sour
1/2 oz. fresh lemon juice
Shake and strain
Lime wedge garnish

TAMARA LVOVA
House specialty glass, chilled
Pour ingredients into blender
1 oz. Stolichnaya Razberi Russian Vodka
1 oz. Appleton Estate V/X Jamaica Rum
1 oz. Dark Crème de Cocoa
1/4 oz. chocolate syrup
2 scoops vanilla ice cream
Blend ingredients (with ice optional)
Whipped cream and strawberry garnish
Drizzle 3/4 oz. Godiva Chocolate Liqueur

TAM-O'-SHANTER
Rocks glass, ice
Build in glass
1 1/2 oz. Kahlúa Coffee Liqueur
1/2 oz. Irish Whiskey
1/2 oz. half & half cream

TANGERINE DROP
Cocktail glass, chilled
Pour ingredients into iced mixing glass
2 1/2 oz. Vincent Van Gogh Oranje Vodka
1/4 oz. grenadine
3/4 oz. grapefruit juice
3/4 oz. cranberry juice
Stir and strain
Orange slice garnish

TARNISHED BULLET
Rocks glass, ice
Build in glass
1 1/2 oz. Tequila
1/2 oz. Green Crème de Menthe

TAVERN SUCKER, THE
Bucket glass, ice
Pour ingredients into iced mixing glass
3/4 oz. Frangelico Liqueur
3/4 oz. DeKuyper Buttershots Schnapps
3/4 oz. Kahlúa Coffee Liqueur
3/4 oz. Baileys Irish Cream
2 oz. chocolate milk
Shake and strain

T-BIRD
Rocks glass, chilled
Pour ingredients into iced mixing glass
1/2 oz. Stolichnaya Russian Vodka
1/2 oz. Grand Marnier Liqueur
1/2 oz. Disaronno Amaretto Liqueur
1 1/2 oz. pineapple juice
Shake and strain

TEATIME
Glass mug, heated
Build in glass
1 oz. Ballylarkin Irish Liqueur
1 oz. Jameson Irish Whiskey
Near fill with hot tea
Serve with lemon wedge

TENDER MERCIES
Coffee mug, heated
Build in glass
1/2 oz. Tuaca
1/2 oz. Tia Maria
1/2 oz. Baileys Irish Cream
Near fill with hot coffee
Whipped cream garnish

DR. MCGILLICUDDY'S®
FIREBALL CINNAMON WHISKY

Think of your childhood and the bright red fireball candy that you would suck on until you could no longer resist the urge to bite into it, and the burst of cinnamon that would fill your mouth when you did. Add a chaser of aged whisky and you have the latest addition to Dr. McGillicuddy's family of innovative libations, FIREBALL CINNAMON WHISKY.

This unique creation from the good Doctor is produced in Canada from a unique infusion of barrel-aged whisky and oil of cinnamon. It is an exhilarating, somewhat fiery liqueur teeming with great taste and a nearly combustible personality.

Dr. McGillicuddy's Fireball Cinnamon Whisky has a true-to-life whisky color and a smooth, extremely light body. Initially, the spicy aroma of cinnamon dominates the bouquet, but within a few minutes the scent of the whisky makes its presence known. Fireball is a fitting name for the whisky, for the flavor of cinnamon immediately raises the temperature in the mouth. The heat and taste of the cinnamon persists for an exceptionally long time, gradually fading away allowing the flavor of the whisky to take center stage.

Dr. McGillicuddy's Fireball Cinnamon Whisky is an ideal bracer for a cold winter night. It is also highly versatile and enjoys scores of creative applications behind the bar.

TENNESSEE GENTLEMAN
Bucket glass, ice
Pour ingredients into iced mixing glass
1 1/4 oz. Gentleman Jack
   Tennessee Whiskey
1 1/4 oz. sweet 'n' sour
Shake and strain
Fill with ginger ale
Orange slice garnish

TENNESSEE MUD
Coffee mug, heated
Build in glass
3/4 oz. Jack Daniel's Tennessee Whiskey
3/4 oz. Disaronno Amaretto Liqueur
Near fill with hot coffee
Whipped cream garnish

TENNESSEE TEA
Highball glass, ice
Build in glass
1 oz. Jack Daniel's Tennessee Whiskey
1/2 oz. Dark Crème de Cacao
Fill with cranberry juice
Lemon twist garnish

TEQUADOR
Bucket glass, ice
Build in glass
1 1/2 oz. Hussong's Reposado Tequila
1/2 oz. Rose's Lime Juice
1/2 oz. Razzmatazz Raspberry Liqueur
Fill with pineapple juice
Lime wedge garnish

TEQUILA A LA BERTITA
Bucket glass, ice
Pour ingredients into iced mixing glass
2 oz. Sauza Tres Generaciones Plata Tequila
3/4 oz. fresh lime juice
1/2 oz. Rose's Lime Juice
2 oz. lemonade
Shake and strain
Fill with Squirt
Lime wedge garnish

TEQUILA DRIVER
Highball glass, ice
Build in glass
1 1/4 oz. Tequila
Fill with orange juice

TEQUILA HIGHLANDER
Rocks glass, ice
Build in glass
1 1/2 oz. Gold Tequila
3/4 oz. Drambuie Liqueur

TEQUILA MARIA

House specialty glass, chilled
Pour ingredients into blender
3/4 oz. Hussong's Reposado Tequila
3/4 oz. Bacardi Gold Rum
1/2 oz. Crème de Banana
1/2 oz. Blackberry Brandy
3/4 oz. grenadine
1/2 cup strawberries
1 1/2 oz. sweet 'n' sour
1 1/2 oz. fresh lime juice
Blend with ice

TEQUILA MOCKINGBIRD (1)

Cocktail glass, chilled
Pour ingredients into iced mixing glass
1 1/2 oz. Tequila
1/2 oz. Green Crème de Menthe
1 1/2 oz. fresh lime juice
Shake and strain
Lime wedge garnish

TEQUILA MOCKINGBIRD (2)

House specialty glass, ice
Pour ingredients into iced mixing glass
1 1/4 oz. Sauza Tres Generaciones
    Añejo Tequila
3/4 oz. Blue Curaçao
2 oz. orange juice
2 oz. sweet 'n' sour
Shake and strain
Lime wedge garnish

TEQUILA QUENCHER

Highball glass, ice
Build in glass
1 1/4 oz. Tequila
1/2 fill orange juice
1/2 fill club soda
Lime wedge garnish

TEQUILA ROSÉ

Bucket glass, ice
Build in glass
1 1/2 oz. Tequila
1/2 oz. Rose's Lime Juice
Near fill with grapefruit juice
Float 1/2 oz. grenadine

TEQUILA SLAMMER/POPPER

Presentation shot glass, chilled
Build in glass
1/2 fill Gold Tequila
1/2 fill ginger ale
Place napkin and palm over glass, slam glass
    down on bar top, drink while foaming

TEQUILA SLIDER

Rocks glass, chilled
Build in glass
1 1/2 oz. Tequila
2 dashes soy sauce
2 dashes Tabasco Sauce
1/2 tsp. horseradish
1/2 oz. fresh lime juice
1 medium raw oyster
1/2 tsp. caviar (optional)

TEQUILA SUNRISE

Bucket glass, ice
Build in glass
1 oz. Tequila
Near fill with orange juice
Float 1/2 oz. grenadine

TEQUILA SUNSET

Bucket glass, ice
Build in glass
1 oz. Tequila
Near fill with orange juice
Float 3/4 oz. Blackberry Brandy

TEQUILIER REAL

Rocks glass, ice
Build in glass
1 1/2 oz. Casa Noble Reposado Tequila
3/4 oz. Grand Marnier 100th Anniversary

TEST-TUBE BABY (1)

Presentation shot glass, chilled
Build in glass
1/2 fill Disaronno Amaretto Liqueur
1/2 fill Tequila
2 drops Baileys Irish Cream

TEST-TUBE BABY (2)

Presentation shot glass, chilled
Build in glass
3/4 oz. Disaronno Amaretto Liqueur
1/2 oz. Southern Comfort Liqueur
3 drops Baileys Irish Cream
    in center with straw

TEXAS TEA

Bucket glass, ice
Build in glass
3/4 oz. Rain Vodka
3/4 oz. Chambord Liqueur
1/2 oz. Jewel of Russia Berry Infusion
Fill with pineapple juice

DEKUYPER®
PEACH PUCKER®

There comes a point in everyone's life when it's time to put work behind you, roll up your sleeves and have a little fun. DEKUYPER PEACH PUCKER is just the kind of lighthearted product that was created for good times and to raise a few smiles in the process.

Peach Pucker is one of a line of similarly concocted sweet 'n' sour schnapps. What differentiates these snazzy liqueurs from the rest of the field is that they are delightfully tart, packing just enough zesty tang to really perk up a cocktail. They are completely devoid of any cloying sweetness that plagues lesser entries. DeKuyper did their homework and created a winner.

Peach Pucker has a light, delicate body and the same golden orange color as tree-ripened peaches. On the palate the liqueur tastes more like peaches picked a touch early, just before the fruit's natural tartness gives way to juicy sweetness. The tangy, peach flavor persists for a remarkably long time.

Here's a low-proof liqueur that was created with drink making in mind. It mixes beautifully with a wide range of juices, spirits and liqueurs. Its tartness is a wonderful counterbalance to the sweeter ingredients often used in cocktails.

Be daring, a little Pucker is nothing to be afraid of.

THAI SMILE
House specialty glass, ice
Pour ingredients into iced mixing glass
1 1/2 oz. Bacardi Light Rum
1 oz. Mount Gay Eclipse Rum
3/4 oz. Blue Curaçao
1 1/4 oz. apple juice
3 oz. pineapple juice
Shake and strain
Float 3/4 oz. Matusalem Classic Black Rum
Pineapple wedge and cherry garnish

38TH PARALLEL
Coffee mug, heated
Build in glass
3/4 oz. Chambord Liqueur
1/2 oz. Baileys Irish Cream
1/2 oz. Dark Crème de Cacao
1/2 oz. Brandy
Near fill with hot coffee
Whipped cream garnish
Sprinkle nutmeg

3D-ELIXIR
Rocks glass, ice
Build in glass
3/4 oz. Dr. McGillicuddy's
   Mentholmint Schnapps
3/4 oz. Dark Crème de Cacao
3/4 oz. DeKuyper Triple Sec

THUG PASSION
Champagne glass, chilled
Pour ingredients into iced mixing glass
2 oz. Alizé de France
2 oz. sweet 'n' sour
Shake and strain
Fill with Champagne
Orange twist garnish

THUMPER
Rocks glass, ice
Build in glass
1 1/2 oz. Brandy
3/4 oz. Tuaca
Lemon twist garnish

TICKLE ME
Rocks glass, ice
Build in glass
1 3/4 oz. VOX Vodka
1/2 oz. Briottet Crème de Cassis
1/2 oz. Villa Massa Limoncello
Lemon twist garnish

TIDAL WAVE (1)
Bucket glass, ice
Build in glass
1 1/2 oz. Laird's Applejack Brandy
Near fill with orange juice
Splash cranberry juice
Orange slice garnish

TIDAL WAVE (2)
Bucket glass, ice
Pour ingredients into iced mixing glass
3/4 oz. Bacardi Gold Rum
3/4 oz. Bacardi Spiced Rum
3/4 oz. Crème de Banana
2 oz. orange juice
Shake and strain
Float 3/4 oz. Galliano Liqueur

TIDAL WAVE (3)
Rocks glass, chilled
Pour ingredients into iced mixing glass
1/2 oz. Vodka
1/2 oz. Gold Rum
1/2 oz. Captain Morgan Spiced Rum
1/2 oz. cranberry juice
1/2 oz. sweet 'n' sour
Shake and strain

TIDY BOWL
Rocks glass, chilled
Pour ingredients into iced mixing glass
1 1/2 oz. Stolichnaya Russian Vodka
1/2 oz. Blue Curaçao
1/2 oz. sweet 'n' sour
Shake and strain
Raisins (2) garnish

TIE ME TO THE BED POST
Rocks glass, chilled
Pour ingredients into iced mixing glass
1/2 oz. Midori Melon Liqueur
1/2 oz. Absolut Citron Vodka
1/2 oz. Malibu Rum
1 oz. sweet 'n' sour
Shake and strain

TIGHTER CIDER
Coffee mug, heated
Build in glass
1 oz. Appleton Special Jamaica Rum
3/4 oz. Calvados Apple Brandy
3/4 oz. Apple Schnapps
1 tsp. apple butter
2 pinches cinnamon
Fill with hot apple cider
Apple wedge garnish

TIGHT SWEATER
Coffee mug, heated
Build in glass
1/2 oz. Frangelico Liqueur
1/2 oz. Kahlúa Coffee Liqueur
1/2 oz. Disaronno Amaretto Liqueur
1/2 oz. Baileys Irish Cream
Near fill with hot coffee
Whipped cream garnish
Dust powdered cocoa

TIJUANA BULLDOG
Bucket glass, ice
Build in glass
1 1/4 oz. Farias Reposado Tequila
3/4 oz. Kahlúa Coffee Liqueur
2 1/2 oz. milk
Fill with cola

TIJUANA SCREW
aka **Tijuana Split**
Highball glass, ice
Build in glass
1 1/4 oz. Tequila
1/2 fill grapefruit juice
1/2 fill orange juice

TIJUANA SUNRISE
Bucket glass, ice
Build in glass
1 oz. Tequila
Fill with orange juice
6 dashes Angostura Bitters

TIKKI DREAM
Cocktail glass, chilled
Rim glass with sugar (optional)
Pour ingredients into iced mixing glass
1 oz. Disaronno Amaretto Liqueur
3/4 oz. Midori Melon Liqueur
1 1/4 oz. cranberry juice
Stir and strain
Orange slice and cherry garnish

TINTED GLASS
Cocktail glass, chilled
Pour ingredients into iced mixing glass
1/2 oz. Vya California Dry Vermouth
1 3/4 oz. Tanqueray № Ten Gin
4-6 drops Chambord Liqueur
Stir and strain
Lemon twist garnish

BAFFERTS® GIN

If you're in the market for a spirit that marches to the beat of a different drummer, then look no further than BAFFERTS GIN, a spry, marvelously twisted gin with a unique outlook on life. Instead of looking to wow the senses with a voluminous bouquet and energized palate, the maker's of this delightful gin took an altogether different approach.

Introduced in 2000, Bafferts Gin is the creation of Hayman Distillers of London. It is crafted with a base of premium, column-distilled grain spirits. During the final distillation, the gin is infused with a mixture of botanicals. The proprietary recipe calls for fewer botanicals than any other premium gin. Therein lies the twist. Bafferts is a light, delicately flavored spirit, which as their marketing suggests, makes it a gin even vodka lovers will enjoy.

Bafferts is an engaging and innovative spirit with a winning personality. It has pristine clarity and a trim, lightweight body. The bouquet is a refined offering of juniper and hints of citrus zest, while the palate merely hints at the principle botanical flavors. Subtle as they are, the flavors add a delightful dimension to the gin. The finish is crisp and fleeting.

Bafferts has a charm unto its own, one best perceived when served straight-up or over ice. Because of its easy going nature, Bafferts is also perfect for any gin-based recipe.

TIP-TOP PUNCH
House specialty glass, ice
Pour ingredients into iced mixing glass
1 1/2 oz. Brandy
1/2 oz. Benedictine
1/2 oz. simple syrup
1 1/2 oz. sweet 'n' sour
Shake and strain
Fill with Champagne

TIRAMISU (1)
House specialty glass, chilled
Pour ingredients into blender
1 oz. Godiva Chocolate Liqueur
1 oz. Disaronno Amaretto Liqueur
1 oz. Kahlúa Coffee Liqueur
2 scoops vanilla ice cream
Blend ingredients (with ice optional)
Whipped cream garnish
Sprinkle shaved chocolate

TIRAMISU (2)
House specialty glass, chilled
Pour ingredients into blender
1 1/4 oz. Appleton Estate V/X Jamaica Rum
3/4 oz. White Crème de Cacao
3/4 oz. Baileys Irish Cream
1/4 oz. chocolate syrup
2 scoops vanilla ice cream
Blend ingredients (with ice optional)
Drizzle 3/4 oz. Tia Maria

TIZIANO
Champagne glass, chilled
Build in glass
1/2 fill white grape juice
1/2 fill Champagne
Lemon twist garnish

T.K.O.
Rocks glass, ice
Build in glass
3/4 oz. Tequila
3/4 oz. Kahlúa Coffee Liqueur
3/4 oz. Ouzo

T. 'N' T.
Highball glass, ice
Build in glass
1 1/4 oz. Tanqueray Gin
Fill with tonic water
Lime wedge garnish

TOASTED ALMOND
Cocktail glass, chilled
Pour ingredients into iced mixing glass
3/4 oz. Disaronno Amaretto Liqueur
3/4 oz. Kahlúa Coffee Liqueur
2 oz. half & half cream
Shake and strain

TOASTED ALMOND CAFÉ
Coffee mug, heated
Build in glass
3/4 oz. Disaronno Amaretto Liqueur
3/4 oz. Kahlúa Coffee Liqueur
Near fill with hot coffee
Whipped cream garnish
Sprinkle nutmeg

TOBOGGAN TRUFFLE
Coffee mug, heated
Build in glass
1 oz. Dr. McGillicuddy's
    Mentholmint Schnapps
1 oz. Godiva Chocolate Liqueur
Near fill with hot coffee
Whipped cream garnish
Sprinkle shaved chocolate

TOKYO SCREAM
House specialty glass, ice
Pour ingredients into iced mixing glass
1 oz. Bacardi Light Rum
3/4 oz. Midori Melon Liqueur
1/2 oz. DeKuyper Peachtree Schnapps
2 oz. pineapple juice
2 oz. orange juice
Shake and strain
Orange slice and cherry garnish

TOM & JERRY
Coffee mug, heated
Build in glass
1 oz. Light Rum
1 oz. Brandy
1 tbsp. Tom & Jerry batter
Fill with hot milk
Sprinkle nutmeg

TOM MIX HIGH
Highball glass, ice
Build in glass
1 1/4 oz. Seagram's 7 Whisky
1 dash Angostura Bitters
1 dash grenadine
Fill with club soda

TOOTSIE ROLL
Highball glass, ice
Build in glass
1 1/4 oz. Van Hoo Belgium Vodka
3/4 oz. Dark Crème de Cacao
Fill with orange juice

TOP HAT
Brandy snifter, heated
Build in glass
1 1/2 oz. Sea Wynde Pot Still Rum
3/4 oz. Grand Marnier 100th Anniversary

TOREADOR
Cocktail glass, chilled
Pour ingredients into iced mixing glass
3/4 oz. Tequila
3/4 oz. White Crème de Menthe
2 oz. half & half cream
Shake and strain

TORONTO
Cocktail glass, chilled
Pour ingredients into iced mixing glass
2 dashes simple syrup
1 dash Angostura Bitters
3/4 oz. Fernet Branca
1 1/2 oz. Canadian Whisky
Stir and strain
Orange twist garnish

TORPEDO SLAM
Shot glass and beer mug, chilled
Build in shot glass
1 1/2 oz. Jim Beam Black Label Bourbon
Build in mug
2/3 fill Draft Beer
Splash Seven-Up
Drop shot glass of bourbon into beer

TORQUE WRENCH
Presentation shot glass, chilled
Build in glass
1/3 fill Midori Melon Liqueur
1/3 fill Champagne
1/3 fill orange juice

TOUR de CARIBBEAN
House specialty glass, ice
Pour ingredients into iced mixing glass
3/4 oz. Bacardi Select Rum
3/4 oz. Mount Gay Eclipse Rum
3/4 oz. Crème de Banana
2 oz. cranberry juice
2 oz. orange juice
Shake and strain
Float 1/2 oz. Tia Maria and
    1/2 oz. Appleton Estate V/X Jamaica Rum
Orange slice and cherry garnish

TOUR de FRANCE
Champagne glass, chilled
Pour ingredients into iced mixing glass
3/4 oz. V.S. Cognac
3/4 oz. Chambord Liqueur
1 1/2 oz. sweet 'n' sour
Shake and strain
Fill with Champagne
Lemon wheel garnish

SAUZA® CONMEMORATIVO® AÑEJO TEQUILA

Long before tequila became fashionable, the brand of choice for aficionados was SAUZA CONMEMORATIVO AÑEJO. This super-premium embodies all of the characteristics a great tequila should possess. Being an extended-aged añejo, Conmemorativo has attained an enviable degree of sophistication, while as a mixto tequila, it has retained a healthy measure of feisty exuberance.

Introduced in 1968, Conmemorativo Añejo is distilled in Jalisco, Mexico, at the Sauza La Perseverancia Distillery. It is a mixto tequila, meaning that it is distilled from a minimum of 51% agave. Sauza ages Conmemorativo Añejo for 2 years in small, white American oak barrels.

Sauza Conmemorativo Añejo is a classically structured tequila. It has a pale yellow hue, a full, rounded body and satiny texture. Its expansive bouquet is laced with the aromas of pepper, caramel, and a hint of oak. The tequila is graced with a complex, semi-sweet palate of vanilla and citrus undertones of white pepper and toasted oak. The finish is long and warming.

While Conmemorativo Añejo is best appreciated neat, you'll thoroughly enjoy what this character-laden tequila does for a cocktail. So don't think using Conmemorativo Añejo in a margarita as diluting a great tequila, consider it rather as an artistic stroke of genius.

TOUR de PANAMA
House specialty glass, ice
Pour ingredients into iced mixing glass
1/2 oz. Bacardi Select Rum
1/2 oz. Crème de Banana
2 oz. pineapple juice
2 oz. orange juice
1/2 oz. Myers's Jamaican Rum
Shake and strain
Float 3/4 oz. Tia Maria
Orange slice and cherry garnish

TOVARICH
Cocktail glass, chilled
Pour ingredients into iced mixing glass
1 1/2 oz. Jewel of Russia Classic Vodka
1/2 oz. Jewel of Russia Berry Infusion
1/2 oz. fresh lime juice
Stir and strain
Lime wedge garnish

TRADE DEFICIT
Coffee mug, heated
Build in glass
3/4 oz. Baileys Irish Cream
3/4 oz. Kahlúa Coffee Liqueur
3/4 oz. DeKuyper Peppermint Schnapps
3/4 oz. Godiva Chocolate Liqueur
Near fill with hot coffee
Whipped cream garnish

TRADE WINDS
House specialty glass, chilled
Pour ingredients into iced mixing glass
3/4 oz. Cruzan Estate Light Rum
3/4 oz. Brandy
3/4 oz. Chambord Liqueur
1 oz. orange juice
2 oz. sweet 'n' sour
Shake and strain
Lemon twist garnish

TRAFFIC LIGHT (1)
Presentation shot glass, chilled
Layer ingredients
1/3 fill Green Crème de Menthe
1/3 fill Crème de Banana
1/3 fill Sloe Gin

TRAFFIC LIGHT (2)
Cordial or sherry glass, chilled
Layer ingredients
1/3 fill Crème de Noyaux
1/3 fill Galliano Liqueur
1/3 fill Midori Melon Liqueur

TRAMONTO SUL GARDA
Champagne glass, chilled
Pour ingredients into iced mixing glass
1 oz. Gin
1/2 oz. Cointreau Liqueur
1/2 oz. pink grapefruit juice
Shake and strain
Fill with Champagne
Lemon twist garnish

TRINITY
Cocktail glass, chilled
Pour ingredients into iced mixing glass
1/2 oz. Dry Vermouth
1 1/2 oz. Jim Beam Black Label Bourbon
2-3 dashes Angostura Bitters
1 dash White Crème de Menthe
Stir and strain
Lemon twist garnish

TRIP TO THE BEACH
House specialty glass, ice
Pour ingredients into iced mixing glass
1 oz. Bacardi Gold Rum
1 oz. Bacardi Limón Rum
1/2 oz. DeKuyper Peachtree Schnapps
3 oz. orange juice
Shake and strain
Orange slice and cherry garnish

TROPHY ROOM
Coffee mug, heated
Build in glass
1/2 oz. Disaronno Amaretto Liqueur
1/2 oz. Vandermint Liqueur
1/2 oz. Myers's Jamaican Rum
Near fill with hot coffee
Whipped cream garnish
Drizzle 1/2 oz. of Tia Maria

TROPICAL DEPRESSION
Coffee mug, heated
Build in glass
1 1/4 oz. Dillon Dark Rhum
1/2 oz. Disaronno Amaretto Liqueur
1/2 oz. Godiva Chocolate Liqueur
Near fill with hot coffee
Whipped cream garnish
Drizzle 3/4 oz. Tia Maria

TROPICAL GOLD
Highball glass, ice
Build in glass
1 oz. Light Rum
1/2 oz. Crème de Banana
Fill with orange juice

TROPICAL HOOTER
Bucket glass, ice
Build in glass
1 1/2 oz. Malibu Rum
1/2 oz. Midori Melon Liqueur
1/2 fill cranberry juice
1/2 fill pineapple juice

TROPICAL HURRICANE
Bucket glass, ice
Build in glass
1 oz. Bacardi Limón Rum
3/4 oz. Midori Melon Liqueur
1 1/2 oz. cranberry juice
1 1/2 oz. pineapple juice
Orange slice and cherry garnish

TROPICAL HUT
House specialty glass, ice
Pour ingredients into iced mixing glass
1 oz. Midori Melon Liqueur
1 oz. Light Rum
1/2 oz. orgeat syrup
1 1/2 oz. sweet 'n' sour
Shake and strain
Pineapple wedge and cherry garnish

TROPICAL ITCH
House specialty glass, ice
Pour ingredients into iced mixing glass
1 oz. Bacardi Gold Rum
1 oz. Mount Gay Eclipse Rum
1/2 oz. grenadine
1 oz. orange juice
1 oz. grapefruit juice
1 oz. pineapple juice
Shake and strain
Float 1/2 oz. Cruzan Banana Rum and
    1/2 oz. Cruzan Pineapple Rum
Orange slice and cherry garnish

TROPICAL JACK
Bucket glass, ice
Build in glass
3/4 oz. Jack Daniel's Tennessee Whiskey
3/4 oz. Crème de Banana
1 dash orange juice
1 dash grenadine
Fill with pineapple juice

TROPICAL MOON
House specialty glass, chilled
Pour ingredients into blender
1 1/2 oz. Myers's Jamaican Rum
3/4 oz. Disaronno Amaretto Liqueur
2 oz. coconut cream syrup
3 oz. pineapple juice
2 scoops vanilla ice cream
Blend with ice
Pineapple wedge and cherry garnish

ALIZÉ® RED PASSION

If literature has taught us anything about
the world in which we live, it's that the
French are masters at the art of seduction.
So it should come as no surprise that the
new sibling of the runaway bestseller
ALIZÉ DE FRANCE should be named
ALIZÉ RED PASSION.

These two, world-class aperitifs are
made from a blend of tropical fruit juices
and premium cognac. The original Alizé
de France features the delectable
combination of passion fruit juice and
brandy, specifically barrel-aged Alizé
Cognac from the L&L Cognac House.
Introduced in 2000, Alizé Red Passion is
an exotic blend of passion fruit juice,
cranberry, natural flavors and Alizé
Cognac. Hugely popular, both versions
of Alizé have been designated "Hot
Brands" in *Impact Magazine*, with the
original having earned the distinction
5 years running.

Alizé Red Passion is marvelously lush
and vibrant. It has a generous bouquet
laced with the succulent aromas of ripe
fruit, and a medium-weight, sensuously
textured body. Its palate is an intriguing
melange of tangy fresh fruit tempered by
the mellow grape character of the brandy.
The finish is refreshing and flavorful.

The original Alizé is equally delightful.
It has an ample bouquet of tart citrus,
and a velvety smooth body with a zesty,
fruity palate. There's a taste of cognac in
each sip. Little wonder it's such a hit.

TROPICAL SENSATION
House specialty glass, ice
Pour ingredients into iced mixing glass
1 1/2 oz. Beefeater London Dry Gin
1/2 oz. Grand Marnier Liqueur
1 oz. Rose's Lime juice
1 oz. orange juice
2 oz. grapefruit juice
Shake and strain
Float 3/4 oz. Vincent Van Gogh
    Citroen Vodka
Lemon wedge garnish

TROPICAL SPECIAL
House specialty glass, ice
Pour ingredients into iced mixing glass
1 1/2 oz. Gin
1/2 oz. Triple Sec
1 oz. orange juice
1 oz. Rose's Lime Juice
2 oz. grapefruit juice
Shake and strain
Orange slice and cherry garnish

TROPICO TANGO
House specialty glass, ice
Pour ingredients into iced mixing glass
2 oz. Tropico
1 oz. Bacardi Limón Rum
2 oz. cranberry juice
2 oz. orange juice
Shake and strain
Orange slice and cherry garnish

TRYST & SHOUT
Champagne glass, chilled
Pour ingredients into iced mixing glass
1 1/2 oz. Disaronno Amaretto Liqueur
2 oz. sweet 'n' sour
Shake and strain
Fill with Champagne
Lemon twist garnish

TURKEY SHOOTER
Presentation shot glass, chilled
Layer ingredients
1/2 fill DeKuyper Peppermint Schnapps
1/2 fill Wild Turkey 80° Bourbon

TUSCANY CHAMPAGNE
Champagne tulip glass, chilled
Build in glass
1 oz. Gran Gala Orange Liqueur
Swirl and coat inside of glass
Fill with Champagne
Orange twist garnish

24-KARAT NIGHTMARE
Presentation shot glass, chilled
Build in glass
1/2 fill Goldschläger
1/2 fill Rumple Minze Schnapps

TWILIGHT MOAN ZONE
Cocktail glass, chilled
Pour ingredients into iced mixing glass
1 1/4 oz. KéKé Beach Cream Liqueur
1 1/4 oz. Zone Melon Italian Vodka
3/4 oz. Chambord Liqueur
Shake and strain
Lime wheel garnish

TWIST de L'ORANGE
Cocktail glass, chilled
Pour ingredients into blender
1 3/4 oz. Ketel One Citroen Dutch Vodka
1/2 oz. Grand Marnier 100th Anniversary
1 scoop orange sorbet
Blend ingredients (with ice optional)
Orange spiral twist garnish

TWISTED LEMONADE
Bucket glass, ice
Build in glass
1 1/4 oz. Bacardi Limón Rum
3/4 oz. Razzmatazz Raspberry Liqueur
Fill with lemonade
Lemon wedge garnish

TWISTED SISTER
aka **Nun in a Blender**
House specialty glass, chilled
Pour ingredients into blender
1 oz. KéKé Beach Cream Liqueur
1 oz. DeKuyper Raspberry Pucker
3/4 oz. Midori Melon Liqueur
1 1/2 oz. sweet 'n' sour
2 scoops vanilla ice cream
Blend ingredients (with ice optional)
Whipped cream and vanilla wafer garnish

TWISTER
House specialty glass, ice
Pour ingredients into iced mixing glass
1 1/2 oz. Light Rum
3/4 oz. DeKuyper Peach Pucker
3/4 oz. DeKuyper Watermelon Pucker
3/4 oz. Malibu Rum
3 oz. orange juice
2 oz. pineapple juice
1 oz. cranberry juice
Shake and strain

UGLY DUCKLING
Brandy snifter, ice
Build in glass
1 3/4 oz. Disaronno Amaretto Liqueur
1/2 fill half & half cream
1/2 fill club soda

ULTERIOR MOTIVE
Cocktail glass, chilled
Pour ingredients into iced mixing glass
2 oz. Old Raj Dry Gin
3/4 oz. Villa Massa Limoncello
Shake and strain
Lemon twist garnish

UPSIDE DOWN IRISH CROWN
Cocktail glass, chilled
Layer ingredients
1 oz. Drambuie Liqueur
1 1/2 oz. Dewar's White Label
  Scotch Whisky
Lemon twist garnish

UP THE CREEK WITH A KICK
Highball glass, ice
Build in glass
1 1/4 oz. Forty Creek Canadian Whisky
3/4 oz. Fireball Cinnamon Canadian Whisky
Fill with ginger ale

UPTOWN
Cocktail glass, chilled
Pour ingredients into iced mixing glass
1 1/2 oz. Myers's Jamaican Rum
1/2 oz. DJ Dotson Triple Sec
1/2 oz. Rose's Lime Juice
2-3 dashes Angostura Bitters
1/4 oz. grenadine
1/2 oz. orange juice
1/2 oz. pineapple juice
Shake and strain

UPTOWN GIRL
Rocks glass, ice
Build in glass
3/4 oz. Extase XO Liqueur
1 1/2 oz. Evan Williams Single Barrel
  Vintage Bourbon
Orange twist garnish

VAMPIRE
Rocks glass, chilled
Pour ingredients into iced mixing glass
1 1/4 oz. Stolichnaya Russian Vodka
3/4 oz. Chambord Liqueur
1 1/2 oz. cranberry juice
Shake and strain

JIM BEAM®
WHITE LABEL BOURBON

Perhaps the most famous name in bourbon, the Beam family has been distilling whiskey since 1795. Their distillery in Clermont, Kentucky is among the largest and most sophisticated in the world. But for all of their technical sophistication, little has changed in how they produce their whiskey.

The benchmark of the brand is JIM BEAM WHITE LABEL BOURBON, the best-selling bourbon in the world. It is distilled from a high proportion of white and yellow corn grown in Indiana and Kentucky, and lesser percentages of rye and malted barley. The other two crucial ingredients are sweet, limestone water from the Long Lick Creek and spontaneous-type yeast, discovered by Jim Beam himself and maintained for over 60 years.

The White Label Jim Beam bourbon is aged a minimum of 4 years in oak barrels. During that time it develops a soft, medium-weight body and an enticing bouquet of vanilla, baking spices, cocoa and toasted oak. On the palate, the whiskey reveals the savory flavors of caramel, vanilla, fruit and a hint of smoke. The finish is warm and relaxed.

Quality, price and versatility make Jim Beam White Label an absolute necessity behind the bar.

VAMPIRO
Bucket glass, ice
Build in glass
Rim glass with salt (optional)
1 1/2 oz. Farias Reposado Tequila
3 oz. Sangrita Mix
3 oz. grapefruit juice
3/4 oz. fresh lime juice
Grapefruit and orange slice garnish
Note: See **Sangrita Mix**

VANDERBILT COCKTAIL
Cocktail glass, chilled
Pour ingredients into iced mixing glass
1 1/2 oz. Brandy
3/4 oz. Cherry Brandy
2 dashes simple syrup
2 dashes Angostura Bitters
Shake and strain

VAN GOOD
Cocktail glass, chilled
Pour ingredients into iced mixing glass
1 1/2 oz. Van Gogh Gin
1/2 oz. Rémy Red
1/2 oz. Dry Sherry
Stir and strain
Lemon twist garnish

VANILLA MAGILLA
Rocks glass, chilled
Pour ingredients into iced mixing glass
1 1/4 oz. Foursquare Spiced Rum
1 oz. Dr. McGillicuddy's
   Mentholmint Schnapps
1/2 oz. Whaler's Hawaiian Vanille Rum

VANILLA SPICE ICE
Rocks glass, ice
Build in glass
2 oz. Chopin Polish Vodka
1/2 oz. Whaler's Hawaiian Vanille Rum
Cinnamon stick garnish

VANIL SENSATION
House specialty glass, chilled
Pour ingredients into blender
1 oz. Stolichnaya Vanil Russian Vodka
3/4 oz. Bombay Gin
3/4 oz. DeKuyper Triple Sec
1 3/4 oz. cranberry juice
2 oz. orange juice
Blend with ice

VELVET HAMMER
Cocktail glass, chilled
Pour ingredients into iced mixing glass
3/4 oz. Triple Sec
3/4 oz. White Crème de Cacao
2 oz. half & half cream
Shake and strain

VELVET SWING
Champagne glass, chilled
Build in glass
1 1/4 oz. Tawny Port
3/4 oz. Armagnac
Fill with Champagne
Lemon wheel garnish

VENETIAN SUNSET
Cocktail glass, chilled
Pour ingredients into iced mixing glass
1 1/2 oz. Grappa
1/2 oz. Campari Aperitivo
1/4 oz. simple syrup
2 oz. orange juice
Shake and strain
Orange slice and mint leaf garnish

VERMOUTH CASSIS
Cocktail glass, chilled
Pour ingredients into iced mixing glass
1 oz. Briottet Crème de Cassis
1 oz. Dry Vermouth
Stir and strain
Lemon twist garnish

VINCENT'S BAUBLES
Cocktail glass, chilled
Pour ingredients into iced mixing glass
1 oz. Vincent Van Gogh Vodka
1 oz. Vincent Van Gogh Oranje Vodka
3/4 oz. Oro di Mazzetti Grappa Liqueur
1/2 oz. Drambuie Liqueur
Stir and strain
Lemon twist garnish

V.I.P. COFFEE
Coffee mug, heated
Build in glass
1 oz. Cruzan Estate Single Barrel Rum
1/2 oz. Kahlúa Coffee Liqueur
1/2 oz. Chambord Liqueur
Near fill with hot coffee
Whipped cream garnish

VODKA GRAND
Cocktail glass, chilled
Pour ingredients into iced mixing glass
1 1/2 oz. Chopin Polish Vodka
1/2 oz. Grand Marnier 100th Anniversary
1/2 oz. Rose's Lime Juice
1/4 oz. fresh lime juice
Stir and strain
Orange slice garnish

VOODOO JUICE
Large house specialty glass, ice
Pour ingredients into iced mixing glass
1 oz. Cruzan Orange Rum
1 oz. Cruzan Banana Rum
1 oz. Cruzan Coconut Rum
1 oz. Cruzan Pineapple Rum
1 1/2 oz. cranberry juice
1 1/2 oz. orange juice
1 1/2 oz. pineapple juice
Shake and strain
Float 3/4 oz. Cruzan Estate Diamond Rum
Orange slice and cherry garnish

VOODOO MOONDANCE
House specialty glass, ice
Pour ingredients into iced mixing glass
1 1/2 oz. Cruzan Estate Diamond Rum
1 oz. Cruzan Estate Light Rum
3/4 oz. grenadine
1 1/2 oz. pineapple juice
1 1/2 oz. orange juice
1 1/2 oz. grapefruit juice
Shake and strain
Splash club soda
Orange slice and cherry garnish

VOODOO SHOOTER
Presentation shot glass, chilled
Layer ingredients
1/3 fill Tia Maria
1/3 fill Cruzan Rum Cream
1/3 fill Bacardi Select Rum

VULCAN
Bucket glass, ice
Build in glass
1/2 oz. Van Gogh Gin
1/2 oz. Vincent Van Gogh Vodka
1/2 oz. Southern Comfort Liqueur
1/2 oz. Malibu Rum
1/2 fill grapefruit juice
1/2 fill Seven-Up

VULCAN MIND PROBE
Presentation shot glass, chilled
Build in glass
1/2 fill Sambuca
1/2 fill Bacardi 151° Rum

WAIKÉKÉ FRATERNITY
House specialty glass, ice
Pour ingredients into iced mixing glass
1 1/2 oz. KéKé Beach Cream Liqueur
3/4 oz. Whaler's Hawaiian Vanille Rum
3/4 oz. Giori Lemoncillo Liqueur
1 oz. sweet 'n' sour
1 oz. limeade
Shake and strain

TROPICO®

One of the first things a mixologist learns about rum is that it marries beautifully with fruit juice. There's just something about the way the flavors complement each other that makes it a timeless taste combination. This was clearly the working premise behind Bacardi's 1999 release of TROPICO, a splendid liqueur ideally suited for the demands of contemporary drink making.

Produced in San Juan, Puerto Rico, Tropico is a blend of Bacardi añejo rum and seven exotic fruit juices, specifically carmabola, passion fruit, mango, pineapple, orange, peach and guarana. It is bottled at 32 proof and should be refrigerated after opening.

Served chilled, it is easy to appreciate why Tropico has found a niche behind American bars. The liqueur has a soft, yellow-gold hue, nearly identical to the color of ripe papaya, and a bouquet redolent with the zesty aromas of fresh, tropical fruit. Its substantial, incomparably lush body is reminiscent of a well-crafted cocktail. The palate is well balanced with a slightly tangy flavor and a tantalizing hint of rum. The finish is lingering and loaded with semi-sweet flavor.

Award winning Tropico has a marvelous, cocktail-like quality when sampled straight-up or on the rocks. Tropico is also excellent in a piña colada, orangesicle and mixed with champagne as a Tropico Mimosa.

WAIST COAT POCKET
House specialty glass, chilled
Pour ingredients into blender
1/2 oz. Kahlúa Coffee Liqueur
1/2 oz. Disaronno Amaretto Liqueur
1/2 oz. Godiva Chocolate Liqueur
1/2 oz. half & half cream
2 scoops vanilla ice cream
Blend ingredients (with ice optional)

WALL STREET WIZARD
Cocktail glass, chilled
Pour ingredients into iced mixing glass
1/2 oz. Tanqueray № Ten Gin
1/2 oz. Original Cristall Russian Vodka
1/2 oz. Light Rum
1/2 oz. Blue Curaçao
1/2 oz. Midori Melon Liqueur
Stir and strain

WANDERER
Bucket glass, ice
Pour ingredients into iced mixing glass
1 oz. Rain Vodka
1/2 oz. Chambord Liqueur
1/2 oz. DeKuyper Cherry Pucker
1/2 oz. Blue Curaçao
1 1/2 oz. pineapple juice
1 1/2 oz. cranberry juice
Shake and strain

WANNA PROBE YA
Bucket glass, ice
Build in glass
1 oz. Captain Morgan Spiced Rum
3/4 oz. Malibu Rum
1/2 fill cranberry juice
1/2 fill pineapple juice

WARD EIGHT
Cocktail glass, chilled
Pour ingredients into iced mixing glass
1 1/2 oz. Bourbon
1/2 oz. grenadine
1 1/2 oz. sweet 'n' sour
Shake and strain

WASHINGTON APPLE
Rocks glass, chilled
Pour ingredients into iced mixing glass
1 oz. DeKuyper Pucker Sour Apple
1 oz. Crown Royal
1 oz. sweet 'n' sour
Shake and strain

WATERGATE
Presentation shot glass, chilled
Layer ingredients
1/4 fill Kahlúa Coffee Liqueur
1/4 fill Baileys Irish Cream
1/4 fill DeKuyper Peppermint Schnapps
1/4 fill Grand Marnier Liqueur

WATERMELON (1)
Rocks glass, ice
Build in glass
3/4 oz. Southern Comfort Liqueur
3/4 oz. orange juice
3/4 oz. Disaronno Amaretto Liqueur

WATERMELON (2)
Presentation shot glass, chilled
Build in glass
1/3 fill Vodka
1/3 fill Midori Melon Liqueur
1/3 fill Baileys Irish Cream
5 drops grenadine

WATERMELON (3)
Presentation shot glass, chilled
Build in glass
1/3 fill VOX Vodka
1/3 fill Sloe Gin
1/3 fill orange juice

WATERMELON (4)
Bucket glass, ice
Build in glass
1 oz. Southern Comfort Liqueur
1/2 oz. Midori Melon Liqueur
2 oz. orange juice
1 dash grenadine

WATERMELON (5)
Rocks glass, chilled
Pour ingredients into iced mixing glass
1 oz. Southern Comfort Liqueur
3/4 oz. Van Hoo Belgium Vodka
1/4 oz. grenadine
2 oz. pineapple juice
Shake and strain

WATKIN'S GLEN
Bucket glass, ice
Pour ingredients into iced mixing glass
1 oz. Absolut Vodka
1/2 oz. Crème de Banana
1/2 oz. Chambord Liqueur
1/2 oz. pineapple juice
1/2 oz. cranberry juice
1/2 oz. orange juice
Shake and strain
Lime wedge garnish

WEEKEND AT THE BEACH (1)
Presentation shot glass, chilled
Build in glass
3/4 oz. DeKuyper Pucker Sour Apple
3/4 oz. DeKuyper Peachtree Schnapps
Splash orange juice
Splash cranberry juice

WEEKEND AT THE BEACH (2)
Rocks glass, chilled
Pour ingredients into iced mixing glass
1 oz. Light Rum
1 oz. DeKuyper Peachtree Schnapps
1 oz. orange juice
1 oz. pineapple juice
Shake and strain

WEEK ON THE BEACH
Rocks glass, chilled
Pour ingredients into iced mixing glass
3/4 oz. DeKuyper Pucker Sour Apple
3/4 oz. DeKuyper Peachtree Schnapps
1/2 oz. orange juice
1/2 oz. pineapple juice
1/2 oz. cranberry juice
Shake and strain

WELLER THAN N.E.1
Bucket glass, ice
Build in glass
1 1/4 oz. W.L. Weller Bourbon
1/2 oz. NapaSaki Saké
1/2 fill lemonade
1/2 fill cranberry juice
Lemon wedge garnish

WET DREAM
Rocks glass, chilled
Pour ingredients into iced mixing glass
3/4 oz. Chambord Liqueur
3/4 oz. Crème de Banana
1/2 oz. orange juice
1/2 oz. half & half cream
Shake and strain

WHALER'S SEASON
House specialty glass, ice
Pour ingredients into iced mixing glass
1 oz. Doorly's XO Barbados Rum
3/4 oz. Foursquare Spiced Rum
3/4 oz. Whaler's Hawaiian Vanilla Rum
1 1/2 oz. orange juice
1 1/2 oz. sweet 'n' sour
Shake and strain
Orange slice garnish

DEKUYPER®
BUTTERSHOTS® SCHNAPPS

No one can call DEKUYPER
BUTTERSHOTS a stuffy or uptight
liqueur. Quite to the contrary, it is a
butterscotch-flavored schnapps born and
bred for fun. While many flavored
schnapps have fallen out of fashion,
Buttershots continues to thrive, primarily
because butterscotch is a timeless favorite
and this schnapps is devoid of the
excessive sweetness that plagues many of
its contemporaries.

DeKuyper Buttershots is produced by
combining pure grain neutral spirits with
butterscotch flavoring. The clear, 30
proof liqueur possesses several
characteristics that make it ideal for
drink making. It is exceptionally
aromatic for a schnapps and the wafting
aroma of butterscotch and vanilla is
downright enticing. It has a light to
medium body brimming with the semi-
sweet flavors of butterscotch and a hint
of caramel.

Versatility must be DeKuyper
Buttershots' middle name. It initially
earned its reputation as a primary
ingredient in numerous shooters, but it
also works perfectly in hot cocoa, coffee
and cappuccinos. It's an ideal flavor to
pair with a wide assortment of liqueurs,
such as Baileys, Kahlúa and Godiva. To
top it off, Buttershots is tailor-made for
milkshakes and ice cream drinks.

WHALE'S TAIL
House specialty glass, chilled
Pour ingredients into blender
1 oz. Vincent Van Gogh Oranje Vodka
1 oz. Whaler's Hawaiian Vanilla Rum
3/4 oz. Blue Curaçao
1 1/2 oz. sweet 'n' sour
3 oz. pineapple juice
Blend with ice
Pineapple wedge garnish

WHAT CRISIS?
Rocks glass, chilled
Pour ingredients into iced mixing glass
1/2 oz. DeKuyper Peach Pucker
1/2 oz. Midori Melon Liqueur
1/2 oz. orange juice
1/2 oz. cranberry juice
Shake and strain

WHAT'S THE RUSH
House specialty glass, ice
Pour ingredients into iced mixing glass
2 oz. Jameson Irish Whiskey
2 oz. lemonade
2 oz. apple juice
Shake and strain
Splash Seven-Up
Orange slice garnish

WHAT'S YOUR HONEY DEW?
Champagne glass, chilled
Pour ingredients into iced mixing glass
1 1/4 oz. Midori Melon Liqueur
3 1/2 oz. lemonade
Shake and strain
Fill with Champagne
Lemon wedge garnish

WHEN HELL FREEZES OVER
House specialty glass, chilled
Pour ingredients into blender
3/4 oz. Hot Damn Cinnamon Schnapps
3/4 oz. Crème de Banana
2 oz. orange juice
2 oz. cranberry juice
Blend with ice

WHERE ARE MY UNDIES?
Bucket glass, ice
Build in glass
1 1/2 oz. KéKé Beach Cream Liqueur
3/4 oz. Whaler's Hawaiian Vanilla Rum
Fill with orange juice

WHIP
Cocktail glass, chilled
Pour ingredients into iced mixing glass
3/4 oz. Pernod
3/4 oz. Brandy
3/4 oz. Hiram Walker Triple Sec
3/4 oz. Dry Vermouth
Stir and strain

WHISKY-ALL-IN
Coffee mug, heated
Build in glass
1 1/2 oz. Scotch Whisky
1 tsp. sugar
1/4 oz. fresh lemon juice
Fill with hot water
Lemon wedge garnish

WHISKY GINGERBREAD
Rocks glass, chilled
Build in glass
3/4 oz. Fireball Cinnamon Canadian Whisky
3/4 oz. Baileys Irish Cream
3/4 oz. DeKuyper Buttershots Schnapps

WHISPER (1)
Brandy snifter, ice
Build in glass
1 oz. Disaronno Amaretto Liqueur
1 oz. Kahlúa Coffee Liqueur
1/2 fill half & half cream
1/2 fill club soda

WHISPER (2)
House specialty glass, chilled
Pour ingredients into blender
3/4 oz. Kahlúa Coffee Liqueur
3/4 oz. Dark Crème de Cacao
3/4 oz. Brandy
1 oz. half & half cream
2 scoops vanilla ice cream
Blend ingredients (with ice optional)
Whipped cream garnish
Sprinkle shaved chocolate

WHITE BULL
Rocks glass, ice
Build in glass
1 1/2 oz. Tequila
3/4 oz. Kahlúa Coffee Liqueur
1/2 oz. half & half cream

WHITE CADILLAC
Highball glass, ice
Build in glass
1 1/4 oz. Scotch Whisky
Fill with half & half cream

WHITE CLOUD
Cocktail glass, chilled
Rim glass with powdered cocoa (optional)
Pour ingredients into iced mixing glass
1 3/4 oz. Jameson Irish Whiskey
3/4 oz. Godiva Chocolate Liqueur
3/4 oz. White Crème de Menthe
1 1/4 half & half cream
Shake and strain

WHITE HEART
Cocktail or house specialty glass, chilled
Pour ingredients into iced mixing glass
3/4 oz. Sambuca
3/4 oz. White Crème de Cacao
2 oz. half & half cream
Shake and strain

WHITE MINNESOTA
Highball glass, ice
Build in glass
1 1/4 oz. White Crème de Menthe
Fill with club soda

WHITE OUT
Cocktail glass, chilled
Pour ingredients into iced mixing glass
1 oz. Cointreau Liqueur
1 oz. Rémy Martin V.S.O.P. Cognac
3/4 oz. DeKuyper Peppermint Schnapps
Stir and strain

WHITE RUSSIAN
Rocks glass, ice
Build in glass
1 1/2 oz. Vodka
3/4 oz. Kahlúa Coffee Liqueur
1/2 oz. half & half cream

WHITE RUSSIAN, PREMIUM
Rocks glass or brandy snifter, ice
Build in glass
1 1/2 oz. Stolichnaya Russian Vodka
3/4 oz. Tia Maria
3/4 oz. Baileys Irish Cream

WHITE SANDS COOLER
House specialty glass, ice
Pour ingredients into iced mixing glass
3/4 oz. Hussong's Reposado Tequila
3/4 oz. Cruzan Estate Light Rum
3/4 oz. Cruzan Banana Rum
2 oz. cranberry juice
2 oz. pineapple juice
Shake and strain
Orange slice and cherry garnish

FORTY CREEK® THREE GRAIN CANADIAN WHISKY

The Kittling Ridge Estate Distillery is a small winery and distillery located near the shores of Lake Ontario in Grimsby, Canada. Eight years ago, veteran winemaker John Hall took over at the helm and set off to create handmade whiskies in a fashion long ago abandoned by larger Canadian distillers.

His tandem of award-winning whiskies leads off with FORTY CREEK THREE GRAIN CANADIAN WHISKY, a skillfully crafted, small batch whisky featuring a combination of rye, maize and malted barley. Each grain is distilled separately in traditional, copper pot stills and aged in charred American oak barrels. The blend contains whiskies up to 8 years in age. The varietal grains contribute individually to the whisky's distinctive, complex character. Forty Creek Three Grain is an aromatic, delicately flavored whisky, well worth a spot on the top shelf.

FORTY CREEK BARREL SELECT also features a blend of small batch rye and maize whiskies distilled in copper alembic stills. Its principal distinction lies in the varying degrees of char in the barrels used to age the whiskies. Much of the blend is aged for up to 6 years in first-fill bourbon barrels with the balance finished in the winery's own sherry casks for 2 years. The result is a whisky brimming with flavor and delicate nuances.

WHITE'S CLUB
Champagne glass, chilled
Rim glass with port and sugar (optional)
Build in glass
2 oz. Tawny Port
Fill with Champagne
Lemon twist garnish

WHITE SPIDER
aka **Cossack**
Rocks glass, ice
Build in glass
1 1/2 oz. Luksusowa Polish Vodka
1/2 oz. White Crème de Menthe

WHITE SWAN
Brandy snifter, ice
Build in glass
1 1/2 oz. Disaronno Amaretto Liqueur
1/2 oz. half & half cream

WHITE WAY
Rocks glass, ice
Build in glass
1 1/2 oz. Gin
1/2 oz. White Crème de Menthe

WHOOTER HOOTER
Bucket glass, ice
Build in glass
1 1/2 oz. Van Hoo Belgium Vodka
1/2 fill cranberry juice
1/2 fill lemonade
Orange slice and cherry garnish

WIDOW WOOD'S NIGHTCAP
Coffee mug, heated
Build in glass
2 oz. Scotch Whisky
1 oz. Dark Crème de Cacao
Near fill with hot milk
Whipped cream garnish
Dust powdered cocoa

WIKI WAKI WOO
House specialty glass, ice
Pour ingredients into iced mixing glass
1 oz. Disaronno Amaretto Liqueur
1/2 oz. Rain Vodka
1/2 oz. Tropico
1/2 oz. Bacardi 151° Rum
1/2 oz. Farias Silver Tequila
1 oz. pineapple juice
1 oz. orange juice
1 oz. cranberry juice
Shake and strain
Orange slice and cherry garnish
Orchid garnish (optional)

WILD ORCHID
Bucket glass, ice
Pour ingredients into iced mixing glass
1 1/4 oz. Ypioca Cachaça
3/4 oz. Crème de Noyaux
1 1/2 oz. fresh lime juice
1/2 oz. grenadine
Shake and strain
Orange slice and cherry garnish

WILE E. COYOTE
Bucket glass, ice
Build in glass
1 1/4 oz. Tuaca
3/4 oz. Jägermeister Liqueur
Fill with pineapple juice
Lemon wedge garnish

WINDEX
Rocks glass, chilled
Pour ingredients into iced mixing glass
1 1/2 oz. Vincent Van Gogh Oranje Vodka
3/4 oz. Light Rum
1/2 oz. Blue Curaçao
1/2 oz. Rose's Lime Juice
Shake and strain

WINE COBBLER
Wine glass or goblet, ice
Build in glass
4 oz. White Wine
1 oz. Triple Sec
1/2 fill orange juice
Near fill with sweet 'n' sour
Splash club soda
Lemon twist garnish

WINE COOLER
aka **Red Wine Cooler, Rosé Cooler**
Wine glass or goblet, ice
Build in glass
1/2 fill Requested Wine
1/2 fill Seven-Up
Lemon twist garnish

WINNIE'S HOT HONEY POT
Coffee mug, heated
Build in glass
1 oz. Drambuie Liqueur
1/2 oz. honey
1/2 oz. lemon juice
Near fill with English Breakfast tea
Serve with lemon

WINSOME WAY
Rocks glass, ice
Build in glass
3/4 oz. Gran Gala Orange Liqueur
3/4 oz. Baileys Irish Cream
3/4 oz. Frangelico Liqueur

WYNBREEZER
House specialty glass, ice
Pour ingredients into iced mixing glass
1 oz. Rhum Barbancourt 3-Star Rum
1 oz. Cockspur V.S.O.R. Rum
3/4 oz. Citrónge Orange Liqueur
3/4 oz. Rose's Lime Juice
2 oz. orange juice
Shake and strain
Near fill with Seven-Up
Float 3/4 oz. Royal Oak Extra Old Rum
Orange slice garnish

XANADU
Champagne glass, chilled
Pour ingredients into iced mixing glass
1/2 oz. Courvoisier V.S.O.P. Cognac
1/2 oz. Cointreau Liqueur
1/2 oz. sweet 'n' sour
Shake and strain
Fill with Champagne
Lemon wheel garnish

XAVIERA
Cocktail or house specialty glass, chilled
Pour ingredients into iced mixing glass
1/2 oz. Kahlúa Coffee Liqueur
1/2 oz. Crème de Noyaux
1/2 oz. Hiram Walker Triple Sec
1 1/2 oz. half & half cream
Shake and strain

YABBA-DABBA-DOO
Rocks glass, chilled
Pour ingredients into iced mixing glass
1 oz. Frangelico Liqueur
1 oz. Kahlúa Coffee Liqueur
1/2 oz. Green Crème de Menthe
Shake and strain

YALE COCKTAIL
Cocktail glass, chilled
Pour ingredients into iced mixing glass
1 1/2 oz. Gin
1/2 oz. Dry Vermouth
2 dashes Angostura Bitters
2 dashes simple syrup
Stir and strain
Lemon twist garnish

YANKEE PANKY
Rocks glass, ice
Build in glass
3/4 oz. Southern Comfort Liqueur
3/4 oz. Disaronno Amaretto Liqueur
3/4 oz. Malibu Rum
3/4 oz. pineapple juice

BEER DRINKS
Blending Lagers and Ales

Mixing different types of beers together has long been standard practice in pubs throughout Europe and Australia, but has only over the past few years become popular in the United States. They're delicious concoctions that look as great as they taste.

The key to their success is blending two beers with appreciably different properties—body, taste, texture, sweetness and bitterness. It is an artful skill that requires balancing the attributes of one brew with the characteristics of another.

An excellent example is the black & tan, a savory blend of stout and ale, typically Guinness and Bass draughts respectively. The Guinness Stout and Bass Ale have different densities, or specific gravities. The beers will layer one on top of the other—the nearly black Guinness floating atop the copper colored Bass—thereby creating a dramatic appearance. The effect is captivating.

The venerable half & half is an equal mix of pilsener and bitter ale drafts. The light, dry lager smoothes the bitter edge of the ale, rendering the combination well suited to American tastes. Another classic concoction is the black velvet, created in 1861 at the Brook's Club in London. It's a superb tasting blend of Guinness draft and chilled champagne. Substitute hard cider for the champagne to create a black velveteen.

The shandy gaff is the refreshing combination of beer and ginger ale. Substitute lemon-lime soda to make a lemon top, or float a jigger of Rose's Lime Juice to make a lager and lime.

Experiment and create your own unique combinations, or consult our beer recipes for inspiration. Tapping into beer's enormous popularity is a dynamic and lucrative way to escape the ordinary.

YELLOW BIRD (1)
Bucket glass, ice
Build in glass
3/4 oz. Light Rum
3/4 oz. Galliano Liqueur
1/2 fill pineapple juice
1/2 fill orange juice

YELLOW BIRD (2)
House specialty glass, chilled
Pour ingredients into blender
1 oz. Light Rum
3/4 oz. Galliano Liqueur
1/2 oz. Crème de Banana
1/4 oz. simple syrup
2 oz. orange juice
2 oz. pineapple juice
Blend with ice
Pineapple wedge and cherry garnish

YELLOW DEVIL
Bucket glass, ice
Build in glass
1 oz. Mount Gay Eclipse Rum
1 oz. Galliano Liqueur
Fill with orange juice
Orange slice garnish

YELLOW JACKET
Rocks glass, chilled
Pour ingredients into iced mixing glass
3/4 oz. Jägermeister Liqueur
3/4 oz. Bärenjäger Honey Liqueur
3/4 oz. Kahlúa Coffee Liqueur
Shake and strain

YELLOW SNOW
House specialty glass, chilled
Pour ingredients into blender
1 1/4 oz. W.L. Weller Bourbon
3 oz. sweet 'n' sour
Blend ingredients (with ice optional)
Lemon wheel pierced with
    pretzel stick garnish

YO HOOTER HOOTER
Rocks glass, chilled
Build in glass
1 1/4 oz. Jack Daniel's Tennessee Whiskey
2 dashes grenadine
1 oz. Seven-Up

YUKON STINGER
Rocks glass, ice
Build in glass
1 3/4 oz. Zubrówka Bison Brand Vodka
1/2 oz. Yukon Jack Liqueur

ZANZIBAR DUNES

House specialty glass, chilled
Pour ingredients into blender
1 1/2 oz. Original Cristall Russian Vodka
1 oz. Midori Melon Liqueur
1 oz. DeKuyper Peach Pucker
1/2 oz. concord grape juice
1 1/2 oz. cranberry juice
2 oz. orange juice
Blend with ice

ZA-ZA

Bucket glass, ice
Pour ingredients into iced mixing glass
1 1/2 oz. Damrak Amsterdam Gin
1 1/2 oz. Dubonnet Rouge
1/2 oz. DJ Dotson Triple Sec
2 oz. orange juice
Shake and strain

ZIPPER HEAD

Rocks glass, ice
Build in glass
1 1/2 oz. Absolut Vodka
3/4 oz. Chambord Liqueur
Splash club soda

ZOMBIE (1)

House specialty glass, ice
Pour ingredients into iced mixing glass
2 oz. Appleton Estate V/X Jamaica Rum
3/4 oz. Crème de Noyaux
3/4 oz. Hiram Walker Triple Sec
1 1/2 oz. sweet 'n' sour
1 1/2 oz. orange juice
Shake and strain
Float 3/4 oz. Bacardi 151° Rum
Orange slice and cherry garnish

ZOMBIE (2)

House specialty glass, ice
Pour ingredients into iced mixing glass
1 1/2 oz. Mount Gay Eclipse Rum
1 oz. Bacardi Light Rum
3/4 oz. Hiram Walker Triple Sec
3/4 oz. grenadine
1 1/2 oz. pineapple juice
1 1/2 oz. orange juice
1 1/2 oz. grapefruit juice
Shake and strain
Splash club soda
Float 3/4 oz. Bacardi Select Rum
Orange slice and cherry garnish

ZOMBIE, PINK

House specialty glass, ice
Pour ingredients into iced mixing glass
1 1/2 oz. Appleton Special Jamaica Rum
3/4 oz. Bacardi Limón Rum
1 oz. Crème de Banana
1/2 oz. grenadine
1 oz. fresh lime juice
2 oz. passion fruit syrup
2 oz. pineapple juice
2 oz. pink grapefruit juice
Shake and strain
Float 3/4 oz. Bacardi 151° Rum
Pineapple wedge and cherry garnish

Z STREET SLAMMER

Rocks glass, chilled
Pour ingredients into iced mixing glass
1 1/4 oz. Appleton Estate V/X Jamaica Rum
3/4 oz. Crème de Banana
1 3/4 oz. pineapple juice
1/2 oz. grenadine
Shake and strain

ZUMA BUMA

Bucket glass, ice
Build in glass
1 1/2 oz. Absolut Citron Vodka
1/2 oz. Chambord Liqueur
Near fill with orange juice
Splash cranberry juice

Glassware

The secret to glassware's success lies in its elegance, transparency and presentation. Its transparency makes it an ideal vehicle for presenting drinks of all types. In addition, glass is an excellent insulator that helps keep cold drinks cold and warm drinks warm. The best way to make a cocktail look as good as it tastes is to present it in a fabulous looking glass. The glass is one of the most important elements in defining the drink's style.

A glassware type recommendation is made with each recipe. The decision as to what size of glass you will use should be based on the size of the drink. For example, if you intend to make a champagne-based cocktail you will need a champagne or wine glass with the capacity to accommodate that size portion. If you already have a glass that you want to serve the cocktail in, but it's not the right size, you can always adjust the recipe ingredients proportionately to fit your glass.

To determine the type of glass for your cocktail, consider that the capacity of the glass when filled with ice is about two or three to one (2-3/1), glass capacity / liquid with ice. Example: A 9 oz. glass will hold approximately 3-4.5 oz. of liquid when filled with cubed ice.

On pages 294 and 295 are a list of beverage, cocktail, wine and beer service glassware to consider for the glassware types recommended in each recipe. The references to Libbey glassware contained in the information are intended as excellent representations of the quality, style, size and shape of glasses that are available today.

For more detailed information on glassware selection, the different types, and handling, see *Successful Beverage Management: Proven Strategies for the On-Premise Operator*, by Robert Plotkin, copyright 2000.

Drink Preparation

Each recipe contains "pouring instructions," which includes the type of glass to use and the steps to take, to make the drink. The following are explanations of the italicized instructions recommended in each recipe. Any other special instructions not listed here are also italicized in the recipe. Additional information about drink preparation can be found in special boxes within the recipe section. A complete directory of these listings is on page 308.

Instructions

1. *Build in glass*
Pour the ingredients directly into the service glass.

2. *Layer ingredients*
Carefully pour each ingredient into the service glass, using the back of a spoon or the side of the glass to slow the pour of the liquid, creating a layered effect.

3. *Pour ingredients into blender*
Blend with ice
Pour a scoop of ice and each of the ingredients into the blender. Use personal judgement when adding ice. These drinks are meant to have a smooth consistency. If the scooped in ice isn't enough to freeze the drink, add another 1/4 -1/3 scoop.

4. *Pour ingredients into blender*
Blend ingredients (with ice optional)
Pour each of the ingredients into the blender. Use personal judgement when adding ice. These drinks are meant to have a smooth consistency. The ice cream or other frozen ingredients may be enough to freeze the drink; if not, add a 1/2 scoop of ice.

5. *Pour ingredients into iced mixing glass*
Shake and strain
Pour a scoop of ice and each of the ingredients into a mixing glass or cocktail shaker. The ingredients are meant to be thoroughly mixed and develop a frothy head of foam. These types of drinks are often prepared both on-the-rocks (over ice), and straight-up (without ice). The same process is used in preparation of either.

6. *Pour ingredients into iced mixing glass*
Stir and strain
Pour a scoop of ice and each of the ingredients, into a mixing glass or cocktail shaker. The ingredients are meant to be thoroughly chilled, and gently mixed. These types of drinks are also sometimes prepared using the "Build in glass" method.

7. **Rim glass with salt**
Moisten the outside edge of the glass rim with lime juice or syrup. Dip in kosher or specialty salt to create a rim.
Rim glass with sugar
Moisten the outside edge of the glass rim with sweetened lime juice or sugar syrup. Dip in sugar to create a rim.

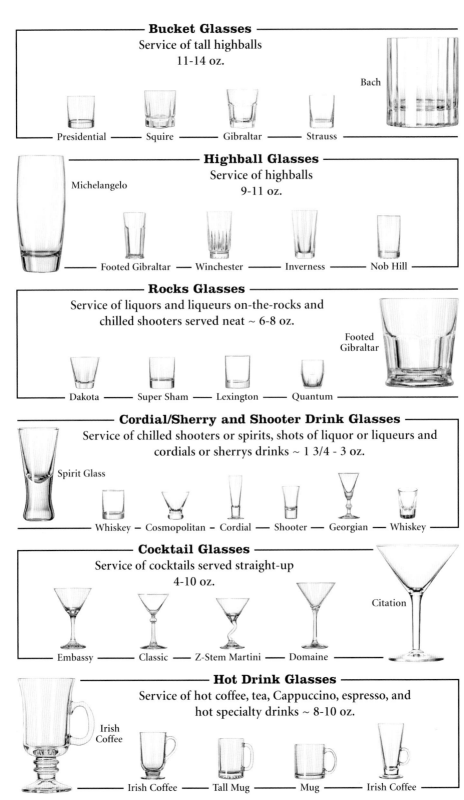

Bucket Glasses
Service of tall highballs
11-14 oz.

Bach

Presidential — Squire — Gibraltar — Strauss

Highball Glasses
Service of highballs
9-11 oz.

Michelangelo

Footed Gibraltar — Winchester — Inverness — Nob Hill

Rocks Glasses
Service of liquors and liqueurs on-the-rocks and
chilled shooters served neat ~ 6-8 oz.

Footed
Gibraltar

Dakota — Super Sham — Lexington — Quantum

Cordial/Sherry and Shooter Drink Glasses
Service of chilled shooters or spirits, shots of liquor or liqueurs and
cordials or sherrys drinks ~ 1 3/4 - 3 oz.

Spirit Glass

Whiskey – Cosmopolitan – Cordial — Shooter — Georgian — Whiskey

Cocktail Glasses
Service of cocktails served straight-up
4-10 oz.

Citation

Embassy — Classic — Z-Stem Martini — Domaine

Hot Drink Glasses
Service of hot coffee, tea, Cappuccino, espresso, and
hot specialty drinks ~ 8-10 oz.

Irish
Coffee

Irish Coffee — Tall Mug — Mug — Irish Coffee

House Specialty Glasses
Service of frozen/blended or tall iced
specialty drinks ~ 10-16 oz.

Squall — Paneled Tumbler — Impressions — Fountainware

Napoli Grande

Chivalry — Super Sham – Coupette/Margarita — Stratus

Snifter Glasses
Service of brandies, whiskies, and liqueurs, neat
6-14 oz.

Citation

Domaine — Citation — Embassy — Michelangelo

Wine Glasses
Service of wine
8-15 oz.

Vina (red)

Vina (white) — Citation (red) – Napa Country (red) · Domaine (white)

Champagne Glasses
Service of champagne ~ 6-9 oz.

Vina

Tiziano Flute — Citation Gourmet — Flute — Domaine

Beer Glasses
Service of beer or draft beer
9-18 oz.

Paneled Mug

Footed Gibraltar — Mug — Heavy Base – Pilsner (Flare)

Glossary

ABERLOUR A'BUNADH SPEYSIDE SINGLE MALT WHISKY — An ultra-premium single malt Scotch whisky distilled in Speyside by Aberlour. 119.2 proof (59.6% abv) Refer to the product review on page 10.

ABSOLUT VODKAS — A line of 100% wheat vodkas made in Ahus, Sweden. The Absolut family also includes CITRON (citrus), PEPPAR (pepper), KURANT (currant) and MANDRIN (mandarine orange). 80 proof (40% abv) Refer to the product review on page 38.

ALIZÉ DE FRANCE — An aperitif made in Cognac, France, from a blend of passion fruit juice and Alizé Cognac. 32 proof (16% abv) Refer to the product review on page 280.

ALIZÉ RED PASSION — An aperitif made in Cognac, France, from a blend of passion fruit juice, cranberry, natural flavors and Alizé Cognac. 32 proof (16% abv) Refer to the product review on page 280.

ALIZÉ V.S.O.P. COGNAC — A brandy made by the L&L Cognac House from an *assemblage* of *eaux-de-vie* from the Grande Champagne, Petite Champagne, Borderies, Fin Bois and Bon Bois regions. 80 proof (40% abv) Refer to the product review on page 222.

AMER PICON — A bitter French cordial from a base of brandy and flavored with oranges, roots, barks, herbs and wine. 78 proof (39% abv)

ANGOSTURA BITTERS — An aromatic bitters made in Trinidad from an infusion of roots, herbs, bark and seeds on a rum base. (45% abv)

ANGOSTURA CARIBBEAN RUM CREAM — A liqueur made from a blend of fresh cream, proprietary flavorings and aged rum. 34 proof (17% abv)

ANISETTE (Anis, Anise) — A sweet, aromatic, licorice-flavored liqueur. 50-60 proof (25-30% abv)

APPLETON ESTATE V/X JAMAICA RUM — A Jamaican rum made from a blend of pot-distilled and continuous-distilled spirits and aged in American oak barrels for 5 to 10 years. 80 proof (40% abv)

APPLETON SPECIAL JAMAICA RUM — A Jamaican rum made from a blend of pot-distilled and continuous-distilled spirits aged in American oak barrels. 86 proof (43% abv)

APRICOT BRANDY
    See Fruit Brandy

AQUAVIT (AKVAVIT) — A double-distilled spirit made in Scandinavian countries from either grain or potatoes, flavored principally with caraway seed. 84-90 proof (42-45% abv)

ARMAGNAC — An aromatic, full-bodied brandy produced in the French province of Gascony with a distinctive, robust flavor and bouquet. 80-86 proof (40-43% abv)

ARTIC VODKA & MELON LIQUEUR — An Italian grain vodka blended with a melon flavored liqueur produced at the Illva Saronno Distillery of Saronno, Italy. 50 proof (25% abv) Refer to the product review on page 264.

ARTIC VODKA & PEACH LIQUEUR — An Italian grain vodka blended with a peach flavored liqueur produced at the Illva Saronno Distillery of Saronno, Italy. 50 proof (25% abv) Refer to the product review on page 264.

ARTIC VODKA & STRAWBERRY LIQUEUR — An Italian grain vodka blended with a strawberry flavored liqueur produced at the Illva Saronno Distillery of Saronno, Italy. 50 proof (25% abv) Refer to the product review on page 264.

BACARDI RUMS — A line of highly successful rums produced in Puerto Rico and the Bahamas from a blend of continuous-distilled and pot-distilled rums. Bacardi Light, the best selling rum in the world, is charcoal filtered and aged a minimum of 1 year in American white oak barrels. The Bacardi family of rums also includes Bacardi Gold (2 years), Bacardi Select (1-4 years), Bacardi 8 (8 years), Bacardi Limón (citrus-infused), Bacardi 151° (75.5% abv) and Bacardi Spice (70 proof). Refer to the product review on page 54.

BAFFERTS GIN — A gin made from a base of premium, column-distilled grain spirits by Hayman Distillers of London. 80 proof (40% abv) Refer to the product review on page 276.

BAILEYS ORIGINAL IRISH CREAM LIQUEUR — A beige-colored cream liqueur made in Ireland from a compound of coffee, chocolate, Irish whiskey and fresh dairy cream. 34 proof (17% abv) Refer to the product review on page 18.

BALLYLARKIN IRISH LIQUEUR — A liqueur made from a base of Irish malt whiskies, cane spirits, and citrus and vanilla flavorings. 80 proof (40% abv) Refer to the product review on page 170.

B & B LIQUEUR — A liqueur made from a blend of Benedictine Liqueur and aged cognac, produced since 1510 at the Benedictine abbey in Fecamp, France. 80 proof (40% abv) Refer to the product review on page 42.

BEEFEATER LONDON DRY GIN — A London dry gin produced since the early 1800s by the House of Burrough. 94 proof (47% abv) Refer to the product review on page 248.

BELVEDERE POLISH VODKA — A vodka quadruple-distilled from rye in both an alembic and continuous still at the Polmos Zyrardów. 80 proof (40% abv) Refer to the product review on page 60.

BENEDICTINE — A monastery liqueur made from a secret recipe of 27 fragrant herbs, spices, plants, tea and fruits, each distilled individually and matured in oak barrels for 3 months before blending. The liqueur is made on a base of aged cognac and rested in oak casks. 80 proof (40% abv) Refer to the product review on page 42.

BLACKBERRY BRANDY
 See FRUIT BRANDY

BLAVOD BLACK VODKA — A vodka triple-distilled from grain with a blackish hue distilled at the Hayman Distillery in London. 80 proof (40% abv) Refer to the product review on page 252.

BLUE CURAÇAO — A blue, orange-flavored liqueur, slightly sweeter than triple sec, produced from the dried peels of oranges. 60 proof (30% abv)

BOMBAY SAPPHIRE LONDON DRY GIN — A London dry gin triple-distilled in uniquely constructed alembic stills and infused with ten botanicals. 94 proof (47% abv) Refer to the product review on page 46.

BOURBON WHISKEY — A full-bodied and full-flavored American straight whiskey. It is distilled from fermented corn mash and, to a lesser degree, from rye, wheat, and barley. Bourbon must be aged a minimum of 2 years in new, charred-oak casks. 80-126 proof (40-63% abv)

BRANDY — A distilled spirit produced in scores of countries from grapes or a fermented mash of fruit. It is often aged in oak, although many are left clear and unaged, such as grappa and *eaux-de-vie*.

BRILLIANT VODKA — A wheat vodka made in the Highlands of Scotland and distilled five times in column stills. 80 proof (40% abv) Refer to the product review on page 134.

BRIOTTET CRÈME DE CASSIS DE DIJON — A liqueur made entirely from Noir de Bourgogne black currants that are macerated in premium grape spirits at the Edmond Briottet Company in Dijon, France. 40 proof (20% abv) Refer to the product review on page 88.

CACHAÇA — A Brazilian spirit distilled from sugar cane molasses. 80 proof (40% abv)

CALVADOS — An apple brandy produced in Calvados, located in Normandy, France. It is distilled in pot stills from a mash of fermented cider apples and aged in oak casks before blending and bottling.

CAMPARI APERITIVO — A bitter Italian aperitif made by an infusion of bitter herbs and orange peels. 48 proof (24% abv)

CANADIAN CLUB WHISKY — A whisky made in Ontario, Canada, from a blend of continuous-distilled corn whisky, and lesser proportions of rye, malted rye and malted barley whiskies that are aged for 6 years. 80 proof (40% abv) Refer to the product review on page 112.

CANADIAN WHISKY — Canadian whisky by law must be blended from cereal grains. It is distilled from a fermented mash of corn, rye and barley. Canadian whiskies are typically light-bodied and aged 6–8 years in oak casks.

CAPTAIN MORGAN SPICED RUM — A Puerto Rican rum made from a blend of continuous-distilled and pot-distilled rums and a proprietary blend of Caribbean spices. 70 proof (35% abv)

CASA NOBLE TEQUILAS — A line of triple-distilled, 100% agave tequilas that include a silver, reposado and limited reserve añejo. 80 proof (40% abv) Refer to the product review on page 84.

CASCADE MOUNTAIN GIN — A gin made from grain and botanicals distilled in a copper alembic still at the Bendistillery in Bend, Oregon. 95 proof (45% abv) Refer to the product review on page 142.

CELTIC CROSSING IRISH LIQUEUR — A liqueur made in Bailieboro, Ireland, from a blend of barrel-aged Irish whiskies, cognac and heather honey. 60 proof (30% abv) Refer to the product review on page 82.

CHAMBORD LIQUEUR — A French framboise liqueur made from black raspberries and various other fruit, herbs and honey. 33 proof (16.5% abv) Refer to the product review on page 12.

CHAMPAGNE — A sparkling wine made in the Champagne region of France located northeast of Paris. Champagne is made from chardonnay, pinot noir and pinot meunier grapes and made effervescent through the *méthode champenoise*, or champagne process.

CHARTREUSE, GREEN — A monastery liqueur made from brandy infused with 130 wild mountain herbs. It is re-distilled four times before aging. 110 proof (55% abv) Yellow Chartreuse is sweeter and less aromatic than the green version. 80 proof (40% abv)

CHERRY BRANDY
    See FRUIT BRANDY

CHOPIN POLISH VODKA — A vodka quadruple-distilled from Stobrawa potatoes. 80 proof (40% abv) Refer to the product review on page 62.

CHRISTIAN BROTHERS BRANDY — A California brandy distilled principally from Thompson Seedless grapes in copper alembic stills, as well as column stills. 80 proof (40% abv) Refer to the product review on page 152.

COCKSPUR V.S.O.R. RUM — A Barbadian rum made from a blend of continuous-distilled and pot-distilled rums aged a minimum of 10 years. 43% abv (86 proof)

COCONUT CREAM SYRUP — A syrup made from the milk and meat of coconuts.

COGNAC — A brandy made since the early 1600s in the region centered around Jarnac, France, made in alembic stills and aged in Limousin oak casks. Cognacs are often identified by their appellation, such a Petite Champagne or Grande Champagne cognac. Fine Champagne cognacs are a blend of Petite Champagne or Grande Champagne cognacs.

COINTREAU LIQUEUR — A liqueur made from a blend of sweet orange peels from Spain, France and Brazil, and bitter, unripe orange peels from South America, double-distilled in copper alembic stills in Angers, France. 80 proof (40% abv) Refer to the product review on page 52.

COURVOISIER COGNAC — One of the preeminent producers of cognac, Courvoisier is located in Jarnac, France. Courvoisier V.S.O.P. is a Fine Champagne cognac comprised of brandies aged a minimum of 8 years in Limousin oak, with most aged in excess of 12 years. Refer to the product review on page 194.

CRATER LAKE VODKA — A small batch vodka made in a copper alembic still from local grain at the Bendistillery in Bend, Oregon. 80 proof (40% abv) Refer to the product review on page 142.

CRÈME DE BANANA — A banana-flavored cordial. 60 proof (30%)

CRÈME DE CACAO — A liqueur flavored with cocoa and vanilla beans, produced in both a light and dark brown version, with little or no difference other than color. 50-60 proof (25-30% abv)

CRÈME DE MENTHE — A cordial flavored by various varieties of mint, principally peppermint. Produced in green and clear versions, the only difference being color. 60 proof (30% abv)

CRÈME DE NOYAUX — A liqueur made from crushed apricot and peach pits with an almond-like flavor. 54–56 proof (27-28% abv)

CROWN ROYAL WHISKY — A blended Canadian whisky that was first introduced in 1939 to celebrate the unprecedented visit of King George VI and Queen Elizabeth to Canada. 80 proof (40% abv)

CRUZAN ESTATE RUMS — A line of rums distilled on Saint Croix in the Virgin Islands from a blend of continuous-distilled rums that are lightly filtered and aged in American oak barrels. The family of Cruzan rums include Cruzan Estate Light (2-3 years), Cruzan Estate Dark (2-4 years) and Cruzan Estate Diamond (5-10 years). 80 proof (40% abv) Refer to the product review on page 232.

CRUZAN SINGLE BARREL ESTATE RUM — A Virgin Island rum made in limited quantities from a blend of old continuous-distilled rums. After blending, the rum is placed in a newly charred, white oak cask for secondary aging. 80 proof (40% abv) Refer to the product review on page 20.

CRUZAN FRUIT-FLAVORED RUMS — A line of Virgin Island rums made from a blend of continuous-distilled rums that are aged 2-3 years in oak barrels, charcoal-filtered and naturally flavored. The Cruzan family of fruit-flavored rums include Banana, Coconut, Orange, Junkanu (citrus) and Pineapple. 55 proof (27.5% abv) Refer to the product review on page 150.

CRUZAN RUM CREAM — A liqueur produced in Ireland made with Irish cream, caramel, vanilla and Cruzan light rum. 34 proof (17% abv)

DAMRAK AMSTERDAM GIN — A grain and malt gin made with 17 fragrant botanicals, distilled five times by the Lucas Bols Company of Amsterdam. 83.6 proof (41.8% abv) Refer to the product review on page 210.

DEKUYPER BUTTERSHOTS SCHNAPPS — A liqueur made from grain spirits with butterscotch flavoring. 30 proof (15% abv) Refer to the product review on page 286.

DEKUYPER HOT DAMN! CINNAMON SCHNAPPS — A liqueur made from grain spirits and oil of cinnamon. 30 proof (15% abv) Refer to the product review on page 250.

DEKUYPER PEACH PUCKER — A sweet and sour, peach-flavored schnapps made from grain spirits and natural flavorings. 30 proof (15% abv) Refer to the product review on page 274.

DEKUYPER PEACHTREE SCHNAPPS — A colorless, peach liqueur made from grain spirits and natural flavorings. 30 proof (15% abv) Refer to the product review on page 148.

DEKUYPER PEPPERMINT SCHNAPPS — A colorless, mint-flavored liqueur with about half the sugar content and twice the alcohol of crème de menthe. It is made from multiple-distilled neutral spirits and pure oil of peppermint. 60 proof (30% abv) Refer to the product review on page 212.

DEKUYPER PUCKER SOUR APPLE — A sweet and sour, apple-flavored schnapps made from pure grain spirits and natural flavorings. 30 proof (15% abv) Refer to the product review on page 110.

DEKUYPER RASPBERRY PUCKER — A sweet and sour, raspberry-flavored schnapps made from grain spirits and natural flavorings. 30 proof (15% abv) Refer to the product review on page 184.

DEKUYPER RAZZMATAZZ RASPBERRY LIQUEUR — A raspberry liqueur made from grain spirits and natural flavorings. 33 proof (16.5% abv) Refer to the product review on page 234.

DEKUYPER TRIPLE SEC — A clear liqueur flavored principally from orange peels grown on the Dutch West-Indies island of Curaçao. 48 proof (24% abv) Refer to the product review on page 178.

DEKUYPER WATERMELON PUCKER — A sweet and sour, watermelon-flavored schnapps made from grain spirits and natural flavorings. 30 proof (15% abv) Refer to the product review on page 258.

DEWAR'S WHITE LABEL SCOTCH WHISKY — A Scotch whisky made in Perth, Scotland, from a blend of malt and grain whiskies. At the core of its blend are the Highland malts of Aberfeldy, Lochnagar and Glen Ord. 80 proof (40% abv) Refer to the product review on page 236.

DIRTY OLIVE — A line of grain, triple-distilled spirits infused with fragrant botanicals and green olive juice from the Spanish province of Andolusia. The family includes Dirty Olive Gin and Dirty Olive Vodka. 70 proof (35% abv) Refer to the product review on page 230.

DISARONNO ORIGINALE AMARETTO — A liqueur made by Illva Saronno in Saronno, Italy, from a base of Italian grape spirits steeped with 17 herbs and fruits, including apricot kernel oil. 56 proof (28% abv) Refer to the product review on page 28.

DJ DOTSON TRIPLE SEC — A colorless, alcohol-free triple sec with a sweet and sour orange flavor. Refer to the product review on page 190.

DR. MCGILLICUDDY'S FIREBALL CINNAMON CANADIAN WHISKY — A Canadian whisky made from an infusion of barrel-aged whisky and oil of cinnamon. 66 proof (33% abv) Refer to the product review on page 272.

DR. MCGILLICUDDY'S MENTHOLMINT SCHNAPPS — A colorless, mint-flavored liqueur made in Canada from a base of grain spirits and infused menthol crystals. 48 proof (24% abv) Refer to the product review on page 226.

DR. MCGILLICUDDY'S VANILLA LIQUEUR — A colorless, vanilla liqueur made in Canada from a base of grain spirits steeped in whole vanilla beans. 48 proof (24% abv) Refer to the product review on page 266.

DOORLY'S XO BARBADOS RUM — A rum produced on the island of Barbados from a blend of barrel-aged, Bajan rums that undergo a second maturation in Oloroso sherry casks. 80 proof (40% abv) Refer to the product review on page 218.

DRAMBUIE LIQUEUR — A liqueur made in Edinburgh, Scotland, from a base of single malt and grain whiskies infused with spice, herbs and heather honey. 80 proof (40% abv) Refer to the product review on page 120.

DRY SHERRY — A blended, fortified wine produced primarily in the Jerez de la Frontera district of Spain from the palomino grape variety and Solera aged in American oak casks. The wine is fortified to about 15% abv with grape spirits.

DRY VERMOUTH — Most closely associated with France, dry vermouth is made from a blend of picpoul and clairette wines aged for 2-3 years, in oak casks exposed to the elements to accelerate maturation. After blending, the wine is infused with botanicals and fortified with grape spirits to about 19% abv. See also Vya Preferred California Vermouth.

DUBONNET BLANC — A fortified aperitif wine made in France from a base of premium white wine that is infused with a proprietary blend of herbs, spices, peels and quinine. The wine is fortified with grape spirits to 19% abv. Refer to the product review on page 44.

DUBONNET ROUGE — A fortified aperitif wine made in France from a base of premium red wine that is infused with a proprietary blend of herbs, spices, peels and quinine. The wine is fortified with grape spirits to 19% abv. Refer to the product review on page 44.

EL JIMADOR TEQUILAS — A line of tequilas made by Herradura from estate-grown blue agaves. El Jimador Silver and Reposado are *mixto* tequilas, meaning that they contain 51% agave. Ultra-premium El Jimador Añejo is a limited edition, 100% agave tequila aged in oak barrels for a minimum of one year. Refer to the product review on page 158.

EL TESORO DE DON FELIPE TEQUILAS — A line of 100% agave tequilas made at the La Altena Distillery outside of Guadalajara. The El Tesoro line includes a silver, reposado and an añejo aged in oak barrels a minimum of 2 years. El Tesoro Paradiso is an añejo further aged in used cognac casks. 80 proof (40% abv) Refer to the product review on page 30.

EVAN WILLIAMS SINGLE BARREL VINTAGE BOURBON — A vintage-dated bourbon made in Bardstown, Kentucky, by Heaven Hill Distilleries. The whiskey is drawn from single barrels after maturing around 10 years. 86.6 proof (43.3% abv) Refer to the product review on page 198.

EXTASE XO LIQUEUR — A liqueur made in Dijon, France, from orange peels grown on Curaçao in the Dutch West Indies and a base of A. Hardy X.O. Fine Champagne Cognac, an *assemblage* of Grande Champagne and Petite Champagne brandies with an average age of 25 years. 80 proof (40% abv) Refer to the product review on page 74.

FARIAS TEQUILAS — A line of 100% agave tequilas double-distilled in the town of Tepatitlan. Farias Añejo is aged a minimum of 2 years in ex-bourbon barrels. 80 proof (40% abv) Refer to the product review on page 186.

FERNET BRANCA — An Italian medicinal bitters. Fernet Branca Menta is flavored with fresh mint leaves. 80 proof (40% abv)

FINLANDIA VODKA — A Finnish vodka triple-distilled in continuous column stills entirely from barley and glacier-fed spring water. 80 proof (40% abv) Refer to the product review on page 156.

FORTY CREEK CANADIAN WHISKIES — A line of small batch whiskies made at the Kittling Ridge Estate Distillery in Grimsby, Canada. Forty Creek Three Grain Whisky is distilled in copper pot stills from rye, maize and malted barley and aged up to 8 years in age. Forty Creek Barrel Select Whisky is a blend of rye and maize whiskies distilled in copper alembic stills, aged in first-fill bourbon barrels and sherry casks. Refer to the product review on page 288.

FOURSQUARE SPICED RUM — A spiced rum made on Barbados at the Foursquare Rum Distillery from a blend of rums barrel-aged a minimum of 2 years and steeped with a mix of ground nutmeg, cinnamon and vanilla. 70 proof (35% abv) Refer to the product review on page 218.

FRANGELICO LIQUEUR — A liqueur made in the Piedmont region of Italy from a base of Italian grape spirits, which are steeped with woodland herbs, berries and hazelnuts. 48 proof (24% abv) Refer to the product review on page 58.

FRUIT BRANDY — Flavored brandy is made by distilling a fermented mash of fruit and brandy. Popular examples include apple, blackberry, cherry, peach, plum, raspberry and strawberry. 70-80 proof (35-40% abv)

GALLIANO LIQUEUR (Liquore Galliano) — An Italian liqueur made from herbs, spices and seeds, with a pronounced flavor of anise. 70 proof (35% abv)

GENTLEMAN JACK RARE TENNESSEE WHISKEY — A Tennessee whiskey made from a recipe created by Jack Daniel at the turn of the 20th century. It is aged in oak barrels for 4 years, and then mellowed twice in sugar maple charcoal. 80 proof (40% abv) Refer to the product review on page 32.

GIN — A spirit distilled typically from a fermented mash of primarily corn and other grains. The spirit is redistilled with flavoring agents called "botanicals," a mixture of roots, herbs, fruits and seeds. Among those frequently used are juniper berries, caraway, anise and coriander seeds, lemon and orange peels, and angelica and orris roots. These botanicals give gin its unique flavor and bouquet. The final distillate is reduced in alcohol to 80-110 proof (40-55% abv).

GINGER BEER — A non-alcoholic, ginger-flavored, carbonated beverage.

GIORI LEMONCILLO CREAM LIQUEUR — A liqueur made in Trentino, Italy, from lemon-infused alcohol and cream. 34 proof (17% abv) Refer to the product review on page 220.

GIORI LEMONCILLO LIQUEUR — A lemon liqueur made in Trentino, Italy, from tree-ripened Sorrento lemons. 60 proof (30% abv) Refer to the product review on page 130.

GLENFARCLAS SINGLE MALT SCOTCH WHISKIES — A line of single malt whiskies distilled in the Speyside of the Highlands. In operation since 1836, Glenfarclas is one of the few distilleries still under private ownership. 80 proof (40% abv) Refer to the product review on page 80.

GODIVA CHOCOLATE LIQUEUR — An American liqueur flavored with Godiva chocolate. 34 proof (17% abv)

GOLDSCHLÄGER — A cinnamon schnapps produced in Switzerland containing 24-carat gold flecks. 90 proof (45% abv)

GOODERHAM & WORTS CANADIAN WHISKY — A Canadian whisky distilled by Corby Distilleries made from a blend of double-distilled rye, barley, malted rye and barley, and wheat whiskies. 90 proof (45% abv) Refer to the product review on page 246.

GOSLING'S BLACK SEAL RUM — A Bermudian rum made from a blend of 3-year-old rums according to the original family recipe from 1860. 80 proof (40% abv) Refer to the product review on page 254.

GRAND MARNIER LIQUEUR — A French liqueur produced by the Lapostolle family since 1880. Its flavor and bouquet is derived from a delicate blend of bitter oranges and well-aged cognac. 80 proof (40% abv) Refer to the product review on page 6.

GRAND MARNIER 100ᵀᴴ ANNIVERSARY — A French liqueur produced by the Lapostolle family since 1927 when it was released to commemorate the company's centenary. It is made on a base of cognacs ranging in age up to 25 years. 80 proof (40% abv) Refer to the product review on page 100.

GRAND MARNIER 150ᵀᴴ ANNIVERSARY — A French liqueur produced by the Lapostolle family since 1977 when it was released to commemorate the company's 150ᵗʰ anniversary. It is made on a base of Grande Champagne cognacs ranging in age up to 50 years. 80 proof (40% abv) Refer to the product review on page 100.

GRAN GALA TRIPLE ORANGE LIQUEUR — An Italian liqueur made from a blend of triple oranges and barrel-aged brandy produced by the Stock Distillery. 80 proof (40% abv) Refer to the product review on page 138.

GRAPPA — A colorless, unaged brandy distilled from the remnants of the winemaking process. Technically grappa is an *eau-de-vie de marc*.

GREEN CHARTREUSE See CHARTREUSE, GREEN

GRENADINE — A sweet, non-alcoholic syrup flavored with pomegranates.

GREY GOOSE VODKA — A French vodka distilled in copper alembic stills from a blend of rye, barley, wheat, and corn, and limestone-filtered water from Provence. 80 proof (40% abv) Refer to the product review on page 96.

GUINNESS STOUT — An ale brewed from roasted, unmalted barley in Dublin, Ireland. It is extremely dark, flavorful and light-bodied. (4.3% abv)

HARDY NOCES D'OR COGNAC — A Grande Champagne cognac made by A. Hardy from a blend of brandies averaging 50 years in age. 80 proof (40% abv) Refer to the product review on page 92.

HERRADURA TEQUILAS — A line of 100% agave tequilas produced entirely on the Herradura Estate in Amatitán. Herradura markets four versions of tequila, including a silver, reposado, and an añejo aged 2 years in American and French oak barrels. Herradura Selección Suprema is a limited-release, 4-year-old añejo. 80 proof (40% abv) Refer to the product review on page 106.

HOT DAMN! CINNAMON SCHNAPPS See DEKUYPER HOT DAMN

HUSSONG'S REPOSADO TEQUILAS — A line of 100% agave tequilas made in Guadalajara at the González González Distillery. Hussong's makes a reposado and an añejo. 80 proof (40% abv) Refer to the product review on page 208.

IRISH MIST — A spicy Irish liqueur made from Irish whiskey, heather honey and a variety of herbs. 80 proof (40% abv)

IRISH WHISKEY — A type of whiskey made in Ireland from a fermented mash of malted and unmalted barley, corn, rye, and lesser amounts of other cereal grains. Irish whiskeys are triple-distilled in pot stills and aged in used bourbon, sherry or port casks. Irish whiskeys are full-bodied and possess a smooth, malty flavor. 80–90 proof (40-45% abv)

JACK DANIEL'S SINGLE BARREL TENNESSEE WHISKEY — A Tennessee whiskey hand-bottled one barrel at a time from select casks of Jack Daniel's whiskey. 90 proof (45% abv) Refer to the product review on page 128.

JACK DANIEL'S TENNESSEE WHISKEY — A Tennessee whiskey distilled in Lynchburg, Tennessee, since 1866 from corn, filtered through sugar maple charcoal. 86 proof (43% abv)

JÄGERMEISTER LIQUEUR — A liqueur made from a blend of 56 roots, herbs and spices macerated in neutral spirits and matured in charred oak barrels prior to blending. 70 proof (35% abv) Refer to the product review on page 124.

JAMESON IRISH WHISKEY — An Irish whiskey made from a blend of grain, malted and unmalted barley whiskies, and triple-distilled in both pot and continuous stills. The blend is aged a minimum of 6 years in American oak barrels and sherry casks. 80 proof (40% abv) Refer to the product review on page 40.

JEWEL OF RUSSIA BERRY INFUSION — A traditional Russian spirit made by steeping super-premium Jewel of Russia Vodka in a mash of fresh, wild cranberries. 44 proof (22% abv) Refer to the product review on page 182.

JEWEL OF RUSSIA CLASSIC VODKA — A Russian vodka continuously distilled from a blend of premium rye, hardy winter wheat and artesian spring water. 80 proof (40% abv) Refer to the product review on page 86.

JEWEL OF RUSSIA WILD BILBERRY INFUSION — A traditional Russian spirit made by steeping super-premium Jewel of Russia Vodka in a mash of fresh, wild bilberries. 40 proof (20% abv) Refer to the product review on page 210.

JIM BEAM BLACK LABEL BOURBON — A Kentucky straight bourbon made by the Beam family in Clermont, Kentucky, since 1795. The whiskey is aged in charred oak barrels for a minimum of 8 years. 80 proof (40% abv) Refer to the product review on page 68.

JIM BEAM WHITE LABEL BOURBON — A Kentucky straight bourbon distilled from a high proportion of white and yellow corn and lesser percentages of rye and malted barley. The whiskey is aged in charred oak barrels for a minimum of 4 years. 80 proof (40% abv) Refer to the product review on page 282.

JOSE CUERVO TEQUILAS — A line of tequilas dating back to 1795. The Jose Cuervo distillery—*La Rojeña*—is located in the town of Tequila and produces many successful labels of *mixto* and 100% agave tequilas. Brands include José Cuervo Especial, 1800 Añejo, Tradicional, José Cuervo Añejo, and Reserva de la Familia de José Cuervo. 80 proof (40% abv)

KAHLÚA COFFEE LIQUEUR — A Mexican liqueur made with coffee beans and cane spirit. 53 proof (26.5% abv) Refer to the product review on page 34.

KÉKÉ BEACH KEY LIME CREAM LIQUEUR — A liqueur made from a base of grain spirits and a blend of cream and natural, key lime flavorings. 30 proof (15% abv) Refer to the product review on page 162.

KELT XO TOUR DU MONDE GRANDE CHAMPAGNE COGNAC — A cognac blended entirely of *eaux-de-vie* distilled in the Grande Champagne district. The cognac finishes its maturation in Limousin oak barrels lashed to a ship's deck for a 3-month sea voyage around the world. 80 proof (40% abv) Refer to the product review on page 24.

KETEL ONE DUTCH VODKA — A vodka from Schiedam, Holland, triple-distilled in small batches entirely from wheat in a 137-year-old, copper alembic still, referred to as "Ketel #1." 80 proof (40% abv) Refer to the product review on page 48.

KNAPPOGUE CASTLE PURE POT STILL IRISH WHISKEY ~ 1951 — A pot still Irish whiskey triple distilled in 1951 at the B. Daly Distillery in Tullamore, and aged in sherry casks for 36 years. 80 proof (40% abv) Refer to the product review on page 140.

KNAPPOGUE CASTLE IRISH SINGLE MALT WHISKEY — A vintage-dated, Irish whiskey triple-distilled at the Bushmill's Distillery and aged in 180-liter white oak barrels. 80 proof (40% abv) Refer to the product review on page 70.

KNOB CREEK SMALL BATCH BOURBON — A small batch Kentucky straight bourbon distilled by Jim Beam and aged for 9 years in new white oak barrels. The barrels are first seared over a low flame, then "flash-fired" to create a deep char. 80 proof (40% abv) Refer to the product review on page 172.

LAIRD'S APPLEJACK APPLE BRANDY — An apple brandy double-distilled in alembic stills and aged 4 years in white oak barrels. 80 proof (40% abv) Refer to the product review on page 162.

LAIRD'S 12-YEAR-OLD RARE APPLE BRANDY — An American apple brandy distilled from a blend of five apple varieties and aged in white oak barrels for a minimum of 12 years. 88 proof (44% abv) Refer to the product review on page 66.

LICOR 43 (Cuarenta y Tres) — A Spanish liqueur made from a base of brandy infused with berries, citrus fruit and fragrant herbs. The "43" in the liqueur's name refers to the number of ingredients used in its proprietary recipe. 62 proof (31% abv) Refer to the product review on page 196.

LILLET — A semi-dry, French fortified aperitif wine with the flavor of oranges, herbs, and quinine, produced in two versions: Lillet Blonde (drier and made with white wine) and Lillet Rouge (sweeter and made with red wine). 18% abv

LOT NO. 40 CANADIAN WHISKY — A Canadian whisky made entirely from prairie rye and malted rye, distilled in small batches in copper alembic stills aged 8 years. 86 proof (43% abv) Refer to the product review on page 176.

LUKSUSOWA POLISH POTATO VODKA — A line of Polish vodkas continuously distilled from potatoes made by the Polmos Poznan Distillery. 80 proof (40% abv) Refer to the product review on page 216.

MAKER'S MARK BOURBON — A Kentucky straight bourbon whisky distilled in small batches, one of only a small number of bourbons to include wheat instead of rye in its mash bill. 90 proof (45% abv) Refer to the product review on page 98.

MALIBU RUM — A liqueur made from Jamaican light rum and coconut. 56 proof (28% abv)

MANDARINE NAPOLÉON LIQUEUR — A Belgian liqueur with a base of well-aged cognac and fresh tangerines grown exclusively in Sicily. 80 proof (40% abv) Refer to the product review on page 116.

MARASCHINO LIQUEUR — A clear liqueur made from Dalmatian Marasca cherries and almonds. 50-60 proof (25-30% abv)

MATUSALEM GRAN RESERVA RUM — A rum of Cuban origin comprised of spirits produced by several West Indies distillers and made around a "blender rum," which is Solera aged about 15 years. 80 proof (40% abv) Refer to the product review on page 122.

METAXA 5 STAR BRANDY — A flavorful brandy produced in Greece.

MIDORI MELON LIQUEUR — A Japanese liqueur produced by Suntory that is made from a base of neutral spirits and proprietary flavors, the most readily identifiable of which is honeydew melon. 42 proof (21% abv) Refer to the product review on page 94.

MOUNT GAY ECLIPSE RUM — A Barbadian rum made in Bridgetown from a blend of continuous-distilled and pot-distilled rums, and aged a minimum of 2 years. 80 proof (40% abv)

MYERS'S JAMAICAN RUM — A dark, Jamaican rum produced in Kingstown, blended from continuous-distilled rums. 80 proof (40% abv)

NAPASAKI SAKÉ — A super-premium *Junmai-Ginjo* saké handcrafted in America from polished *Akitakomachi* rice, water, yeast and koji, an enzyme that converts the rice's starches into glucose. (15% abv) Refer to the product review on page 102.

OLD RAJ DRY GIN — A super-premium, alembic-distilled gin made by the Scottish firm of Cadenhead's. Its botanical mix contains saffron, a spice that endows the gin with an intriguing pale yellow tint. 110 proof (55% abv) Refer to the product review on page 180.

OPAL NERA BLACK SAMBUCA — A black, opaque liqueur made from anise, elder flower and lemon produced in Theme, Italy. 80 proof (40% abv)

ORANGE BITTERS — A bittersweet, orange-flavored bitters.

ORANGE FLOWER WATER — A French, non-alcoholic perfumed water with the scent of orange blossoms.

ORGEAT SYRUP — A French, non-alcoholic almond-flavored syrup.

ORIGINAL CRISTALL RUSSIAN VODKA — A vodka triple-distilled from winter wheat and glacier water by the Cristall Distillery in Moscow. 80 proof (40% abv) Refer to the product review on page 26.

ORIGINAL POLISH VODKA — A 100% rye vodka distilled six times in column stills produced at the Polmos Bielsko-Biala Distillery. 80 proof (40% abv) Refer to the product review on page 108.

ORO DI MAZZETTI — A grappa-based liqueur made from moscato grapes by Mazzetti d'Altavilla in the Piedmont region of Italy. 60 proof (30% abv) Refer to the product review on page 260.

OTARD XO COGNAC — A Fine Champagne cognac made with a blend of brandies distilled in the Grande Champagne, Petite Champagne and Borderies, some aged more than 35 years. 80 proof (40% abv) Refer to the product review on page 126.

OUZO — A liqueur made in Greece and Cyprus from anise, drier and stronger than anisette. 90-92 proof (45-46% abv)

PEARL VODKA — A Canadian vodka distilled in small batches from soft, winter wheat and spring water from the Rockies. 80 proof (40% abv) Refer to the product review on page 192.

PERNOD — A pastis liqueur made in France from anise seeds, herbs, and flavorings on a base of brandy. 80.2 proof (40.1% abv)

PEYCHAUD BITTERS — A New Orleans bitters with a pronounced anise flavor. 35% abv

PIKE CREEK CANADIAN WHISKY —
A whisky made from a blend of column-distilled, grain whiskies aged in re-charred oak barrels for a minimum of 10 years, then further matured in Cockburn port pipes. 80 proof (40% abv) Refer to the product review on page 202.

PLYMOUTH GIN — An alembic-distilled gin made in Plymouth, England, at the historic Black Friars Distillery of Coates & Co. 82.4 proof (41.2% abv) Refer to the product review on page 76.

POIRE WILLIAM (*Eau-de-vie de Poires*) — A dry *eau-de-vie* made in Germany, Switzerland and France from the fermented mash of William, Bartlett or Anjou pears. Some versions are aged for 1 to 2 years and bottled with a whole pear. 80-90 proof (40-45% abv)

PORT — A sweet red or white fortified wine made primarily in Portugal, although the number of American vineyards making quality port wine is steadily increasing.

PUSSER'S BRITISH NAVY RUM — A naval rum made from a blend of six pot-distilled rums produced at several West Indies distilleries. Pusser's Blue Label is bottled at 95.5 proof (47.75% abv) and the Red Label is 80 proof (40% abv).

PYRAT RUM — A line of super-premium rums made on the island of Anguilla from barrel-aged, alembic rums produced by 7 Caribbean distillers. The rums in the blend range in age from 8-40 years. The line includes Pyrat Pistol, Pyrat XO and the ultra-premium Pyrat Cask 32. 80 proof (40% abv)

RAIN VODKA — A vodka made at the historic Buffalo Trace Distillery in Frankfort, Kentucky, quadruple-distilled in three different column stills from organically grown yellow corn and Kentucky limestone spring water. 80 proof (40% abv) Refer to the product review on page 204.

RAZZMATAZZ RASPBERRY LIQUEUR
See DEKUYPER RAZZMATAZZ

RÉMY RED — A liqueur made with a base of Fine Champagne Rémy Martin cognac infused with red currants, apricots, peaches and the flavors of South American guarana and Chinese ginseng. 32 proof (16% abv) Refer to the product review on page 224.

RHUMS BARBANCOURT — A line of Haitian agricole rhum double-distilled, first in a column still and then in a copper pot still, and matured in Limousin oak vats. The line includes Rhum Barbancourt Three Star (4 years), Five Star Réserve Spéciale (8 years) and Réserve du Domaine (15 years). 80 proof (40% abv)

R.L. SEALE 10-YEAR-OLD BARBADOS RUM —
A rum produced on the island of Barbados from a blend of Bajan rums barrel-aged a minimum of 10 years. 80 proof (40% abv) Refer to the product review on page 218.

ROSE'S LIME JUICE — A sweetened lime juice made since the late 18th century from West India limes in St. Albans, England.

RUM — A distilled spirit produced from a mash of fresh sugar cane juice or cane molasses. Rums are distilled in virtually every country that grows and exports sugar. 75-152 proof (37.5-76% abv)

RUMPLE MINZE SCHNAPPS —
A peppermint schnapps made in the Black Forest of Germany. 100 proof

SAINT JAMES RHUMS — A line of Martinique agricole rhums made in a continuous still and aged in Limousin oak barrels. The Saint James family includes Imperial Blanc (unaged), Rhum Paille (12 months), Royal Ambre (18 months), Extra Old (3 years), Hors D'Age (6 years), and the unaged, pot-distilled Coeur de Chauffe. 84-120 proof (42-60% abv)

SAKÉ — A Japanese beer brewed from rice and often served warm. (14-18% abv) See also NAPASAKI SAKÉ

SAMBUCA — An Italian anise-flavored liqueur made from wild elderbush berries. 70-84 proof (35-42% abv)

SAUZA TEQUILAS — A line of tequilas with a heritage dating back to 1873. The Sauza distillery—*La Perseverancia*—is situated in the Town of Tequila and produces a highly successful range of *mixto* and 100% agave tequilas. The line includes Sauza Silver, Hornitos Reposado, Conmemorativo, Tres Generaciones Plata, and Tres Generaciones Añejo. 80 proof (40% abv) Refer to the product review of Sauza Hornitos on page 56, the review of Conmemorativo on page 278, the review of Tres Generaciones Plata on page 136, and the review of Tres Generaciones Añejo on page 4.

SCOTCH WHISKY — A whisky distilled primarily from barley, which is allowed to germinate, or malt. The principle appellations in Scotland are the Highlands, Lowlands, Campbeltown, Islay, Skye, Orkney and Mull. There are essentially three types of Scotch whisky—malt, grain, and blended. A single malt is a whisky distilled at a single distillery entirely from malted barley. Blended Scotch whiskies are combinations of grain and malt whiskies. The difference between various blended Scotches comes from both proportion and quality of the component whiskies.

SEAGRAM'S 7 WHISKY — A blended whiskey made in Lawrenceburg, Indiana, since the 1930s. 80 proof (40% abv)

SEA WYNDE POT STILL RUM — A Caribbean rum made in the traditional style of the British Royal Navy comprised of five pot still rums from Jamaica and Guyana, ranging in age between 5 to 11 years. 80 proof (40% abv) Refer to the product review on page 90.

SHERRY — A fortified and blended wine made principally in Spain that is matured according to the Solera aging system. (17-22% abv)

SIGNATORY SCOTCH WHISKIES — A line of independently bottled, rare malt whiskies. Founded in Edinburgh, Signatory has a large selection of malt whiskies from distilleries throughout Scotland, including the Signatory Regionals, a collection of malts from each of the whisky producing appellations. Refer to the product review on page 164.

SLOE GIN — A liqueur flavored with the sloe berry, a small wild plum that grows on the Blackthorn bush. 40-60 proof (20-30% abv)

SMIRNOFF VODKA — An American vodka distilled from corn, based on the recipe of Piotr Smirnoff, the purveyor of vodka to the czars. 80 proof (40% abv)

SOUTHERN COMFORT LIQUEUR — An American liqueur produced since 1874 from a base of grain neutral spirits and flavored with peach liqueur, fresh peach and citrus extracts. 80 proof (40% abv) Refer to the product review on page 154.

STOLICHNAYA RUSSIAN VODKAS — A highly successful line of Russian vodkas made in the heart of Moscow, double-distilled from hearty winter wheat. Stolichnaya Gold Vodka is quadruple-distilled from late harvest wheat and glacial water. The Stolichnaya family of vodkas also includes Vanil (vanilla), Strasberi (strawberry), Persik (peach), Limonnaya (lemon), and Ohranj (orange). 80 proof (40% abv) Refer to the product review on page 14.

SWEET VERMOUTH — Most closely associated with Italy, sweet vermouth is made from a blend of Apulia and Moscato di Canelli wines. These wines are infused with secret formulas of flavoring agents consisting of herbs, roots, seeds, quinine, and various botanicals, then aged 1 to 2 years and fortified with distilled spirits to 16–18% abv. See also Vya Preferred California Vermouth on page 166.

TANQUERAY NO. TEN GIN — A gin made in London, quadruple-distilled in small batches from a fresh botanical mix. 94.6 proof (47.3% abv) Refer to the product review on page 16.

TEQUILA — A spirit produced in Mexico from the Agave Tequilana Weber, a variety of aloe better known as the blue agave. The plant requires 8-12 years to reach maturity. After harvesting, the agave is baked, shredded, fermented and then double-distilled, most often in copper pot stills. *Mixto* tequilas are blended from 51% blue agave. Silver tequilas are bottled without aging. A reposado tequila is aged a minimum of 3 months in oak barrels, but less than a year. Añejo tequila is aged a minimum of a year. 80–92 proof (40-46% abv)

TEQUILA ROSE STRAWBERRY CREAM LIQUEUR — An American liqueur made from a blend of cream, tequila and natural strawberry flavorings. 34 proof (17% abv) Refer to the product review on page 206.

TIA MARIA — A liqueur produced from a blend of Blue Mountain coffee beans, chocolate and Jamaican rum. 53 proof (26.5% abv)

TROPICO — A liqueur made from a blend of Bacardi añejo rum and seven exotic fruit juices produced in San Juan, Puerto Rico. 32 proof (16% abv) Refer to the product review on page 284.

TUACA — An Italian liqueur made with herbs, fruit peels and brandy. 84 proof (42% abv)

VANDERMINT LIQUEUR — A Dutch chocolate and mint liqueur. 60 proof (30% abv)

VAN GOGH GIN — A gin made in Schiedam, Holland, double-distilled from grain and a mix of 10 herbs and botanicals. The final distillation is in a copper alembic still designed specifically for producing gin. 94 proof (47% abv) Refer to the product review on page 114.

VAN HOO VODKA — A Belgian grain vodka distilled first in an alembic still, then triple-distilled in a column still at the Van Hoorebeke Distillery, makers of Mandarine Napoléon Liqueur. 80 proof (40% abv) Refer to the product review on page 168.

VILLA MASSA LIMONCELLO — An Italian liqueur made on a base of grain spirits infused with lemons in Sorrento, Italy. 60 proof (30% abv) Refer to the product review on page 244.

VINCENT VAN GOGH VODKA — A Dutch vodka handcrafted at the Dirkswager Distillery in Schiedam, Holland, column-distilled from a proprietary blend of premium grains and purified water. The distillery also produces Citroen (citrus), Oranje (orange) and Wild Appel (apple) vodkas. 70-80 proof (35-40% abv) Refer to the product review on page 72.

VODKA — A spirit distilled from a fermented mash of potatoes, rice, beets, grapes, and most frequently grain. The fermented mash is distilled to a high-proof, then filtered and reduced to 80-100 proof. The majority of vodkas are unaged and bottled immediately after distillation.

VOX VODKA — An ultra-premium vodka made in the Netherlands entirely from wheat and distilled five times. 80 proof (40% abv) Refer to the product review on page 2.

VYA PREFERRED CALIFORNIA DRY VERMOUTH — A super-premium vermouth made at the Quady winery in Madera, California, from a blend of French Colombard and Orange Muscat white wines infused with aromatic herbs, flowers and plants. (18% abv) Refer to the product review on page 166.

VYA PREFERRED CALIFORNIA SWEET VERMOUTH — A super-premium vermouth made at the Quady winery in Madera, California, from a blend of Orange Muscat, French Colombard and Valdepenas varietal wines infused with herbs, spices, flowers, and citrus. (16% abv) Refer to the product review on page 166.

WHALER'S HAWAIIAN RUMS — A line of Hawaiian rums distilled in Honolulu in continuous stills from locally grown sugar cane molasses. The Whaler's line includes Original Vanille (vanilla-infused), Great White (silver), Rare Reserve (dark añejo), Spiced and Killer Coconut (coconut-infused). 70 proof (35% abv) Refer to the product review on page 188.

WILD TURKEY 80° BOURBON WHISKEY — A Kentucky straight bourbon whiskey produced in Lawrenceburg, Kentucky, since 1855. 80 proof (40% abv)

WILD TURKEY 101° BOURBON WHISKEY — A straight bourbon whiskey produced in Lawrenceburg, Kentucky, distilled from sweet corn, rye and barley malt before being aged in heavily charred oak barrels. 101 proof (50.5% abv) Wild Turkey also produces Rare Breed, a bourbon bottled undiluted, unfiltered and at barrel-proof; Kentucky Spirit, a single barrel bourbon bottled unblended and at 101 proof; and Russell Reserve, a small batch, 101 proof bourbon aged for 10 years. Refer to the product review on page 238.

W.L. WELLER SPECIAL RESERVE BOURBON — A line of Kentucky straight bourbon whiskies made at the Buffalo Trace Distillery in Franklin County, Kentucky. This bourbon is one of only a few Kentucky whiskies distilled with a mash bill containing wheat instead of rye. It is aged 7 years and bottled at 90 proof. The W.L. Weller line also includes W.L. Weller Centennial, a 10-year-old bourbon; Old Weller Antique, a 107 proof bourbon aged 7 years; W.L. Weller 12-year-old Bourbon, (90 proof) and limited release W.L. Weller 19-year-old. Refer to the product review on page 268.

X.O. CAFÉ COFFEE LIQUEUR — A Mexican liqueur made with a base of premium tequila and flavored with coffee. 70 proof (35% abv)

YPIOCA CACHAÇA — An ultra-premium Brazilian cachaça distilled from cane sugar. 80 proof (40% abv)

YUKON JACK LIQUEUR — A Canadian liqueur made with herbs, orange peels and Canadian whisky, 100 proof (50% abv).

ZONE ITALIAN VODKA — A line of ultra-premium, Italian vodkas column-distilled entirely from locally grown wheat and infused with natural flavorings. The Zone family of vodkas includes the flavors of melon (cantaloupe), tangerine, lemon, and banana. 50 proof (25% abv) Refer to the product review on page 240.

ZUBRÓWKA BISON BRAND VODKA — A traditional Polish vodka made at the Polmos Poznan from potatoes triple-distilled in column stills and infused with the essential oils of buffalo grass. 82 proof (41% abv) Refer to the product review on page 144.

Product Review and Mixology Index

Find a Drink — Special Index

Introduction

BarMedia has created an easy to use, alphabetically listed set of the best recipes you will find anywhere on the planet. And we have created a special index for you to use when finding a recipe.

1. Every drink that has the drink type in its name is listed alphabetically by the main drink type listing.

Example: A *Horny Margarita* would be found by looking up *Margarita, Horny*. Go to the main body of recipes to the *m's* and find Margarita, Horny.

2. If you are looking for a specific brand or type of liquor used in a recipe, go to the liquor name or type. There, you will find all of the recipes made with this type of product.

Example: *Sauza Hornitos Tequila* would be found by looking up *Sauza Hornitos Tequila*. *Vodka* would be found by looking up *Vodka*. Listed under the heading will be all of the recipes using each product. Use the main list of alphabetical recipes to find the drink you are looking for.

3. If you are looking for a specific drink type, you will find it alphabetically listed by the main drink category.

Example: *Blended and Frozen* drinks will be found by looking up *Blended and Frozen*. Every blended and frozen drink listed in the book will be found under this heading. Every drink category within the book is listed in our special index.

Peruse, have fun, and find great drinks!

A

ABSOLUT CITRON VODKA
Absolut Samurai
Absolut Trouble
Ali-Tron
Blue Lemonade
Capers Cocktail
Cement Mixer
Citron Neon
Collins, Jeff
Cosmopolitan
Cosmopolitan, Alizé
Cosmopolitan, Dubonnet
Done & Bradstreet
Jolly Rancher (2)
Kamikaze, Citron
Mama Citron
Margarita, Kamikaze
Martini, Cajun King
Martini, Citrus
Martini, Dirty Citrus
Martini, Lemon Grove
Martini, Sapphire Sin
Pink Baby
Province Town
Recession Depression
Reggae Sunsplash
Ruby Red
Salty Dogitron
Take the 'A' Train
Tie Me to the Bed Post
Zuma Buma
ABSOLUT KURANT VODKA
Bank Shot
Kurant Affair
Mind Bender
Side Shot
Sweet Red Kiss

ABSOLUT MANDRIN VODKA
Absolut Mandrinade
Absolut Mandrin Mimosa
Martini, Absolut Mandrin
Martini, Passion
ABSOLUT PEPPAR VODKA
Blood Mary,
 Bloody Nose (2)
Fahrenheit 5000
Hasta la Vista, Baby
Louisiana Shooter
Margarita Picante
Martini, Blood Shot
Martini, Cajun (2)
Martini, Cajun King
Martini, Creole
Martini, Raving Rhino
Martini, Star's Jewel
ABSOLUT VODKA
Absolut Grand
Ball Joint
Dona & Bradstreet
Island Sunset
Jackie Special
Jolly Rancher (1)
Madonna's Brassiere
Martini, Black (2)
Martini, Black (3)
Province Town
Purple Hooter (2)
Rigor Mortis
Roxanne
Somosa Bay
Sunstroke
Take the 'A' Train
Watkin's Glen
Zipper Head

ALCOHOL-FREE RECIPES
A.S. Macpherson
Bloody Mary, Virgin
Bloody Mary,
 What? Me Worry
Blueberry Lemon Fizz
Cardinali
Cardinal Punch
Cartland Cure
Cinderella
Coco Mocha
Frosted Strawberry Tea
Georgia's Own
Himbeersaft
Jersey Lilly
Jogger
Kiddy Cocktail
Margarita, Virgin (1)
Margarita, Virgin (2)
Miami Vice (2)
Montego Bay (2)
Nicolas
Parson's Particular
Pom Pom
Princess Margaret
Raspberry Kiss
Rosy Pippin
Roy Rogers
San Francisco
Sangrita Mix
Shirley Temple
Sonoma Nouveau
Southern Belle
ALIZÉ DE FRANCE
Alizé Day
Alizé Dream Maker
Black Diamond
Desert Passion
Floating Heart
Margarita, Passion
Mariachi Loco
Martini, Caribbean

Martini, Fourth Degree
Martini, Tropical
Martini, Willy Nilly
Passionate Sunset
Passion Punch
Pineapple Smooch
Summer in the Park
Thug Passion
ALIZÉ RED PASSION
Ali-Tron
Alizé Cocktail
Ariana's Dream
Bellisimo
Culture Shock
Defroster (1)
Desert Passion
Floating Heart
Magic Potion
Manhattan,
 Tennessee Blush
Mint Julep, On the Mark
Passionate Fruit
Pink Moment
Saké Passion
Saké Passion Club
Sex in the Tropics
ALIZÉ V.S.O.P. COGNAC
Alizé Orchid Cocktail
Club Macanudo
French Mountie
Martini, Diamond
Passion Royalé
AMARETTO
See Disaronno Amaretto
ANGOSTURA CARIBBEAN RUM CREAM
Café Kingston
Julia
Monkey Juice
Shore Boat

APPLETON ESTATE V/X JAMAICA RUM
Appleton Blast
Artificial Intelligence
Bahama Mama (1)
Black Jamaican
Blue Marlin
Café Kingston
Caribbean Cruise (1)
Caribbean Gridlock
Chocolate Covered
    Banana (1)
City Tavern Cooler
Daiquiri, Calypso
Daiquiri, Mulatta
Dharama Rum
Drunken Monkey
Florida T-Back
Heat Wave
Hot Buttered Rum
Independence Swizzle
Jackalope
Jamaica Juice
Jamaica Me Crazy (1)
Jamaica Me Crazy (2)
Jamaican Barbados Bomber
Jamaican Coffee
Jamaican Crawler
Jamaican Fever
Jamaican Planter's Punch
Jamaican Rum Cow
Jamaican Shake
Jamaican Spice
Jamaican Tennis Beads
Jamba Juice
Kiss of the Islands
Mai Tai, Mobay
Mango Mingle
Margarita, Caribbean
Margarita, Jamaican
Margarita, Montego
Melon Moose
Mel's Chocolate
    Butterscotch Shake
Mel's Choc/PB/Nana Shake
Mobay Runner
Mocha Jamocha
Peter Prescription
Piña Colada, Kingston
Piña Colada, Monkalada
Piña Colada,
    Tropical Moon
Piña Colada,
    Tropical Splashes
Pink Paradise
Planter's Punch (2)
Planter's Punch (3)
Quarter Deck
Rancho Valencia
    Rum Punch
Rum Runner (1)
Shark Bite
Shore Boat
Smooth Screw
Tamara Lvova
Tiramisu (2)
Tour de Caribbean
Zombie (1)
Z Street Slammer

APPLETON SPECIAL JAMAICA RUM
Appleton Breeze
Jamaica Juice
Jamaican Fever
Jamaican Planter's Punch
Jamaican Rose
Jamaican Rum Cow
Montego Bay (1)

Piña Colada, Port Royal
Tighter Cider
Zombie, Pink

APRICOT BRANDY
Alizé Cocktail
Frappé, Apricot Brandy
Katinka
Periodista (1)
Periodista (2)
Pousse Café (2)

AQUAVIT
Bay Bridge Commuter (2)
Bay Bridge
    Commuter Shooter
Bloody Mary, Danish (1)
Bloody Mary, Danish (2)
Bloody Mary,
    Wharf Popper
Manhattan, Tivoli
Martini, Rosalind Russell

ARMAGNAC
Cesar Ritz
French Mandarine
Gentleman's Boilermaker
Velvet Swing

ARTIC MELON VODKA
Blue Bayou (1)
Bomb Pop
Cosmopolitan, Melon
Death of a Virgin

ARTIC PEACH VODKA
Blended Frog
Champagne Cornucopia
Comfortable Crush
Cosmopolitan, Artic Peach
Cosmopolitan, Chi Chi
Massappeal
Pink Moment
Son of a Peach

ARTIC STRAWBERRY VODKA
Alizé Dream Maker
Californian
Cartel Shooter
Ecstasy Shooter
Martini, Strawberry (1)

B

BACARDI 8 RESERVA RUM
Ancient Mariner (1)
Andalusia
Golden Dragon
Havana Sidecar (2)
Jacqueline
Larchmont (1)
Martini, Havana
Midnight Express (1)
Reserva Cocktail

BACARDI GOLD RUM
Acapulco Gold
Alpine Glow
Amaretto Cruise
Bacardi Tropico Dream
Badda-Bing
Banana Fruit Punch
Banana Milkshake
Big Bacardi Bamboo
Blast-Off Punch
Boina Roja
Café Reggae
Caribbean Berry
Caribe Surfsider
Cocomacoque
Cocomotion
Cork Street Coffee (1)
Daiquiri, Lechthaler's

Deathwish
Deep Sea Diver
Four Wise Men
Frappé, Mulatta
Frappé, Tricontinental
Goom Bay Smash (1)
Hawaiian Hurricane
Honey Rum Toddy
Hot Rum Cow
Hummer
Infusion, Brazilian Daiquiri
Italian Sunrise (1)
Kapalua Butterfly
Killer Whale
Lounge Lizard
Love Potion #9
Maraschino Rum Mist
Midway Manhattan
Mincemeat Mocha
Nácional
Otter Water
Piña Colada, Black Pearl
Piña Colada, Choco
Piña Colada, Chocolate
Piña Colada,
    Golden Bacardi
Piña Colada, Italian
Piña Colada, Kokomo Joe
Piña Colada, Stramaretto
Piña Colada,
    Toasted Almond
Purple Piranha
Riviera Nights
Rumscapes
Sassafras Sunset
Screaming Good Times
Slopped Disk
Strawberry Smash
Tequila Maria
Tidal Wave (1)
Trip to the Beach
Tropical Itch

BACARDI LIGHT RUM
Acapulco
A Day at the Beach
Adios Mother
Amangani
    Indian Paintbrush
American Graffiti
Apple Brandy Cooler
Apple Works
Ariana's Dream
Bacardi Cocktail
Bahama Mama (1)
Bahama Mama (2)
Beach Blonde
Beachcomber (2)
Blast-Off Punch
Blue Bayou (2)
Blue Hawaiian
Bog Fog
Boina Roja
Burgundy Bishop
Bushwacker
Caipirissma
Calypso Coffee
Caribbean Champagne
Caribbean Gridlock
Caribbean Romance
Caribe Surfsider
Cecil's Dream
Coconut Breeze
Creole
Daiquiri, Berry
Daiquiri, Charles
Daiquiri, Coconut
Daiquiri, de Piña
Daiquiri, Don Roland

Daiquiri, Florida
Daiquiri, La Floridita
Daiquiri, Lechthaler's
Daiquiri, Papa hemingway
Daiquiri, Passion
Dingo
Down Under Snowball
Ed Sullivan
Elixir of Love
El Presidenté Cocktail (2)
El Presidenté Cocktail (3)
.44 Magnum
Frappé, Banana Rum
Fruit Stripe
Funky Monkey
Gangbuster
Gang Green
Glass Tower
Gorilla Milk
Green Monster
Green Reef
Gulf Stream Scream
Halekulani Sunset
Hawaiian Hurricane
Iced Tea, Terminal
Infusion, Brazilian Daiquiri
Isleña
Jade
Jamaican Tennis Beads
Jealousy
Julia
Kamikaze, Radioactive
Lethal Injection
Lost Lovers
Martini, El Presidenté
Melon Moose
Midway Rat (1)
Midway Rat (2)
Neon Twister
New Orleans Jazz Time
Otter Water
Papa Dobles
Parple Thunder
Pilgrim
Pilgrim's Pride
Piña Colada, Amaretto
Piña Colada, Aussie
Piña Colada, Brazilian
Piña Colada,
    Golden Bacardi
Piña Colada, Kahlúa
Piña Colada, Kokomo Joe
Piña Colada,
    Tropical Moon
Pink Slipper
Planter's Punch (2)
Plymouth Rocks
Primal Shooter
Purple Piranha
Rancho Valencia
    Rum Punch
Raspberry Cream
R. F. & E.
Rhododendron
Rhumba Escapades
Riviera Days
Rum Alexander
Rum Runner (1)
Rusty Nickel
Sand Blaster
Santiago (2)
Shark Attack
Shark's Tooth
Shore Breeze
Sloppy Joe's Cocktail
South of France
Spats Columbo
Spilt Milk (1)

Straw House Hummer
Suffering Bastard
Thai Smile
Tokyo Scream
Zombie (2)

BACARDI LIMÓN RUM
Bellisimo
Bossa Nova
Catherine was Great
Cheesy Cheerleader
Cosmopolitan, Disaronno
Cosmopolitan, Limón
Daiquiri, Prickly Pear
Dark Waters
Electric Lemonade
Gauguin
Iced Tea, jesse's Shocking
Italian Punch
Knickerbocker
Knickerbocker
    Special Cocktail
laughing Bacardi Cow
Lemon Squeeze
Limón Fitzgerald
Limón Orange Breeze
Limón Runner
Martini, Caribbean
Martini, Emerald
New England
    Summer Spritzer
New Orleans Buck
N'Orleans Chiller
Nymphomaniac (1)
Passionate Screw
Piña Colada, Lemonada (1)
Piña Colada, Midori
Pink Lemonade (2)
Screaming Good Times
Sneak & Peak Cocktail
Starburst
Trip to the Beach
Tropical Hurricane
Tropico Tango
Twisted Lemonade
Zombie, Pink

BACARDI 151° RUM
Bahama Mama (2)
Big Bacardi Bamboo
Calypso Highway
Colombian Necktie
Firecracker
Gangbuster
Habana Libre
Jet Fuel (1)
Kamikaze, Radioactive
Pain in the Butt
Pazzo Grand
    Spanish Coffee
Piña Colada, Holiday Isle
Piranha Club Initiation
Purple Piranha
Razorback Hogcaller
Strawberry Smash
Vulcan Mind Probe
Wiki Waki Woo
Zombie (1)
Zombie, Pink

BACARDI SELECT RUM
Artificial Intelligence
Bat Bite
Betty Grable
Big Chill
Black Maria
Black Orchid
Bossa Nova
Bush Tickler
Café Foster
Calypso Highway

Cappa 21
Cappo de Tutti Cappi
Caribbean Cruise (2)
Daiquiri, Derby
Deep Sea Diver
Duke of Earl
Flaming Armadillo
Flamingo (2)
.44 Magnum
Gangbuster
Infusion, Brazilian Daiquiri
Ithmus Buffalo Milk
Jump Me
Lifesaver (1)
Love Potion #9
Pain in the Butt
Parple Thunder
Pilgrim's Pride
Piña Colada, Chocolate
Piña Colada, Stramaretto
Pineapple Fizz
Pink Creole
Pink Gator
Piranha Club Initiation
Planter's Punch (3)
Rain Man
R. F. & E.
Riviera Nights
Rum Runner (2)
San Andreas Fault
Santiago (1)
Shot Thru the Heart
Starburst
Sun Seeker
Sunrise
Swimming Naked at Sunset
Tour de Caribbean
Tour de Panama
Voodoo Shooter
Zombie (2)

BACARDI SPICED RUM
Bermuda Triangle (1)
Blackbeard's Treasure
Firecracker
Flamingo (1)
Gang Green
Jamba Juice
Lost Lovers
Lounge Lizard
Piña Colada, Choco
Slipped Disk
Tidal Wave (1)

BAFFERTS GIN
Bafferts Reviver
Eau de Gin
Fitzgerald Cocktail
London Gold
London Redhead
Looking for Trouble
Magic Potion
Martini, Amadora
Martini, Buckeye
Martini, Cajun (2)
Martini, Infused
Martini, London Dry
Martini, Marseilles

**BAILEYS ORIGINAL
IRISH CREAM LIQUEUR**
After Five
Aspen Coffee
Baby Grand Cocktail
Baileys Butterball
Baileys Comet
Baileys Express
Baileys Fizz
Baileys Malibu Rum Yum
Baileys Mint Kiss
Bam Be

Banana Sandwich
BBC
Beam Me Up, Scottie
Beautiful Thing
Belvedere Milk Chocolate
Berlin Wall
B-52
Bleacher's Twist
Bloody Brain
Blow Job (2)
Bobsledder's Banshee
Bottom Bouncer
Brain Shooter
Bukhara Coffee
Busted Rubber
Butterfinger
Butterscotch Slide
Café Chocolate (1)
Café Chocolate (2)
Canyon Quake (1)
Canyon Quake (2)
Car Bomb
Carmalita
Celtic Kiss
Cement Mixer
Cherry Bomb
Chicago Times
Chocolate Covered
    Banana (2)
Cork Street Coffee (2)
Cruzan Glide Slide
Cyrano
Dactyl Nightmare
Death by Chocolate
Debonair
Deep Throat
Designer Jeans
Dragoon
Duck Fart
Dusty Rose
Dying Nazi from Hell
Electrical Storm
Embolism
Emerald Isle
Erie Canal
E.T.
Eye to Eye
French Dream
Frozen Cappuccino
F-16
Fuzzy Mussy
G-Boy
German Chocolate Cake
Gingerbread Man
Gorilla Milk
Hot Irish Dream
Iacocca
Il Duce
International Affair
International Cappuccino
International Velvet Café
I.R.A.
Irish Car Bomb
Irish Chocolate Kiss
Irish-Choco-Orange
Irish Coffee Royale (2)
Irish Float
Irish Headlock
Irish Maria
Irish Raspberry
Jack Benny
Jane's Milk
Jelly Fish
Julio's Butterscotch
Jumper Cables
Jungle Milk
Koala Float
Koolo

Landslide
Left Bank
Liquid Gold
Madonna's Brassiere
Madtown Milkshake
Malibu Fizz
Martini,
    Elisa's Martini of Love
Martini, Irish
Mellow Dramatic
Mighty Kong
Milk of Amnesia
Millionaire's Coffee
Milwaukee River
Monsoon
Mr. Murphy
Mrs. Baileys' Bush
Mrs. Baileys' Favor
Mud Puddle
Mudslide (1)
Mudslide (2)
Navy Grog, Nor'easter
Neutron Bomb
Nun Out of Habit
Nut Cream Coffee
Nut 'n' Holli
Nut 'n' Honey
Nutty Irishman
Nutty Mexican
Oatmeal Cookie (1)
Oatmeal Cookie (2)
Opulent Coffee
Orgasm (1)
Orgasm (2)
Pot o' Gold
Pousse Café, Four-Way
Presidential Juice
Quaalude, Iranian
Quaalude, Irish
Quaalude, Russian
Rasta Man
Rose Petal
Russian' About
Russian Polar Bear
Scottish Tan
Screaming Orgasm
Seven Twenty-Seven (727)
Sex on the Beach
    on a Cloudy Day
Sexual Chocolate
Shot Thru the Heart
Sky High
Slippery Banana
Slippery Greek
Slippery Nipple
Sno-Cap
Sperm Bank
Spilt Milk (1)
Spilt Milk (2)
Stiff Dick
Strawberry Quickie
Sugar Baby
Sweet (Irish) Dreams
Tavern Sucker, The
Tender Mercies
Test-Tube Baby (1)
Test-Tube Baby (2)
38th Parallel
Tight Sweater
Tiramisu (2)
Trade Deficit
Watergate
Watermelon (2)
Whisky Gingerbread
White Russian, Premium
Winsome Way

BALLYLARKIN
IRISH LIQUEUR
Café Chopin
C-Note A-Float
Debonair
Hot Irish Dream
Let Us Alone
Manhattan, Vintage
Margarita, Emerald Isle
O'Brain Freeze
Pillowtalk
Teatime
B & B LIQUEUR
Baby Grand Cocktail
Bam Be
Banilla Boat
BBC
Beauty and the Beast
Beverly Hills Cooler
Brainstorm Cocktail
B-Sting
Buzz Bomb
Champs Elysees
   Cocktail (1)
Champs Elysees
   Cocktail (2)
Creamy Dreamy Isotope
De Gaulle's Dessert
Foreign Legion
French Consulate
Golden Dream
   with Double Bumpers
Gypsy
Hasta la Vista, Baby
Honeymoon
Le Bistro
Manhattan, Biscayne
Manhattan, Loretto
Manhattan, Preakness
Manhattan,
   Sheepshead Bay
Marquis
Martini, Bentley
Martini, Monastery
Martini, Rolls Royce
Merry Widow (1)
Midnight Lace
Monk's Coffee
Palace Guard
South of France
BEEFEATER
LONDON DRY GIN
After Hours Cocktail
Barbary Coast
Blue Duck
Cosmopolitan, London
Cream of Gin
Gimlet, Soho
Infusion, Beefeater
   Bloody Caesar
Infusion, Beefeater Deli
Margarita Britannia (2)
Martini, Blue Moon (2)
Martini, Copper Illusion
Martini, 008
Martini, Fourth Degree
Martini, Jaded
Martini, Lemoneater
Martini, San Francisco
Martini, Shagged
Morning Sun
Purple People Beefeater
Rin Tin Gin Tonic
Tropical Sensation
BEER
Baltimore Zoo
Beer Buster
Belgian Waffle

Bismark
Black and Brown
Black and Tan
Black Ape
Black Death
Black Velvet
Black Velveteen
Bloody Mary, Michilata
Boilermaker
Brown Drink
Brown Velvet
Bumble Bee
Car Bomb
Dead Eye Dick's Red Eye
Depth Charge
Dr. Pepper (2)
Dr. Pepper from Hell
Ginger Beer Shandy
Gold and Lager
Grandfather
Half & Half
Irish American
Irish Car Bomb
Koala Bear (2)
Lager and Black
Lager and Lime
Lemon Top
Michelada, Sauza
Midnight Oil
110 Degrees in the Shade
Pink Panther (1)
Purple Death
Rabid Dog
Red Beer
Reverend Craig
Rock 'n' Bock
Run, Skip and Go Naked
Sex in the Coal Region
Shandy Gaff
Skip and Go Naked
Snake Bite (2)
Torpedo Slam
BELVEDERE
POLISH VODKA
Blush
Caipiroshka
Doubt Raiser
Grapes of Wrath
Gumby
Kamikaze, Melon
Lemon Tart
Martini, Bel-Air
Martini, Belvedere Startini
Martini, Pear
Orange Delight
BLACKBERRY BRANDY
Black Hooter
Caribe Surfsider
Houndstooth
Jelly Bean
Pin in the Butt
Rum Runner (1)
Rum Runner (2)
Sex in the Coal Region
Steeplechase
Tequila Maria
Tequila Sunset
BLAVOD BLACK VODKA
Black & Blue Bayou
Black Beauty
Black Cat
Cosmopolitan, Black
Dark Water
Jungle Juice
Late-Nite Lemon Drop
Martini, Black Apple
Martini, Gotham
Martini, Midnight (1)

Nosferatu
Nosferatu's Shooter
Octopus Ink
Sex on a Black Sand Beach
BLENDED AND
FROZEN RECIPES
Alizé Day
Alizé Dream Maker
Amangani
   Indian Paintbrush
Amaretto Cruise
Ariana's Dream
Bacardi Tropico Dream
Bafferts Reviver
Balashi Breeze
Banana Fruit Punch
Banana Popsicle
Bananas Barbados
Berries Jubilee
Big Chill
Blackbeard's Treasure
Blizzard (1)
Blushing Berry Cooler
Borinquen
Bush Tickler
Bushwacker
Butterscotch Slide
Caribbean Berry
Caribbean Cruise (1)
Caribbean Gridlock
Caribe Surfsider
Cartland Cure
Catherine was Great
Cecil's Dream
Cheap Shades
Chi-Chi
Chiquita Punch
Chocolate Milk Cooler
Cinderella
Citron Neon
Coco Loco
Coco Mocha
Cocomotion
Crimson Rose
Culture Shock
Defroster (1)
Delicias de la Habana
Down Under Snowball
Ed Sullivan
El Conquistador
Frostbite
Frosted Peach Freeze
Frosted Strawberry Tea
Frozen Rose
Fruit Stripe
Gauguin
Georgia's Own
Golden Ram
Goom Bay Smash (1)
Goom Bay Smash (2)
Gorky Park Cooler (2)
Ithmus Buffalo Milk
Jamaica Juice
Jamaica Me Crazy (2)
Jamaican Planter's Punch
Jardinera
Kapalua Butterfly
Key Isla Morada
Koala Float
Lasting Passion
Latin Love
Latin Lover (2)
Lemon Parfait
Liam's Passion
Lost Lovers
Love Potion #9
Margarita, Cranberry (1)
Margarita, Cranberry (2)

Margarita de Fruta
Margarita, Hawaiian
Margarita, Honeydew this
Margarita, Mango
Margarita, Maui (1)
Margarita, Meltdown
Margarita,
   Midnight Madness
Margarita,
   Neon Watermelon
Margarita, Normandy
Margarita, Pear
Margarita, Pineapple
Margarita, Prickly Pear (1)
Margarita, Prickly Pear (2)
Margarita, Raspberry
Margarita, Raspberry Torte
Margarita, Red Cactus
Margarita,
   Strawberry Lover's
Margarita, Two-Toned
   Watermelon
Maui Breezer
Meadow Snow
Mediterranean Freeze
Meister-Bation
Mexican Runner
Miami Vice (1)
Morning Sun
Mother Mason's Delight
Mystic Runner
Navy Grog, Modern
Offenburg Flip
Orsini
Pain in the Butt
Papa Dobles
Pink Cadillac
Pink Slipper
Princess Margaret
Purple People Beefeater
Pusser's Pain Killer
Reggae Walker
Rhododendron
Rhum Barbancourt Freeze
Rock Lobster
Sea Side Liberty
Sex in the Woods
Sheilaberry
Sky High
Slipped Disk
Smooth Screw
Sneaky Peach
Socialite Prize Fight
South of France
South-of-the-Border
   Mango Mash
Starburst
Strawberries 'n' Cream
Strawberry Smash
Straw House Hummer
Strummer Hummer
Summer Tonic
Sweaty Betty
Sweet Tart (1)
Tequila Maria
Twisted Sister
Vanil Sensation
Whale's Tail
When Hell Freezes Over
Yellow Bird (2)
Zanzibar Dunes
BLOODY MARY RECIPES
   See Alphabetized Recipes
   Bloody Mary,
BLUE CURAÇAO
Adios Mother
Aqua Zest
Balashi Breeze

Beach Bum Blue
Big Blue Shooter
Black & Blue Bayou
Black 'n' Blue
Black Orchid
Blast-Off Punch
Blue Bayou (1)
Blue Bayou (2)
Blue Devil
Blue Duck
Blue Flute
Blue Hawaii
Blue Hawaiian
Blue Lady
Blue Lagoon (1)
Blue Lagoon (2)
Blue Lemonade
Blue Marlin
Blue Moon Café
Blue Tail Fly
Blue Wave
Blue Whale
Calypso Highway
Citron Neon
Cold Gold
Cool Mint Listerine
Crypto Nugget
Curaçao Cooler
Damrak Blue Lady
Delicias de la Habana
Desert Sunrise
Done & Bradstreet
Electric Jam
Eve's Apple
Flaming Blue Blaster
Gang Green
Gator Juice
Halekulani Sunset
Iced Tea, Alaskan
Iced Tea, Bimini
Iced Tea, Blue Kangaroo
Iced Tea, Dirty Ashtray
Infusion, Ice
   Blue Margarita
Infusion, Pineapple
   Purple Passion
Infusion, Sky Blue
Infusion, Summer
   Shades Margarita
Island Flower
Island Sunset
Jamaica Me Crazy (2)
Jealousy
Jewel
Kamikazi, Blue
Kamikazi, Radioactive
Kentucky Swamp Water
Kiss of the Islands
L.A.P.D.
Lemon Lavender
Leprechaun
Loch Lomond (2)
Manhattan,
   Blue Grass Blues
Margarita, Azul
Margarita, Blue
Margarita, Blue
   Maestro Gran
Margarita, Blue Moon
Margarita, Catalina
Margarita, Hawaiian
Margarita, Luna Azul
Margarita, Mad Russian
Margarita,
   Midnight Madness
Margarita, Purple (1)
Margarita, Teal
Margo Moore

Martini, Blue Moon (1)
Martini, Blue Moon (2)
Martini, Blue Pacific
Martini Blues
Martini, Blue Shock
Martini, Sakétini
Miami Vice (1)
Milwaukee River
Monster Appeaser
Octopus Ink
Piña Colada, Emerald Isle
Piña Colada,
   Tropical Moon
Piranha Club Initiation
Pousse Café (3)
Purple Flirt
Purple Piranha
Rhum Barbancourt Freeze
Ritz Fizz
St. Patrick's Day
Sea Water
Shark Attack
Shark's Tooth
Smurf Piss
Soyer-au-Champagne
Spanish Fly
Stars & Stripes
Stealth Bomber (1)
Summer Lemonade
Surf Sider (1)
Swamp Water Stinger
Tequila Mockingbird (2)
Thai Smile
Tidy Bowl
Wall Street Wizard
Wanderer
Whale's Tail
Windex

BOMBAY SAPPHIRE
LONDON DRY GIN
Aviation Cocktail
Blue Lady
Bombay Grand
Bombay Spider
Gimlet, Sapphire
Gin & Sin
Gran Bombay
London Lemonade
Martini, Alexander Nevsky
Martini, Blue Moon (1)
Martini, Dragon's Breath
Martini, Paisley
Martini, Princeton
Martini, Rolls Royce
Martini, Sakétini
Martini, Sapphire Sin
Martini, Star's Jewel
Martini, Yellow Rattler
Negroni, uptown
Old Flame
Sidecar in Bombay
Vanil Sensation

BOURBON WHISKEY
Boilermaker
City Tavern Cooler
Collins, John
Depth Charge
Frappé, Lagniappe
French 95
Highball
Horse's Neck with a Kick
Hot Toddy
Iced Tea, Manhattan
Mamie's Southern Sister
   Manhattan
Manhattan, Dry
Manhattan, Perfect
Mint Julep

Old Fashion
Old Fashion, Muddled
Ward Eight
BRANDY
Aching Bach
Apple Brandy Cooler
Basin Street Balm
B & B
Benson Bomber
Betsy Ross
Between the Sheets
Blizzard (2)
Bosom Caresser
Brandy Alexander
Brandy Egg Nog (2)
Brandy Gump
Café Correcto
Canyon Quake (2)
Cappa 21
Cappo de Tutti Cappi
Cherry Blossom
Chicago
Chocolate Squirrel
Classic Vette
Corpse Reviver (2)
Creamy Dreamy Isotope
Diablo
Dire Straits
Dirty Mother
East India
Fogcutter
Fogcutter, Royal Navy
Forever Amber
Frappé, Apricot Brandy
French Consulate
French Maid's Café
Freudian Slip
Golden Dream
   with Double Bumpers
Grand Sidecar
Great Lakes Trapper
Green Hornet
Harvard
Heartbreak
Hemingway's
   Flambé Coffee
Hot Toddy
Imperial Sidecar
Inoculation
Irish Headlock
Italian Stinger
Jamaican Fever
Japanese Cocktail
Keoki Coffee
Keoki Shooter
Le Bistro
Let Us Alone
Manhattan,
   Blood and Sand
Manhattan, Brandy
Manhattan, Dry Brandy
Manhattan, Perfect Brandy
Margarita, Mezcal
Margo Moore
Maui Breezer
Maxim's a Londres
Ménage à Trois
Mexican Cocoa
Midori Stinger
Montmarte
Mother
Navy Grog, Original
Persuader
Port in a Storm
Pousse Café (1)
Pousse Café (2)
Pousse Café (3)
Prairie Oyster (1)

Run, Skip and Go Naked
Scorpion
Separator (1)
Separator (2)
Siberian
Sidecar (2)
Soyer-au-Champagne
Stinger
Strawberry Alexandra
38th Parallel
Thumper
Tip-Top Punch
Tom & Jerry
Trade Winds
Vanderbilt Cocktail
Whip
Whisper (2)

BRILLIANT VODKA
Alabama Slammer (3)
Brilliant Sonic
Crystal Clear
Iceberg (2)
Kamikaze, Apple
Madame Butterfly
Martini, Amber Skies
Martini, Diamond
Martini, 008
Martini, Rosalind Russell
Martini, Starlight
Martini, Topaz

BRIOTTET CRÈME
DE CASSIS DE DIJON
Blush
Bull and Bear
Chimayo Cocktail
Daiquiri, French (1)
El Cajon Sunrise
El Diablo
Italian Sunrise (2)
Kir
Kir Royale
Knickerbocker
   Knee Knocker
Lillet Champagne Royale
Manhattan, Dijon
Manhattan, Rose
Martini, Black (2)
Martini, Brazen
Martini, Gotham
Moulin Rouge
Naked Pretzel
Piña Colada, French
Reggae Sunsplash
Sangria, New World Punch
Summer Tonic
Tickle Me
Vermouth Cassis

BUTTERSCOTCH
SCHNAPPS
See DeKuyper Butershots

CAMPARI APERITIVO
Americano
Americano Highball
Campari Soda
DC-3 Shooter
Lena Cocktail
Manhattan, Tivoli
Martini, Becco
Martini, Black Tie (2)
Martini, Blood Orange
Martini, Blood Shot
Martini, Copper Illusion
Martini, Fantino
Martini, Romana

Martini, Rosebud
Negroni
Negroni, Uptown
Old Flame
Venetian Sunset
CANADIAN CLUB WHISKY
Club Sherry
Doctor's Orders
Dog Sled
Empire State Slammer
Heartbreak
Infusion, Lumberjack
King Midas
Midori Canuck
Mother Lode
Saké Passion
Saké Passion Club
Smiles for Miles
Sour, Sparkling
   Sweet Apple
Spilt Milk (1)
Sunknee Delite
CANADIAN WHISKY
Canadian
Canadian Stone Fence
Manhattan, Maple Leaf
Manhattan, Mets
Manhattan, Park Paradise
Manhattan, Quebec
Manhattan, Roman
Toronto
**CAPPUCCINO AND
ESPRESSO RECIPES**
Apple Grand Marnier
Baileys Express
Blast from the Past
Café Correcto
Cappa 21
Cappo de Tutti Cappi
Emerald Isle
Foreign Legion
Gran Cappuccino
Hot Chambord Dream
Iacocca
Il Duce
International Cappuccino
International Velvet Café
Le Bistro
Louvre Me Alone
Martini, Espresso
Mrs. Baileys' Favor
Philippi Creek
River Seine Cappuccino
Sovereignty
**CAPTAIN MORGAN
SPICED RUM**
Big Blue Shooter
Captain's Coffee (2)
Captain's Cooler
Cool Captain
Gorky Park Cooler (2)
Jamaican Spice
Knicker Knocker
Leaning Tower
Margarita, Captain
Nymphomaniac (2)
Pink Passion
R. F. & E.
Suntan Teaser
Tidal Wave (3)
Wanna Probe Ya
**CASA NOBLE
GOLD TEQUILA**
Margarita, Champagne
Reconsider
Saké-Rama
Take the Prize

**CASA NOBLE
REPOSADO TEQUILA**
Lickety-Split
Margarita, Luna Azul
Margarita, My Baby Grand
Noble Holiday
Rodéo Driver
Sicilian Sunrise
Tequilier Real
CASCADE MOUNTAIN GIN
All American Whistler
Collins, Beverly
Gimlet, Cher's
Gulf Breeze
Kamikazi,
   Cascade Mountain
Lockhart Zoo
Martini, All American (1)
Martini, All American (2)
Martini, Bootlegger
Martini, Boston
Martini, Bubblegum
Meadows Snow
Mountain Retreat
Presumption Cocktail
Sax with Bill
**CELTIC CROSSING
IRISH LIQUEUR**
Castle Coffee
Celtic Kiss
Chopin's River
Emerald Isle
Erie Canal
Irish Boggle
Limerick
Manhattan,
   Spice Apple Brandy
Martini, Celtic
Martini, Irish
Spirit of Erie Coffee
Sweet (Irish) Dreams
**CHAMBORD
LIQUEUR DE FRANCE**
Abbey Road
Absolut Mandrinade
Alizé Dream Maker
Alizé Orchid Cocktail
Aviation Cocktail
Banilla Boat
Bank Shot
Beachcomber (1)
Bellinisimo
Berries Jubilee
Betty Grable
Big Bacardi Bamboo
Bikini Line
Black and White
Blackbeard's Treasure
Black Hooter
Black Stockings
Blast from the Past
Bleacher's Twist
Brut 'n' Bogs
Burgundy Cocktail
Burnt Sienna
Café Contenté
Caribbean Sunset
Caribe Sunset
Cartel Shooter
C.C. Rider
Chambord Dream
Chambord Repose
Champagne Framboise
Cherrillo
Cocaine Shooter (1)
Cocaine Shooter (2)
Colorado Avalanche
Comfortable Crush

Crab House Shooter
Cranberry Squeeze
Cyrano
Daiquiri, Berry
Daiquiri, Rhum
De Gaulle Cocktail
Doctor's Elixir
Doubt Raiser
Dream Catcher
Dry Arroyo
Dusty Rose
East River
Ecstasy Shooter
E Pluribus Unum
Express Mail Drop
Fat Cat Fizz
Federal Express
Five Dollar Margaret
Framboise Kiss
French Dream
French Toast Royale
Fruity Tutti
Fun in the Sun
Gimlet, Raspberry
Glasnost
Guava Martinique
Harvest Grog
Heather Blush
Holland's Opus
Hollywood
Holy Hand Grenade
Hot Chambord Dream
Hot Irish Dream
Iced Tea, Jesse's Shocking
Iced Tea, Raspberry
Imperial Duo
Irish Raspberry
Jar Juice
Jewel of Russia
Kamikazi, Purple (1)
Kamikazi, Purple (2)
Kamikazi, Raspberry
Knickerbocker
   Special Cocktail
Latin Lover (2)
Left Bank
Lobotomy
Lookout Point
Lost Lovers
Madtown Milkshake
Mandarine Dream
Manhattan,
   Blood and Sand
Manhattan, Poor Tim
Manhattan, Raspberry
Margarita, Black Gold
Margarita, El Conquistador
Margarita, Meltdown
Margarita,
   Midnight Madness
Margarita, Purple (1)
Margarita, Red Cactus
Margarita, Santa Rita
Margarita, Tres Compadres
Margarita, Two-Toned
Margarita, Zinful
Maritime Sunrise
Martini, Alexander Nevsky
Martini, Black (1)
Martini, Bubblegum
Martini, Crème Brûlée (3)
Martini, French (2)
Martini, Harper's
Martini, Imperial
Martini, Medici
Martini, Metropolis
Martini, Midnight (2)
Martini, Nitelife

Martini, Passion
Martini, Poinsettia
Martini, Tartini (2)
Martini, Ty-Won-On
Mellow Dramatic
Mexican Melon
Mikhail Cocktail
Mind Bender
Miss Ube Darn
Orange Cranberry Toddy
Otter Water
Pain in the Butt
Paris Burning
Passionate Screw
Peter Prescription
Piña Colada,
   Hawaiian Lion
Piña Colada, Port Royal
Pink Cadillac
Pink Coconut
Pink Creole
Pink Slipper
Pope on Vacation
Primo Bacio
Purple Death
Purple Hooter (1)
Purple Hooter (2)
Purple Matador
Raspberry Banana Split
Raspberry Cream
Raspberry Sour
Raspberry Sweet Tart
Raspberry Torte
Raztini
Red Eclipse
Rendezvous Punch
Restoration
Riviera Days
Riviera Nights
Royal Bay Breeze
Royal Flush
Rue de la Paix
Rumscapes
Saint Moritz
Sandy Beach Bay
Say Hey Marseilles
1701 Fog
Sex on a Black Sand Beach
Sex on the Beach (1)
Sex on the Beach (2)
Sex on the Beach (3)
Sex on the Beach (4)
Sex on the Beach (5)
Sex with an Alligator (1)
Sneak & Peak Cocktail
Somosa Bay
Sovereignty
Storm-a-Long Bay
Strawberry Smash
Summer Hummer
Sweet Red Kiss
Sweet Tart (2)
Sweet Tart (3)
Take the Prize
Texas Tea
38th Parallel
Tinted Glass
Tour de France
Trade Winds
Twilight Moan Zone
Vampire
V.I.P. Coffee
Wanderer
Watkin's Glen
Wet Dream
Zipper Head
Zuma Buma

CHAMPAGNE RECIPES

Absolut Mandrin Mimosa
Ambrosia (1)
Ambrosia (2)
April in Paris
Ball Bearing
Banalini
Bellini
Bellisimo
Betelgeuse
Beverly Hills Cooler
Bismark
Black Velvet
Blood Orange
   Champagne Cocktail
Blue Flute
BLue Train Special
Blushing Angel
Bogs & Bubbles
Brut 'n' Bogs
Bubble Zaza
Buzz Bomb
Cajun Mimosa
Caribbean Champagne
Caribbean Contessa
C.C. Rider
Celestial Fizz
Cesar Ritz
Champagne Cocktail
Champagne Cornucopia
Champagne Framboise
Champagne Imperial
Champagne Jubilee
Champagne Marseille
Champagne Normande
Champs Elysees cocktail (2)
Cherry Amore
Chicago
Code Red
Cognac Ritz
Concorde
Damrak 75 (1)
De Gaulle Cocktail
Doubt Raiser
Down Under
Dream Catcher
Dry Arroyo
Du Monde
East River
Ed Sullivan
Eiffel Tower
Estes Fizz
Express Mail Drop
Fedora Express
Floating Heart
French Consulate
French 95
French 75 (1)
French 75 (2)
Freudian Slip
Glenda
Gran Bliss
Grand Alliance
Griffin, The
Heather Blush
Hemingway
Honeydew
Ice Cream Bellini
Imperial Fuzz
Jewel of Russia
Kir Royale
Lillet Champagne Royale
Lobotomy
Margarita, Champagne
Margarita, Mimosa
Maxim's a Londres
Metro Cocktail
Mikhail Cocktail

Mimosa
Montmarte
Nelson's Blood (3)
New Orleans Jazz Time
Ocho Rios
Pacific Rim
Passion Royalé
Pink Cadillac
Pink Panther (2)
Pizzetti
Poire-Suisse
Primo Bacio
Puccini
Ritz Americana
Ritz Fizz
Ritz Pick-Me-Up
Room Service at the Ritz
Ruddy Mimosa
Rue de la Paix
Russian Nights
Sandy Beach Bay
Santiago (1)
Savoy Champagne Cocktail
Soyer-au-Champagne
Sputnik
Summer in the Park
Thug Passion
Tip-Top Punch
Tiziano
Tour de France
Tramonto Sul Garda
Tryst & Shout
Tuscany Champagne
Velvet Swing
What's Your Honey Dew?
White's Club
Xanadu

CHARTREUSE, GREEN

C. & C.
Green Lizard
Manhattan, St. Moritz
Martini Thyme
Pousse Café (2)
Pousse Café (3)
Razorback Hogcaller
Swamp Water

CHARTREUSE, YELLOW

Alaska
Frappé, Parisian
Pousse Café (2)

CHERRY BRANDY

Blood and Sand (1)
Blood and Sand (2)
Cherry Bean
Cherry Blossom
Singapore Sling (1)
Singapore Sling (2)
Vanderbilt Cocktail

CHOPIN POLISH VODKA

Black Stockings
Café Chopin
Chocolate Almond Kiss
Chopin's River
Cookie
Knickerbocker
   Knee Knocker
Martini, Nutcracker
Sonoma Chiller
Vanilla Spice Ice
Vodka Grand

CHRISTIAN
BROTHERS BRANDY

Alpine Glow
Aunt Bea's Cure-All
   Hot Milk Punch
Barcelona Coffee
Blue Train Special
Brandy Egg Nog (1)

Canyon Quake (1)
Carte Blanche
Champs Elysees
   Cocktail (1)
Cherry Amore
Chocolate Milk Cooler
Dangerous Liaisons
Fedora
Foreign Legion
Heavenly Toddy
Iced Tea, Havana
Randy Brandy Egg Nog
Restoration
Sacrifice Fly

CINNAMON SCHNAPPS

See DeKuyper Hot Damn!

COCKSPUR V.S.O.R. RUM

Apple Brandy Cooler
Banana Fruit Punch
Beach Blonde
Caribbean Cruise (1)
Cocomacoque
Fruit Stripe
Otter Water
Santiago (2)
Smooth Screw
Wynbreezer

COCKTAIL AND
STRAIGHT-UP RECIPES

Absolut Grand
Absolut Trouble
Adam's Apple
After Hours Cocktail
Alaska
Ali-Tron
Alizé Cocktail
Alizé Orchid Cocktail
Appendectomy
Appendicitis
Appetizer
Apple a Go-Gogh
Apple Cart
Apple Tinker
Autumn Sidecar
Aviation Cocktail
Bacardi Cocktail
Balalaika
Ball Joint
Banana Monkey
Banana Nuts
Banana Stigma
Barbary Coast
Basin Street Balm
Bearing Strait
Bee's Knees
Belvedere Milk Chocolate
Bermuda Triangle (3)
Betsy Ross
Bettor's Dream
Bible Belt (1)
Bible Belt (2)
Black Diamond
Black 'n' Blue
Black Stockings
Blood and Sand (2)
Blue Devil
Blue Lady
Blue Marlin
Blush
Bobby Burns
Bombay Grand
Bosom Caresser
Brainstorm Cocktail
Brandy Gump
Brass Monkey
Brazil
Brilliant Lemon Drop
Brooklyn

B-Sting
Bull and Bear
Byrrh Cocktail
Cadenhead's Knight
Café Chopin
Canadian
Caribbean Cruise (3)
Castle in the Clouds
Cayman Cocktail
Champs Elysees
   Cocktail (1)
Cherry Blossom
Cillo Amore
Cillo Blanco
Classic Vette
Clover Club
Club Macanudo
C-Note A-Float
Coconut Coffee Pot
Commodore
Corpse Reviver (1)
Corpse Reviver (2)
Cosmopolitan, Chi Chi
Cuban Cocktail
Cuban Peach
Cuban Sidecar
Cuban Special
Dale's Sour Apple
Damrak Blue Lady
Dangerous Liaisons
Deauville
Debutante
Dewar's Tango
Desert Passion
Diablo
Diki-Diki
Diplomatic Immunity
Doctor's Advice
Dollar Bill
Done & Bradstreet
Dubonnet Cocktail
East India
Eau de Gin
El Presidenté Cocktail (1)
El Presidenté Cocktail (2)
El Presidenté Cocktail (3)
Eve's Peach
Fatmancillo
Fedora
Finlandia Lime Light
Fitzgerald Cocktail
Fortress of Singapore
French Mountie
Fu Manchu
Fuzzy Wuzzie
Gin and It
Gin & Sin
Gloomraiser
Gold Rush (1)
Gold Rush (3)
Goose Down
Gran Bombay
Grand Marshall Sour
Grand Orange Blossom
Grand Sidecar
Grapes of Wrath
Gypsy
Habanos Havana
Half & Half (1)
Harvard
Havana
Havana Club
Havana Cocktail
Havana Sidecar (1)
Havana Sidecar (2)
Heavyweight Sailor
Highland Cocktail
Holland's Opus

Honey Bee
Honeymoon
Hot Honey Pot
Hot Tropico Mama
Hourglass
Hunker Punker
Ideal Cocktail
Imperial Duo
Imperial Sidecar
Irish Chocolate Kiss
Irish-Choco-Orange
Irish Dish
Irish Shillelagh
Irish Wish
Island Ditty
Island Dream
Island Fever
Island Flower
Jackarita
Jack Rose Cocktail
Jacqueline
Jade
Jameson Cannes-Style
Japanese Cocktail
Jersey Devil
Jewels and Gold
John Wayne
Joke Juice
Jumby Bay Punch
Kamikaze, Italian
Katinka
Kentucky Shuffle
Key Lime Cooler
Killer Koolaid
Klondike
Knickerbocker
    Special Cocktail
Knockout
Larchmont (1)
Larchmont (2)
Larchmont (3)
Late-Nite Lemon Drop
Lemon Drop (1)
Lemon Drop (3)
Lemon Heaven
Lemon Lavender
Lena Cocktail
Let Us Alone
Limón Fitzgerald
Loch Lomond (1)
London Gold
London Lemonade
London Redhead
Lookout Point
Lover's Lane
Madame Butterfly
Madame Mandarine
Made in the Shade
Maiden's Prayer
Massappeal
Maui Wowie
Meadowlark Lemon
Mellonaire
Merry Window (1)
Midnight Express (1)
Midnight Express (2)
Midnight Express (3)
Midnight Orchid
Midorable
Millionaire Cocktail
Monkey Gland
Mountain Retreat
Mount Gay Café
Mud Puddle
Nácional
Native Sun
Negroni
Negroni, Uptown

Noble Nymph
Nosferatu
Nuts & Berries
Octopus Ink
Old Flame
Opera Cocktail
Orange Blossom (1)
Orange Delight
Orange Dream
Orange-U-Glad-2-C-Me
Original Monk
Paddy
Palace Guard
Peach Cobbler
Perfect 10
Periodista (1)
Periodista (2)
Pineapple Fizz
Pineapple Smooch
Pink Baby
Pink Creole
Pink Gin
Pink Lady (2)
Pink Moment
Pisco Sour
Poireisse
Presidenté
Presumption Cocktail
Purple Hooter (1)
Putting on the Ritz
Rainbow
    International Cocktail
Razzle Dazzle Rose
Recession Depression
Red Lion
Reserva Cocktail
Rio Rita
Rolls Royce
Royal Bay Breeze
Russian' About
Sail of the Century
St. Patrick's Day
Saké Passion
Sauza Threesome
Savannah
Sax with Bill
Scurvey Abator
Seattle's 6.3
Sea Water
1701 Fog
Sex with an Alligator (1)
Sex with an Alligator (2)
Sherry's Blossom
Sidecar (1)
Sidecar (2)
Sidecar in Bombay
Sidecar, Irish
Sidecar Royale
Simply Crimson
Sin in Hawaii
Sloppy Joe's Cocktail
Sneak & Peak Cocktail
Sour
Sour Mint
Splendid Gin
Starlight
Stone Sour
Summer Hummer
Summer Memories
Sunburnt Señorita
Sunday Brunch
    Punch Cocktail
Sunflower
Sunglow
Sunstroke
Surf Sider (1)
Sweet Red Kiss
Taj Majal

Tangerine Drop
Tequila Mockingbird (1)
Tikki Dream
Tinted Glass
Toronto
Tovarich
Trinity
Twilight Moan Zone
Ulterior Motive
Upside Down Irish Crown
Uptown
Vanderbilt Cocktail
Van Good
Venetian Sunset
Vermouth Cassis
Vincent's Baubles
Vodka Grand
Wall Street Wizard
Ward Eight
Whip
White Cloud
White Out
Yale Cocktail
Yellow Snow
COCOA RECIPES
Cabin Fever Cure
Canadian Foot Warmer
Carte Blanche
Chicago Times
Colorado Avalanche
French Kiss
Great Lakes Trapper
Jungle Milk
Mad Hatter
Mexican Cocoa
Pusser's Stalemate
Sacrifice Fly
COFFEE RECIPES
Abbey Road
Ambush
Aspen Coffee
Baileys Mint Kiss
Barcelona Coffee
Bay Area Garter
Black Jack
Black Maria
Black Ruby
Café a la Cabana
Café Amore
Café Brûlot
Café Charles
Café Chocolate (1)
Café Chocolate (2)
Café Contenté
Café Diablo
Café Dublin
Café Foster
Café Kingston
Café Reggae
Café Royale
Café St. Armands
Calypso Coffee
Capo di Sopranos
Captain's Coffee (1)
Captain's Coffee (2)
Caribbean Dream
Castle Coffee
Chambord Repose
Chicago Times
Chill-out Café
Ciao Bello
Coco Mocha
Cork Street Coffee (1)
Cork Street Coffee (2)
Duke of Earl
Dutch Coffee
Electrode Overload
French Maid's Café

Fuzzy Dick
Fuzzy Mussy
Greek Coffee
Hemingway's
    Flambé Coffee
Hot Irish Dream
Hunter's Coffee
International Affair
Irish Boggle
Irish Coffee
Irish Coffee Royale (1)
Irish Coffee Royale (2)
Italian Coffee
Jamaican Coffee
Jumper Cables
Keoki Coffee
Keoki Shooter
Leave Us Alone
Lemon Nog
Mexican Coffee
Mexican Monk
Midnight Lace
Millionaire's Coffee
Mincemeat Mocha
Mocha Jamocha
Monk's Coffee
Monte Cristo Shooter
Montego Bay (1)
Navy Grog, Nor'easter
Nina's Coffee
Northern Lights (1)
Nut Cream Coffee
Opulent Coffee
Pazzo Grand
    Spanish Coffee
Peter Prescription
Royal Street Coffee
San Andreas Fault
Say Hey Marseilles
Scotch Coffee
Shore Boat
Spirit of Erie Coffee
Tender Mercies
Tennessee Mud
38th Parallel
Tight Sweater
Toasted Almond Café
Toboggan Truffle
Trade Deficit
Trophy Room
Tropical Depression
V.I.P. Coffee
COGNAC
Amber Cloud
Andalusia
Apple Grand Marnier
Burgundy Cocktail
Buzz Bomb
Café Amore
Café Diablo
Café Royale
C. & C.
Celestial Fizz
Collins, Pierre
Corpse Reviver (1)
De Gaulle Cocktail
Frappé, Parisian
French Connection
French 75 (2)
Gran Cappuccino
Louvre Me Alone
Paris Burning
Philippi Creek
Piña Colada, French
Ritz Pick-Me-Up
River Seine Cappuccino
Savoy Champagne Cocktail
Sidecar (1)

CRÈME DE CACAO, DARK
After Tan (1)
Alexander the Great
Almond Joy
Angel's Kiss
Benson Bomber
Black Beauty
Black Maria
Brandy Alexander
Brandy Egg Nog (2)
Brown Squirrel
Bush Tickler
Café Chocolate (1)
Café Chocolate (2)
Café Gates
Café Reggae
Café St. Armands
Caribe Sunset
Chambord Dream
Chambord Repose
Chill-Out Café
Chocolate Almond Kiss
Chocolate Squirrel
Coffee Nutcake
Colorado Avalanche
Cookies 'n' Cream
Daiquiri, Mulatta
Dharama Rum
Dirty Banana
Frappé, Mulatta
Frappé, Tricontinental
Frosted Coke
Frozen Monk
Hot Chambord Dream
Hummer
Irish Alexander (2)
Jackalope
Keoki Coffee
Keoki Shooter
King Alfonse
Koala Bear (1)
Martini, Topaz
Mexican Monk
Mocha Jamocha
Mother Mason's Delight
Ninja
Orange Frappé
Pusser's Stalemate
Quaalude
Quaalude, Irish
Sexual Chocolate
Shark's Tooth
Silver Cloud
Tamara Lvova
Tennessee Tea
38th Parallel
3D-Elixir
Tootsie Roll
Whisper (2)
Widow Wood's Nightcap

CRÈME DE CACAO, WHITE
After Tan (2)
Ariana's Dream
Bananas Over You
Banana Split
Banshee
Barbary Coast
Blue Hawaii
Blue Tail Fly
Bukhara Coffee
Caribbean Dream
Cecil's Dream
Cillo Blanco
Corpse Reviver (2)
Cream of Gin
Doctor's Advice
Elixir of Love
Fire and Ice (1)

Frappé, Mocha
French Crush
Gin Alexander
Golden Cadillac
Grasshopper
Green Reef
Houndstooth
Irish Alexander (1)
Irish Chocolate Kiss
Jelly Fish
Martini, Palm Island
Mellow Dramatic
Mexican Grasshopper
Nuts to You
Passion Alexander
Peppermint Pattie
Pink Squirrel
Quaalude, Alaskan
Raspberry Cream
Rum Alexander
Savannah
Scotch Bounty
Silver Bullet
Snake Bite (3)
Sovereignty
Sperm Bank
Strawberry Alexandra
Strawberry Rose
Tiramisu (2)
Velvet Hammer
White Heart

CRÈME DE MENTHE, GREEN
After Eight
Carte Blanche
C-Note A-Float
Daiquiri, Don Roland
Emerald Ice
Grasshopper
Green Hornet
Green Mint Float
Green Spider
Highland Golfer
Irish Chocolate Kiss
Jade
Manhattan, Shamrock
Mexican Flag
Mexican Grasshopper
Mint Freeze
Mint Julep, Pineapple
Nina's Coffee
Pistachio Mint Ice Cream
Pousse Café (1)
Shillelagh
Tarnished Bullet
Tequila Mockingbird (1)
Traffic Light (1)
Yabba-Dabba-Doo

CRÈME DE MENTHE, WHITE
Banana Split
Carte Blanche
Cream of Gin
Debutante
Frappé, Mocha
Fu Manchu
Galliano Stinger
Goal Post
Great Lakes Trapper
Kahlúa Mint
Knockout
Martini, Bitchin'
Martini, Godiva Mint
Martini, Iceberg
Midori Stinger
Pousse Café (2)
Pousse Café (3)
Pousse Café Four-Way

Pousse Café, Tuaca
Rainbow Shooter (1)
Silver Spider
Smoothy
Stinger
Toreador
Trinity
White Cloud
White Minnesota
White Spider
White Way

CRÈME DE NOYAUX
'57 Chevy
Frappé, Apricot Brandy
Hasta la Vista, Baby
Hawaiian Punch (2)
Hawaiian Shooter
Killer Koolaid
Lethal Injection
Mai-Tai (1)
Pink Squirrel
Rainbow Shooter (1)
Rainbow Shooter (2)
Rhododendron
Scorpion
Spilt Milk (1)
Suffering Bastard
Traffic Light (2)
Wild Orchid
Xaviera
Zombie (1)

CRISTALL LEMON TWIST RUSSIAN VODKA
Cosmopolitan, Cristall Lemon Twist
Lemon Heights
Lemon Lavender

CROWN ROYAL CANADIAN WHISKY
Duck Fart
Koolo
Manhattan, Moon Over Manhattan
Martini, Blue Shock
Monster Appeaser
Royal Canadian
Royal Flush
Spilt Milk (2)
Washington Apple

CRUZAN BANANA RUM
Banalini
Banana Bay
Banana Cow
Banana Nuts
Banana Popsicle
Banana Stigma
Big Bamboo, The
Calypso Highway
Chocolate Banana (2)
Chocolate Covered Banana (1)
Culture Shock
Daiquiri, Banana
Diplomatic Immunity
Funky Monkey
Ithmus Buffalo Milk
Jamaican Ten Speed
Jane's Milk
Kiwi
Latin Love
Latin Lover (2)
Margarita, Camino Real
Margarita, Conga
Martini, Fidel's
Mellonaire
Mexican Runner
Mighty Kong
Monkey Bite

Montego Bay (1)
Mystic Runner
Ocho Rios
Offenburg Flip
Piña Colada, Lt. Kije's
Piña Colada, Monkalada
Piña Colada, Strawberry Banana
Pink Highliter
San Andreas Fault
Strummer Hummer
Suntan Teaser
Tropical Itch
Voodoo Juice
White Sands Cooler

CRUZAN COCONUT RUM
A Day at the Beach
After Tan
Artificial Intelligence
Bahama Mama (2)
Big Chill
Blue Lagoon (1)
Coconut Breeze
Coconut Coffee Pot
Come-on-I-Wanna-Lei-Ya
Cosmopolitan, Chi Chi
Cruzan Glide Slide
Culture Shock
Daiquiri, Coconut
Drunken Monkey
Florida T-Back
Funky Monkey
Goom Bay Smash (2)
Gorky Park Cooler (1)
Gorky Park Cooler (2)
Jumper Cables
Kamikaze, Kokonut (1)
Key Isla Morada
Key Largo
Latin Love
Lethal Injection
Maui Wowie
Mobay Runner
Mystic Runner
Offenburg Flip
Paranoia
Piña Colada, Canne Bay
Piña Colada, Emerald Isle
Pink Coconut
Screaming Weebies
Sea Side Liberty
Spirit of Erie Coffee
Voodoo Juice

CRUZAN ESTATE DIAMOND RUM
Big Bamboo, The
Café Contenté
Culture Shock
Electrode Overload
Frozen Devotion
Honeybunch Punch
Looking for Trouble
Mango Mingle
Mexican Runner
Outrigger
Pucker-Up
Rendezvous Muumuu
Voodoo Juice
Voodoo Moondance

CRUZAN ESTATE LIGHT RUM
Beachcomber (1)
Bloody Mary, Bloody Wright
Blue Hawaii
Borinquen
Ithmus Buffalo Milk
Martini, Black Devil

Miami Ice
Rendezvous Muumuu
Trade Winds
Voodoo Moondance
White Sands Cooler

CRUZAN ESTATE
SINGLE BARREL RUM
Barn Raiser
Hula Skirt
Island Dream
Island Fever
Island Flower
Jungle Cream
Larchmont (3)
V.I.P. Coffee

CRUZAN ORANGE RUM
After Tan (1)
Banana Cow
Blast-Off Punch
Cold Gold
Come-on-I-Wanna-Lei-Ya
Lemon Heaven
Martini, Virgin Island
Miniskirt Limbo
N'Orleans Chiller
Pilgrim's Pride
Voodoo Juice

CRUZAN PINEAPPLE RUM
Blue Lagoon (1)
Daiquiri de Piña
Desert Storm
Green Reef
Ground Zero
Key Isla Morada
Margarita, Conga
Martini, Piña
Passionate Screw
Piña Colada, Canne Bay
Tropical Itch
Voodoo Juice

CRUZAN RUM CREAM
Blizzard (2)
Cork Street Coffee (1)
Jungle Cream
Mocha Jamocha
Pucker-Up
Voodoo Shooter

D

DAIQUIRI RECIPES
See Alphabetized Recipes
Daiquiri,

DAMRAK
AMSTERDAM GIN
Adios Mother
Appendectomy
Collins, Rodeo Drive
Damrak Blue Lady
Damrak 75 (1)
Gimlet, Cobbler's
Hunker Punker
Ideal Cocktail
Jungle Juice
Margarita, Damrak 'Rita
Martini, Cupid's Bow
Martini, Dutch (1)
Martini, Iceberg
Martini, Journalist
Stock Market Zoo
Za-Za

DEKUYPER BUTTERSHOTS
SCHNAPPS
Baileys Butterball
Blonde Teaser (1)
Blonde Teaser (2)
Bottom Bouncer

Butterfinger
Butterscotch Hop
Butterscotch Slide
Dr. Vanilla Wafer
Gingerbread Man
I.R.A.
Julio's Butterscotch
Koolo
Lifesaver (2)
Martini, Crème Brûlée (3)
Neutron Bomb
Oatmeal Cookie (2)
Sacrifice Fly
Slippery Dick
Stiff Dick
Strawberry Quickie
Sugar Baby
Tavern Sucker, The
Whisky Gingerbread

DEKUYPER CHERRY
PUCKER
Black Cat
Cherry Bomb
Cowboy Killer
Nuckin Futs
Wanderer

DEKUYPER HOT DAMN!
CINNAMON SCHNAPPS
Apple Spice
Bananas Foster
Cinnamon Sling
Colombian Necktie
Emerald Ice
Eve's Apple
Fahrenheit 5000
Fire and Ice (1)
Fire and Ice (2)
Hot Times
Jamaican Spice
Kamikaze, Bloody
Margarita, Diablo
Orchard Haze
Rainbow Holiday Cup
Red Death
Santa Claus is Coming
When Hell Freezes Over

DEKUYPER PEACH
PUCKER
Banalini
Beach Bum Blue
Bloody Brain
Cayman Cocktail
Censored on the Beach
Crystal Clear
Death of a Virgin
Eve's Peach
'57 T-Bird
   with Arizona Plates
Georgia Peach (1)
Golden Ram
Gullet Pleaser
Jolly Rancher (1)
Kamikaze, Fuzzy
Malibu Sunset
Martini, Citrus
Miami Ice
Midori Cooler
Neon Twister
Passionate Fruit
Peach Bomb
Peach Breeze
Pitless Shot
Purple Passion
Twister
What Crisis?
Zanzibar Dunes

DEKUYPER PEACHTREE
SCHNAPPS
Acapulco Gold
All American Whistler
Amaretto Cruise
Appleton Blast
Basin Street Balm
Bermuda Triangle (2)
Big Fat Monkey Kiss
Blue Whale
Cesar Ritz
Champagne Cornucopia
Cheap Shades
City Tavern Cooler
Cosmopolitan, Cosmorita
Cuban Peach
Debutante
Down Under Snowball
Frosted Peach Breeze
Frosty Navel
Fruity Tutti
Fuzzy Navel
Fuzzy Wuzzie
Georgia Peach (2)
Georgia Turnover
Glass Tower
Glenda
Golden Peach
Gran Bliss
Gulf Stream Scream
Hasta la Vista, Baby
Heat Wave
Imperial Fuzz
Jewel
Knickerbocker Knocker
Leprechaun
Loch Lomond (2)
Margarita, Catalina
Margarita, Georgia
Margarita, Georgia Peach
Margarita, Sangrita
Margarita, Santa Rita
Mediterranean Freeze
New Orleans Jazz Time
Northern Lights (2)
Nymphomaniac (2)
Pacific Rim
Passionate Point
Peach Blaster
Peach Cobbler
Peaches and Dreams
Peaches 'n' Berries
Peach Fuzz
Peachie Keen
Pink Moment
Piranha Club Initiation
Putting on the Ritz
Reggae Walker
Roxanne
Royal Flush
Ruddy Mimosa
St. Patrick's Day
Sangria
Sangria, Margarita
Sangria, New World Punch
Sangria Punch, Berry New
Screaming Fuzzy Navel
Sex at the Beach
Sex on the Beach (4)
Sex on the Beach (5)
Silk Panties (1)
Silk Panties (2)
Skinny Dipping
Sneaky Peach
Swamp Water Stinger
Tokyo Scream
Trip to the Beach
Weekend at the Beach (1)

Weekend at the Beach (2)
Week on the Beach
DEKUYPER PEPPERMINT
SCHNAPPS
After Five
Apple Sting
Area 151
Brain Shooter
B-Sting
Cookie
Cool Captain
Cool Mint Listerine
Deathwish
Electrode Overload
Flaming Blue Blaster
Flaming Blue Jeans
Frappé, Derby Mint
Frostbite
Iceberg (1)
Jet Fuel (2)
Mother Lode
Orgasm (2)
Russian Polar Bear
Slippery Dick
Smiles for Miles
Snowshoe (1)
Trade Deficit
Turkey Shooter
Watergate
White Out
DEKUYPER RASPBERRY
PUCKER
Berry Cooler
Blended Frog
Busted Rubber
Cosmopolitan, Raspberry
Daiquiri, Raspberry
Designer Jeans
El Conquistador
Electric Watermelon (2)
Embolism
Flaming Blue Jeans
Guava Cooler
Hairy Sunrise
Key West
Killer Whale
Madonna's Brassiere
Midori Cooler
Pink Flamingo
Pucker-Up
Sex in the Coal Region
Twisted Sister
DEKUYPER RAZZMATAZZ
RASPBERRY LIQUEUR
Alizé Day
Badda-Bing
Black Tequila Rose
Bomb
Dr. Berry Vanilla
Dr. Seuss Go-Go Juice
Fruit Burst
Island Sunset
Jackie Special
Jäger Monster
Kiwi
La Bamba
L.A.P.D
Leaning Tower
Lifesaver (2)
Loco en la Cabeza (1)
Malibu Runner
Malibu Sunset
Margarita, Purple (2)
Mexican Runner
Midnight Orchid
Pink Gator
Poppycock Rock
Purple Passion

Purple People Beefeater
Razzle Dazzle
Razzle Dazzle Rose
Razzmatazz
Razzputenee
Release Valve
Root Canal
Royal Godiva
Satin Pillow
Sex with an Alligator (2)
Tequador
Twisted Lemonade
DEKUYPER PUCKER
SOUR APPLE
Adam's Apple
Apple a Go-Gogh
Apple Cooler
Apple Spice
Apple Tinker
Candy Apple
Crabapple
Crypto Nugget
Dale's Sour Apple
Eve's Apple
Green Sneakers
Hot Times
Jolly Rancher (3)
Kamikaze, Apple
Kuwaiti Cooler
Macintosh Press
Martini, Appletini (1)
Martini, Appletini (2)
Martini, Appletini (3)
Martini, Black Apple
Martini, Green Apple
Orchard Haze
Pearl Diver
Sex at the Beach
Sex with an Alligator (2)
Sour, Sparkling
   Sweet Apple
Spider Cider
Weekend at the Beach (1)
Week on the Beach
Washington Apple
DEKUYPER TRIPLE SEC
Bafferts Reviver
Baltimore Zoo
Beachcomber (2)
Bible Belt (1)
Canadian
Cosmopolitan, Black
Creamsicle (1)
Crimson Rose
Cuban Sidecar
Cuban Special
Dale's Sour Apple
Dirty Lemonade
El Conquistador
'57 T-Bird
   with Arizona Plates
.44 Magnum
Glass Tower
Green Sneakers
Hairy Sunrise
Hasta la Vista, Baby
Irish Alexander (2)
Jamaican
Barbados Bomber
Joke Juice
Kamikaze, Apple
Looking for Trouble
Manhattan, Biscayne
Margarita, Agave Juice
Margarita, Coyote (1)
Margarita, Coyote (2)

Margarita, Floridita
Margarita, Georgia Peach
Margarita, Horny (2)
Margarita, Key Lime
Margarita, Mount Fugi
Margarita,
   Neon Watermelon
Margarita, Picante
Margarita, Picosita
Margarita, Prickly Pear (1)
Margarita, Red Cactus
Margarita, Sangrita
Margarita, Shootah
Margarita, Tea-Arita
Margarita, Two-Toned
Margarita, Watermelon
Martini, Journalist
Martini, Muscovy
Mellonaire
Mexican Blackjack
Millionaire Cocktail
Panama Red
Raspberry Sweet Tart
Rhett Butler
Satin Pillow
Stealth Bomber (2)
Sunrise
Suntan Teaser
3D-Elixir
Vanil Sensation
DEKUYPER WATERMELON
PUCKER
Bafferts Reviver
Bomb Pop
Bubble Zaza
Electric Watermelon (1)
Madonna's Brassiere
Margarita, Watermelon
Martini, Watermelon
Twister
DEWAR'S WHITE LABEL
SCOTCH WHISKY
Aberdeen Angus
Barbary Coast
Black Watch
Bomb
Dewar's Highland Cooler
Dewar's Tango
Earl of Grey
Heather Blush
Highland Highball
Jolly Rancher (1)
Loch Lomond (2)
Martini, Paisley
Rob Roy, Highland Fling
Scotch Bounty
Silk Tie
Upside Down Irish Crown
DILLON DARK RUM
Cecil's Dream
Cocomotion
Gimlet, Martinique (2)
Rum and Black
Straw House Hummer
Tropical Depression
DIRTY OLIVE GIN
Dirty Bull
Dirty Gin 'n' Juice
Dirty Lemonade
Martini, Dirty Gin Twist
Martini, Dirty Olive Gin
DIRTY OLIVE VODKA
Bloody Mary,
   Bloody Tex-Mex
Bloody Mary, Dirty
Bloody Mary,
   Dirty Bloody Cajun

Dirty Dog
Martini, Dirty Olive Vodka
Martini, Dirty Citrus
DISARONNO
ORIGINALE AMARETTO
Abbey Road
A Day at the Beach
After Tan (1)
After Tan (2)
Alabama Slammer (2)
Alabama Slammer (4)
Alabama Slammer (5)
Almond Joy
Amaretto Cruise
Ambush
American Dream
Appleton Blast
August Moon
Bacardi Tropico Dream
Banana Frost
Beach Blonde
Benson Bomber
Berry Cooler
Betty Grable
Big Fat Monkey Kiss
Black Widow
Blueberry Tea
Blue Flute
Bocci Ball
Bocci Shooter
Brown Squirrel
Bubble Gum
Cactus Juice
Café Amore
Canyon Quake (2)
Caribbean Berry
Caribbean Romance
Catherine was Great
Cecil's Dream
Champagne Jubilee
Champagne Marseille
Chicago Times
Chill-Out Café
Chip Shot
Chocolate Squirrel
Cillo Amore
Cillo Fellow
Come-on-I-Wanna-Lei-Ya
Cosmopolitan, Disaronno
Cowboy Killer
Crab House Shooter
Creamsicle (2)
Desert Storm
Dingo
Down Under
Dreamsicle (1)
Dreamsicle (2)
Dr. Pepper (1)
Dr. Pepper (2)
Dr. Pepper From Hell
Dubonnet Fuzzy
Duke of Earl
Dunham Good
Ed Sullivan
Elixir of Love
Express Mail Drop
Federal Express
'57 Chevy
'57 T-Bird
   with Arizona Plates
'57 T-Bird
   with Florida Plates
'57 T-Bird
   with Hawaiian Plates
Five Dollar Margaret
Flaming Armadillo
Foreign Legion

French Kiss
Frozen Devotion
Full Moon
Godchild
Godfather
Godmother
Golden Ram
Grand Alliance
Hawaiian Punch (1)
Hawaiian Punch (2)
Iced Tea, Italian
International Cappuccino
Irish Headlock
Italian Coffee
Italian Punch
Italian Sunrise (1)
Italian Sunrise (2)
Italian Surfer
Italian Valium
Jackalope
Jackie Special
Jäger Monster
Jamaican Shake
Jelly Fish
John Wayne
Jolly Rancher (2)
Julia
Jumper Cables
Key Largo
King's Cup
Kool Aid (1)
Kool Aid (2)
Lake Street Lemonade
Lemon Nog
Lobotomy
Lounge Lizard
Love Canal
Lunch Box
Malibu Runner
Mama Citron
Manhattan Beach
Manhattan, Italian
Manhattan, Moon
   Over Manhattan
Margarita Azul
Margarita, Hawaiian
Margarita, Italian
Margarita, Oscarita
Martini, Amber Skies
Martini, Blue Shock
Martini, Full Moon (1)
Martini, Full Moon (2)
Martini, Kentucky
Martini, Nuttini
Martini, Tiramisu
Martini, Toasted Nuts
Marz Bar
Maui Breezer
Midway Manhattan
Midway Rat (1)
Midway Rat (2)
Monsoon
Monster Appeaser
Mooseberry
Mother Mason's Delight
Multiple Orgasm
Native Sun
Navy Grog, Nor'easter
New York Nut
Nina's Coffee
Nuckin Futs
Nut 'n' Holli
Nutty Professor
Oatmeal Cookie (1)
Orange Frappé
Orange Julius
Orgasm (1)

Outrigger
Paddy O'Rocco
Paranoia
Peckerhead
Persuader
Piña Colada, Amaretto
Piña Colada, Italian
Piña Colada, Lemonada (2)
Piña Colada, Stramaretto
Piña Colada,
   Toasted Almond
Piña Colada,
   Tropical Moon
Pink Panther (2)
Pink Paradise
Pirate Love
Purple Matador
Quaalude, Iranian
Rabid Dog
Razzmatazz
Red Devil
Rigor Mortis
Ritz Fizz
Roasted Toasted Almond
Rose Petal
Roxanne
Royal Canadian
Royal Street Coffee
St. Petersburg Sundae
Screaming Orgasm
Seventh Avenue
Seventh Heaven
Sex in the Woods
Sex on the Beach
   on a Cloudy Day
Sicilian Kiss
Silver Cloud
Silver Shadow
Skinny Dipping
Slipped Disk
Smiles for Miles
Smooth Gentleman
Sperm Bank
Spilt Milk (2)
Stiletto
Strawberry Shake
Straw House Hummer
Strummer Hummer
Sweet Tart (3)
T-Bird
Tennessee Mud
Test-Tube Baby (1)
Test-Tube Baby (2)
Tight Sweater
Tikki Dream
Tiramisu (1)
Toasted Almond
Toasted Almond Café
Trophy Room
Tropical Depression
Tropical Moon
Tryst & Shout
Ugly Duckling
Waist Coat Pocket
Watermelon (1)
Whisper (1)
White Swan
Wiki Waki Woo
Yankee Panky

DJ DOTSON TRIPLE SEC
Absolut Samurai
August Moon
Balalaika
Beachcomber (1)
Canadian Stone Fence
Captain's Cooler
Cold Fusion
Dew Drop Dead

Dreamsicle (2)
Gotham Lemonade
Honeymoon
Iced Tea, Havana
Jade
Kamikaze, Citron
Kamikaze,
   Southern Comfort
Magic Potion
Mai Tai, Mobay
Margarita, Bahama Mama
Margarita, Captain
Margarita, Caribbean
Margarita, Cranberry (2)
Margarita, Ice Cream
Margarita, Raspberry
Margarita, Sunny
Margarita, Virgin (1)
Margarita, Virgin (2)
Uptown
Za-Za

DR. MCGILLICUDDY'S
FIREBALL CINNAMON
CANADIAN WHISKY
Canadian Foot Warmer
Celeste's Cocktail
Fire-It-Up
Fool's Gold
Hell on Ice
Hot Honey Pot
International Dream
Sleigh Ride
Up the Creek with a Kick
Whisky Gingerbread

DR. MCGILLICUDDY'S
MENTHOLMINT
SCHNAPPS
Andes Summit
Bobsledder's Banshee
Canyon Slider
Doctor's Advice
Doctor's Elixir
Frappé, Doctor
   Chocolate Mint
Inoculation
Molotov's Cocktail
Nosferatu
Nosferatu's Shooter
No Tell Motel
Poppycock Rock
Snowshoe (2)
Sweaty Betty
3D-Elixir
Toboggan Truffle
Vanilla Magilla

DR. MCGILLICUDDY'S
VANILLA LIQUEUR
Aunt Bea's Cure-All
   Hot Milk Punch
Bananas Foster
Candy Apple
Coconut Cream Pie
Doctor's Orders
Dr. Berry Vanilla
Dr. Vanilla Dreamsicle
Dr. Vanilla Peanut
   Butter Cup
Dr. Vanilla Wafer
Key Lime Pie (2)
McGillicuddy's
   Cream Soda
Orange Dream
Sugar Baby

DOORLY'S XO
BARBADOS RUM
Daiquiri, Sweet Tart
Happy Hour
Mad Hatter

Sherry's Blossom
Socialite Prize Fight
Whaler's Season

DRAMBUIE LIQUEUR
Aberdeen Angus
Black Jeweled Russian
Bobby Burns
Golden Nails
Inverted Nail
Irish Dish
Rusty Nail®
Scotch Coffee
Scottish Dreams
Seventh Avenue
Tequila Highlander
Upside Down Irish Crown
Vincent's Baubles
Winnie's Hot Honey Pot

DUBONNET BLANC
London Redhead
Martini, Cupid's Bow
Martini, 008
Martini, Dutch (1)
Martini, Elephant's Ear
Martini, Fourth Degree
Martini, Marseilles

DUBONNET ROUGE
Appetizer
Blushing Angel
Castle in the Clouds
Club Macanudo
Dollar Bill
Dubonnet Cocktail
Dubonnet Fuzzy
Fat Cat Fizz
Lady Madonna
London Redhead
Manhattan, Dubonnet
Manhattan, Lafayette
Manhattan, Mazatlan
Manhattan, Mellow
Manhattan, Twin Peaks
Martini, Harper's
Martini, Napoleon
Merry Widow (1)
Opera Cocktail
Rob Roy, Oh Joy
St. Tropez
Silken Veil
Splendid Gin
Sweet Red Kiss
Za-Za

E

EL JIMADOR
AÑEJO TEQUILA
Dead Grizzly
Dead Grizzly Shooter
Looking for Trouble
Margarita, Cillo Italian

EL JIMADOR
REPOSADO TEQUILA
Blue Wave
El Diablo
Margarita, Black Forest
Margarita Diablo
Margarita, Jalapeño
Margarita, Purple (2)
Piña Colada, Acapulco
South-of-the-Border
   Mango Mash
Star Gazer

EL TESORO
AÑEJO TEQUILA
Alice in Wonderland
Gran Sonoran Sunset
Margarita Mas Fino
Margarita Primero Clase
Mexican Itch
Sonoran Sunset
Sunburnt Señorita

EL TESORO
SILVER TEQUILA
Cactus Juice
Margarita, Camino Real
Margarita, Georgia
Margarita Mas Fino
Martini, Cozumel
Martini, Los Altos
Martini, Star's
Nutty Mexican

ESPRESSO RECIPES
See Cappuccino and
   Espresso Recipes

EVAN WILLIAMS SINGLE
BARREL VINTAGE
BOURBON WHISKEY
Manhattan, Cherbourg
Manhattan, Vintage (1)
Manhattan, Vintage (2)
Old Fashion, Evan's
Uptown Girl

EXTASE XO LIQUEUR
Bettor's Dream
Choco Laté Orange
French Harvest
Gin & Sin
Hula Skirt
Leave Us Alone
Lover's Lane
Made in the Shade
Marseilles Stockings
Martini, Everglades
Martini, Moscow Chill
Martini, Shagged
Orange Delight
Scurvey Abator
Sherry's Blossom
Uptown Girl

F

FARIAS REPOSADO
TEQUILA
Dr. Seuss Go-Go Juice
Margarita, Anita
Peach Cobbler
River Madness
Tijuana Bulldog
Vampiro

FARIAS SILVER TEQUILA
Acapulco
Lockhart Zoo
Margarita, Coyote (1)
Margarita, Tuaca
Perfect Fit
Razzputenee
Stock Market Zoo
Wiki Waki Woo

FINLANDIA VODKA
Cabin Fever Cure
Cillo Fellow
Clam Fogger
Crypto Nugget
Downeaster
Finlandia Lime Light
Glacier Breeze
Hoochie KéKé Mama
Limerick

Martini, Green Lantern
Sky High
Sno-Cap
South Beach Twist
FIREBALL CINNAMON
CANADIAN WHISKY
See Dr. McGillicuddy's
Fireball Cinnamon
FORTY CREEK THREE
GRAIN CANADIAN
WHISKY
Celeste's Cocktail
Defroster (1)
Dudley Does Right
Fresh Squeezed Bat Juice
Looking for Trouble
Up the Creek with a Kick
FOURSQUARE
SPICED RUM
Aunt Bea's Cure-All
Hot Milk Punch
Bomb
Cabin Fever Cure
Flaming Blue Blaster
Fool's Gold
Ginger Snap
Hell on Ice
Mad Hatter
Peach Cobbler
Stock Market Zoo
Vanilla Magilla
Whaler's Season
FRANGELICO LIQUEUR
American Dream
Angel Kiss
Aspen Coffee
Autumn Sidecar
Banana Nuts
Bananas Over You
Bay Area Garter
Black Beauty
Carmalita
Chicago Times
Chocolate Almond Kiss
Chocolate Squirrel
Coffee Nutcake
Cork Street Coffee (1)
Cork Street Coffee (2)
E Pluribus Unum
Fatmancillo
Foreign Legion
Frangelico Freeze
Friar Tuck
Frozen Cappuccino
Frozen Monk
F-16
Fuzzy Mussy
G-Boy
German Chocolate Cake
Hemingway's
Flambé Coffee
Hot Irish Dream
Iacocca
Il Duce
Madtown Milkshake
Manhattan, New Orleans
Margarita, Rio Grande
Martini, Amber Skies
Martini, Crème Brûlée (1)
Martini, Crème Brûlée (2)
Martini,
Elisa's Martini of Love
Martini, Nutcracker
Martini, Nuttini
Martini, Snickertini
Martini, Topaz
Mexican Monk
Millionaire's Coffee

Monsoon
Mrs. Baileys' Favor
Mud Puddle
New York Nut
Ninja
Nut Cream Coffee
Nut 'n' Holli
Nut 'n' Honey
Nuts & Berries
Nuts to You
Nutty Irishman
Nutty Mexican
Oatmeal Cookie (1)
O'Brain Freeze
Opulent Coffee
Pistachio Mint Ice Cream
Pope on Vacation
Quaalude
Quaalude, Alaskan
Quaalude, Iranian
Quaalude, Irish
Quaalude, Russian
Russian' About
Satin Pillow
Say Hey Marseilles
Sky High
Strawberry Nut
Tavern Sucker, The
Tight Sweater
Winsome Way
Yabba-Dabba-Doo
FRAPPÉ RECIPES
See Alphabetized Recipes
Frappé,
FROZEN RECIPES
See Blended and
Frozen Recipes

G

GALLIANO LIQUEUR
Amber Cloud
Café Charles
California Root Beer
Creamy Dreamy Isotope
Dire Straits
Dreamsicle (1)
Freddy Fudpucker
Galliano Stinger
Golden Cadillac
Golden Dream
Golden Dream
with Double Bumpers
Golden Ram
Golden Screw
Harvey Wallbanger
International Stinger
Italian Stallion
Italian Stinger
Jenny Wallbanger
Jersey Root Beer
Joe Canoe
King's Cup
Leisure Suit
Manhattan, Galliano
Peachie Keen
Pearl Diver
Piña Colada, Aussie
Piña Colada,
Golden Bacardi
Sloe Comfortable Screw
Up Against the Wall
Summer Slammer
Pousse Café (3)
Pousse Café, Four-Way
Red Zipper
Root Beer

Root Beer Float
Tidal Wave (2)
Traffic Light (2)
Yellow Bird (1)
Yellow Bird (2)
Yellow Devil
GENTLEMAN JACK RARE
TENNESSEE WHISKEY
See Jack Daniel's
Gentleman Jack
GIBSON RECIPES
See Alphabetized Recipes
Gibson,
GIMLET RECIPES
See Alphabetized Recipes
Gimlet,
GIN
Alaska
Appendicitis
Bee's Knees
Bloody Mary, Gin
Blue Devil
Byrrh Cocktail
Cinnamon Sling
Clam Digger
Clover Club
Collins, Tom
Dubonnet Cocktail
English Mule
Fogcutter
Fogcutter, Royal Navy
Foghorn
French 75 (1)
Gibson
Gibson, Dry
Gibson, Extra Dry
Gimlet
Gin Alexander
Gin and It
Gin Rickey
Gloomraiser
Golden Fizz
Gulf Tide
Iced Tea, Afterburner
Iced Tea, Alaskan
Iced Tea, Bimini
Iced Tea, Blue Kangaroo
Iced Tea, California
Iced Tea, Dirty Ashtray
Iced Tea, Florida
Iced Tea, Green Tea
Iced Tea, Hawaiian
Iced Tea, Italian
Iced Tea, Long Beach
Iced Tea, Long Island
Iced Tea, Manhattan
Iced Tea, Raspberry
Iced Tea, Strawberry
Iced Tea, Tahiti
Iced Tea, Terminal
Iced Tea, Texas
Iced Tea, Tropical
Infusion, Lemoneater
Italian Valium
Knockout
Mamie's Sister
Margarita Britannia (1)
Martini
Martini, Bald Head
Martini, Bitchin'
Martini, Bronx
Martini, Cajun (1)
Martini, 007
Martini, Dry
Martini, Extra Dry
Martini, F.D.R.
Martini, Fino
Martini, French (3)

Martini, Infused
Martini, Italian (3)
Martini, Newbury
Martini, Palm Island
Martini, Perfect
Martini, Romana
Martini, Saké
Martini, Smoked (2)
Martini, Spanish
Martini Thyme
Merry Widow (2)
Minnehaha
Monkey Gland
Negroni
New Orleans Fizz
Opera Cocktail
Orange Blossom (1)
Orange Blossom (2)
Orsini
Passion Potion
Pink Lady (1)
Pink Lady (2)
Ramos Fizz
Red Lion
Red Tail Dragon
Rolls Royce
Root Canal
Rosy Pippin
Royal Fizz
Rumba
Run, Skip and Go Naked
Savannah
Scorpion
Sheilaberry
Silver Fizz
Singapore Sling (1)
Singapore Sling (2)
Skip and Go Naked
Snowball
Spy's Demise
Tramonto Sul Garda
Tropical Special
White Way
Yale Cocktail
GIORI LEMONCILLO
LIQUEUR
Capers Cocktail
Capo di Sopranos
Castle in the Clouds
Cheesy Cheerleader
Cillo Blanco
Classic Vette
Collins, Jamie
Daiquiri, Sweet Tart
El Toro
Fatmancillo
Frappé, Lemon
Fruit Burst
Gimlet, Cobbler's
Irish Wish
Island Dream
Lemon Heaven
Lemon Heights
Lemon Parfait
Lemon Squeeze
Margarita, Cillo Italian
Martini, Fantino
Martini, Jaded
Martini, Shade Tree
Piña Colada, Lemonada (2)
Rin Tin Gin Tonic
South Beach Twist
Summercillo
Summer Tonic
Sunknee Delite
Waikéké Fraternity

GIORI LEMONCILLO CREAM LIQUEUR
A Cillo Mia
Capo di Sopranos
Cherrillo
Ciao Bello
Cillo Amore
Cillo Fellow
Cosmopolitan, Cillo
Dreamsicle (4)
Goose Down
Lemon Heaven
Lemon Heights
Lemon Nog
South Beach Twist
Summercillo
Summer Tonic

GLENFARCLAS SINGLE MALT SCOTCH WHISKY
Irish Dish
Mahogany Gold
Scottish Tan

GODIVA CHOCOLATE LIQUEUR
All Star Cast
American Dream
Andes Summit
Bay Area Garter
Belvedere Milk Chocolate
Black Stockings
Butterfinger
Café a la Cabana
Café Amore
Café Foster
Carte Blanche
Chocolate Banana (2)
Chocolate Covered
   Banana (1)
Chocolate Cream Soda
Choco Laté Orange
Chocolate White Russian
C-Note A-Float
Death by Chocolate
Electrode Overload
Frangelico Freeze
Gold and Riches
Guava Martinique
Helene
Ice Chocolate
Imperial Duo
International Dream
Irish-Choco-Orange
Jamaican Rose
Leave Us Alone
Martini, Chocolate
Martini,
   Chocolate Cranberry
Martini,
   Elisa's Martini of Love
Martini, Godiva Mint
Martini, Moscow Chill
Martini, Pyrat
Martini, Snickertini
Martini, Tiramisu
Martini, Toasted Nuts
Martini, Tropical
Marz Bar
Mud Puddle
Nosferatu
Nosferatu's Shooter
Nun Out of Habit
Poire-Suisse
Rasta Man
Rosebud
Royal Godiva
Rumball
Sacrifice Fly
San Andreas Fault

Seventh Avenue
Socialite
Tamara Lvova
Tiramisu (1)
Toboggan Truffle
Trade Deficit
Tropical Depression
Waist Coat Pocket
White Cloud

GOLDSCHLÄGER LIQUEUR
Beverly Hillbilly
Dunham Good
Electrical Storm
Fool's Gold
French Tickler
Gingerbread Man
Gold and Lager
Gold Furnace
Gold Rush (2)
Margarita, Triple Gold
Oatmeal Cookie (1)
Oatmeal Cookie (2)
Pot O' Gold
Stars at Night
24-Karat Nightmare

GOODERHAM & WORTS CANADIAN WHISKY
Bettor's Dream
French Mountie
Sleigh Ride

GOSLING'S BLACK SEAL RUM
Alpine Glow
Bahama Mama (1)
Banana Milkshake
Bermuda Triangle (1)
Bermuda Triangle (2)
Black Orchid
Bushwacker
Caribbean Berry
Caribbean Gridlock
Daiquiri, Flight of Fancy
Daiquiri, Raspberry
Dark'n Stormy®
Dingo
Flamingo (1)
Goom Bay Smash (2)
Halekulani Sunset
Jamaican Tennis Beads
Jet Fuel (1)
Julia
Jump Me
Kiss of the Islands
Knickerbocker
Lethal Injection
Maui Wowie
Navy Grog, Nor'easter
Paranoia
Periodista (2)
Piña Colada, Bermuda
Piña Colada, Black Pearl
Piña Colada, Emerald Isle
Piña Colada,
   Strawberry Banana
Purple Flirt
Rhododendron
Rum Swizzle
Surf Sider (1)

GRAND MARNIER LIQUEUR
Absolut Grand
Absolut Trouble
A.M.F.
Appendectomy
Apple Grand Marnier
Ball Joint
Bearing Strait
B-52

Bible Belt (2)
Big Bacardi Bamboo
Blast from the Past
Blow Job (1)
Blow Job (2)
Blueberry Tea
Body Warmer
Bombay Grand
Busted Rubber
Café Chocolate (1)
Café Diablo
Café Gates
Caribbean Contessa
Cartel Buster
Celestial Fizz
Champagne Marseille
Concorde
Cosmopolitan,
   Margarita Cosmo
Dirty Harry
Doubt Raiser
'57 T-Bird
   with Florida Plates
'57 T-Bird
   with Hawaiian Plates
Flaming Armadillo
Frappé, Coffee Marnier
French Connection
French Maid's Café
French Tickler
Freudian Slip
Full Moon
Fuzzy Dick
Fuzzy Mussy
G-Boy
Glenda
Gold Rush (1)
Grand Orange Blossom
Grand Sidecar
Iacocca
Iced Tea, Terminal
Iced Tea, Texas
International Affair
Killer Whale
Landslide
Larchmont (1)
Larchmont (2)
Larchmont (3)
Lifesaver (1)
Loco en la Cabeza (1)
Louvre Me Alone
Manhattan, Boulevard
Manhattan, Satin
Margarita,
   Blue Maestro Gran
Margarita, Britannia (2)
Margarita, Cadillac
Margarita, French/Russian
Margarita, Jalapeño
Margarita, Kentucky
Margarita, Mad Russian
Margarita, Maui (2)
Margarita, Meltdown
Margarita, My Baby Grand
Margarita,
   Prickly Pineapple
Margarita, Rosarita
Margarita, Saké
Margarita, Sonoran
Margarita, Teal
Martini, Belvedere Startini
Martini, French (1)
Martini, Full Moon (1)
Martini, Jalisco
Martini, Lemon Grove
Martini, Napoleon
Mexican Itch
Mexican Siesta

Millionaire's Coffee
Monk's Coffee
Monte Cristo Shooter
Mooseberry
Mount Gay Café
Northern Lights (1)
Orange Cranberry Toddy
Passionate Point
Passionate Sunset
Peter Prescription
Piña Colada, Holiday Isle
Presumption Cocktail
Raspberry Sour
Red Lion
Rock-a-Fellow's Fancy
Room Service at the Ritz
Savoy Champagne Cocktail
Seven Twenty-Seven (727)
Sex at the Beach
Shot in the Dark
Shot Thru the Heart
Sky High
Slipped Disk
Somosa Bay
Stolichnaya Lemonade
Sunflower
Sunstroke
Surf Sider (1)
Swimming Naked at Sunset
T-Bird
Tropical Sensation
Watergate

GRAND MARNIER 100TH ANNIVERSARY
Alice in Wonderland
Ancient Mariner (1)
Ancient Mariner (2)
April in Paris
Champagne Imperial
Cyrano
Gold and Riches
Grand Ball
Grand Marshall Sour
Jacqueline
Kamikaze, French
Kamikaze, Purple (1)
Kentucky Shuffle
Margarita Framboise
Martini, Cozumel
Sail of the Century
Sidecar in Bombay
Sonoran Sunset
Tequilier Real
Top Hat
Twist de L'Orange
Vodka Grand

GRAN GALA TRIPLE ORANGE LIQUEUR
Alpine Glow
Badda-Bing
Café Chocolate (2)
Caribbean Cruise (2)
Caribbean Cruise (3)
Cosmopolitan, Chi Chi
Creamsicle (2)
Diplomatic Immunity
Dream Catcher
Gimlet, Cher's
Gimlet, Sapphire
Gimlet, Soho
Gran Bliss
Gran Bombay
Gran Cappuccino
Gran Sonoran Sunset
Hawaiian Sunburn
Imperial Sidecar
International Velvet Café
Irish-Choco-Orange

Jackarita
Kamikaze, Italian
Lickety-Split
Liquid Gold
Margarita, Rose
Margarita, Sea Breeze
Martini, Full Moon (2)
Martini, Italian (1)
Opulent Coffee
Orange Frappé
Sonoran Sunrise
South Beach Twist
South-of-the-Border
   Mango Mash
Tuscany Champagne
Winsome Way

GRAPPA RECIPES
Margarita,
   Malta's Grapparita
Martini, Medici
Venetian Sunset

GREY GOOSE VODKA
Black Widow
Bloody Mary,
   Bloody French Goose
Brass Monkey
Club Macanudo
Goose Down
Kamikaze, French
Madame Mandarine
Martini, Crème Brûlée (1)
Martini,
   Elisa's Martini of Love
Martini, French (1)
Martini, French (2)
Martini, Monastery
Martini, Tartini (1)
Martini, Willy Nilly

H

HERRADURA
  REPOSADO TEQUILA
Bloody Mary, Michilata
El Cajon Sunrise
Liquid Gold
Margarita, Chapala
Margarita, Santa Rita
Margarita, Señorita
Margarita, Spanish
Mexican Melon

HIGHBALL RECIPES
Acapulco Gold
Americano Highball
Baileys Fizz
Bat Bite
Batida
Baybreeze
Berry Cooler
Black-Eyed Susan
Black Widow
Blood and Sand (1)
Bocci Ball
Bog Fog
Brilliant Sonic
Buck
Buckhead Root Beer
Bullfrog (1)
Californian
California Root Beer
California Screw
Campari & Soda
Cape Codder
Censored on the Beach
Chiller
Cinnful Apple
Clam Fogger

Cold Gold
Comfortable Screw
Cuba Libre
Dingy Ginger
Downeaster
Dreamsicle (1)
Dr. Pepper (1)
English Mule
Foghorn
Fresh Squeezed Bat Juice
Fuzzy Navel
Georgia Peach (1)
Gin Rickey
Golden Nail
Golden Screw
Greyhound
Gulf Tide
Highball
Hiland Highball
Hollywood
Horse's Neck with a Kick
Isle of Pines
Jaundice Juice
Jersey Root Beer
Kahlúa Club
Kiwi
Lemongrad
Leprechaun
London Nightclub
Macintosh Press
Mackenzie Gold
Madras
Mamie's Sister
Mamie's Southern Sister
Mamie Taylor
Mango Monsoon
Melon Ball (1)
Melon Breeze
Mexican Bullfrog
Midori Driver
Mind Eraser (2)
Moose Milk
Moscow Mule
Northern Lights (2)
Orange Blossom (2)
Orange Chiller
Peach Blaster
Peach Breeze
Pearl Harbor
Peppermint Cooler
Persuader
Presbyterian
Razzle Dazzle
Release Valve
Rickey
Root Beer Tooter
Royal Godiva
Rum Screw
Saoco
Salty Bull
Salty Dog
Scarlett O'Hara
Screaming Fuzzy Navel
Screwdriver
Seabreeze
Seven & Seven
Seventh Heaven
Sex on the Beach (1)
Sex on the Beach (2)
Silk Panties (1)
Skyscraper
Sloe Comfortable Screw
Sloe Poke
Sloe Screw
Smooth Driver
Sonoran Sunset
Summer Breeze
Susie Taylor

Swamp Water
Tahitian Apple
Tennessee Tea
Tequila Driver
Tequila Quencher
Tijuana Screw
T. 'n' T.
Tom Mix High
Tootsie Roll
Tropical Gold
Up the Creek with a Kick
Weller Than N.E. 1
White Cadillac
White Minnesota

HIGHBALL RECIPES, TALL
Absolut Mandrinade
Acapulco Sunburn
Alabama Slammer (3)
Alabama Slammer (4)
Alien Secretion
All American Whistler
Apple Cooler
Apple Spice
Appleton Blast
Appleton Breeze
Aqua Zest
Banana Bay
Barn Raiser
Bay Bridge Commuter (1)
Bay Bridge Commuter (2)
Benson Bomber
Bermuda Triangle (1)
Bermuda Triangle (2)
Between the Sheets
Black & Blue Bayou
Black Cat
Black Orchid
Black Sun
Blonde Teaser (1)
Blonde Teaser (2)
Blue Bayou (1)
Blueberry Tea
Blue Duck
Blue Lagoon (1)
Blue Lagoon (2)
Blue Lemonade
Blue Wave
Blue Whale
Bombay Spider
Bomb Pop
Bullfrog (2)
Burgundy Bishop
Cactus Juice
Cactus Moon
California Lemonade
Canadian Stone Fence
Candy Apple
Cannonball
Capers Cocktail
Cheap Sunglasses
Chihuahua
Chimayo Cocktail
Chocolate Cream Soda
Cillo Fellow
Cinnamon Sling
City Tavern Cooler
Clam Digger
Collins, Rodeo Drive
Colorado Bulldog
Comfortable Crush
Comfort Kit
Congo Cooler
Cove Cooler
Crabapple
Cranberry Squeeze
Creamy Dreamy Isotope
Cruzan Glide Slide
Dark'n Stormy®

Death of a Virgin
Desert Sunrise
Dewar's Highland Cooler
Dew Drop Dead
Dirty Bull
Dirty Dog
Dirty Gin 'n' Juice
Dirty Lemonade
Dizzy Lizzy
Dr. Berry Vanilla
Dreamsicle (3)
Dreamsicle (4)
Dubonnet Fuzzy
Dudley Does Right
El Cajon Sunrise
El Diablo
Electric Watermelon (2)
El Toro
Encinada Hill Climber
Face Eraser
Fat Cat Fizz
'57 Chevy
'57 T-Bird
   with Arizona Plates
'57 T-Bird
   with Florida Plates
'57 T-Bird
   with Hawaiian Plates
Firecracker
First Aid Kit
Flamingo (1)
Freddy Fudpucker
French Crush
French Sweetheart
Frosted Coke
Gator Juice
Ginger Snap
Glacier Breeze
Glass Tower
Golden Fizz
Gotham Lemonade
Gran Sonoran Sunset
Green Monster
Green Sneakers
Ground Zero
Gulf Breeze
Gumby
Habana Libre
Hairy Sunrise
Happy Hour
Harvey Wallbanger
Hawaiian Punch (2)
Hawaiian Sunburn
Heartbreak
Heat Wave
Hell on Ice
Highland Golfer
Hoochie KéKé Mama
Independence Swizzle
In the Red
Isleña
Italian Punch
Italian Sunrise (1)
Italian Sunrise (2)
Jäger Monster
Jamaica Me Crazy (1)
Jamaican Crawler
Jamaican Spice
Jar Juice
Jenny Wallbanger
Jet Fuel (1)
Joe Canoe
Jump Me
Jungle Juice
KéKé Kicker
Kentucky Swamp Water
Key Largo
King Midas

Dharama Rum
Dreamsicle (2)
Dr. Vanilla Dreamsicle
Dr. Vanilla Peanut
    Butter Cup
Emerald Ice
E Pluribus Unum
Eve's Apple
Fire and Ice (1)
Frangelico Freeze
Frosty Navel
Frozen Cappuccino
Frozen Devotion
Frozen Monk
Gorilla Milk
Hummer
Ice Cream Bellini
Il Duce
Irish Float
Irish Raspberry
Jamaican Rum Cow
Jamaican Shake
Julia
Julio's Butterscotch
Knickerbocker
    Knee Knocker
Koala Bear (1)
Laughing Bacardi Cow
Lemon Tree Tantalizer
Madtown Milkshake
Mango-A-Gogo
Mango in the Wynde
Margarita, Blue Moon
Margarita, Ice Cream
Margarita, Sunny
Melon Scoop
Mel's Chocolate
    Butterscotch Shake
Mel's Choc/PB/Nana Shake
Mint Freeze
Mocha My Eye
Nuckin Futs
O'Brain Freeze
Orange Frappé
Parfait
Peachie Keen
Pilgrim
Pilgrim's Pride
Piña Colada, Choco
Piña Colada, Chocolate
Piña Colada, Emerald Isle
Piña Colada, Holiday Isle
Piña Colada, Kahlúa
Piña Colada, Monkalada
Piña Colada,
    Tropical Moon
Piña Colada,
    Tropical Splashes
Pirate Love
Pistachio Mint Ice Cream
Pullman Porter
Raspberry Banana Split
Raspberry Cream
Red Sky
Rhumba Escapades
Rosebud
Rose Petal
Rum Alexander
St. Petersburg Sundae
Screaming Good Times
Shark's Tooth
Sno-Cap
Storm-A-Long-Bay
Strawberry Alexandra
Strawberry Banana Split
Strawberry Nut
Strawberry Rose
Strawberry Shake

Tamara Lvova
Tiramisu (1)
Tiramisu (2)
Tropical Moon
Twist de L'Orange
Waist Coat Pocket
Whisper (2)

ICED TEA RECIPES
See Alphabetized Recipes
    Iced Tea,

INFUSION RECIPES
See Alphabetized Recipes
    Infusion,

IRISH MIST LIQUEUR
Café Dublin
Irish Alexander (1)
Irish Brogue
Irish Coffee Royale (2)
Irish Stinger
Irish Tea
Mr. Murphy
Nut 'n' Holli
Paddy O'Rocco

IRISH WHISKEY
Café Dublin
Collins, Joe
I.R.A.
Irish Coffee
Irish Coffee Royale (1)
Irish Coffee Royale (2)
Irish Headlock
Irish Shillelagh
Irish Stinger
Irish Tea
Manhattan, Irish
Mrs. Baileys' Favor
Nut Cream Coffee
Paddy
Tam-O'-Shanter
Brainstorm Cocktail

JACK DANIEL'S
GENTLEMAN JACK
TENNESSEE WHISKEY
Brooklyn
Manhattan, Poor Tim
Manhattan, Satin
Manhattan, Twin Peaks
Mint Julep, Gentleman's
Rainbow
    International Cocktail
Smooth Gentleman
Tennessee Gentleman
JACK DANIEL'S SINGLE
BARREL TENNESSEE
WHISKEY
Frappé, Derby Mint
Grand Marshall Sour
Manhattan Glitz
Manhattan, Jack's Best
Manhattan,
    Tennessee Blush
Martini, All American (1)
JACK DANIEL'S
TENNESSEE WHISKEY
Bible Belt (2)
Black Jack
Chocolate Ice Cream Float
Four Wise Men
Happy Jacks
Jackarita
Jack Benny
Jack Tail
Lynchburg Lemonade
Mexican Blackjack

Mint Julep, Pineapple
No Tell Motel
Southern Suicide
Tennessee Mud
Tennessee Tea
Tropical Jack
Yo Hooter Hooter

JÄGERMEISTER LIQUEUR
Afterburner
Beverly Hillbilly
Bitches from Hell
Bloody Mary, Jäger Salsa
Buckhead Root Beer
Bucking Bronco
Dying Nazi From Hell
Electrical Storm
Freddy Kruger
Jägerita
Jäger Monster
Jäger My Worm
Jet Fuel (2)
Meister-Bation
Mexican Nazi Killer
Milk of Amnesia
Oatmeal Cookie (2)
Rumplemeister
Sammy Jäger
Sand Blaster
Sexual Chocolate
Sex with an Alligator (1)
Sex with an Alligator (2)
Stars at Night
Surfers on Acid
Wile E. Coyote
Yellow Jacket

JAMESON IRISH WHISKEY
Black Diamond
Dollar Bill
Eye to Eye
Golden Peach
Irish Alexander (2)
Irish Brogue
Irish Car Bomb
Irish Raspberry
Irish Wish
Jameson Cannes-Style
Jewel
Mint Freeze
Raspberry Sour
St. Patrick's Day
Silk Tie
Sour Melon Patch
Teatime
What's the Rush
White Cloud
J. BALLY RHUM
Big Chill
Daiquiri, French
Gimlet, Martinique (2)
JEWEL OF RUSSIA
BERRY INFUSION
Catherine was Great
Cosmopolitan, Dirty
Double Agent
Dream Catcher
Kool Aid (1)
Metro Cocktail
Texas Tea
Tovarich
JEWEL OF RUSSIA
CLASSIC VODKA
Black Jeweled Russian
Chocolate White Russian
Gorky Park Cooler (1)
Green Russian
Jewels and Gold
Katinka
Martini, New Bond

Martini, Russian Tea Room
Martini, Tartini (2)
Metro Cocktail
Mooseberry
Tovarich
JEWEL OF RUSSIA WILD
BILBERRY INFUSION
Balalaika
Congo Cooler
DC-3 Shooter
Gorky Park Cooler (1)
Gotham Lemonade
Hawaiian Punch (1)
Hollywood
Jewel of Russia
Mooseberry
Piña Colada, Lt. Kije's
JIM BEAM BLACK LABEL
BOURBON WHISKEY
Black-Eyed Susan
Bomb
Collins, Jamie
Hell on Ice
Kentucky Swamp Water
Manhattan, Algonquin
Manhattan, Marianne
Manhattan, St. Moritz
Ritz Americana
Stock Market Zoo
Torpedo Slam
Trinity
JIM BEAM WHITE LABEL
BOURBON WHISKEY
Apple Spice
Blizzard (1)
Burnt Sienna
Canyon Slider
Fedora
Four Wise Men
Jaundice Juice
Manhattan, Biscayne
Manhattan, Dijon
Manhattan, Dubonnet
Manhattan, Galliano
Manhattan, Rosebud
Manhattan, Shamrock
Manhattan, Waldorf
Reverend Craig
Skyscraper
JOSE CUERVO TEQUILA
A.M.F.
Brahma Bull
Cartel Buster
Four Wise Men
Gold Rush (1)
Hangin' on a Stick
Hasta la Vista, Baby
Iced Tea, Terminal
Jägerita
KéKé Kicker
Margarita, Cadillac
Margarita la Reyna
    del Playa
Margarita, Rocky Point
Margarita, Pink Cadillac
Mexican Blackjack
Panama Red

KAHLÚA COFFEE LIQUEUR
Abbey Road
Aching Bach
Afterburner
After Eight
After Five
Aggravation

American Dream
Apple a Go-Gogh
Area 151
Aspen Coffee
Bahama Mama (2)
Baileys Butterball
Baileys Mint Kiss
Banana Sandwich
Bay Area Garter
Beam Me Up, Scottie
Benson Bomber
B-52
Black and White
Black Beauty
Black Russian
Black Jeweled Russian
Black Watch
Bleacher's Twist
Blushing Berry Cooler
Brave Bull
Bullfighter
Bush Tickler
Bushwacker
Butterscotch Hop
Butterscotch Slide
Café Charles
Café Chocolate (1)
Café Chocolate (2)
Café Chopin
Café Contenté
Café Dublin
California Root Beer
Canadian Foot Warmer
Canyon Quake (1)
Capo di Sopranos
Captain's Coffee (2)
Caribbean Cruise (1)
Caribbean Sunset
Carmalita
Castle Coffee
Cherry Bomb
Chill-Out Café
Chip Shot
Chiquita Punch
Chocolate Milk Cooler
Ciao Bello
Cillo Amore
C-Note A-Float
Coffee Nutcake
Colorado Avalanche
Colorado Bulldog
Cookie
Creamy Bull
Cruzan Glide Slide
Dire Straits
Dirty Mother
Doctor's Advice
Dragoon
Duck Fart
Emerald Isle
E Pluribus Unum
Face Eraser
Fatmancillo
Fire-It-Up
Five Dollar Margaret
Flaming Armadillo
Frangelico Freeze
Frappé, Coffee Marnier
Frappé, Mocha
Frappé, Sambuca Mocha
French Kiss
French Maid's Café
Frosted Coke
Frozen Cappuccino
Frozen Monk
F-16
Fun in the Sun
Fuzzy Dick

German Chocolate Cake
Girl Scout Cookie
Good & Plenty
Gorilla Milk
Gran Cappuccino
Harbor Lights
Hoochie KéKé Mama
Hummer
Iacocca
Il Duce
International Cappuccino
International Dream
International Velvet Café
I.R.A.
Irish Boggle
Irish Coffee Royale (1)
Irish Raspberry
Ithmus Buffalo Milk
Jackalope
Jack Benny
Jamaican Rum Cow
Julio's Butterscotch
Kahlúa Club
Kahlúa Mint
KéKé Kicker
Keoki Coffee
Keoki Shooter
Koala Float
Lemon Nog
Lighthouse
Liquid Gold
Malibu Slide
Marquis
Martini, Espresso
Martini, Tartini (1)
Martini, Tiramisu
Melon Scoop
Mel's Chocolate
   Butterscotch Shake
Mel's Choc/PB/Nana Shake
Ménage à Trois
Mexican Cocoa
Mexican Coffee
Mexican Grasshopper
Mexican Monk
Mighty Bull Shooter
Mighty Kong
Millionaire's Coffee
Milwaukee River
Mind Eraser (1)
Mind Eraser (2)
Mint Freeze
Mocha My Eye
Monsoon
Monte Cristo Shooter
Moose Milk
Mother
Mudslide (1)
Mudslide (2)
Neutron Bomb
Noblé Holiday
Nuckin Futs
Nut 'n' Honey
Nutty Professor
Nutty Mexican
O'Brain Freeze
Opulent Coffee
Orgasm (1)
Piña Colada, Choco
Piña Colada,
   Hawaiian Lion
Piña Colada, Kahlúa
Piña Colada,
   Strawberry Banana
Piña Colada,
   Toasted Almond
Pirate's Hiccup
Pistachio Mint Ice Cream

Poppycock Rock
Pousse Café (3)
Pousse Café, Four-Way
Presidential Juice
Quaalude
Quaalude, Iranian
Quaalude, Russian
Raspberry Banana Split
Reverse Russian
River Seine Cappuccino
Roasted Toasted Almond
Rock-a-Fellow's Fancy
Root Beer
Root Beer Float
Rose Beam
Royal Canadian
Royal Street Coffee
Russian Bear
Russian Polar Bear
St. Petersburg Sundae
Say Hey Marseilles
Scottish Tan
Screaming Orgasm
Separator (1)
Separator (2)
Seven Twenty-Seven (727)
Sexual Chocolate
Shore Boat
Shot Thru the Heart
Siberian
Silver Cloud
Sky High
Slippery Banana
Smith & Kerns
Smith & Wesson
Sno-Cap
Sombrero
Star Gazer
Sugar Baby
Sugar Daddy
Tam-O'-Shanter
Tavern Sucker, The
Tight Sweater
Tijuana Bulldog
Tiramisu (1)
T.K.O.
Toasted Almond
Toasted Almond Café
Trade Deficit
V.I.P. Coffee
Waist Coat Pocket
Watergate
Whisper (1)
Whisper (2)
White Bull
White Russian
Xaviera
Yabba-Dabba-Doo
Yellow Jacket

KAMIKAZE RECIPES
See Alphabetized Recipes
   Kamikaze,

**KÉKÉ BEACH KEY LIME
CREAM LIQUEUR**
Big Bamboo, The
Cheesy Cheerleader
Green Monster
Hoochie KéKé Mama
KéKé Kicker
Ké Largo
Martini, KéKé V
Miniskirt Limbo
Piña Colada, KéKé Colada
Twilight Moan Zone
Twisted Sister
Waikéké Fraternity
Where are My Undies?

**KETEL ONE
  DUTCH VODKA**
Blonde Teaser (1)
Coconut Coffee Pot
Gypsy
Kamikaze, Fuzzy
Lizard Bitch
Manhattan Smoky
Martini, Ketel One
Martini, Mandarine
Martini, Midnight (3)
Martini, Moro
Martini, Snickertini
Melon Breeze
**KNAPPOGUE CASTLE
IRISH WHISKEY**
Ambush
Castle Coffee
Castle in the Clouds
Diplomatic Immunity
Emerald Isle
Erie Canal
Fun in the Sun
Green Mint Float
Hourglass
Irish Boggle
Irish-Choco-Orange
Martini, Irish
Peaches and Dreams
Sidecar, Irish
Spirit of Erie Coffee
Sweet (Irish) Dreams
**KNOB CREEK SMALL
BATCH BOURBON
WHISKEY**
Kentucky Shuffle
Knob Creek
Lena Cocktail
Manhattan, Boulevard
Manhattan,
   Continental Perfect
Manhattan, Preakness
Manhattan, Rose
Manhattan,
   Sheepshead Bay
Manhattan, Westchester
Old Fashion, Knob Creek

L

**LAIRD'S APPLEJACK
APPLE BRANDY**
Ambrosia (2)
Applejack Cream
Apple Sting
Apple Toddy
Aprés Ski
Chef Dieter's
   Apple Pie Cocktail
Collins, Jack
Deauville
Diki-Diki
Happy Jacks
Harvest Grog
Hole-in-One
Honeymoon
Jack Rose Cocktail
Jersey Devil
Klondike
Manhattan, Big Apple
Old Fashion, Apple
Pink Lady (2)
Steeple Jack
Tidal Wave (1)

LAIRD'S 12-YEAR-OLD
RARE APPLE BRANDY
Apple Cart
Apple Works
Aprés Ski
Café Brûlot
International Affair
Manhattan, Spiced
Apple Brandy
LAYERED CORDIAL
RECIPES
See Shooter and Cordial
Recipes, Layered
LAYERED SHOOTER
RECIPES
See Shooter and Cordial
Recipes, Layered
LICOR 43
(CUARENTA Y TRES)
Barcelona Coffee
Café a la Cabana
Café St. Armands
Caipirinha (2)
Dreamsicle (3)
Dreamsicle (4)
Gold Rush (3)
Key Lime Cooler
Key Lime Pie (1)
Margarita, Spanish
Mini Beer
Piña Colada, Spanish
Sex on a Black Sand Beach
LILLET BLONDE
Lillet Champagne Royale
Margarita la Reyna
del Playa
Martini, 007
Martini, Mystical
Martini, New Bond
LOT NO. 40
CANADIAN WHISKY
Canadian Bliss
Canadian Foot Warmer
LUKSUSOWA POLISH
POTATO VODKA
Dale's Sour Apple
Face Eraser
Green Sneakers
Kamikaze, Bloody
Lake Street Lemonade
Martini, Bleu
Martini, Chocolate
Cranberry
Martini, Fantino
Martini, Medici
Martini, Poinsettia
Melon Ball Cooler
Monster Appeaser
Razzle Dazzle Rose
White Spider

M

MAKER'S MARK
BOURBON WHISKEY
Dizzy Lizzy
John Wayne
Manhattan, Italian
Manhattan, Lafayette
Manhattan, Loretto
Manhattan, Mazatlan
Manhattan, Raspberry
Manhattan, Smoky
Manhattan, Tivoli
Margarita, Kentucky
Martini, Kentucky
Mint Julep, On the Mark

MALIBU RUM
After Tan (2)
Alien Secretion
Baileys Malibu Rum Yum
Big Blue Shooter
Blue Lagoon (2)
Coconut Cream Pie
Goom Bay Smash (1)
Infusion, Alien Secretion
Island Sunset
Italian Surfer
Jackie Special
Jet Fuel (1)
Ju Ju Bee
Kamikaze, Kokonut (2)
Lifesaver(2)
Luau
Malibu Beach
Malibu Fizz
Malibu Runner
Malibu Slide
Malibu Sunset
Margarita, Bahama Mama
Martini, Tropical
Monkey Bite
Nymphomaniac (2)
Piña Colada,
Malibu Orange
Pink Passion
Piranha
Pope on Vacation
Rainbow Shooter (2)
Reggae Sunsplash
R. F. & E.
Rock Lobster
Scotch Bounty
Screaming Hawaiian
Sex in the Coal Region
Sex in the Tropics
Sex on the Beach
on a Cloudy Day
Ship Wreck
Spring Break
Suntan Teaser
Surfers on Acid
Surf Sider (2)
Tie Me to the Bed Post
Tropical Hooter
Twister
Vulcan
Wanna Probe Ya
Yankee Panky
MANDARINE
NAPOLÉON LIQUEUR
All Star Cast
Bonaparte
Bull and Bear
Cactus Moon
Castle Coffee
Electric Lemonade
French Mandarine
French Twist
Happy Hour
Honeybunch Punch
Let Us Alone
Madame Mandarine
Mandarine Dream
Margarita, Anita
Margarita, Cranberry (1)
Margarita, El Conquistador
Margarita, Normandy
Margarita, Santiago
Margarita,
Strawberry Lover's
Marquis
Martini, Dry Rain
Martini, Mandarine
Noble Nymph

Orange Dream
Pink Sunset
Raztini
Rodéo Driver
Sea Dew
Star Gazer
Sunday Brunch
Punch Cocktail
MANHATTAN RECIPES
See Alphabetized Recipes
Manhattan,
MARGARITA RECIPES
See Alphabetized Recipes
Margarita,
MARTINI RECIPES
See Alphabetized Recipes
Martini,
MATUSALEM CLASSIC
BLACK RUM
Black Mass
Blizzard (2)
Cool Carlos
Cruzan Glide Slide
Manhattan Beach
Melon Scoop
Piña Colada, Bellevue
Piña Colada, Choco
Piranha Punch
Planter's Punch (3)
Rum Runner (1)
Stealth Bomber (1)
Storm-a-long Bay
Thai Smile
MATUSALEM
GOLDEN DRY RUM
Delicias de la Habana
Habanos Havana
Havana Cocktail
Havana Sidecar (1)
Iced Tea, Havana
Manhattan Beach
Piña Colada, Bellevue
Pink Slipper
Stealth Bomber (1)
MATUSALEM
GRAN RESERVA RUM
Café a la Cabana
Daiquiri, Whale Smooch
Dark Waters
Florida
Island Ditty
Lover's Lane
Rock-a-Fellow's Fancy
MATUSALEM
LIGHT DRY RUM
Cuban Cocktail
Cuban Peach
Cuban Sidecar
Cuban Special
Delicias de la Habana
Habana Libre
Iced Tea, Havana
Isla de Piños
Manhattan Beach
Manhattan, Cuban
Manhattan,
Cuban Medium
Manhattan, Latin
Maui Wowie
Naval Commission
Screaming Weebies
Stealth Bomber (1)
MATUSALEM
RED FLAME RUM
Borinquen
Naval Commission
Piranha Punch

METAXA 5 STAR BRANDY
Alexander the Great
Café Charles
Greek Coffee
International Stinger
MEZCAL
Margarita,
Blue Maestro Gran
Margarita, Mezcal
Martini, Mystical
MIDORI MELON LIQUEUR
Acapulco Breeze
Acapulco Sunburn
Alien Secretion
Artificial Intelligence
Balashi Breeze
Bomb Pop
Bullfrog (2)
Burnt Sienna
Cheap Shades
Circus Peanut
Citron Neon
Cold Fusion
Colorado River Cooler
Crystal Clear
Dactyl Nightmare
Delicias de la Habana
Desert Passion
Done & Bradstreet
Drunken Monkey
Electric Watermelon (1)
Electric Watermelon (2)
E.T.
'57 T-Bird
with Arizona Plates
Finlandia Lime Light
Fruity Tutti
Gang Green
Green Monster
Green Reef
Green Russian
Green Sneakers
Ground Zero
Gulf Stream Scream
Gumby
Hole-In-One
Honeydew
Iced Tea, Green Tea
Infusion, Alien Secretion
Infusion, Beach
Infusion, Ice
Blue Margarita
Infusion, Pool Water
Infusion, Summer
Shades Margarita
Infusion, Vodka Crocodile
Jamaican Crawler
Jamaican Tennis Beads
Jamaican Ten Speed
Jealousy
Jolly Rancher (1)
Jolly Rancher (2)
Jolly Rancher (3)
Ju Ju Bee
Kamikaze, Melon
Ké Largo
Killer Koolaid
Knickerbocker Knocker
Kool Aid (1)
Kool Aid (2)
Kuwaiti Cooler
Leaf
Limerick
Lizard Bitch
Luau
Malibu Fizz
Margarita la Reyna
del Playa

P

PEARL VODKA
Adios Mother
Cool Mint Listerine
Cosmopolitan, Raspberry
Electric Lemonade
'57 T-Bird
    with Arizona Plates
Frosted Coke
Jar Juice
Lockhart Zoo
Martini, KéKé V
Martini, Pearl Jam
Martini, Piña
Marz Bar
Orange Dream
Pearl Diver
Royal Bay Breeze
PEACH SCHNAPPS
See DeKuyper Peachtree
PEPPERMINT SCHNAPPS
See DeKuyper Peppermint
PERNOD
Brazil
Gloomraiser
Hemingway
Iceberg (2)
Knockout
Manhattan, Paparazzi
Manhattan, Waldorf
Martini, Bald Head
Martini, Bitchin'
Merry Widow (1)
Minnehaha
Monkey Gland
Sazerac
Suissesse
Whip
PIKE CREEK
    CANADIAN WHISKY
Canadian Tart
Dry Creek
Friar Tuck
Grand Ball
PIÑA COLADA RECIPES
See Alphabetized Recipes
    Piña Colada,
PLYMOUTH GIN
Diki-Diki
Martini, Blue Pacific
Martini Blues
Martini, Friar Paul
Martini, Full Nelson
Martini, Half Nelson
Martini, Mayflower
Martini, Rivers
Martini, Virgin Island
Pink Gin
Scurvey Abator
PORT AND SHERRY
    RECIPES
Adonis
Alaska
Andalusia
Betsy Ross
Bloody Mary, Bloodhound
Brazil
Brown Velvet
Club Sherry
Coronation
Dizzy Lizzy
Fogcutter
Fogcutter, Royal Navy
Gentleman's Boilermaker
Havana
Martini, Amadora

Martini, Bel-Air
Martini, Fino
Martini, Golden Girl
Martini, Havana
Martini, San Francisco
Martini, Spanish
Midnight Oil
Moulin Rouge
Nelson's Blood (3)
Port and Lemon
Port in a Storm
Port O' Call
Quarter Deck
Rainbow
    International Cocktail
Rob Roy, Oh Joy
Van Good
Velvet Swing
White's Club
POUSSE CAFÉ RECIPES
See Alphabetized Recipes
    Pousse Café,
PRESIDENTÉ BRANDY
See Brandy, Presidenté
PUSSER'S BRITISH
    NAVY RUM
Café Reggae
Cannonball
Captain's Coffee (1)
Cove Cooler
Flamingo (2)
Fogcutter, Royal Navy
Naval Commission
Navy Grog, Modern
Navy Grog, Nor'easter
Nelson's Blood(1)
Nelson's Blood (2)
Painkiller
Piña Colada, Pusser's Island
Pusser's Daily Ration
Pusser's Pain Killer
Pusser's Stalemate
Shore Boat
PYRAT RUMS
Ancient Mariner (2)
Big Blue Shooter
Daiquiri, Derby
Daiquiri, Pyrat
Gimlet, Pyrat
Heavyweight Sailor
Larchmont (2)
Latin Lover (1)
Martini, Pyrat
Pirate Love
Planter's Rum Punch
Rumball

R

RAIN VODKA
Electric Jam
Mango Monsoon
Martini, Dry Rain
Martini, Hot Marti
Martini, Louisiana Rain
Martini, Red Rain
Mediterranean Freeze
Midnight Orchid
Monsoon
Mud Puddle
Orange Frappé
Sweet Tart (1)
Texas Tea
Wanderer
Wiki Waki Woo

RAZZMATAZZ
    RASPBERRY LIQUEUR
See DeKuyper Razzmatazz
RÉMY MARTIN
    V.S. COGNAC
Cosmopolitan,
    Rémy Colada
Golden Max
Imperial Duo
RÉMY RED
Alabama Slammer (3)
Canadian Tart
Celeste's Cocktail
Code Red
Collins, Red Turkey
Dingy Ginger
Dudley Does Right
Manhattan, Rosebud
Margarita, Purple (2)
Martini, Red Rain
Orange-U-Glad-2-C-Me
Red Eclipse
Red Sky
Rémy Red Punch
Rémy Red Sunrise
Seven of Hearts
Van Good
RHUM BARBANCOURT
Borinquen
Daiquiri, Calypso
Daiquiri, Rhum
Guava Martinique
Lasting Passion
Martini, Smoked (2)
Midnight Express (3)
Rhum Barbancourt Freeze
Wynbreezer
ROB ROY RECIPES
See Alphabetized Recipes
    Rob Roy,
ROCKS RECIPES
Absolut Samurai
Aggravation
Alabama Slammer (2)
All Star Cast
Almond Joy
Americano
Ancient Mariner (1)
Ancient Mariner (2)
Angel Kiss
Apple Sting
Area 151
Baileys Comet
Bananas Foster
Beautiful Thing
Berlin Wall
Black Beauty
Black Jamaican
Black Russian
Black Jeweled Russian
Black Tequila Rose
Black Watch
Brahma Bull
Brave Bull
Brown Cow
Caipirinha (1)
Caipirinha (2)
Caipirissma
Caipiroshka
Canadian Bliss
Canadian Tart
Celtic Kiss
Choco Laté Orange
Chocolate White Russian
Chopin's River
Club Sherry
Cookie
Creole

Dead Grizzly
Debonair
Dire Straits
Dirty Mother
Doctor's Elixir
Dry Creek
Erie Canal
Fire-It-Up
Flaming Blue Blaster
Flaming Blue Jeans
French Dream
Friar Tuck
Fruity Tutti
Galliano Stinger
Godchild
Godfather
Godmother
Good & Plenty
Grand Ball
Grape Nehi
Green Hornet
Green Mint Float
Green Russian
Green Spider
Helene
Houndstooth
Hula Skirt
Iceberg (1)
Iceberg (2)
International Stinger
Irish Brogue
Irish Maria
Irish Stinger
Italian Stallion
Italian Stinger
Italian Valium
Jack Benny
Jungle Cream
Knob Creek
Krakow Witch
Lady Madonna
Left Bank
Lemon Heights
Lemon Tart
Lighthouse
Liquid Gold
Mama Citron
Marquis
Midori Canuck
Midori Stinger
Mind Bender
Mind Eraser (1)
Mint Julep, Gentleman's
Mist
Molotov's Cocktail
Monkey Juice
Mother
Mother Lode
Mr. Murphy
Mrs. Baileys' Bush
Mudslide (2)
Nelson's Blood (1)
Noble Holiday
Nutty Professor
Nutty Irishman
Nutty Mexican
Old Fashion
Old Fashion, Apple
Old Fashion, Evan's
Old Fashion, Knob Creek
Old Fashion, Muddled
Panther
Peaches 'n' Berries
Pillowtalk
Prairie Oyster (1)
Presidential Juice
Quaalude, Alaskan
Quarter Deck

Razorback Hogcaller
Razzmatazz
Red Russian
Rock-a-Fellow's Fancy
Rum and Black
Rum Old-Fashioned
Rusty Nail®
Sazerac
Scottish Dreams
Scottish Tan
Separator (2)
Seven Twenty-Seven (727)
Sex on a Black Sand Beach
Sex on the Beach on a
  Cloudy Day
Siberian
Sicilian Kiss
Silken Veil
Silk Panties (2)
Silver Bullet
Smiles for Miles
Smith & Kerns
Smith & Wesson
Smoothy
Snake Bite (1)
Snowshoe (1)
Snowshoe (2)
Socialite
Sombrero
Star Gazer
Stinger
Sugar Daddy
Sweet (Irish) Dreams
Tam-O'-Shanter
Tarnished Bullet
Tequila Highlander
Tequilier Real
3D-Elixir
Thumper
Tickle Me
T.K.O.
Top Hat
Ugly Duckling
Uptown Girl
Vanilla Spice Ice
Watermelon (1)
Whisper (1)
White Bull
White Russian
White Russian, Premium
White Spider
White Swan
White Way
Winsome Way
Yankee Panky
Yukon Stinger
Zipper Head

ROYAL OAK
  EXTRA OLD RUM
Banana Cow
Banana Monkey
Caribbean Cruise (2)
Daiquiri, Charles
Jet Fuel (1)
Lasting Passion
Monkey Juice
Nevada Pete Cocktail
Rendezvous Punch
Strawberry Banana Split
Wynbreezer

RUM, LIGHT
Balashi Breeze
Barn Raiser
Between the Sheets
Caipirinha (2)
Caribbean Cruise
Collins, Pedro
Cuba Libre

Daiquiri
Daiquiri, Banana
Daiquiri, Fruit (Basic)
Daiquiri, Hemingway
Electric Watermelon (1)
El Presidenté Cocktail (1)
'57 Chevy
Florida
Fogcutter
Guava Cooler
Hot Times
Hurricane (1)
Hurricane (2)
Iced Tea, Afterburner
Iced Tea, Alaskan
Iced Tea, Bimini
Iced Tea, Blue Kangaroo
Iced Tea, California
Iced Tea, Dirty Ashtray
Iced Tea, Florida
Iced Tea, Green Tea
Iced Tea, Hawaiian
Iced Tea, Italian
Iced Tea, Long Beach
Iced Tea, Long Island
Iced Tea, Manhattan
Iced Tea, Raspberry
Iced Tea, Strawberry
Iced Tea, Tahiti
Iced Tea, Texas
Iced Tea, Tropical
Infusion, Barrier Reef
Infusion, Cherry Bomb
Irish Shillelagh
Isle of Pines
Joe Canoe
Leaf
Mai Tai (1)
Mai Tai (2)
Mai Tai (3)
Margo Moore
Martini, Maritime
Melon Grind
Mojito (1)
Mojito (2)
Navy Grog
Ocho Rios
Orchard Haze
Passion Potion
Periodista (1)
Piña Colada
Piña Colada, Fruit (Basic)
Piña Colada, KéKé Colada
Piña Colada,
  Liqueur-Flavored
Pink Highliter
Piranha
Presidenté
Rainbow Holiday
Red Tail Dragon
Release Valve
Root Canal
Rumba
Rum Fix
Rum Milk Punch
Rum Mint Julep
Rum Old-Fashioned
Rum Screw
Run, Skip and Go Naked
Saoco
Scorpion
Sheilaberry
Shillelagh
Silver Spider
Smurf Piss
Sour Mint
Spy's Demise
Strummer Hummer

Summer Breeze
Susie Taylor
Tahitian Apple
Tom & Jerry
Tropical Gold
Tropical Hut
Twister
Wall Street Wizard
Weekend at the Beach
Windex
Yellow Bird (1)
Yellow Bird (2)

RUM, GOLD
Commodore
Cork Street Coffee (2)
Fu Manchu
Havana
Havana Club
Hurricane (1)
Hurricane (2)
Jumby Bay Punch
Mai Tai (2)
Mai Tai (3)
Navy Grog, Original
Piña Colada, Spanish
Piranha
Planter's Punch (1)
Rum Toddy
Scorpion
Tidal Wave (3)

RUM, 151 PROOF
Afterburner
Area 151
Dr. Pepper from Hell
Flaming Blue Jeans
Green Lizard
Harbor Lights
Hawaiian Hurricane
Hurricane (2)
Iced Tea, Afterburner
Jet Fuel (2)
Lighthouse
Mai Tai (2)
Mai Tai (3)
Mexican Flag
Red Death
Rocket
Rum Old-Fashioned
Rum Punch

RYE WHISKEY
Brainstorm Cocktail
Manhattan, Prohibition
Sazerac

S

ST. JAMES
  EXTRA OLD RHUM
Chocolate Covered
  Banana (1)
Cool Carlos
Curaçao Cooler
Daiquiri, French
Drunken Monkey
Gimlet, Martinique (1)
Guava Martinique
Love Potion #9
Martini, Martinique
Offenburg Flip
Piña Colada, French
Sassafras Sunset
Suffering Bastard

SAKÉ
Martini, Saké
Saké-Rama

SAMBUCA
Black Mass

Café Diablo
Capo di Sopranos
Freddy Kruger
Glass Tower
Italian Coffee
La Mosca
Martini, Tartini (1)
Philippi Creek
Sammy Jäger
Slippery Nipple
Vulcan Mind Probe
White Heart

SAMBUCA ROMANO
Frappé, Sambuca Mocha
Hemingway's
  Flambé Coffee
Manhattan, Roman

SAUZA BLANCO TEQUILA
Infusion,
  Lemontree Margarita
Infusion, Lime-Tequila
Margarita, Black Gold
Margarita, Blue
Margarita, Cranberry (1)
Margarita, Cranberry (2)
Margarita, Hawaiian
Margarita, Key Lime
Margarita, Meltdown
Margarita,
  Neon Watermelon
Margarita, Normandy
Margarita, Pear
Margarita, Pineapple
Margarita, Prickly Pear (1)
Margarita, Prickly Pear (2)
Margarita, Raspberry Torte
Margarita, Sangrita
Margarita Splash
Margarita,
  Strawberry Lover's
Margarita, Tea-Arita
Margarita, Watermelon

SAUZA CONMEMORATIVO
  AÑEJO TEQUILA
Acapulco Sunburn
Alizé Day
Area 151
Chimayo Cocktail
El Conquistador
El Toro
Encinada Hill Climber
Eve's Peach
In the Red
La Bamba
Loco en la Cabeza (1)
Margarita, Bahama Mama
Margarita, Black Gold
Margarita, Blue Moon
Margarita, Coyote (2)
Margarita, DC 3
Margarita, El Conquistador
Margarita, Eleganté
Margarita, Georgia Peach
Margarita, Herba Buena
Margarita, La Bamba
Margarita,
  Prickly Pineapple
Margarita, Rosarita
Margarita, Sea Breeze
Margarita, Tres Compadres
Mexican Siesta
Native Sun
Nutty Professor
Osmosis
Sauza Sunrise
Sea Water
Sonoran Sunrise

Test-Tube Baby (1)
Tijuana Screw
Tijuana Sunrise
T.K.O.
Toreador
White Bull
TEQUILA, GOLD
Gold Rush (2)
Infusion, Pepper-Tequila
Infusion, Sonoran Spittoon
Margarita, Catalina
Margarita, Italian
Prairie Fire
Tequila Highlander
Tequila Slammer/Popper
TEQUILA ROSE
STRAWBERRY
CREAM LIQUEUR
Black Tequila Rose
Crimson Rose
Frozen Rose
Hot Apple Rose
Jamaican Rose
Margarita, Rose
Peaches 'n' Berries
Rose Beam
Rosebud
Strawberry Quickie
Strawberry Rose
TIA MARIA
Alice In Wonderland
A.M.F.
Bam Be
Bikini Line
Black Jamaican
Black Maria
Blast from the Past
Blow Job (1)
Brahma Bull
Café Amore
Café Gates
Café Kingston
Café Reggae
Calypso Coffee
Cappa 21
Cappo de Tutti Cappi
Caribbean Sunset
Caribe Sunset
Cartel Buster
Chambord Repose
Cocomotion
Coconut Coffee Pot
Deep Throat
Dirty Harry
Dry Arroyo
French Dream
Heavyweight Sailor
Hunter's Coffee
Irish Maria
Jamaica Me Crazy (1)
Jamaican Coffee
Jamaican Dust
Jamaican Holiday
Jamaican Shake
Jungle Cream
Louvre Me Alone
Margarita, Rio Grande
Martini, Espresso
Midway Manhattan
Midway Rat (1)
Midway Rat (2)
Mocha Jamocha
Montego Bay (1)
Mount Gay Café
Multiple Orgasm
Navy Grog, Nor'easter
New York Nut
Peter Prescription

Piña Colada, Black Pearl
Piña Colada, Kingston
Piña Colada, Monkalada
Piña Colada, Port Royal
Pirate Love
Rasta Man
Reggae Walker
Russian' About
Satin Pillow
Sex in the Woods
Sex on the Beach (1)
Smooth Screw
Sovereignty
Tender Mercies
Tiramisu (2)
Tour de Caribbean
Tour de Panama
Trophy Room
Tropical Depression
Voodoo Shooter
White Russian, Premium
TROPICO
Bacardi Tropico Dream
Bucking Bronco
Celeste's Cocktail
Creamy Dreamy Isotope
Hot Tropico Mama
Iced Tea, Jesse's Shocking
Margarita, Rocky Point
Primo Bacio
Slow Tropico Cruise
Tropico Tango
Wiki Waki Woo
TUACA
Autumn Sidecar
Black Maria
Chicago Times
Forever Amber
Frappé, Lemon
Gimlet, Tuaca
Gimlet, Whaler
Hot Apple Pie
Margarita, Tuaca
Mincemeat Mocha
Nina's Coffee
Nut 'n' Honey
Pousse Café, Tuaca
Tender Mercies
Thumper
Wile E. Coyote

V

VAN GOGH GIN
Holland's Opus
Maiden's Prayer
Martini, Imperial
Martini, Marguerite
Martini, Napoleon
Martini, Star's
Miami Ice
Van Good
Vulcan
VAN HOO VODKA
Beer Buster
Bullfrog (1)
Cheap Sunglasses
.44 Magnum
Grape Nehi
Hairy Sunrise
Looking for Trouble
Naked Pretzel
Swamp Water Stinger
Tootsie Roll
Watermelon (5)
Whooter Hooter

VILLA MASSA
LIMONCELLO
Bafferts Reviver
Cactus Moon
Canadian Bliss
Defroster (1)
Du Monde
Kamikaze, Italian
Late-Nite Lemon Drop
Lemon Tart
Limón Fitzgerald
Martini, Italian (1)
Martini, Lemoneater
Massapeal
Mint Julep, Gentleman's
Mojito, Massa
Perfect 10
Splendid Gin
Tickle Me
Ulterior Motive
VINCENT VAN GOGH
CITRON VODKA
Eiffel View
Fortress of Singapore
Ice Pick Iced Tea
Lemon Drop (2)
Tropical Sensation
VINCENT VAN GOGH
ORANJE VODKA
Choco Laté Orange
Eiffel View
Tangerine Drop
Vincent's Baubles
Whale's Tail
Windex
VINCENT VAN GOGH
VODKA
Choco Laté Orange
Green Spider
Houndstooth
Martini, Chocolate
Martini, Espresso
Miami Ice
Raztini
Sunflower
Vincent's Baubles
Vulcan
VINCENT VAN GOGH
WILD APPEL VODKA
Martini, Green Apple
Apple a Go-Gogh
Sin in Hawaii
Original Sin
VODKA
Angel Kiss
Baybreeze
Belvedere Milk Chocolate
Bikini Line
Black Russian
Bloody Mary
Bloody Mary, Bloody Bull
Bloody Mary, Bloody Cajun
Bloody Mary,
      Bloody Italian
Bloody Mary, Mango
California Screw
Cape Codder
Chi-Chi
Cocaine Shooter (1)
Cocaine Shooter (2)
Collins, Vodka
Colorado Bulldog
Death By Chocolate
'57 Chevy
Gibson, Vodka
Gimlet, Tuaca
Gimlet, Vodka
Godchild

Godmother
Greyhound
Harvey Wallbanger
Hawaiian Hurricane
Iced Tea, Afterburner
Iced Tea, Alaskan
Iced Tea, Bimini
Iced Tea, Blue Kangaroo
Iced Tea, California
Iced Tea, Dirty Ashtray
Iced Tea, Florida
Iced Tea, Green Tea
Iced Tea, Hawaiian
Iced Tea, Italian
Iced Tea, Long Beach
Iced Tea, Long Island
Iced Tea, Manhattan
Iced Tea, Raspberry
Iced Tea, Strawberry
Iced Tea, Tahiti
Iced Tea, Texas
Iced Tea, Tropical
Infusion, Astral Apricot
Infusion, Beach
Infusion, Cosmic Coconut
Infusion, Lime Lights
Infusion, Mars Mango
Infusion, Pineapple
Purple Passion
Infusion,
      Planetary Pineapple
Infusion,
      Roxbury Pineapple
Infusion, Sicilian Martini
Infusion, Spice Satellite
Infusion, Venus Vanilla
Infusion, Vodka Crocodile
Jenny Wallbanger
Kamikaze
Kamikaze, Cranberry
Kamikaze, Italian
Kamikaze, Purple (1)
Kamikaze, Purple (2)
Knicker Knocker
Kool Aid (2)
Lemon Drop (3)
Madras
Martini, Appletini (1)
Martini, Dirty (1)
Martini, 007
Martini, Dry Vodka
Martini, Extra Dry Vodka
Martini, Maritime
Martini, Sicilian (1)
Martini, Sicilian (2)
Martini, Strawberry (1)
Martini, Vodka
Martini, Zorbatini
Melon Ball (1)
Melon Ball (2)
Midori Canuck
Mind Eraser (1)
Mocha My Eye
Molotov's Cocktail
Moscow Mule
Mudslide (1)
Mudslide (2)
Nut 'n' Honey
Ocean Breeze
110 Degrees in the Shade
Orange Julius
Passion Potion
Peach Bomb
Peach Breeze
Peach Fuzz
Pearl Harbor
Piña Colada, Aussie
Pink Lemonade (1)

Pink Sunset
Pitless Shot
Prairie Oyster (2)
Primo Bacio
Pullman Porter
Purple Hooter (1)
Quaalude
Quaalude, Alaskan
Quaalude, Iranian
Quaalude, Irish
Raspberry Torte
Red Devil
Red Russian
Red Sky
Red Zipper
Release Valve
Reverse Russian
Roasted Toasted Almond
Root Beer
Root Beer Float
Root Beer Tooter
Root Canal
Russian Bear
Russian Sunrise
Salty Dog
Screaming Fuzzy Navel
Screaming Hawaiian
Screaming Orgasm
Screwdriver
Seabreeze
Sex at the Beach
Sex in the Coal Region
Sex in the Woods
Sex on the Beach (1)
Sex on the Beach (4)
Sex with an Alligator (2)
Sheilaberry
Sherry's Blossom
Siberian
Silken Veil
Silk Panties (1)
Silk Panties (2)
Silver Cloud
Silver Spider
Skinny Dipping
Smooth Driver
Spanish Fly
Spider Cider
Spy's Demise
Starlight
Straight Shooter
Tidal Wave (3)
Watermelon (2)
White Russian

VOX VODKA
Baltimore Zoo
Barn Raiser
Bay Bridge Commuter (1)
Bloody Mary,
     Bloody Caesar
Martini, Appletini (2)
Martini, Appletini (3)
Martini, Flirtini (1)
Martini, Metropolis
Martini, Rosebud
Martini, Toasted Nuts
Mind Eraser (1)
New York Nut
Sweet Tart (2)
Tickle Me
Watermelon (3)

VYA PREFERRED
CALIFORNIA
DRY VERMOUTH
Black Diamond
Ideal Cocktail
Lena Cocktail
Manhattan, Cherbourg
Manhattan,
     Continental Perfect
Manhattan, Dubonnet
Manhattan, Poor Tim
Manhattan, Raspberry
Manhattan, Smoky
Manhattan,
     Spiced Apple Brandy
Manhattan, Westchester
Martini, All American (1)
Martini, All American (2)
Martini, Dragon's Breath
Martini, Dry Rain
Martini, Elephant's Ear
Martini, Friar Paul
Martini, London Dry
Martini, Mighty
Martini, Moro
Martini, Paisley
Martini, Rolls Royce
Martini, Sapphire Sin
Palace Guard
Taj Majal
Tinted Glass

VYA PREFERRED
CALIFORNIA
SWEET VERMOUTH
Golden Dragon
Irish Wish
Lena Cocktail
Manhattan, Cherbourg
Manhattan,
     Continental Perfect
Manhattan, Jack's Best
Manhattan, Loretto
Manhattan, Napoleon
Manhattan, Satin
Manhattan, Tivoli
Martini, All American (2)
Martini, Becco
Martini, Rolls Royce
Negroni, Uptown
Old Flame
Rob Roy, Highland Fling
California Dry

WHALER'S ORIGINAL
VANILLE RUM
Banana Frost
Betelgeuse
Blonde Teaser (2)
Butterscotch Hop
Come-on-I-Wanna-Lei-Ya
Daiquiri, Whale Smooch
Gimlet, Whaler
Jardinera
Mango Mingle
New York Nut
Peach Cobbler
Peaches and Dreams

Piña Colada, Lemonada (2)
Pirate's Hiccup
Randy Brandy Egg Nog
Sandy Beach Bay
Sleigh Ride
Vanilla Magilla
Vanilla Spice Ice
Waikéké Fraternity
Whaler's Season
Whale's Tail
Where are My Undies?

WILD TURKEY 80°
BOURBON WHISKEY
Snowshoe (1)
Snowshoe (2)
Turkey Shooter

WILD TURKEY 101°
BOURBON WHISKEY
Buffalo Sweat
Collins, Red Turkey
Deathwish
Dingy Ginger
Flaming Blue Blaster
Jealousy
Jet Fuel (2)
Manhattan,
     Blue Grass Blues
Manhattan, Paparazzi
Rabid Dog

WINE RECIPES
Burgundy Bishop
Burgundy Cocktail
Colorado River Cooler
Coronation
Hot Mulled Wine
Kir
Margarita, Cantina Wine
Margarita, Vintner's
Margarita, Zinful
Maria Sangrita
Martini, Black (3)
New England
     Summer Spritzer
Port in a Storm
Restoration
Sangria
Sangria, Margarita
Sangria, New World Punch
Sangria Punch, Berry New
Sonoma Chiller
Spritzer
Wine Cobbler
Wine Cooler

W.L. WELLER SPECIAL
RESERVE BOURBON
WHISKEY
Brown Cow
Brown Cow Milkshake
Bull and Bear
Dead Grizzly
Dead Grizzly Shooter
Hot Milk Punch
Manhattan, Danish
Manhattan, New Orleans
Millionaire Cocktail
Orange-U-Glad-2-C-Me
Smoothy
Steeplechase
Weller Than N.E.1
Yellow Snow

YUKON JACK LIQUEUR
Burnt Sienna
Dead Grizzly
Dead Grizzly Shooter
Frostbite
Mackenzie Gold
Northern Lights (1)
Northern Lights (2)
Panama Jack
Peckerhead
Red Death
Rocket
Shot in the Dark
Snake Bite (1)
Sweaty Betty
Yukon Stinger

Z

ZONE MELON VODKA
Apple Cooler
Electric Watermelon (1)
Ju Ju Bee
Martini, Hawaiian
Melon Grind
Twilight Moan Zone

ZONE PEACH VODKA
Bubble Zaza
Cayman Cocktail
Censored on the Beach
Crabapple
Frosted Peach Breeze
Glass Tower
Martini, Gummie Bare
Peachy Congo Cooler
Summercillo

ZUBRÓWKA BISON
BRAND VODKA
Bloody Mary, Bloodhound
Bloody Mary, Bloody Bison
Bloody Mary,
     Bloody Moose
Bloody Mary,
     Bloody Nose (1)
Brawny Broth
Krakow Witch
Martini, Brazen
Martini, Mighty
Martini, Ty-Won-On
Yukon Stinger

Resources

A. Hardy Cognac
9575 W. Higgins, Ste. 802
Rosemont, IL 60018
PH.847.698.9860
www.ahardyusa.com
Extase XO Liqueur,
Hardy Noces d'Or Cognac,
    Original Polish Vodka

A. V. Imports
6450 Dobbin Rd., Ste. G
Columbia, MD 21045
PH.800.638.7720
www.avimports.com
Giori Lemoncillo Liqueur,
    Giori Lemoncillo Cream
    Liqueur

AdamBa Imports
585 Meserole St.
Brooklyn, NY 11237
PH. 718.628.9700
www.adamba.com
Luksusowa Polish Potato
    Vodka, Bak's Zubrówka
    Bison Brand Vodka

**Allied Domecq Spirits
& Wine USA, Inc.**
355 Riverside Ave.
Westport, CT 06880
PH.203.221.5400
www.adsw.com
Beefeater London Dry Gin,
    Canadian Club Whisky,
    Courvoisier Cognacs,
    Kahlúa Coffee Liqueur,
    Maker's Mark Bourbon,
    Midori Melon Liqueur,
    Sauza Tequilas, Stolichnaya
    Vodkas

Austin Nichols & Co.
105 Corporate Park Dr.
    Ste. 200
West Harrison, NY 10604
PH.914.539.4500
www.austin-nichols.com
Aberlour a'bunadh Speyside
    Single Malt Whisky,
    Jameson Irish Whiskey, Wild
    Turkey 101° Bourbon

BMC Imports
76 Elm St.
New Canaan, CT 06840
PH.203.972.6529
www.jewelofrussia.com
Jewel of Russia Classic Vodka,
    Jewel of Russia Infusions

Bacardi USA
2100 Biscayne Blvd.
Miami, FL 33137
PH.305.573.8600
www.bacardi.com
B & B Liqueur, Bombay
    Sapphire London Dry Gin,
    Dewars White Label Scotch
    Whisky, Disaronno
    Originale Amaretto,
    Drambuie Liqueur

Bacardi USA
The Baddish Group
552 Seventh Ave., Ste. 6C
New York, NY 10018
PH.212.221.7611
www.bacardi.com
Bacardi Límon Rum, Tropico,
    Otard XO Cognac

Bartolomeh, Inc.
308 W. 89th St., #5A
New York, NY 10024
PH.212.799.7398
www.dirtyolive.com
Dirty Olive Vodka,
    Dirty Olive Gin

Bendistillery
1470 NE 1st St., Ste. 800
Bend, OR 97701
PH.541.318.0200
www.bendistillery.com
Cascade Mountain Gin

Better Beverage Importers
275 Grand Blvd.
Westbury, NY 11590
PH.516.334.2222
www.vhl.co.uk
Forty Creek Three Grain
    Canadian Whisky

Bishop Wines & Spirits, Inc.
10810 Inland Ave.
Miraloma, CA 91792
PH.909.681.8600
www.bishopbrands.com
Bafferts Gin, Whaler's Original
    Vanille Rum

Black Vodka Company
2421 Geneva Ave.
Daly City, CA 94014
PH.415.252.8039
www.blackvodka.com
Blavod Black Vodka

Brown-Forman
850 Dixie Hwy
Louisville, KY 40210
PH.502.585.1100
www.brown-forman.com
Finlandia Vodka, Gentleman
    Jack Rare Tennessee
    Whiskey, Jack Daniel's
    Single Barrel Tennessee
    Whiskey, Southern Comfort
    Liqueur

Buffalo Trace Distillery
1001 Wilkinson Blvd.
Frankfurt, KY 40601
PH.502.223.7641
www.buffalotrace.com
Glenfarclas Single Malt Scotch
    Whisky, W.L. Weller Special
    Reserve Bourbon

Charles Jacquin
2633 Trenton Ave.
Philadelphia, PA 19125
PH.800.523.3811
Royale Chambord
    Liqueur de France

**Dime Group
International, Inc.**
100 Fairway Dr., Ste. 128
Vernon Hills, IL 60061
PH.847.573.0009
Signatory Single Malt
    Scotch Whisky

Distillerie Stock USA, Ltd.
58-58 Laurel Hill Blvd.
Woodside, NY 11377
PH.800.323.1884
www.stockusaltd.com
Gran Gala Triple
    Orange Liqueur

Frank Pesce
    International Group
902 Clint Moore Rd., Ste. 142
Boca Raton, FL 33487
PH.561.997.0400
www.vodka@cristall.com
Original Cristall Russian
    Vodka

Gosling Brothers
17 Dundonald St.
Hamilton, HM10, Bermuda
PH.441.295.1123
www.goslings.com
Gosling's Black Seal Rum

Great Spirits Co.
1331 Lamar, Ste. 1125
Houston, TX 77010
PH.713.750.0033
www.greatspirits.com
Celtic Crossing Irish Liqueur,
    Knappogue Castle Irish
    Whiskies, Sea Wynde Pot
    Still Rum

Heaven Hill Distilleries
1064 Loretto Rd.
Bardstown, KY 40004
PH.502.348.3921
www.hhdmarketing
    @heaven-hill.com
Christian Brothers Brandies,
    Dubonnet, Evan Williams
    Single Barrel Vintage
    Bourbon

International Beverage Co.
7730 Roswell Rd., Ste. 207
Atlanta, GA 30350
PH.770.390.9714
www.interbevusa.com
Kelt XO Tour du Monde
    Grand Champagne Cognacs

Jerry Adler Company
1199 Oxford Court
Highland Park, IL 60035
PH.847.432.5080
DJ Dotson Triple Sec

Jim Beam Brands
510 Lake Cook Rd.
Deerfield, IL 60015
PH.847.948.8888
DeKuyper Liqueurs and
    Pucker Schnapps, El Tesoro
    Tequilas, Jim Beam
    Bourbons, Knob Creek
    Small Batch Bourbon,
    VOX Vodka

Kobrand Corp.
134 E. 40th St.
New York, NY 10016
PH.212.490.9300
www.kobrandwine.com
Alizé Aperitifs and
    Alizé Cognacs

Laird & Co.
One Laird Rd.
Scobeyville, NJ 07724
PH.732.542.0312
www.lairdandcompany.com
Artic Flavored Vodkas, Laird's
    Applejack Brandy, Laird's
    12-year-old Rare Apple
    Brandy, Oro di Mazzetti
    Liqueur, Villa Massa
    Limoncello

Liquid International
    Premium Spirits Co.
334 E. 74th St., Ste. 6B
New York, NY 10021
PH.212.717.2901
www.lipsimport.com
NapaSaki Saké

Luctor International
9635 A Gateway Dr.
Reno, NV 89511
PH.888.539.3361
www.vincentvodka.com
Vincent Van Gogh Vodkas,
    Van Gogh Gin

Majestic Distilling Company
2200 Monumental Rd.
P. O. Box 7372
Baltimore, MD 21227
PH.410.242.0200
www.majesticdistilling.com
Ballylarkin Irish Liqueur,
    Farias Tequilas

Ron Matusalem
1205 SW 37th Ave., Ste. 300
Miami, FL 33135
PH.305.448.8255
www.matusalem.com
Matusalem Gran Reserva Rum

McCormick Distilling Co.
17817 Coit Rd., #4106
Dallas, TX 75252
PH.816.640.2276
www.mccormickdistilling.com
Gooderham & Worts Canadian
    Whisky, Hussong's Tequilas,
    KéKé Beach Key Lime
    Cream Liqueur, Lot No. 40
    Canadian Whisky, Pike
    Creek Canadian Whisky,
    Tequila Rose Strawberry
    Cream Liqueur

Millennium Import Company
c/o Clarity Coverdale Fury
120 S. 6th St., Ste. 1300
Minneapolis, MN 55402
PH.612.339.3902
www.ccf-ideas.com
Belvedere Polish Vodka,
    Chopin Polish Vodka

Motts North America
6 High Ridge Park
P.O. Box 3800
Stamford, CT 06905
PH.203.968.7812
www.motts.com
Rose's Lime Juice

Nolet Spirits
30 Journey
Aliso Viejo, CA 92656
PH.800.243.3618
www.ketelone.com
Ketel One Dutch Vodka

Pearl Spirits Inc.
655 Redwood Highway
Ste. 120
Mill Valley, CA 94941
PH.415.380.3730
Pearl Vodka

Preiss Imports
P. O. Box 2172
Ramona, CA 92065
PH.800.745.5042
www.preissimports.com
Briottet Liqueurs, Mandarine
Napoléon Liqueur, Old Raj
Dry Gin, Van Hoo Vodka

Quady Winery
P. O. Box 728
Madera, CA 93639
PH.559.673.8068
www.quadywinery.com
Vya Preferred California
Vermouths

R & A Imports, Inc.
P. O. Box 1133
Pacific Palisades, CA 90272
PH.310.454.2247
www.zonevodka.com
Zone Vodkas

Rémy Amerique
1350 Avenue of the Americas
New York, NY 10019
PH.212.399.4200
www.remycointreau.com
Cointreau Liqueur, Rémy Red

Sazerac, Inc.
803 Jefferson Hwy
New Orleans, LA 70121
PH.504.831.9450
www.sazerac.com
Dr. McGillicuddy's Schnapps
and Vanilla Liqueur,
El Jimador Tequilas,
Dr. McGillicuddy's Fireball
Cinnamon Canadian
Whisky, Herradura Tequilas,
Rain Vodka

Schieffelin and Somerset
2 Park Ave., 17th floor
New York, NY 10016
PH.212.251.8200
www.trade-pages.com
Grand Marnier Liqueurs,
Tanqueray No. Ten Gin

Seagram North America
800 Third Ave., 12th Floor
New York, NY 10022
PH.212.572.7000
www.seagram.com
Absolut Vodka

Sidney Frank Importing Co.
20 Cedar St., Ste. 203
New Rochelle, NY 10801
PH.914.633.5630
www.jagermeister.com
Grey Goose Vodka,
Jägermeister Liqueur

Spirit of Hartford
P.O. Box 260730
Hartford, CT 06126
PH.860.404.1776
www.spiritofhartford.com
Damrak Amsterdam Gin,
Foursquare Spiced Rum

Todhunter Imports, Ltd.
222 Lakeview Ave.
West Palm Beach, FL 33401
PH.561.837.6300
www.todhunter.com
Cruzan Estate Rums, Cruzan
Flavored Rums, Cruzan
Single Barrel Rum,
Plymouth Gin

UDV North America
333 W. Wacker Dr., Ste. 1100
Chicago, IL 60606
PH.312.279.3400
www.baileys.com
Baileys Original Irish
Cream Liqueur

Vamonos Rap
747 N. La Brea Av
Los Angeles, CA 90..
PH.323.939.7999
www.casanoble.com
Casa Noble Tequilas

White Diamond Spirits, Inc.
701 N. Green Valley Parkway
Henderson, NV 89014
PH.702.990.3050
www.brilliantvodka.com
Brilliant Vodka

Wm. Grant & Co.
130 Fieldcrest Ave.
Edison, NJ 08837
PH.732.225.9000
www.grantusa.com
Frangelico Liqueur, Licor 43
(Cuarenta y Tres)

GLASSWARE
Libbey
300 Madison Ave.
Toledo, OH 43604
PH.419.325.2100
www.libbey.com
Libbey Glassware

PHOTOGRAPHY
Erik Hinote Photography
Contact Publisher
for information